# Knowing Him by Heart

# KNOWING HIM BY HEART

## African Americans on Abraham Lincoln

Edited by
FRED LEE HORD
and
MATTHEW D. NORMAN

Published by
the Knox College Lincoln Studies Center
and the
University of Illinois Press
Urbana, Chicago, and Springfield

Library of Congress Cataloging-in-Publication Data
Names: Hord, Fred L., editor. | Norman, Matthew D., editor.
Title: Knowing him by heart: African Americans on Abraham
    Lincoln / edited by Fred Lee Hord and Matthew D. Norman.
Other titles: African Americans on Abraham Lincoln
Description: Urbana : University of Illinois Press, 2022. | Series:
    The Knox College Lincoln studies center series | Includes
    bibliographical references and index.
Identifiers: LCCN 2022016204 (print) | LCCN 2022016205 (ebook) |
    ISBN 9780252044687 (cloth) | ISBN 9780252053702 (ebook)
Subjects: LCSH: Lincoln, Abraham, 1809–1865—Relations with
    African Americans. | Lincoln, Abraham, 1809–1865—Influence. |
    African Americans—Attitudes—History. | American literature—
    African American authors. | Presidents—United States—
    Biography—Anecdotes.
Classification: LCC E457.2 .K585 2022 (print) | LCC E457.2 (ebook) |
    DDC 973.7092 [B]—dc23/eng/20220513
LC record available at https://lccn.loc.gov/2022016204
LC ebook record available at https://lccn.loc.gov/2022016205

# CONTENTS

# ACKNOWLEDGMENTS

We are very grateful for the kind and generous support that we have received during the long life of this project. We thank the staff at the University of Illinois Press for their hard work and assistance. We appreciate the series editors, Douglas Wilson and the late Rodney Davis, for their early encouragement, steadfast support, and for generously sharing their files at the Lincoln Studies Center. We appreciate the support of Knox College, Northern Illinois University, and the University of Cincinnati: Provosts Kai Campbell and Michael Schneider of Knox College; NIU Provost and current President Lisa Freeman; and Krista Sigler, chair of the History Department at UC Blue Ash College. We appreciate the assistance of Joel Ward; and all the work-study students at Northern Illinois University and Knox College. Librarians from many institutions have been of invaluable assistance, particularly Jeff Douglas of the Henry M. Seymour Library at Knox College, the interlibrary loan staff at the University of Cincinnati Libraries, and a special thanks to Laurie Sauer, reference librarian extraordinaire at Seymour Library and compiler of the index.

This book is dedicated to our families, especially Heather Norman, Terry Lee Hord, and the Hord and White children and grandchildren.

# FREQUENTLY CITED SOURCES

AANB: Henry Louis Gates Jr. and Evelyn Brooks Higginbotham, eds. *African American National Biography*. 2nd ed. 12 vols. New York: Oxford University Press, 2013.

ANB: John A. Garraty and Mark C. Carnes, eds. *American National Biography*. 24 vols. New York: Oxford University Press, 1999.

Collected Works: Roy P. Basler, ed. *The Collected Works of Abraham Lincoln*. 9 vols. New Brunswick: Rutgers University Press, 1953–1955.

DANB: Rayford W. Logan and Michael R. Winston, eds. *Dictionary of American Negro Biography*. New York: Norton, 1982.

Lincoln Papers: Lincoln, Abraham. Abraham Lincoln Papers. Series 1–4, spanning the years 1774–1948. Manuscript/mixed material. Washington, DC: Library of Congress. https://www.loc.gov/collections/abraham-lincoln-papers/.

# Knowing Him by Heart

# INTRODUCTION

Langston Hughes, celebrated African American poet in the Harlem Renaissance and beyond, began to compose poetry when he was attending Lincoln Central School in Lincoln, Illinois. Later, as a student at Lincoln University in Pennsylvania during the mid-1920s, the new Lincoln Memorial in Washington, DC, served as the inspiration for a poem in which he proposed to "go see Old Abe/ Sitting in the marble and moonlight." Although Daniel Chester French's sculpture of Lincoln would remain "Quiet for a million, million years," Hughes could still hear Lincoln's "voice forever/Against the/Timeless walls/Of time." As the words chiseled above French's sculpture assert, "the memory of Abraham Lincoln is enshrined forever" in both Henry Bacon's Greek temple and in "the hearts of the people." Hughes's "Lincoln Monument: Washington" attests to the deeply profound symbolic significance of Abraham Lincoln. He continues to speak and has a special place in the hearts of Black people long after his death. While Hughes does not reveal what Lincoln said to him, this anthology provides an opportunity to see Lincoln reflected in the voices of African Americans. Whether they actually saw him and heard him or he only resided in their hearts and minds, these voices, like the voice Hughes heard at the Lincoln Memorial, reverberate and reveal a different type of monument to the sixteenth president.[1]

In his seminal book, *Lincoln and the Negro*, Benjamin Quarles suggested that "Lincoln became Lincoln because of the Negro," and he quoted a revealing statement from Frederick Douglass regarding the primacy of Lincoln's place in the consciousness of African Americans that serves as a central theme of this anthology:

"We all know Lincoln by heart." The documents in this collection enable readers to interrogate Quarles's conclusion and Douglass's statement, as these sources provide an opportunity to view the scaffolding of a monument to Lincoln that has been constructed from words rather than marble or bronze. Beginning in the late 1850s, when African Americans first took serious notice of Lincoln, to the 1920s when Lincoln helped inspire Langston Hughes, to the most recent example of President Barack Obama, the architecture of this monument is fluid, complex, and wide-ranging. Far from being a monolith, the voices collected here offer a variety of African American responses to Lincoln. Assembling these voices has been a task of excavation, for while some of the contributors will be familiar, others may not. Recovering forgotten voices and including them with the better-known serves to demonstrate not only the breadth and depth of feelings on Lincoln but also provides a unique opportunity to examine the critical role that African Americans have played in shaping Lincoln's place in our collective memory. A work that spans one hundred and fifty years and contains a diverse array of contributions further facilitates an exploration of how perceptions of Lincoln remained consistent or shifted as time passed, circumstances changed, and analyses proliferated, and to understand why.[2]

While African Americans initially viewed Lincoln with skepticism and were quite critical of his views on racial equality and his willingness to prioritize the preservation of the Union over the abolition of slavery, the Emancipation Proclamation elevated him to a special place in many of their hearts. The words that comprise this edifice suggest that Lincoln's status as a venerated symbol has weighed heavily on both the hearts and minds of African Americans as they struggled with the various meanings and consequences of emancipation. Some voices uncritically praised "Father Abraham" as their savior and were willing to overlook the limitations of the Emancipation Proclamation, yet others were more circumspect. This persistent ambivalence indicates an intricately evolving historical tension between apprehending Lincoln by heart and by head. In speeches, essays, books, editorials, sermons, poems, and other forms of expression, African American commentaries on Lincoln reflect a variety of hopes, fears, aspirations, frustrations, memories, and assessments. Whether they viewed him as the heroic "Great Emancipator," a "reluctant" emancipator, an anti-Black racist, vacillating, or just "big enough to be inconsistent," African Americans have grappled with Lincoln's legacy and expressed a complex, nonlinear array of thoughts and feelings about him. Black responses to Lincoln reveal, in part, incongruity between a sense of African American agency in securing their freedom and the image of Lincoln as a messiah who bestowed emancipation as a gift to passive, but grateful recipients. As the Civil War receded into history and memory, faltering progress toward full equality and a growing sense of self-determination affected how many African Americans understood and assessed Lincoln.

The purpose of this book is to present an extensive anthology of African American views on Lincoln that represents the complexity of these head-heart perceptions. Our aim has been to excavate African American assessments of Lincoln from the late 1850s, a decade that witnessed Lincoln's rise to national prominence, to the bicentennial of Lincoln's birth in 2009—an anniversary that coincided with the inauguration of Barack Obama, who embraced Lincoln's legacy to support his candidacy and frame his presidency. This anthology is distinctive for being the first collection solely devoted to African American writings on Abraham Lincoln, and it offers readers an opportunity to contemplate a new type of monument that further attests to Lincoln's significance on the landscape of American memory. Unpacking Quarles's notion that Lincoln became Lincoln because of the Negro and Douglass's conception of Black Americans knowing Lincoln by heart, this work provides substantive evidence of how these processes occurred over the span of one hundred and fifty years.

While *Knowing Him by Heart* is the first work of its kind to uncover, compile, and present an extensive selection of African American writings on Lincoln, John E. Washington (1880–1964), a dentist, educator, collector of Lincolniana, and member of Washington, DC's Black community, made an initial effort to register African American views on Lincoln in his book, *They Knew Lincoln* (1942). Growing up in the neighborhood near Ford's Theater, Washington was captivated by stories from family members and others who recalled their encounters with Lincoln. Washington began to cultivate a serious interest in Lincoln that culminated with the publication of the first book that focuses exclusively on Lincoln's relationships with African Americans. *They Knew Lincoln* is an amalgam of Washington's reminiscences of the stories he heard and a history of the African Americans who served and witnessed Lincoln during his presidency. Although limited by its focus and methodology, *They Knew Lincoln* is a valuable resource, as it provides compelling evidence of the strong feelings African Americans had for Lincoln, and in addition to documenting Lincoln's place in the folklore of Washington, DC's African American community, Washington's work brought to light many people whom previous Lincoln scholars had largely ignored. *Knowing Him by Heart* includes documents from some of the persons Washington discusses in his book, such as William Florville, Elizabeth Keckly, and William Slade, and demonstrates that the connection between Lincoln and African Americans that Washington initially explored in his work runs deep and has profound consequences.[3]

Spanning one hundred fifty years and including people who not only knew Lincoln but also reflected on his significance during his lifetime and in the decades that followed, the editors hope *Knowing Him by Heart* will appeal not only to scholars in the fields of Lincoln Studies, African American history, and Civil War memory, but also to students and general readers. Black Americans understood Lincoln's imperfections perhaps better than anyone, yet as soon as he was assassinated, they laid claim to his legacy for a variety of purposes, not the least of which was a desire to mold an image of him that would serve their interests. To cement this connection, a monument to Lincoln was proposed and eventually realized with Thomas Ball's *Emancipation Group*. Unveiled in Washington, DC, in 1876, the monument depicts Lincoln emancipating a slave who is rising from his knees. H. Cordelia Ray's poem that was composed for the ceremony offered a "loving tribute" to the "martyred chief," but Frederick Douglass's dedication address reflects the ambivalence and complexity that exemplify many of the voices assembled here. Although Douglass referred to Lincoln as "pre-eminently the white man's president" and Black people as "only his step-children," he also described Lincoln as "our friend and liberator" who was "near and dear to our hearts." As the documents reveal, Douglass was not alone in embracing Lincoln's legacy for the purpose of advancing the cause of racial equality, but there was also tension between this desire to enlist Lincoln in the continuing struggle and frustration with the insufficient progress toward that goal.[4]

Ball's sculpture epitomizes the image of emancipation as a gift that Lincoln gave to the enslaved and figuratively depicts what historians David Brion Davis, Marcus Wood, and others have referred to as the "emancipation moment." Certainly, Lincoln's signing of the Final Emancipation Proclamation on January 1, 1863, marked the seminal emancipation moment for the United States, and many of the documents in this collection afford readers an opportunity to examine how African Americans immediately responded to and later reflected upon this singular moment in time. Collectively, these sources help illuminate a contradictory tendency that, as David Brion Davis has observed, hails emancipation as a "glorious moment of national rebirth" that proved in "many ways a failure." Just months after Lincoln issued the Emancipation Proclamation, James H. Hudson criticized it as a "half-way measure" that applied only to areas "beyond the reach" of federal authority and continued to allow slavery in states or portions of states that remained loyal to the Union. Frustrated by the lack of progress toward full equality, Frederick Douglass declared in 1888 that the "so-called emancipation" was a "stupendous fraud," and Martin Luther King Jr. reiterated this sentiment on the steps of the Lincoln Memorial in 1963, when he asserted that Black Americans were still not free in the centennial year of Lincoln's Emancipation Proclamation. While the failure to finish the work of emancipation did not diminish Lincoln's stature in the eyes of either Douglass or King, the voices in this collection speak to a larger issue that illustrates a process of reinterpreting and reinventing the emancipation moment for the purpose of constructing a usable past that would serve the needs of the present and future. These endeavors kept memories of emancipation alive and produced a monument in words far more nuanced and complex than Ball's sculpture.[5]

Even though Ball's monument suggests that the issue of emancipation has been settled, and freedom was a gift Lincoln bestowed upon the enslaved, many of the sources collected here suggest otherwise and reveal a dialectical struggle between what Marcus Wood has termed the "liberation fantasy" and the conception of freedom as a natural right that cannot be given but "can only be returned to those who have been robbed of it." The idealized slave kneeling at Lincoln's feet in Ball's *Emancipation Group* is at odds with the nearly two hundred thousand Black men who took up arms to secure their freedom and the Black voices that criticized Lincoln during his presidency and exhorted him to take action against slavery and on behalf of racial equality. The excavated words collected here therefore problematize the notion of a single emancipation narrative in which Lincoln performed the role of a White messiah, for while some expressed unequivocal gratitude for what Lincoln did, others complicate this trope by seeking to emancipate themselves from the perception that their freedom was solely the result of Lincoln's beneficence. Such a dialectic has profound implications for understanding persistent themes that the texts address, such as Lincoln's ambivalence in issuing the Emancipation Proclamation; Lincoln's contradictory statements on racial equality and whether or not he came to believe African Americans would make good citizens; Lincoln's role as a messiah and martyr to the cause of Black freedom; and the belief that if freedom was a gift from Lincoln then African Americans had to achieve mainstream success as a means of paying the debt owed to Lincoln's memory and justifying the sacrifices made in their behalf during the Civil War.[6]

Whether freedom was a gift from Lincoln, a natural right that was restored through Black agency, or a combination of factors indicates that this fundamental question remains unsettled, just as the status of formerly enslaved persons remained a bitter point of contention following Lincoln's assassination. African American responses to Lincoln, be it from their hearts or their heads, reflect all these complexities and expose an ongoing discourse over the meanings of freedom. In celebrating Emancipation Day and Lincoln's birthday, and at other commemorative events and in various publications, African Americans seized terrain in the contest over Lincoln's legacy and the memory of the Civil War. Their words on these occasions revivified the emancipation moment into a series of moments that in effect produced a living monument to Lincoln. This monument could serve a variety of purposes, such as paying tribute to the Great Emancipator, making the case for racial equality, building a sense of community, demonstrating respectability, or as Frantz Fanon observed in *Black Skin, White Masks*, revealing a desire for recognition.

Fanon remarked on the tendency to commemorate the emancipation moment by erecting monuments that depict passive, grateful slaves and suggested that members of the oppressed race must receive recognition in order to invert this hierarchy, for "as long as he has not been effectively recognized by the other, it is this other who remains the focus of his actions. His human worth and reality depend on this other and on his recognition by the other." Commemorating Lincoln was an opportunity to complicate the emancipation narrative, and thereby provided a potential means to receive recognition. Fanon asserted that African Americans not only fought for their freedom but were "fought against." Indeed, though African American soldiers fought in the Civil War, this opportunity only came after a struggle with the Lincoln administration. Black soldiers faced the enemy on the battlefield and opponents on the home front who resented their service and resisted efforts to use their military service as a path to equal citizenship. Lincoln recognized the valuable contribution of African American soldiers, and concluded that they should be treated as citizens, but many White Americans refused to do so, particularly those on the losing side. As the struggle for equality and recognition continued in the decades following Lincoln's assassination, his signature increasingly came to be seen as conferring the gift of emancipation, with the defeated vicariously owning the gift. Fanon made the grisly observation that the freedom that resulted from fighting was tempered by the "scores of Negroes hanged by their testicles" during and after the war, yet he envisioned a "grandiose" monument "slowly rising" from this sanguinary battlefield that featured "a white man and a black man *hand in hand*" at the top. Such a monument depended upon the recognition of Blacks and Whites as equals and the voices excavated and presented in this work are figurative building blocks in this edifice that reveal the architecture of African American memory of Lincoln and emancipation.[7]

The centennial of Lincoln's birth in 1909 prompted efforts to construct a new monument to him, and amidst the celebrations of his life it was becoming increasingly evident that a growing number of White Americans, regardless of whether they were from the North or the South, were seeking to elide discussion of the unfinished work of the Emancipation Proclamation in the interest of sectional reconciliation. What had once been a day for African Americans to celebrate, Lincoln's birthday was more and more being coopted by Whites who had little interest in remembering Lincoln for emancipation and instead sought to exclude Blacks from their Lincoln Day events. This trend dovetailed with Jim Crow laws and a systematic effort to deprive African Americans of their voting rights in the South that effectively reversed the achievements of Reconstruction. The strong comments Lincoln made in the 1850s against the political and social equality of the races and the most egregious racial miscues during his presidency gave pause to some Black Americans, yet appealed to those who enlisted Lincoln as an ally in their efforts to condemn "Radical" Reconstruction as a tragic error and enforce a legalized system of White supremacy. In speculating on what Lincoln's racial policies would be if he were alive in 1909, William Pickens offered a counter-memory to this increasingly prevalent White supremacist image of Lincoln. Though Lincoln's support for compensated emancipation, Black Laws, and colonization signified that he had "no special love for the Negro," his belief in the natural equality of all men and ability to alter his positions led Pickens to conclude that Lincoln would favor equal rights for Black Americans.[8]

Albert Enoch Pillsbury, a White civil rights activist, was also alarmed by the trend that downplayed the significance of emancipation and the unfinished work of racial equality. In a 1913 address at Howard University that was delivered to mark the fiftieth anniversary of the Emancipation Proclamation, Pillsbury observed that too many Americans were "politely ignoring historical truth" by dismissing slavery as the cause of the Civil War and minimizing Lincoln's role in ending it. For Pillsbury, this "political perversion of history" was being conducted to further the cause of "national harmony" and "justify new bondage of the oppressed race." David Blight's seminal work on the memory of the Civil War details the extent to which a desire for sectional reconciliation had surpassed a commitment to finish the work of emancipation by 1913. As many White Americans embraced a commemoration of the Civil War that emphasized reunion and sectional harmony, they came to believe that it had been a mistake to grant African Americans political rights during Reconstruction. In refusing to support federal intervention in the South, a blind eye was turned to segregation, political disenfranchisement, and the wanton violence employed to enforce this system. Lincoln functioned as a prominent icon in this reconciliationist narrative of Civil War memory and helped bridge the sectional divide.[9]

As monuments to the defeated rebellion increasingly dotted the landscape in the South, the Lincoln Memorial in Washington was designed as a symbol of sectional reconciliation and it was dedicated in 1922 before a racially segregated audience. Virtually ignoring Lincoln's role as Great Emancipator, the monument instead burnished his image as savior of the Union, despite the efforts of Robert Moton, president of Tuskegee Institute and the lone African American speaker at the dedication ceremony. The Lincoln enshrined in this memorial was a Lincoln that many Whites, regardless of section, had come to embrace. A Lincoln that was, in Pillsbury's words, "indifferent to slavery" and whose Emancipation Proclamation was, as President Warren Harding stated in his speech at the Lincoln Memorial dedication, solely "a means to the great end—maintained union and nationality." African Americans recognized this muting of an emancipationist memory of Lincoln and the Civil War as part of an agenda for national reunion on terms largely dictated by the side that had lost the war. As the *Chicago Defender* editorialized following the dedication of the Lincoln Memorial: "The conquered have become the victorious." In a radio address on Lincoln's birthday, William Lloyd Imes cited a Bible passage, "Ye kill the prophets, and then build monuments to them," to illustrate the irony of this trend to honor Lincoln while failing to uphold his principles. The Baltimore *Afro-American* observed that the South was indeed "in the saddle" and had succeeded in creating a situation that perverted the true meaning of Lincoln's Gettysburg Address, yet following the controversy surrounding the Lincoln Memorial's dedication, the *Afro-American* criticized the extent to which "unthinking colored folks have made of Abraham Lincoln a great hero and ideal."[10]

The editor of the *Afro-American* was not alone in decrying the extent to which African Americans expressed uncritical admiration and gratitude for Lincoln, as the documents reveal a tension between the perception of Lincoln as a heaven-sent savior and a practical politician. For many, especially those who had endured enslavement, Lincoln and his Emancipation Proclamation appeared to fulfill an expectation that stemmed from a theodicy that engendered hope for a Christian messiah who would come to earth and free them. Lincoln was therefore often likened to deliverers, such as Moses and Jesus, elevated to the status of a demigod, or at the very least had his hand guided by divine intervention. African American Christianity was antithetical to enslavement and even when some, like Harriet Tubman, referred to Lincoln as "Massa," it designated a master they could trust because he broke their chains of bondage. By the early twentieth century, some condemned this view of Lincoln as a vestige of slavery. Writing in the year before the Lincoln Memorial was dedicated, Hubert H. Harrison perhaps best captured this tension when he asserted that Lincoln was not only a great man but the greatest president, yet he was neither a god nor a friend of Black people.

Clearly, Lincoln remained central in African American memories of the Civil War, and the documents in this anthology indicate not only a variety of opinions, but as Hubert Harrison's interpretation suggests, Black people could memorialize Lincoln without necessarily venerating him. The Emancipation Proclamation was itself a special monument of words in that many African Americans who recognized its limitations saw its possibilities, while others perceived the proclamation principally through the lens of what it did not do and had no room left in so many shattered dreams to consider it more than another rhetorical edifice of those in authority. African Americans who believed the document would replace the ignominy of what Lincoln termed in his Second Inaugural Address, "two hundred and fifty years of unrequited toil," converted the imperfect millennial proclamation to the best stepping-stone yet to actual freedom. For so many years, Blacks had built verbal and symbolic monuments to honor their persistence in the everlasting storm of time, yet this welcomed document on New Year's Day 1863 stood not only on the flat thick page, but also suggested much about its future shape as a monument. From Frederick Douglass to Mary Church Terrell to W. E. B. Du Bois to Benjamin Quarles, African Americans have—with or without reticence—claimed that Lincoln was, in the balance, worthy of memorializing, his ambiguities and objectionable behaviors notwithstanding. Just months after the

Lincoln Memorial's dedication, Du Bois argued that "when habit and convention were torn away there was something left to Lincoln." In the centennial year of Lincoln's Preliminary Emancipation Proclamation, Quarles submitted that Lincoln "became a symbol and hence a product of something more than memory alone," as African Americans created "their own authorized version of the Lincoln Testament . . . 'Out of the house of bondage.' "[11]

Allen Guelzo has argued that "one of the most dramatic transformations in American historical self-understanding" during the twentieth century was "the slow, almost unnoticed withdrawal of African Americans from what was once the great consensus of Blacks' admiration of Abraham Lincoln." Merrill Peterson's comprehensive examination of Lincoln's place in American memory suggests that by the 1960s, African Americans had abandoned Lincoln as their hero and savior and transferred their love and admiration to Martin Luther King Jr. This shift in sentiment seemingly reached its apogee in 1968 with the publication of Lerone Bennett Jr.'s biting critique of Lincoln in *Ebony* magazine, which argued that Lincoln was little more than a White supremacist who did not care much for the welfare of African Americans. Clearly, a lot had happened between the issuance of the Emancipation Proclamation and the publication of Bennett's piece. As several of the following selections illustrate, the debate over whether Lincoln merited the title of Great Emancipator did not begin in the late 1960s. There had long been a strong connection between adherence to the Republican Party and veneration of Lincoln. When African Americans began to leave the "Party of Lincoln" in the 1930s and support the Democratic Party, John E. Washington and other Republican loyalists worried that this would result in Black people abandoning Lincoln as well. While Washington envisioned an unrealized book project that would persuade African Americans to remain both Republicans and Lincoln admirers, readers will be able to see how the shift in voting behavior influenced perceptions of Lincoln. The primary sources excavated and collected here therefore indicate that it would be inaccurate to conclude that African American views on Lincoln and the Emancipation Proclamation followed a straight-line trajectory that went from uncritical adulation in the 1860s to bitter disillusionment by the 1960s. Rather, the documents support a very different conclusion than has been often assumed, and instead offer a much more complicated and nuanced set of African American views of Lincoln.[12]

This anthology of readings about African American views of Abraham Lincoln does not seek to settle anything about Black views on Lincoln for this time, much less all time, but rather we hope the voices assembled here will lead readers to reexamine their own positions and provide another window to see Lincoln. While our focus is neither Lincoln's views on race nor the views of White Americans on Lincoln, we believe the documents offer valuable insight into how African Americans perceived Lincoln's views on race and proposed alternatives to the dominant White perceptions of Lincoln. Our intention is not to offer a definitive Black view of Lincoln, whether it be positive or negative. At this point, we do not find any neat demarcations in the time, gender, or occupation of the contributors. Selections have been culled from newspapers, magazines, books, and manuscript collections. Although the heft of this volume might suggest otherwise, not every document we found has been included and some difficult decisions were made in determining what to include and what to exclude. These decisions were guided by the goal to present an extensive, diverse, and rich selection of documents that reflect a variety of perspectives from across the span of one hundred fifty years. In addition to including well-known political and religious leaders, writers, and intellectuals, the reader will encounter people who may not be prominent today, yet they offered insightful, compelling, and thoughtful reflections on Lincoln. Insofar as the available sources permit, we have included the voices of men and women from throughout the United States who offer a variety of views on Lincoln that range from uncritical adulation to severe criticism. Above all else, we want these voices to speak for themselves, yet it is important to give attention to the historical contexts of these perceptions. Accordingly, each selection has a headnote that identifies the author and provides historical context for the document. Assessments by African American historians from different time periods are also included as a way to further contextualize the opinions of that period.

A primary, inescapable problem in examining the voices of African Americans from the forming of this nation to at least the 1960s is the paucity of sources from women. This phenomenon has been tempered some in the last fifty years or so by feminist/womanist initiatives but was incredibly systematic before then. Beginning in the late 1850s, this project covers more than one hundred years when men largely controlled access to opportunities for publication and Black women had precious little space in the public sphere with often neither a room nor a pen of their own. Although Emancipation Day celebrations are a rich source for gauging how Lincoln was remembered and commemorated, as Leslie Schwalm notes in her history of these events in the Midwest, until the 1890s Black women were often limited to the role of "costumed female symbols." When women formed organizations, such as the National Association of Colored Women, they began to be featured as speakers at these events, and they also took an active interest in commemorating Lincoln's legacy, as some of the following selections will illustrate. Almost all women's voices before the modern Freedom Movement were either ignored or barely accorded recognition. From the inception of this project, the editors have made a concerted effort to include the voices of women by searching lesser-known publications and fairly recent, less sexist sources to ameliorate this problem, but it is a formidable one. While an anthology of African American voices on Lincoln that included men and women in equal numbers would not be an accurate representation of available sources, readers will encounter several

# Introduction

significant pieces from women, including Frances Ellen Watkins Harper, Elizabeth Keckly, Sojourner Truth, Harriet Tubman, Ida B. Wells, Alice Dunbar-Nelson, and Gwendolyn Brooks. In addition to selections from publications, manuscripts from the papers of Mary McLeod Bethune, Mary Church Terrell, Daisy Bates, and Edith Sampson are also included.

Unearthing the voices of African American women is further complicated by another problem that frustrates students of African American history and culture, and that was the failure to preserve sources that are known to have existed. For example, one can find references to various African American newspapers, yet search library catalogs in vain for extant copies. Another instance of a lost source is from Katherine D. Tillman, a writer active in the early twentieth century, who published *Lincoln's Proclamation*. One can only wonder what she made of the Emancipation Proclamation because this work has not been located. We hope that this first effort to present a collection of African American voices on Lincoln will inspire others to search for and uncover additional sources that have been lost or forgotten.[13]

The documents focus on six major issues regarding African American responses to Abraham Lincoln: Lincoln's views on Black enslavement; the Emancipation Proclamation, including its motives and meanings, as well as Lincoln's proposal for gradual, compensated emancipation; Lincoln's proposals to colonize African Americans; his decision to employ Blacks as soldiers in the Civil War, especially the controversies over recruitment, pay, and status; Lincoln's positions on social and political equality for African Americans; and African American views of personal relationships or exchanges (or both) with Lincoln. Selections reveal how African Americans remembered and commemorated Lincoln through collective celebrations of Emancipation; Lincoln's birthday; and the appropriation of Lincoln's legacy in other public events. Starting with celebrations immediately following the Emancipation Proclamation, we give special attention to the centennial of Lincoln's birth in 1909; the fiftieth anniversary commemorations of emancipation in 1913; activities to mark the centennial of emancipation; and other celebrations that received national publicity. Second, Lincoln birthday celebrations, frequently connected with Frederick Douglass, certainly assumed prominence in African American life, especially during the centennial year of Lincoln's birth in 1909. Third, Lincoln legacy celebrations—meaning both those held after his death and those of the modern Black Freedom Movement—have been especially significant. Even when Lincoln seems to be only a reference, the historical resonance of his life and legacy is unmistakable.

At bedrock level, the editors hope that uncovering and making these documents accessible to scholars, students, and general readers will encourage informed discourse regarding the legacies of slavery and the Civil War, and Lincoln's place in American memory. African Americans sought to stake out ownership of the war's legacy by constructing and maintaining an emancipationist memory of the war even in the face of a dominant reconciliationist narrative that minimized emancipation and its consequences. This monument of words offered a counter-memory to a Lincoln that was either indifferent or hostile to the cause of racial equality, as African Americans struggled among themselves to determine whether they were more than mere objects of Lincoln's gift of freedom.

Additionally, we hope the documents will provoke some reflection on an especially elusive but critically important question of how the image of Abraham Lincoln impacted—and still impacts—Black and White American identity. Why, for instance, do Americans seem mesmerized under the spell of the Lincoln Memorial that Robert Moton helped dedicate and that inspired Langston Hughes? What are the implications of Blacks and Whites alike claiming Lincoln as their own? As Lerone Bennett asserted, one's identity "is based, at least in part, on what you think about Lincoln, the Civil War, and slavery." Though very critical of Lincoln, Bennett sees Lincoln as "a key, perhaps the key to the American personality and what we invest in him, and *hide* in him, is who we are." Interrogating Bennett's claims, this book offers a variety of ways Blacks have expressed their investment in Lincoln, as the excavated documents reveal the intersection between memories of Lincoln and African American identities. The implications of these connections are national, for the assembled voices will aid in crystallizing the meanings of freedom, explore the legacy of emancipation, and provide insights into the construction of historical memory and "memory's ownership."[14]

Finally, the editors hope that one additional issue gets raised in the intricacies of the analyses above. We believe that even in the face of Lincoln's iconic nature, we have not yet identified his largest possibilities for signaling better race relations, or at least enabling a sober reappraisal of them. Our hope is that this anthology of African American perceptions of Lincoln will help contribute to and perhaps invigorate an informed dialogue that furthers greater understanding of both past and present race relations in this country. The Emancipation Proclamation, Lincoln's suggestion that African Americans were citizens, his employment of Blacks as soldiers, and the proposal that at least some freedmen should vote were all affronts to the notion that Blacks were inherently inferior and had been fortunate to be enslaved. The meanings of the iconic sixteenth president crossing paths with a dark-skinned people whose ascribed status was lower than the lowliest of Whites remain evasive and contested, yet we believe that the documents we have uncovered provide an opportunity for readers to examine this relationship in greater depth and from a multitude of perspectives. If Quarles was correct that Lincoln became Lincoln because of African Americans, then perhaps an anthology that traces the trajectory of this evolution will reinforce this vital connection between Lincoln and African Americans and all the implications this relationship has for understanding American race relations. If this occurs at any level, we all shall benefit.

## Editorial Note

Selections in this volume come from both manuscript and printed sources. Each item has been transcribed word for word and letter for letter. The sometimes-idiosyncratic nature of spelling, syntax, capitalization, and punctuation in manuscripts has been preserved and the editorial *sic* is not used. Editorial intrusion has been kept to a minimum and all editorial matter is enclosed in brackets. Omitted words are indicated with an ellipsis. In the case of printed sources, typographical errors such as transposed letters and missing terminal punctuation have been silently corrected. Paragraph indentations are standardized, as are the salutation, closing, and signature in letters, which are flush left. Interlineations are brought into line at the point where the writer intended to insert them.

## NOTES

1. Langston Hughes's "Lincoln Monument: Washington" was first published in the March 1927 issue of *Opportunity* and is included in this volume. For details on Hughes's early life, see Arnold Rampersad, *The Life of Langston Hughes*, vol. 1 (New York: Oxford University Press, 1986).

2. Benjamin Quarles, *Lincoln and the Negro* (New York: Oxford University Press, 1962; reprinted, New York: Da Capo Press, 1990), page three of unpaginated foreword. In a draft of a speech on Lincoln from late 1865, Frederick Douglass stated: "You all know his life by heart." See Douglass, Draft of A Speech on Lincoln, c. December 1865, below.

3. Originally published by E. P. Dutton in 1942, *They Knew Lincoln* was long out of print until a recent and most welcome new edition was published in 2018 by Oxford University Press that includes a lengthy and very informative introduction by Kate Masur. See John E. Washington, *They Knew Lincoln* (New York: E. P. Dutton, 1942; reprinted, New York: Oxford University Press, 2018).

4. For analysis of Ball's sculpture, see Kirk Savage, *Standing Soldiers, Kneeling Slaves: Race, War, and Monument in Nineteenth-Century America* (Princeton, NJ: Princeton University Press), 89–128. Douglass's remarks at the unveiling of the monument on April 14, 1876, are included in their entirety below.

5. David Brion Davis, "The Emancipation Moment" in *Lincoln the War President: The Gettysburg Lectures*, edited by Gabor S. Boritt (New York: Oxford University Press, 1992), 66; James H. Hudson, Letter to Editor of *Pacific Appeal*, Feb. 25,1863; Frederick Douglass, Speech in Washington, April 16, 1888, in John W. Blassingame et al., eds., *The Frederick Douglass Papers*, Series One, 5 volumes (New Haven: Yale University Press) 5: 712–724; Martin Luther King Jr., *A Call to Conscience: The Landmark Speeches of Dr. Martin Luther King, Jr.*, edited by Clayborne Carson and Kris Shepard (New York: Warner Books, 2001), 75–88.

6. Marcus Wood, *The Horrible Gift of Freedom: Atlantic Slavery and the Representation of Emancipation* (Athens: University of George Press, 2010), 2–3.

7. Frantz Fanon, *Black Skin, Whites Masks,* translated by Richard Philcox (1952; New York: Grove Press, 2008), 191, 195–96.

8. William Pickens, "What Would Lincoln Do," Feb. 1909, below. For Lincoln's popularity with White supremacists in the early twentieth century, see Matthew Norman, "'Had Mr. Lincoln Lived': Alternate Histories, Reconstruction, Race and Memory," *Journal of the Abraham Lincoln Association* 38, no. 1 (2017): 43–69.

9. Albert E. Pillsbury, *Lincoln and Slavery* (Boston: Houghton Mifflin Company, 1913) 12; David W. Blight, *Race and Reunion: The Civil War in American Memory* (Cambridge, MA: Harvard University Press, 2001).

10. Pillsbury, *Lincoln and Slavery,* 12; [Warren G. Harding], *President Harding's Address at the Dedication of the Lincoln Memorial* (Washington, DC: Government Printing Office, 1922), 3; J. LeCount Chestnut, "Mock Ideal of Lincoln at Memorial," *Chicago Defender,* June 10, 1922; "A Government of the People," *Afro-American* (Baltimore, MD), July 5, 1913; "The Lincoln Memorial," *Afro-American* (Baltimore, MD), June 9, 1922. For Robert Moton's remarks at the dedication of the Lincoln Memorial and William Lloyd Imes's radio address on Feb. 12, 1935, see below.

11. For the July 1922 statement from W. E. B. Du Bois that was published in *The Crisis* and the excerpt from Quarles's *Lincoln and the Negro,* see below.

12. Allen C. Guelzo, "How Abe Lincoln Lost the Black Vote: Lincoln and Emancipation in the African American Mind," *Journal of the Abraham Lincoln Association* 25, no. 1 (2004): 1–22; Merrill D. Peterson, *Lincoln in American Memory* (New York: Oxford University Press, 1994), 55–60, 167–76, 348–58, 382–85. Lerone Bennett Jr.'s "Was Abe Lincoln a White Supremacist" from the Feb. 1968 issue of *Ebony* is included in its entirety below. John E. Washington's politics and plans for a book to vindicate Lincoln and the Republican Party are discussed in Kate Masur's introduction to the reprint edition of *They Knew Lincoln,* lx-lxi. For a recent examination of attitudes regarding Lincoln and the Emancipation Proclamation that appreciates the complexity of African Americans views, see Chandra Manning, "The Shifting Territory of Attitudes Toward Abraham Lincoln and Emancipation," *Journal of the Abraham Lincoln Association* 34, no. 1 (2013): 18–39.

13. Leslie A. Schwalm, *Emancipation's Diaspora: Race and Reconstruction in the Upper Midwest* (Chapel Hill: University of North Carolina Press, 2009), 230, 233–36.

14. Lerone Bennett Jr., *Forced into Glory: Abraham Lincoln's White Dream* (Chicago: Johnson Publishing Company, 2000).

## FREDERICK DOUGLASS, Emancipation Day Address at Poughkeepsie, New York, August 2, 1858

*When Frederick Douglass (1818–1895) first took notice of Lincoln during the 1858 US Senate campaign in Illinois, he was a leading figure in the abolition movement who had gained international attention for autobiographies chronicling his early life as a slave in Maryland. In addition to delivering lectures and sharing his own experiences with slavery, Douglass was editor of an abolitionist newspaper in Rochester, New York. As the nominee of the recently formed Republican Party, Lincoln challenged the incumbent Stephen A. Douglas. Given Senator Douglas's national prominence as the architect of the controversial Kansas-Nebraska Act, which repealed a prohibition on slavery in these territories and instead allowed White settlers to determine the issue for themselves, the campaign was extensively covered in newspapers throughout the country. Even though Lincoln lost the election, the attention he received during the campaign and from subsequent speaking engagements outside the state made him a nationally recognized figure and helped propel him to the Republican presidential nomination in 1860. Here, Douglass commends Lincoln for the address he delivered in Springfield on June 16, when he accepted his party's nomination for the Senate—best known today as his "House Divided" Speech. Douglass appreciated Lincoln's assertion that the country could not survive permanently divided over the slavery issue, and it must become all one thing or all the other since there was no middle ground or possibility to compromise this fundamental moral question. The passage that Douglass quoted from Lincoln's speech was perhaps the most radical statement Lincoln had made on slavery and served as a major point of contention in the subsequent joint debates that Lincoln and Douglas held in seven Illinois towns. Senator Douglas viewed slavery as a political issue and rejected Lincoln's belief that slavery was a moral evil that unjustly deprived African Americans of fundamental rights. The fact that Lincoln was praised by a prominent Black abolitionist was used against him by Democrats in Illinois, as he was accused of being a radical who supported complete racial equality. While Douglass applauded Lincoln's moral opposition to slavery, he would not have approved of Lincoln's attempts to refute the charge that he supported racial equality by making a distinction between natural rights as expounded in the Declaration of Independence—life, liberty, and the pursuit of happiness—and the civil and political rights that governments conferred. While Lincoln believed all men were entitled to the former, he claimed it did not necessarily follow that African Americans should be able to vote, hold political office, or marry White people. Lincoln's House Divided Speech and his subsequent statements during the campaign on African Americans have been subjected to much analysis and commentary ever since, as the selections in this volume will demonstrate. Douglass himself would offer a variety of interpretations of Lincoln over more than thirty-five years. The documents that follow will detail Douglass's shifting views both throughout Lincoln's presidency and after.*

---

The contest going on just now in the State of Illinois is worthy of attention. STEPHEN A. DOUGLAS, the author of the Kansas-Nebraska bill, is energetically endeavoring to hold his seat in the American Senate, and Mr. ABRAM LINCOLN is endeavoring as energetically to get that seat for himself. This, however, is only a partial view of the matter. The truth is, that Slavery and Anti-Slavery is at the bottom of the contest. As matters now stand, DOUGLAS has a desperate case on his hands. [. . .]

He [Stephen A. Douglas] is one of the most restless, ambitious, boldest and most unscrupulous enemies with whom the cause of the colored man has to contend. [. . .] It seems to me that the white DOUGLAS should occasionally meet his deserts at the hands of a black one. Once I thought he was about to make the name respectable, but now I despair of him, and must do the best I can for it myself. (Laughter.) I now leave him in the hands of Mr. LINCOLN, and in the hands of the Republican Party of Illinois, thanking both the latter, because they have nobly upheld and made prominent the principles of the Republican Party in Illinois, which seemed about to be compromised and sacrificed at the very heart of the Government.

The key-note of Republicanism in that State, at present, is given in the following extract from the great speech of Mr. LINCOLN:

"We are now far into the fifth year since a policy was initiated with the avowed object and confident promise of putting an end to Slavery agitation. Under the operation of that policy, that agitation has not only not ceased, but has constantly augmented. In my opinion it will not cease until a crisis shall have been reached and passed. 'A house divided against itself cannot stand.' I believe this government *cannot endure permanently half Slave and half Free*. I do not expect the Union to be dissolved—I do not expect the house to fall—*but I do expect it will cease to be divided*. It will become all one thing, or all the other. Either the opponents of

Slavery *will arrest the further spread of it,* and place it where the public mind shall rest in the belief *that it is in the course of ultimate extinction;* or its advocates *will push it forward till it shall become alike lawful in all the States*—old as well as new, North as well as South."

Well and wisely said. One system or the other must prevail. Liberty or Slavery must become the law of the land.

In "Commemoration of Negro Emancipation in the British West Indies," *New York Times,* August 3, 1858.

## FREDERICK DOUGLASS, "The Chicago Nominations," June 1860

*Like many other observers, Douglass was surprised that the Republican convention in Chicago nominated Lincoln for the presidency. While Lincoln had gained national attention as a result of his debates with Stephen A. Douglas during the 1858 campaign for US Senate, he had not won election and his only experience at the national level was a single term in the US House of Representatives from 1847 to 1849. The favorite going into the convention was William H. Seward, a US Senator and former governor of New York. Seward was one of the leaders of the Republican Party, but in an October 1858 speech he had asserted that an "irrepressible conflict" existed between the free labor North and the slave labor South. While Lincoln had made a similar statement in his June 1858 House Divided Speech, Seward's speech generated more controversy at the time, and some Republicans feared he was too radical. Lincoln not only seemed moderate in comparison, but as Douglass suggests, his relative inexperience at the national level could be an advantage. Lincoln also came from a key state that Republicans had to win in 1860 if they were to take control of the White House. Lincoln's old rival, Senator Stephen A. Douglas, received the nomination of one faction of the Democratic Party, while Vice President John C. Breckinridge was nominated by another faction, largely from the South, that deemed Douglas insufficiently pro-slavery. A new Constitutional Union Party nominated Senator John Bell of Tennessee for president and Edward Everett of Massachusetts for vice president. Although the Republican Party platform opposed the expansion of slavery to the federal territories rather than the abolition of slavery throughout the United States, Douglass concluded that Lincoln was preferable over the alternatives.*

The nomination of Mr. LINCOLN has taken the people of this part of the Country by surprise. The popular feeling in favor of Mr. SEWARD was no where stronger, or more earnest, than in this part of the State. The people felt that he had a stronger claim upon his party than any other man, having done more to give that party shape, and to systematise the elements composing it, and to furnish it with ideas, than any other man in the nation.

The Republican party is justly proud of Mr. SEWARD, proud of his history, proud of his talents, and proud of his attainments as a statesman, and it is not without strong feeling that it sees him shoved aside to make room for a man whose abilities are untried, and whose political history is too meagre to form a basis on which to judge of his future. [...]

Mr. LINCOLN is a man of unblemished private character; a lawyer, standing near the front rank at the bar of his own State, has a cool well balanced head; great firmness of will; is perseveringly industrious; and one of the most frank, honest men in political life. He cannot lay claim to any literary culture beyond the circle of his practical duties, or to any of the graces found at courts, or in diplomatic circles, but must rely upon his "good hard sense" and honesty of purpose, as capital for the campaign, and the qualities to give character to his administration. His friends cannot as yet claim for him a place in the front rank of statesmanship, whatever may be their faith in his latent capacities. His political life is thus far to his credit, but it is a political life of fair promise rather than one of rich fruitage.

It was, perhaps, this fact that obtained for him the nomination. Our political history has often illustrated the truth that a man may be too great a statesman to become President. The failure of Webster, Clay and Silas Wright in the Presidential race, is in point here, and the success of Harrison, Polk, Taylor and Pierce, tends to prove the same proposition.

If, therefore, Mr. LINCOLN possesses great capacities, and is yet to be proved a great statesman, it is lucky for him that a political exigency moved his party to take him on trust and before his greatness was ripe, or he would have lost the chance. But when once elected it will be no longer dangerous for him to develop great qualities, and we hope that in taking him on a "profession of his faith," rather than on the recommendations of his political life, his party will witness his continual "growth in grace," and his administration will redound to the glory of his country, and his own fame.

As to his principles, there is no reason why the friends of Mr. SEWARD should not heartily support him. He is a radical Republican, and is fully committed to the doctrine of the "irrepressible conflict." In his debates with Douglas, he came fully up to the highest mark of Republicanism, and he is a man of will and nerve, and will not back down from his own assertions. He is not a compromise candidate by any means. [...]

The Presidential contest, this fall, is likely to be rather sharply defined. If Mr. DOUGLAS is put on the course, the old personal rivalry between him and Mr. LINCOLN will render the campaign especially spicy. [...]

The nomination of BELL and EVERETT will tend to divert strength from the Democracy, and give advantage to LINCOLN, but will have no great influence on the general result. [ . . . ]

For ourselves, we are sorry that the hosts of freedom could not have been led forth upon a higher platform, and have had inscribed upon their banners, "Death to Slavery," instead of "No more Slave States." [ . . . ]

But as between the hosts of Slavery propagandism and the Republican party— incomplete as is its platform of principles—our preferences cannot hesitate.

While we should be glad to co-operate with a party fully committed to the doctrine of "All rights, to all men," in the absence of all hope of rearing up the standard of such a party for the coming campaign, we can but desire the success of the Republican candidates.

It will be a great work accomplished when this Government is divorced from the active support of the inhuman slave system. To pluck executive patronage out of the hands of the pliant tools of the whip and the chain; to turn the tide of the National Administration against the man-stealers of this country and in favor of even a partial application of the principles of justice, is a glorious achievement, and we hope for its success.

*Douglass' Monthly* (Rochester, NY), June 1860.

## H. FORD DOUGLAS, Address at Framingham, Massachusetts, July 4, 1860

*Born a slave in Virginia, Douglas (1831–1865) escaped to Ohio, where he became a leader in the abolition movement and a proponent of Black emigration. After moving to Illinois in the mid-1850s, Douglas was able to observe Lincoln first-hand. During the 1860 political campaign, Douglas addressed abolition meetings in the Midwest and New England, where he spoke of his knowledge of Lincoln. During the war, Douglas served in the 95th Illinois and was either able to pass as a White man or his comrades were indifferent to his complexion. Following the Emancipation Proclamation, Douglas's opinion of Lincoln changed from the one offered below. Once the federal government officially accepted Black men into the military Douglas became one of the very few African American commissioned officers when he was appointed captain of an independent light artillery battery in 1865. Shortly after being discharged from the army Douglas died from malaria contracted while he was serving in the South. In the following speech, Douglas relates his personal encounter with Lincoln during the 1858 Senate campaign and argues that a wide chasm separates true anti-slavery principles from Lincoln and his Republican Party's positions on slavery and racial equality. After Lincoln accepted the presidential nomination, there was renewed interest in a bill he had prepared during his single term as a member of the US House of Representatives that would have gradually abolished slavery in Washington, DC, by providing financial compensation to slaveholders. Lincoln did not present his bill once he learned that leading White residents in Washington opposed it. Abolitionists like Douglas were critical of Lincoln's proposal because it included a provision that required municipal authorities to apprehend fugitive slaves (ANB).*

---

We have four parties in this country that have marshalled themselves on the highway of American politics, asking for the votes of the American people to place them in possession of the government. We have what is called the Union party, led by Mr. Bell, of Tennessee; we have what is called the Democratic party, led by Stephen A. Douglas, of Illinois; we have the party called the Seceders, or the Slave-Code Democrats, led by John C. Breckinridge, of Kentucky, and then we have the Republican party, led by Abraham Lincoln, of Illinois. All of these parties ask for your support, because they profess to represent some principle. So far as the principles of freedom and the hopes of the black man are concerned, all these parties are barren and unfruitful; neither of them seeks to lift the negro out of his fetters, and rescue this day from odium and disgrace.

Take Abraham Lincoln. I want to know if any man can tell me the difference between the anti-slavery of Abraham Lincoln, and the anti-slavery of the old Whig party, or the anti-slavery of Henry Clay? Why, there is no difference between them. Abraham Lincoln is simply a Henry Clay Whig, and he believes just as Henry Clay believed in regard to this question. And Henry Clay was just as odious to the anti-slavery cause and anti-slavery men as ever was John C. Calhoun. In fact, he did as much to perpetuate negro slavery in this country as any other man who has ever lived. Henry Clay once said, 'That is property which the law declares to be property,' and that 'two hundred years of legislation have sanctioned and sanctified property in slaves'! [. . .]

I know Abraham Lincoln, and I know something about his anti-slavery. I know the Republicans do not like this kind of talk, because, while they are willing to steal our thunder, they are unwilling to submit to the conditions imposed upon that party that assumes to be anti-slavery. [. . .] They say, 'We must not be in too great a hurry to overthrow slavery; at least, we must take half a loaf, if we cannot get the whole.' Now, my friends, I believe that the very best way to overthrow slavery in this country is to occupy the highest possible anti-slavery ground. [. . .]

I do not believe in the anti-slavery of Abraham Lincoln, because he is on the side of this Slave Power of which I am speaking, that has possession of the Federal Government. What does he propose to do? Simply to let the people and the Territories regulate their domestic institutions in their own way. In the great debate between Lincoln and Douglas in Illinois, when he was interrogated as to whether he was in favor of the admission of more slave States into the Union, he said, that so long as we owned the territories, he did not see any other way of doing than to admit those States when they made application, WITH OR WITHOUT SLAVERY. Now, that is Douglas's doctrine; it is stealing the thunder of Stephen A. Douglas.

In regard to the repeal of the Fugitive Slave Law, Abraham Lincoln occupies the same position that the old Whig party occupied in 1852. They asserted then, in their platform, that they were not in favor of the repeal of that law, and that they would do nothing to lessen its efficiency. What did he say at Freeport? Why, that the South was entitled to a Fugitive Slave Law; and although he thought the law could be modified a little, yet, he said, if he was in Congress, he would have it done in such a way as *not to lessen its efficiency!* Here, then, is Abraham Lincoln in favor of carrying out that infamous Fugitive Slave Law, that not only strikes down the liberty of every black man in the United States, but virtually the liberty of every white man as well; for, under that law, there is not a man in this presence who might not be arrested to-day upon the simple testimony of one man, and, after an *ex parte* trial, hurried off to slavery and to chains. *Habeas corpus*, trial by jury,—those great bulwarks of freedom, reared by the blood and unspeakable woe of your English ancestors, amidst the conflicts of a thousand years,—are struck down by this law; and the man whose name is inscribed upon the Presidential banner of the Republican party is in favor of keeping it upon the statute-book!

Not only would I arraign Mr. Lincoln, in regard to that law, for his pro-slavery character and principles, but when he was a member of the House of Representatives, in 1849, on the 10th day of January, he went through the District of Columbia, and consulted the prominent pro-slavery men and slaveholders of the District, and then went into the House of Representatives, and introduced, on his own responsibility, a fugitive slave law for the District of Columbia. It is well known that the law of 1793 did not apply to the District, and it was necessary, in order that slaveholders might catch their slaves who sought safety under the shadow of the capitol, that a special law should be passed for the District of Columbia; and so Mr. Lincoln went down deeper into the pro-slavery pool than even Mr. Mason of Virginia did in the Fugitive Slave Law of 1850. Here, then, is the man who asks for your votes, and for the votes of the anti-slavery people of New England, who, on his own responsibility, without any temptation whatever, introduced into the District of Columbia a fugitive slave law! That is a fact for the consideration of anti-slavery men.

Then, there is another item which I want to bring out in this connection. I am a colored man; I am an American citizen; and I think that I am entitled to exercise the elective franchise. I am about twenty-eight years old, and I would like to vote very much. I think I am old enough to vote, and I think that, if I had a vote to give, I should know enough to place it on the side of freedom. (Applause.) No party, it seems to me, is entitled to the sympathy of anti-slavery men, unless that party is willing to extend to the black man all the rights of a citizen. [. . .] Men of my complexion are not allowed to testify in a court of justice, where a white man is a party. If a white man happens to owe me anything, unless I can prove it by the testimony of a white man, I cannot collect the debt. Now, two years ago, I went through the State of Illinois for the purpose of getting signers to a petition, asking the Legislature to repeal the 'Testimony Law,' so as to permit colored men to testify against white men. I went to prominent Republicans, and among others, to Abraham Lincoln and Lyman Trumbull, and neither of them dared to sign that petition, to give me the right to testify in a court of justice! ('Hear, hear.') In the State of Illinois, they tax the colored people for every conceivable purpose. They tax the negro's property to support schools for the education of the white man's children, but the colored people are not permitted to enjoy any of the benefits resulting from that taxation. We are compelled to impose upon ourselves additional taxes, in order to educate our children. The State lays its iron hand upon the negro, holds him down, and puts the other hand into his pocket and steals his hard earnings, to educate the children of white men; and if we sent our children to school, Abraham Lincoln would kick them out, in the name of Republicanism and anti-slavery!

I have, then, something to say against the anti-slavery character of the Republican party. Not only are the Republicans of Illinois on the side of slavery, and against the rights of the negro, but even some of the prominent Republicans of Massachusetts are not acceptable anti-slavery men in that regard. In the Senate of the United States, some of your Senators from the New England States take special pains to make concessions to the Slave Power, by saying that they are not in favor of bringing about negro equality; just as Abraham Lincoln did down in Ohio two years ago. When he went there to stump that State, the colored people were agitating the question of suffrage in that State. The *Ohio Statesman*, a paper published in Columbus, asserted, on the morning of the day that Mr. Lincoln made his speech, that he was in favor of negro equality; and Mr. Lincoln took pains at that time to deny the allegation, by saying that he was not in favor of bringing about the equality of the negro race; that he did not believe in making them voters, in placing them in the jury-box, or in ever bringing about the political equality of the races. He said that so long as they lived here, there must be an inferior and superior position; and that he was, as much as anybody else, in favor of assigning to white men the superior position.

The *Liberator* (Boston), July 13, 1860.

## FREDERICK DOUGLASS, "The Inaugural Address," April 1861

*Inauguration Day in Washington on March 4, 1861, was fraught with tension. Since Lincoln's election in November, seven southern states had renounced their allegiance to the Union, formed the so-called Confederate States of America, and elected Mississippi senator Jefferson Davis as the president of this new government. President James Buchanan had denounced secession as illegal and unconstitutional, yet he had also stated that the federal government could not force a state to remain in the Union. As Lincoln traveled by train to Washington in February 1861, an alleged assassination plot in Baltimore led him to alter his travel plans and he took an earlier train to Washington. Some criticized Lincoln for being a coward by sneaking into Washington at night. Threats against Lincoln's life continued, and General Winfield Scott took every precaution to ensure that the inauguration occurred without incident. Douglass believed Lincoln's Inaugural Address was ambiguous at best and at worst expressed pro-slavery sentiments akin to those of his Democratic predecessors, Buchanan and Franklin Pierce. Douglass was puzzled by Lincoln's claim that the Union was perpetual on the one hand and his assertion on the other hand that a conflict was not necessary to resolve the differences between North and South. Douglass was especially galled by Lincoln's claim that he would enforce the Fugitive Slave Act and not interfere with slavery in the states where it existed. He therefore devoted much of his criticism to Lincoln's willingness to return fugitive slaves to their masters and noted the recent case of Lucy Bagley, a fugitive living in Cleveland, Ohio, who was arrested, brought to trial, and returned to slavery. For Douglass, the one glimmer of hope in Lincoln's address was his recommendation that measures be put in place to protect free African Americans from being falsely arrested and tried as fugitives. Douglass feared that the first anti-slavery president was not sufficiently committed to the cause and Jefferson Davis would prove his superior in the coming conflict.*

---

Elsewhere in the columns of our present monthly, our readers will find the Inaugural Address of Mr. Abraham Lincoln, delivered on the occasion of his induction to the office of President of the United States. The circumstances under which the Address was delivered, were the most extraordinary and portentous that ever attended any similar occasion in the history of the country. Threats of riot, rebellion, violence and assassination had been freely, though darkly circulated, as among the probable events to occur on that memorable day. The life of Mr. Lincoln was believed, even by his least timid friends, to be in most imminent danger. No mean courage was required to face the probabilities of the hour. He stood up before the pistol or dagger of the sworn assassin, to meet death from an unknown hand, while upon the very threshold of the office to which the suffrages of the nation had elected him. The outgoing Administration, either by its treachery or weakness, or both, had allowed the Government to float to the very verge of destruction. A fear, amounting to agony in some minds, existed that the great American Republic would expire in the arms of its newly elected guardian upon the very moment of his inauguration. For weeks and months previously to the 4th of March, under the wise direction and management of General Scott, elaborate military preparations were made with a view to prevent the much apprehended outbreak of violence and bloodshed, and secure the peaceful inauguration of the President elect. [...] No doubt exists that to him, rather than to any forbearance of the rebels, Washington owes its salvation from bloody streets on the fourth of March. The manner in which Mr. Lincoln entered the Capital was in keeping with the menacing and troubled state of the times. He reached the Capital as the poor, hunted fugitive slave reaches the North, in disguise, seeking concealment, evading pursuers, by the underground railroad, between two days, not during the sunlight, but crawling and dodging under the sable wing of night. He changed his programme, took another route, started at another hour, travelled in other company, and arrived at another time in Washington. We have no censure for the President at this point. He only did what braver men have done. It was, doubtless, galling to his very soul to be compelled to avail himself of the methods of a fugitive slave, with a nation howling on his track. It is hard to think of anything more humiliating. [...]

Once in Washington, Mr. Lincoln found himself in the thick atmosphere of treason on the one hand, and a cowardly, sentimental and deceitful profession of peace on the other. With such surroundings, he went to work upon his Inaugural Address, and the influence of those surroundings may be traced in the whole character of his performance. Making all allowance for circumstances, we must declare the address to be but little better than our worst fears, and vastly below what we had fondly hoped it might be. It is a double-tongued document, capable of two constructions, and conceals rather than declares a definite policy. No man reading it could say whether Mr. Lincoln was for peace or war, whether he abandons or maintains the principles of the Chicago Convention upon which he was elected. The occasion required the utmost frankness and decision. Overlooking the whole field of disturbing elements, he should have boldly rebuked them. He saw seven States in open rebellion, the Constitution set at naught, the national flag insulted, and his own life murderously sought by slave-holding assassins. Does he expose and rebuke the enemies of his country, the men who are bent upon ruling or ruining the country? Not a bit of it. But at the very start he seeks to court their favor, to explain himself where nobody misunderstands him, and to deny intentions of which nobody had accused him. He turns away from his armed enemy and deals his blows on the head of an innocent bystander. He knew, full well, that the grand objection to him and his party respected the one great question of slavery extension. The South want to extend slavery, and the North want to confine it where it is, 'where the public mind shall rest in the belief of its ultimate extinction.' This was the question which carried the North and defeated the South in the election which made Mr. Abraham Lincoln President. Mr. Lincoln knew this, and the South has known it all along; and yet this subject only gets the faintest allusion, while others, never seriously in dispute, are dwelt upon at length.

Mr. Lincoln opens his address by announcing his complete loyalty to slavery in the slave States, and quotes from the Chicago platform a resolution affirming the rights of property in slaves, in the slave States. He is not content with declaring that he has no lawful power to interfere with slavery in the States, but he also denies having the least '*inclination*' to interfere with slavery in the States. This denial of all feeling against slavery, at such a time and in such circumstances, is wholly discreditable to the head and heart of Mr. Lincoln. Aside from the inhuman coldness of the sentiment, it was a weak and inappropriate utterance to such an audience, since it could neither appease nor check the wild fury of the rebel Slave Power. Any but a blind man can see that the disunion sentiment of the South does not arise from any misapprehension of the disposition of the party represented by Mr. Lincoln. The very opposite is the fact. The difficulty is, the slaveholders understand the position of the Republican party too well. Whatever may be the honied phrases employed by Mr. Lincoln when confronted by actual disunion; however silvery and beautiful may be the subtle rhetoric of his long-headed Secretary of State, when wishing to hold the Government together until its management should fall into other hands; all know that the masses at the North (the power behind the throne) had determined to take and keep this Government out of the hands of the slave-holding oligarchy, and administer it hereafter to the advantage of free labor as against slave labor. The slaveholders knew full well that they were hereafter to change the condition of rulers to that of being ruled; they knew that the mighty North is outstripping the South in numbers, and in all the elements of power, and that from being the superior, they were to be doomed to hopeless inferiority. This is what galled them. They are not afraid that Lincoln will send out a proclamation over the slave States declaring all the slaves free, nor that Congress will pass a law to that effect. They are no such fools as to believe any such thing; but they do think, and not without reason, that the power of slavery is broken, and that its prestige is gone whenever the people have made up their minds that Liberty is safer in the hands of freemen than in those of slaveholders. To those sagacious and crafty men, schooled into mastery over bondmen on the plantation, and thus the better able to assume the airs of superiority over Northern doughfaces, Mr. Lincoln's disclaimer of any power, right or inclination to interfere with slavery in the States, does not amount to more than a broken shoe string! [. . .]

The slaveholders, the parties especially addressed, may well inquire if you, Mr. Lincoln, and the great party that elected you, honestly entertain this very high respect for the rights of slave property in the States, how happens it that you treat the same rights of property with scorn and contempt when they are set up in the Territories of the United States?—If slaves are property, and our rights of property in them are to be so sacredly guarded in the States, by what rule of law, justice or reason does that property part with the attributes of property, upon entering into a Territory owned in part by that same State? The fact is, the slaveholders have the argument all their own way, the moment that the right of property in their slaves is conceded under the Constitution. It was, therefore, weak, uncalled for and useless for Mr. Lincoln to begin his Inaugural Address by thus at the outset prostrating himself before the foul and withering curse of slavery. The time and the occasion called for a very different attitude. Weakness, timidity and conciliation towards the tyrants and traitors had emboldened them to a pitch of insolence which demanded an instant check. Mr. Lincoln was in a position that enabled him to wither at a single blast their high blown pride. The occasion was one for honest rebuke, not for palliations and apologies. The slaveholders should have been told that their barbarous system of robbery is contrary to the spirit of the age, and to the principles of Liberty in which the Federal Government was founded, and that they should be ashamed to be everlastingly pressing that scandalous crime into notice. Some thought we had in Mr. Lincoln the nerve and decision of an Oliver Cromwell; but the result shows that we merely have a continuation of the Pierces and Buchanans, and that the Republican President bends the knee to slavery as readily as any of his infamous predecessors. Not content with the broadest recognition of the right of property in the souls and bodies of men in the slave States, Mr. Lincoln next proceeds, with nerves of steel, to tell the slaveholders what an excellent slave hound he is, and how he regards the right to recapture fugitive slaves a constitutional duty; and lest the poor bondman should escape being returned to the hell of slavery by the application of certain well known rules of legal interpretation, which any and every white man may claim in his own case, Mr. Lincoln proceeds to cut off the poor, trembling negro who had escaped from bondage from all advantages from such rules. He will have the pound of flesh, blood or no blood, be it more or less, a just pound or not, The Shylocks of the South, had they been after such game, might have exclaimed, in joy, an Abraham come to judgment! But they were not to be caught with such fodder. The hunting down a few slaves, the sending back of a few Lucy Bagleys, young and beautiful though they be, to the lust and brutality of the slaveholders and slave-breeders of the Border States, is to the rapacity of the rebels only as a drop of water upon a house in flames. The value of the thing was wholly in its quality. 'Mr. Lincoln, you will catch and return our slaves if they run away from us, and will help us hold them where they are;' what cause, then, since you have descended to this depth of wickedness, withholds you from coming down to us entirely? Indeed, in what respect are you better than ourselves, or our overseers and drivers who hunt and flog our negroes into obedience?'—Again; the slaveholders have a decided advantage over Mr. Lincoln, and over his party. He stands upon the same moral level with them, and is in no respect better than they. If we held the Constitution, as held by Mr. Lincoln, no earthly power could induce us to swear to support it. The fact is, (following the lead of the Dred Scott decision, and all the Southern slaveholding politicians, with all the doughfaces of the North who have been engaged in making a Constitution, for years, outside of the Constitution of 1789,) Mr. Lincoln has taken everything at this point in favor of slavery for granted. He is like the great mass of his countrymen, indebted to the South for both law and gospel.

But the Inaugural does not admit of entire and indiscriminate condemnation. It has at least one or two features which evince the presence of something like a heart as well as a head. Horrible as is Mr. Lincoln's admission of the constitutional duty of surrendering persons claimed as slaves, and heartily as he seems determined that that revolting work shall be performed, he has sent along with his revolting declaration a timid suggestion which, tame and spiritless as it is, must prove as unpalatable as gall to the taste of slaveholders. He says: 'In any law on this subject, ought not all the safeguards of liberty known in humane and civilized jurisprudence be introduced, so that a free man be not in any case surrendered as a slave.' For so much, little as it is, let the friends of freedom thank Mr. Lincoln. This saves his Address from the gulf of infamy into which the Dred Scott decision sunk the Supreme Court of the United States. Two ideas are embraced in this suggestion: First, a black man's rights should be guarded by all the safeguards known to liberty and to humane jurisprudence; secondly, that slavery is an inhuman condition from which a free man ought by all lawful means to be saved. [ . . .] Thanking Mr. Lincoln for even so much, we yet hold him to be the most dangerous advocate of slave-hunting and slave-catching in the land.

He has laid down a general rule of legal interpretation which, like most, if not all general rules, may be stretched to cover almost every conceivable villainy. *'The intention of the law-giver is the law,'* says Mr. Lincoln. But we say that this depends upon whether the intention itself is lawful. If law were merely an arbitrary rule, destitute of all idea of right and wrong, the intention of the lawgiver might indeed be taken as the law, provided that intention were certainly known. But the very idea of law carries with it ideas of right, justice and humanity. [ . . .]

But the case is not murder, but simply the surrendering of a person to slavery who has made his or her escape from slavery into a free State. But what better is an act of this kind than murder? Would not Mr. Lincoln himself prefer to see a dagger plunged to the hilt into the heart of his own daughter, than to see that daughter given up to the lust and brutality of the slaveholders of Virginia, as was poor, trembling Lucy Bagley given up a few weeks ago by the Republicans of Cleveland? What is slavery but a slow process of soul murder? What but murder is its chief reliance? [...]

How sadly have the times changed, not only since the days of Madison—the days of the Constitution—but since the days even of Daniel Webster. Cold and dead as that great bad man was to the claims of humanity, he was not sufficiently removed from the better days of the Republic to claim, as Mr. Lincoln does, that the surrender of fugitive slaves is a plain requirement of the Constitution.

But here comes along a slight gleam of relief. Mr. Lincoln tremblingly ventures to *inquire* (for he is too inoffensive to the slaveholders to assert and declare, except when the rights of black men are asserted and declared away) if it 'might not be well to provide by law for the enforcement of that clause in the Constitution which guarantees that the citizens of each State shall be entitled to all the privileges and immunities of citizens in the several States.'

Again we thank Mr. Lincoln. He has, however, ventured upon a hazardous suggestion. The man has not quite learned his lesson. He had not been long enough in Washington to learn that Northern citizens, like persons of African descent, have no rights, privileges or immunities that slaveholders are bound to respect. [...] Yes, this is something to be thankful for and is more than any other American President has ever ventured to say, either in his Inaugural Speech or Annual Message. It is perhaps, this latter fact that gives Mr. Lincoln's casual remark its chief importance.—Hitherto our Presidents had pictured the South as the innocent lamb, and the greedy North as the hungry wolf, ever ready to tear and devour.

From slave-catching, Mr. Lincoln proceeds to give a very lucid exposition of the nature of the Federal Union, and shows very conclusively that this Government, from its own nature and the nature of all Governments, was intended to be perpetual, and that it is revolutionary, insurrectionary and treasonable to break it up. His argument is excellent; but the difficulty is that the argument comes too late. When men deliberately arm themselves with the avowed intention of breaking up the Government; when they openly insult its flag, capture its forts, seize its munitions of war, and organize a hostile Government, and boastfully declare that they will fight before they will submit, it would seem of little use to argue with them. If the argument was merely for the loyal citizen, it was unnecessary. If it was for those already in rebellion, it was casting pearls before swine. [...]

It remains to be seen whether the Federal Government is really able to do more than hand over some John Brown to be hanged, suppress a slave insurrection, or catch a runaway slave—whether it is powerless for liberty, and only powerful for slavery. Mr. Lincoln says, 'I shall take care that the laws of the Union shall be faithfully executed in all the States'—that is, he will do so as *'as far as practicable*,' and *unless* the American people, his masters, shall, in some authoritative manner direct the contrary. To us, both these provisos had better have been omitted. They imply a want of confidence in the ability of the Government to execute its own laws, and opens its doors to all that border tribe who have nothing but smiles for the rebels and peace lecturers for the Government. The American people have placed the Government in the hands of Abraham Lincoln for the next four years, and his instructions are in the Constitution. He had no right to suppose that they will reverse those instructions in a manner to give immunity to traitors; and it was a mistake to admit such a possibility, especially in the presence of the very traitors themselves. [ . . . ] Mr. Lincoln has avowed himself ready to catch them [slaves] if they run away, to shoot them down if they rise against their oppressors, and to prohibit the Federal Government *irrevocably* from interfering for their deliverance. With such declarations before them, coming from our first modern anti-slavery President, the Abolitionists must know what to expect during the next four years, (should Mr. Lincoln not be, as he is likely to be, driven out of Washington by his rival, Mr. Jeff. Davis, who has already given out that should Mr. Lincoln attempt to do, what he has sworn to do—namely, execute the laws, fifty thousand soldiers will march directly up on Washington!).

*Douglass' Monthly* (Rochester, NY), April 1861: 433–435.

## THOMAS HAMILTON, "President Lincoln's Inaugural," March 16, 1861

*Thomas Hamilton (1823–1865), a New York native, began publishing the* Anglo-African Magazine *and* Weekly Anglo-African *newspaper in 1859. Hamilton published the literary magazine until early 1860 and the newspaper until the spring of 1861. Thomas's brother, Robert (1819–1870), resumed publication of the* Anglo-African *newspaper in August 1861 and it became one of the leading African American newspapers during the Civil War. In the following editorial, Thomas Hamilton expresses his disappointment with Lincoln's Inaugural Address that had been delivered at the US Capitol on March 4, 1861. Like Frederick Douglass, Hamilton found Lincoln's commitment to anti-slavery deficient, especially in reference to the sections of the address where Lincoln pledged to enforce the odious Fugitive Slave Act and endorsed an amendment to the Constitution that Congress had approved just prior to his inauguration, which would have prohibited the federal government from interfering with or abolishing slavery in any state. Though Lincoln submitted this proposed Thirteenth Amendment to the states for ratification, it was not ratified by the requisite number of states. In 1865 it was replaced with a very different amendment that abolished slavery throughout the nation.*

———————

Of the millions who, on the [4]th of March, awaited the words of Abraham Lincoln, few looked so anxiously for them as the people whom we represent. An isolated class, with the mark of caste placed upon them by the Godless will of a criminal nation; with millions of brethren in bonds; many of us fugitives from the American Egypt; denied the commonest need of political and social right; ourselves branded, and our children growing up pariahs; yet ever working with a will to win manhood's recognition, and imbued with hope perennial in its freshness, it was natural we should regard with interest the day which inaugurated a new party, a new President, and a new power into the various departments of this government. We remembered that it was called the party of freedom, that its supporters were almost exclusively in the Northern States, and that its platform, in spite of other and contradictory passages, contained the ever glorious utterances of the Declaration of Independence. With the buoyancy common to our humanhood, (and in this as to other things we differ not from the fairer-skinned) we put aside other words of the triumphant—that it was only the party of free labor, not freedom; that its aims were for the whites, but not for MAN; that its slogan was not against slavery, but only its extension; that its oft-reiterated creed was for Free Territories, Free Homes, and Free Labor for *white* men—lands, laws, and recognition for the fair skin, but none for the dark, unless it was in the scorn and contumely wherewith the baseness of this nation has *polarized* into a word when speaking of the latter. Forgetting all these shadows, we remembered the light, letting our vision rest there only.

Well, the hour has passed and gone. Through its elected chief the "white man's" party stands acknowledged. Its dicta have authoritatively gone forth from the steps of the national capitol. What hope does President Lincoln's Inaugural hold for us? Let us see.

One thing must strike the observant reader, and that is the plain, terse, and simple expression of the speaker. There is no equivocation, no double-dealing. How far he will or will not go is very directly said. We are the more convinced by this, Mr. Lincoln's first State Paper, that he not inaptly has won the cognomen of "Honest Abe." His right to this we acknowledge, and it is because of that belief that our sorrow is the more profound, our hope the more shattered, and our gloom the more assured. In examining a document of this kind, we naturally look to ascertain if there shines one ray through it to light our path. At this crisis, brought about because of the wrongs brought upon us as a people, we search for some desirable expression. Coming to the perusal of this paper, with renewed hopes, believing that the auguries were favorable, and that a grain of comfort would be ours, we turn away with a heaving heart and with a more dead despair of our future here. We see a man of warm and generous impulses, uncorrupted by the chicanery of parties, fresh from the people, out of the bosom of the Great West, where, in forms yet uncrystalized, lies so much that is noble in humanity, universally conceded to be honest—we see such a man, elected in the hour of peril to direct the affairs of the nation—not as in the case of the slave-hound, Millard Fillmore, with swift alacrity ready to shed the blood of the innocent— but slowly, sadly, with evident reluctance, though in stern sincerity, expressing his determination to assume and maintain *with all his power*, the functions of National Kidnapper; this, too, not out of love for the task, but because it is *written*. Read his words, and see how much we may hope. We give those portions of the Inaugural relative to the Fugitive Slave enactment. The reader will mark a few points. The only statute upon which President Lincoln felt it necessary to explicitly dwell is this infamous law—this, too, in the face of the fact that traitors have undermined the government, that revolution stalks unbidden through the land, and scorn and disgrace have for months past been heaped upon the Union and its supporters throughout the South. General vagueness seems to be the rule in speaking of this state of things throughout the remainder of the document. This we say not in any up[b]raiding sense, but to show the strong and definite contrast presented when *our* liberties are in peril. Again, the President passes over in a slighting manner, as immaterial, the constitutional question of Federal or State kidnapping, to express the hope that all "safeguards" will be introduced to protect the liberty of freemen, &c. This latter might have some meaning, had we not had late cases wherewith to measure the "safeguards" which Republican legislation will give. The late Cleveland (Ohio) slave case offers a pertinent illustration, as does also the amendment to the Constitution lately passed by the Republican majority in Congress, and which, it will be seen, without having read, President Lincoln hastens to approve. [ . . . ]

"The only substantial dispute," when the history of the contest is fairly written, will be found to be something more than a mere question of extension. It is slavery, President Lincoln—the wrong done to four and a half millions of human beings; it is to the oppression heaped upon them—in the denial of human rights, the scorn, contumely, and degradation which is constantly heaped on them, that all this fraternal strife and internecine war is due, and not to the question of extending the crime over a few thousand square leagues more of territory. It is the *existence*, not the *extension* of slavery that is at issue. The latter is but one of the collateral questions, magnified by adroit politicians into importance to divert and distract the nation from the only vital position—shall slavery live at all? [ . . . ].

We gather no comfort from the Inaugural of President Lincoln. Its force is strengthened by our conviction of his own earnestness and honesty. Actively oppressed in the one section of this country, and in the other as actively rejected, we can see but little left us. Our hope must be in ourselves—in the energy and vigor, the ability and courage we claim to possess, and for all of which we shall have a full use. We must throw off the yoke of policy, of subserviency, of submission, mark out a line of conduct, and pursue it manfully to the end. "It is the fear of death alone makes oppression possible," and it behooves us to act in that spirit. We must put the question plainly. The Republican party is for the *white* man. We must rely on ourselves.

Editorial in the *Weekly Anglo-African* (New York), March 16, 1861.

## ROBERT HAMILTON, "The Fatal Step Backward," September 21, 1861

*Despite the hope Lincoln expressed in his Inaugural Address for a peaceful solution to the secession crisis, he made the momentous decision for war following the firing upon Fort Sumter in April. Initially, Lincoln hoped the war would be short and limited to the single objective of preserving the Union. On August 30, 1861, General John C. Fremont, commander of the Department of the West, issued a proclamation that freed the slaves of rebels in Missouri. Believing that a general had no authority to free slaves and fearing that such an emancipation edict would alienate Union supporters in the border slave states that had not seceded, Lincoln ordered Fremont to revise his proclamation so that it conformed with the Confiscation Act that Congress had approved in August 1861, which authorized the government to institute legal proceedings for the purpose of confiscating any property, including slaves, that was used to aid the rebellion. Lincoln's order was published in the newspapers and provoked the ire of abolitionists who believed that a decisive blow against slavery must be struck. Robert Hamilton (1819–1870) had recently revived the* Anglo-African *newspaper when he published the following editorial condemning Lincoln's action. Hamilton was frustrated with not only Lincoln's revocation of Fremont's emancipation decree but also the overall federal policy of not interfering with slavery. Despite the recently enacted Confiscation Act, military officers, such as General Nathaniel Banks and Colonel Abram Duryee of the Fifth New York, had allowed slaveholders to reclaim fugitive slaves. Although Hamilton is dismissive of the president's war powers, Lincoln would ultimately invoke those powers when he issued the Emancipation Proclamation.*

---

The reverse at Bull Run was a slight affair compared with the letter of Abraham Lincoln which hurls back into the hell of slavery the thousands in Missouri rightfully set free by the proclamation of Gen. Fremont, which deprives the cause of

the Union of its chiefest hold upon the heart of the public, and which gives to
the rebels "aid and comfort" greater than they could have gained from any other
earthly source.

Fremont, the pathfinder, deserves eternal gratitude from the just and the true,
for having found a way to expose to the public gaze the real source of the hesitation, vacillation and the half-and-half policy which has distinguished the government in the conduct of this war: now, we all know whom to blame; we can *see*
why officers in the army from major-generals (Banks) down to colonels (Duryea)
betrayed such indecent haste to send back to the enemy their fugitive slaves—it
was the sure road to Presidential favor, and to army promotion.

And yet we do not despair. The anti-slavery sentiment, the anti-slavery men
must see their course clearly and follow it out. They must appeal from the President to the people, and the people will sustain them. Mr. Lincoln rests upon the
Act of Congress as his authority for curtailing the "war power" which Fremont
exercised in accordance with the well ascertained public law, in such cases often
acted upon before. We must force Congress up to the proper platform and to an
Act of universal emancipation, by petition upon petition, such as will command
their action.

We have earnestly endeavored by letters and through friends, to urge upon
Gerrit Smith on the one hand, and the prominent members of the Garrison party
on the other hand, to take up the labor of urging upon the people to petition
Congress for IMMEDIATE EMANCIPATION. We have urged that *now* is the
time, when the nation is reeling under the blows of slavery, *now* is the time to
preach successfully their life-long doctrines of Immediate Emancipation, and to
load the tables of the coming Congress with the petitions of millions demanding
freedom for the slave as the only means of putting down rebellion and saving the
republic.

They have all replied in nearly the same strain. Some fear the excitement of
counter petitions, and all rely upon the "*war power*" to accomplish emancipation.
The war power indeed! Where is the war power now? A broken reed, dashed to
atoms with one stroke of the President's pen. Now then Abolition friends will
you suffer your own eyes to teach you? Will you take up the cause of Emancipation by a bold appeal to the people, by an overwhelming voice forcing Congress
to Act, or will you desert the slave when you may secure his freedom?

It is idle to trust any longer to the "war power," or to events for the accomplishment of Emancipation. The President is "set" upon upholding the slave system,
and is stubborn as a mule. The South is not slow to perceive this and can and
will manage him in such a way as to stave off emancipation. He would sooner die
than proclaim emancipation, unless overwhelmingly forced to do so by an Act of
Congress. To Congress, then let us appeal. Rouse the people.

This is the day's duty of all true abolitionists, and not an hour should be lost.

The forlorn hope of insurrection among the slaves may as well be abandoned. They are too well informed and too *wise* to court destruction at the hands of the combined Northern and Southern armies—for the man who has reduced back to slavery the slaves of rebels in Missouri would order the army of the United States to put down a slave insurrection in Virginia or Georgia.

Editorial in the *Anglo-African* (New York), September 21, 1861.

## JABEZ P. CAMPBELL, "The President and the Colored People," Trenton, New Jersey, October 1, 1861

*A native of Delaware, Campbell (1815–1891) was serving in New Jersey as a minister of the AME Church when he wrote the following response to Lincoln's August 12, 1861, proclamation that declared September 26 a day of fasting and prayer. In his proclamation, Lincoln suggested that the Civil War was a form of divine punishment and urged people to observe the day by praying "that our arms may be blessed and made effectual for the re-establishment of law, order and peace, throughout the wide extent of our country; and that the inestimable boon of civil and religious liberty, earned under His guidance and blessing, by the labors and sufferings of our fathers, may be restored in all its original excellence." Campbell shared the frustrations of Frederick Douglass and others who believed Lincoln was lagging behind Republicans in Congress and his generals, such as Benjamin F. Butler and John C. Fremont, who had taken action against slavery. Given the War Department's rejection of Black men who attempted to enlist in the army and Lincoln's determination to restore the Union without abolishing slavery, as evidenced by his recent rebuke of General Fremont's order freeing the slaves of rebels in Missouri, Campbell questioned whether African Americans were included when Lincoln urged "all the people of the nation" to participate in the fast day. In 1864, Campbell was elected a bishop of the AME Church* (Richard R. Wright Jr., Centennial Encyclopedia of the African Methodist Episcopal Church [Philadelphia: A. M. E. Book Concern, 1916], 58–59; Collected Works, 4: 482).

---

On the 12th of August, 1861, the President of these United States issued a proclamation setting apart the last Thursday in September, as a day of humiliation, prayer and fasting for all the people of the nation, and he earnestly recommended to all the people, and especially to all ministers and teachers of religion of all denominations, and to all heads of families, to observe and keep that day according to their several creeds and modes of worship, in all humility, and with all religious solemnity, to the end that the united prayer of the nation may ascend to the throne of grace, and bring down plentiful blessings upon our country.

Now, the question arises, Did the President, in all of this proclamation, or in any part of it, mean and intend to include the colored people? Did he intend the terms, "all the people of the nation," "all the people—all the ministers and teachers of religion, and heads of families,"—that the use of all these terms should, without distinction, embrace the two classes of white and black men? This is the greatest question upon which we are to give judgment. [...] To this question we return the emphatic answer: No, never! He intended no such thing; the class of black men were never intended by the President's proclamation. But some men will say, Why do you say so? What is the reason you have to assign, for saying or presuming to say, that he did not intend to include the class of black men? To the question in this shape we answer there are many reasons to be assigned, but we shall name only a few out of the many.

1st. The President is not now, and never was, either an abolitionist, or an anti-slavery man.

2d. He has no quarrel whatever with the south, upon the slavery question.

3d. He, his cabinet, and all of his official organs most steadily proclaim that this is not a war against slavery, but a war for the Union, to save slavery in the Union. The President intends that the Union shall be preserved as it was, when he came into power, the chief corner-stone of which was slavery.

4th. The President believes the Constitution of the United States to be a compromise, or an instrument of compromises between slavery and freedom.

5th. He holds the Dred Scott decision, which says that "Black men have no rights that white men are bound to respect," to be a part and parcel of the organic law of the land, which he is bound faithfully to execute. And for that very reason he would not treat slave property as suggested by General Butler, contraband in war, before the Special Congress took action upon the question. For that reason, after Congress met and took action, and passed an act by which the property of rebels shall become confiscated to the United States, he interfered with the proclamation of General Fremont, when he attempted to carry into effect the intention of the act of Congress, upon the slave property of rebels.

6th. It is to be most clearly seen in the refusal of the government to receive black men to be soldiers in the army, and absolutely refusing to let them bear arms against the rebels under the government.

7th. It is to be just as clearly seen in the recent order from the War Department commanding that no black man shall be allowed to wear soldier clothes, and those servants who are found with any regiment or company, being black men and having soldier clothes upon their backs, shall forthwith take them off. By all these acts the President means to show to the nation, both Union men and rebels, that he does not recognize black men, either expressly nor impliedly to be a part of this nation. But the proclamation for a day of humiliation, prayer, and fasting was addressed to all the people of this nation, especially ministers and teachers of religion, and heads of families, and to no other class of people or persons under the whole heaven. Foreign nations, aliens and negroes are not intended, and it would be doing violence to language, and offering an insult to common sense for an intelligent man to press the President's proclamation into any such service. [ . . . ]

If the President and his people would be heard and accepted, they must take their black brothers with them to the throne of grace.

*Christian Recorder* (Philadelphia, PA), Oct. 12, 1861.

## ROBERT HAMILTON, "The President's Message," December 7, 1861

*Lincoln sent his first Annual Message to Congress on December 3, 1861. Editor Robert Hamilton (1819–1870) was unimpressed, and he focused his criticism on two particular aspects of the message: Lincoln's recommendation that the United States offer diplomatic recognition to Haiti and Liberia and his endorsement of a federally funded plan to colonize slaves freed under the Confiscation Act that Congress had approved the previous August. The United States had refused to recognize Haiti and Liberia because the prospect of dealing with dark-skinned diplomats from those nations had been too much for most White Americans to stomach. Having gained its independence as a result of a successful slave uprising made recognition of Haiti all the more objectionable, especially to Southern slaveholders. With most slave states unrepresented in Congress during the rebellion, Republicans believed the time was opportune to offer recognition to the two nations. Congress followed Lincoln's recommendation and formal relations with the two countries began in 1862. The Confiscation Act, passed the previous summer, allowed the federal government to confiscate slaves that had been used to directly aid the rebellion. In his Annual Message, Lincoln suggested that those freed slaves be sent outside the United States at federal expense. While Hamilton doubted Lincoln's sincerity in recommending diplomatic recognition for Haiti and Liberia, he was convinced that the president genuinely desired to rid the nation of persons of color. In criticizing Lincoln's position on race, Hamilton referred to the fact that some of Lincoln's Kentucky in-laws supported the rebellion.*

One of the most amusing aspects of American caste-hate, is, when a white American not entirely free from its influence is placed in a position in which he is obliged to introduce a black, as a man, a gentleman, or a brother. It works against the grain most frightfully, and the contortions of face wherewith words are uttered which the soul believes out, are a perfect study. President Lincoln "makes mouths" after this fashion:

"If any good reason exists why we should remain longer in withholding our recognition of the independence and sovereignty of Hayti and Liberia, I am unable to discern it. Unwilling, however, to inaugurate a novel policy in regard to them without the approbation of Congress, I submit for your consideration the expediency of an appropriation for maintaining a Charge d'Affaires near each of those new States. It does not admit of doubt that important commercial advantages might be secured by favorable treaties with them."

In this paragraph the President evidently squirms as wretchedly in introducing two negro states into the family of nations, as he will one of these days when Mr. Seward shall introduce the black minister of Hayti to the chief magistrate of our Union. For we earnestly hope that both Hayti and Liberia will accede to no treaty of amity, &c., unless one of their citizens (who must be black) shall be accredited to this government. What does the President mean by "these *new* States?" Surely Hayti is a government at least sixty years old, and there is nothing new nor novel in the fact of its recognition by one of the great powers of the earth. [. . .]

*[The editorial then turns to Lincoln's colonization proposal and quotes a lengthy passage from the message.]*

Which means, being interpreted, "Gentlemen, I really don't know what to do with the irrepressible negro. I have said my say, and done the best I could. I cannot be too hard on my wife's relations. They are in rebellion to be sure; but they cannot, when conquered, live on equal terms with their former slaves. They are the government, I feel it, daily, and nightly. If you would have them perpetual this necessity must occur, the negro must be moved out of their sight. I say no more. You are wiser; do as you please about it, but, I beg you, spare their feelings. A few hundred or thousand millions, to pay them for slaves they have forfeited will be cheerfully borne by the Northern mudsills. A short war to acquire more territory to settle these freed negroes upon will just keep our hands in." As free colored men, we thank Mr. Lincoln for nothing, when he asks Congress to provide for the expatriation of such of us as may be desirous to leave the country. We are decidedly of the opinion that we will stay: any surplus change Congress may have can be appropriated "with our consent" to expatriate and settle elsewhere the surviving slaveholders.

Editorial in the *Anglo-African* (New York), December 7, 1861.

## ROBERT HAMILTON, "The Hanging of Gordon for Man Stealing," March 1, 1862

*On February 21, 1862, Nathaniel Gordon became the first and only American to be executed for participating in the international slave trade. Despite receiving numerous appeals to commute Gordon's sentence, Lincoln refused and instead only granted a temporary stay of execution so that Gordon would have adequate time to make "the necessary preparations for the awful change which awaits him." Editor Robert Hamilton (1819–1870) believed the execution of Gordon was just, and as the following indicates, he hoped that this symbolic statement against human trafficking would lead to further steps against slavery, regardless of the impact such action might have on border slave states, namely Kentucky. Hamilton also made reference to the death of the Lincolns' son, Willie, who had passed away on February 20.*

---

The firmness of President Lincoln in this affair is the most solid indication of character he has yet manifested. Whatever, in the coming hours, he may do to put down slavery, it is enough for the present that he has planted his broad foot squarely down upon the slave-trade; he need not move that foot, but only heft it a little more, and slavery already pale and trembling and laboring under self-induced convulsion will be squelched out also. God give him the grace, and keep away Kentucky advisers from him. It has pleased God at this hour to take from his household one little one who was the light and life thereof. O may the same power grant him to see and feel and alleviate the multiplied agonies of the millions to whom slavery says "you have no rights—your children are mine!"

Editorial in the *Anglo-African* (New York), March 1, 1862.

## HENRY MCNEAL TURNER on Lincoln's Proposal for Compensated Emancipation, March 16, 1862

*Born to free parents in South Carolina, Turner (1834–1915) was a minister of the AME Church when he penned the following letter to the editor of the* Christian Recorder *from Baltimore. On March 6, 1862, Lincoln had sent a message to Congress recommending that the federal government offer pecuniary assistance to any state that adopted a plan for the gradual abolition of slavery. While Lincoln's message marked the first time a president had proposed an abolition measure to Congress, Turner was not impressed, as he doubted its feasibility and believed the language of the message obfuscated the issue. Instead, he favored a more immediate and direct solution. After Congress failed to adopt Lincoln's*

*plan, the president drafted the Emancipation Proclamation. Appointed chaplain*
*of the 1st US Colored Infantry in September 1863, Turner served in the army*
*until September 1865. Turner was a member of the Georgia legislature during*
*Reconstruction and eventually became so disillusioned with race relations in the*
*United States that he advocated Black emigration to Africa in the 1890s (ANB;*
*Compiled military service record, Henry McNeal Turner, Chaplain, 1st US Col-*
*ored Infantry, M1819, Record Group 94, National Archives, Washington, DC).*

---

The late Message of President Lincoln to Congress, relative to emancipation, has given rise to more speculations, and created more surmises than any other document ever issued from the mansion halls of the White House; and likely no other Message ever, for the moment, was productive of so surreptitious suspense since this nation had its name. Its annunciation seems to benumb the most active intellects, and paralyze the most flippant tongues.

Both Houses of Congress were thrown into a mazy wonder, as to how they would unwind the intricate strata of its apparent preternatural syllabication. Collegiate sons, who had been reared on the bread of literature, and had prowled through the fields of classic lore, gleaning from every source language, constructibility, and how its convoluted reticulations should be dismembered, were paradoxically magnetized, from all appearance, or else logic, rhetoric, and analysis, were proving recreant to the noble trust for which they had been procured.

But passing on from Congressmen to the lower grades of society, we behold governors, State legislatures, mayors, City counsellors, police officers, political petit-maitres, Irishmen, Germans, women, children, and, last of all in God's universe, the Ethiopian, all making terrible strides to get the paper. The newspaper boys are flitting up and down the streets as on India rubber toes and wiry springing heels, proclaiming, as they go, *President Lincoln on emancipation!* Silence, say the inmates of many houses, (who never think of a paper.) What's that? The boy shrills out again—*President Lincoln on emancipation!* Get the paper, get the paper! say the rich, poor, white or colored, whoever he may be, for all must see. Accordingly, the paper is bought, regardless of price; and the way they go at reading it!—every one is spell-bound, the children all come around, with eager anxiety, to see what is the matter, they look as though a death-warrant had arrived, the old folks are all breathless, the reader proceeds to chatter out the message,—listen—be quiet,—

"*Resolved*, The United States ought to co-operate with any State which may adopt gradual abolishment of slavery, giving to such State pecuniary aid to be used by such State in its discretion, to compensate for the inconveniences, public and private, produced by such a change of system."

But at this juncture the baby wakes up, and countermands the silence by a few sonorous yells, (great confusion.) Every solace is offered, and unless the irritated child soon learns the art of muteness, it is hurried away to some sphere where its interrupting loquacity breaks not the incorporate charm that enshrines every fibre of the mind.

The Ethiopian, too, with all his untutoredness, verges out of his dreary iceberg cavern as if touched by the thawing sun of a freer day. Laying hold of the Message, he grapples, with Herculean strength, in untwisting its most technical terminologies, hoping to congratulate in the person of the President a Moses waving a mace of independence, with a voice waxing louder and louder, exclaiming, *Let my people go,*—hoping to hear freedom's birth heralded in tones of volcanic mutterings,—hoping it (the Message,) to be the Jesus of liberty coming to dethrone the Herod of tyranny,—hoping to hear the Jubilee trumpet, *Arise, ye slaves, and come to freedom!* but, alas, alas, *not yet*, is the echo. [...]

But what is the conclusion arrived at in relation to the true spirit of the Message? Sir, it is this:—A great many here have been blinded and made to believe that it portends hope for a brighter day; but I look at it as one of the most ingenious subterfuges, to pacify the humane and philanthropic hearts of the country, that was ever produced, and I believe it will result to the North what Senator Douglas's Squatter Sovereignty did to South Carolina. I have not time nor space to analyze the Message; but how some of our people can see so much in it to elate them, I cannot find out; for, after recommending it, it denies that Congress has any power to legislate on slavery—leaving it under the absolute control of individual States, with which control they have ever been invested. Before we raise our joys too high, mark this phrase,—*giving to such State pecuniary aid to be used by such State in its discretion*. In that phrase there is a broad field, a wide space, an ocean of thought.

"Turner on the President's Message," *Christian Recorder* (Philadelphia), March 22, 1862.

## ROBERT HAMILTON, "The Emancipation Message," March 22, 1862

*On March 6, 1862, President Lincoln sent a message to Congress recommending that the federal government provide financial assistance to any state that adopted a plan for gradual, compensated emancipation. Reaction to this proposal varied. While Henry McNeal Turner criticized the proposal for being vague and indirect (see above), the following editorial from the* Weekly Anglo-African *suggested the opposite. For editor Robert Hamilton (1819–1870), Lincoln's message offered a radical change in federal policy and portended the ultimate demise of slavery. This apparent sudden change of course led the editor to ask whether he was dreaming, and while it was easy for some to dismiss Lincoln's proposal, Hamilton noted the contrast between Lincoln suggesting a means of ending slavery and his predecessors in office who took steps to protect and strengthen the institution.*

———————

That the President of these United States sent a message to Congress proposing a means of securing the emancipation of the slaves, was an event which sent a thrill of joy throughout the North, and will meet with hearty response throughout christendom. The quiet manner in which this matter was laid before the national Legislature, and the utter unpreparedness of the public mind for this most important step, was a stroke of policy, grandly reticent on the part of its author, yet most timely and sagacious, which has secured for Abraham Lincoln a confidence and admiration on the part of the people, the whole loyal people, such as no man has enjoyed in the present era.

We could hardly believe the news. We dared not take up the message for a day or two, satisfied with the simple glory of the announcement, yet fearful that a reading of the document might send some shuddering doubt through a willingly rejoicing spirit. How many thousands there are, who exclaimed with the faithful man of old, "now lettest thou thy servant depart in peace!" But any doubts, all doubts were removed on the third or fourth reading of the message—for it will bear a close scrutiny—and now, when it is more than a week old it seems better and stronger than ever. It is not only cased in impregnable armor, but gives half silent evidence of power and will to blast the institution of slavery at any moment. It is the monitor which that rebellion had better heed.

The message contains a recommendation, an affirmation and a threat.

The recommendation is that Congress shall pass the following resolution:

"Resolved, That the United States ought to co-operate with any State which may adopt a gradual abolishment of slavery, giving to such State pecuniary aid, to be used by such State in its discretion to compensate for the inconveniences, public and private, produced by such change of system."

It is our opinion that Old Abe "cooned it on de log," when he produced that resolution. It passes the subtlety of Seward, the straight-forwardness of Stanton, or the skill of Chase. It is plainly home-spun, most definite in its indefiniteness. It is a solid offer of aid in well doing, yet requiring proof of "inconveniences" before the aid shall be forthcoming. Of course if no "inconveniences" arise, no pecuniary aid will be needed. Then again, the resolution once passed by Congress, quietly, but effectually places Congress along with the President on the side of emancipation, as willing aiders and abettors thereof. The moral sense of the nation will have found vent in a legislative decree in behalf of emancipation. Who would have been crazed enough, eighteen months ago, to have predicted such things? [ . . . ]

The affirmation in the message is, "The Federal Government would find its highest interest in such measure (the gradual abolishment of slavery) as one of the most efficient measures of self preservation." Is this a *"kalon oneiron,"* a spe-cious dream, or a sunshine reality? Can it be that the walls of that Cabinet in which Van Buren bowed down to slavery, in which Tyler nestled with the guilty upholders of slavery, in which Fillmore signed the damnable Fugitive Slave Bill, in which Buchanan paled and drivelled over the cups which treason held to his lips—can it be possible that the same four walls reverberated to the slight but portentious scratchings of the pen which wrote that grand sentence of freedom to four million of blacks and twenty-six millions of whites? If thousands have visited with awe the chambers at Fontainbleau in which the greatest genius of modern times abdicated an empire, with what reverence will they who come after us look upon the room where a plain single-minded but earnest man, elect of the people, signed the dethronement of the greatest evil which has cursed all time! That resolution, and this short sentence will be memorable in all time. It marks the grandest revolution of the ages, a revolution from barbarism to civilization, of darkness to light, of slavery into freedom. Of all the lands in which the sunshine rests where is there to day a nobler for the lover of freedom to dwell upon, be he black or white, bond or free?

But the crowning glory of this message is that it grows as it goes. When we get towards the last sentences they ring like an organ peal from the skies. "Such means as may seem indispensable, or may absolutely promise great efficiency towards ending the struggle, must and will come!" Which means, without inter-pretation, "I Abraham Lincoln, in order to crush this rebellion, will exercise the power invested in me as Commander-in-Chief of the army and navy of the United States—to abolish slavery!" Who could have prophesied this three months ago? Who? Why the down-trodden, degraded, beaten, bruised, crushed slaves all the way down South—wise with the inspiration of the good time coming who all give this one testimony: "I knowed it was a comin." Who? why the slaves whose dream of liberty blazed into a reality when they heard of Lincoln's election. They knew him better than he knew himself; their sight was keener than Seward's or Garrison's. Can we longer doubt that among the hidden things of Providence there must be an inspiration among men of their coming fortunes?

Editorial in the *Weekly Anglo-African* (New York), March 22, 1862.

## DANIEL ALEXANDER PAYNE, Account of Meeting with Lincoln, April 1862

*Born free in South Carolina, Payne (1811–1893) commenced his career as a Lutheran minister. By the time he met with Lincoln in April 1862, he was a bishop in the AME Church. Lincoln had long been a supporter of eliminat-ing slavery in the nation's capital. During his single term in the US House of*

*Representatives, he drafted a plan for compensated emancipation in Washington, DC, but he never formally introduced the proposal due to Southern opposition. In April 1862, Congress approved a District emancipation bill that made loyal slaveholders eligible to apply for compensation and appropriated funds to colonize freed persons who wished to leave the country. Payne wanted to make sure Lincoln signed the bill, and when he did on April 16, he informed Congress that he had "ever desired to see the national capital freed from the institution." The law freed over three thousand persons, and Lincoln appointed a three-member commission that reviewed petitions and determined the amount of compensation each slaveholder received. Payne later became president of Wilberforce University, wrote a history of the AME Church, and published his autobiography from which the following is an excerpt. A brief contemporary report of the meeting corroborates the favorable impression that Lincoln made upon the bishop (ANB; "District of Columbia Correspondence," Christian Recorder [Philadelphia, PA], April 26, 1862).*

---

Among the political wonders of the year was the emancipation of the slaves in the District of Columbia. [. . .] On Friday afternoon, April 11, 1862, Congress passed the bill abolishing slavery in the District of Columbia. The following Monday night I called on President Lincoln to know if he intended to sign the bill of emancipation, and thereby exterminate slavery in the District of Columbia? Having been previously informed of my intention to interview him, and having on my arrival at the White House sent in my card, he met me at the door of the room in which he and Senator Washburn were conversing. Taking me by the hand, he said: "Bishop Payne, of the African M. E. Church?" I answered in the affirmative; so with my hand in his he led me to the fireplace, introduced me to Senator Washburn, and seated me in an armchair between himself and the Senator. At that moment Senator Carl Schurz entered the room and seated himself on the right of Senator Washburn. With these preliminaries, I will now state the substance of our conversation. I said: "I am here to learn whether or not you intend to sign the bill of emancipation?" He answered and said: "There was a company of gentlemen here to-day requesting me by no means to sign it." To which Senator Schurz replied: "But, Mr. President, there will be a committee to beg that you fail not to sign it; for all Europe is looking to see that you fail not." Then said I: "Mr. President, you will remember that on the eve of your departure from Springfield, Ill., you begged the citizens of the republic to pray for you." He said, "Yes." Said I: "From that moment we, the colored citizens of the republic, have been praying: 'O Lord just as thou didst cause the throne of David to wax stronger and stronger, while that of Saul should wax weaker and weaker, so we beseech thee cause the power at Washington to grow stronger and stronger, while that at Richmond shall grow weaker and weaker.'" Slightly bending his head, the President said: "Well, I must believe that God has led me thus far, for I am conscious that I never would have accomplished what has been done if he had not been with me to counsel and to shield." But neither Carl Schurz nor I could induce him to say "Yes" or "No" to our direct question.

I had now consumed about three-quarters of an hour of his time, and felt that it was my duty to withdraw. So, putting into his hand copies of the Christian Recorder and our monthly magazine, I told him that if he could find a leisure moment to look over them he would be able to see what the AME Church was doing to improve the character and condition of our people in the republic. There was nothing stiff or formal in the air and manner of His Excellency—nothing egotistic. [ . . . ] President Lincoln received and conversed with me as though I had been one of his intimate acquaintances or one of his friendly neighbors. I left him with a profound sense of his real greatness and of his fitness to rule a nation composed of almost all the races on the face of the globe.

In Daniel Alexander Payne, *Recollections of Seventy Years* (Nashville: A. M. E. Sunday School Union, 1888), 146–148.

## HENRY HIGHLAND GARNET on Emancipation in Washington, DC, May 12, 1862

*Born to enslaved parents in Maryland, Garnet (1815–1882) escaped with his family to New York. He studied at the Oneida Institute and became a Presbyterian minister. In addition to being an abolitionist, Garnet helped found the African Civilization Society and promoted emigration to Africa. During the Civil War, Garnet was minister at the Fifteenth Street Presbyterian Church in Washington, and he became the first African American to speak in the House Chamber of the US Capitol when he delivered a sermon there in February 1865 to commemorate Congress's approval of the Thirteenth Amendment. African Americans in New York celebrated the emancipation of slaves in Washington on May 12 with a series of events that culminated with an evening program at the Cooper Institute, where Garnet and others spoke. Garnet perceived great significance in Lincoln signing the District emancipation bill and believed that it was part of a larger strategy that would ultimately result in the complete abolition of slavery throughout the nation (ANB; the* Liberator *[Boston], May 23, 1862).*

---

Mr. Garnet said that he stood before the largest colored audience ever assembled in the great metropolis of the Empire State. A stranger looking on would be led to ask, What means this great gathering of joyful souls? He would tell them that they had come together to commemorate the abolition of slavery in the

National Capital, for the Capital of our country is now free. (Applause and continued cheering.) On the 16th of April, about 2 o'clock, the President dipped his pen in ink, moved it upon a parchment, and the shackles fell from the limbs of every bondman within the limits of that beautiful spot bearing the sacred name of Washington. At this hour, slavery fell prostrate; opened her lank jaws, snapped her snaggy teeth, and with a spasmodic kick gave up the ghost. He believed President Lincoln's mind was made up to sign the bill long before it was passed. He believed President Lincoln to be one of the first statesmen and rulers in the nation, whose tardiness he belikened to a hostler with a vicious horse, who first cautiously slicks down the animal and then takes him with a master's hand by the mane. By the act of Emancipation in the District of Columbia the death blow has been struck upon the head of Slavery and though its tail, like the snakes, may wriggle about for a while, it must die before sundown.

*Pacific Appeal* (San Francisco, CA ), July 12, 1862.

## PHILIP A. BELL on Lincoln's Revocation of Gen. Hunter's Emancipation Decree, June 14, 1862

*Philip A. Bell (1809–1889) was an abolitionist who worked for an African American newspaper in New York City before moving to San Francisco in the late 1850s. Bell was editor of the* Pacific Appeal *when it commenced publication in 1862. He later became editor of* The Elevator, *another African American newspaper in San Francisco that competed with the* Appeal. *Here, Bell is critical of Lincoln's decision to revoke General David Hunter's General Orders No. 11, issued on May 9, 1862. Hunter was commander of the Department of the South, an area that included the states of South Carolina, Georgia, and Florida, and his order declared that all slaves in those states were "forever free." Hunter had issued the order without consulting authorities in Washington. In revoking Hunter's order, Lincoln asserted that generals did not have the legal authority to emancipate slaves, as that war power belonged solely to the president. Bell and other abolitionists were frustrated by what they perceived as yet another act by Lincoln to forestall emancipation. Edward Stanly, the military governor of occupied North Carolina, was also under scrutiny for allegedly preventing the education of Black children (DANB).*

---

We have refrained, hitherto, from commenting on President Lincoln's Pro-Slavery Proclamation in reference to the proclamation issued by Gen. Hunter, declaring the slaves free in the department of the South, over which he had military command, in hopes that the President only denied that Gen. Hunter had "been authorized by the Government to make any proclamation declaring slaves free," in order that action in the premises might come from the highest source, *i.e.* the President himself, moreover, he intimates in his proclamation that he is yet undecided. He says, "whether it is competent for him, as Commander-in-Chief of the army and navy, to declare slaves in any State free, and whether at any time it shall become necessary and indispensable for the maintenance of Government to exercise such supposed power, are questions which he reserves to himself, and which he cannot feel justified in leaving to the decision of commanders in the field."

The President exhibits as much tergiversation as ever did our New York Magician, as Martin Van Buren was called, in former days. He is as non-committal as that "Northern man with Southern principles."

Recent dispatches, however, have given us to understand that the Cabinet has revoked Gen. Hunter's proclamation, and hence slavery is still recognized in the department of the South. We thought from President Lincoln's confiscation messages, his emancipation recommendations and other liberal actions, that it was his intention to strike at the root of the tree of strife. We supposed he was possessed of judgment sufficient to know that it was useless to lop off the extraneous branches, and leave the trunk of the Upas of discord and disunion—slavery—still standing to branch forth again and diffuse its malignant and pestiferous poison over the land; and we still hope he will abide by the principles he has hitherto avowed, on the strength of which he was elected. [ . . . ]

We fear the Administration is pursuing a course detrimental to the best interests of the country, and encouraging the Rebels in their efforts to overthrow the Union, and perpetuate slavery. [ . . . ]

We also fear, by the course he is pursuing, the President will alienate his ablest generals from him, and he will be unable to find capable men to take command of departments most infected with the evil. He must either grant them unrestricted power, or appoint such ingrates as Edward Stanly.

Editorial in the *Pacific Appeal* (San Francisco), June 14, 1862.

## EDWARD M. THOMAS to Abraham Lincoln, Washington, DC, August 16, 1862

*A leader in the Washington, DC, African American community, Thomas (c. 1820–1863) chaired a delegation of Black men from Washington that had met with Lincoln on August 14 to hear the president's proposal to colonize former slaves in Central America. The meeting and Lincoln's address received extensive press coverage. Thomas's willingness to give serious consideration to Lincoln's plan put him at odds with many in the community. While a response from Lincoln to the following letter has not been located, Jacob Van Vleet, an editor of the Wash-ington* National Republican, *provided one hundred dollars to Thomas and a colleague for the purpose of visiting northern cities and discussing Lincoln's plan. Thomas's acceptance of money from Van Vleet provoked further controversy (see Lincoln Papers, Series 1, General Correspondence, 1833 to 1916: "Jacob R. S. Van Vleet to Abraham Lincoln, Sunday, August 17, 1862, [Introduction]" https:// www.loc.gov/item/mal1772900; "Defence of Edward M. Thomas," the* Anglo-African *[New York], Jan. 3, 10, 1863; "Died,"* Christian Recorder *[Philadelphia, PA], March 21, 1863; Kate Masur, "The African American Delegation to Abra-ham Lincoln: A Reappraisal,"* Civil War History *56, no. 2 (2010): 117–144; for Lincoln's remarks on the occasion, see* Collected Works *V: 370–75; additional responses to Lincoln's proposal are included in this volume).*

---

Sir

We would respectfully Suggest that it is necessary that we Should confer with leading colored men in Phila New York and Boston upon this movement of emi-gration to the point reccommended in your address

We were entirely hostile to the movement until all the advantages were so ably brought to our views by you and we believe that our friends and co-laborers for our race in those cities will when the Subject is explained by us to them join heartily in Sustaining Such a movement

It is therefore Suggested in addition to what is Stated that you authorize two of us to proceed to these cities and place your views before them to facilitate and promote the object. We desire no appointment only a letter from your hand Say-ing you wish us to consult with our leading friends. As this is part of the move-ment to obtain a proper plan of colonization we would respectfully Suggest to your Excellency that the necessary expenses of the two (or more if you desire) be paid from the fund appropriated.

It is our belief that Such a conference will lead to an active and zealous Support of this measure by the leading minds of our people and that this Support will lead to the realization of the fullest Success, within the Short time of two weeks from our departure the assurance can be Sent you of the result of our mission and that a Success

I have the honor to be your
Excellencies Obt St
Edward M. Thomas
chairman

Lincoln Papers, Series 1, General Correspondence, 1833 to 1916: "Edward M. Thomas to Abraham Lincoln, Saturday, August 16, 1862 (Seeks Interview)," https://www.loc.gov /item/mal1771700/.

## FREDERICK DOUGLASS, "The President and His Speeches," September 1862

*Many African Americans felt compelled to respond to the White House meeting that occurred on August 14, 1862, when Lincoln urged a delegation of free Black men from Washington to give serious consideration to colonization. Lincoln hoped they would help start a colony in Central America that would be sustained by mining coal and selling it to the US Navy. Not only did the subject and tone of Lincoln's remarks outrage Douglass but he was also particularly incensed by Lincoln's claim that the mere presence of persons of African descent in the country was the cause of the war. The other speech Douglass commented upon was delivered at a Union rally in front of the Capitol on August 6, where Lincoln stated that both Secretary of War Edwin Stanton and General George McClellan wanted the army to succeed, and that the secretary was not responsible for withholding any supplies or reinforcements from the general. Douglass further criticized Lincoln's handling of the war by noting that Congress had enacted measures against slavery, yet Lincoln and his generals, Henry W. Halleck in particular, were apparently failing to enforce those measures.*

---

The President of the United States seems to possess an ever increasing passion for making himself appear silly and ridiculous, if nothing worse. Since the publication of our last number he has been unusually garrulous, characteristically foggy, remarkably illogical and untimely in his utterances, often saying that which nobody wanted to hear, and studiously leaving unsaid about the only things which the country and the times imperatively demand of him. Our garrulous and joking President has favored the country and the world with two speeches, which if delivered by any other than the President of the United States, would attract no more attention than the funny little speeches made in front of the arcade by our friend John Smith, inviting customers to buy his razor strops.—One of the speeches of the President was made at a war meeting in Washington in vindication of Mr. Stanton, and in justification of himself against the charge that he had failed to send reinforcements to Gen. McClellan. [ . . . ]

The other and more important communication of the President it appears was delivered in the White House before a committee of colored men assembled by his invitation. In this address Mr. Lincoln assumes the language and arguments of an itinerant Colonization lecturer, showing all his inconsistencies, his pride of race and blood, his contempt for negroes and his canting hypocrisy. How an honest man could creep into such a character as that implied by this address we are not required to show. The argument of Mr. Lincoln is that the difference between the white and black races renders it impossible for them to live together in the same country without detriment to both. Colonization therefore, he holds to be the duty and the interest of the colored people. Mr. Lincoln takes care in urging his colonization scheme to furnish a weapon to all the ignorant and base, who need only the countenance of men in authority to commit all kinds of violence and outrage upon the colored people of the country. Taking advantage of his position and of the prevailing prejudice against them he affirms that their presence in the country is the real first cause of the war, and logically enough, if the premises were sound, assumes the necessity of their removal.

It does not require any great amount of skill to point out the fallacy and expose the unfairness of the assumption, for by this time every man who has an ounce of brain in his head—no matter to which party he may belong, and even Mr. Lincoln himself must know quite well that the mere presence of the colored race never could have provoked this horrid and desolating rebellion. Mr. Lincoln knows that in Mexico, Central America and South America, many distinct races live peaceably together in the enjoyment of equal rights, and that the civil wars which occasionally disturb the peace of those regions never originated in the difference of the races inhabiting them. A horse thief pleading that the existence of the horse is the apology for his theft or a highway man contending that the money in the traveler's pocket is the sole first cause of his robbery are about as much entitled to respect as is the President's reasoning at this point. No, Mr. President, it is not the innocent horse that makes the horse thief, not the traveler's purse that makes the highway robber, and it is not the presence of the negro that causes this foul and unnatural war, but the cruel and brutal cupidity of those who wish to possess horses, money and negroes by means of theft, robbery, and rebellion. Mr. Lincoln further knows or ought to know at least that negro hatred and prejudice of color are neither original nor invincible vices, but merely the offshoots of that root of all crimes and evils—slavery. [ . . . ]

Illogical and unfair as Mr. Lincoln's statements are, they are nevertheless quite in keeping with his whole course from the beginning of his administration up to this day, and confirms the painful conviction that though elected as an anti-slavery man by Republican and Abolition voters, Mr. Lincoln is quite a genuine representative of American prejudice and negro hatred and far more concerned for the preservation of slavery, and the favor of the Border Slave States, than for any sentiment of magnanimity or principle of justice and humanity. This address of his leaves us less ground to hope for anti-slavery action at his hands than any of his previous utterances. Notwithstanding his repeated declarations that he considers slavery an evil, every step of his Presidential career relating to slavery proves him active, decided, and brave for its support, and passive, cowardly, and treacherous to the very cause of liberty to which he owes his election. This speech of the President delivered to a committee of free colored men in the capital explains the animus of his interference with the memorable proclamation of

General Fremont. A man who can charge this war to the presence of colored men in this country might be expected to take advantage of any legal technicalities for arresting the cause of Emancipation, and the vigorous prosecution of the war against slaveholding rebels. To these colored people, without power and without influence the President is direct, undisguised, and unhesitating. He says to the colored people: I don't like you, you must clear out of the country. So too in dealing with anti-slavery Generals the President is direct and firm. He is always brave and resolute in his interferences in favor of slavery, remarkably unconcerned about the wishes and opinions of the people of the north; apparently wholly indifferent to the moral sentiment of civilized Europe; but bold and self reliant as he is in the ignominious service of slavery, he is as timid as a sheep when required to live up to a single one of his anti-slavery testimonies. He is scrupulous to the very letter of the law in favor of slavery, and a perfect latitudinarian as to the discharge of his duties under a law favoring freedom. When Congress passed the Confiscation Bill, made the Emancipation of the slaves of rebels the law of the land, authorized the President to arm the slaves which should come within the lines of the Federal army, and thus removed all technical objections, everybody who attached any importance to the President's declarations of scrupulous regard for law, looked at once for a proclamation emancipating the slaves and calling the blacks to arms. But Mr. Lincoln, formerly so strict and zealous in the observance of the most atrocious laws which ever disgraced a country, has not been able yet to muster courage and honesty enough to obey and execute that grand decision of the people. He evaded his obvious duty, and instead of calling the blacks to arms and to liberty he merely authorized the military commanders to use them as laborers, without even promising them their freedom at the end of their term of service to the government, and thus destroyed virtually the very object of the measure. Further when General Halleck issued his odious order No 3, excluding fugitive slaves from our lines, an order than which none could be more serviceable to the slaveholding rebels, since it was a guarantee against the escape of their slaves, Mr. Lincoln was deaf to the outcry and indignation which resounded through the north, and west, and saw no occasion for interference, though that order violated a twice adopted resolution of Congress. When General McClellan employed our men guarding rebel property and even when Gen. Butler committed the outrage paralleled only by the atrocities of the rebels—delivering back into bondage thousands of slaves—Mr. Lincoln again was mute and did not feel induced to interfere in behalf of outraged humanity.

The tone of frankness and benevolence which he assumes in his speech to the colored committee is too thin a mask not to be seen through. The genuine spark of humanity is missing in it, no sincere wish to improve the condition of the oppressed has dictated it. It expresses merely the desire to get rid of them, and reminds one of the politeness with which a man might try to bow out of his house some troublesome creditor or the witness of some old guilt. We might also criticize the style adopted, so exceedingly plain and coarse threaded as to make the impression that Mr. L. had such a low estimate of the intelligence of his audience, as to think any but the simplest phrases and constructions would be above their power of comprehension. As Mr. Lincoln however in all his writings has manifested a decided awkwardness in the management of the English language, we do not think there is any intention in this respect, but only the incapacity to do better.

*Douglass' Monthly* (Rochester, NY), Sept. 1862.

## Resolutions of Newtown, New York Meeting on Lincoln's Colonization Proposal, August 20, 1862

*Lincoln's August 14, 1862, meeting at the White House with a delegation of free Black men from Washington for the purpose of urging them to consider a colonization plan evoked many responses. The following reply from a meeting of African Americans in New York highlights the primary obstacle to colonization: the overwhelming conviction that the United States was home, and it was insulting to assume that African Americans were any less attached to the country than persons of European descent. This response also highlights the vital role Black people had played in both building and defending the nation and notes their willingness to take up arms to defend the Union, abolish slavery, and make the promise of equality in the Declaration of Independence a reality for all Americans.*

At a mass meeting of the colored people of Newtown, L.I., held on the 20th ult., the following reply to the President's Address on Colonization was read and adopted:—

We, the colored citizens of Queen's Co., N.Y., having met in mass meeting, according to public notice, to consider the speech of Abraham Lincoln, President of the United States, addressed to a Committee of Free Colored Men, called at his request at the White House in Washington, on Thursday, Aug. 14, 1862, and to express our views and opinions of the same; and whereas, the President desires to know in particular our views on the subject of being colonized in Central America or some other foreign country, we will take the present opportunity to express our opinions most respectfully and freely, since as loyal Union colored Americans and Christians we feel bound to do so.

*First.* We rejoice that we are colored Americans, but deny that we are a "different race of people," as God has made of one blood all nations that dwelt on the face of the earth, and has hence no respect of men in regard to color, neither ought men to have respect to color, as they have not made themselves or their color.

*Second.* The President calls our attention particularly to this question—"Why should we leave this country?" This, he says, is perhaps the first question for proper consideration. We will answer this question by showing why we should remain in it. This is our country by birth, consequently we are acclimated, and in other respects better adapted to it than to any other country. This is our native country; we have as strong attachment naturally to our native hills, valleys, plains, luxuriant forests, flowing streams, mighty rivers, and lofty mountains, as any other people. Nor can we fail to feel a strong attachment to the whites with whom our blood has been commingling from the earliest days of this our country. Neither can we forget and disown our white kindred. This is the country of our choice, being our fathers' country.

*Third.* Again, we are interested in its welfare above every other country; we love this land, and have contributed our share to its prosperity and wealth. This we have done by cutting down forests, subduing the soil, cultivating fields, constructing roads, digging canals. We have, too, given our aid in building cities and villages, in building and supporting churches and schools. We have aided in procuring its mineral resources, as coal, iron, and the precious metals; helped in the construction of railroads, bridges, telegraph lines, steamboats and ships; assisted in cattle-breeding, raising various kinds of produce, as corn, wheat, oats, potatoes, cotton, rice, tobacco, the leading staples of the country, &c. In these ways, and many others too numerous to be named here, have we aided the nation in her growth and progress, and contributed to her general prosperity.

*Fourth.* Again, we believe, too, we have the right to have applied to ourselves those rights named in the Declaration of Independence, "that all men are born free and equal, and have certain inalienable rights, among which are life, liberty, and the pursuit of happiness,"—rights which we have derived from the Creator,— since we helped to gain our country's independence, under Washington, on her battle-fields as well as in the corn-fields, and we helped to maintain the same in 1814 under General Jackson at New Orleans, and are willing and ready even now to fight our country's battles against slaveholding traitors and rebels, who are slaying thousands of freemen, and seeking the very life-blood of the nation; and we hope and believe that the time is not far distant when, instead of being called upon to leave our country, the loyal and just people of the country will pass judgment on the men who stopped the million of our brave hearts, strong arms and willing hands, desiring to fight our country's battles in her most trying hour and sorest need. While bleeding and struggling for her life against slaveholding traitors, and at this very time, when our country is struggling for life, and one million freemen are believed to be scarcely sufficient to meet the foe, we are called upon by the President of the United States to leave this land, and go to another country, to carry out his favorite scheme of colonization. But at this crisis, we feel disposed to refuse the offers of the President, since the call of our suffering country is too loud and imperative to be unheeded.

Again, the President says that Congress has placed a sum of money at his disposition for the purpose of aiding the colonization of the people of African descent, or some portion of them, in some country; therefore making it his duty, as it had been a long time his inclination, to favor that course. Our answer is this: There is no country like our own. Why not declare slavery abolished, and favor our peaceful colonization in the rebel States, or some portion of them? We are all in favor of this, and we believe the majority of those who elected you to the office of the chief magistrate of the nation are in favor, also, of this measure. We believe that this would be a wise and just policy, and would receive the approbation of God and all good men. We would cheerfully return there, and give our most willing aid to deliver our loyal colored brethren and other Unionists from the tyranny of rebels to our Government.

We colored people are all loyal men, which is more than any other class of people in the country can say. There are Yankee, English, Scotch, German and French rebels, but no colored rebels; and let us add, Mr. President, that no one suffers by our presence but rebels and traitors: and if we were permitted to fight our country's battles, and an army of colored men were permitted to march into those rebel States, well armed and equipped, we believe, with your Excellency, that the rebels would suffer from our presence, but the Union would be saved without spades and shovels.

Congress has also passed the Confiscation and Emancipation bill. Now, if the President is disposed to give the colored people the benefits guaranteed by that bill, and declare the Rebel States Free States, we would colonize ourselves in our native States, without the aid of the Government, and the President might use the money to defray the expenses of the war.

In conclusion, we would say that, in our belief, the speech of the President has only served the cause of our enemies, who wish to insult and mob us, as we have, since its publication, been repeatedly insulted, and told that we must leave the country. Hence we conclude that the policy of the President toward the colored people of this country *is a mistaken policy.*

"Reply to the President by the Colored People of Newtown, L.I.," the *Liberator* (Boston), Sept. 12, 1862.

## ALFRED P. SMITH, Letter to President Lincoln in Response to Colonization Proposal, Saddle River, New Jersey, September 5, 1862

*Smith (1832–1901) was a New Jersey native who edited a newspaper in his hometown of Saddle River after the Civil War. Here, Smith takes issue with a statement Lincoln had made during the August 14 colonization meeting that asserted White people and Black people were of separate races. Smith also refers to the recent opening of official diplomatic relations between the United States and Haiti. The prospect of receiving a dark-skinned Haitian diplomat had long been an obstacle to the United States' recognition of Haiti, and Lincoln had allegedly claimed that he would have no objections if President Fabre Geffrard sent a Black diplomat to Washington. Like others who objected to Lincoln's proposal, Smith viewed the United States as his home, and the notion that African Americans should leave to mine coal in Central America was as absurd as suggesting that Lincoln and his generals do the same (Maxine N. Lurie, ed.,* The Encyclopedia of New Jersey *[New Brunswick, NJ: Rutgers University Press, 2004], 750).*

———————

As you are awaiting a reply from the negroes of the country to your recent colonization proposition, you will not, I trust, think it strange that an humble person like myself should venture to address you. Not long since, I was highly gratified by the assurance you, sir, are reported to have given President Geffrard, that you will not tear your shirt even if he does send a negro to Washington. This assurance is also very encouraging to me at the present time, as I am unable to see why a native American negro should be more objectionable to you than one belonging to a foreign country. Should I, however, manifest extraordinary stupidity in my remarks, please, sir, to extend your gracious pardon, and be kind enough to attribute all my perversity to the tightness of my hair, which may render my cranium impervious to your most cogent reasoning.

In the outset, good Mr. President, permit me to congratulate you on your good fortune in having a sum of money placed at your disposal in times like these. In this respect, sir, (especially if it is in specie,) you are highly favored above ordinary mortals. Could you now but, also, enjoy the luxury of spending it, for the benefit of those philanthropic coal speculators you refer to, I can well believe that you might feel yourself raised to the highest pinnacle of human happiness.

The simplicity, good sir, with which you assume that colored Americans should be expatriated, colonized in some foreign country, is decidedly rich—cool and refreshing as the breezes of "Egypt," or the verdure of your prairie home. The assertions, however, you do make in favor of your assumption, are worthy of a passing notice. If admitted, they would make sad havoc with the doctrines that have been cherished by the good and great of all ages. Different races, indeed! Let me tell you, sir, President though you are, there is but one race of men on the face of the earth:—One Lord, one faith, one baptism, one God and Father of all, who is above all, and through all, and in all. Physical differences no doubt there are; no two persons on earth are exactly alike in this respect; but what of that? In physical conformation, you, Mr. President, may differ somewhat from the negro, and also from the majority of white men; you may even, as you intimate, feel this difference on your part to be very disadvantageous to you; but does it follow that therefore you should be removed to a foreign country? Must you and I and Vice-President Hamlin, and all of us, submit to a microscopic examination of our hair, to determine whether the United States or Central America should be our future home? [. . .]

Pray tell us, is our right to a home in this country less than your own, Mr. Lincoln? Read history, if you please, and you will learn that more than two centuries ago, Mr. White-man and Mr. Black-man settled in this country together. The negro, sir, was here in the infancy of the nation, he was here during its growth, and we are here to-day. If, through all these years of sorrow and affliction, there is one thing for which we have been noted more than all else, it is our love of country, our patriotism. In peace, the country has been blessed with our humble labor, nor have we ever been found wanting in the times that have tried the souls of men. We were with Warren on Bunker Hill, with Washington at Morristown and Valley Forge, with LaFayette at Yorktown, with Perry, Decatur, and McDonough in their cruisings, and with Jackson at New Orleans, battling side by side with the white man for nationality, national rights, and national glory. And when the history of the present atrocious insurrection is written, the historian will record: "Whoever was false, the blacks were true." Would you, then, in truckling subserviency to the sympathizers with this bloody rebellion, remove the purest patriotism the country affords? If you would, let me tell you, sir, you cannot do it. Neither fraud nor force can succeed, but by the fatal ruin of the country. Are you an American? So are we. Are you a patriot? So are we. Would you spurn all absurd, meddlesome, impudent propositions for your colonization in a foreign country? So do we.

I trust, good Mr. President, you will not rend your garments when I tell you that the question of colonization, so persistently thrust upon us by the heartless traders in the woes of a bleeding people, has long been settled by a unanimous determination to remain, and survive or perish, rise or fall with the country of our birth. In our conventions, conferences, &c., again and again, in the most emphatic language, we have declared our utter detestation of this colonization scheme, whatever form it may assume.

In holy horror, disinterested sir, you may hold up your hands at what you choose to denominate the "selfishness" of the unalterable resolution; but pray tell us, is it any more selfish than your own determination to remain here, instead of emigrating to some petty foreign country; and it is as selfish as the desire to exclude us from a country where there is room enough for ten times the present population; or is it, think you, as selfish as the coal traders, and the swarms of contractors, agents, &c., for whose benefit you are so anxious to spend some of the money our liberal Congress has placed at your disposal? If it is selfishness, please, sir, to remember your own plea for the coal speculations, &c., viz.: all persons look to their self-interest.

But say, good Mr. President, why we, why anybody should swelter, digging coal, if there be any, in Central America? In that country where the sun blazes with a fervor unknown in these high latitudes, where a broad-brimmed Panama, a cigar and a pair of spurs are considered a comfortable costume for the natives, why should we, why should anybody dig coal? Do tell. Might we not just as well dig ice on the coast of Labrador? But, say you: "Coal land is the best thing I know of to begin an enterprise." Astounding discovery! Worthy to be recorded in golden letters, like the Luna Cycle in the temple of Minerva. "Coal land, sir!" Pardon, Mr. President, if my African risibilities get the better of me, if I do show my ivories whenever I read that sentence! Coal land, sir! If you please, sir, give McClellan some, give Halleck some, and by all means, save a little strip for yourself.

Twenty-five negroes digging coal in Central America! Mighty plan! Equal to about twenty-five negroes splitting rails in Sangamon!

It was my intention to have shown you, sir, the necessity of retaining the labor of the negroes in the South as freemen, but space will not permit. According to theory, white men can't stand it, can't live *honestly* in the South: we can. Henceforth, then, let this be the motto: "The Gulf States, purged of traitors, the home of the loyal, emancipated blacks!" And then, good sir, if you have any nearer friends than we are, let them have that coal-digging job.

"A Colored Man's Reply to President Lincoln on Colonization," the *Liberator* (Boston), Sept. 5, 1862.


## FRANCES ELLEN WATKINS HARPER on Lincoln's Colonization Proposal, September 27, 1862

*A Maryland native, Harper (1825–1911) was a poet and novelist who played an active role in a variety of reform organizations, including the American Anti-Slavery Society and the Women's Christian Temperance Union, and she was one of the founders of the National Association of Colored Women. In addition to writing and lecturing, she also worked as a teacher. Here, Harper dismisses Lincoln's colonization proposal and suggests that the leader of the nation must possess a heart that values the abolition of slavery more than preserving a Union with slavery. In suggesting that the war was a form of divine punishment for the sin of slavery, Harper anticipates a theme that Lincoln would explore in his Second Inaugural Address (ANB).*

---

Heavy is the guilt that hangs upon the neck of this nation, and where is the first sign of national repentance? The least signs of contrition for the wrongs of the Indian or the outrages of the negro? As this nation has had glorious opportunities for standing as an example to the nations leading the van of the world's progress, and inviting the groaning millions to a higher destiny; but instead of that she has dwarfed herself to slavery's base and ignoble ends, and now, smitten of God and conquered by her crimes, she has become a mournful warning, a sad exemplification of the close connexion between national crimes and national judgments. [...]

The country needs a leader, high and strong, and bold and brave: his heart the home of great and noble purposes, who would count the greatest victory worse than a shameful defeat if resubjugation of the South should only mean a reconstruction of the Union on its old basis.

As to the colonization scheme, give yourself no uneasiness. If Jeff. Davis does not colonize Lincoln out of Washington, let him be thankful. The President's dabbling with colonization just now suggests to my mind the idea of a man almost dying with a loathsome cancer, and busying himself about having his hair trimmed according to the latest fashion. I anticipate no fresh trouble to our people from this movement. Let the President be answered firmly and respectfully, not in the tones of supplication and entreaty, but of earnestness and decision, that while we admit the right of every man to choose his home, that we neither see the wisdom nor expediency of our self-exportation from a land which has been in a measure enriched by our toil for generations, till we have a birth-right on the soil, and the strongest claims on the nation for that justice and equity which has been withheld from us for ages—ages whose accumulated wrongs have dragged the present wars that overshadow our head. And even were we willing to go, is the nation able to part with us? What Christian land under heaven is able to part with four millions of its laboring population? And should this country ever emerge from this dreadful war, with its resources diminished, its strength crippled, and industry paralyzed, will it not want our labor to help rebuild the ravages of war and the wastes of carnage? [...]

O, be hopeful, my friend! Upon our side of the controversy stands God himself, and this gives us a solemn and sublime position. A people thus situated may lift up their heads and take courage in the hope of a sure and speedy redemption.

*Christian Recorder* (Philadelphia), Sept. 27, 1862.

## PHILIP A. BELL on the Preliminary Emancipation Proclamation, September 27, 1862

*Editor Philip A. Bell (1809–1889) welcomed the news of Lincoln's Preliminary Emancipation Proclamation that had been issued on September 22. While Bell regretted that the proclamation did not indicate Black men would be used as soldiers, he hoped that the* New York Herald *and other skeptics would be proven wrong in suggesting that the White population of the northern and western states would not support this revolutionary new policy.*

The great principles embodied in this astounding document were flashed across the continent with the news of Tuesday last. Being somewhat anticipated, from recent rumors and unofficial reports, its reception was not marked by any very great degree of surprise or amazement on the part of the public press or the people generally. But though no firing of cannon was heard from the hill-tops, and no flags were displayed for this special occasion, the Proclamation was, nevertheless, read and discussed with intense interest. A murmur might have been heard, here and there, from the groups that could be seen in earnest conversation, apparently discussing the merits of the great topic which the telegraph had just announced, but there was not much excitement and no noisy demonstration of any kind. But still the subject increases in interest, as its mighty import becomes more thoroughly comprehended, and day by day, new consequence is added to the Proclamation.

The city press has already been bold in expressing its approbation of the President's intended course; but the enthusiasm of the people is in contrast with that manifested on the announcement, some time ago, that the President would not accept the services of colored men as soldiers, but would as laborers. "Straws sometimes signify which way the wind blows." [...]

The opinion expressed above by the New York *Herald*, with regard to the revolutionizing effect upon labor, in carrying out this great emancipation measure of the President, applies, to a great extent, to the Northern States, including California, and intimates that those States are not in favor of emancipation as a war measure. This, if true, is to be regretted; but we believe the *Herald* to be mistaken, that it will live to correct its own opinions in this matter, and see the entire concurrence of the North and West in the policy of the President as being statesmanlike, as well as patriotic and humane. While to our race it is the harbinger of so much that is gratifying, our joy would be tinged with a sadness insufferable to think that the American people at large were not eventually to be blessed thereby. It will help immensely in crushing the rebellion, and saving the

Union, and put the nation immeasurably forward of its former self in the path of civilization and progress.

*Pacific Appeal* (San Francisco), Sept. 27, 1862.

## FREDERICK DOUGLASS, "Emancipation Proclaimed," October 1862

*Douglass (1818–1895) had been among Lincoln's harshest critics for failing to take decisive action against slavery and for endorsing colonization. Douglass opened the October 1862 issue of his monthly newspaper with the following response to Lincoln's Preliminary Emancipation Proclamation that had been issued on September 22. In addition to assessing the impact that this new policy would have upon the war effort, Douglass attempted to allay the reservations of his readers, and perhaps his own as well, by expressing confidence in Lincoln's resolve to follow through with the proclamation despite widespread opposition. Apparently willing to set aside his reservations concerning Lincoln, Douglass perceived the revolutionary implications of the Emancipation Proclamation and hoped the president would couple this policy with a call for Black men to serve in the army. Douglass also realized this policy would cost Lincoln support from those who found emancipation too radical a deviation from the initial limited war aim of preserving the Union and he claimed that the cause would be better off without the likes of those in the military who had opposed emancipation, such as George McClellan, and Dixon Miles, who had recently surrendered a garrison of over twelve thousand soldiers at Harpers Ferry to Stonewall Jackson.*

———

Common sense, the necessities of the war, to say nothing of the dictates of justice and humanity have at last prevailed. We shout for joy that we live to record this righteous decree. *Abraham Lincoln,* President of the United States, Commander-in-Chief of the army and navy, in his own peculiar, cautious, forbearing and hesitating way, slow, but we hope sure, has, while the loyal heart was near breaking with despair, proclaimed and declared: "THAT ON THE FIRST OF JANUARY, IN THE YEAR OF OUR LORD ONE THOUSAND, EIGHT HUNDRED AND SIXTY-THREE, ALL PERSONS HELD AS SLAVES WITHIN ANY STATE OR ANY DESIGNATED PART OF A STATE, THE PEOPLE WHEREOF SHALL THEN BE IN REBELLION AGAINST THE UNITED STATES, SHALL BE THENCEFORWARD AND FOREVER FREE." "Free forever" oh! long enslaved millions, whose cries have so vexed the air and sky, suffer on a few more days in sorrow, the hour of your great deliverance draws nigh! oh! ye millions of free and loyal men who have earnestly sought to free your bleeding country from the dreadful ravages of revolution and anarchy, lift up now your voices with joy and thanksgiving, for with freedom to the slave will come peace and safety to your country. President Lincoln has embraced in this proclamation the law of Congress passed more than six months ago, prohibiting the employment of any part of the army and naval forces of the United States, to return fugitive slaves to their masters commanded all officers of the army and navy to respect and obey its provisions. He has still further declared his intention to urge upon the Legislature of all the slave States not in rebellion the immediate or gradual abolishment of slavery. But read the proclamation, for it is the most important of any to which the President of the United States has ever signed his name.

Opinions will widely differ as to the practical effect of this measure upon the war. All that class at the North who have not lost their affection for slavery will regard the measure as the very worst that could be devised, and as likely lead to endless mischief. All their plans for the future have been projected with a view to a reconstruction of the American Government upon the basis of compromise between slaveholding and non-slaveholding States. The thought of a country unified in sentiments, objects and ideas, has not entered into their political calculations, and hence this newly declared policy of the Government, which contemplates one glorious homogeneous people, doing away at a blow with the whole class of compromisers and corrupters will meet their stern opposition. Will that opposition prevail? Will it lead the President to reconsider and retract[?] Not a word of it. Abraham Lincoln may be slow, Abraham Lincoln may desire peace even at the price of leaving our terrible national sore untouched, to fester on for generations, but Abraham Lincoln is not the man to reconsider, retract and contradict words and purposes solemnly proclaimed over his official signature.

The careful, and we think, the slothful deliberation which he has observed in reaching this obvious policy, is a guarantee against retraction. But even if the temper and spirit of the President himself were other than what they are, events greater than the President, events which have slowly wrung this proclamation from him may be relied on to carry him forward in the same direction. To look back now would only load him with heavier evils, while diminishing his ability, for overcoming those with which he now has to contend. To recall his proclamation would only increase rebel pride, rebel sense of power and would be hailed as a direct admission of weakness on the part of the Federal Government, while it would cause heaviness of heart and depression of national enthusiasm all over the loyal North and West. No, Abraham Lincoln, will take no step backward. His word has gone out over the country and the world, giving joy and gladness to the friends of freedom and progress wherever those words are read, and he will stand by them, and carry them out to the letter. If he has taught us to confide in nothing else, he has taught us to confide in his word. The want of Constitutional power, the want of military power, the tendency of the measure to intensify Southern hate, and to exasperate the rebels, the tendency to drive from him all that class of Democrats at the North, whose loyalty has been conditioned on his restoring the union as it was, slavery and all, have all been considered, and he has taken his ground notwithstanding. The President, doubtless saw, as we see, that it is not more absurd to talk about restoring the union, without hurting slavery, than restoring the union without hurting the rebels. As to exasperating the South, there can be no more in the cup than the cup will hold, and that was full already. The whole situation having been carefully scanned, before Mr. Lincoln could be made to budge an inch, he will now stand his ground. Border State influence, and the influence of half loyal men have been exerted and have done their worst. The end of these two influences is implied in this proclamation. Hereafter, the inspiration as well as the men and the money for carrying on the war will come from the North, and not from half loyal border States.

The effect of this paper upon the disposition of Europe will be great and increasing. It changes the character of the war in European eyes and gives it an important principle as an object, instead of national pride and interest. It recognizes and declares the real nature of the contest, and places the North on the side of justice and civilization, and the rebels on the side of robbery and barbarism. It will disarm all purpose on the part of European Government to intervene in favor of the rebels and thus cast off at a blow one source of rebel power. All through the war thus far, the rebel ambassadors in foreign countries have been able to silence all expression of sympathy with the North as to slavery. With much more than a show of truth, they said that the Federal Government, no more than the Confederate Government, contemplated the abolition of slavery.

But will not this measure be frowned upon by our officers and men in the field? We have heard of many thousands who have resolved that they will throw up their commissions and lay down their arms, just so soon as they are required to carry on a war against slavery. Making all allowance for exaggeration there are doubtless far too many of this sort in the loyal army. Putting this kind of loyalty and patriotism to the test, will be one of the best collateral effects of the measure. Any man who leaves the field on such a ground will be an argument in favor of the proclamation, and will prove that his heart has been more with slavery than with his country. Let the army be cleansed from all such pro-slavery vermin, and its health and strength will be greatly improved. But there can be no reason to fear the loss of many officers or men by resignation or desertion. We have no doubt that the measure was brought to the attention of most of our leading Generals, and blind as some of them have seemed to be in the earlier part of the war, most of them have seen enough to convince them that there can be no end to this war that does not end slavery. At any rate, we may hope that for every pro-slavery man that shall start from the ranks of our loyal army, there will be two anti-slavery men to fill up the vacancy, and in this war one truly devoted to the cause of Emancipation is worth two of the opposite sort.

Whether slavery will be abolished in the manner now proposed by President Lincoln, depends of course upon two conditions, the first specified and the second implied. The first is that the slave States shall be in rebellion on [or] after the first day of January 1863, and the second is we must have the ability to put down that rebellion. About the first there can be very little doubt. The South is thoroughly in earnest and confident. It has staked everything upon the rebellion. Its experience thus far in the field has rather increased its hopes of final success than diminished them. Its armies now hold us at bay at all points, and the war is confined to the border States slave and free. If Richmond were in our hands and Virginia at our mercy, the vast regions beyond would still remain to be subdued. But the rebels confront us on the Potomac, the Ohio, and the Mississippi. Kentucky, Maryland, Missouri, and Virginia, are in debate on the battlefields and their people are divided by the line which separates treason from loyalty. In short we are yet, after eighteen months of war, confined to the outer margin of the rebellion. We have scarcely more than touched the surface of the terrible evil. It has been raising large quantities of food during the past summer. While the masters have been fighting abroad, the slaves have been busy working at home to supply them with the means of continuing the struggle. They will not down at the bidding of this Proclamation, but may be safely relied upon till January and long after January. A month or two will put an end to general fighting for the winter. When the leaves fall we shall hear again of bad roads, winter quarters and a spring campaign. The South which has thus far withstood our arms will not fall at once before our pens. All fears for the abolition of slavery arising from this apprehension may be dismissed. Whoever therefore, lives to see the first day of next January, should Abraham Lincoln be then alive and President of the United States may confidently look in the morning papers for the final proclamation, granting freedom, and freedom forever, to all slaves within the rebel States. On the next point nothing need be said. We have full power to put down the rebellion. Unless one man is more than a match for four, unless the South breeds braver and better men than the North, unless, slavery is more precious than liberty, unless a just cause kindles a feebler enthusiasm than a wicked and villainous one, the men of the loyal States will put down this rebellion and slavery, and all the sooner will they put down that rebellion by coupling slavery with that object. Tenderness towards slavery has been the loyal weakness during the war. Fighting the slaveholders with one hand and holding the slaves with the other, has been fairly tried and has failed. We have now inaugurated a wiser and better policy, a policy which is better for the loyal cause than an hundred thousand armed men. The Star Spangled banner is now the harbinger of Liberty and the millions in bondage, inured to hardships, accustomed to toil, ready to suffer, ready to fight, to dare and to die, will rally under that banner wherever they see it gloriously unfolded to the breeze. Now let the Government go forward in its mission of Liberty as the only condition of peace and union, by weeding out the army and navy of all such officers as the late Col. Miles, whose sympathies are now known to have been with the rebels. Let only the men who assent heartily to the wisdom and the justice of the anti-slavery policy of the Government, be lifted into command, let the black man have an arm as well as a heart in this war, and the tide of battle which has thus far only waved backward and forward, will steadily set in our favor. The rebellion suppressed, slavery abolished, and America will, higher than ever, sit as a queen among the nations of the earth.

Now for the work. During the interval between now and next January, let every friend of the long enslaved bondman do his utmost in swelling the tide of anti-slavery sentiment, by writing, speaking, money and example. Let our aim be to make the North a unit in favor of the President's policy, and see to it that our voices and votes, shall forever extinguish that latent and malignant sentiment at the North, which has from the first cheered on the rebels in their atrocious crimes against the union, and has systematically sought to paralyze the national arm in striking down the slaveholding rebellion. We are ready for this service or any other, in this, we trust the last struggle with the monster slavery.

*Douglass' Monthly* (Rochester, NY), Oct. 1862.

## GEORGE B. VASHON, Open Letter to President Lincoln on Colonization, October 1862

*A native of Pennsylvania, Vashon (1824–1878) was the first African American graduate of Oberlin College. Prior to the Civil War, he taught school, practiced law in New York, and lived for a time in Haiti. For Vashon, Haiti represented a potential refuge from American racial prejudice, and his experiences there made him well qualified to comment on Lincoln's support for colonization. His open letter to Lincoln, published in Frederick Douglass's newspaper, offered a somewhat detached assessment, for Vashon realized the appeal emigration had for some African Americans, yet he thought it unrealistic to expect most others to feel the same way and he deemed such an enterprise impracticable. Vashon noted the role that African Americans had played in helping to secure American independence and took issue with Lincoln's claim that the mere presence of persons of African descent had caused the war (ANB).*

---

Highly Honored and Respected Sir,—The papers announce, that on the 14th of August you had an interview with a committee of colored men, and addressed them in reference to the propriety of the expatriation of their class. As a colored man, I am deeply interested in this matter; and feel that under the circumstances, I ought to be excused for the liberty which I take in making answer to you personally.

In the first place, sir, let me say, that I do not put myself in opposition to the emigration of Colored Americans, either individually, or in large masses. I am satisfied, indeed, that such an emigration will be entered upon, and that too, to no inconsiderable extent. Liberia, with the bright and continually growing promise for the regeneration of Africa, will allure many a colored man to the shores of his motherland. Haiti with her proud boast, that, she, alone, can present an instance in the history of the world, of a horde of despised bondmen becoming a nation of triumphant freemen, will by her gracious invitation, induce many a dark hued native of the United States, to go and aid in developing the treasures stored away in her sun-crested hills and smiling savannahs. And, Central America, lying in that belt of empire which Destiny seems to promise to the blended races of the earth, will, no doubt, either with or without federal patronage, become the abiding place of a population made up, in great measure, of persons who will have taken refuge there from the oppression which they had been called upon to undergo in this country.

But, entertaining these views, and almost persuaded to become an emigrant myself, for the recollections of a thirty months' residence in Haiti still crowd pleasantly upon my memory[,] I am confident that, in thus feeling, I am not in sympathy with the majority of my class,—not in sympathy either with the great body of them. Those men are doubtless aware, that many comforts and advantages which they do not now enjoy here, await them elsewhere. No feeling of selfishness, no dread of making sacrifices, (as you intimate,) detains them in the land of their birth. They are fully conscious of the hatred to which you have adverted, they endure its consequences daily and hourly;—tremblingly too, perhaps, lest the utterances of their Chief Magistrate may add fuel to the fire raging against them, but buoyed up by the knowledge, that they are undeserving of this ill usage, and sedulously endeavoring to perform the various duties that are incumbent upon them, they enjoy, amid all their ill, a species of content, and echo back, by their conduct, your own words, that "It is difficult to make a man miserable while he feels he is worthy of himself, and claims kindred to the great God who made him." Thus, they have schooled themselves "to labor and to wait," in the hope of the coming of a better time. [. . .]

These men too, have another reason for clinging to the land of their nativity; and that is, the gross injustice which inheres even in the slightest intimation of a request, that they should leave it, an injustice which must necessarily be, in the highest degree, revolting to their every sense of right. Who and what are these men? Their family records in this land, in almost every instance, antedate our revolutionary struggle, and you, sir, will read in your country's history, unlike the ignorant and rapid reporters, who, from time to time, in their marketless and pen free calumny of a race, detail from our camps the lie, that "the negro will not fight,"—you, Sir, know, that black Americans fighting shoulder to shoulder with white Americans, in the contest which confirm our nationality, merited and received the approbation of Washington; and, that the zealous and fleet-footed slave of that time, did, for the partisan bands of Sumter and Marion, the same kind offices which the travel worn and scarcely tolerated "contraband" of our days has done for the armies of Burnside and McClellan. [...]

But setting aside the injustice of a policy which would expatriate black Americans, let us examine for a moment, its expediency. [...] Has not the experience of our heart stricken armies—an experience which has prompted the yielding up of the spade to the black man, while the musket is withheld from him—sufficiently indicated, that negro cultivators are absolutely required for that portion of the Union?

But, sir, it is not enough, that the policy which you suggest, should be expedient. It must also, be feasible. You have, doubtless, looked at this matter with the eye of a statesman. You have reflected, that, to remove entirely this "bone of contention," demands the expatriation of nearly one-sixth portion of the Union. You have after mature thought, settled the physical possibility of so large an expatriation; and calmly calculated the hundreds of millions of dollars which its accomplishment will add to our national liabilities,—large now, and growing larger daily under the exigencies of our civil war. Have you also considered, that the meager handful of negroes under Federal rule, constitutes, so to speak, only the periosteum, while "the bone" itself projects over into territory arrayed against your authority, and may yet be employed by unhallowed Rebellion, grown desperate in its extremity, as a vast and terrible weapon for the attainment of its ends? Whether this be a probability, or not, it is clear, that the difficulties in the way of your suggested enterprise are such as entitle it to be termed Herculean. [...]

President of the United States, let me say in conclusion, that the negro may be "the bone of contention" in our present civil war. He may have been the occasion of it; but he has not been its cause. That cause must be sought in the wrongs inflicted upon him by the white man. The white man's oppression of the negro, and not the negro himself, has brought upon the nation the leprosy under which it groans. The negro may be the scab indicative of the disease but his removal, even if possible, will not effect a cure. Not until this nation, with hands upon its lips, and with lips in the dust shall cry repentantly, "Unclean! unclean!" will the beneficent Father of all men, of whatever color, permit its healing and purification.

*Douglass' Monthly* (Rochester, NY), Oct. 1862.

## HENRY MCNEAL TURNER, Response to Preliminary Emancipation Proclamation, September 26, 1862

*While Turner (1834–1915) had reacted to Lincoln's proposal for compensated emancipation with much skepticism (see above), he believed the Preliminary Emancipation Proclamation that Lincoln issued on September 22, 1862, was nothing short of revolutionary. For Turner, the day of deliverance so long antici-pated was at hand, as the proclamation represented a dramatic shift in Lincoln's conduct of the war. However much this event was cause for rejoicing, Turner pointed out a sobering practical problem that he urged African Americans to confront. While the war had thus far resulted in thousands of so-called con-trabands—enslaved people who fled their masters and sought refuge within US military lines—the Emancipation Proclamation proposed to free millions of persons, and Turner knew the government was not prepared to handle this situation. He therefore tempered his joy with a call for action to address this looming crisis.*

---

The time has arrived in the history of the American African, when grave and solemn responsibilities stare him in the face. The proclamation of President Lin-coln, promising in the short space of a hundred days, to liberate thousands, and hundreds of thousands of human beings, born under, and held in subjection to the most cruel vassalage that ever stained a nation's garment, has opened up a new series of obligations, consequences, and results, never known to our honored sires, nor actually met with through the long chain of a glorious ancestry. We live in one of the most eventful periods of the world's revolutions—a period virtually speaking, that "kings and prophets waited for, but never saw."

A generation has passed from among the living since men upon this continent first dared to speak in the defence of human rights. But generations have passed since the God of heaven was first besieged by billions of entreaties, despatched from the earnest hearts of millions of tortured souls, from every vale, hill and dale, where defrauded humanity felt the grind of oppression's wheel. And amid all the din and dash of legislative and congressional enactments, determined upon the consummate extension of its transitive duration, a circle of darkness shrouded the scheme, and hurled the traffic to the ground, amid a dense rolling fog of dismal confusion, for which a parallel is not to be found.

But now, while many of these warm-hearted philanthropists, prompted by considerations purely divine, are lying in their graves, and while thousands of thousands of prayer-offering saints, whose supplications were heard in the skies as a mixture of anxiety, torture, want and grief, have passed from the trouble-some scenes of earth to the land of immortal birth, their labors, toils, and efforts combined, have, by gradual incursions upon the powers of injustice, through the instrumentality of their continuous and circumfluent lash, pushed on despite the oppositions, the dawn of freedom and the morn of liberty.

And now, we are verging upon a time very unlike the previous days of our American existence. The great quantity of contrabands, (so called,) who have fled from the oppressor's rod, and are now thronging Old Point Comfort, Hilton Head, Washington City, and many other places, and the unnumbered host who shall soon be freed by the President's proclamation, are to materially change their political and social condition. The day of our inactivity, disinterestedness, and irresponsibility, has given place to a day in which our long cherished abilities, and every intellectual fibre of our being, are to be called into a sphere of requisition. The time for boasting of ancestral genius, and prowling through the dusty pages of ancient history to find a specimen of negro intellectuality is over. Such useless noise should now be lulled, while we turn our attention to an engagement with those means which must, and alone can, mould out and develop those religious, literary, and pecuniary resources, adapted to the grave expediency now about to be encountered.

Thousands of contrabands, now at the places above designated, are in a condition of the extremest of suffering. We see them in droves every day perambulating the streets of Washington, homeless, shoeless, dressless, and moneyless. And when we think of the cold freezing days of a coming winter, at which time the surface of the earth not unfrequently will be concreted into a solid mass of congelation, our sensibilities of humanity sink under the dreadful apprehensions consequent upon such direful privations.

Every man of us now, who has a speck of grace or bit of sympathy, for the race that we are inseparably identified with, is called upon by force of surrounding circumstances, to extend a hand of mercy *to bone of our bone and flesh of our flesh.* And no one can now screen himself behind the nice matured scrupulosities which have in so many instances redounded to a plausible excuse, to the ever garrulous but never performers, in that, after giving assistance to the contrabands, they would again be returned back to slavery, and thus we would be found as having lavished our charitable expenditures upon a human chattel, destined to a state of perpetual vassalage; the morality of that thing, however, has not only been questionable but grievously condemnable.

But the proclamation of President Lincoln has banished the fog, and silenced the doubt. All can now see that the stern intention of the Presidential policy is, to wage the war in favour of freedom, till the last groan of the anguished heart slave shall be hushed in the ears of nature's God. This definition of the policy bids us rise, and for ourselves think, act, and do. We have stood still and seen the salvation of God, while we besought him with teary eyes and bleeding hearts; but the stand-still day bid us adieu Sept. 22, 1862. A new era, a new dispensation of things, is now upon us—*to action, to action*, is the cry. We must now begin to think, to plan, and to legislate for ourselves.

"A Call to Action," *Christian Recorder* (Philadelphia), Oct. 4, 1862.

## THOMAS STROTHER on Lincoln's Colonization Proposal, October 4, 1862

*Strother (c. 1810–1872) an AME minister and regular contributor to the* Christian Recorder, *was serving at Terre Haute, Indiana, when he wrote the following letter in opposition to Lincoln's colonization proposal. Strother correctly predicted that opposition from Central American leaders, including President Tomas Martinez of Nicaragua, would prove to be a major obstacle to Lincoln's plan to establish a colony on the Isthmus of Chiriqui (in present-day Panama) for the purpose of mining coal. In reflecting on the war and the racial situation in the United States, Strother suggested that the conflict was a form of divine punishment for sins committed against persons of color. Strother later served as minister at Cairo, Illinois, and attended the 1866 convention of Black men that was held in Galesburg, Illinois.*

It does seem, sir, like mockery in President Lincoln to say, as he does, that he wishes to colonize the colored people of this country in Central America. Has President Lincoln made any arrangements with President Martinez, the President of Central America, for a colony of colored people from the United States? I would suppose that no understanding of this kind had taken place between these two chieftains. I see an extract from a private letter from Martinez, stating that not only he himself is opposed to the scheme, but that his people are bitterly opposed to any thing of the kind. Where, then, are the grounds of President Lincoln's plan for a colored colony to be taken to Central America? Now, seeing that this is the case, as two other letters from two reliable gentlemen, (one living in Nicaragua, the other in Chinandaga, towns of Central America,) fully establish, does it not seem like mockery to offer to colonize colored people in any number in such a region? It is but to add insult to injury.

But it is asked—What shall we do with the negro? I would answer—Give them their rights, and they will do for themselves. To me, there would be just as much reason and sense in asking what the Almighty made them for. I believe that there would be just as much presumption in asking one of these questions as the other. Where is it written that the Lord holds the white man accountable for the welfare of the colored man, after that the white man shall have done justice to the colored man? Is it anywhere so written? If so, I have never been so fortunate as to find it. Then why should the whites put themselves to so much trouble about the country in which we shall live? Let them but give us justice, and Providence and we will attend to the balance. I do not suppose it will be asked our white friends in the great assize, whether they had done their duty in selecting good countries for us, and in colonizing us in them, and shifting us from one place to another in order to have us conveniently and happily situated. I do not suppose that any such question will be asked, but rather—Did you do unto the colored man as you would have him do unto you? This will be the great question which will be asked. And where does the white friend live in this whole nation, that will be able to answer this question in the affirmative? Because of injustice, which has been so alarmingly practised toward the colored man by those who consider themselves his superiors, is it that the judgments of the Almighty have at last been let loose in this nation. We need not be at a loss to know why these have been let loose, for when we notice who they are upon whom these judgments are falling, we are satisfied about the cause of their coming. The colored race does not seem to be the object of the thunderbolts displayed in the judgments which are now abroad in the land, but the so-considered superior race, who have lived so long on the unpaid labor of the colored man, is feeling now these awful fulminations from East to West, and from North to South; and it seems strange that with all these heavy judgments which now are extant throughout this doomed nation, that the very people who are suffering under the awful weight of these scourges, should be anxious still to inflict additional wrongs upon the very people that the Almighty is now punishing them for having wronged. I say this, because it would be an everlasting wrong, in my opinion, to throw any number of colored people into a colony in Central America; because, in the first place, the Central American people do not want us there, for I see by private letters from responsible and intelligent gentlemen living in that country, that the Government there is so opposed to President Lincoln's colonization scheme, that they are determined to take steps against it, and I am not the least surprised at it. Why drive us from North America, or urge us in any way to leave here, after having sucked our life-blood for more than two hundred years?

*Christian Recorder* (Philadelphia), Oct. 4, 1862.

## EZRA R. JOHNSON, "The Liberty Bells are Ringing," October 4, 1862

*A native of Massachusetts, Johnson (1814–1870) was a sailmaker and abolitionist in New Bedford before moving to San Francisco, California, where he speculated in land, practiced medicine, worked for equal rights, and was a regular contributor to the* Pacific Appeal. *In a speech on September 3, Johnson had predicted that the president would soon take decisive action against slavery, and Lincoln's Preliminary Emancipation Proclamation, issued on September 22, proved Johnson's prescience. In the following response to the proclamation, Johnson reasoned that Lincoln had little choice but to expand the war aims to include the destruction of slavery. For Johnson and many other African Americans, the war was God's punishment for the sin of slavery, and he correctly forecast that Lincoln would soon turn to Black men to help fill the need for additional soldiers to bring the war to a successful conclusion (Pacific Appeal [San Francisco], Sept. 6, 1862; Oct. 1, 1870).*

---

Intelligence has been received by telegraph that President Lincoln has issued a Proclamation, in which he gives notice that he will urge upon Congress the passage of laws providing for the emancipation of slaves, and declaring all slaves free, in States which, on the 1st of January next, shall still be in rebellion against the Government.

The Chief of our Nation is not insensible of the fact that we have reached a stern crisis in our struggle for national existence. The grave anxiety imprinted on every loyal face, the activity and energy displayed by the military leaders of the disunion forces[,] the successes they have achieved in Virginia, Tennessee, and even in Kentucky, all attest to a change in the aspect of the struggle. Our armies pause, content to hold their own and fortunate if unassailed, while the North puts forth its best efforts to raise three hundred thousand men, deemed necessary to crush out the rebellion. [ . . . ]

All the world see, with astonishment and confusion, a war carried on for freedom, in which the only right preserved is the right of a man to his slaves, and where the one side strikes without fear or mercy, and the other dares not touch his enemy's weakness, though that weakness has caused all the trouble. But, at length, the time has come when, as many of us have expected, God has appointed that we must either ask the help of the despised slave, or see the proud Republic fall in miserable ruin. Government has no weapon now remaining but the armed slave. We are on the brink of destruction. Proclamations, Confiscation Bills, levies of hundreds of thousand will be useless, unless we do justice—free the slave and arm him.

In all probability the war cannot be speedily brought to a termination. Whenever all the available material for white soldiers has been exhausted, the President will be compelled to conquer his prejudices and make a virtue of necessity by inviting colored men to enlist in the army. The next effort to enroll 300,000 men, under the regulations of the drafting process, will test the patriotism of the people to their utmost tension. Truly the Almighty, as with the curses of Egypt, is showing the Americans what is the sin of caste, and what shall be its punishment. Their hatred and unchristian prejudices against us is returning home to them, and is scattering pestilence and death on either side. If they turn from the error of their ways and do us justice, it will wipe out the crimson from their bloody fields, and bid the flowers spring in spotless beauty from an unstained sod. It will roll back to the womb of the past the groans and sighs and piteous cries of the poor slaves who have done no evil to their countrymen, and are ready to die in defence of their liberty.

Let Government do these things, and then we will feel a natural pride and glory for a Free Union, as it should be. Then we will have a home and birthright in a free land for ourselves and children, and we will pledge our highest vow to strive to make the Union what it ought to be, after the terrible ordeal through which it is called to pass. It will then be redeemed, purified and exalted in the estimation of the whole civilized world, and traitors will never again be entrusted with its destinies. It will march on in all the greatness of its power and grandeur of its destiny. We will then blot out the records of time the story of ten thousand wrongs—of a nation's dishonor and a world in woe.

*Pacific Appeal* (San Francisco), Oct. 4, 1862.

## C. P. S., "The President on Emancipation," October 4, 1862

*The Appeal's correspondent in Benicia, California, was identified in the paper only as "C. P. S." and may have been Simon P. Clanton (b. 1830), a Virginia-born barber who worked as an agent for the* Appeal. *C. P. S. defended Lincoln's Preliminary Emancipation Proclamation from critics who believed it did not go far enough. Anticipating what Frederick Douglass and others would later argue regarding Lincoln's alleged vacillation and slowness to act against slavery, C. P. S. suggested that the president could not get too far ahead of public opinion. If Lincoln made an error, it would be one of the head, not the heart.*

---

To many of our people who entertain more radical views, the course of the President on the emancipation question seems rather equivocal. They believe that Mr. Lincoln does not want to abolish Slavery, and that he will not do it, except, through stress of circumstances, he is forced to adopt it as a military necessity; that he would much rather leave that cancer gnawing at the vitals of the Government than remove it, if he could crush the rebellion without it. My first hasty conclusions were the same, but a sober second thought makes me believe otherwise. Upon reviewing the past course of Mr. Lincoln dispassionately, I find that, though many of his acts have been mystified by diplomatic expressions and legal phraseology, to give the old ship of State the appearance of steering in the old constitutional channel, yet, by a close observation, there could be seen a constant under-current in favor of freedom. It must not be thought, at such a time as this, that the simple stroke of the President's pen will knock the shackles off of every bondsman. It will require more than that; and let me tell you that, without the co-operation of the people of the United States, Mr. Lincoln cannot do any more than the lamented John Brown. The President sees and feels the pernicious influences of the "institution" as we do, but how to get rid of it is quite another question, and unless he can surround himself with men who think as he does, and see as he sees, would it be wise in him to adopt measures ahead of public sentiment, and thereby destroy his chances for doing good among the whole people, disorganize his cabinet, create dissension in the ranks of the army, and, in the general chaos, open the doors and let the enemy come in and subvert the government, undo all that he has done, paralyze his arms and rivet the chains of oppression faster upon the people? No, sir; I think the President is doing the very best he knows how, considering the material he has to work with, to save the country and restore freedom; and it is my opinion that if he does not do that which is humane, just and equitable in the end, it will be an error of the head and not of the heart. I believe he means to do that which is right, and if he fails, there will be others more to blame than he. Surrounded as he is, by men whom it may not be safe to trust too far; besieged on every hand by men with all kinds of schemes, emigration, subjugation, colonization, confiscation, and what not, all of which they individually claim are the only means of saving the country, is it strange that he should seem at times to waver? If Mr. Lincoln can wade safely through all these obstacles, save the country and do us justice, he will have accomplished a herculean task, and win for himself the lasting gratitude of mankind, and a name worthy of a place in the highest niche of fame. I am as radical as any man need be on the subject of emancipation, but I do not think it politic at such a time as this—powerless as we are—to be hasty in declaring what we will and will not do in this emergency, except that we are ready and willing to do all we can to aid the Administration in its laudable efforts to save the country, and do justice between man and man. We will not now stop to discuss whether it be the stubborn endurance of Jeff. Davis and his horde, or Mr. Lincoln's calm and dispassionate convictions of the wrongs of human bondage, that brought forth his emancipation manifesto. [ . . . ]

The President may have been actuated by some benevolent design toward us, which we have no idea of. The fact is, we are on the outside and cannot see what is going on within. We are not in a position to know what opposition the President may have to contend with in carrying out any measure calculated to benefit our race; therefore, when he *seems* to be wrong, I think we should give him the benefit of the doubt. In the position we occupy we are not competent to arrive at important conclusions, no more than a man would be competent to sit in a jury on his own trial.

*Pacific Appeal* (San Francisco), Oct. 4, 1862.

## FREE BLACK PEOPLE OF WASHINGTON, DC, Letter to
## President Lincoln on Colonization, November 2, 1862

*While Lincoln's August 14, 1862, meeting at the White House with a commit-
tee of Black men from Washington had provoked widespread protests against
Lincoln's plea for colonization, the following letter indicates that there were
some Black people in Washington not only willing to consider Lincoln's plan
but also participate in it. Lincoln had been in negotiations with a company that
owned land on the Isthmus of Chiriqui, located in present-day Panama. The
proposed plan involved sending African American colonists to Chiriqui where
they would mine coal that the federal government would purchase for the navy.
Senator Samuel C. Pomeroy of Kansas acted as a special agent responsible for
helping to organize the logistics of establishing the colony. Lincoln approved a
contract with the company on September 11, 1862, but opposition from neighbor-
ing countries led Lincoln to abandon the venture. Lincoln did not meet with the
anxious prospective colonists and had one of his secretaries inform them that he
too was eager for them to depart for Chiriqui. With the collapse of the Chiriqui
plan, Lincoln entered into an agreement on December 31, 1862, that involved
colonizing Vache Island off the coast of Haiti. In the spring of 1863, nearly five
hundred colonists sailed for the island. The colony proved to be a disaster, and
less than a year later the government brought the remaining colonists back to
the United States.*

---

To the President: Sir—The undersigned, on behalf of their colored brethren
and themselves, have called on your Excellency to learn when we can take our
departure to the land promised us by you in the address you made to us in this
your Executive mansion. We have learned from the Hon. Senator Pomeroy, the
Agent of Emigration, whom you appointed to conduct us to Chiriqui, that he
is ready, his equipments engaged, his provisions for the emigrants bought, that
a vessel suitable has been found, that the consent of the Government with its
agreement to receive us as citizens with equal rights and obligations has been
obtained, and that he only waits your orders to announce the day of sailing, and
that he can sail within a week, if your order is given.

Many of us, acting upon your promise to send us so soon as one hundred
families were ready, have sold our furniture, have given up our little homes to go
on the first voyage, and now, when more than five times that number have made
preparations to leave, we find that there is uncertainty and delay, which is greatly
embarrassing us, and reducing our scanty means, until fears are being created that
these means are being exhausted. Poverty in a still worse form than has yet met
us may be our winter prospect.

We have seen it stated in the newspapers that you do not intend to let us depart. We are not willing to believe that your Excellency would make arrangements for us to go—would tell us that we could not live prosperously here—would create hopes within us, and stimulate us to struggle for national independence and respectable equality, and then, when we had made ourselves ready for the effort, in confident belief of the integrity of your promise, that its realization will be withheld.

Congress has placed the power and the means solely in the hands of your Excellency to aid in removing us. You begun the movement. You appointed Senator Pomeroy—in whom not only the colored people, but the whole country, have confidence—to see that justice should be done us in our removal. He has said that he is ready. We therefore earnestly beg that your Excellency will now give him explicit orders to sail before the cold weather sets in to pinch us here—before the storms of winter shall make our voyage a dangerous one.

Published in several newspapers, including *National Republican* (Washington, DC, November 3); and the *Liberator* (Boston, November 7).

## FREDERICK DOUGLASS, "January First 1863"

*While Douglass (1818–1895) had initially expressed great confidence in Lincoln after the Preliminary Emancipation Proclamation was issued (see above), subsequent events led him to wonder whether Lincoln would follow through and issue the final proclamation on January 1. Republicans had suffered losses in the midterm elections, and these defeats were attributed to the unpopularity of Lincoln's proclamation. In his Annual Message to Congress in early December, Lincoln had urged Congress to approve measures providing federal funds to compensate slaveholders and colonize former slaves. These developments, combined with Lincoln's seeming reluctance to take decisive action against slavery and the emotionless, legalistic justification for emancipation in the preliminary proclamation, led Douglass to have serious concerns about what Lincoln would do, or perhaps not do, on New Year's Day. Douglass ruminated on the consequences of emancipation. What if Lincoln faltered on January 1? Douglass spent New Year's Day in Boston, where he spoke at a large gathering to commemorate the momentous occasion. He later recalled anxiously waiting until late in the evening before official word arrived that Lincoln had signed the proclamation.*

---

The first of January, which is now separated from us only by a few days and hours, is properly looked forward to with an intense and all surpassing interest, by all classes of the American people and from the most opposite reasons and motives. The slave hopes to gain his liberty, the slaveholders fear the loss of Slaves, and northern doughfaces fear the loss of political power. It is a pivotal period in our national history—the great day which is to determine the destiny not only of the American Republic, but that of the American Continent. [...] Unquestionably, for weal or for woe, the first of January is to be the most memorable day in American Annals. The fourth of July was great, but the first of January, when we consider it in all its relations and bearings is incomparably greater. [...] We may well stay before it and amplify it. It is an occasion which can happen but seldom in the life of any nation. It is not the creation of individual design and calculation, but the grand result of stupendous all controlling wide sweeping national events. Powerful as Mr. Lincoln is, he is but the hands of the clock. He cannot change the pivotal character of the day. The word has gone forth—and no system of balancing, of props here, or weight there, can possibly anchor the national ship in anything like a stationary position after the first day of January. [...] The tide is reached which must be taken at the flood—For the present the Angel of Liberty has one ear of the nation and the demon of Slavery the other. One or the other must prevail on the first of January. The national head swings, pendulum like, now to the one side and now to the other. Alas, no man can tell which will prevail—and we are compelled to wait, hope, labour and pray.

It is of but little use to speculate as to probabilities, when events are at the door which will dispel all doubt and make all certain—yet we may even now glance at the probable effects which may be looked for as certain to follow any one of other the three courses—open to the President of the United States on the first of January. We say *three courses* although in a radical point of view there are but *two*. One is the issuing, according to promise of his proclamation abolishing slavery in all the States and parts of States which shall be in rebellion on the first of January and the second is, not to issue it at all. Any postponement, any apology—any plan of compromise which saves the guilty neck of slavery one hour beyond the first of January, will be in effect a suppression of the proclamation altogether. And now supposing that Mr. Lincoln shall fail, supposing that the hour comes and the man is missing, what will be the effect upon him? Thus far the loyal north has trusted him, less for his ability than his honesty. They have supported him with patience rather than enthusiasm. His word though clumsily uttered has been esteemed his bond, good for all, and more than all it has promised. But what, as we have already said, if the President fails in this trial hour, what if he now listens to the demon slavery—and rejects the entreaties of the Angel of Liberty? Suppose he cowers at last before the half loyal border Slave States, which have already nearly ruined his administration, and have been of more service to Richmond than to Washington from the beginning—withholds his proclamation of freedom—disappoint the just hopes of his true friends, dispels the fear and dismay of his enemies—and thus gives a new lease of life to the slaveholder's rebellion? Where then will stand Mr. Abraham Lincoln? We know not what will become of him. The North has been so often betrayed and trifled with that it has become unsafe to predicate anything spirited, resolute and decided on her part. But this we will say, if Mr. Lincoln shall thus trifle with the wounds of his bleeding country—thus fiddle, while the cold earth around Fredericksburg is wet with the warm blood of our patriot soldiers—every one of whom was slain by slaveholding rebels, he will be covered with execrations as bitter and as deep as any that ever settled upon the head of any perjured tyrant ancient or modern. His name would go down in history scarcely less loathsome than that of Nero. Such a course, on the part of Mr. Lincoln would justly make him the distrust and scandal of his friends, the scorn of the world and the contempt of his enemies. Henceforth none but fools will believe in him and his protestations of honesty and patriotism will be hailed but as the deceitful utterances of another Iago.

To the country, a failure to issue the Emancipation proclamation would prove the most stunning and disastrous blow received during the war. It would well nigh break the loyal heart of the nation, and fill its enemies North and South, with a demoniacal enthusiasm.— [ . . . ] The most hopeful of all our prophets would wilt in despair. For who could trust to presidential promises or in any arm or department of Government when the central pillar had fallen? Who but a fool can believe that any grace shown the rebels at this moment after nearly two years of patience will not be construed into conscious weakness, into a base and cowardly spirit, as another proof of the unfitness of the Northern "round heads" to rule, and of the necessity of rebel dominion? The natural and inevitable effect of the suppression or postponement of the proclamation will be to cheer the hopes and intensify the determination and efforts of the rebels to break up and destroy the Union. Mr. Lincoln might threaten in the event of continued resistance, to send out another decree on the fourth of July 1863, but the North would gain no hope from it and the South would be caused no fear by it for the moral constitution of the Government more solemn than all paper ones would be broken down beyond repair.

But on the other hand let the President promptly on the morning of the first of January, with the truthful steadiness and certainty of the movement of the heavenly bodies send forth his glorious proclamation of Liberty, and a shout like the voice of many waters will rise to heaven from three millions of robbed and plundered bondmen, while a groan of despair, will [be] heard in every rebel Hall South of Mason and Dixon's line. It will add four millions to the strength of the Union with a single dash of the pen, establish the moral power of the Government, kindle anew the enthusiasm of the friends of freedom, number the days of Northern doughfaceism, strengthen the hearts of our brave troops in the field, convince the world of our sincerity, give a fuller meaning to the Declaration of

Independence, and put peace forever between the conscience and the patriotism of the people. [. . .]

But will that deed be done? Oh! that is the question. There is reason both for hope and fear. The promise is yet unretracted, the rebels are still in arms, bold, active, unyielding, strong and defiant. [. . .] The being in rebellion was the ground for the promised proclamation. This ground within nine days of the first of January holds good. Not a single rebel State has grounded its weapons since the twenty second of September. Thus far the President is dared to do his worst, thus far the villainy of the South is a spur to the virtue of the North, and affords reason to hope that we shall have the promised proclamation of freedom to all the Inhabitants of the rebel States.

On the 22d of September, as we have said, the President declared that he would issue, on the first of January 1863, a proclamation of Emancipation Abolishing Slavery in all the Slave States which should then be in rebellion. But alas, he made these a burden of what should have been a joy. He reached that point like an ox under the yoke, or a Slave under the lash, not like the uncaged eagle spurning his bondage and soaring in freedom to the skies. His words kindled no enthusiasm. They touched neither justice nor mercy. Had there been one expression of sound moral feeling against Slavery, one word of regret and shame that this accursed system had remained so long the disgrace and scandal of the Republic, one word of satisfaction in the hope of burying slavery and the rebellion in one common grave, a thrill of joy would have run round the world, but no such word was said, and no such joy was kindled. He moved but was moved by necessity.—Emancipation—is put off—it was made f[u]ture and conditional—not present and absolute.

While however, there are strong grounds for supposing that President Lincoln will duely issue his proclamation on the morning of the first of January[,] [t]he absence of all mention of his purpose to do so, in his recent message, his reported saying that the rebellion is already substantially suppressed, his parliaing with the border State men, his avowed readiness to change his opinion, whenever he should be convinced, the tremendous pressure likely to be brought to bear upon him, by the conservators of slavery, the apparent lack in him of any vital hostility towards slavery, the declared motives for the measure being only military, not moral or political necessity, the democratic pro-slavery gains obtained at the North since the 22d of September[,] [t]he space given in his late message to compensated Emancipation, all served to cast a doubt upon the promised and hoped for proclamation, which only the event can remove or confirm. So stands the case within one week of the first of January. The suspense is painful, but will soon be over.

*Douglass' Monthly* (Rochester, NY), January 1863.

# Resolutions from Emancipation Celebration at Beaufort, South Carolina, January 1, 1863

*The following resolutions were enclosed in a letter to Lincoln from Solomon Peck, a White Baptist missionary and abolitionist from New England who was among the first missionaries to go to the Sea Islands after they were occupied by US military forces. Peck ministered to African Americans and established a school for them at Beaufort. Lincoln did not exempt the Sea Islands from the Final Emancipation Proclamation, as he did with other parts of rebellious states that had come under US authority, and Peck reported that this resulted in the freedom of over 1,100 members of his church. Although only one member of the committee that prepared the resolutions was able to write his name, their esteem for Lincoln was such that they would not be deterred from conveying their words of thanks and well wishes to the president, so they requested Peck to record the resolutions as they were spoken. For them, Lincoln was an instrument of Divine will whom they hoped to meet in the afterlife (Lincoln Papers, Series 1, General Correspondence, 1833 to 1916: "S. Peck to Abraham Lincoln, Thursday, January 1, 1863 [Sends Resolutions Supporting Emancipation Proclamation from Church in Beaufort, South Carolina]," https://www.loc.gov/ item/mal2087700/; John McClintock and James Strong,* Cyclopedia of Biblical, Theological, and Ecclesiastical Literature, *vol. 7 [New York: Harper and Brothers, 1877], 862; E. L. Pierce,* The Negroes of Port Royal *[Boston: R. F. Walcutt, 1862], 32–33).*

Extract from the Minutes of the Baptist Church of Christ in Beaufort, S.C.—"Beaufort, Jany 1. 1863.

"1. <u>Resolved,</u> That we all unite, with our hearts & minds, to give thanks to God for this great thing that He has done for us; that He has put into his (Mr. Lincoln's) mind—that all should come to this very stand, according to the will of God, in freeing all the colored people. We believe that Jesus Christ will now see of the travail of his soul, in what he has done for us.

"2. <u>Resolved,</u> That we all unite together to give Mr. President Lincoln our hearty thanks for the Proclamation. We are more than thankful to him & to God, & pray for him & ourselves. May the blessing of God rest upon you. May grace, mercy & peace sustain you. May you go on conquering & to conquer this rebellion. We have gathered together two or three times a week for the last five months, to pray that the Lord might help you & all your soldiers, hoping that the Almighty would bless you in all your goings, & crown you with a crown of glory & a palm of victory. We never expect to meet your face on earth; but may we meet in a better world than this;—this is our humble prayer.

"<u>Voted,</u> That the Committee sign the Resolutions for us,—& that we request our Pastor Dr. Peck to send them to Mr. Lincoln."

Jacob Robinson (by his mark) +
Daniel Mifflin " " " +
Joseph Jenkins " " " +
Jime Harrison " " "+
January " " " +
Harry Simmons " " " +
Caesar Singleton " " " +
Thomas Ford " " " +
Kit Green Kit Green
Charles Pringle " " " +
Peter White " " " +
Elias Gardner " " " +
Moses Simmons " " "

Lincoln Papers, Series 1, General Correspondence. 1833 to 1916: "Beaufort South Carolina Baptist Church to Abraham Lincoln, Thursday, January 1, 1863 (Resolutions Supporting Emancipation Proclamation)," https://www.loc.gov/item/mal2084200/.

## PHILIP A. BELL, "The Year of Jubilee Has Come!" January 3, 1863

*Editor Philip A. Bell (1809–1889) welcomed the Final Emancipation Proclamation with great hope and enthusiasm. While he had lamented that the Preliminary Emancipation Proclamation contained no provision indicating that Blacks would be welcomed into the army as fighting men, such was not the case with the final version of the proclamation. For Bell and many others, January 1, 1863, was indeed the year of Jubilee, for it marked the beginning of a new era in which the federal government was no longer complicit in the crime of slavery and instead was committed to a policy of freeing millions.*

The anxiously looked-for day has arrived. It has brought freedom, under the President's Proclamation, to untold numbers of slaves on American soil, who have writhed in agony under the galling chains of slavery, crying, with deep lamentations, "How long, how long, O Lord, before our deliverance shall come to pass?" To-day they are permitted, under the broad shield of the United States Government, to stand erect as men. To-day they arise above the status of mere bondsmen, allied to the brute creation in a property sense, by the soulless political theories of the impious slaveocracy. To-day the Government has washed its hands clean of the stains of slavery in the States and parts of States that are in rebellion. America, henceforth, looms up with grandeur. She has burst the bands that have bound her, from her infancy to her maturity, and declares, before High Heaven, she must be free! Giant-like, she now appears, with her implements of war, not only to strike terror to traitors and domestic foes at home, but, with added strength from her loyal colored sons, she may with confidence hurl defiance at her enemies abroad. America, to-day, takes a proud stand, confronting the world with unabashed majesty.

*Pacific Appeal* (San Francisco), January 3, 1863.

## ROBERT HAMILTON, "The Great Event," January 3, 1863

*For editor Robert Hamilton (1819–1870), the Final Emancipation Proclamation was nothing less than the greatest event of the nineteenth century. While Hamilton noted that the proclamation was a war measure and not necessarily motivated by humanitarian concern for the enslaved, he nevertheless praised Lincoln for issuing it and predicted that it would doom the rebellion. In assessing the power of the proclamation, Hamilton offered a critique of one of the most common and enduring pro-slavery arguments which held that the enslaved were well-treated and therefore happy and content with their situation. For Hamilton, the Emancipation Proclamation placed much of the burden on the enslaved themselves, for he believed they were ultimately responsible for taking advantage of the opportunity the proclamation afforded by seizing their freedom in running away to the US military lines.*

———————

THE GREAT EVENT Of this century was done at Washington, January 1st, 1863. By the President's Proclamation so large a proportion of slaves are declared free, that the freedom of the remainder is a forgone conclusion. And movements in Missouri, Maryland, and even North Carolina confirm this view.

What does the Proclamation mean? How far will it go towards setting the slaves free?

The Proclamation is simply a war measure. It is an instrument for crushing, hurting, injuring, and crippling the enemy. It is *per se* no more humanitarian than a hundred pounder rifled cannon. It seeks to deprive the enemy of arms and legs, muscles and sinews, used by them to procure food and raiment and to throw up fortifications.

There is this difference, however, between the cannon and the proclamation. The former does its work according to the skill and position of our artillerymen, and the strength of the powder and projectiles. The latter depends for its success on the disposition and will of the owners of the legs, arms, and muscles within the hostile lines—it is an appeal to the slaves, to make such use of themselves as will secure their own freedom and the salvation of the republic!

It is freely admitted that this proclamation is not only a war measure, it is also a necessary war measure; that is to say the issue of the war, in other words, the fate of the whole country, depends on the success of this measure. The skill of our generals has been tried, the bravery of our soldiers has been tried, the strength of our resources pushed to the utmost—we have in the field an army as large as that of Xerxes, and on the water, ships in thousands, and yet all these do not prevail and our tried and trusted ruler calls upon the negro to "come to the rescue!"

This is what the proclamation means. It is an appeal from physical force to ideal forces; from matter to mind; it holds up to the slave a single idea which has been the food of his soul through centuries of gloom and suffering! There it stands a pillar of flame beckoning them to this dreamed of promise of freedom! Bidding them leap from chattel-hood to manhood, from slavery to freedom!

Will the slaves respond to this call? Will they grasp this proffered freedom? It is strange that men can even ask the question. Has it not been answered again and again? [ . . . ] Whenever our armies have penetrated a thickly populated slave district, have not the slaves, in their eager enthusiasm, rushed towards them with their bundles, in search of liberty? Will the knowledge, which they will soon gain of this proclamation, cause them to turn their backs upon liberty?

Some among us assert, that the slaves' love of their masters and of their homes will triumph over their desire for liberty; why not add that their love of being lashed, of having their children sold from their sight will also triumph over their passion for freedom?

We believe that the effects of this great and glorious proclamation will surprise every body. The slaveowners will wake up from a dream which they have indulged in all their lives, about the content and happiness of their youthful slaves; the rebel generals will be surprised and all their officers who are slaveholders will be seeking leave to go home; the stomach of the rebel army will be surprised by starvation; the government at Washington will be astonished at the first great victory of this war; the people of the North will be surprised at the sound common sense wherewith the slaves will choose liberty and take most excellent care of themselves besides; and the world will be surprised to see the backbone of the rebellion broken without a battle.

Editorial in the *Anglo-African* (New York), January 3, 1863.

# Emancipation Celebration at Trenton, New Jersey, January 1, 1863

*In early 1863, the pages of the* Anglo-African *were filled with reports from various communities of how news of the Final Emancipation Proclamation was welcomed. January 1 was now the beginning of not only a new year but also a new era, and the resolutions approved at the meeting in Trenton, New Jersey, indicated the profundity of the occasion.*

---

On Thursday evening, January 1st, the colored citizens of Trenton met at the African M.E. Church, Perry street, and organized by the election of Rev. Mr. Moore as Chairman. The meeting was opened with prayers by Rev. Mr. Gaseway.

The Chairman stated the object of the meeting, and after some remarks by Rev. Mr. Moore, Rev. Mr. Gould, Rev. Mr. Walker, and others, the following preamble and resolutions were offered by Rev. W.E. Walker, and unanimously adopted:

WHEREAS, In view of the forthcoming proclamation of the President of the United States, which recognizes the right of nearly four millions of our brethren in bonds to their personal liberty we recognize in it the hand of Almighty God, who executeth righteousness and judgment for all that are oppressed; therefore—

*Resolved,* That we hail Abraham Lincoln, our present Chief Magistrate, as the instrument in the hand of God in executing his righteous purpose.

*Resolved,* That we will continue to offer up our earnest prayers and supplications in behalf of the President and all others in authority, for their aid in the furtherance of this great, glorious and just measure.

*Resolved,* That we regard this war as only the judgment of God, inflicted on this nation for her great national sin of slaveholding, and not until she turns to righteousness, and learns to do justice and love mercy, will peace reign in her borders.

*Resolved,* That we (in the strength of God) will so demean ourselves as to show that our brethren deserve this precious boon.

The *Anglo-African* (New York), Jan. 10, 1863.

# JAMES SMITH, Report on Emancipation Celebration at Elmira, New York, January 5, 1863

*In early 1863, the pages of the* Anglo-African *were filled with reports from various locales that described how the news of the Final Emancipation Proclamation was celebrated. Reverend James Smith reported that in addition to speeches, music, and singing, the Methodist Episcopal Zion Church at Elmira, New York,* marked the occasion by raising the American flag for the first time, and it bore an inscription honoring Lincoln. For this congregation, Lincoln's Emancipation Proclamation had transformed a symbol associated with oppression into one that now held out the promise of freedom.

———————

A grand celebration in honor of the President's Proclamation of Freedom was held in the M.E. Zion Church of Elmira on Monday, Jan. 5th, by the friends of impartial liberty. For the first time since our church organization we raised the American flag, and it is now streaming in the breeze, bearing, in large letters, the heartfelt inscription: "GOD BLESS ABRAHAM LINCOLN!" Every abolitionist in that large assemblage heartily greeted the old flag with earnest and enthusiastic applause as the emblem of protection for the oppressed of this guilty and suffering land [...] It was a grand jubilee in honor of the greatest event of the nineteenth century—the liberation of our race and the permanent ascendancy of republican principles.

The *Anglo-African* (New York), Jan. 17, 1863.

## ALEXANDER T. AUGUSTA to Abraham Lincoln, Toronto, Canada, January 7, 1863

*A native of Virginia, Augusta (1825–1890) was a medical doctor in Toronto when he read the Emancipation Proclamation and its call for Black men to serve in the military. As Augusta indicates in the following letter, he had moved to Canada because he was unable to gain admission to a medical school in the US. Eager to serve, he also wrote to Secretary of War Stanton and received an invitation to appear before the board that examined candidates for army surgeon. When Augusta first appeared before the board, he was denied an examination because he was of African descent. He successfully appealed, passed the exam, and was appointed a surgeon with the rank of major, thereby becoming the first African American surgeon in the army. His officer rank made him a target for violence; during a train trip he was assaulted and one of the shoulder straps was torn from his uniform. Augusta met Lincoln at a White House reception in February 1864 and was "kindly received" by the president. Augusta's refusal to follow segregationist practices on a Washington streetcar inspired Congress to pass a bill that Lincoln signed which prohibited discrimination on the city's streetcars. After being discharged from the army at the end of the war, Augusta remained in Washington, where he practiced medicine and was a member of the faculty at Howard University's medical school (AANB; "The Late Outrage Upon Surgeon Augusta, In Baltimore," the Liberator, May 29, 1863; Congressional Globe,*

*38th Cong., 1st Sess., 553–555; "The Reception at the White House," Evening Star [Washington], Feb. 24, 1864; "Negroes at the President's Levee," Detroit Free Press, March 4, 1864).*

―――――――――

Sir,

Having seen that it is intended to garrison the U.S. forts &c with coloured troops, I beg leave to apply to you for an appointment as surgeon to some of the coloured regiments, or as physician to some of the depots of "freedmen." I was compelled to leave my native country, and come to this on account of prejudice against colour, for the purpose of obtaining a knowledge of my profession; and having accomplished that object, at one of the principle educational institutions of this Province, I am now prepared to practice it, and would like to be in a position where I can be of use to my race.

If you will take matters into favorable consideration, I can give satisfactory references as to character and qualification from some of the most distinguished members of the profession in the city where I have been in practice for about six years.

I remain Sir

Yours Very Respectfully

A. T. Augusta

Bachelor of Medicine

Trinity College Toronto

Compiled Military Service Record, Alexander T. Augusta, Surgeon, 7th US Colored Infantry, M1820, Record Group 94, National Archives, Washington, DC.

## JEREMIAH B. SANDERSON, Address at Emancipation Jubilee in San Francisco, January 14, 1863

*African Americans in San Francisco gathered on January 14, 1863, to celebrate the Emancipation Proclamation. The hall where the event was held was decorated with life-sized portraits of Lincoln and William Lloyd Garrison. A native of Massachusetts, Sanderson (1821–1875) worked as a barber in New Bedford and was active in the abolition movement prior to moving to California in the early 1850s. Once in California, Sanderson taught school and became a leading advocate of equal rights. As a young abolitionist in New England, Sanderson had known Garrison and worked with him, so it was only fitting that he paid tribute to both Garrison and Lincoln in his remarks. In noting Garrison's contribution to the anti-slavery cause, Sanderson was among the first Emancipation Day speakers to not only rank Lincoln with abolitionists but also place the Emancipation Proclamation within the larger context of the decades-long struggle to make the promise of equality in the Declaration of Independence a reality (Ralph M. Lapp, "Jeremiah Sanderson: Early California Negro Leader," The Journal of Negro History 53, no. 4 [Oct. 1968]: 321–33).*

———

In behalf of 5000 Colored people of California, I greet you, and welcome you to a participation in this day's celebration. In behalf of the millions of our brethren, whose emancipation from slavery was proclaimed by the President of the United States on the 1st of January, 1863, I salute you. In behalf of the descendants of Africa throughout our country, the Western Continent and the world, I congratulate you.

This is a day of thanksgiving and rejoicing to us. The day which our fathers desired to see, and for which we have prayed. They died without the sight;—we are permitted to behold the dawning and the light of the advancing day of freedom to our race.

Our thanks are due unto God, who ruleth from everlasting to everlasting. [...]

Our thanks are next due to *Abraham Lincoln*, the President of the U. States—the minister of God and the servant of the people, in carrying out the Proclamation of Emancipation. Let him be praised. "Honor be given to whom honor is due." Mr. Lincoln was placed at the head of this Government in troublous times—placed at the helm of the ship of state in a violent storm. He has been required to do a work more difficult than has devolved upon any chief magistrate since the organization of the American Federal Union. And nobly thus far has he discharged his duties. [...]

We are aware of the dangers which have threatened this Government with destruction since Mr. Lincoln's election and which threatens it now. The prime cause of that danger is found in the existence of slavery. No fact in the history of our country has been made plainer than that slavery has been the cause of constant strife and bad blood between the people of the country, and is the cause of the present war. Slavery presided at the birth of the Government. [...] [S]lavery has grown stronger as the Government grew older—from the beginning i[t] has controlled the legislative, judiciary and executive departments of the Government. [...]

For the perpetuation of slavery the South are fighting in [t]his war; for its destruction the North are fighting—the result of the contest involves the liberties, not of the colored people alone, but of all the people, white and black.

This is the golden hour for the nation. Slavery may now be destroyed. Mr. Lincoln sees and feels its importance—his position is grand and full of solemn responsibility. If slavery is destroyed, the course of this nation in future will be onward and upward to a degree of wealth, power, intelligence and glory hardly to be conceived. Should the slave power succeed, (which cannot be,) the nation will go backward and downward.

Mr. Lincoln may be compared to St. Peter, holding the key of heaven. If he will continue to stand firmly by his Proclamation, this declaration of faith, and the people, as they have, continue to sustain him with heart, voice, hand, purse, the prosperity of the nation in future is sure—"the gates of hell shall not prevail against her." The Colored people of the United States by this Act of Emancipation, are now bound to stand by this Government—the American Federal Union—with Abraham Lincoln at its head—by every solemn tie that can bind men to their country, and the Government under which they were born, and which secures to them the enjoyment of "life, liberty, and the pursuit of happiness." I think I can say, without boasting, for the colored people of California, that when the Government requires and calls upon them, they will stand beside you and defend the Government and with their lives. [...] The event which we celebrate to-day will forever embalm the name of Abraham Lincoln in the hearts of the descendants of Africa on this continent and throughout the world. There is another name which is always to be mentioned in this connection—the name of WM. LLOYD GARRISON. If there is a man in this nation to whom we owe obligations for sacrifices, for sufferings and for services rendered, more than to others, that man is Wm. Lloyd Garrison. In early youth he made a vow giving himself to labor for the destruction of slavery—he has kept that vow—for more than thirty years, amid obloquy, threats, persecution, imprisonment, mob-violence; through tears of blood he has come to the slave, to the interests and rights of the nominally free Colored people, "ever faithful among the faithless found." [...] I rejoice to believe that he has been permitted to live to see this day—to hear the President's Proclamation of Emancipation, the day and event for which he has labored so long and faithfully. Our gratitude and love are his.

Fellow Citizens: Permit me to say, in closing, we cannot more effectually shew our sense of the value of the service rendered to our people throughout the country—our gratitude to God—our thankfulness to the President—our obligations to the Government and People—than by giving heed to good counsel, and preparing for the discharge of those duties which will grow out of the new relations we are entering upon.

*Pacific Appeal* (San Francisco), Jan. 17, 1863.

## OSBORNE P. ANDERSON, Remarks at Emancipation Celebration in Chicago, January 1, 1863

*The following account of how African Americans in Chicago celebrated January 1, 1863 indicates the high esteem in which Lincoln was held. A resolution approved during the evening portion of the program proclaimed that Lincoln's actions were "embalmed in the hearts of his countrymen," while another resolution made it clear that Black men were willing to shed their blood to uphold the Emancipation Proclamation and the Declaration of Independence. The highlight of the celebration was the appearance of Osborne P. Anderson (1830–1872), one of only a handful of men who survived abolitionist John Brown's 1859 raid on Harpers Ferry, Virginia. Anderson eluded capture and published a memoir of his experiences:* A Voice from Harper's Ferry *(1861). For Anderson, Lincoln's proclamation was the culmination of the work Brown had begun and represented nothing less than the single greatest event in the history of the country. In suggesting that the bloody conflict was God's punishment for slavery, Anderson echoed sentiments Brown had expressed on his way to the gallows and anticipated how Lincoln explained the cost and duration of the war in his Second Inaugural Address.*

---

*Remarks of Mr. O.P. Anderson*

Mr. President and friends: Approaching this hour in which we have assembled, I confess to you that I feel overwhelmed by the occasion which has shook not only this continent, but arrested the attention of mankind everywhere, who have been enquiring what was the cause of this war. It has been a mighty problem to solve, and I am glad to know that the first day of the new year gives us a solution of the problem. Not only in the United States, but across the great deep, men have watched for the solution of the problem.

This war is not unnatural. It results from natural causes. It dates back to the revolution—to when the colonies met in convention to adopt the constitution. It was then the first concession was made to slavery, and the government was founded upon a compromise, and there dates the commencement of the war.

The speaker then rapidly showed what he thought was the foolishness of attributing the war to the election of Mr. Lincoln. The war was rather the expression of an antagonism beyond the mere election of a president.

This war, he said, is the all absorbing question. Battles have been fought, some have been successful, and some have not, and in all we recognize the hand of Almighty God moulding and shaping the destinies of a downtrodden race. Even anti-slavery men have at times doubted and trembled; I have never. I believe in God's just judgment. To-day this war is nothing more than the accumulated wrath of God. I am hopeful, and believe in a mysterious outpouring of vengeance, and I rejoice to-day that Abraham Lincoln, after trying all other means, on the 22d of September last declared that all slaves should be free. The people everywhere rejoice at this consummation, and it is no matter what the politicians say, it was brought about after all other means were tried. The President is a cool, calculating, shrewd man, and notwithstanding the opposition papers and politicians, he aimed straight at the source of the difficulty. The very conflict which is raising to-day is to me only the doom of slavery, and the perpetuation of liberty. It is God vindicating the principles of that old man, John Brown, who fought and died for the right. (Applause.)

Some writers had said that the discovery of America by Columbus was the greatest event in our history. Others had said that the signing of the Declaration of Independence was the greatest, but if this proclamation is carried out, to-day, said the speaker, will be the most memorable in the annals of the country.[...]

*[Resolutions approved at evening meeting:]*

Whereas, the President of the United States of America has issued a proclamation of freedom to all states and parts of states in rebellion against the government on this the first day of January in the year of our Lord 1863; and whereas, it has pleased Almighty God to select Abraham Lincoln as his instrument through which his justice is to be rendered to all men in this country; therefore,

*Resolved*, That we hail with deep emotion the auspicious event, and as good and loyal colored Americans we tender to Abraham Lincoln our sincerest thanks in the name of the republic, of God, and of humanity.

*Resolved*, That in the President of the United States we recognize the Christian patriot and honest man, who, since his inauguration as chief magistrate, his acts have been blessed of God, and will be embalmed in the hearts of his countrymen, and when some future historian shall come to write the history they will find a document that will go down to posterity beside the immortal Declaration of Independence.

*Resolved*, We also congratulate all lovers of the rights of man upon this auspicious and glorious result of their labors; they have secured for themselves endearing immortality, viz: liberty to four millions of slaves, privileges never heretofore enjoyed by 650,000 nominal freemen of the north, and to untold thousands of the poorer whites in the states now in rebellion.

*Resolved*, That we will ever hold this, the first day of January, 1863, as abolishment day, the day that four millions of Africo-Americans were redeemed from the thraldom of American slavery into the noonday of universal life, by the single shake of the pen of one man, big Abraham Lincoln.

*Resolved*, That, amidst our happiness, we reflect with sadness upon the fact that so many soldiers of freedom have fallen in the struggle, but their cenotaph will ever be in the hearts of a grateful people.

*Resolved*, That as heretofore so hereafter, we being loyal to the government, should they give us the rights of man, we will pledge our lives, our fortunes and our sacred honor to sustain the true declaration of Jefferson and Adams recognizing as a self-evident truth the right of all men to the pursuit of happiness, and to this end we will not sheath the sword of truth until we have unfurled our banner dipped in the blood of millions to the breeze on the Gulf coast, and proclaim to the bondsman your chains are severed, every yoke is broken, under the American sky redeemed, regenerated, and disenthralled by the sacred genius of universal emancipation.

"Rejoicing Over the Emancipation Proclamation," the *Anglo-African* (New York), Jan. 17, 1863.

## H. FORD DOUGLAS to Frederick Douglass, Colliersville, Tennessee, January 8, 1863

*Though he had been a harsh critic of Lincoln during the 1860 presidential campaign (see above), H. Ford Douglas (1831–1865) began to alter his view of Lincoln after the president issued the Emancipation Proclamation and called for Black men to serve in the army. Douglas had not waited for Lincoln's call and was serving in an Illinois regiment when he penned the following to Frederick Douglass. Douglas was either able to pass as a White man or his comrades in the 95th Illinois Infantry were indifferent to his complexion. Douglas believed the war was educating Lincoln to such an extent that he was optimistic further progress towards racial equality would be made and there would soon be no more talk of colonization. For Douglas and thousands of others, one of the surest ways to accelerate the process was for Black men to take up arms.*

---

Abraham Lincoln has crossed the Rubicon and by one simple act of Justice to the slave links his memory with immortality.

The slaves are *free!* How can I write these precious words? And yet it is so unless twenty millions of people cradled in christianity and civilization for a thousand years commits the foulest perjury that ever blackened the pages of history. In anticipation of this result I enlisted six Months ago in order to be better prepared to play my part in the great drama of the Negroe's redemption. I wanted its drill, its practical details for mere theory does not make a good soldier. I have learned something of war for I have seen war in its brightest as well as its bloodiest phase and yet I have nothing to regret. For since the stern necessities of this struggle have laid bare the naked issue of freedom on one side and slavery on the other—freedom shall have in the future of this conflict if necessary my blood as it has had in the past my earnest and best words. It seems to me that you can have no good reason for withholding from the government your hearty cooperation. This war will educate Mr. Lincoln out of his idea of the deportation of the Negro quite as fast as it has some of his other proslavery ideas with respect to employing them as soldiers.

Hitherto they have been socially and politically ignored by this government, but now by the fortunes of war they are cast morally and mentally helpless (so to speak) into the broad sunlight of our Republican civilization there, to be educated and lifted to a higher and nobler life. National duties and responsibilities are not to be colonized, they must be heroically met and religiously performed. This mighty waste of manhood resulting from the dehumanizing character of slave institutions of America is now to be given back to the world through the patient toil and self-denial of this proud and haughty race. They must now pay back to the negro in Spiritual culture in opportunities for self-improvement what they have taken from him for two hundred years by the constant over-taxing of his physical nature. This law of supply and demand regulates itself. And so this question of the colonization of the negro will be settled by laws over which war has no control. Now is the time for you to finish the crowning work of your life. Go to work at once and raise a Regiment and offer your services to the government and I am confident they will be accepted. They say we will not fight. I want to see it tried on. You are the one to me of all others, to demonstrate this fact.

I belong to company G, 95th Regiment Illinois Volunteers—Captain Eliot N. Bush—a christian and a gentleman.

*Douglass' Monthly* (Rochester, NY), Feb. 1863.

## THOMAS MORRIS CHESTER, Speech at Cooper Institute, New York, January 20, 1863

*A native of Pennsylvania, Chester (1834–1892) became so frustrated by the depth of racial prejudice that he advocated colonization and moved to Liberia in the 1850s. He returned to the United States during the Civil War, and as the following address indicates, the Emancipation Proclamation gave Chester hope and optimism regarding the future. For Chester, the war was a form of divine punishment, and he believed "Father Abraham" was successfully leading the country into a new age of freedom. Chester was later employed as a war correspondent by a Philadelphia newspaper and covered African American soldiers in Virginia. After the war, Chester studied law and moved to Louisiana in the early 1870s, where he became involved in Reconstruction politics (ANB).*

On the morning of the first of January, the Arbiter of nations moved the heart and nerved the hand of President Lincoln, and he issued the grandest proclamation that ever came from any source beneath the Throne of God. (Applause.) It breaks the shackles of hereditary bondmen and loosens the fetters of every slave. It raises from the level of chattels millions of our race to the standard of manhood.

It protects the sanctity of the marriage relationship and lays the foundation for domestic purity. It releases from licentious restraint our cruelly treated women and defends them in the maiden chastity which instincts suggest. It justifies the natural right of the mother over the disposition of her daughters, and gives to the father the only claim which Almighty God intended should be exercised by man over his son. (Applause.) It demolishes the auction-block, where so many tears of blood have been shed and lays the foundation for morality and religion. It destroys the slave-pens, which have been the scene of so many sufferings and deaths, and begins the erection, on their site, of good schools, which will illuminate the dark minds of the south with wisdom and genuine philosophy. It puts an end to blasphemy and the perversion of the scriptures, and inaugurates those higher and holier influences which will prosper all the people and bless the land from the Atlantic to the Pacific. It breaks up forever the system of slavery with its blasting iniquities and secures the blessings of religion and liberty, which shall immortalize the glory of the republic. It ends the days of oppression, cruelty and outrage, founded on complexion, and introduces an era of emancipation, humanity and virtue, founded upon the principles of unerring justice. This act, which terminates so many evils flowing out of a vile system, and inaugurates so many blessings by a bold dash of Father Abraham's pen, should be written in letters of gold upon heaven's blue canopy. (Applause.)

The glorious results of the proclamation will be no less beneficial to the six millions of whites than to the three millions of blacks. Actuated by a false idea of interest, they have reared an institution which has cursed the country and made its advocates traitors. The blood and prayers of millions of our race, crying from the cotton-fields and rice-swamps, accompanied with the earnest supplication of holy men of every clime, have reached the Throne of God and been answered back in the grand proclamation of freedom. (Applause.) [...]

The magnitude of America's crimes against God and man has brought down upon this nation a terrible retribution. We have reason, however, to believe that this severely scourged country will yet be brought safely through the ordeal under the wise and just administration of Father Abraham. The hopes of all good men are centered in the great truths and sublime principles which the government has so cheerfully supported. This period marks an era in American history, which opens with the morning of freedom and will be perpetuated with an unrivaled glory that will challenge admiration. The government at last is brought back to the principles of the fathers of the republic, and on the basis of Christianity and universal liberty a superstructure will be reared that will transcend the greatness of ancient or modern nationalities. As Washington heads the first page of the nation's history, which has made him memorable throughout the land, so Lincoln marks the next brighter and grander era which has immortalized his name all over creation. [...]

Let us all rejoice that the good times so long and so often promised are beginning to light up the land, and may your efforts conspire to hasten on the glorious period to its full meridian. [...] Let your principles be as honest as Lincoln's, as loyal as Cameron's, and as firm as the ridge of rocks beyond the prairies of the west. Let us all exult that the soil of this great empire, extending from ocean to ocean, is consecrated to freedom under the genial glow of those rays of civilization which dissolve every fetter and raises the bondman, though Afric's sun may have burnt his brow, to dignity of manhood.

The *Anglo-African* (New York), Feb. 7, 1863.


## JAMES H. HUDSON Criticizes Lincoln and the Emancipation Proclamation, February 25, 1863

*Hudson was an agent for the* Pacific Appeal *in Suisun City, California. While many praised Lincoln and rejoiced at the news of the Emancipation Proclamation, Hudson chastised Lincoln for being slow to take action against slavery and criticized the proclamation for applying only to areas in rebellion and thus beyond the reach of the federal government. The phrase "Put not your trust in princes" is from Psalm 146.*

I object. I think our view of the Freedom Proclamation, its significance and its consequences, is incorrect [...] I am one of those who think the President has been too dilatory in seizing, for the use of the public, such potent means of oppressive warfare as a declaration of emancipation would have been 12 months ago, and even now, so far from perceiving the full requirements of the occasion— as, for instance, the necessity for complete and decisive measures for reducing the strength of the rebellion,—our honest but incompetent President adopts a halfway measure, which purports to give freedom to the bulk of the slave population beyond the reach of our arms, while it ignores or defies justice, by clinching the rivets of the chain which binds those whom alone we have present power to redeem. The proclamation should have been made to include every bondsman on the soil of America; every chain should have been broken, and the oppressed bidden to go free. Then, indeed, believing we were obeying the divine law, we might have invoked God's blessing upon our arms, and we could then have boldly claimed the services of every loyal man, white or black, in suppressing this hell-born and heaven-defying rebellion. The proclamation has been brought forth by timid and heaven-doubting midwives, and proved an incompetent and abominable abortion. "Put not your trust in princes," says the inspired writer, and he might have added with truth, acknowledged by the wrongs of a long-suffering people, "nor in the rule of republics—their strength is nought, and burnt-offerings are offensive in my sight." Oh that the scales might drop from their eyes, and that they could pray, and work, and rule and fight with the fervor, the steadfastness, the wisdom and the righteousness that have characterized God's chosen people in olden times.

Letter to the editor of the *Pacific Appeal* (San Francisco), March 7, 1863.

## FRANCES ELLEN WATKINS HARPER, "The President's Proclamation," March 7, 1863

*While Harper (1825–1911) had been quite critical of Lincoln's colonization policy and believed he had been slow to act against slavery (see above), the following poem suggests that the Emancipation Proclamation brought light to the world and offered the "dawn of freedom" to those who were enslaved.*

It shall flash through coming ages,
It shall light the distant years;
And eyes now dim with sorrow
Shall be brighter through their tears.

It shall flush the mountain ranges,
And the valleys shall grow bright;
It shall bathe the hills in radiance,
And crown their brows with light.

It shall flood with golden splendor,
All the huts of Caroline;
And the sun kissed brow of labor,
With lustre new shall shine.

It shall gild the gloomy prison,
Darkened with the age's crime;
Where the dumb and patient millions,
Wait the better coming time.

By the light that gilds their prison,
They shall seize its mouldering key;
And the bolts and bars shall vibrate,
With the triumphs of the free.

Like the dim and ancient Chaos,
Shuddering at Creation's light;
Oppression grim and hoary,
Shall cower at the sight.

And her spawn of lies and malice,
Shall grovel in the dust;
While joy shall thrill the bosoms
Of the merciful and just.

Though the morning seems to linger,
O'er the hill tops far away,
The shadows bear the promise,
Of the quickly coming day.

Soon the mists and murky shadows,
Shall be fringed with crimson light;
And the glorious dawn of freedom,
Break resplendent on the sight.

The *Anglo-African* (New York), March 7, 1863.

## JOHN PROCTOR to Abraham Lincoln, Beaufort, South Carolina, April 18, 1863

*Proctor enlisted in the 2nd South Carolina Infantry (later designated the 34th US Colored Infantry) on March 20, 1863. John Hay, one of Lincoln's secretaries, had evidently met Proctor during his visit to South Carolina in the spring of 1863 and promised to give his letter, written without the benefit of a formal education, to President Lincoln. Proctor attained the rank of sergeant and was discharged from the service on February 28, 1866. Captain Edward W. Hooper of General Rufus Saxton's staff enclosed Proctor's letter in a note to John Hay (see Lincoln Papers, Series 1, General Correspondence, 1833 to 1916: "Edward W. Hooper to John Hay, Monday, Monday, May 25, 1863 [Cover Letter]," https:// www.loc.gov/item/mal2366900; Compiled military service record, John Proctor, Sergeant, Company H, 34th US Colored Infantry, M1992, Record Group 94, National Archives, Washington, DC).*

---

Deare sir I have had the onner of righting to you these fue lines hoping that tha may find you in A most Perfic state of helte as it left me the saim. Deare sir I have had the oner of righting to you By the request of capt. hoopper of genrel saxten staff and I then think that it was the Greateist oner that I cold have had. sir I wold that I only cold have right Better so that I cold Ex spriss my word Better—tho wat little I have got I stold it when I wer with my rebble master so that I hav never had the right schooling. But I hope that you ma under stand wat little I have sed. sir sence I have got a way from the rebbles I hav throne my self in to the collard

regemint so that I may have the Pleger of capttor my master Bueregaurd—as I hav
Binn sirvin under him so long I think know is the time for me to let him spinte
sum of his time under me and my hot shot.

I only wish that I only cold have the Pleger of coming to Be hold you—with
mine eyes I am verry much longing to see you remember me to all of my Brothers felow cittysons of the united states

I am now your humble
sirvant. John. Proctor.
of the 2 So Ca. V. C.o. C

Lincoln Papers, Series 1, General Correspondence, 1833 to 1916: "John Proctor to Abraham
Lincoln, Saturday, April 18, 1863 (Former Slave of General Beauregard Has Joined Union
Army)," https://www.loc.gov/item/mal2304400.

## WILLIAM SLADE to Abraham Lincoln, Washington, DC, April 28, 1863

*Slade (1815–1868) served in the Lincoln White House as the president's usher
and valet. A leader of the African American community in Washington, Slade
was an elder at the Fifteenth Street Presbyterian Church, involved in various
philanthropic endeavors, and helped organize a celebration of the first anniversary of the District emancipation law in April 1863. Eager to have Black men
serve in the military, Slade sent the following note to Lincoln that enclosed a
petition signed by him and over fifty other African American citizens in Washington that requested Secretary of War Stanton to authorize the recruitment of
a regiment of Black soldiers from Washington, DC, and Alexandria, Virginia.
Robert Dale Owen was a member of the recently appointed American Freedmen's Inquiry Commission that was charged with examining the condition of
persons freed by the Emancipation Proclamation. The petitioners recommended
that J. D. Turner, former chaplain of the 4th Pennsylvania Cavalry, and William
G. Raymond, a former lieutenant in the 86th New York and hospital chaplain,
be commissioned as the commanding officers of the regiment. Lincoln followed
Slade's recommendation and authorized Turner and Raymond to begin recruiting a regiment that eventually came to be known as the 1st US Colored Troops.
Raymond recalled in his memoirs that there was such hostility to the prospect
of accepting Black men as soldiers that armed guards were required at recruiting meetings and on one occasion someone fired a pistol at him. After Lincoln's
death, Mrs. Lincoln reportedly gave Slade one of her husband's canes. Slade
served as President Johnson's White House steward until his death (Natalie
Sweet, "A Representative 'of our people': The Agency of William Slade, Leader*

*in the African American Community and Usher to Abraham Lincoln," Journal of the Abraham Lincoln Association 34, no. 2 [2013]: 21–41; W. G. Raymond, Life Sketches and Faith Work [Boston: George E. Crosby & Co., 1891];* Evening Star *[Washington, DC], Apr. 17, 1863).*

Sir

The foregoing petition was suggested to me By the Honl Robert Dale Owen and had we not deemd It of the utmost importance to have it before your Excellency at the earliest practicable moment, I could just as easily have had this paper filld with Names, as to have got what we have, as I beleive To the best of my knowledge, these men are the universal choice of our people and if it is Necessary we will increase the List.

Your obedient servant
William Slade

Lincoln Papers, Series 1, General Correspondence, 1833 to 1916: "Washington D. C. Black Citizens to Edwin M. Stanton, Wednesday, April 22, 1863 (Petition Recommending Officers for a Black Regiment; with Note from William Slade to Lincoln [. . .])," https://www.loc.gov/item/mal2310200/.

## ROBERT PURVIS, Address to the American Anti-Slavery Society, New York, May 12, 1863

*The son of a White father and a free woman of color, Purvis (1810–1898) was a prominent leader of the abolition movement who helped found the American Anti-Slavery Society, organized opposition to the Fugitive Slave Act, and fought for the equal treatment of African Americans in his home state of Pennsylvania. Purvis had long opposed colonization and condemned Lincoln's proposal as an insane scheme doomed to fail. As the following speech indicates, Purvis's attitude toward Lincoln had changed rather dramatically by early 1863, largely as a result of the Emancipation Proclamation and the enlistment of Black men into the army. Purvis was also encouraged by other actions of the Lincoln administration, especially the November 1862 opinion of Attorney General Edward Bates that argued African Americans were citizens and thus repudiated a key tenet of Chief Justice Roger Taney's opinion in the 1857 Dred Scott case. While some abolitionists remained skeptical of Lincoln and criticized the Emancipation Proclamation for not going far enough, Purvis had faith in Lincoln and was optimistic about the future of race relations (ANB; the* Liberator *[Boston], Sept. 12, 1862).*

[T]his is a proud day for the "colored" man. For the first time since this Society was organized, I stand before you a recognized citizen of the United States (applause). And let me add, for the first time since your government was a government is it an honor to be a citizen of the United States! Sir, old things are passing away, all things are becoming new. Now a black man has rights, under this government, which every white man, here and everywhere, is bound to respect (applause). The damnable doctrine of the detestable Taney is no longer the doctrine of the country. The Slave Power no longer rules at Washington. [ . . . ] I forget the past; joy fills my soul at the prospect of the future. I leave to others the needful duty of censure. But, I hear some of my hearers saying, "It is too soon to begin to rejoice; don't halloo till you are out of the woods; don't be too sure of the future—wait and see." No, sir, I will not wait—I cannot be mistaken. My instincts, in this matter at least, are unerring. The good time which has so long been coming is at hand. I feel it, I see it in the air, I read it in the signs of the times; I see it in the acts of Congress, in the abolition of slavery in the District of Columbia, in its exclusion from the Territories, in solemn treaties for the effectual suppression of the infernal foreign slave trade, in the acknowledgment of the black republics of Hayti and Liberia. I see it in the new spirit that is in the army; I see it in the black regiment of South Carolina (applause); I see it in the 54th Regiment of Massachusetts; I see it in the order of Adjnt.-Gen. Thomas, forming a Black Brigade at Memphis; I see it, above all, and more than all, in the GLORIOUS AND IMMORTAL PROCLAMATION OF ABRAHAM LINCOLN, ON THE FIRST OF JANUARY, 1863 (cheers). By that imperishable instrument the three million of slaves in the rebel States are legally and irrevocably free! [ . . . ] By that immortal document all the remaining slaves of the country are in effect promised their freedom. In *spirit* and in *purpose*, thanks to *Almighty God!* this is no longer a slaveholding republic. The fiat has gone forth which, when this rebellion is crushed—and it will be crushed as sure as there is a God in heaven—the fiat has gone forth which, in the simple but beautiful language of the President, "will take all burdens from off all backs, and make every man a freeman."

The *Anglo-African* (New York), May 23, 1863.

## HANNAH JOHNSON to Abraham Lincoln, Buffalo, New York, July 31, 1863

*Hannah Johnson's son was a soldier in the 54th Massachusetts, one of the first regiments of Black soldiers raised in the free states. She was one of many, including Frederick Douglass and Senator Charles Sumner, who urged Lincoln to respond to threats from rebel authorities that captured Black soldiers and their*

*White officers would not be treated as prisoners of war. Instead, Black soldiers would be treated like escaped slaves and White officers prosecuted for fomenting servile insurrection. This meant either enslavement or execution for the soldiers and almost certain death for their officers. By July 1863, these threats were becoming reality as the first Black units engaged in combat. While Hannah Johnson's son survived the July 18, 1863, assault on Fort Wagner, his commanding officer, Colonel Robert Gould Shaw, was killed. On the same day that Hannah Johnson wrote to Lincoln, Colonel Shaw's father, Francis George Shaw, also wrote to the president and expressed his wish to see "immediate measures taken to extend the protection of the United States over his surviving officers & men." On the same day these letters were written, the War Department issued General Orders No. 252 that published an order from President Lincoln directing that for every US prisoner that was killed or enslaved a like number of rebel prisoners be executed or put to hard labor. Lincoln indicated it was the obligation of the federal government to protect all "citizens" regardless of their "class, color, or condition." Despite these orders, numerous atrocities were committed against Black soldiers and their White officers (see Lincoln Papers, Series 1, General Correspondence, 1833 to 1916: "Charles Sumner to Abraham Lincoln, Wednesday, May 20, 1863 [Recommends Presidential Proclamation Promising to Retaliate against Threatened Treatment of Black Troops and Their Officers (...)]," https://www.loc.gov/item/mal2359700; Lincoln Papers, Series 1, General Correspondence, 1833 to 1916: "Francis George Shaw to Abraham Lincoln, Friday, July 31, 1863 [Protection for Officers of Black Soldiers]," https://www .loc.gov/item/mal2522200; Collected Works, VI: 357).*

---

Excellent Sir

My good friend says I must write to you and she will send it[.] My son went in the 54th regiment. I am a colored woman and my son was strong and able as any to fight for his country and the colored people have as as much to fight for as any. My father was a Slave and escaped from louisiana before I was born morn forty years agone I have but poor edication but I never went to schol but I know just as well as any what is right between man and man. Now I know it is right that a colored man should go and fight for his country, and so ought to a white man. I know that a colored man ought to run no greater risques than a white, his pay is no greater his obligation to fight is the same. So why should not our enemies be compelled to treat him the same, made to do it.

My son fought at Fort Wagoner but thank God he was not taken prisoner, as many were I thought of this thing before I let my boy go but then they said Mr. Lincoln will never let them sell our colored solders for slaves, if they do he will get them back quck he will rettallyate and stop it. Now Mr Lincoln dont you think you oght to stop this thing and make them do the same by the colored men they have lived in idleness all their lives on stolen labor and made savages of the colored people but they now are so furious because they are proving themselves to be men, such as have come away and got some edication. It must not be so, you must put the rebels to work in State prisons to making shoes and things, if they sell our colored soldiers, till they let them all go, and give their wounded the same treatment, it would seem cruel, but their no other way, and a just man must do hard things sometimes, that shew him to be a great man. They tell me some do you will take back the Proclamation, don't do it. When you are dead and in Heaven, in a thousand years that action of yours will make the Angels sing your praises I know it. Ought one man to own another, law for or not, who made the law, surely the poor slave did not, so it is wicked, and a horrible outrage, there is no sense in it, because a man has lived by robbing all his life and his father before him, should he complain because the stolen things found on him are taken. Robbing the colored people of their labor is but a small part of the robbery their souls are almost taken, they are made bruits of [oxen?]. You know all about this

Will you see that the colored men fighting now, are fairly treated. You ought to do this, and do it at once, not let the thing run along meet it quickly and manfully, and stop this, mean cowardly cruelty. We poor oppresed ones, appeal to you, and ask fair play.

Yours for Christ sake

Hannah Johnson

Record Group 94, Entry 360, Letters Received by the Colored Troops Division, Box 19, National Archives, Washington, DC.

## FREDERICK DOUGLASS, "The Commander-in-Chief and His Black Soldiers," August 1863

*Frederick Douglass had two sons serving in the 54th Massachusetts Infantry, and here he expressed his concern for the treatment of Black soldiers and dismay at Lincoln's apparent indifference to their plight. The 54th had participated in the ill-fated assault on Fort Wagner on July 18, and rebel authorities, including Jefferson Davis, had indicated that captured Black soldiers would be treated like slaves engaged in servile insurrection rather than prisoners of war. This meant either enslavement or execution for any Black soldier who was captured. Though Douglass's sons had not been captured, he was worried about the fate of the soldiers who had fallen into enemy hands and was disturbed by reports of atrocities committed against Black soldiers who not only fought at Fort Wagner but also in prior engagements at Milliken's Bend and Port Hudson in Louisiana.*

*Lincoln received personal appeals from politicians and parents of soldiers to take action, and on July 31, he issued an order of retaliation that threatened to execute or put to hard labor a like number of rebel prisoners for every US soldier that was executed or enslaved. Douglass also alluded to the inequality of pay between Black and White soldiers. His concerns about the equal treatment of Black soldiers were directly expressed to the president when he met Lincoln for the first time in August 1863.*

---

Whatever else may be said of President Lincoln, the most malignant Copperhead in the country cannot reproach him with any undue solicitude for the lives and liberties of the brave black men, who are now giving their arms and hearts to the support of his Government. When a boy, on a slave plantation the saying was common: "Half a cent to kill a negro and half a cent to bury him."—The luxury of killing and burying could be enjoyed by the poorest members of Southern society, and no strong temptation was required to induce white men thus to kill and bury the black victims of their lust and cruelty—With a Bible and pulpit affirming that the negro is accursed of God, it is not strange that men should curse him, and that all over the South there should be manifested for the life and liberty of this description of man, the utterest indifference and contempt. Unhappily the same indifference and contempt for the lives of colored men is found wherever slavery has an advocate or treason an apologist. In the late terrible mobs in New York and elsewhere, the grim features of this malice towards colored men was every where present. Beat, shoot hang, stab, kill, burn and destroy the negro, was the cry of the crowd. Religion has cursed him and the law has enslaved him, and why may not the mob kill him?—Such has been our national education on this subject, and that it still has power over Mr. Lincoln seems evident from the fact, that no measures have been openly taken by him to cause the laws of civilized warfare to be observed towards his colored soldiers. The slaughter of blacks taken as captives, seems to affect him as little as the slaughter of beeves for the use of his army. More than six months ago Mr. Jefferson Davis told Mr. Lincoln and the world, that he meant to treat blacks not as soldiers but as felons. The threat was openly made, and has been faithfully executed by the rebel chief. At Murfreesboro twenty colored teamsters in the Federal service, were taken by the rebels, and though not soldiers, and only servants, they were in cold blood—every man of them—shot down. At Millikens Bend, the same black flag with its death's head and cross-bones was raised. When Banks entered Port Hudson he found white federal prisoners, but no black ones. Those of the latter taken, were no doubt, in cold blood put to the sword. Today, news from Charleston tells us that negro soldiers taken as prisoners will not be exchanged, but sold into slavery—that some twenty of such prisoners are now in their hands. Thousands of negroes are now being enrolled in the service of the Federal Government. The Government calls them, and they come. They freely and joyously rally around the flag of the Union, and take all the risks ordinary and extraordinary, involved in this war. They do it not for office, for thus far, they get none; they do it not for money, for thus far, their pay is less than that of white men. They go into this war to affirm their manhood, to strike for liberty and country.—If any class of men in this war can claim the honor of fighting for principle, and not from passion, for ideas, not from brutal malice, the colored soldier can make that claim preeminently. He strikes for manhood and freedom, under the forms of law and the usages of civilized warfare. He does not go forth as a savage with tomahawk and scalping knife, but in strict accordance with the rules of honorable warfare. Yet he is now openly threatened with slavery and assassination by the rebel Government—and the threat has been savagely executed.

What has Mr. Lincoln to say about this slavery and murder? What has he said?—Not one word. In the hearing of the nation he is as silent as an oyster on the whole subject. If two white men are threatened with assassination, the Richmond Rebels are promptly informed that, the Federal Government will retaliate sternly and severely. But when colored soldiers are so threatened, no word comes from the Capitol. What does this silence mean? Is there any explanation short of base and scandalous contempt for the just rights of colored soldiers?

For a time we tried to think that there might be solid reasons of state against answering the threats of Jefferson Davis—but the Government has knocked this favorable judgment from under us, by its prompt threat of retaliation in the case of the two white officers at Richmond who are under sentence of death. Men will ask, the world will ask, why interference should be made for those young white officers thus selected for murder, and not for the brave black soldiers who may be flung by the fortunes of war into the hands of the rebels? Is the right to "life, liberty and the pursuit of happiness" less sacred in the case of the one than the other?

It may be said that the black soldiers have enlisted with the threat of Jefferson Davis before them, and they have assumed their position intelligently, with a full knowledge of the consequences incurred. If they have, they have by that act shown themselves all the more worthy of protection. It is noble in the negro to brave unusual danger for the life of the Republic, but it is mean and base in the Republic if it rewards such generous and unselfish devotion by assassination, when a word would suffice to make the laws of war respected, and to prevent the crime. Shocking enough are the ordinary horrors of war, but the war of the rebels, toward the colored men is marked by deeds which well might "shame extremest hell." And until Mr. Lincoln shall interpose his power to prevent these atrocious assassinations of negro soldiers, the civilized world will hold him equally with Jefferson Davis responsible for them. The question is already being asked: Why is it that colored soldiers which were first enlisted with a view to "Garrison forts and arsenals, on the Southern coast,"—where white men suffer from climate, should never be heard of in any such forts and arsenals? Was that a trick? Why is it that they who were enlisted to fight the fevers of the South, while white soldiers fight the rebels are now only heard of in "forlorn hopes," in desperate charges, always in the van, as at Port Hudson, Milliken Bend, James Island and Fort Wagner? Green colored recruits are called upon to assume the position of veterans. They have performed their part gallantly and gloriously, but by all the proofs they have given of their patriotism and bravery we protest against the meanness, ingratitude and cruelty of the Government, in whose behalf they fight, if that Government remains longer a silent witness of their enslavement and assassination. Having had patience and forbearance with the silence of Mr. Lincoln a few months ago, we could at least imagine some excuses for his silence as to the fate of colored troops falling by the fortunes of war into the hands of the rebels, but the time for this is past. It is now for every man who has any sense of right and decency, to say nothing of gratitude, to speak out trumpet-tongued in the ears of Mr. Lincoln and his Government and demand from him a declaration of purpose, to hold the rebels to a strict account for every black federal soldier taken as a prisoner. For every black prisoner slain in cold blood, Mr. Jefferson Davis should be made to understand that one rebel officer shall suffer death, and for every colored soldier sold into slavery, a rebel shall be held as a hostage. For our Government to do less than this, is to deserve the indignation and the execration of mankind.

*Douglass' Monthly* (Rochester, NY), August 1863.

## LEONARD A. GRIMES to Abraham Lincoln, Washington, DC, August 21, 1863

*Grimes (1815–1873), a Boston minister and abolitionist, was serving as president of the American Baptist Missionary Convention that was holding its annual meeting in Washington, when the convention appointed him to lead a committee to call on Lincoln. The purpose of the interview was to obtain protection for missionaries sent to the South who ministered to Black people that had come within the lines of US military forces. Lincoln met with the delegation, listened to Grimes, and granted the request by providing a letter stating that he would "be glad for all facilities to be afforded them which may not be inconsistent with or a hindrance to our military operations" (see "An Interview with the President of the United States," the Anglo-African, Sept. 5, 1863; Collected Works, VI: 401).*

To His Exilancy,
President Lincoln
Your petitioner would, respectfully beg an interview of a few moments, for a deligation of Ministers of the Gospel, now in session in the City of Washington, as the "American Baptist Missionary Convention, and if an interview should be granted please name the hour.
Yours most respectfully
L. A. Grimes
of Boston Mass
Pres. American Bap. Miss. Convention

Lincoln Papers, Series 1, General Correspondence, 1833 to 1916: "American Baptist Missionary Convention to Abraham Lincoln, Friday, August 21, 1863 (Request Interview)", https://www.loc.gov/item/mal2573000.

## JEREMIAH ASHER to Abraham Lincoln, Philadelphia, Pennsylvania, September 7, 1863

*Asher (1812–1865) was a Connecticut native whose grandfather had been a slave who received his freedom through military service in the Revolutionary War. Asher condemned both slavery in the South and racial prejudice in the North while serving as pastor of the Shiloh Baptist Church in Philadelphia. Although there was no law prohibiting the appointment of Black chaplains, military regulations required chaplains to be appointed by regimental officers. Since there were no Black commissioned officers until near the end of the war and White officers in Black regiments generally preferred White chaplains, Asher was among the fewer than twenty African Americans who were appointed during the war. Commissioned chaplain of the 6th US Colored Infantry in December 1863, Asher remained in the service until his death from typhoid fever at Wilmington, North Carolina on July 27, 1865 (Compiled military service record, Jeremiah Asher, Chaplain, 6th US Colored Infantry, M1820, Record Group 94, National Archives, Washington, DC).*

Dear Sir
In behalf of the Colerd Clergy and Churches of Philadelphia I write to ask you if there is any Law of Congress Prohibiting the appointment of Cole. Chaplains to the Colerd Regiments of United States volunteers.
The Soldiers are anxious to hav Colerd Ministers as their Spiritual Teachers Applications have been made at the War Department but have not been considered if there is no Legal obstruction will you be Pleased to use your influence in this matter and thus oblige the Colerd Regiments who are anxious to have

Religious instruction and the Colerd People in general who ever have been and ever will be Loyal Subjects to the government This your Petitioner will ever Pray

I have the honor to be your most obedient Servant

Jeremiah Asher

Pastor of the Shiloh Church 1013 Rodman St

Record Group 94, Entry 360, Letters Received by the Colored Troops Division, Box 2, National Archives, Washington, DC.

## ROBERT HAMILTON on Lincoln's Letter to James C. Conkling, September 12, 1863

*James C. Conkling, a Springfield, Illinois, political colleague of Lincoln, had invited the president to attend a mass meeting in his hometown on September 3. Although unable to attend, Lincoln sent a letter to Conkling, dated August 26, which was read at the meeting and published in the newspapers. In his letter to Conkling, Lincoln offered a vigorous defense of the Emancipation Proclamation and his decision to allow Black men to serve in the armed forces. While some urged Lincoln to retract the proclamation, Lincoln asserted in his letter to Conkling that the proclamation was a promise that could not be broken "any more than the dead can be brought to life." Lincoln also praised the vital contribution that African American soldiers were making to the war effort and noted that his generals felt the same way. Editor Robert Hamilton (1819–1870) praised Lincoln's letter and quoted from near the conclusion of the document where the president claimed that victory in the war would vindicate republican government and predicted that while Black veterans would take pride in the role they had played in helping to save the nation they would continue to face challenges from Whites who refused to abandon their prejudices.*

---

We know not when we have arisen from the perusal of a document with greater pleasure than from that of the President's letter, which will be found in another column. We believe that we have a right to be proud of, and rejoice over the fact that our good President has written such a letter. There are those who will cavil at it, not only because of the principles upon which it is based, but from its peculiar construction. Its construction, to us, is one of its virtues. The President might have written such a letter as only the most polished and erudite could comprehend; but he has not done so, and we are very glad of it. The understanding of the wayfaring man was to be enlightened and satisfied, and to do this, plain language had to be used, and now everybody understands just what Mr. Lincoln means. There is an air of sincerity running through the letter which must carry conviction to every heart not previously seared by the infernal spirit of Copperheadism. But what gives us peculiar pleasure, is the manner in which it confirms our every assertion concerning Mr. Lincoln. While others were halting and doubting in reference to the policy of the government, we have urged our friends to have full faith in it and its head, for we felt well assured that he could not turn his back upon the principles which were involved in the struggle which the nation is engaged in for its existence.

For the perpetuity of the nation he has worked, and for that alone. Where he has erred, it has been the work of his head and not of his heart, and he has always corrected the error when he found himself in the wrong. The manner in which he argues the case with those who differ from him is his own; nevertheless, it is very effectual. He sees very clearly what must be the end of this contest if the Union is to survive, and come squarely up to the work. He comprehends very clearly that the destiny of the colored man in this country is intimately connected with the life of the nation, and he therefore makes this the burthen of his whole letter. The frank and manly acknowledgment in reference to the services of colored troops is as generous as it is true; and while it fixes forever this important fact upon the page of history, *that they have struck one of the heaviest blows yet dealt against the rebellion*, it also gives them a position as soldiers, before this and all the nations of the earth, which others will try in vain to parallel.

What the President says in regard to his great proclamation will send a thrill of joy through many a doubting and trembling heart and afford great satisfaction to every loyalist in the land.

The concluding sentences of this noble letter ought to be printed in letters of gold and hung in the house of every colored man in the land. Read it:

"Peace does not appear so distant as it did. I hope it will come soon and come to stay; and so come as to be worth the keeping in all future time. It will then have been proved that among freemen there can be no successful appeal from the ballot to the bullet, and that they who take such appeal are sure to lose their case and pay the cost. *And then there will be some black men who can remember that, with silent tongue, and clenched teeth, and steady eye, and well poised bayonet, they have helped mankind on to this great consummation; while I fear that there will be some white ones unable to forget that with malignant heart and deceitful speech they have striven to hinder it.*"

Editorial in the *Anglo-African* (New York), Sept. 12, 1863.

## JOHN WILLIS MENARD to Abraham Lincoln, New York, September 16, 1863

*A native of Illinois, Menard (1838–1893) was a leading advocate of African American emigration because he believed the United States was "a land of*

*caste, of injustice and oppression." He worked as a clerk for James Mitchell,
Lincoln's Commissioner of Emigration, and initially planned to emigrate to
Liberia. With Mitchell's support, Menard visited British Honduras (present-
day Belize) and explored its potential as a site for African American colonization. The following was written shortly after Menard returned from this mission. Neither a response from Lincoln nor a pamphlet copy of Menard's report
has been located, but the* Anglo-African *printed Menard's report to Lincoln.
Menard concluded that the "prospects of the colored man are very flattering"
in British Honduras because "his color is not a social barrier to positions of
trust and honor." Despite Menard's favorable report, the Lincoln administration did not act on his recommendation. After the Civil War, Menard moved
to Louisiana and became the first African American elected to the US House
of Representatives, but he was not allowed to take his seat due to a dispute over
the election results. Menard moved to Florida, where he held a federal patronage
appointment, edited a newspaper, and served in the state legislature. A volume
of poetry that Menard published in 1879 included a poem that paid tribute to
Lincoln for issuing the Emancipation Proclamation ("Honduras. Report of J.
Willis Menard," the* Anglo-African *[New York], Oct. 24, 1863; Bess Beatty,
"John Willis Menard: A Progressive Black in Post-Civil War Florida,"* Florida
Historical Quarterly *59, no. 2 [Oct. 1980]: 123–142; John Willis Menard,* Lays
in Summer Lands *[Washington, DC: Enterprise Publishing, 1879]; Phillip
W. Magness and Sebastian N. Page,* Colonization After Emancipation: Lin-
coln and the Movement for Black Resettlement *[Columbia: University of
Missouri Press, 2011]).*

---

Sir:

Having just returned from an exploration of British Honduras, in Central
America, with a view to lay the basis of a <u>permanent home</u> for myself and those
of my colored race who, from unfavorable circumstances in this country, may be
disposed to emigrate, I respectfully ask that your Excellency will be good enough
to let me report, in pamphlet form, to your Excellency. Should you approve, I will
forward some few copies to your Excellency. I am sorry not to be able to have as
many copies printed as I need for general distribution among my race.
I am Sir, Your Excellency's most obedt. Servt.
J. W. Menard

Records of the Office of the Secretary of the Interior Relating to the Suppression of the Afri-
    can Slave Trade and Negro Colonization, 1854–1872, M160, Record Group 48, Microfilm
    Roll 8, National Archives, Washington, DC.

# ROBERT HAMILTON Endorsing Lincoln for a Second Term as President, October 24, 1863

*With the presidential election of 1864 over a year away, editor Robert Hamilton (1819–1870) offered an unqualified endorsement of Lincoln for a second term. Though Lincoln had yet to propose voting rights for African Americans, Hamilton was optimistic that Lincoln would eventually embrace this policy and oversee the complete abolition of slavery.*

---

We should not be "American citizens of African" or any other "descent," if we failed to think about "our next President." Never was this important matter so late getting on the *tapis* as in the present term. We are within thirteen months of the next election, and nobody has fairly started a candidate. How absorbing this war must be when it overshadows and supplants our quadrennial excitement!

There is one man who has, so far, succeeded in keeping the next Presidency out of the people's minds. He keeps them so thoroughly exercised with *this* that they have little time to bestow on the *next* President. He has a long, shrewd head, and he knows the people better than any live man ever knew them on this side of the Atlantic. Even Louis Napoleon does not know the French better than this man knows the American people. He has taken more than two years to convince the American people that he had that quality which they most lack and therefore greatly respect—honesty; and now he will, within another year, convince the same people that he possesses what their need is most urgent to have—ability. As no man, to day, in all the Americas denies his honesty, so shortly will all admit his transcendent ability.

Everyone who has come in contact with him, whether successful or unsuccessful in their special mission—every one gives the same testimony in behalf of his transparent, simple-minded honesty! All have seen straight through him alike; he is a man open, sincere, and without guile! To be sure, he has done a little "seeing through" the while himself; but how wonderful the uniformity of his testimony, and what "gifts" he must have to win it! How vastly spread, how deeply ingrained the sympathy he must have with all classes; even the rebels, stubborn in arms, are evidently infected with this "Northern sympathy," for they have ceased, to a great extent, to apply bitter epithets to his name. Such sympathy is, of course, a stepping-stone to whatever the object of it may desire. He has simply to signify his willingness to be re-elected President, and the people will re-elect him by acclamation. Politicians, ordinary and extraordinary, evidently take this view of the matter, or, in spite of war's alarms, they would have trotted another candidate into the field. They see that "it's no use," and lay their noses for the spoils which may be got from a continuation of the present government for another term.

And we also, whose all is staked in the future of this great nation, we may as well pray for long life to "Honest Old Abe." There will be trials for us in store—dark days may yet frown upon us; but, under God's good will, we may depend on there being carried out a liberal and enlightened policy of emancipation and affranchisement, if the same hand which now directs shall continue to guide the helm of the ship of State.

Editorial in the *Anglo-African* (New York), Oct. 24, 1863.

## AFRICAN CIVILIZATION SOCIETY, Address to Abraham Lincoln, Washington, DC, November 5, 1863

*James Mitchell, Lincoln's commissioner of emigration, arranged for the president to meet with a committee of Black men from the African Civilization Society. Formed in New York in the late 1850s, the society's initial focus was on sending missionaries to Africa and promoting economic growth there. To further its mission, the society explored the possibility of establishing a colony in Africa. This dovetailed with Mitchell's mission to encourage and support colonization efforts. However, the changing circumstances of the war led the society to shift its focus to assisting newly freed persons in the South. George W. Le Vere (1820–1886), a Congregational minister in Brooklyn, was president of the society and acted as spokesperson for the delegation during the interview. Lincoln reportedly indicated that he would consider the request for five thousand dollars, but he did not sign the executive order that Mitchell had prepared for this purpose (see Lincoln Papers, Series 2, General Correspondence, 1858 to 1864: "[James Mitchell] to John P. Usher, Thursday, November 5, 1863 [Draft of Order to Release Funds to African Civilization Society]," https://www.loc.gov/item/mal4266500; "African Colonization," Brooklyn Daily Eagle, Nov. 12, 1863).*

Mr President

The present Delegation in whose name I now speak, are men who love and fear God. We have often earnestly prayed, that he alone would choose your changes; suit you to circumstances: bless you, and direct you, and all your associate counsellors. We deem it a great privilege at this time to be permitted to submit the fact; that our society is fully organized and with one exception: quite prepared to develope our great scheme of modern civilization and christian benevolence; or as it is more fully expressed: in Art Second of The Constitution: The object of this society shall be, the civilization and christianization of Africa; and of African ancestors in any portion of the earth where-ever dispersed; also the destruction of the african slave trade, by the introduction of lawful commerce into Africa, the promotion of the growth of cotton, and other products there whereby the natives may become industrious producers, as well as consumers of articles of commerce; and generally the elevation of the condition of the coloured population of our own country and of other lands.

Our field of operation is as wide as the world. We have the requisites for its proper cultivation, except money. Of this important medium we are quite destitute.

Our faith in the living God amid the great and peculiar events transpiring under the present administeration prompts us to beleive that your Excellency was raised up in the wisdom of Jehovah to reform this great nation and deliver millions of captives, just as trully and certainly as Moses (once an exiled Hebrew) was to deliver God's ancient covenant people the Jews from Egyptian bondage. As Representatives of the African civilization society we hereby greatfully acknowledge your many timely services recently rendered a suffering portion of our race in this land. Your acts have so fully demonstrated the Problems of national mercy and righteousness that we cannot tell in which they exell. Mindful of the account which we are to render to both God and man, we here submit the singular fact; that this is only Institution of the kind on our globe managed wholly by coloured gentlemen. We beleieve ourselves to be the proper, if not the only legal applicants for suitable portions of the funds; so wisely and liberally appropriated by the present Administration: For the benefit of certian portions of coloured people in this land as well as other parts of the earth.

The Society is universal in its tendences and designs, and under a fourfold Idea in due time we hope to be able to give civilization, the Gospel, science and commerce to our people where-ever they may need them.

In order that we may at once enter upon, and continue this work without interruption we earnestly pray that the President of these United States may—find it in harmony with a good conscience, and most excellent judgment, and within his Executive descretion to place the sum of $5000 or more Dollars to the credit of the African civilization society; with such arrangements that we may draw on the proper Department, for similar amounts as the progress of our work sall require the same.

All of with is most respectfully submitted

George. W. Le Vere

Peter S Porter

William Anderson

Richard H. Cain

Henry. M. Wilson

Secretary

Lincoln Papers, Series 1, General Correspondence, 1833 to 1916: "African Civilization Society to Abraham Lincoln, Thursday, November 5, 1863, (Seek Funds in Order to "Civilize" Africa)", https://www.loc.gov/item/mal2784000.

## FREDERICK DOUGLASS, Address to the American Anti-Slavery Society, Philadelphia, Pennsylvania, December 4, 1863

*The American Anti-Slavery Society marked its thirtieth anniversary with a meeting held in Philadelphia in early December 1863. In calling for the meeting, William Lloyd Garrison, the longtime president of the organization, promised that the meeting would not only reflect on the Society's work over the past three decades but also celebrate Lincoln's Emancipation Proclamation. Abolitionists had been among Lincoln's strongest critics, and many remained skeptical following the Emancipation Proclamation. Prior to Douglass's speech, members of the convention had vigorously debated Lincoln's anti-slavery policies and intentions. Just as Lincoln had spoken of "unfinished work" in his Gettysburg Address two weeks prior, here Douglass suggests that the work will not be done until slavery has been completely abolished and persons of color accorded equal rights—an "Abolition war" followed by an "Abolition peace." Douglass also details his first meeting with Lincoln that had taken place at the White House the previous August. Douglass had met with the president to discuss his concerns regarding the treatment of Black soldiers. Douglass's public account accords with the private letter he had written to George L. Stearns shortly after the meeting. Douglass wrote Stearns that Lincoln impressed him with his honesty and determination to uphold his emancipation policy. Both Lincoln and Douglass had no illusions about the difficulties of ending slavery and convincing the country to accept Black people as citizens.*

---

We live to see a better hope tonight. I participate in the profound thanksgiving expressed by all, that we do live to see this better day. I am one of those who believe that it is the mission of this war to free every slave in the United States. I am one of those who believe that we should consent to no peace which shall not be an Abolition peace. I am, moreover, one of those who believe that the work of the American Anti-Slavery Society will not have been completed until the black men of the South, and the black men of the North, shall have been admitted, fully and completely, into the body politic of America. I look upon slavery as going the way of all the earth. It is the mission of the war to put it down. But a mightier work than the abolition of slavery now looms up before the Abolitionist. This Society was organized, if I remember rightly, for two distinct objects; one was the emancipation of the slave, and the other the elevation of the colored people. When we have taken the chains off the slave, as I believe we shall do, we shall find a harder resistance to the second purpose of this great association than we have found even upon slavery itself.

I am hopeful; but while I am hopeful, I am thoughtful withal. If I lean to either side of the controversy to which we have listened today, I lean to that side which implies caution, which implies apprehension, which implies a consciousness that our work is not done. Protest, affirm, hope, glorify as we may, it cannot be denied that Abolitionism is still unpopular in the United States. It cannot be denied that this war is at present denounced by its opponents as an Abolition war; and it is equally clear that it would not be denounced as an Abolition war, if Abolitionism was not odious. It is equally clear that our friends, Republicans, Unionists, Loyalists, would not spin out elaborate explanations and denials that this is the character of the war, if Abolition were popular. [ . . . ]

I look at this as an Abolition war instead of being a Union war, because I see that the lesser is included in the greater, and that you cannot have the lesser until you have the greater. You cannot have the Union, the Constitution, and Republican institutions, until you have stricken down that damning curse, and put it beyond the pale of the Republic. For, while it is in this country, it will make your Union impossible; it will make your Constitution impossible. I therefore call this just what the Democrats have charged it with being, an Abolition war. Let us emblazon it on our banners, and declare before the world that this is an Abolition war, (applause,) that it will prosper precisely in proportion as it takes upon itself this character. (Renewed applause.) [ . . . ]

When this rebellion shall have been put down, when the arms shall have fallen from the guilty hands of traitors, you will need the friendship of the slaves of the South, of those millions there. Four or five million men are not of inconsiderable importance at any time; but they will be doubly important when you come to reorganize and reestablish republican institutions in the South. Will you mock those bondmen by breaking their chains with one hand, and with the other giving their rebel masters the elective franchise, and robbing them of theirs? I tell you the negro is your friend. You will make him your friend by emancipating him. But you will make him not only your friend in sentiment and heart by enfranchising him, but you will make him your best defender, your best protector against the traitors and the descendants of those traitors, who will inherit the hate, the bitter revenge which will crystallize all over the South, and seek to circumvent the Government that they could not throw off. You will need the black men there, as a watchman and patrol; and you may need him as a soldier. You may need him to uphold in peace, as he is now upholding in war, the star-spangled banner. (Applause.) [ . . . ]

I have been down there [Washington] to see the President; and as you were not there, perhaps you may like to know how the President of the United States received a black man at the White House. I will tell you how he received me—just as you have seen one gentleman receive another (great applause); with a hand and a voice well-balanced between a kind cordiality and a respectful reserve. I tell you

I felt big there! (Laughter.) Let me tell you how I got to him; because everybody can't get to him. He has to be a little guarded in admitting spectators. The manner of getting to him gave me an idea that the cause was rolling on. The stairway was crowded with applicants. Some of them looked eager; and I have no doubt some of them had a purpose in being there, and wanted to see the President for the good of the country! They were white; and as I was the only dark spot among them, I expected to have to wait at least half a day; I had heard of men waiting a week; but in two minutes after I sent in my card, the messenger came out, and respectfully invited "Mr. Douglass" in. I could hear, in the eager multitude outside, as they saw me pressing and elbowing my way through, the remark, "Yes, damn it, I knew they would let the nigger through," in a kind of despairing voice—a Peace Democrat, I suppose. (Laughter.) When I went in, the President was sitting in his usual position, I was told, with his feet in different parts of the room, taking it easy. (Laughter.) Don't put this down, Mr. Reporter, I pray you; for I am going down there again tomorrow! (Laughter.) As I came in and approached him, the President began to rise, (laughter,) and he continued rising until he stood over me (laughter); and, reaching out his hand, he said, "Mr. Douglass, I know you; I have read about you, and Mr. Seward has told me about you;" putting me quite at ease at once.

Now, you will want to know how I was impressed by him. I will tell you that, too. He impressed me as being just what every one of you have been in the habit of calling him—an honest man. (Applause.) I never met with a man, who, on the first blush, impressed me more entirely with his sincerity, with his devotion to his country, and with his determination to save it at all hazards. (Applause.) He told me (I think he did me more honor than I deserve) that I had made a little speech, somewhere in New York, and it had got into the papers, and among the things I had said was this: That if I were called upon to state what I regarded as the most sad and most disheartening feature in our present political and military situation, it would not be the various disasters experienced by our armies and our navies, on flood and field, but it would be the tardy, hesitating, vacillating policy of the President of the United States; and the President said to me, "Mr. Douglass, I have been charged with being tardy, and the like;" and he went on, and partly admitted that he might seem slow; but he said, "I am charged with vacillating; but, Mr. Douglass, I do not think that charge can be sustained; I think it cannot be shown that when I have once taken a position, I have ever retreated from it." (Applause.) That I regarded as the most significant point in what he said during our interview. I told him that he had been somewhat slow in proclaiming equal protection to our colored soldiers and prisoners; and he said that the country needed talking up to that point. He hesitated in regard to it, when he felt that the country was not ready for it. He knew that the colored man throughout this country was a despised man, a hated man, and that if he at first came out with such a proclamation, all the hatred which is poured on the head of the negro race would be visited on his administration. He said that there was preparatory work needed, and that that preparatory work had now been done. And he said, "Remember this, Mr. Douglass; remember that Milliken's Bend, Port Hudson and Fort Wagner are recent events; and that these were necessary to prepare the way for this very proclamation of mine." I thought it was reasonable, but came to the conclusion that while Abraham Lincoln will not go down to posterity as Abraham the Great, or Abraham the Wise, or as Abraham the Eloquent, although he is all three, wise, great and eloquent, he will go down to posterity, if the country is saved, as Honest Abraham (applause); and going down thus, his name may be written any where in this wide world of ours side by side with that of Washington, without disparaging the latter. (Renewed applause.)

But we are not to be saved by the captain, at this time, but by the crew. We are not to be saved by Abraham Lincoln, but by that power behind the throne, greater than the throne itself.

*Proceedings of the American Anti-Slavery Society at its Third Decade, Held in the City of Philadelphia, Dec. 3d and 4th, 1863* (New York: American Anti-Slavery Society, 1864), 111, 112, 115, 116–118, 110–118.

## PHILIP A. BELL on President Lincoln's Annual Message, December 12, 1863

*In his third Annual Message, dated December 8, 1863, President Lincoln claimed that his Emancipation Proclamation and decision to permit Black men to serve in the armed forces had made vital contributions to the war effort and the cause of freedom. In a separate Proclamation of Amnesty and Reconstruction, issued on the same date, Lincoln offered pardons to rebels who were willing to take an oath of allegiance and abide by all laws and proclamations regarding slavery. While certain categories of rebels were excluded, such as high-ranking officers and those who had abused prisoners of war, Lincoln's proclamation was seen as a magnanimous effort to restore the Union. Editor Philip A. Bell (1809–1889) praised Lincoln's Annual Message and his amnesty proclamation for their commitment to upholding and furthering the cause of emancipation. By 1864, Lincoln's lenient plan for reconstruction had earned many critics among abolitionists who demanded a punitive policy towards the rebels and a more concrete commitment from the president on equal rights for African Americans.*

---

The President's Message was delivered to Congress on Wednesday last, Dec. 9th, and telegraphed to the Associated Press, and published in the *Alta*, on Thursday morning, the 10th. We consider it the most important state paper ever sent to congress and the nation since the formation of the Government. It is important to us as a people. No executive of the nation has ever stood up so unflinchingly in behalf of the rights of our down-trodden race as President Lincoln. He who dared issue the great Emancipation Proclamation deserves the world's regard and is entitled to our everlasting gratitude. In the greater part of his Message the President dwells upon Emancipation as the foundation of his future policy for the good of the country. Appended to the Message is a conciliating Proclamation, humane yet stringent and just, developing a plan for the return of rebeldom to its allegiance, conceived in the spirit which has so signally character-ized his every official act since his inauguration. His Emancipation policy is set forth in bold relief, and with a seriousness which will cause the most experienced statesman to pause and reflect, ere he opposes the several recommendations he has made for the consideration of Congress.

Editorial in the *Pacific Appeal* (San Francisco), Dec. 12, 1863.

## WILLIAM FLORVILLE to Abraham Lincoln, Springfield, Illinois, December 27, 1863

*Florville (c. 1806–1868) was a Haitian immigrant who settled in Springfield, Illinois, and became Lincoln's friend, barber, and legal client. In addition to expressing his support and gratitude for the president's emancipation policy, Florville offers some words of condolence for Willie Lincoln who had died on February 20, 1862. Florville also lets Lincoln know that his house and dog were apparently in good hands, as the home was being rented by Lucian Tilton and his family, while the Lincolns' dog was staying with one of their neighbors. (DANB)*

Dear sir—I, having for you, an irrisisteble feeling of gratitude for the kind regards shown, and the manifest good wishis exhibited towards me, since your residence in Washington City; as Communicated by Doctor Henry sometime ago, and lately by his Exelency Governor Yates, have for the above reasons and our long acquaintance, thought it might not be improper for one so humble in life and occupation, to address the President of the United States—

Yet, I do so, feeling that if it is received by you (and you have time for I know you are heavily Tax) it will be read with pleasure as a communication from Billy the Barber. this I express and feel. for the truly great man regards with corresponding favor the poor, and down troden of the Nation, to those more favored in Color, position, and Franchise rights. And this you have shown, and I and my people feel greatful to you for it. The shackels have fallen, and Bondmen have become freeman to some extent already under your Proclamation. And I hope ere long, it may be universal in all the slave states. That your authority may soon extend over them all, to all the oppressed, releiving them from their Bondage, and cruel masters; who make them work, and fight, against the Goverment. And when so released, they would be glad I have no doubt, to assist in putting down this infamous Rebellion—May God grant you health, and strength, and wisdom, so to do, and so to act, as shall redown to his Glory, and the Good, peace, prosperity, Freedom, and hapiness of this Nation. So that war shall be known no more, that the cause or pretext for war be removed, that Rebellion and secession shall have no plea to make, and nothing to ask for, that all the states may not have an equal right to demand. then, and not till then, will the Government be steadfast and abiding. and for that reason, I hope and trust, that you may be chosen for a second term to administer the affairs of this Government. I think, after a four years experiance, you are posted in matters relating thereto. and better calculated to carry out your own designs, and the wishes of the people, than any other man in this Nation. And the people here so think.

And if it shall be the wish of the men, who support the Goverment, anxious to put down the Rebellion, sustaining the army, loving Freedom and the union, and who sustain your acts, and your Administration, that you should again accept the office of Chief Magistrate of this Nation, I hope you will not decline: but accept it, and put things and matters through, to their termination and when these troubles shall end, the Nation will rejoice, the oppressed will shout the name of their deliverer, and Generations to come, will rise up and call you blessed. (so mote it be) I was sorry to hear of your illness, and was glad when I learned that your health was improving. I hope by this time, you are able, or soon will be, to attend to your arduous buisness

I was surprised at the announcement of the death of your son Willy. I thought him a smart boy for his age, so considerate, so manly: his Knowledge and good sence, far exceeding most boys more advanced in years. yet the time comes to all, all must die.

I should like verry much, to see you, and your family, but the priviledge of enjoying an interview, may not soon, if ever come.

My family are all well. My son William is married and in buisness for himself. I am occupying the same place in which I was at the time you left. Tell Taddy that his (and Willys) Dog is alive and Kicking doing well he stays mostly at John E Rolls with his Boys who are about the size now that Tad & Willy Ware When they left for Washington

your Residence here is Kept in good order. Mr Tilton has no children to ruin things. Mrs Tilton and Miss Tilton are verry strong union Ladies and do a great deal for the soldiers who are suffering so much for us & to sustain the Goverment please accept my best wishis for yourself and family. and my daily desires for yourself that your administration may be prosperous, wise, and productive of Good results to this Nation, and may the time soon come, when the Rebellion shall be put down; and Traitors, receive their just recompence of reward. and the People be at Peace, is the Sincere feelings of your obt servant

William Florville the Barber

Lincoln Papers, Series 1, General Correspondence, 1833 to 1916: "William Florville to Abraham Lincoln, Sunday, December 27, 1863 (Appreciation)," https://www.loc.gov/item/mal2892300.

## HENRY JOHNSON on Meeting Lincoln at the White House, January 1, 1864

*Johnson (?–1865) was minister of the St. James AME Zion church in Ithaca, New York, when he traveled to Washington in late 1863, where he witnessed the final piece of the Statue of Freedom being placed atop the recently completed dome of the US Capitol. On New Year's Day he was among the first group of African Americans to be admitted to the president's reception at the White House. Although Lincoln had met privately with African Americans, the New Year's Day reception in 1864 was the first time Black people were admitted with the public. Johnson and the other African Americans in attendance were the subject of newspaper commentary, as supporters of the Lincoln administration viewed it as a sign of progress, while critics believed it was further evidence that Lincoln favored complete social equality, including interracial marriage. After meeting Lincoln, Johnson participated in a celebration to mark the first anniversary of the Emancipation Proclamation ("The News," Chicago Tribune, Jan. 3, 1864; "The New Year's Reception at the White House," New York Herald, Jan. 3, 1864; "The President Receiving Negroes," Cincinnati Enquirer, Jan. 11, 1864; "Emancipation Anniversary," Evening Star [Washington, DC], Jan. 2, 1864; "Died," Christian Recorder [Philadelphia], April 8, 1865).*

---

I had the privilege also, without molestation, of calling upon the President, Hon. A. Lincoln, on new year's day, which was his reception day. I found him to be a gentleman, straight and tall, modest, with pleasing features; firm and determined doth he look, and as I think he is.

"A Trip to Washington," the *Anglo-African* (New York), January 23, 1864.

## THOMAS R. STREET, Emancipation Day Address, Virginia City, Nevada Territory, January 1, 1864

*While little is known about Street (?-1873), the following Emancipation Day address is an excellent example of how African Americans shaped popular perception of the Emancipation Proclamation. Willing to overlook the proclamation's limitations, Street instead welcomed freedom as a gift from Lincoln that marked the beginning of a new era. Echoing sentiments Lincoln had expressed in the 1850s, Street asserted that slavery contradicted the nation's founding creed, as expressed in the Declaration of Independence, and was a stain upon the republican robe. Like Lincoln, Street made a distinction between natural rights, civil rights, and social equality. While the Emancipation Proclamation promised to fulfill the Declaration's proposition that all men would enjoy their natural right to liberty, Street hoped it would also lead to civil rights, yet made it clear that he was not advocating complete social equality between the races. Street was optimistic that newly freed people would prove themselves worthy, and in doing so he anticipated a prominent theme in subsequent Emancipation Day orations where speakers would catalog the progress made since January 1, 1863. Unlike the successful slave revolution in Haiti that Toussaint Louverture helped lead or Denmark Vesey's abortive slave rebellion in South Carolina during the early 1820s, Street pointed out that emancipation and the enlistment of Black men into the army had the full sanction of Lincoln's administration. At an event in Virginia City that was held to commemorate the ratification of the Fifteenth Amendment in 1870, Street again expressed his gratitude for Lincoln and claimed that voting rights were an "outgrowth" of the Emancipation Proclamation (Elevator [San Francisco], May 6, 1870).*

---

This is the first anniversary of a day destined to become memorable in the annals of the world. (applause.) The beginning of the New Year has, for centuries, been celebrated throughout Christendom with feasts and songs, as the dawning of a new era, the commencement of a new life. It has lately been made, to our race, a day of rejoicing and jubilee indeed, for it is a day on which was lifted from us the burden of centuries of oppression and wrong; it is a day when the shadows and darkness were driven from above us by the tempest blows of war, and the colored people of America were raised into the sunlight of a broader and freer manhood. (applause.) A thousand hearts to-day are moved by the same new and untried emotion, as the great waters are moved by the same breath from God. [ . . .] If our race are unskilled in the arts of modern civilization, it is only because the oppressor has purposely prevented us from becoming familiar with them. If they are ignorant, it is only because they are debarred the ordinary institution, such as are extended to the child of the poorest and meanest criminal. But I will not on this occasion advert to the disadvantages under which we have labored, or the unfairness of censuring us for not achieving results without means. It is rather my pleasant task today, to express our joy and gratitude at the issuance and the practical benefits of the great philanthropist's free measure of the age, the *magna charta* of our race, the Emancipation Proclamation of Abraham Lincoln, which was issued on January 1st, 1863. (applause.) The Emancipation Proclamation was brought out by the dire necessities of war, acted upon by the impelling principle of justice. The principle which it embodies and utilizes, is the outgrowth of the advancement of the age, but it is none the less welcome to its recipients, none the less generous in its gift of joy, and none the less gratefully and thankfully received by all of our race, because of its being acquiesced in by a majority of the American people as a military necessity. [ . . . ]

The republic which began its existence with the declamation that all men are created equal, falsified its own assumption of universal freedom. [ . . . ] The growth of the American republic might fitly be compared to the construction of a mighty edifice, the title deed to the land on it was constructed, was acquired by toil and privation, by combat with the savages and the elements, and the seal by which it passed to its present possessors, was reddened with blood and sacrifice. [ . . . ] The fair-haired Saxon and the dusky son of Ethiopia, alike, labored upon its walls, but while the former enjoyed its shelter, gloried in its grandeur and exulted in its greatness; the latter was unjustly deprived of the fruits of his labor, and the God of Justice is rocking that temple to its foundation stones as a consequence. The tyrants who held the African in bondage, are being swept away by pestilence, by famine, and by terrific blasts which Azrael the death-angel moves with his beating wings, and the robes of justice are being purified by the bath of blood, into which, those who have so long disgraced her sacred name have recklessly plunged her. (applause.) I speak of the rights of the colored race; it is a subject about which there has been much misrepresentation and much of unseemly ridicule. We do not ask from the Anglo-Saxon what he calls social equality. We have as little desire for social equality with him, as he can have for social equality with us. (That is so.) We prefer to mix with our own people, to form our own society, to have our own customs, our own manners and our own destiny. (Good.) The rights we ask are those which properly belong to every member of the human family, of whatever country or race, the right to eat what we earn, to enjoy unmolested our lives, liberty and property, and to be justly protected in the exercise of those rights by the Government which we aid in supporting and preserving. (Applause.)

We demand for ourselves and for our posterity only that liberty which is our God-given, inalienable right. [ . . . ]

It is fortunate for us and for our children, that the Emancipation of the colored race occurred because of, and simultaneously with the reconstruction of the great

American republic. No second *Toussaint L'Ouverture,* or Denmark Vesey, has arisen to lead our brethren in the South to a freedom in which the horrors and excesses of Saint Domingo might have been repeated. It is the Federal Government itself, and not an insurrectionary leader that has declared freedom to the slave, and encouraged the freedmen to fight for the liberty of his enslaved kindred and race. (Applause.) [. . .] And can the reproach of cowardice be longer laid upon a suffering and patient people? The gallant conduct of the 2d Louisiana regiment at Port Hudson, and the fearless bravery of the South Carolina Volunteers, have shown how desperately even slaves can fight when their swords are sharpened by the thought that they are battling for their own freedom as well as for the freedom of their country. (Loud applause.)

President Lincoln—God bless him!—has declared that, when this slaveholders' rebellion is crushed, no man freed by the operation of the Emancipation Proclamation shall ever be returned to slavery. (Applause.) We believe that the great loyal American people will keep faith with us and with our enslaved brethren, and therefore for the present and for the hopeful future. This day, upon the first anniversary of our independence, we give our joyous praises to the Giver of all good and perfect gifts. (Applause.) [. . .] The influence of this triumph of justice and right has extended beyond the theatre of the immediate conflict. California, at the last session of her Legislature, wiped out the reproach which had for many years rested upon her laws, by removing the disability, which had previously existed, against receiving the evidence of colored men in Courts of Justice, and we hope that the first Legislature of the dawning State of Nevada will adopt a similar measure for our civil and criminal Code. It is true that the Emancipation of our race has been accomplished through a mighty civil convulsion, accompanied by much of blood and sorrow, but such has been the history of every great movement in favor of liberty.[ . . .]

We have, indeed, great cause for rejoicing here to-day. The spirit of adventure and desire for wealth has brought many of our people to these western deserts, where we possess a facility to develop and advance seldom vouchsafed to our race. It should be our duty, and doubtless be our purpose to so conduct ourselves as to achieve our own good opinion as well as the respect of all others. We have here an opportunity to attain alike material, intellectual and moral advancement unmolested by despotic exactions, and unhampered by tyrannical restrictions. When I look over this assemblage and see how much of intelligence, industry, morality and religion is represented among our own people, I am proud of my race and my country, and I am led to believe that we shall not prove unworthy of our advancement and our destiny.

*Pacific Appeal* (San Francisco, CA), Jan. 23, 1864.

## PHILIP A. BELL Endorses Lincoln for a Second Term in Office, January 9, 1864

*The start of 1864 witnessed many celebrations to mark the first anniversary of the Emancipation Proclamation. The following reports on such an event in San Francisco, where African Americans not only commemorated the Emancipation Proclamation but also endorsed Lincoln for another term as president. Editor Philip Bell (1809–1889) argued that such an endorsement was merited, given Lincoln's support for emancipation and the progress he had made on the issue of racial equality. Though Black men could not vote in most states, including California, Bell suggests that they could play an important role in the campaign.*

The nomination of Mr. Lincoln by acclamation, at the celebration held on January 1st, at Platt's Music Hall, on Montgomery [S]t., in commemoration of the Emancipation Proclamation issued by President Lincoln, Jan. 1, 1863, was a tribute of respect and the high appreciation felt by the colored citizens of San Francisco for him. They were made happy in this opportunity to bestow a humble mark of their approbation. He is the man who, of all others who have occupied the Presidential chair, since the formation of the Government or the adoption of the Constitution, has stood up in defiance of the slave-power, and dared officially to maintain the doctrine, by his official actions, that we are citizens, though of African descent—that the army and navy shall protect and defend such citizens in common with all others—that provision ought to be made for the education of freedmen—that he will not withhold his official sanction from any measure which has for its object the amelioration of the condition of the freedmen in the States which may hereafter return to their allegiance under free State Constitutions, in accordance with his recent Proclamation of Amnesty. For these, and other more weighty reasons, we have duly considered him to be the right man in the right place in the present crisis, and also the man to fill the Presidential chair in 1864. It might be said, what have colored men to do with politics? The answer is this: They are subjects, under the Government where they were born and live. The slave-power, heretofore, has been permitted to wield the sceptre of might over right. Its influence has disfranchised us in State after State, both before and since it obtained its meridian height. Its glory is about setting, as does the sun in the west—ours is about rising, as does the sun in the east. Under the Proclamation of Freedom, our sun is just rising,—the slaveholders' power is fast setting. It will soon be dark with them. It is now quite light with us. They will soon have to get candles to see to read the dark deeds they have committed against a defenceless, outraged and once enslaved people.

Our light of day has now commenced, by the will of Nature's God, to shine with brightness and beauty. That light is the light of civilization, as now evinced in Liberia, Africa, and Hayti, represented by their ministers at Washington—the light evinced by our restoration to citizenship—the light apparent in our progress in domestic and political economy, in literature, the arts, science, and an encouraging knowledge of all the elements which are calculated to constitute a prosperous, happy, and a great as well as grateful people. These reasons may be considered an answer as to what colored men have to do with politics. But it may be interrogated again, what can we effect, even if Mr. Lincoln should be nominated by a political convention, when we cannot vote? To which we would answer, If Mr. Lincoln should receive the nomination, which we believe he will, over all other aspirants, colored men can do just as much or more than they did in the last presidential campaign. By fair argument, by reason, and by clear demonstration, they have convinced untold numbers of naturalized citizens (those with whom they were acquainted and on friendly or familiar terms) of the utter folly of their voting a ticket which had for its object not only the perpetual enslavement of the black man, but the injuring and degrading of themselves, by helping to establish and perpetuate a power that denied the right of free speech to freemen, etc. We have thus heretofore sought, and would still seek, to convince others that free, republican principles, which are our principles, are the only ones which can relieve all from the wrong and debasement which the slave-power engenders.

Editorial in the *Pacific Appeal* (San Francisco), Jan. 9, 1864.

## JOHN H. MORGAN ET AL. to Abraham Lincoln, Pensacola, Florida, January 16, 1864

*A native of Virginia, Morgan enlisted in the 14th Infantry Regiment, Corps d'Afrique (later designated the 86th US Colored Infantry) on September 21, 1863. Black soldiers initially received seven dollars per month, while White soldiers were paid thirteen dollars per month. Congress approved a measure in June 1864 that made the pay and benefits of Black soldiers equal to White soldiers. The law was retroactive to January 1, 1864, and also stipulated that soldiers like Morgan, who were free men when the rebellion started, were entitled to back pay from the time of their enlistment. Morgan rose to the rank of sergeant major but was demoted to private in early 1865. After being wounded in the assault on Fort Blakely, Morgan was deemed disabled and discharged on May 20, 1865 (Compiled military service record, John H. Morgan, Private, Company K, 86th US Colored Infantry, Record Group 94, National Archives, Washington, DC).*

Sir

we the undersign non commissioned offerciers So called and your most humble Servant off The fourteenth Regiment Corps de Afrique we ask off you to gain
information wether we Ar to have the Same treatment bestowed on ous As all off
the Regtiments that is now fighting In the field to bestow the union as it was

Please Your Honor we inlisted to fight For our Country and for the laws off the
Land we have tryed to do So ever sence we Have been in the Service and that has
been Six Months, and ever Sence we landed on this peninsula we have done our
utmost in pretecting goverment property Thare has not been a call for defending The cause that we ar fighting for Sence we Have been on this peninsula that
we refused To do, thay tell ous for working quality we ar fare Surperior to all the
white regtment and for fighting we will never faulter From that

Please Your Honor Sence we have Been on this peninsula for the defence off
The navy yard we have thowing up breats Works from the bay to the buyio and
all off the fettige duty is preformed by this By this regiment and the grand out
post is preformed by ous also the line off pickets Exstend for nine miles

Please Your Honor when we inlisted in the united States Service the understanding was that we Should recieve the Same pay and rattion as the white Soldiers
we have the Same felling For our Wifes and Chrildrens at home and we Study the
wellfare off them as much so as the white Soldiers, the majoyity off the Men in
this Regtiment have familys in New Orleans and from letters recieved here Thay
ar in a Starving condistion thare are Some four or five oderly Sergant that have
wife In the North how is exspecting to desired off ous Some thing to live on we
cant Seport Them on Seven dollas per a month—

Please Your Honor

all we ask for is Justist Bestowed on ous and thare Shant be one Star on the
Glourious banner off liberty that wont Shine out Brightly over all off the patriots
Fighting to montaining your most Just law Please Your Honor we dont looke
for Eney better treatment than the white Soldiers but the Same the Cannon and
Rifles ball have not a bit off respects off person in action our lives is as Sweet to
ous as it is to them that recieves thirteen Dollars per month

Please Your Honor when you called for Soldiers off african desent I John. H.
Morgan the writeter off this letter was in the western army off the united States in
the capasity off A Servant I left and went home to Cincinnati to inlist to fight for
My Country me and my nefphew thought our Serviceses would be more needed in
this department as soon vickburg and Port Hudson was takeing we come to New
Orleans to inlist in army off the Gulf If Congress has passed a law to pay the black
Soldiers Seven dollas per month I would like transferd to a northing regiment—

Please Your Honor for drill this regiment Can not be exceled for the time that
we have Been in the Service, thare ar five off the first Sergents that can read and
write and can Preform all off the dutys off a Sergent—

Please Your Honor this letter is from the sergants Fourteenth Regtment Corps
de Afrique Writting by John. H. Morgan first Sergant Company K
Wm J Barcroff first Sergent Co H.
William. D. Mayo first Sergent Co D
John Talor first Sergant Co A

Record Group 94, Entry 360, Letters Received by the Colored Troops Division, Box 44,
National Archives, Washington, DC.

## MATTILD BURR to Abraham Lincoln, January 18, 1864

*Mrs. Burr's husband, Charles, was born a free man in Pennsylvania and enlisted
in the 3rd US Colored Troops on July 18, 1863. Like other Black soldiers, Burr
was paid only $7 per month until Congress approved a measure in June 1864
that made the pay and benefits of Black soldiers equal to White soldiers. This
law was retroactive to January 1, 1864, and also stipulated that those soldiers
who were free men when the rebellion started were entitled to back pay from the
time of their enlistment (Compiled military service record, Charles Burr, Private,
Company K, 3rd US Colored Infantry, M1820, Record Group 94, National
Archives, Washington, DC).*

---

sir i with mutch plasur set daun to adress you with A few lines to let you know
that my husband is in the army and left me hear with A helpless famely and he has
not recived any pay and i get no reliefe i woudd like to know if you please what
will be done he is in the third U S Colard troops Co K on morris island his name
is Charles Burr pleas rite and let me know
   yours truly
   mattild Burr

Record Group 94, Entry 360, Letters Received by the Colored Troops Division, Box 43,
National Archives, Washington, DC.

## AMOS G. BEMAN on the First Anniversary of the Emancipation Proclamation, January 23, 1864

*A native of Connecticut, Beman (1812–1874) was a Congregational minister,
missionary, and civil rights activist who had been involved in the abolition movement for over thirty years when he wrote the following. While Beman offered
high praise to Lincoln and the Emancipation Proclamation, he also noted that
Lincoln was not fully committed to the equality of the races. Beman therefore*

*paid tribute to those who had long been toiling in the abolition movement and credited them for essentially paving the way for the success of Lincoln's proclamation. Beman's essay is an early example of crediting Lincoln while at the same time noting that his views on race were not as progressive as abolitionists (ANB).*

---

The first day of January 1863, will ever be regarded as the colored man's day. The Proclamation of President Abraham Lincoln will be read, and studied, while one of the race effected by it shall remain upon the face of the globe—in this connection, as in no other, President Lincoln's name will shine forth as "one of the immortal names that were not born to die." Much will be said—much will be written. A large page in the world's history will be occupied with an account of his government, and of the events which transpired during his administration; but his glorious Proclamation of Emancipation will stamp the First Day of January 1863, as the day of days—the Great Day of Jubilee to millions of immortal men—made in the image of God! Upon this anniversary day the concentrated gaze of the civilized world will be turned. The more the circumstances which called forth the proclamation are studied—the more its effects are developed—the more it will commend itself to the intelligence of the wise, and the good. All honor to President Lincoln! All honor to the heroism of those spirits whose inspiring councils strengthened him in his purpose of sending forth the proclamation, which broke the chains from so many limbs.

Who made Abraham Lincoln as far as he is developed, into a "perfect man" in the science of human freedom—of the rights and immunities of human nature? It is never said, it is never thought, it is never pretended, by his bitterest enemies, that in anything which he has done—he has been self-moved—that he has acted from the spontaneous impulses of a great and noble heart—for there is no proof that he accepts the solemn and sublime idea of the perfect equality, and equal brotherhood of the whole human race—upon the Rock, he has never appeared to stand nor is he prepared to install the colored man in all his rights, and therein defend him on sea and land—clothed and invested in all the immunities of an American citizen; but while we say this, and could say much more, we have no disposition to criticize our noble President at the present time, or to detract an iota from the just meed of praise which is his due. We desire that all which truth and justice demands should be freely and heartily accorded to him—let his name be written as with a diamond—let the historian stamp it with letters of fire upon tablets of gold—let the poet sing it in strains sweeter than Mar's verse—let the orator with "star-eyed science," and the scholar with the graces of literature embalm it—let the great heart of humanity enshrine it.

Yet when unfolding that volume of truth, which the past *forty* years has been preparing, as the history of the Anti-Slavery Enterprise, there is presented to the eye of intelligence, the names of many men and women, colored and white, who have toiled and suffered, and died for these truths of which the Proclamation was born. These have under God created that omnipresent and omnipotent public sentiment in which the President "lives and moves, and has his being," and in which he is as "clay in the hands of the potter."

Neither does he yet come up to the scholarship in the Philosophy of Human Rights as announced in the Sacred Volume of Truth and the Divine principles of civil government and Constitutional Freedom as defined in the Declaration of Independence, and the Constitution of the United States. No, a voice from the tomb of Alvin Stewart, or from the granite resting-place of the sage of Quincy, hath power to instruct him; the writings of Beriah Green, of Lysander Spooner, and last but not *least*, that now the "old man eloquent" with logic on fire, and whose linked thunderbolts no man dare meet (see the correspondence between Henry Ward Beecher and Geo. B. Cheever,) we mean the old Nestor of Christian Constitutional Liberty, and righteous civil government Wm. Goodell, or the Phelpses, the Garrisons, the Phillipses, the Thea. S. Wrights and the Cornishes, the Lydia Maria Childs, the Abby Kelley Fosters, and a multitude of others, which no man can number whose voices and pens in Church and State, in all places where "men do most congregate," have by "line upon line, and by precept upon precept" poured floods of light, upon the public mind and heart, and conscience, "through evil as well as through good report," until they have created under God, and developed that moral and religious influence which has in part accomplished the work to which they consecrated themselves, and for which they have with a devotion as constant as truth, and with an industry and zeal as unwavering as justice, and with a fidelity as pure and generous as their cause was patriotic, and sacred, they and their compeers created the Niagara, the voice of whose thunder rolled over the land on the First Day of January, 1863!

Let their deeds find a trumpet tongue in the orator, amid the glorious celebration of President Lincoln's Emancipation Proclamation. Let their names be held in grateful remembrances, let them shine as stars of the first magnitude in the galaxy of Freedom.

The *Anglo-African* (New York), Jan. 23, 1864.

## RICHARD H. CAIN to Abraham Lincoln, Washington, DC, January 27, 1864

*Cain (1825–1887) was a minister in the AME church with a congregation in Brooklyn when the Civil War began. He went to South Carolina at the end of the war, where he took charge of the Emanuel AME Church in Charleston and became involved in politics. In addition to serving in the state legislature, Cain served two terms in the US House of Representatives during Reconstruction. Cain wrote to Lincoln on behalf of the African Civilization Society, an organization founded in the late 1850s for the purpose of promoting economic development and Christian missionary efforts in Africa. As Cain's letter indicates, during the Civil War the society began to focus its efforts on building schools for newly freed persons in the South. Lincoln referred Cain's letter to the War Department (ANB; DANB).*

---

Sir the accumulating intrests which are clustering arround our race, amid the revolutions in this country, prompts us to believe that we have a great work to perform, in assisting in ellivating our people made free by your proclaimation. You will see, by the accompanying circular, the motives which prompt us in making a so reasonable request, <u>For Permission and Authority, to establish schools for the instruction of the Freedmen, within the lines of our Armies,</u> that we may qualify them for citizenship, and the high duties of moral, and social, as well as spiritual life by leading them to comprehend their high destiny in the future. We seek a general permit from the Government to enter and establish schools and churches among our Brethren throughout the southern states, always subject to the regulations proscribed by the laws, and in harmony with the intrests of the People, and the maintainence of the Authority of the General Government. The society and the friends of humanity, will highly appreciate such consideration from you, as will be, favourable to the objects contemplated by the society, for which we will ever pray.

R. H. Cain, in behalf of the society. An early answer will greatly assist us in our good work.

Record Group 94, Entry 360, Letters Received by the Colored Troops Division, Box 50, National Archives, Washington, DC.

## JEAN BAPTISTE ROUDANEZ AND ARNOLD BERTONNEAU,
## Memorial to Abraham Lincoln, March 10, 1864

*Roudanez (1815–1895) and Bertonneau (1834–1912) were free persons of color who traveled to Washington from New Orleans in early 1864 for the purpose of presenting a petition to President Lincoln and Congress that urged the federal government to ensure that persons of color who were free before the start of the war be granted suffrage in Louisiana. The petition was signed by over a thousand persons of color. After Roudanez and Bertonneau arrived in Washington, they determined that all persons of color, including those who were enslaved when the rebellion began, should have the right to vote. The following document is the memorial reflecting this more expansive demand for equal voting rights. Lincoln received Roudanez and Bertonneau at the White House and reportedly informed them that he "saw no reason why intelligent black men should not vote," but this was not a military question and therefore a matter for the Louisiana constitutional convention to decide. Following his meeting with Roudanez and Bertonneau, Lincoln wrote a confidential letter to Michael Hahn, the recently elected governor of Louisiana, and suggested that the new Louisiana constitution permit some Black men to vote, namely military veterans and those who were "very intelligent." Lincoln believed these men "would probably help, in some trying time to come, to keep the jewel of liberty within the family of freedom." Lincoln's letter to Hahn was made public in the weeks following his assassination and is a vital piece of evidence regarding his views on racial equality. A draft of Lincoln's March 15, 1864 letter to Hahn is in the Abraham Lincoln Papers at the Library of Congress (Lincoln Papers, Series 1, General Correspondence, 1833 to 1916: "Abraham Lincoln to Michael Hahn, Tuesday, March 15, 1864 [Hahn Invested with Powers of Governor]," https://www.loc.gov/item/mal3158300). For accounts of his meeting with Roudanez and Bertonneau, see* The Principia *(New York), March 10, 1864; and the* Liberator *(Boston), April 15, 1864.*

---

Your memorialists respectfully show that they are loyal citizens of Louisiana, of African descent, born free.

That they have been appointed a Committee by the signers of the accompanying petition, to which this memorial is supplementary, for the purpose of presenting the said petition, and of urging, in person, the—as your memorialists believe—just claims therein contained.

That your memorialists desire to present, for your favorable consideration, the following statement and prayer in addition to the accompanying petition—namely:

That, whereas, it may be urged that the United States has no authority to change the laws and Constitution of the State of Louisiana, as to the qualification of voters at State elections. This has already been done by the authority of the United States in respect to white citizens of Louisiana employed in the military and naval service of the United States, as will more clearly appear by what follows.

That the Constitution of Louisiana, title 2, article 12, excludes soldiers, seamen, or marines in the army or navy of the United States from the right of suffrage.

That, by General Order No. 24, from Headquarters, Department of the Gulf, Maj.-Gen. N.P. Banks ordered that the citizens who had volunteered for the defence of the country in the army or navy, and who were otherwise qualified voters, should be allowed to vote in the election precincts in which they might be found on the day of election; thereby enfranchising those who were, by the Constitution and laws of Louisiana, disfranchised.

And your memorialists further show that the Constitution and laws of Louisiana have been altered by the authority of the United States in other respects and more particularly.

That by the proclamation of Gen. N.P. Banks, dated New Orleans, January 11, 1864, it was declared that the officers chosen in the election then approaching should constitute the civil government of the State, under the Constitution and laws of Louisiana, except so much of the said Constitution and laws as *recognize, regulate, or relate to slavery.*

And your memorialists further show that, though in their accompanying petition they have only asked the right of suffrage for those citizens of Louisiana of African descent born free before the rebellion, yet that justice, and the principles for which they contend, require also the extension of this privilege to those born slaves, with such qualifications as should affect equally the white and the colored citizen, and that this is required not only by justice, but also by expediency, which demands that full effect should be given to all the Union feeling in the rebel States, in order to secure the permanence of the free institutions and loyal governments now organized therein.

And your memorialists pray that the right of suffrage may be extended, not only to natives of Louisiana of African descent born free, but also to all others, whether born slave or free, especially those who have vindicated their right to vote by bearing arms, subject only to such qualifications as shall equally affect the white and colored citizens.

And your memorialists will ever pray.

The *Anglo-African* (New York), April 2, 1864; the *Liberator* (Boston), April 1, 1864.


# Petition of North Carolina Freedmen to Abraham Lincoln, April or May 1864

*Just weeks after meeting with a Louisiana delegation to discuss the suffrage issue, Lincoln met with a group of men from North Carolina who also petitioned the president for voting rights. According to Clinton D. Pearson (or Pierson), a member of the delegation, the interview with Lincoln went well, as the president "gave the committee full assurances of his sympathy in the struggle the colored people of North Carolina are now making for their rights." In addition to appealing to the principles embodied in the Emancipation Proclamation and Declaration of Independence, the petition noted that some free African American men had been able to vote in North Carolina prior to the state constitution being amended in 1835. Abraham H. Galloway (1837–1870) and Clinton Pierson*

served as delegates to the North Carolina constitutional convention in 1868, and
Galloway was subsequently elected to the state senate ("Reception of the North
Carolina Delegation," the Anglo-African [New York], May 14, 1864; AANB;
Journal of the Constitutional Convention of the State of North Carolina,
at its Session 1868 [Raleigh: Joseph W. Holden, 1868]).

———————————

*To His Excellency the President of these United States:*

We, the colored citizens of North Carolina, composed alike of those born
in freedom and those whose chains of bondage were severed by your gracious
proclamation, cherishing in our hearts and memories that ever to be remembered sentence, embodied in the Declaration of Independence, that "all men are
created free and equal," being well aware that the right of suffrage was exercised,
without detriment, by the colored freemen of this State previous to 1835, and that
some of the Northern States, most advanced in arts, sciences, and civilization,
have extended that right to the colored citizens with eminent success and good
results, do most earnestly and respectfully petition your Excellency to finish the
noble work you have begun, and grant unto your petitioners that greatest of
privileges, when the State is reconstructed, to exercise the right of suffrage, which
will greatly extend our sphere of usefulness, redound to your honor, and cause
posterity, to the latest generation, to acknowledge their deep sense of gratitude.
We feel proud in saying that we have contributed moral and physical aid to our
country in her hour of need and expect so to continue to do until every cloud of
war shall disappear, and your administration stand justified by the sure results
that will follow. Feeling sanguine of the success of this our petition, and that you
will, with pleasure confer upon us this inestimable boon prayed for; we, with the
most profound respect, remain, yours, respectfully, in behalf of the people,

Abraham H. Galloway,
Clinton D. Pearson,
John R. Good,
Isaac K. Felton,
Jarvis M. Williams.

"Freeman of North Carolina Striking for Their Rights," the *Anglo-African* (New York), May
14, 1864.

## DON CARLOS RUTTER to Abraham Lincoln, Saint Helena Island, South Carolina, May 29, 1864

*The following letter indicates not only the esteem that newly freed persons had
for Lincoln but also how keen they were to possess property of their own. The
Sea Islands off of Georgia and South Carolina were seized by US forces early*

*in the war and immediately attracted the interest of Northern philanthropists who came to the islands in order to build churches, schools, and otherwise aid former slaves in their transition to freedom. Laura Towne (1825–1901), a teacher and abolitionist who had attended a medical college for women in Philadelphia, established a school on St. Helena Island, where she worked to assist African Americans for the remainder of her life. Some freed persons had an opportunity to purchase land that the federal government had confiscated for failure to pay taxes while many others were able to obtain land under Special Field Orders No. 15 that General William T. Sherman issued in January 1865. This order enabled thousands of Black families to settle on forty-acre plots with the promise that they would eventually be able to purchase the land. Lincoln approved this order, but his successor, Andrew Johnson, did not, and directed that captured land be returned to its original owners once those planters had been pardoned. The vast majority of families were removed from the land because they did not have an adequate opportunity to obtain a clear title through purchase (ANB; Rupert S. Holland, ed.,* Letters and Diary of Laura M. Towne *[Cambridge, MA: Riverside Press, 1912]).*

My name is Don Carlos, and I hope my letter will find you and your family in perfect health.

Will you please to be so kind Sir, as to tell me about my little bit of land. I am afraid to put on it a stable, or cornhouse, and such like, for fear it will be taken away from me again. Will you please to be so kind as to tell me whether the land will be sold from under us or no, or whether it will be sold to us at all. I should like to buy the very spot where I live. It aint but six acres, and I have got cotton planted on it, and very fine cotton too; and potatoes and corn coming on very pretty. If we colored people have land I know we shall do very well—there is no fear of that. Some of us have as much as three acres of corn, besides ground-nuts, potatoes, peas, and I don't know what else myself. If the land can only be sold, we can buy it all, for every house has its cotton planted, and doing well, and planted only for ourselves. We should like to know how much we shall have to pay for it—if it is sold.

I am pretty well struck in age Sir, for I waited upon Mrs. Alston that was Theodosia Burr, daughter of Aaron Burr, and I remember well when she was taken by pirates,—but I can maintain myself and my family well on this land. My son got sick on the Wabash (Flagship at Hilton Head) and he will never get well, for he has a cough that will kill him at last. He cannot do much work, but I can maintain him. I had rather work for myself and raise my own cotton than work for a gentleman for wages, for if I could sell my cotton for only .20 cts a pound it would pay me.

What ever you say I am willing to do, and I will attend to whatever you tell me.
Your most obedient servant,
don carlous Rutter

P. S. After the Government Superintendent gave me leave to pick one of the new houses, I pitch upon the one I live in. Then I fill up the holes in the garden, and in the house, I lath it & fill in with moss till it is comfortable in the winter. I did a heap of work on it, and now it would hurt my heart too much to see another man have it. I should not like it at all.

The letter above was dictated to me by a Freedman on St. Helena Island who is a refugee from Edisto, and who was formerly confidential servant in the Alston family. He can read & write, but is too old to do it with ease. He, with others of the Freedmen, often expresses a wish to speak to Massa Linkum, feeling sure that he will listen to their plea for land & do what is best for them. At Carlos desire, I took down from his own lips the words he was restless to speak to the President, intending to hand the letter to him at the Sanitary Fair, but I refrained from so doing that business might not be thrust in upon pleasure. I have given my promise to Carlos that I will do my best to let his "own word" reach the ear in which he has unbounded trust & hope, and therefore I forward this letter to Washington, begging no one to prevent its reaching its destination.

Very respectfully
Laura Towne
Teacher of Freedmen on St. Helena Is.

Lincoln Papers, Series 1, General Correspondence, 1833 to 1916: "Laura Towne to Abraham Lincoln, Sunday, May 29, 1864 (Sends Dictated Letter of Don Carlos Rutter, a Freedman at St. Helena, South Carolina)," Manuscript/Mixed Material, https://www.loc.gov/item/mal3339100.

## GEORGE E. STEPHENS Criticizes Lincoln's Policies on Race, May 26, 1864

*A native of Philadelphia, Stephens (1832–1888) worked as a cabinetmaker and sailor before becoming a servant to an officer in a Pennsylvania regiment at the beginning of the Civil War. Stephens was a regular correspondent of the* Anglo-African *throughout the war, and once Black men were permitted to serve in the army he enlisted in the 54th Massachusetts and was soon promoted to sergeant. While many were willing to overlook the limitations of the Emancipation Proclamation and Lincoln's past support for colonization, Stephens was not. Even though Lincoln's attorney general, Edward Bates, had issued an opinion that repudiated Chief Justice Taney's finding in the 1857* Dred Scott *case that African Americans could never become US citizens, Stephens believed the*

*Lincoln administration had done more to protect the interests of slaveholders than to advance the cause of equal rights. At the end of the war Stephens was commissioned as a lieutenant but his commission was only recognized by Massachusetts and not recognized by the federal government until 1884. After the war, he started a school for freed persons in Virginia, was active in the Grand Army of the Republic, and attended reunions with other Black veterans (Compiled military service record, George E. Stephens, First Lieutenant, Company K, 54 Massachusetts Infantry, M1898, Record Group 94, National Archives, Washington, DC; Donald Yacovone, ed.,* A Voice of Thunder: The Civil War Letters of George E. Stephens *[Urbana: University of Illinois Press, 1997]).*

---

Now, we cannot ride in the city passenger cars unless they legislate to that effect; we cannot even buy public lands, unless some act or order is promulgated, extending the privilege; we could not be employed upon the public works, unless some provisional law or order was appended to it, and when our so-called masters ran away from us, and went to the war to "break the glorious Union," we could not go out into the world, free, without meeting at every footstep legislative obstructions—laws and rules for the government of not men, but contrabands; and when we volunteered in the army to fight for the country, after serving a year, we must accept the insulting, starving pay which, it is presumed, legislation had imposed; and legislation must step forward and award us full pay. Is this not a triumphant argument that the policy of the Administration is based on the Dred Scott decision—that "black men had no rights that white men are bound to respect"?

We knew, of course, that the President of the United States distinctly said that his proclamation of Emancipation was issued purely and solely on the ground of military necessity, hence, the exception of part of Kentucky, Tennessee, Virginia, and Louisiana, and so forth from its provisions. Another prominent Republican "only wanted to use the colored man against the rebellion," that "he would rather see the waves of the broad Atlantic roll between the races," etc. Such we knew to be the drift of sentiment in high quarters. But why, if military necessity could wring this proclamation, was there not accompanying it a policy that would make it available against the rebellion? If there was a necessity for the first, it follows there was for the second. Why did not the Administration, when it was compelled to substitute the military for the civil law, ignore that accursed dictum of Taney?

Military necessity has proclaimed martial law from the St. Lawrence to the Dry Tortugas, yet the cardinal precept of the slave-driver is held sacred and inviolate. [ . . . ]

The Administration has so compromised itself with the Border slave-States' interest that it threatens to maintain the system in every region not affected by the proclamation. One of the most fatal mistakes of this war has been the false and indefinite policy of the Administration. The Emancipation proclamation should have been based as much on the righteousness of emancipation as on the great need of the measure, and then let the people see that the war for slavery and secession could be vigorously met only by war for the Union against slavery [...].

Mr. Lincoln and Mr. Blair must tell the poor negro, "You had better leave the country—the races cannot exist together." "If there had been no colored people, there would have been no war." He turned to the traitors South, who hate him with a vengeance that every drop of blood in his body could not satiate, "If you do not lay down your arms, I will issue a proclamation." They, of course, did not lay down their arms. They knew that the back-bone of their antagonist was too weak, and was too full of conciliation to make emancipation so plain and positive that the black millions could know it of a truth. The heart of the Administration is bent on reconstruction, but I fear there will never be any reconstruction under President Lincoln, and his satellites mean another lease to slavery. [...]

Did not President Lincoln offer the bait to the Southerners, "If you want to save your slaves, lay down your arms"? If this war is maintained by the North with a view to the restoration of the system, God, being just, will never prosper its stupendous villainy, and its criminality would make the North a bye-word and a disgrace; for it would then be a war for power and for conquest. Make it a war for the liberty of the human race, not liberty only for the slave, but liberty for the master and for every proscribed man; and for breaking every image of the slave-master's fetisch.

Letter to the editor of the *Anglo-African* (New York), June 18, 1864.

## JAMES W. C. PENNINGTON Supports the Reelection of Lincoln, June 9, 1864

*Born a slave in Maryland, Pennington (1807–1870) ran away and became a prominent abolitionist and minister in New York and Connecticut. Prior to the war, Pennington helped found the American Missionary Association, wrote an autobiography, published a history of African Americans, and lectured throughout Europe. After the war, he worked with freed persons in the South. Lincoln's party had nominated him for a second term at its national convention that was held in Baltimore in early June. Pennington enthusiastically endorsed Lincoln's candidacy and explained why Black men should vote for him in November (ANB).*

The prospect of having HIS EXCELLENCY ABRAHAM LINCOLN for our next President, should awaken in the inmost soul of every American of African descent emotions of the most profound and patriotic enthusiasm. There was a kind and wise Providence in bringing Mr. Lincoln into the Presidential chair, and I believe that the same all wise Providence has directed him in everything he has done as our President. I say our President, because he is the only American President who has ever given any attention to colored men as citizens. I believe that his renomination by the Convention is not only sound policy, but that it is equivalent to re-election, and especially if colored men will do their duty at the ballot-box next November.

It lies with colored men now to decide this great issue. The wisest, the safest, and the soundest policy for colored Americans is to exert all our influence to keep our present Chief Magistrate where he is for four years from next March.

There are many reasons why we, as colored men, should prefer Mr. Lincoln for our next President. Among the many I may say: 1. He is an honest President. 2. He is faithful to the whole nation. 3. He commands the respect of the world. 4. He is more cordially hated by the Copperheads of the North and the rebels of the South than any other living man. 5. His re-election will be the best security that the present well begun work of negro-freedom and African redemption will be fully completed. May God grant us four long years more of the judicious administration of that excellent man, ABRAHAM LINCOLN, and when I speak thus I believe I speak the sentiments of nine-tenths of my colored fellow-citizens. What say you, Mr. Editor?

Letter to the editor of the *Anglo-African* (New York), June 25, 1864.

## "AFRICANO" Opposes the Reelection of Lincoln, Point Lookout, Maryland, July 18, 1864

*"Africano" was a pseudonym for a solider in the 5th Massachusetts Cavalry who corresponded with the* Anglo-African *newspaper. While Lincoln's Emancipation Proclamation had won him the hearts of many African Americans, "Africano" remained skeptical, for he was not convinced that Lincoln had given up on his plans for colonization and he questioned Lincoln's commitment to abolition by noting that Lincoln placed preservation of the Union first and had exempted loyal slave states from the Emancipation Proclamation. A convention met in Cleveland at the end of May and nominated John C. Fremont for the presidency on a platform that called for constitutional amendments providing for the abolition of slavery and equality before the law for all men. Given Lincoln's clash with Fremont at the beginning of the war over Fremont's proclamation freeing the slaves of rebels in Missouri, some abolitionists believed Fremont was more committed to racial equality and a strong Reconstruction policy than Lincoln. Fremont eventually withdrew from the presidential race in September,*

*and "Africano" changed his mind about Lincoln after the Democrats held their convention (see below).*

———————

Coinciding with my brother soldier of the 54th Mass., I would say a few words as to the necessity of colored men, soldiers particularly, voting, if such is allowed, for the creator of the Emancipation proclamation. Many of our intelligent colored men believe in Mr. Lincoln; but *we*, who have studied him thoroughly, know him better, and as *we* desire to conglomerate in the land of our nativity, and not be severed from the ties we hold most dear, we hail the nomination of one of liberty's most radical sons—John C. Fremont. Mr. Lincoln's policy in regard to the elevation and inseparability of the negro race, has always been one of a fickle-minded man—one who, holding anti-slavery principles in one hand and colonization in the other, always gave concessions to slavery when the *Union* could be preserved without touching the peculiar institution. Such a man is not again worthy the votes of the voting portion of the colored race, when the intrepid Fremont, explorer of the Maraposa Valley, the well-known freedom-cherishing, negro-equalizing patriot, is the competitor. The press, like Mr. Lincoln, has always been, and will ever be, in favor of negro colonization; for, like him, they fear competition, and it is not extraordinary if the press should now uphold Mr. Lincoln, though dissatisfied with his vacillating administration, to keep John C. Fremont from occupying the presidential chair. The loyal and true-hearted people of the North will, no doubt, weigh the two men now before the public, and choose the one not found wanting. We are within ourselves satisfied that the Cleveland Convention will carry its object—that of electing Freedom's son—while the Baltimore Convention, with its nominee for re-election, will return to the plowshare.

While we thank Mr. Lincoln for what the exigencies of the times forced him to do, we also censure him for the non-accomplishment of the real good this accursed rebellion gave him the power to do, and which if he had done, instead of bartering human sinews and human rights with slaveholding Kentucky, the world would have looked upon him as the magnanimous regenerator of American institutions, and the benevolent protector of human freedom.

Letter to the editor of the *Anglo-African* (New York), August 6, 1864.

## ANNIE DAVIS to Abraham Lincoln, Bel Air, Maryland, August 25, 1864

*The following letter illustrates some of the confusion that stemmed from the Emancipation Proclamation, as Lincoln's proclamation only applied to areas that were in rebellion on January 1, 1863. Since Maryland remained loyal to the Union, it was exempt from the proclamation. Maryland voters went to the polls in October 1864 and ratified a new state constitution that abolished slavery. Prior to the referendum, Lincoln expressed his desire to see the constitution ratified and reiterated his wish that all people were free. Annie Davis and other enslaved persons in Maryland were emancipated on November 1, 1864, when the new constitution went into effect.*

---

Mr president

It is my Desire to be free. to go to see my people on the eastern shore. my mistress wont let me you will please let me know if we are free. and what i can do. I writte to you for advice. please send me word this week. or as soon as possibl.

and oblidge

Annie Davis

Record Group 94, Entry 360, Letters Received by the Colored Troops Division, Box 59, National Archives, Washington, DC.

## FREDERICK DOUGLASS to Abraham Lincoln, Rochester, New York, August 29, 1864

*Douglass wrote the following letter shortly after his second meeting with Lincoln. When they met, Lincoln was worried that he would not win reelection in November and he feared that one of the first acts of his Democratic successor would be to negotiate a peace with the Confederacy and revoke the Emancipation Proclamation. During their interview, Lincoln consulted with Douglass on a potential plan that would facilitate the movement of as many Black people as possible from the slave states to the free states before a new Democratic administration could take power on March 4, 1865. The reasoning was that it would be far more difficult to return these people to a state of slavery if they were on free soil. As Lincoln's prospects for reelection improved, the plan he had discussed with Douglass became unnecessary and was never implemented. David Blight notes that if the proposed plan had been enacted, "it would have forged an unprecedented alliance between black leadership and federal power for the purpose of emancipation" (David W. Blight,* Frederick Douglass' Civil War *[Baton Rouge: Louisiana State University Press, 1989], 183–184).*

---

Sir: Since the interview with wh. Your Excellency was pleased to honor me a few days ago, I have freely conversed with several trustworthy and Patriotic colored men concerning your suggestion that something should be speedily done to inform the slaves in the Rebel states of the true state of affairs in relation to them and to warn them as to what will be their probable condition should peace be concluded while they remain within the Rebel lines: and more especially to urge upon them the necessity of making their escape. All with whom I have thus far spoken on the subject, concur in the wisdom and benevolence of the Idea, and some of them think it practicable. That every slave who escapes from the Rebel states is a loss to the Rebellion and a gain to the Loyal cause, I need not stop to argue the proposition is self evident. The negro is the stomach of the rebellion. I will therefore briefly submit at once to your Excellency—the ways and means by which many such persons may be wrested from the enemy and brought within our lines:

1st Let a general agt. be appointed by your Excellency charged with the duty of giving effect to your Idea as indicated above: Let him have the means and power to employ twenty or twenty five good men, having the cause at heart, to act as his agents: 2d Let these agents which shall be selected by him, have permission to visit such points at the front as are most accessible to large bodies of slaves in the Rebel states: Let each of the said agts have power—to appoint one sub agent or more in the locality where he may be required to operate: the said sub agent shall be thoroughly acquainted with the country—and well instructed as to the representations he is to make to the slaves:—but his chief duty will be to conduct such squads of slaves as he may be able to collect, safely within the Loyal lines: Let the sub agents for this service be paid a sum not exceeding two dolls. per day while upon active duty.

3dly In order that these agents shall not be arrested or impeded in their work— let them be properly ordered to report to the Generals commanding the several Departments they may visit, and receive from them permission to pursue their vocation unmolested. 4th Let provision be made that the slaves or Freed men thus brought within our lines shall receive subsistence until such of them as are fit shall enter the service of the country or be otherwise employed and provided for: 5thly Let each agent appointed by the General agent be required to keep a strict acct of all his transactions, of all monies received and paid out, of the numbers and the names of slaves brought into our lines under his auspices, of the planta-tions visited, and of everything properly connected with the prosecution of his work, and let him be required to make full reports of his proceedings—at least, once a fortnight to the General Agent.

6th Also, let the General agt be required to keep a strict acct of all his transac-tions with his agts and report to your Excellency or to an officer designated by you to receive such reports: 7th Let the General agt be paid a salary sufficient to enable him to employ a competant clerk, and let him be stationed at Washing-ton—or at some other Point where he can most readily receive communications from and send communications to his agents: The General agt should also have a kind of roving commission within our lines, so that he may have a more direct and effective oversight of the whole work and thus ensure activity and faithfulness on the part of his agents.

This is but an imperfect outline of the plan—but I think it enough to give your Excellency an Idea of how the desirable work shall be executed.

Your Obedient Servant

Fredk Douglass

*[Douglass enclosed the following on a separate sheet of paper. Lincoln endorsed this request by directing that Charles Douglass be discharged from the service. Orders discharging Sergeant Douglass were issued on September 10, 1864. Frederick Douglass's note is in Record Group 94, Records of the Adjutant General's Office, National Archives, Washington, DC. A copy of the order discharging Charles R. Douglass is in Compiled military service record, Charles R. Douglass, Sergeant, Company I., 5th Massachusetts Cavalry, M1817, Record Group 94, National Archives, Washington, DC.]*

Private

Now, Mr President—I hope I shall not presume to much upon your kindness—but I have a very great favor to ask. It is not that you will appoint me General Agent to carry out the Plan now proposed—though I would not shrink from that duty—but it is, that you will cause my son Charles R Douglass. 1st Sergeant of Company I. 5th Massachusetts dismounted cavalry—now stationed at "Point Lookout" to be discharged. He is now sick. He was the first colored volunteer from the State of New York—having enlisted with his Older Brother in the Mass. 54th partly to encourage enlistments. He was but 18 when he enlisted—and has been in the service 18. months. If Your Excellency can confer this favor—you will lay me under many obligations

Again Your Obedient Servant

Fredk Douglass

Lincoln Papers, Series 1, General Correspondence, 1833 to 1916: "Frederick Douglass to Abraham Lincoln, Monday, August 29, 1864 (Plan for Helping Slaves Escape from Rebel States)," https://www.loc.gov/item/mal3565200.

## ROBERT HAMILTON on the Presidential Election, September 24, 1864

*Despite issuing the Emancipation Proclamation and calling on Black men to serve in the military, Lincoln still had many critics among the abolitionists. Some of them favored an alternative candidate in the 1864 presidential election, such as John C. Fremont who had received the nomination from a convention held in Cleveland at the end of May. As soon as the Democratic Party held its convention in Chicago and nominated General George B. McClellan on a platform denouncing the war as a failure, it became apparent to editor Robert Hamilton (1819–1870) that while Lincoln had faults, he was far more preferable than McClellan. Any split among those who favored anti-slavery could aid in electing McClellan. Hamilton therefore sought to make it clear that while Lincoln was not perfect, his policies had done a great deal for the anti-slavery cause and he must be the choice, for McClellan would likely negotiate a peace settlement with the rebels and revoke the Emancipation Proclamation.*

---

We know that there are Democrats who honestly believe that Abraham Lincoln is a tyrant, desirous of the overthrow of American liberty, but they are the exception. The leaders and a vast majority of the party desire his removal because they deem him too honest. They think he wants to do justice to the black man, and, *therefore*, they want to defeat him. Shall they be permitted?

You and we may have thought that Mr. Lincoln has not done what *we think* he could have done for the overthrow of oppression in our land; *but that is not the question now. The great and overshadowing inquiry is, do you want to see the many noble acts which have been passed during Mr. Lincoln's administration repealed, and slavery fastened again upon Maryland, Louisiana, Tennessee, Virginia and portions of States now free?* This is the only question now, and if you are a friend of liberty you will give your influence and cast your vote for Abraham Lincoln, who, under God, is the only hope of the oppressed.

These are the sentiments we gave utterance to at Poughkeepsie and Hudson, and we entreat our readers everywhere, who are voters, nay, who are not voters, to give them a thought. If the enemies of God and humanity have united against him, surely the friends of God and liberty ought to combine to secure the reelection of our freedom-loving President.

There is no middle course left. We must either vote to preserve what has been secured for liberty, or we must vote for the men who are ready to trample her in the dust, and spread slavery broadcast over the whole continent. That God will give us wisdom to see our duty, and will and energy to do what we can in this trying hour to save our country, is our earnest prayer.

Editorial in the *Anglo-African*, New York, September 24, 1864.

## "AFRICANO" Prefers Lincoln over George B. McClellan in the Presidential Election, Point Lookout, Maryland, September 2, 1864

*"Africano" was a pseudonym for a soldier in the 5th Massachusetts Cavalry. In a letter to the editor written in July (see above), "Africano" had endorsed John C. Fremont for the presidency. Those who supported Fremont believed he*

*was more committed to abolition, racial equality, and a firm policy of Recon-*
*struction than Lincoln. Once the Democrats held their national convention in*
*Chicago at the end of August, "Africano," Frederick Douglass, and others who*
*were not enthusiastic about the prospect of a second term for Lincoln took a*
*more pragmatic approach and concluded that another four years of Lincoln*
*would be far preferable to a Democratic administration led by General George*
*B. McClellan. In addition to nominating the popular general for president, the*
*Democrats adopted a platform that proclaimed the war a failure. If McClellan*
*defeated Lincoln, he would likely seek a negotiated peace to end the war, and*
*such a move would probably be accompanied by a revocation of the Emancipa-*
*tion Proclamation. "Africano" reiterated his reasons for opposing Lincoln but*
*concluded that a seriously flawed Lincoln would be better than the alternative.*

---

This Republic has for the last four years past undergone agonies and tribula-
tions commensurate to her crimes which no other government of her age now on
the face of the world would have been capable of undergoing, but her long and
prosperous peace had not led her to the conviction that the olive branch would
have perpetually lived green in the garden of her wide-spread domain. No! In
her prosperity she accumulated riches, and these, coupled with her sons' undying love for their country's altar, has saved her from being precipitated into that
abyss in which governments fall but to live in history. It is now an established
fact that her means are exhausted—her sons, where are they? Turn your eyes to
that vast plain watered by the Potomac; there they lie cold in death, in honor of
their country's name—turn your eyes to gory battlefields too numerous and too
painful to retrace, there you will find them expiating the crimes practiced on inoffensive negroes by their departed sires. [. . .] Will you, notwithstanding all these,
by nominating and electing George B. McClellan, hurl into fresh dishonor your
country, by compromising with children of your own rearing—with domestic
foes whose life—whose all—now depends on your leniency and fatherly protection? Now that victory on every side is perching on our banners, will you degrade
Freedom's sons with a dishonorable compromise with that treason with which
they have so long and so vigorously contended? By electing George B. McClellan, the only man on whom the South looks with anxious eye for protection,
President of the United States, you close the avenues to a vigorous prosecution
of this dying rebellion [. . .].

McClellan and his party have ever been the chief instruments in giving aid
and assistance to the common enemy of the country, inaugurators of this bloody
conflict for the erection of the temple of Slavery on the rightful domains of
Freedom. [. . .]

When Mr. Lincoln stabbed slavery, had he followed up his political victory by
stabbing the monster to death, and eternally hiding its foul stain, by immediately

eradicating it from the entire country, to-day it would have been dead, buried and grown out of the memory even of those who fostered, idolized and made it the centre of their affections; and the Union would have been restored, the chivalry made to repent of their audaciousness, and the *beloved institution* would have perished without having found so many thousands of "poor white trash" to rally in her defence, to the detriment of the pride and glory of this great country, seeing that the foundation of the political fabric of the so-called confederacy had crumbled to ruin. In this, as in many other things, Mr. Lincoln has shown his inefficiency as a statesman, and though we abhor him when we consider the many injustices he has allowed to be practiced on colored men, we cannot but think him a better object than George B. McClellan. We do not in the least pretend to be a Lincolnite, for these reasons: 1st, Mr. Lincoln's unjust policy towards the negro soldiers in not enforcing upon the rebel authorities the necessity of acknowledging and treating them as prisoners of war. 2d, His partial freedom and his colonization scheme. 3d, His ordering the enlistment of slaves and paying bounty to their so-called masters, under pretence of being loyal men, thereby recognizing, to a certain extent, the right of property in man. 4th, His protecting disloyal Kentucky and parts of greater disloyal States from the liberating influence of his double-sided instrument; but for the time being we shall carefully avoid intermingling him with baser coin, and come more closely to the subject under consideration. [...]

Why should the Chicago Convention, in its blindness, be permitted to thus triumph in overruling the country? Why should the highest gift in the nation's power be lavished so profusely, so transcendently on the traitor of but yesterday, who bought his popularity by spilling the best blood of the country? Union men of the North! Republicans! rally your whole strength. This is your time; forget party strifes and personal animosities [...].

Now to you blackmen, I appeal, scatter not yourselves but for the good of our race, sustain the principles founded on Justice, Humanity, and Freedom!!

Letter to the editor of the *Anglo-African* (New York), Sept. 24, 1864.

## S. W. CHASE, Remarks to Abraham Lincoln upon Presenting a Bible, September 7, 1864

*Reverend Chase was part of a delegation that met with Lincoln at the White House and presented him with a Bible on behalf of the African American community in Baltimore. In arranging the meeting, R. Stockett Matthews, a Baltimore attorney and Republican politician, suggested to Lincoln that the "colored people are quite as eager to present to you the very handsome expression of their gratitude" and such a meeting would "be productive of some good in the public sense." Matthews may have been referring to a constitutional referendum in*

*Maryland that was scheduled for October 12. The primary issue in the election was a provision in the new constitution that abolished slavery. In accepting the Bible, Lincoln reiterated his belief "that all mankind should be free" and referred to the Bible as "the best Gift God has given to man." Today the Bible is part of the collections at the Fisk University Library (Lincoln Papers, Series 1, General Correspondence, 1833 to 1916: "R. Stockett Mathews to Abraham Lincoln, Wednesday, July 6, 1864 [Meeting with Committee of Black Men and Women from Baltimore, Maryland; Endorsed by John Hay]," https://www .loc.gov/item/mal3430000).*

---

Mr. President: The loyal colored people of Baltimore have dedicated to us the authority to present this Bible, as a token of their appreciation of your humane part towards the people of our race. While all the nation are offering their tribute of respect, we cannot let the occasion pass by without tendering our respect. Since we have been incorporated in the American family we have been true and loyal, and we now stand by, ready to defend the country. We are ready to be armed and trained in military matters, in order to protect and defend the Star-spangled Banner.

Our hearts will ever feel the most unbounded gratitude towards you. We come forward to present a copy of the Holy Scriptures as a token of respect to you for your active part in the cause of emancipation. This great event will be a matter of history. In future, when our sons shall ask what mean these tokens, they will be told of your mighty acts, and rise up and call you blessed.

The loyal colored people will remember your Excellency at the throne of Divine Grace. May the King Eternal, an all wise Providence, protect and keep you, and when you pass from this world, may you be borne to the bosom of your Saviour and God.

*Daily National Republican* (Washington, DC), Sept. 7, 1864.

## SOJOURNER TRUTH, Account of October 29, 1864 Meeting with Abraham Lincoln

*Born a slave named Isabella Baumfree in New York, Truth (c. 1799–1883) was a well-known abolitionist and activist for women's rights when she met with Lincoln at the White House. Truth had traveled to Washington from her home in Michigan and was assisting freed persons at the settlement established in Arlington on the plantation where Robert E. Lee had lived before the war. Truth was determined to meet Lincoln in person and congratulate him for issuing the Emancipation Proclamation. The "Mrs. C" referred to in the letter is Lucy*

*Colman, a White abolitionist who was also working with freed persons. Colman helped arrange the meeting and gave a favorable account of the interview in a letter written shortly after the event occurred. In her autobiography published nearly thirty years later, Colman offered a very different version of the story. In the later version, Colman claimed that Lincoln was brusque and treated Truth like "his washerwoman." The 1875 edition of Truth's* Narrative *includes the following account of the meeting along with some additional dialogue where Truth states that she had never heard of Lincoln prior to his candidacy for president, while Lincoln responds that he had heard of her "many times before that." Lucy N. Colman,* Reminiscences *(Buffalo: H.L. Green, 1891), 66–67; Carleton Mabee, "Sojourner Truth and President Lincoln,"* The New England Quarterly 61, No. 4 (Dec. 1988), 519–529.

———

It was about 8 o'clock, a.m., when I called on the President. Upon entering his reception room we found about a dozen persons in waiting, among them two colored women. I had quite a pleasant time waiting until he was disengaged, and enjoyed his conversation with others; he showed as much kindness and consideration to the colored persons as to the whites—if there was any difference, more. One case was that of a colored woman, who was sick and likely to be turned out of her house on account of her inability to pay her rent. The President listened to her with much attention, and spoke to her with kindness and tenderness. He said he had given so much he could give no more, but told her where to go and get the money, and asked Mrs. C—n to assist her, which she did.

The President was seated at his desk. Mrs. C. said to him, "This is Sojourner Truth, who has come all the way from Michigan to see you." He then arose, gave me his hand, made a bow, and said, "I am pleased to see you."

I said to him, "Mr. President, when you first took your seat I feared you would be torn to pieces, for I likened you unto Daniel, who was thrown into the lions' den; and if the lions did not tear you into pieces, I knew that it would be God that had saved you; and I said if He spared me I would see you before the four years expired, and he has done so, and now I am here to see you for myself."

He then congratulated me on my having been spared. Then I said: "I appreciate you, for you are the best President who has ever taken the seat." He replied thus: "I expect you have reference to my having emancipated the slaves in my proclamation. But," said he, mentioning the names of several of his predecessors (and among them emphatically that of Washington), "they were all just as good, and would have done just as he had done if the time had come. If the people over the river (pointing across the Potomac) had behaved themselves, I could not have done what I have; but they did not, and I was compelled to do these things." I then said: "I thank God that you were the instrument selected by him and the people to do it."

He then showed me the Bible presented to him by the colored people of Baltimore, of which you have no doubt seen a description. I have seen it for myself, and it is beautiful beyond description. After I had looked it over, I said to him: "This is beautiful indeed; the colored people have given this to the Head of the government, and that government once sanctioned laws that would not permit its people to learn enough to enable them to read this Book. And for what? Let them answer who can."

I must say, and I am proud to say, that I never was treated by any one with more kindness and cordiality than were shown to me by that great and good man, Abraham Lincoln, by the grace of God President of the United States for four years more. He took my little book, and with the same hand that signed the death-warrant of slavery, he wrote as follows:

"For aunty Sojourner Truth,

Oct. 29, 1864.

A. LINCOLN."

As I was taking my leave, he arose and took my hand, and said he would be pleased to have me call again. I felt that I was in the presence of a friend, and I now thank God from the bottom of my heart that I always have advocated his cause, and have done it openly and boldly. I shall feel still more in duty bound to do so in time to come. May God assist me.

"Letter from Sojourner Truth," *National Anti-Slavery Standard* (New York), Dec. 17, 1864. A slightly different version was published in the *Liberator* (Boston), Dec. 23, 1864. Unable to write, Truth dictated her account in a letter addressed to Rowland Johnson, Freedmen's Village, VA, Nov. 17, 1864.

## ROBERT HAMILTON Gives Thanks for Lincoln's Reelection, November 19, 1864

*Although Lincoln had initially worried about his prospects for reelection to the point where he had consulted with Frederick Douglass and made other preparations to save the Union between the election and inauguration of his successor, he overwhelmingly defeated his Democratic challenger, George B. McClellan, in the election held on November 8. Robert Hamilton (1819–1870) rejoiced at the results. For Hamilton, Lincoln's victory represented not only the triumph of anti-slavery principles and all but guaranteed the rebellion's ultimate defeat, but it also vindicated the republican principle of civilian rather than military control of the government. In making the latter point he quoted from the famed Roman orator Cicero: "Toga cedant arma," the military yields to the civil power.*

There are many more "Thank God's" than "Huzza's" over this great event. The great National heart beats soberly and solemnly over what it feels to be the great triumph of a great principle, involving the existence and perpetuity of the Republic. There are novel features about this event well worth our consideration. Three years ago, we happened to meet a distinguished writer and historian, who assented to the remark "that we would soon be thoroughly under military rule, and that from President down to Town Constable, no man would stand any chance of success unless with an army handle to his name." This opinion was a sound one then, according to the lights of history concentrated into the apothegm—"*armis cedat toga.*" But look at the result! The army leaders went in with characteristic dash to conquer a peace and a nation according to their view. It may be said that, to all intents and purposes, the military dictator of the South held full command of both armies in the field. At all events, military power commanded the "situation."

In the good old times of Greece and Rome, such circumstances would have led to an easy descent from civil to military rule. But here we are to-day utterly belying history in this, that "*toga cedant arma.*" "Arms yielded to civil law." A plain civilian is chosen by the people, instead of a soldier, in the fourth year of a terrible war. Of the two candidates before the people for their choice, the military man represented an inglorious peace, the plain citizen represented the continuance of the war until a reliable, honorable, national peace shall be obtained. Each of these men holds up their trophies. The one held up the Western Virginia Mountains; the "iron hand" to put down servile insurrection; the magnificent army gathered before Washington, from which (the army) he drove the Hutchinsons and John Brown's song; the seven days' battle before Richmond; Antietam. The other man holds up the Emancipation proclamation, *free Missouri, free Louisiana,* and FREE MARYLAND!!! And lo! the people, with a vast, overflowing majority, vote for freedom!—vote for the civilian. In full view of all the pains, sufferings, and losses, which the continuance of this war entails, they vote to maintain it; and not only to maintain it, but also to maintain it after the fashion in which Abraham Lincoln had carried it on—the sword in one hand, and the proclamation of Freedom in the other; a method so sound and effective that Jeff Davis himself seems disposed to emulate it. What "winning ways" that same "OLD ABE" must have about him.

And so we go on for the next four years: supported by the moral power of the people, upheld by the promise of their best endeavors. At the helm, a strong hand, a vigorous arm, a cool head and sagacious; a soul pledged to freedom in any event—a man whose experience has made him thoroughly acquainted with all the ropes, the masts, the sails, and the sound old hull, who knows all the officers and crew—and they know him!—and the enemy know him too.

"Da seen a smoke way down de ribber,
Whar de Linkum gunboat lay."

We are willing, for one, to take passage in that gunboat, satisfied she will work her way up stream and across swamps, until the re-united Union, glorious in its purification, shall not contain a foothold for tyrant or slave!

The *Anglo-African* (New York), Nov. 19, 1864.

## MARTIN DELANY, Account of Meeting with Abraham Lincoln, February 8, 1865

*Born to a free woman and an enslaved father in Virginia, Delany (1812–1885) grew up in Pennsylvania and briefly attended Harvard Medical School before racial prejudice compelled him to leave. Active in the abolition movement, Delany was perhaps the leading proponent of African American emigration before the Civil War, and he scouted a location for a proposed colony in West Africa. The following account details Delany's February 1865 meeting with Lincoln, where he proposed the creation of a Black military force commanded by Black officers. At this point all regiments of United States Colored Troops were under the command of White officers. While Delany's plan was not implemented, shortly after meeting with Lincoln, he was commissioned a major in the 104th US Colored Troops and became the first African American field officer in the army. Delany remained in the army until August 1868. During Reconstruction he was assigned to the Freedmen's Bureau in South Carolina, and he remained there for a time following his discharge from the army and was active in politics (ANB; Compiled military service record, Martin R. Delany, Major, 104th US Colored Infantry, Record Group 94, National Archives, Washington, DC).*

---

We give in Major Delany's own language his interview with President Lincoln.

He tells us, "On entering the executive chamber, and being introduced to his excellency, a generous grasp and shake of the hand brought me to a seat in front of him. No one could mistake the fact that an able and master spirit was before me. Serious without sadness, and pleasant withal, he was soon seated, placing himself at ease, the better to give me a patient audience. He opened the conversation first.

"'What can I do for you, sir?' he inquired.

"'Nothing, Mr. President,' I replied; 'but I've come to propose something to you, which I think will be beneficial to the nation in this critical hour of her peril.' I shall never forget the expression of his countenance and the inquiring look which he gave me when I answered him.

"'Go on, sir,' he said, as I paused through deference to him. I continued the conversation by reminding him of the full realization of arming the blacks of the

South, and the ability of the blacks of the North to defeat it by complicity with those at the South, through the medium of the *Underground Railroad*—a measure known only to themselves.

"I next called his attention to the fact of the heartless and almost relentless prejudice exhibited towards the blacks by the Union army, and that something ought to be done to check this growing feeling against the slave, else nothing that we could do would avail. And if such were not expedited, all might be lost. That the blacks, in every capacity in which they had been called to act, had done their part faithfully and well. To this Mr. Lincoln readily assented. I continued: 'I would call your attention to another fact of great consideration; that is, the position of confidence in which they have been placed, when your officers have been under obligations to them, and in many instances even the army in their power. As pickets, scouts, and guides, you have trusted them, and found them faithful to the duties assigned; and it follows that if you can find them of higher qualifications, they may, with equal credit, fill higher and more important trusts.'

" 'Certainly,' replied the president, in his most emphatic manner. 'And what do you propose to do?' he inquired.

"I responded, 'I propose this, sir; but first permit me to say that, whatever I may desire for black men in the army, I know that there exists too much prejudice among the whites for the soldiers to serve under a black commander, or the officers to be willing to associate with him. These are facts which must be admitted, and, under the circumstances, must be regarded, as they cannot be ignored. And I propose, as a most effective remedy to prevent enrolment of the blacks in the rebel service, and induce them to run to, instead of from, the Union forces—the commissioning and promotion of black men now in the army, according to merit.'

"Looking at me for a moment, earnestly yet anxiously, he demanded, 'How will you remedy the great difficulty you have just now so justly described, about the objections of white soldiers to colored commanders, and officers to colored associates?'

"I replied, 'I have the remedy, Mr. President, which has not yet been stated; and it is the most important suggestion of my visit to you. And I think it is just what is required to complete the prestige of the Union army. I propose, sir, an army of blacks, commanded entirely by black officers, except such whites as may volunteer to serve; this army to penetrate through the heart of the South, and make conquests, with the banner of Emancipation unfurled, proclaiming freedom as they go, sustaining and protecting it by arming the emancipated, taking them as fresh troops, and leaving a few veterans among the new freedmen, when occasion requires, keeping this banner unfurled until every slave is free, according to the letter of your proclamation. I would also take from those already in the service all that are competent for commission officers, and establish at once in the South a camp of instructions. By this we could have in about three months an army of

forty thousand blacks in motion, the presence of which anywhere would itself be
a power irresistible. You should have an army of blacks, President Lincoln, commanded entirely by blacks, the sight of which is required to give confidence to
the slaves, and retain them to the Union, stop foreign intervention, and speedily
bring the war to a close.'

"'This,' replied the president, 'is the very thing I have been looking and hoping
for; but nobody offered it. I have thought it over and over again. I have talked about
it; I hoped and prayed for it; but till now it never has been proposed. White men
couldn't do this, because they are doing all in that direction now that they can;
but we find, for various reasons, it does not meet the case under consideration.
The blacks should go to the interior, and the whites be kept on the frontiers.'

"'Yes, sir,' I interposed; 'they would require but little, as they could subsist on
the country as they went along.'

"'Certainly,' continued he; 'a few light artillery, with the cavalry, would comprise your principal advance, because all the siege work would be on the frontiers and waters, done by the white division of the army. Won't this be a grand
thing?' he exclaimed, joyfully. He continued, 'When I issued my Emancipation
Proclamation, I had this thing in contemplation. I then gave them a chance by
prohibiting any interference on the part of the army; but they did not embrace
it,' said he, rather sadly, accompanying the word with an emphatic gesture.

"'But, Mr. President,' said I, 'these poor people could not read your proclamation, nor could they know anything about it, only, when they did hear, to know
that they were free.'

"'But you of the North I expected to take advantage of it,' he replied.

"'Our policy, sir,' I answered, 'was directly opposite, supposing that it met your
approbation. To this end I published a letter against embarrassing or compromising the government in any manner whatever; for us to remain passive, except in
case of foreign intervention, then immediately to raise the slaves to insurrection.'

"'Ah, I remember the letter,' he said, 'and thought at the time that you mistook
my designs. But the effect will be better as it is, by giving character to the blacks,
both North and South, as a peaceable, inoffensive people.' Suddenly turning, he
said, 'Will you take command?'

"'If there be none better qualified than I am, sir, by that time I will. While it
is my desire to serve, as black men we shall have to prepare ourselves, as we have
had no opportunities of experience and practice in the service as officers.'

"'That matters but little, comparatively,' he replied; 'as some of the finest offi-
cers we have never studied the tactics till they entered the army as subordinates.
And again,' said he, 'the tactics are easily learned, especially among your people.
It is the head that we now require most—men of plans and executive ability.'

"'I thank you, Mr. President,' said I, 'for the—'

"'No—not at all,' he interrupted.

" 'I will show you some letters of introduction, sir,' said I, putting my hand in my pocket to get them.

" 'Not now,' he interposed; 'I know all about you. I see nothing now to be done but to give you a line of introduction to the secretary of war.'

"Just as he began writing, the cannon commenced booming.

" 'Stanton is firing! listen! he is in his glory! noble man!' he exclaimed.

" 'What is it, Mr. President?' I asked.

" 'The firing!'

" 'What is it about, sir,' I reiterated, ignorant of the cause.

" 'Why, don't you know? Haven't you heard the news? Charleston is ours!' he answered, straightening up from the table on which he was writing for an instant, and then resuming it. He soon handed me a card, on which was written,—

'February 8, 1865.

'Hon. E.M. Stanton, *Secretary of War*.

'Do not fail to have an interview with this most extraordinary and intelligent black man.

'A. LINCOLN'

"This card showed he perfectly understood my views and feelings; hence he was not content that my color should make its own impression, but he expressed it with emphasis, as though a point was gained. The thing desired presented itself; not simply a man that was *black*, because these had previously presented themselves, in many delegations and committees,—men of the highest intelligence,— for various objects; but that which he had wished and hoped for, their own proposed measures matured in the council-chamber had never been fully presented to them in the person of a black man."

Frank A. Rollin, *Life and Public Services of Martin R. Delany* (Boston: Lee and Shepard, 1883), 166–171.

## GEORGE WASHINGTON to Abraham Lincoln, Hilton Head, South Carolina, March 19, 1865

*Washington dictated this letter to a teacher at one of the schools that had been organized to educate freed persons on the Sea Islands. While Washington's motives for traveling from where his family lived in Georgia to Hilton Head are unclear, the Sea Islands would have been an attractive destination due to the support, assistance, and opportunities available there. In addition to churches and schools that northern philanthropic organizations were operating, General William T. Sherman's Special Field Orders No. 15, issued in January 1865, provided Black families the opportunity to settle on forty-acre plots of land.*

Most respected friend

I take this opportunity this holy Sabbath day to try to express my gratitude and love to you. With many tears I send you this note through prayer and I desire to render you a thousand thanks that you have brought us from the yoke of bondage. And I love you freely. I am now 53 years old. Inauguration day was also my Birthday. I have come 278 miles from Savannah and from there to Hilton Head. I have lain awake four nights and my mind so bore upon you that I could not rest till I sent you a letter. I lived in Butts Co. Ga. I am obliged to send you this to satisfy my mind. I wish you all the blessings that can be restored by the Almighty.

I would be glad to go back to see my family. I do love my wife and children. I have been a Baptist member for 25 years and I have been praying for this for 17 years. At that time I had a vision and you was made known to me in a dream. I saw a comet come from the North to the South and I said good Lord what is that? I heard a voice "There shall be wars & rumors of wars" I saw many signs and wonders. My soul is filled with joy at the pleasure of letting you know. I have had a heap of high mountains and deep waters to cross. My master threatened my life if I should talk about this. But I just put all my trust in the Lord and I believe he has brought me conqueror through. I give my mind to pray for you the balance of my days. It would satisfy me if you would condescend to send me an answer to this on account of my fellow servants. If you should answer please direct to Mrs Luther Fowler. Stono plan—

Hilton. Head. S.C.

Yours with the greatest esteem

George Washington.

P.S. I have written the above precisely as dictated by a poor colored man who came to me in a flood of tears and begged me to write to the President for him. It is so entirely expressive of the feelings of all "Freedmen" that I send it. We have a large mission school in our house attended by nearly 800 people. A large number of them are adults and if it would not be too great an intrusion on your time I would be happy to receive a note from you for the "Freedmen" of the island.

Yours with respect

Mrs L Fowler

Lincoln Papers, Series 1, General Correspondence, 1833 to 1916: "Mrs. Luther Fowler [George Washington] to Abraham Lincoln, Sunday, March 19, 1865 (Writes on behalf of freedman at Hilton Head)," https://www.loc.gov/item/mal4137000.

## THOMAS MORRIS CHESTER, Report on Lincoln's Visit to Richmond, Virginia, April 4, 1865

*In 1864, Chester (1834–1892) was hired by the Philadelphia* Press *as a war correspondent. This was notable because the* Press *was not an African American newspaper and Chester was the only African American war correspondent for a daily newspaper during the Civil War. Chester covered the war in Virginia and was with the first troops that occupied Richmond on April 3, 1865—Gen. Godfrey Weitzel's 25th Corps, comprised entirely of United States Colored Troops. Chester was therefore well situated to report on Lincoln's visit to Richmond the following day, and he took particular interest in how the African American community responded to Lincoln's presence (R. J. M. Blackett, ed.,* Thomas Morris Chester, Black Civil War Correspondent *[Baton Rouge: Louisiana State University Press, 1989]).*

---

The great event after the capture of the city was the arrival of President Lincoln in it. He came up to Rocket's wharf in one of Admiral Porter's vessels of war, and, with a file of sailors for a guard of honor, he walked up to Jeff Davis' house, the headquarters of General Weitzel. As soon as he landed the news sped, as if upon the wings of lightning, that "Old Abe," for it was treason in this city to give him a more respectful address, had come. Some of the negroes, feeling themselves free to act like men, shouted that the President had arrived. This name having always been applied to Jeff, the inhabitants, coupling it with the prevailing rumor that he had been captured, reported that the arch-traitor was being brought into the city. As the people pressed near they cried "Hang him!" "Hang him!" "Show him no quarter!" and other similar expressions, which indicated their sentiments as to what should be his fate. But when they learned that it was President Lincoln their joy knew no bounds. By the time he reached General Weitzel's headquarters, thousands of persons had followed him to catch a sight of the Chief Magistrate of the United States. When he ascended the steps he faced the crowd and bowed his thanks for the prolonged exultation which was going up from that great concourse. The people seemed inspired by this acknowledgment, and with renewed vigor shouted louder and louder, until it seemed as if the echoes would reach the abode of those patriot spirits who had died without witnessing the sight.

General Weitzel received the President upon the pavement, and conducted him up the steps. General Shepley, after a good deal of trouble, got the crowd quiet and introduced Admiral Porter, who bowed his acknowledgments for the cheering with which his name was greeted. The President and party entered the mansion, where they remained for half an hour, the crowd still accumulating around it, when a headquarters' carriage was brought in front, drawn by four horses, and Mr. Lincoln, with his youngest son, Admiral Porter, General Kautz, and General Devens entered. The carriage drove through the principal streets, followed by General Weitzel and staff on horseback, and a cavalry guard. There is no describing the scene along the route. The colored population was wild with enthusiasm. Old men thanked God in a very boisterous manner, and old women shouted upon the pavement as high as they had ever done at a religious revival.

But when the President passed through the Capitol yard it was filled with people. Washington's monument and the Capitol steps were one mass of humanity to catch a glimpse of him. [ . . . ]

It must be confessed that those who participated in this informal reception of the President were mainly negroes. [ . . . ]

I visited yesterday (Tuesday) several of the slave jails, where men, women, and children were confined, or herded, for the examination of purchasers. The jailors were in all cases slaves, and had been left in undisputed possession of the buildings. The owners, as soon as they were aware that we were coming, opened wide the doors and told the confined inmates they were free. The poor souls could not realize it until they saw the Union army. Even then they thought it must be a pleasant dream, but when they saw Abraham Lincoln they were satisfied that their freedom was perpetual. One enthusiastic old negro woman exclaimed: "I know that I am free, for I have seen Father Abraham and felt him."

When the President returned to the flag-ship of Admiral Porter, in the evening, he was taken from the wharf in a cutter. Just as he pushed off, amid the cheering of the crowd, another good old colored female shouted out, "Don't drown Massa Abe, for God's sake!"

*The Press* (Philadelphia), April 11, 1865.

## ISAAC J. HILL, Account of Lincoln's Visit to Richmond, April 4, 1865

*A native of Pennsylvania, Hill (1826–?) enlisted in the 29th Connecticut Infantry (Colored) in January 1864 and served until October 1865, when he was mustered out as a private. Hill's regiment was part of General Godfrey Weitzel's 25th Corps and among the first units to occupy Richmond, Virginia, when the city fell in early April 1865. The following eyewitness account of Lincoln's April 4 visit to Richmond is from Hill's history of the 29th Connecticut that was published shortly after the war ended. Although Hill mistakenly had Lincoln visiting the city on April 3, his poignant account captures the emotional reception Lincoln received from Richmond's African American residents. In addition to writing a history of his regiment, Hill served as an AME minister in Virginia and New York following the war (Compiled military service record, Isaac J. Hill, Private, Company D, 29th Connecticut Infantry [Colored], M1824, Record Group 94, National Archives, Washington, DC; Israel L. Butt, History of African Methodism in Virginia [Norfolk: Hampton Institute Press, 1908]).*

The 3d instant President Lincoln visited the city. No triumphal march of a conqueror could have equalled in moral sublimity the humble manner in which he entered Richmond. I was standing on the bank of the James river viewing the scene of desolation when a boat, pulled by twelve sailors, came up the stream. It contained President Lincoln and his son, Admiral Porter, Captain _____, of the Army, Captain _____, of the Navy, Lieut. W.W. _____, of the Signal Corps. In some way the colored people on the bank of the river ascertained that the tall man wearing the black hat was President Lincoln. There was a sudden shout and clapping of hands. I was very much amused at the plight of one officer who had in charge fifty colored men to put to work on the ruined buildings; he found himself alone, for they left work and crowded to see the President. As he approached I said to a woman, "Madam, there is the man that made you free." She exclaimed, "Is that President Lincoln?" My reply was in the affirmative. She gazed at him with clasped hands and said, "Glory to God. Give Him the praise of his goodness," and she shouted till her voice failed her.

When the President landed there was no carriage near, neither did he wait for one, but leading his son, they walked over a mile to Gen'l Weitzel's headquarters at Jeff Davis' mansion, a colored man acting as guide. Six soldiers dressed in blue, with their carbines, were the advanced guards. Next to them came President Lincoln and son, and Admiral Porter, flanked by the other officers right and left. Then came a correspondent, and in the rear were six sailors with carbines. Then followed thousands of people, colored and white. What a spectacle! I never witnessed such rejoicing in all my life. As the President passed along the street the colored people waved their handkerchiefs, hats and bonnets, and expressed their gratitude by shouting repeatedly, "Thank God for his goodness; we have seen his salvation." The white soldiers caught the sound and swelled the numbers, cheering as they marched along. All could see the President, he was so tall. One woman standing in a doorway as he passed along shouted, "Thank you, dear Jesus, for this sight of the great conqueror." Another one standing by her side clasped her hands and shouted, "Bless the Lamb—Bless the Lamb." Another one threw her bonnet in the air, screaming with all her might, "Thank you, Master Lincoln." A white woman came to the window but turned away, as if it were a disgusting sight. A few white women looking out of an elegant mansion waved their handkerchiefs. President Lincoln walked in silence, acknowledging the salute of officers and soldiers, and of the citizens, colored and white. It was a man of the people among the people. It was a great deliverer among the delivered. No wonder tears came to his eyes when he looked on the poor colored people who were once slaves, and heard the blessings uttered from thankful hearts and thanksgiving to God and Jesus. They were earnest and heartfelt expressions of gratitude to Almighty God, and thousands of colored men in Richmond would have laid down their lives for President Lincoln. After visiting Jeff Davis' mansion he proceeded to the rebel capitol and from the steps delivered a short speech and spoke to the colored people as follows:

"In reference to you, colored people, let me say God has made you free. Although you have been deprived of your God-given rights by your so-called masters, you are now as free as I am, and if those that claim to be your superiors do not know that you are free, take the sword and bayonet and teach them that you are—for God created all men free, giving each the same rights of life, liberty and the pursuit of happiness."

The gratitude and admiration amounting almost to worship, with which the colored people of Richmond received the President must have deeply touched his heart. He came among the poor unheralded, without pomp or pride, and walked through the streets, as if he were a private citizen more than a great conqueror. He came not with bitterness in his heart, but with the olive leaf of kindness, a friend to elevate sorrow and suffering, and to rebuild what had been destroyed. [...]

This good and God-fearing President died on the morning of the 15th of April at half-past seven o'clock, and he bore to heaven the fetters of four millions of slaves, and I think I can hear him say to the Father of all good spirits, "These are they that came up through great tribulation." He was meek, like the Lord and Savior, and forgave his enemies to the last. I fancy I can almost hear him say in his dying moments, "Father, forgive them for they know not what they do." No class of people feel his death as the colored people do, for we have lost the best friend we had on our earth, our great deliverer. He had done all a President could do for the poor colored race.

In I. J. Hill, *A Sketch of the 29th Regiment of Connecticut Colored Troops* (Baltimore: Daugherty, Maguire & Co., 1867), 26–28.

## ALEXANDER H. NEWTON, Account of Lincoln's Visit to Richmond, April 4, 1865

*Born to a free mother and an enslaved father in North Carolina, Newton (1837–1921) enlisted in the 29th Connecticut Infantry (Colored) in December 1863 and attained the rank of commissary sergeant. Like Isaac J. Hill (see above), Newton witnessed Lincoln's visit to Richmond, and the following account is from Newton's autobiography. After being mustered out of the army in October 1865, Newton served as a minister for the AME Church (Compiled military service record, Alexander H. Newton, Sergeant, Company E, 29th Connecticut Infantry [Colored], M1824, Record Group 94, National Archives, Washington, DC; AANB).*

We were present in Richmond when President Lincoln made his triumphal entry into the city. It was a sight never to be forgotten. He passed through the main street. There were multitudes of Colored people to greet him on every hand. They received him with many demonstrations that came from the heart, thanking God that they had seen the day of their salvation, that freedom was theirs, that now they could live in this country, like men and women, and go on their way rejoicing. Orderly I.J. Hill said that he saw a colored woman trying to get a look at the president, at last he came along and Orderly Hill said to her: "Madame, there is the man that made you free." She shouted, "Is that President Lincoln? Glory to God, give Him praise for His goodness." The President, with his son, and Admiral Porter, together with others walked over a mile to the headquarters of General Weitzel, at the mansion of Jeff Davis. A colored man acted as the guide. There were six Union soldiers as advance guard, then came President Lincoln, his son, and Admiral Porter, while on his right and his left were other officers. He was followed by six sailors with their carbines. This march created the wildest enthusiasm of the Colored people. They had lived to see the day of their liberty dawning. I was reminded of what had been done for the ancient Hebrews by Moses when he led them out of the land of their bondage, into the land of their promised liberty. Lincoln was indeed our Moses. He led us forth. He gave us our freedom. I noticed one white lady in a window, who turned away from the whole scene as if in utter disgust. There were still two sides to the question, then and there are two sides to it today. How long will these two sides remain, is the question. As the President looked out upon the poor Colored people and remembered how many lives had been lost in working out their salvation, he was not able to keep the tears from his eyes. They were tears of gladness and sorrow, of regret and delight; but the tears of my own people were the tears of the greatest joy.

The President went to the state capitol where he made a short address in which he said: "Now you Colored people are free, as free as I am. God has made you free and if those who are your superiors are not able to recognize that you are free, we will have to take the sword and musket and again teach them that you are free. You are as free as I am, having the same rights of liberty, life and the pursuit of happiness. [...]"

On April 16th, 1865, we were painfully shocked to hear of the death of President Lincoln, at the hands of an assassin. No one can measure the consternation which struck our hearts. This great and wonderful man who had guided the Ship of State through four years of such perilous waves and winds, that he should thus pass away and in such an infamous manner, was more than we could stand.

In Alexander H. Newton, *Out of the Briars: An Autobiography and Sketch of the Twenty-ninth Regiment Connecticut Volunteers* (Philadelphia: A. M. E. Book Concern, 1910), 65–67.

## JACOB THOMAS, Sermon Preached in Memory of Abraham Lincoln at AME Zion Church, Troy, New York, April 16, 1865

*A native of Philadelphia, Thomas (1823–?) spent a long and active career as a minister of the African Methodist Episcopal Zion Church in New York. At the time of the following sermon, Thomas was serving in Troy, where he had raised funds to build a church and parsonage. Delivered on Easter Sunday, one day after Lincoln's death, Thomas's sermon reveals how news of the assassination was met with profound shock and grief. Thomas notes the purity of Lincoln's heart, and in apotheosizing Lincoln as a martyr and savior he helped establish Lincoln's unique place in the hearts of African Americans (J. W. Hood, One Hundred Years of the African Methodist Episcopal Zion Church [New York: A. M. E. Zion Book Concern, 1895]).*

---

*Know ye not that there is a prince and a great man fallen this day in Israel?*
—2 Samuel, iii, 38.

My friends, we meet at this hour with sad hearts. We have been stricken. The blow has fallen heavily upon us, and a nation mourns today. Truly a prince and a great man in Israel has fallen. We cannot but weep bitter tears that so great and good a man as Abraham Lincoln, has been cut down in the midst of his usefulness by a death so cruel. At the moment he was about to realize the great results of his four years labor, just as victory had perched upon our banners, he fell a martyr to freedom. We shall never look upon his like again.

A few days ago joy and gladness filled every heart. All who were loyal to the government rejoiced and gave thanks to Almighty God because of the victory won, the downfall of the rebel capital. This intelligence was too glorious to be unalloyed. Ere our joy had subsided, sorrow overtook us. News reached us from Washington of the bloody deed perpetrated there. We would not believe it. It could not be possible that a creature in the form of man could be found so God-forsaken, as to take the life of the man who had malice for none but charity for all! The hours between the first rumor and the confirmation of the report, were hours of dreadful suspense. But the truth came at last. There was no longer room for doubt. It was too true, that on last Friday evening, whilst enjoying at a place of amusement a few moments of relaxation from toil, accompanied by his wife and a few friends, unconscious of danger near, he was brutally murdered—shot down by the cowardly hand of an assassin. Palsied be the tongue, withered be the arm of the guilty, execrable wretch who committed this, the blackest of all crimes. Yes, our dear President is no more. The beloved of his country, the father and friend of the oppressed, the champion of universal freedom, has fallen victim to southern malice and revenge. Kind heaven weeps to-day over the bloody spectacle.

We, as a people, feel more than all others that we are bereaved. We had learned to love Mr. Lincoln as we have never loved man before. We idolized his very name. We looked up to him as our saviour, our deliverer. His name was familiar with our children, and our prayers ascended to God in his behalf. He had taught us to love him. The interest he manifested in behalf of the oppressed, the weak and those who had none to help them, had won for him a large place in our heart. It was something so new to us to see such sentiments manifested by the chief magistrate of the United States that we could not help but love him. Is it wondered that we mourn to-day? Nay, we have seen old gray-headed men and young maidens weep because of this affliction. Had disease attacked him and he had passed away according to the natural course of nature, we could have consoled ourselves with the thought that it was God's will it should be so. But falling as he did by the hand of the wicked, we derive our consolation only from the assurance that by his uprightness, his honesty and his principles of Christianity, he is now enjoying that rest that remains for the just.

Our text is a fitting one for the occasion. A great man has fallen. From whatever standpoint we view Mr. Lincoln, we find in him the marks of true greatness. A few years ago this plain, homely lawyer was scarcely known outside of his own state. But how soon did he become the point of attraction. Not only was he the center of observation in this country, but the civilized world was watching him. He far exceeded the expectations of all men. He became as the ark of safety to his country, the praise and glory of his fellow men. To us as a despised people, he was a second Moses—a second Daniel in wisdom. From a humble position in life he reached the very summit of honor, occupied the highest seat that it was in the power of the American people to give him, and filled that seat as no man ever filled it before him. The mind that conceived and drew up the Proclamation of Emancipation was a great mind. The results of this grand deed are patent to all. He was a philanthropist in the most extensive sense of the word—benevolent, kind, and ever ready to make others happy. One of the most prominent features in the character of our departed friend was his merciful disposition even towards his foes. He was strictly honest; this is admitted by his worst enemies. "Honest Abe," he was familiarly called by all classes. He was honest with his people, honest to himself, honest to his God. This is what God requires of all men, to be honest in heart. The exterior of this great man may have been plain, homely and awkward, but the interior was beautifully finished and furnished with Christian graces. It was his reliance upon God that carried him safely through the storm of four years duration. It was this that has made him blessed in the favor of God, forever.

Yes, Abraham Lincoln is no more, and we mingle our tears with those of the mourning widow and bereaved friend. We feel that in his loss our punishment is more than we can bear, yet in God is our consolation. Let us hope for the best. An all-wise God has permitted this great grief to come upon us. Let us look to him for deliverance in the time of our distress. We are humbled, we are mortified, we are brought very low. Our trust must be in God. Whilst we mourn, he whose death we deplore, is enjoying the reward of his labor, happy with his God, mingling with those kindred spirits who went before him. The two truest and greatest men that ever lived on earth, John Brown and Abraham Lincoln, have met in glory, and they cease not to give praise and honor to him that liveth forever and ever. The memory of Abraham Lincoln will ever be dear to us. It is engraved upon our hearts. It can never be effaced. He has been our true friend and we can never forget him. We feel as though God had raised him up for a special purpose, and that having accomplished the labor assigned him, he has gone to his rest. May God protect us and keep us from farther evils.

In *A Tribute of Respect by The Citizens of Troy, to the Memory of Abraham Lincoln* (Albany: J. Munsell, 1865), 43–47.

## Resolutions Passed on Lincoln's Assassination in Middletown, Connecticut, April 20, 1865

*The following resolutions were adopted at a public meeting held at the AME church in Middletown, Connecticut, to mourn the assassinated president. Reverend J. F. Lloyd led the meeting that featured several speeches, including one that compared Lincoln to an oak tree that had withstood a storm until being struck down by lightning at the very end of the storm when the crisis had passed. The resolutions indicated the high esteem in which Lincoln was held shortly after his death, as he was memorialized as a Moses-like father figure who had been martyred for his devotion to the cause of equality.*

---

Resolved, That our thanks be returned unto God for sparing unto us Abraham Lincoln, who, like Moses, was permitted to view the promised land from Pisgah's top, but not permitted to take the children over until he had in a great measure accomplished the work appointed him, viz:—the subduing of the rebellion, and giving freedom to a long down-trodden race and peace to a suffering nation.

Resolved, That the foul deed which deprived us of him whom we had come to look upon as a father, shall be the means of uniting loyal citizens of every party in eradicating that dark blot (slavery) from our nation's otherwise bright escutcheon. [...]

Resolved, That we, as a people, feel the blow which struck down our friend Abraham Lincoln, as though meant for us, for we, of the African race looked upon our late President as our best friend, and the champion of our rights which he has sealed with his blood, and we will cherish his name and memory to remotest generations as a martyr to our cause.

The *Anglo-African* (New York), May 6, 1865.

## MARTIN DELANY, Proposal for a Monument to Abraham Lincoln, April 20, 1865

*Delany (1812–1885) was a major in the 104th US Colored Infantry when he made the following proposal in the immediate aftermath of Lincoln's assassination. Although Delany had been a leading proponent of emigration prior to the war, the Emancipation Proclamation and the opportunity to serve as an army officer had evidently altered his views at least temporarily. As the nation mourned Lincoln, Delany called on African Americans to show their gratitude for Lincoln by contributing money for a monument to be built in his memory. Since Lincoln's actions had benefited all African Americans, Delany called for donations in the amount of one cent so that all could be invested in the project. Other African Americans had similar ideas in the wake of Lincoln's death. The Colored People's National Lincoln Monument Association was organized in Washington on April 25, 1865, with all of the persons mentioned in Delany's proposal serving as officers: Henry H. Garnet was president; Stephen Smith the treasurer; James McCune Smith was a director; and Daniel A. Payne and Delany were life directors. This organization sought to establish a school in Washington whose primary purpose was the education of freed persons. The extent of Delany's involvement with this organization is unknown, and it did not deter him from writing a follow-up letter to the* Anglo-African, *where he offered a detailed description of the monument he hoped to see erected. While Delany's proposed monument was not built, Charlotte Scott, a former slave living in Ohio, donated $5 to start a fundraising drive for a monument to Lincoln that ultimately culminated in Thomas Ball's* Emancipation Group *that Frederick Douglass delivered the dedication address for in April 1876 (*Christian Recorder *[Philadelphia], July 15, 1865; the* Anglo-African *[New York], June 10, 1865).*

---

A calamity such as the world never before witnessed—a calamity the most heart-rending, caused by the perpetration of a deed at the hands of a wretch the most infamous and atrocious—a calamity as humiliating to America as it is infamous and atrocious—has suddenly brought our country to mourning by the untimely death of the humane, the benevolent, the philanthropic, the generous, the beloved, the able, the wise, great and good man, the President of the United

States, Abraham Lincoln, the Just. In his fall, a mighty chieftain and statesman has passed away. God, in his inscrutable providence, has suffered this, and we bow with meek and humble resignation to his Divine will, because He does all things well. God's will be done!

I suggest that, as a just and appropriate tribute of respect and lasting gratitude from the colored people of the United States to the memory of President Lincoln, the Father of American Liberty, every individual of our race contribute *one cent*, as this will enable each member of every family to contribute, parents paying for every child, allowing all who are able to subscribe any sum they please above this, to such national monument as may hereafter be decided upon by the American people. I hope it may be in Illinois, near his own family residence.

This penny or one cent contribution would amount to the handsome sum of forty-thousand ($40,000) dollars, as a tribute from the black race (I use the genitive term), and would be not at all felt; and I am sure that so far as the South is concerned, the millions of freedmen will hasten on their contributions.

To this end, then, let proper and well-selected committees be appointed in every community, to whom such contributions will be made, with a record of the name of every family and the number of inmates, the name of husband and wife simply, and so many children, as—"George and Elizabeth Parker and five children, 7 cents."

I would to this end name, as the common Treasurer for the funds, to be paid over to the proper officers at the proper time, in their order, Rev. Stephen Smith, Philadelphia, who will make weekly acknowledgments of the aggregate amount received, with the names of the places where received from, simply.

I am certain that every loyal editor in Philadelphia and elsewhere will gladly publish without cost such an item.

Will the Rt. Rev. Dr. Payne, President of Wilberforce University, Rev. Dr. H. H. Garnet, and James McCune Smith, M.D., sanction this proposition?

"Monument to President Lincoln," the *Anglo-African* (New York), May 13, 1865.


## ROBERT HAMILTON, "Thy Will Be Done," April 22, 1865

*In the weeks that followed the shock of Lincoln's assassination, Hamilton's Anglo-African mourned Lincoln by printing thick black columns throughout the newspaper. He eulogized Lincoln by comparing him to George Washington and suggesting that the nation had supreme faith in his leadership. While Hamilton expressed grief, he also believed that the assassination served as a powerful warning that a lenient Reconstruction policy like the one Lincoln favored should not be implemented, as the rebels needed to be punished and African Americans must be able to vote.*

Since that cold night in December nearly seventy years ago, when a grief-stricken rider rushed from Mount Vernon laden with the sad news of the death of Washington, no event has shed so profound a grief over [t]he land as the murder of Abraham Lincoln. Then the nation all told, was a little over three million, now, it counts up thirty millions of souls; spaces over which the news travelled, then in days and weeks, it reaches now in minutes and hours, so that the sudden news and extent of the shock, is, in the latter event tenfold the greater. Washington's career, moreover, to mortal eyes had run its course, and he was cut off rather from the comforts and delights of a well-earned retirement than arrested in the midst of his usefulness to mankind. With Abraham Lincoln it was different. He was still in the midst, and apparently an indispensable part of great events daily transpiring, and was really leaned upon by the best hopes of an immense majority of the people. Within a week of his death, a newspaper (*The N.Y. Express*) which has most bitterly opposed him, his party and his policy, uttered the remark that it "*had learned to pray for the preservation of his life.*" Men had learned to trust the future of the nation to his keeping. So calmly had he met, so quietly and wisely had he overcome all past difficulties that we all regarded him as more than equal to any coming emergencies, and in the joy of our hearts were forgetting past afflictions, in the joyous sunlight of a golden peace in which he figured as the grand central peacemaker. No matter what course he had chosen, we would have cheerfully acquiesced in it—sure that his wise instincts had led to what was best.

It was at this stage of his career that Abraham Lincoln was suddenly removed from our midst, and the nation aroused from that almost dreary confidence wherewith it had shifted to one poor mortal brain the responsibilities which really rested upon the intelligent millions. In the darkest hours of the rebellion, when the yelling hosts of the insurgents pressed triumphantly on the soil of a free State, the people came to the rescue, and above and beyond the free devotion of their means, their time and their lives to the common safety, they helped him *think* the way out of danger. But now, that the immediate dangers and horrors of war have passed away, and there is only peace to be negotiated, the masses have suddenly stopped their helpful thinking, and left the conditions of peace or reconstruction to the unaided judgment and discretion of one man, to whom, if Providence had not kindly removed him, the gigantic task would have been an impossible duty; who would have gone down under a more dismal fate than the assassin's bullet. [ . . . ]

There should not be any hurry in welcoming back to our outstretched hands and fervent breasts, the wolves, serpents and savage barbarians who yet constitute the head and front of the Southern people, whose hearts are now dancing the scalp dance over the remains of our murdered President [ . . . ].

If the franchise be withheld from the freedmen, then the old slaveholding class will, as before, fill all the offices and return to Congress as before in one compact body. Such will be the result of the reconstruction on the principles which seemed uppermost in the mid of our late deeply lamented President.

We think there is now an end to this policy. In a way which could have been compassed by no less a sacrifice, the North has been awakened to the danger into which it was drifting. The dreams of early peace[,] easy reconstruction and grand material prosperity have been rudely broken by one dreadful reality. [ . . . ]

If the slaveholding class be awarded a milder punishment than banishment, then let it be entire disfranchisement during their natural lives. And not only the officers, but all the soldiers engaged in the rebellion should be disfranchised [ . . . ].

In view, then, that this terrible awakening was required by this great nation in order to change its course of conduct, in view of the real peace [ . . . ] which will follow this change of policy, we can only, with uncovered heads and reverent hearts, [ . . . ] exclaim, THY WILL BE DONE.

The *Anglo-African* (New York), April 22, 1865.


## JAMES W. C. PENNINGTON on Lincoln's Funeral Procession through New York City, April 27, 1865

*While the nation mourned Lincoln's death, the struggle over how he would be remembered commenced. As this letter from Pennington (1807–1870), a well-known abolitionist and clergyman, indicates, one of the first questions concerning Lincoln's place in American memory was the extent to which African Americans would be able to participate in the formal funeral ceremonies that occurred during the process of returning Lincoln's body to Springfield. Thousands of people participated in a procession through the streets of New York on April 25 as Lincoln's body was moved from City Hall, where it had lain in state for a day, to the train station. In making arrangements for the procession the Common Council determined that only White people could participate. Despite protests from African Americans and the city's commissioner of police, the council refused to allow Black people to march. On the evening before the event, a telegram from the War Department in Washington directed that "no discrimination respecting color should be exercised in admitting persons to the funeral procession." The next day, Pennington led a hastily assembled group of a few hundred African Americans who marched in the rear of the procession with police protection. Recently freed slaves from the South carried a banner in the procession that paid tribute to "Abraham Lincoln our Emancipation" ("Obsequies of the Martyred President," National Anti-Slavery Standard [New York], April 29, 1865).*

The Common Council of New York had certainly no more right to rule the societies of colored men out of the funeral procession, than they would have to decide that a certain part of a man's family should not attend his funeral through the street.

One story is that the Common Council was influenced in their action by an intimation that the Irish societies had determined not to join in the procession if colored societies were assigned a place.

This is simply ridiculous. Was Mr. Lincoln the President of the Irish only? Of all other classes, was he not emphatically the President of the colored man? Have we not had it thrown in our teeth by the Irish that our father was dead? The spirit that would exclude colored men from the President's funeral, is the same that murdered him, from whomsoever it may come. [ . . . ]

The action of the Common Council was an insult to the memory of the President.

The *Anglo-African* (New York), May 13, 1865.

## ANGELINE R. DEMBY, Poem in Memory of Abraham Lincoln, April 29, 1865

*A resident of Philadelphia, Demby (c.1848–?) was an aspiring young poet who responded to Lincoln's assassination with a tribute that memorialized him as a Christlike martyr whose death was so deeply felt that it caused bleeding and broken hearts. Demby was confident that Lincoln's role as emancipator had secured him a place in paradise, and despite the pain of his passing, the people whom he freed would help finish his work (Eric Gardner, "African American Women's Poetry in the 'Christian Recorder,' 1855–1865: A Bio-Bibliography with Sample Poems," African American Review 40 [winter 2006]: 813–831).*

We mourn to learn that we are struck
With such appalling wo;
We bow beneath the mighty stroke;
Twas God who willed it so.

A martyr to sweet Freedom's laws,
A patriot true and brave,
With noble brow and form erect,
Is stricken to the grave.

The grave shall not environ him;
His spirit is with God;

It took its flight at early morn,
When Jesus spoke the word.

"Come unto me, beloved Son,
You filled your place of trust;
I call you hence, come unto me;
I'll raise you from the dust."

The nation mourns a patriot slain!
Lord, heal the broken heart.
We cannot bear this staggering pain,
Unless thou heal the smart.

Thy balm supply to bleeding hearts;
Our comfort Thou shall be.
It was thy will that we should part
With him who made us free.

In bondage dark, oppressed with shame,
We long were made to stand,
Till Abraham Lincoln did proclaim
Freedom throughout the land.

God bless the true Republican!
His name shall ever live,
Till God shall unto every man
Perpetual freedom give.

Though we still weep, we will not stand,
With folded hands and mourn—
But, with all friends of Abraham,
We'll trample treason down.

"Lines Respectfully Dedicated to the Memory of our Much Beloved and Martyred President, Abraham Lincoln," *Christian Recorder* (Philadelphia), April 29, 1865; *Poetical Tributes to the Memory of Abraham Lincoln* (Philadelphia: J. B. Lippincott, 1865), 220–221.

## Reaction to Lincoln's Assassination, Baltimore, Maryland, April 1865

*The following account from a correspondent in Baltimore indicates the profound sorrow that Lincoln's assassination evoked. The report of people openly weeping accords with Secretary of the Navy Gideon Welles's diary entry that noted a similar phenomenon in Washington, including a large crowd of Black people*

*in front of the White House who were crying. The suddenness of the event was
stunning and came at a time when the correspondent believed Lincoln was just
beginning to exhibit "the best qualities of the human heart." It was as though
people had lost a close friend or family member, for the correspondent likened
Lincoln to a father and hoped that the blood of the martyred president would
help make the nation whole again.*

---

How feeble words seem to express the profound grief of a nation! how inad-
equate its language to paint the overwhelming sorrow of a horror-stricken people!
ABRAHAM LINCOLN, President of the United States, has been brutally murdered—meanly, cowardly, treacherously assassinated.

We at this time have no words to express the deep feeling that this fiendish and
diabolical act has exercised over this community. Its awful suddenness, coupled
with its utter fiendishness, has overwhelmed us, as it has the nation at large. [. . .]

[I]t was but yesterday that the National heart pulsated with the most intense
exultation over the victories which had perched upon the banners of the Republic. To-day, the keenest anguish, the most profound sorrow, and grief the most
overwhelming, paralyzes all.

Oh! it is too distressing, too heart-sickening to think of. Just at the time when
the President was exhibiting the best qualities of the human heart; when he was
bending all the energies of mind, and the nobler feelings of his better nature, in
bringing the four years carnage of fire and blood to a close—when he was extending the most kind and liberal forgiveness to the rebels—his head is pierced with
the shot of the assassin, who exclaims, as he gloats over his work of death—*"Sic
semper tyrannis!"* But the devil-possessed assassin, as well as the entire South,
will soon realize the fact that, instead of killing a tyrant, they have taken the life
of one of decidedly the most humane and magnanimous rulers who ever sat at
the head of a government.

The effect of the news upon the people of this city beggars description. Strong
men cried like children, while the women were frantic with sorrow; for in the
death of the President they realize the death of a friend—a father. The whole
city is draped in mourning, the church and fire bells dolefully toll, while knots
of grave and sorrow-stricken men are to be seen at this corner and that, heaping
curses deep and dark upon the head of the guilty one. All places where liquor is
sold are closed by order of the military authorities, while the entire police force
is on duty. The effect of the murder of the President has converted many hitherto
red-hot Secessionists to strong out-and-out Union men.

We are one of those who see the finger of God in all things, and while no one
laments the death of our most excellent President more than we, yet we believe
that when the tears which now blind us shall have ceased their flowing, and when

we are enabled to look into matters calmly and religiously, that we will then perceive that this act of blood will do much to cement the nation in one solid, compact Union. For as the blood of the martyrs was the seed of the Church, even so will the blood of Abraham Lincoln be the seed out of which will come tens and hundred of thousands of righteous men, who are to Christianize and evangelize this guilty and perverse nation, and make it indeed the "land of the free and the home of the brave."

The *Anglo-African*, April 22, 1865.

## HENRY O. WAGONER, Report on Lincoln's Funeral Procession in Chicago, May 2, 1865

*Wagoner (1816–1901), an abolitionist and civil rights leader in Chicago, detailed how the Chicago Black community mourned the martyred Lincoln and participated in the funeral procession as his body moved through the city on May 1. In addition to holding a mass meeting and approving resolutions, several hundred Black citizens marched in the procession. While the War Department had to intervene in order for African Americans to be able to participate in the New York funeral procession, Wagoner optimistically reported that the appointment of John Jones, another prominent Chicago Black leader, to a committee that accompanied Lincoln's body to Springfield was further "cheering evidence of progress."*

Resolved, That we have no words with which adequately to express our profound gratitude for the great boon he has been the instrument of conferring on our people, in breaking the bonds of the bondmen, and in freeing over three millions of our people by the force of his memorable proclamation—thus, not only in freeing their limbs, but in putting arms in their hands with which to help themselves in swelling beyond the measure of their chains and aiding in crushing the rebellion. [ . . . ]

Resolved, That we believe the honored name of Abraham Lincoln will ever be cherished and dear to the hearts of our people, not alone to the colored people of this Republic, but also to those of other lands and especially to those who shall fully understand the man and his character.

Resolved, That while we do not wish to be understood as mitigating the crime of assassination, we *do* believe, however, that the fact and circumstances of his death, like that of all martyrs for a cause, will tend ultimately to promote that cause and to defeat its enemies.

Resolved, That as a further testimonial of our interest, love and affection for the illustrious dead, we will turn out *en masse* to attend the funeral ceremonies which will take place in this city to-morrow. [...]

The funeral procession of the remains of our Moses-like late President, took place yesterday in our city, and was one of the grandest and most imposing demonstrations, at the same time one of the most solemn and orderly assemblies of the vastest multitudes that has ever taken place in Chicago—or, indeed, in the great North-west. The remains were escorted through the streets by not less than 40,000 people. The colored citizens were promptly on hand to take the position assigned them, and were about five hundred strong, bearing appropriate banners and mottoes, such as— "We mourn our loss," "Rest in peace with a nation's tears," etc.

"The Funeral of President Lincoln and the Colored People," the *Anglo-African* (New York), May 13, 1865.

## GEORGE W. LE VERE, Eulogy of Abraham Lincoln, New Orleans, Louisiana, May 22, 1865

*Le Vere (1820–1886), a Congregationalist minister in Brooklyn, New York, and president of the African Civilization Society, had met Lincoln in November 1863, when the president received a committee from the society (see above). In January 1864, Le Vere was appointed chaplain of the 20th US Colored Infantry and he served in the army until October 1865. In his eulogy of Lincoln, Le Vere focused on Lincoln's character, and in urging people to write Lincoln's name in their family Bibles he was in effect suggesting that Lincoln had become a member of all their families (Compiled military service record, George W. Le Vere, Chaplain, 20th US Colored Infantry, M1823, Record Group 94, National Archives, Washington, DC).*

---

Know ye not that there is a Prince and a great man fallen—ii. Samuel, 3d, 38v.

We meet today to mingle our kindred voices in a solemn dirge. And to pray to the God of our fathers for our distracted and our sorrow stricken country. And I, your humble servant, have been selected to speak some fitting words in commemoration of the somewhat mysterious and yet noble and sublime career of that "Great and good Man," Abraham Lincoln our very highly esteemed and much beloved President, who in the glory of his days has been taken from us; amidst the shouts of joy and thanksgivings that were bursting forth from every loyal heart and ascending the skies, East, West, North and South.

And just as the backbone of the Hydra-headed monster "Rebellion" had been broken by the irresistible power of the Union arms and the surrender of Robt. E. Lee and his shattered forces, who had transformed themselves into traitors and rebels against their country, its constitution and laws, and when peace appeared to be near at hand, the nation is convulsed by the solemn and heart-rendings of the assassination of its Chief Magistrate.

We have not chosen the words of our text as above quoted, to attempt to contrast the life and character of our noble President, with the life and character of Abner, who is referred to by the King of Israel, in the words we have chosen.

But believe that they can be truthful as well as the words of our choice, for the present solemn occasion. There needs to be a combination of elements in a character, to produce what may be called truly a great man. [ . . . ]

He was persevering, though poor; he had, burning in his nature, the fire of respiration, which urged him to seek for a clerkship in a law office which he obtained; and by his close application to study, he made himself a proficient lawyer and was admitted to plead at the bar.

Still comparatively unknown, he yet advances further, and obtains the nomination as the republican candidate for the United States Senate. His opponent was Stephen A. Douglas, one of the most able politicians of the democratic party, with whom he canvasses the State of Illinois, and discusses the merit and demerits of the principles of both parties, in which he showed that he possessed very rare abilities; thus he was brought out of obscurity to be a prominent man in our great nation.

At the convention held in the city of Chicago in 1860, he was chosen as the representative of true republican principles, and as such, he was elected by the people President of the United States of America. And like king Solomon, he did not pray for riches, honor, or glory; but wisdom to govern the people. And this God granted to him.

And with a masterly mind, and a superior knowledge, he brought into requisition the power and strength of the Government, for the suppression of the rebellion.

Being honest, he could not fail to be just; therefore he remembered the poor, the down-trodden, the outraged, and the despised and proclaimed liberty to the bondman and said, "thou art free."

With discretion, he was prepared to meet those branded rebels at Fortress Monroe, who sought to inveigle him into a scheme for a dishonorable peace. Yet in charity he sympathized with them in their sad and forlorn condition; he had suffered long with, and manifested kindness toward them; he did not envy their position, neither did he vaunt or puff up himself; nor behave unseemly but gentle and dignified.

Being firm, he was unalterable in his purposes for justice and the right. And thus he lived and died; truly a "prince and a great man has fallen."

Let us go to our homes and write upon the records of our family Bible the name of Abraham Lincoln, the great and good man, the President of the United States of America, who was assassinated on the evening of the 14th day of April, 1865, in the city of Washington, D.C.

And leave it to be handed down to our children, and to their children's children.

*New Orleans Tribune*, July 7, 1865.

## FREDERICK DOUGLASS, Speech at Cooper Institute, New York, June 1, 1865

*Less than two months after Lincoln's assassination, Douglass delivered an address on Lincoln at the Cooper Institute. A complete transcript of Douglass's speech was evidently not reported in the newspapers, but the following is taken from a manuscript in the Douglass Papers at the Library of Congress that was likely the basis of Douglass's address on June 1. Douglass offered a panegyric and urged other Blacks to do the same, especially in the wake of the controversy over African American participation in Lincoln's funeral procession through New York City (see James W. C. Pennington's remarks above). For Douglass, it was vital for African Americans to not only mourn Lincoln but also play an active role in keeping his memory alive in the future. Lincoln, according to Douglass, was unequivocally the "blackmans president," as his presidency accomplished so much for them even though he did not always do as they wished. Lincoln's importance to African Americans could not be forgotten, as Douglass realized that much work remained to finish what Lincoln had begun. The stakes involved in shaping how Lincoln and the Civil War would be remembered were therefore very high. Just as Lincoln's connection to African American freedom and citizenship must be remembered and immortalized with monuments, Douglass also emphasized that it could not be forgotten that the forces responsible for slavery were also responsible for atrocities during the war, such as the Andersonville prison camp, and those same forces had been responsible for Lincoln's murder. Douglass therefore concluded that there was no difference between assassination conspiracists John Wilkes Booth, Lewis Payne, and George Atzerodt and Confederate leaders such as Robert E. Lee, Jefferson Davis, and John C. Breckinridge. At the outset of the struggle over how Lincoln would be remembered, Douglass claimed Lincoln as an ally in the cause of racial equality. Douglass concluded his address with a favorite anecdote about the time when Lincoln had made Connecticut Governor William A. Buckingham wait while he met with Douglass.*

I come before you this Evening with much diffidence: The rarest gifts, the best eloquence, the highest order of genius to which the nation has given birth, might well be employed here and now, and yet fail of justice to the dignity and solemnity of this occasion.

The character of the illustrious deceased, the position he occupied at the head of our Government, the extraordinary manner of his death, with all the attendant circumstances of the country, are fruitful themes, of the most interesting nature;—themes which must depend upon the historian, rather than upon the orator, for elaborate and appropriate celebration.

Had Abraham Lincoln died, from any of the numerous ills to which flesh is heir, and by which men are removed from the scenes of life; Had he reached that good old age, of which his vigorous constitution, and his temperate habits gave promise; Had he seen the end of the great work which it was his good fortune to inaugurate; Had the curtain of death been but gradually drawn around him;—our task this Evening, though sad, and painful would be very simple.

But dying as he did die, by the red hand of violence, snatched suddenly away from his work without warning;—killed, murdered, assassinated, not because of personal hate, for no man, who knew Abraham Lincoln, could hate him; but solely because he was the President, the faithful, loyal President of the United States—true to his country, and true to the cause of human freedom, taking care that the constitution and the laws were obeyed; for this reason he was slain, murdered, assasinated, and for this all commanding reason—he to day commands our homage and the homage of good men everywhere as a glorious martyr—one who must be viewed if viewed rightly, in connection with his country and with all that pertains to his country. Very evidently here is a large field opened, but the most any man can do, with a subject like this, and at a time like this, when every faculty of thought and feeling, is intensely active, when the press, the pulpit and the platform, when poetry and art in all her departments has been occupied with this one great Event for weeks: I say, the most I can do, the most any man can do, is in some humble measure, to give back to the country, the thoughts and feelings which are derived from the country [...].

To day all over this country men have been thinking of Abraham Lincoln: Our Statesmen scholars and poets—have been celebrating as never before the memory of our martyred President. It is well. He is worthy of it all—and it is becoming in all—to join however, humbly in these tokens of respect and veneration.

One thing will be at once conceded by all generous minds; No people or class of people in this country, have a better reason for lamenting the death of Abraham Lincoln, and for desiring to honor and perpetuate his memory, than have the colored people; and yet we are about the only people, who have been in any case forbidden to exhibit our sorrow, or to show our respect for the deceased president publicly. The attempt to exclude colored people from his funeral procession in

New York—was one of the most disgraceful, and sickening manifestations of moral emptiness, ever exhibited by any nation or people professing to be civilized: But what was A. Lincoln to the colored people or they to him? As compared with the long line of his predecessors, many of whom were merely the facile and servile instruments of the slave power; Abraham Lincoln, while unsurpassed in his devotion, to the welfare of the white race, was also in a sense hitherto without example, emphatically the blackmans President: the first to show any respect for their rights as men.

To our white fellow country men therefore we say, follow your martyred president to his grave, lay the foundation of his monument broad and strong—let its capstone rise towards the sky—do homage to his character, forever perpetuate his memory; but as you respect genuine sorrow, unfeigned grief, and sincere bereavement, let the colored people of this country—for whom he did so much, have space at least, for one stone in that monument—one which shall tell to after-coming generations the story of their love and gratitude to Abraham Lincoln.

Those love most to whom most is forgiven. One of the most touching scenes connected with the funeral of our lamented President, occurred at the gate of the Presidential mansion: A colored woman standing at the gate weeping, was asked the cause of her tears; Oh! sir she said we have lost our Moses: But said the gentleman, the Lord will send you another: That may be, said the weeping woman—but Oh! we had him. To her mind one as good; or better might come in his stead—but no such possibility to her was equal to the reality, actual possession in the person of Abraham Lincoln.

The colored people, from first to last, and through all, whether through good or through evil reports, fully believed in Abraham Lincoln. Even though he sometimes smote them, and wounded them severely, yet they firmly trusted in him: This was however, no blind trust unsupported by reason: They early caught a glimpse of the man, and from the evidence of their senses, they believed in him. They viewed him not in the light of separate individual facts—but in the light of his mission—in his manifest relation to events—and in the philosophy of his statesmanship—Viewing him thus they trusted him—as men are seldom trusted. They did not care what forms of expression the President adopted, whether it were justice, expediency, or military necessity so that they saw slavery abolished—and Liberty was established in the country.

Under Abraham Lincolns beneficent rule, they saw themselves being gradually lifted to the broad plain of equal manhood: Under his rule, and by measures approved by him, they saw gradually fading the hand writing of ages which was against them: Under his rule, they saw millions of their brethren proclaimed free and invested with the right to defend their freedom: Under his rule, they saw the confederate states—that boldest of all conspiracies against the just rights of human nature, broken to pieces, overpowered conquered, shattered to fragments—ground to powder and swept from the face of existence: Under his rule, they saw the Independence of Hayti and Liberia recognized—and the whole colored race steadily rising into the friendly consideration of the American people. [. . .]

Here after when men think of slavery, they will think of murder. Here after when men think of slaveholders, they will think of assassins; Here after when men think of southern chivalry they will think of our starving prisoners at Andersonville. Here after when men think of southern honor, they will think of the assassination of Abraham Lincoln. [. . .]

The beginning of the rebellion is assassination. [T]he end of the rebellion is assassination. It is consistent throughout. It ends as it began. Not a line of analogy is missing. Booth and Beauregard, Payne and President Davis[,] Adzerot and Breckenridge, were servants of a common cause, and will go down in history as clansmen and kinsmen—and brothers beloved in a common conspiracy and a common crime. It has been sometimes regretted that Booth was not captured alive, that he might have been regularily tried, condemned, sentenced and executed. [. . .]

But let us turn away from the hateful assassin, and think of the loved and honored martyr who fell by the hand of the assassin.

The world is old, an[d] its experiences vast, but was there ever such an hour, caused by the announcement of the death of any monarch, as was caused by the news of the death of Abraham Lincoln? Was ever any people so instantly and so universally overwhelmed with grief? Did ever a great and victorious nation so suddenly pass from triumph to tears—from exaltation and joy to the very dust and ashes of mourning[?] I know of none and the world knows of none [. . .].

The gentle, the amiable, character of the man—the man, with malice towards none, but charity towards all—the last man in the world—one could think to tempt the assassins dagger—The thought was full of astonishment as well as horror. The event itself, was so sudden, so tragic, and so out [of] joint with all seeming probability, so in contradiction to all our feelings that few could at the first believe the dreadful news[.] You remember all the circumstances, and yet it seems fit in an address like this that we reiterate their leading features. The story is soon told: while seated with his wife, in a private box at Ford's Theatre, set apart by its proprietor, for the President and his family;—while putting off the burdens of State for the moment, observing the play entitled Our American Cousin, which he had been specially invited to witness—all unconscious of danger to himself or to the State: Abraham Lincoln was shot down by an assassin who stood behind him—and died from the wound the ensuing morning: Such was the shocking news flashed from Washington on the Fifteenth April [. . .].

Men everywhere recognized in it the hand and heart of the rebellion: The life taken was not the life the murderers saught. It was not the President but, the

Country they would strike down through him. But what a day! What a day to the American people was that fourteenth of April. For the moment we seemed suspended over the howling abyss of Anarchy and social chaos. At that moment a breath or an atom—might have detached us from the moorings [of] civil order—and plunged us into Nation[al] ruin. [...]

Had the solid earth opened and swallowed up one of our chief cities, had the tombs, burst beneath our feet, and the sheeted dead walked forth from the dust of ages, the sensation of astonishment and horror could not have been more profound and all pervading. [...]

I shall not undertake to describe the grand tumult of emotions that throbbed in all loyal hearts that day. A thought of the assassin caused a shudder, as if one had in the darkness of a lonely way come upon the fierce glaring eyes of a ferocious beast—or trodden upon a poisonous reptile. We were smitten with a feeling of shame for the fiendish possibilities of human nature. For a moment there stole through men's hearts a strange distrust of each other. They looked at their fellow citizens with a searching glance, which said not so much who are you but what are you and how do you feel at this mournful hour? [F]or none could tell how far the dark spirit of assassination had travelled north nor where the blow would next fall.

Still as I look back to that day, and analize the emotions every where excited, I must say, the one sentiment, the one feeling,—vastly more intense, more prominent and all pervading, than all others; the one that stirred deepest, the hearts of men, and caused their eyes to alternate between tears at one moment, and sparks of fire at another, was a feeling of sorrow a sense of personal bereavement in the death of Abraham Lincoln. This one great feeling—overtapped and interlaced all others—and colored every object to the eye and spirit.

What was the real cause of this deep sorrow? Who can explain whence the hold this man had upon the American people? His high official character, no doubt had something to do with it—but very evidently this was not all. Other Presidents have died, though none have been assassinated before President Lincoln—Yet none were ever so mourned. [...]

What then was the cause of our grief? [W]hence our bereavement: I affirm that it was not because the country had lost a president, but because the world had lost a man—one whose like we may not see again.

The fact is the people in the very depths of their souls loved Abraham Lincoln. They knew him, and knew him as one brother knows another, and they loved him as one brother loves another. He was not only the President of the Country, but a member of each loyal family—in the country. The very picture of his plain American face was loved—as the picture of a dear relation.

Abraham Lincoln was no exotic,—no imported growth of king craft or of Priest craft. He was no imitator of foreign customs or copiest of foreign manners, but thoroughly American in all that distinguished his character—There was not a fibre in his whole composition that did not identify him with his country to the fullest extent. He was a self made man, the architect of his own fortune. And the American people—indebted to themselves for themselves, saw in him, a full length portrait of themselves. In him they saw their better qualities represented— incarnated, and glorified—and as such they loved him.

Other men have, perhaps, been as much honored, but no American has been so much loved—by the American people. But we stand even yet, too near the newly made grave of Abraham Lincoln, either for a just analyses of his character—or for a dispassionate review of his official life. The wound caused by his death is yet too deep—too fresh, the sorrow too lasting, and the mind too excited—with the scenes of sorrow for just criticism or unbiased Eulogy.

The sad and solemn pageantry of his funeral has not yet faded from our vision: The long and imposing procession winding its way through distant states, towards the setting sun is still in sight. The sable drapery of mourning has scarcely ceased to sadden in dwellings or streets. The booming of distant cannon proclaiming a nation's grief, has hardly ceased to reverberate. Muffled drums are still beating funeral marches to his grave, the national flag still waves sadly at half mast against the hollow sky, while the image of him who has gone, lingers in our hearts, like the last smile of a loving mother—just quitting the shores of time.

It was my privilege to know Abraham Lincoln and to know him well. I saw and conversed with him at different times during his administration, and upon two occasions at least, by his special invitation. He was the first American President, who thus rose above the prejudice of his times, and Country.

I mention it as a proof of his independence. He knew that he could do nothing—which would call down upon him more fiercely the ribaldry of the vulgar— than by showing any respect to a colored man. I found him as you all know him to have been a plain man. There was neither paint nor varnish about him. His manners were simple, unaffected unstudied. His language was like himself— plain strong, sinewy—and earnest. He stated his views with great clearness and strength. Few men could state a case so strongly and convincingly. His utterances were always to the point and without ornament. Though a western man—he was entirely free from extra[va]gance or exaggeration in thought or speech: He was conscious of the vast responsibilities resting upon him, but bore himself as one able to bear them successfully. His dignity as the President, never stood in the way of his amiability as a man. He was like his pictures, the same man from whichever side you viewed him. He neither awed by his silence nor silenced by the volubility or authority of his speech. While willing to give, he was equally willing to receive; and so far from feeling restrained, in his presence, he acted upon me as all truly great men act upon their fellow men, as a Liberator,—He set me at perfect Liberty—to state where I differed from him as freely, as where

I agreed with him. From the first five minutes I seemed to myself, to have been acquainted with [him] during all my life. He was one of the most solid men I ever met, and one of the most transparent.

What Mr Lincoln was among white men; How he bore himself towards them, I do not know, but this much I am bound to say, that he was one of the very few white Americans who could converse with a Negro without any thing like conde-cension, and without in anywise reminding him of the unpopularity of his color. If you will pardon the seeming egotism I will mention a fact or two in further illustration of the character of President Lincoln and of his kindly disposition towards colored people. He seemed to want to know them thoroughly. Born in Kentucky—living in Illinois—accustomed to seeing the colored man in most unfavorable conditions it was natural to expect from him at the first—as those made to the colored people he called about him during the first years of the war. But Mr Lincoln soon outgrew his colonization ideas and schemes—and came to look upon the Blackman as an American citizen.

On one occasion while conversing with him, his messenger twice announced that Governor Buckenam of Connecticut was in an adjoining room, and was very desirous of seeing him. Tell the Governor to wait—said Mr Lincoln—I want to have a long talk with my friend Douglass. I remained a full hour after this with the President, while Governor Buckenham waited patiently in an adjoining room the Presidents pleasure to see.

This was probably the first time in the history of the country when the Gov-ernor of a state, was required to wait for an interview, because the President of the United States, was engaged in conversation with a Negro.

*Frederick Douglass Papers* (Washington, DC: Library of Congress), https://www.loc.gov /collections/frederick-douglass-papers/.

## FREDERICK DOUGLASS, Draft of a Speech on Lincoln, circa December 1865

*Internal evidence suggests that this draft of a speech on the consequences of Lin-coln's assassination was begun in late 1865, as Douglass (1818–1895) delivered an address, "The Assassination and Its Lessons," during a speaking tour in 1866. It is in this draft where Douglass stated that everyone knew Lincoln's "life by heart." In the excerpt below, Douglass contended that the last part of Lincoln's life was his zenith. In seeking to draw a sharp contrast between Lincoln and his successor, Andrew Johnson, Douglass emphasized that Lincoln was prepared to extend the vote to some African Americans and suggested that his timorousness in doing so was the product of his philosophy of not assailing unnecessarily the prejudices of people to make his point. In using the rail-splitter analogy, Douglass asserted that Lincoln's initial proposal for limited Black voting rights was merely the starting point, as he realized not only the contradiction of denying the vote to those who fought to preserve the Union, but also foresaw a future where there would be no legal distinctions between Blacks and Whites. Douglass wanted his audience to realize that, if Lincoln had lived, Reconstruction would not be failing in the egregious ways it was under Johnson's leadership.*

---

You all know his life by heart. [. . .] The last days of Mr Lincoln were his best days. If he did not control events he had the wisdom to be instructed by them. When he could no longer withstand the current he swam with it. What he said on the steps of the Capital four years ago did not determine what the same lips should utter four years afterward. No two papers are in stronger contrast than his first and his last Inaugural addresses. The first was intended to reconcile the rebels to the Government by argument and persuasion, the second was a recognition of the operation [of] inevitable and universal laws. In this he was willing to let justice have its course. You all remember with what solemn emphasis he expressed this on the fourth March—six weeks before his assassination:

"Fondly do we hope, fervently do we pray that this mighty scourge of war shall soon pass away. Yet if God wills it continue till all the treasure piled by two hundred and fifty years of the bondman's unrequited toil shall have been wasted [every] drop of blood drawn by the lash shall have been paid for by one drawn by the sword, we must still say, as was said three thousand years ago—the judgements of the Lord are true and rightious altogether."

Had Mr Lincoln lived, we might have looked for still greater progress. Learning wisdom by war—he would have learned more from Peace. Already he had expressed himself in favor of extending the right of sufferage to two classes [of] colored men, first to the brave colored soldiers who had fought under our flag—and second to the very intelligent part of the colored population south. This declaration on his part though it seemed to mean but little meant a great deal. It was like Abraham Lincoln. He never shocked prejudices unnecessarily. Having learned statesmanship while splitting rails, he always used the thin edge of the wedge first—and the fact that he used this at all meant that he would if need be, use the thick as well as the thin. He saw the absurdity of asking men to fight for a Government which should degrade them—and the meanness of enfranchising enemies and disfranchising friends. He was a progressive man, a humane man, an honorable man, and at heart an antislavery man. He had exhausted the resources of conciliation upon rebels and slaveholders and now looked to the principles of Liberty and justice, for the peace, security happ[i]ness and prosperity of his country. I assume therefore, had Abraham Lincoln been spared to see this day— the negro of the south would have more than a hope of enfranchisement and no rebels would hold the reins of Government in any one of the late rebellious states.

Whosoever else have cause to mourn the loss of Abraham Lincoln, to the colored people of the country—his death is an unspeakable calamity.

*Frederick Douglass Papers* (Washington, DC: Library of Congress), https://www.loc.gov/collections/frederick-douglass-papers/.

## Address of the Illinois Convention of Colored Men to the American People, Galesburg, Illinois, October 16–18, 1866

*Over fifty men from Illinois responded to a call to convene at Galesburg in the fall of 1866 for the purpose of discussing the challenges that African Americans faced both in Illinois and nationally. The following is an excerpt from the convention's address to the American people that was prepared by a committee of seven men, including Joseph H. Barquet, a noted orator, civil rights activist, and veteran of the 54th Massachusetts. In invoking Lincoln's name to support Black suffrage, the committee quoted from Lincoln's 1862 Annual Message to Congress and his March 13, 1864, letter to Governor Michael Hahn of Louisiana. Although Lincoln's letter was confidential, it was widely published in the months following his assassination.*

---

A voice from the tomb of the martyred Lincoln seems now to reach the national ear, saying, "The hour is come in which to enfranchise the colored American people, that they may 'help you keep the jewel of liberty in the family of freedom.'" To the test of man's fitness for self-government, as presented by "the model republic," the oppressed of every clime still fondly look. To cleanse and purify it—to make it a light casting its rays of grandeur and stability in the redemption of the nations, from whatever tyrannizes over man—the image of his Maker—is your great work. And in the memorable words of departed excellence and worth, it is within your competency to "meanly lose, or nobly save, the last best hop[e] of the earth!"

*Proceedings of the Illinois Convention of Colored Men, Assembled at Galesburg [...]* (Chicago: Church, Goodman and Donnelly, 1867), 36.

## Elizabeth Keckley, *Behind the Scenes*, 1868

*Born a slave in Virginia, Keckley—or Keckly (1818–1907)—purchased her freedom and settled in Washington, where she became Mary Lincoln's dressmaker and friend. Keckly's son was killed early in the war, as he had been able to pass as White and enlist in a Missouri regiment. The Lincolns lost their son, Willie, to*

*illness in February 1862, and the shared grief over their lost sons brought Keckly
and Mrs. Lincoln closer together. Keckly was a prominent member of the African
American community in Washington and helped form the Contraband Relief
Association that assisted newly freed persons who had been displaced by the war.
Following President Lincoln's assassination, Mary Lincoln became consumed
by fear over her financial situation and enlisted Keckly in an ill-fated scheme
to sell her clothing. Keckly also reached out to prominent Black leaders, such as
Frederick Douglass and Henry Highland Garnet, who were willing to assist Mrs.
Lincoln, but she declined these overtures. Having been a frequent visitor at the
White House and a close confidante of Mrs. Lincoln, Keckly published a memoir,
Behind the Scenes, in the wake of the "old clothes scandal." While Keckly hoped
it would vindicate Mrs. Lincoln, the tell-all nature of the book outraged the Lin-
coln family and ended their friendship. The following excerpts offer glimpses of
life at the White House that few were in a position to observe (Jennifer Fleischner,
Mrs. Lincoln and Mrs. Keckly [New York: Broadway Books, 2003]).*

---

I was worn out with watching, and was not in the room when Willie died, but
was immediately sent for. I assisted in washing him and dressing him, and then
laid him on the bed, when Mr. Lincoln came in. I never saw a man so bowed down
with grief. He came to the bed, lifted the cover from the face of his child, gazed at
it long and earnestly, murmuring, "My poor boy, he was too good for this earth.
God has called him home. I know that he is much better off in heaven, but then
we loved him so. It is hard, hard to have him die!"

Great sobs choked his utterance. He buried his head in his hands, his tall frame
was convulsed with emotion. I stood at the foot of the bed, my eyes full of tears,
looking at the man in silent, awe-stricken wonder. His grief unnerved him, and
made him a weak, passive child. I did not dream that his rugged nature could be
so moved. I shall never forget those solemn moments—genius and greatness
weeping over love's idol lost. There is a grandeur as well as a simplicity about the
picture that will never fade. [ . . . ]

In 1863 the Confederates were flushed with victory, and sometimes it looked
as if the proud flag of the Union, the glorious old Stars and Stripes, must yield
half its nationality to the tri-barred flag that floated grandly over long columns
of gray. These were sad, anxious days to Mr. Lincoln, and those who saw the man
in privacy only could tell how much he suffered. One day he came into the room
where I was fitting a dress on Mrs. Lincoln. His step was slow and heavy, and his
face sad. Like a tired child he threw himself upon a sofa, and shaded his eyes with
his hands. He was a complete picture of dejection. Mrs. Lincoln, observing his
troubled look, asked:

"Where have you been, father?"

"To the War Department," was the brief, almost sullen answer.

"Any news?"

"Yes, plenty of news, but no good news. It is dark, dark everywhere."

He reached forth one of his long arms, and took a small Bible from a stand near the head of the sofa, opened the pages of the holy book, and soon was absorbed in reading them. A quarter of an hour passed, and on glancing at the sofa the face of the President seemed more cheerful. The dejected look was gone, and the countenance was lighted up with new resolution and hope. The change was so marked that I could not but wonder at it, and wonder led to the desire to know what book of the Bible afforded so much comfort to the reader. Making the search for a missing article an excuse, I walked gently around the sofa, and looking into the open book, I discovered that Mr. Lincoln was reading that divine comforter, Job. He read with Christian eagerness, and the courage and hope that he derived from the inspired pages made him a new man. I almost imagined that I could hear the Lord speaking to him from out the whirlwind of battle: "Gird up thy loins now like a man: I will demand of thee, and declare thou unto me." What a sublime picture was this! A ruler of a mighty nation going to the pages of the Bible with simple Christian earnestness for comfort and courage, and finding both in the darkest hours of a nation's calamity. [ . . . ]

Mr. Lincoln, as every one knows, was far from handsome. He was not admired for his graceful figure and finely moulded face, but for the nobility of his soul and the greatness of his heart. His wife was different. He was wholly unselfish in every respect, and I believe that he loved the mother of his children very tenderly. He asked nothing but affection from her, but did not always receive it. When in one of her wayward impulsive moods, she was apt to say and do things that wounded him deeply. If he had not loved her, she would have been powerless to cloud his thoughtful face, or gild it with a ray of sunshine as she pleased. We are indifferent to those we do not love, and certainly the President was not indifferent to his wife. She often wounded him in unguarded moments, but calm reflection never failed to bring regret.

*[The following exchange occurred in the summer of 1864, when Lincoln's prospects for reelection seemed bleak.]*

"Mr. Lincoln will be re-elected. I am so confident of it, that I am tempted to ask a favor of you."

"A favor! Well, if we remain in the White House I shall be able to do you many favors. What is the special favor?"

"Simply this, Mrs. Lincoln—I should like for you to make me a present of the right-hand glove that the President wears at the first public reception after his second inaugural."

"You shall have it in welcome. It will be so filthy when he pulls it off, I shall be tempted to take the tongs and put it in the fire. I cannot imagine, Lizabeth, what you want with such a glove."

"I shall cherish it as a precious memento of the second inauguration of the man who has done so much for my race. He has been a Jehovah to my people—has lifted them out of bondage, and directed their footsteps from darkness into light. I shall keep the glove, and hand it down to posterity."

"You have some strange ideas, Lizabeth. Never mind, you shall have the glove; that is, if Mr. Lincoln continues President after the 4th of March next."

I held Mrs. Lincoln to her promise. That glove is now in my possession, bearing the marks of thousands of hands that grasped the honest hand of Mr. Lincoln on that eventful night. Alas! it has become a prouder, sadder memento than I ever dreamed—prior to making the request—it would be.

[*On the evening of April 11, 1865, Lincoln made what proved to be his final public address. Keckly was present and offered the following recollection of the event.*]

About 7 o'clock that evening I entered the White House. As I went up-stairs I glanced into Mr. Lincoln's room through the half-open door, and seated by a desk was the President, looking over his notes and muttering to himself. His face was thoughtful, his manner abstracted, and I knew, as I paused a moment to watch him, that he was rehearsing the part that he was to play in the great drama soon to commence.

Proceeding to Mrs. Lincoln's apartment, I worked with busy fingers, and in a short time her toilette was completed.

Great crowds began to gather in front of the White House, and loud calls were made for the President. The band stopped playing, and as he advanced to the centre window over the door to make his address, I looked out, and never saw such a mass of heads before. It was like a black, gently swelling sea. [ . . .] It was a grand and imposing scene, and when the President, with pale face and his soul flashing through his eyes, advanced to speak, he looked more like a demi-god than a man crowned with the fleeting days of mortality.

The moment the President appeared at the window he was greeted with a storm of applause, and voices re-echoed the cry, "A light! a light!"

A lamp was brought, and little Tad at once rushed to his father's side, exclaiming:

"Let me hold the light, Papa! let me hold the light!"

Mrs. Lincoln directed that the wish of her son be gratified, and the lamp was transferred to his hands. The father and son standing there in the presence of thousands of free citizens, the one lost in a chain of eloquent ideas, the other looking up into the speaking face with a proud, manly look, formed a beautiful and striking tableau.

There were a number of distinguished gentlemen, as well as ladies, in the room, nearly all of whom remarked the picture.

I stood a short distance from Mr. Lincoln, and as the light from the lamp fell full upon him, making him stand out boldly in the darkness, a sudden thought struck me, and I whispered to the friend at my side:

"What an easy matter would it be to kill the President, as he stands there! He could be shot down from the crowd, and no one would be able to tell who fired the shot."

I do not know what put such an idea into my head, unless it was the sudden remembrance of the many warnings that Mr. Lincoln had received. [...]

*[On the day of Lincoln's death, Mrs. Lincoln called for Keckly to visit her at the White House.]*

I asked and received permission to go into the Guests' Room, where the body of the president lay in state. When I crossed the threshold of the room, I could not help recalling the day on which I had seen little Willie lying in his coffin where the body of his father now lay. I remembered how the President had wept over the pale beautiful face of his gifted boy, and now the President himself was dead. The last time I saw him he spoke kindly to me, but alas! the lips would never move again. The light faded from his eyes, and when the light went out the soul went with it. What a noble soul was his—noble in all the noble attributes of God! Never did I enter the solemn chamber of death with such palpitating heart and trembling footsteps as I entered it that day. No common mortal had died. The Moses of my people had fallen in the hour of his triumph. Fame had woven her choicest chaplet for his brow. Though the brow was cold and pale in death, the chaplet should not fade, for God had studded it with the glory of the eternal stars.

When I entered the room, the members of the Cabinet and many distinguished officers of the army were grouped around the body of their fallen chief. They made room for me, and, approaching the body, I lifted the white cloth from the white face of the man that I had worshipped as an idol—looked upon as a demi-god. Notwithstanding the violence of the death of the President, there was something beautiful as well as grandly solemn in the expression of the placid face. There lurked the sweetness and gentleness of childhood, and the stately grandeur of god-like intellect. I gazed long at the face, and turned away with tears in my eyes and a choking sensation in my throat. Ah! never was man so widely mourned before. The whole world bowed their heads in grief when Abraham Lincoln died.

Elizabeth Keckley, *Behind the Scenes* (New York: G. W. Carleton & Co., 1868), 103–104, 118–120, 146–47, 153–154, 175–178, 189–191.

## PAUL TREVIGNE on Emancipation Day, January 1, 1869

*A New Orleans Creole, Trevigne (1825–1907) was an editor of the New Orleans Tribune, a bilingual newspaper owned and published by Dr. Charles L. Roudanez. A forceful advocate of abolition and equal rights, the Tribune had once been very critical of Lincoln for his "tame, vacillating, halting policy" and had refused to endorse him for president in 1864. The following editorial indicates a rather marked difference in tone, as Trevigne marveled at the changes brought by emancipation. Rather than solely credit Lincoln for emancipation, Divine Providence and the victories won on the battlefield by General Grant were also cited. Trevigne looked forward to even further progress under the new administration of President Grant that would commence on March 4. At the end of the piece Trevigne quoted from Lincoln's ever-popular House Divided Speech (AANB; "The Next President," New Orleans Tribune, Sept. 22, 1864).*

---

Six years of freedom!—freedom not alone to four millions of slaves, but to the whole nation. For that nation cannot itself be free, which enslaves any portion of the human family. In doing so, it must put fetters upon itself. Personal liberty, the liberty of speech and of the press are abridged. Free discussion cannot exist. Prejudice, which is a bondage, is intensified. "Slavery," said Mr. Mason of Virginia, "discourages arts and manufactures [. . .] It brings the judgment of Heaven on a country. By an inevitable chain of causes and effects, Providence punishes national aims by national calamities."

Such, for a long period, was the national bondage and disgrace. But on the first day of January 1863, by the stern yet gracious compulsion of Providence, mingling mercy with judgment, the United States of America became free. What the nation had professed before, with no little hypocrisy, certainly with a gross inconsistency, now became a reality. She no longer stood up before the world and high Heaven with "a lie in the right hand." Casting off at length the fetters of prejudice, and exempted from constitutional guarantees by an overpowering "military necessity," the nation decreed universal liberty. Henceforth there should not be a slave within the national jurisdiction.

On the 22d September, 1862, by proclamation, Mr. Lincoln had announced to the rebellious States, that on condition of renewing their allegiance to the Government within one hundred days, their domestic institutions would be undisturbed; but otherwise their slaves would be declared free.

These terms, which were all that the President, at that time, felt himself authorized, by his oath of office, to propose to the States in rebellion, having been disregarded by them, he accordingly, at the expiration of the prescribed time, on the 1st day of January, 1863, issued that memorable proclamation, the anniversary of whose publication occurs today. But it had to be enforced by the military arm, through more than two years of terrible conflict, until the final surrender of the Confederate army under Gen. Lee, at Appomattox, Va., on the 9th day of April, 1865, made freedom universal, as a fact. What the nation had decreed, what President Lincoln had announced, was consummated by Gen. Grant. And his election to the Presidency—the first election to that office by the people since the death of Lincoln—is the public sanction of that act of emancipation, and the public pledge that it shall be made good in every particular.

Therefore may we rejoice today. Freedom is not a mere proclamation or promise. The nation is solemnly committed to freedom, universal and unfettered. And if aught remains to be done by further legislation to bring this question to its logical conclusion, it will be done. The nation cannot go back—rather must it advance. The day of compromises, patched up mixtures of principle and policy, of honesty and expediency, is, we trust, over. Freedom is the all-conquering law.

How different, the position of the four millions of colored people of the South today, from what it was six years ago. Those of us who were slaves are free, and those who were free, are freer—all are American citizens, invested with the right of suffrage, with the way open before us to make the most of our manhood. It becomes us to show our gratitude to God, who is truly the author of our freedom, by putting that freedom to honorable uses; by the promotion of education, by cultivating the great virtues of industry, economy, and integrity, and by cherishing our homes and the altars of our religion. Freedom involves its solemn responsibilities as well as its enjoyments and privileges. A great work is before us, and the eyes of the nation, of the world, are upon us. If we are true to ourselves, if we stand together, God will bless us, and a glorious future awaits us. Therefore this day is not only for congratulations and rejoicings, but for serious reflections and good resolutions.

How different the present position of the American Republic in the eyes of the world from what its position was before the war. Then indeed we were a great and powerful nation, but the world justly mocked at our boastings, and taunted us with our slavery. A Republic with four millions of bondmen! But America is free. The foul blot is no longer upon her name.

And now how potent and beneficent her influence. She can open her mouth without shame, and plead for the oppressed of other lands. The silent influence of her example is felt all over the world. It breathes its benediction upon the sons of toil, whom despotisms and aristocracies have robbed of their rights, inspiring them with new hopes for themselves and their children. Never did America stand so high, exert so wide, so beneficent an influence, or have before her the promise of so bright a future, as today. Not the great North and West alone should rejoice in this day. The South has even more reason for thanksgiving, as she is already beginning to discover; and the period will come when this day shall be celebrated as the nation's second birthday, by the people of all the States.

In 1858, a little more than ten years ago, at Springfield, Illinois, Mr. Lincoln, in replying to Mr. Douglas, used these memorable words: "The result is not doubtful. We shall not fail; if we stand firm, we shall not fail. Wise counsels may accelerate, or mistakes delay, it, but, sooner or later, the victory is sure to come." He lived to see his prophecy fulfilled. But with triumph to freedom, came death to the great Liberator. Today he sleeps in the cemetery at Springfield, the martyr-president; but his name is revered wherever freedom is honored, and is specially a household word among those to whom his Proclamation came as an Evangel from heaven.

Editorial in the *New Orleans Tribune,* Jan. 1, 1869.

## THOMAS N. C. LIVERPOOL, Address on Lincoln's Birthday, Cincinnati, Ohio, February 12, 1873

*Shortly after Lincoln's assassination, a group of African American men in Cincinnati formed the Lincoln Memorial Club for the purpose of annually commemorating Lincoln's birthday. The festivities included a banquet at one of the member's homes that featured toasts and speeches. Liverpool (1836–1874) was a barber, former newspaper editor, and a leader of the Black community known for his skill as an orator. In his 1873 tribute to Lincoln, Liverpool asserted that the Emancipation Proclamation was by no means inevitable, and he hoped that African Americans throughout the nation would always remember to give thanks to Lincoln for the gift of freedom by celebrating February 12. The following year, Liverpool joined with other members of the Lincoln Memorial Club in petitioning Congress to make Lincoln's birthday a national holiday ("Death of a Prominent Colored Man," Cincinnati Enquirer, April 16, 1874; 43rd Cong., 1 Sess.,* House Miscellaneous Document No. 148*).*

---

This is the sixty-fourth anniversary of the birth of Abraham Lincoln, who, while President of the United States, liberated millions of our brethren. It is the purpose of the members of this Club to meet on each recurring anniversary to show that they hold in grateful remembrance the man who struck the death-blow to the institution that degraded and brutalized and kept in ignorance an entire race.

In contemplating this, the grandest act in the history of this or any other country—the act which has caused us to assemble around this festive board tonight, and will send the name of Abraham Lincoln down to the latest posterity—my admiration of the man is increased by the fact that he belonged to a different race of people, a large and influential number of whom believed that the black man was of an inferior race, whose normal condition was slavey; that if liberated and thrown upon his own resources he would become worthless, revel in vice and idleness, and finally lapse back into a barbarous state.

The author of the Emancipation Proclamation did not sympathize with this idea, but believed that out of one blood God created all nations, and, desiring to see every man the equal with the other, proclaimed slavery abolished.

It is generally claimed that the liberation of the slaves was the necessary result of the war; that it was inevitable; but, sir, I incline to the opinion that, had Mr. Lincoln favored it, slavery would be more secure in this country to-day than ever. To those who have given this subject but little thought this assertion appears strange and, perhaps, startling, but when it is remembered that, at the time the Proclamation was issued, loyal and patriotic men everywhere were oppressed, and entertained grave doubts as to whether this Union would be saved, and our armies were meeting with as many defeats as victories, Lincoln's recommendations were readily accepted and acted upon, the assertion appears less strange, and by no means startling.

I feel, therefore, that I hazard nothing in saying that, had Lincoln willed it, slavery would still be in existence. Holding this opinion, I rejoice in being a member of this memorial club, which has been organized to assist in keeping his memory green. I would rejoice still more if similar clubs were organized in every state, city and town in this Union.

Peering through the dim vista of the future, I see a sight, as the 12th day of February rolls around, that fills me with enthusiasm; it is our people, who have come to fully understand to whom they are indebted for the great boon they enjoy, coming up from every quarter, and assembling themselves in mass-meeting for the purpose of honoring the memory of our hero, and thanking God for the gift of such a benefactor. All over this land Washington's birthday is celebrated because he is the father of his country; so will Lincoln's be because he is the savior of our race.

"Abraham Lincoln. The 64th Anniversary of His Birth—Celebrated by the Lincoln Memorial Club," *Cincinnati Enquirer*, Feb. 13, 1873.

## FREDERICK DOUGLASS, Address at Dedication of the Freedmen's Monument, Washington, DC, April 14, 1876

*If a single speech could express the ambivalence of African Americans regarding Lincoln, this oration by Douglass (1818–1895) might well be that document. It had been eighteen years since Douglass first took notice of Lincoln, and the dedication of Thomas Ball's sculpture depicting Lincoln emancipating a slave provided an opportunity for reflection. His personal relationship with the martyred president, the passage of time, and the failures of Reconstruction evoked a complex array of thoughts and feelings. In 1865, Douglass asserted that Lincoln was emphatically the Black man's president, yet in 1876 he claimed Lincoln was essentially the White man's president. Douglass's claim that African Americans were merely Lincoln's "step-children" is often taken out of context, as his interpretation was more nuanced. If Lincoln had not put the Union and the interests of White people first then the destruction of slavery and progress towards equality would not have been possible. While abolitionists believed Lincoln was slow to take action against slavery, Douglass observed that within the broader historical context—over two hundred years of enslavement of a people whose ascribed status was based on the lie of racial inferiority—Lincoln's Emancipation Proclamation was swift and revolutionary. The unveiling of the Freedmen's Monument was a signal tribute indicative of the centrality of African Americans in shaping Lincoln's legacy. That a Black man was the keynote speaker at an event honoring Lincoln, where President Grant and other dignitaries were present, indicates how far the country had come, yet Lincoln's work remained unfinished. Nevertheless, Lincoln accomplishments were so significant that Douglass believed he had earned a permanent place in the hearts of Americans, whether they were Black or White.*

---

I warmly congratulate you upon the highly interesting object which has caused you to assemble in such numbers and spirit as you have to-day. This occasion is in some respects remarkable. Wise and thoughtful men of our race, who shall come after us, and study the lesson of our history in the United States; who shall survey the long and dreary spaces over which we have travelled; who shall count the links in the great chain of events by which we have reached our present position, will make a note of this occasion; they will think of it and speak of it with a sense of manly pride and complacency.

I congratulate you, also, upon the very favorable circumstances in which we meet to-day. They are high, inspiring, and uncommon. They lend grace, glory, and significance to the object for which we have met. Nowhere else in this great country, with its uncounted towns and cities, unlimited wealth, and immeasurable territory extending from sea to sea, could conditions be found more favorable to the success of this occasion than here.

We stand to-day at the national centre to perform something like a national act—an act which is to go into history; and we are here where every pulsation of the national heart can be heard, felt, and reciprocated. A thousand wires, fed with thought and winged with lightning, put us in instantaneous communication with the loyal and true men all over this country.

Few facts could better illustrate the vast and wonderful change which has taken place in our condition as a people than the fact of our assembling here for the purpose we have to-day. Harmless, beautiful, proper, and praiseworthy as this demonstration is, I cannot forget that no such demonstration would have been tolerated here twenty years ago. The spirit of slavery and barbarism, which still lingers to blight and destroy in some dark and distant parts of our country, would have made our assembling here the signal and excuse for opening upon us all the floodgates of wrath and violence. That we are here in peace to-day is a compliment and a credit to American civilization, and a prophecy of still greater national enlightenment and progress in the future. I refer to the past not in malice, for this is no day for malice; but simply to place more distinctly in front the gratifying and glorious change which has come both to our white fellow-citizens and ourselves, and to congratulate all upon the contrast between now and then; the new dispensation of freedom with its thousand blessings to both races, and the old dispensation of slavery with its ten thousand evils to both races—white and black. In view, then, of the past, the present, and the future, with the long and dark history of our bondage behind us, and with liberty, progress, and enlightenment before us, I again congratulate you upon this auspicious day and hour.

Friends and fellow-citizens, the story of our presence here is soon and easily told. We are here in the District of Columbia, here in the city of Washington, the most luminous point of American territory; a city recently transformed and made beautiful in its body and in its spirit; we are here in the place where the ablest and best men of the country are sent to devise the policy, enact the laws, and shape the destiny of the Republic; we are here, with the stately pillars and majestic dome of the Capitol of the nation looking down upon us; we are here, with the broad earth freshly adorned with the foliage and flowers of spring for our church, and all races, colors, and conditions of men for our congregation—in a word, we are here to express, as best we may, by appropriate forms and ceremonies, our grateful sense of the vast, high, and pre-eminent services rendered to ourselves, to our race, to our country, and to the whole world by Abraham Lincoln.

The sentiment that brings us here to-day is one of the noblest that can stir and thrill the human heart. It has crowned and made glorious the high places of all civilized nations with the grandest and most enduring works of art, designed to illustrate the characters and perpetuate the memories of great public men. It is the sentiment which from year to year adorns with fragrant and beautiful flowers the graves of our loyal, brave, and patriotic soldiers who fell in defence of the Union and liberty. It is the sentiment of gratitude and appreciation, which often, in presence of many who hear me, has filled yonder heights of Arlington with the eloquence of eulogy and the sublime enthusiasm of poetry and song; a sentiment which can never die while the Republic lives.

For the first time in the history of our people, and in the history of the whole American people, we join in this high worship, and march conspicuously in the line of this time-honored custom. First things are always interesting, and this is one of our first things. It is the first time that, in this form and manner, we have sought to do honor to an American great man, however deserving and illustrious. I commend the fact to notice; let it be told in every part of the Republic; let men of all parties and opinions hear it; let those who despise us, not less than those who respect us, know that now and here, in the spirit of liberty, loyalty, and gratitude, let it be known everywhere, and by everybody who takes an interest in human progress and in the amelioration of the condition of mankind, that, in the presence and with the approval of the members of the American House of Representatives, reflecting the general sentiment of the country; that in the presence of that august body, the American Senate, representing the highest intelligence and the calmest judgment of the country; in presence of the Supreme Court and Chief-Justice of the United States, to whose decisions we all patriotically bow; in the presence and under the steady eye of the honored and trusted President of the United States, with the members of his wise and patriotic Cabinet, we, the colored people, newly emancipated and rejoicing in our blood-bought freedom, near the close of the first century in the life of this Republic, have now and here unveiled, set apart, and dedicated a monument of enduring granite and bronze, in every line, feature, and figure of which the men of this generation may read, and those of after-coming generations may read, something of the exalted character and great works of Abraham Lincoln, the first martyr President of the United States.

Fellow-citizens, in what we have said and done to-day, and in what we may say and do hereafter, we disclaim everything like arrogance and assumption. We claim for ourselves no superior devotion to the character, history, and memory of the illustrious name whose monument we have here dedicated to-day. We fully comprehend the relation of Abraham Lincoln both to ourselves and to the white people of the United States. Truth is proper and beautiful at all times and in all places, and it is never more proper and beautiful in any case than when speaking of a great public man whose example is likely to be commended for honor and imitation long after his departure to the solemn shades, the silent continents of eternity. It must be admitted, truth compels me to admit, even here in the presence of the monument we have erected to his memory, Abraham Lincoln was not, in the fullest sense of the word, either our man or our model. In his interests, in his associations, in his habits of thought, and in his prejudices, he was a white man.

He was pre-eminently the white man's President, entirely devoted to the welfare of white men. He was ready and willing at any time during the first years of his administration to deny, postpone, and sacrifice the rights of humanity in the colored people to promote the welfare of the white people of this country. In all his education and feeling he was an American of the Americans. He came into the Presidential chair upon one principle alone, namely, opposition to the extension of slavery. His arguments in furtherance of this policy had their motive and mainspring in his patriotic devotion to the interests of his own race. To protect, defend, and perpetuate slavery in the States where it existed Abraham Lincoln was not less ready than any other President to draw the sword of the nation. He was ready to execute all the supposed constitutional guarantees of the United States Constitution in favor of the slave system anywhere inside the slave States. He was willing to pursue, recapture, and send back the fugitive slave to his master, and to suppress a slave rising for liberty, though his guilty master were already in arms against the Government. The race to which we belong were not the special objects of his consideration. Knowing this, I concede to you, my white fellow-citizens, a pre-eminence in this worship at once full and supreme. First, midst, and last, you and yours were the objects of his deepest affection and his most earnest solicitude. You are the children of Abraham Lincoln. We are at best only his step-children; children by adoption, children by force of circumstances and necessity. To you it especially belongs to sound his praises, to preserve and perpetuate his memory, to multiply his statues, to hang his pictures high upon your walls, and commend his example, for to you he was a great and glorious friend and benefactor. Instead of supplanting you at this altar, we would exhort you to build high his monuments; let them be of the most costly material, of the most cunning workmanship; let their forms be symmetrical, beautiful, and perfect; let their bases be upon solid rocks, and their summits lean against the unchanging blue, overhanging sky, and let them endure forever! But while in the abundance of your wealth, and in the ful[l]ness of your just and patriotic devotion, you do all this, we entreat you to despise not the humble offering we this day unveil to view; for while Abraham Lincoln saved for you a country, he delivered us from bondage, according to Jefferson, one hour of which was worse than ages of the oppression your fathers rose in rebellion to oppose.

Fellow-citizens, ours is no new-born zeal and devotion—merely a thing of this moment. The name of Abraham Lincoln was near and dear to our hearts in the darkest and most perilous hours of the Republic. We were no more ashamed of him when shrouded in clouds of darkness, of doubt, and defeat than when we saw him crowned with victory, honor, and glory. Our faith in him was often taxed and strained to the utter-most, but it never failed. When he tarried long in the mountain; when he strangely told us that we were the cause of the war; when he still more strangely told us to leave the land in which we were born; when he refused to employ our arms in defence of the Union; when, after accepting our services as colored soldiers, he refused to retaliate our murder and torture as colored prisoners; when he told us he would save the Union if he could with slavery; when he revoked the Proclamation of Emancipation of General Frémont; when he refused to remove the popular commander of the Army of the Potomac, in the days of its inaction and defeat, who was more zealous in his efforts to protect slavery than to suppress rebellion; when we saw all this, and more, we were at times grieved, stunned, and greatly bewildered; but our hearts believed while they

ached and bled. Nor was this, even at that time, a blind and unreasoning super-
stition. Despite the mist and haze that surrounded him; despite the tumult, the
hurry, and confusion of the hour, we were able to take a comprehensive view of
Abraham Lincoln, and to make reasonable allowance for the circumstances of his
position. We saw him, measured him, and estimated him; not by stray utterances
to injudicious and tedious delegations, who often tried his patience; not by isolated facts torn from their connection; not by any partial and imperfect glimpses,
caught at inopportune moments; but by a broad survey, in the light of the stern
logic of great events, and in view of that divinity which shapes our ends, rough
hew them how we will, we came to the conclusion that the hour and the man of
our redemption had somehow met in the person of Abraham Lincoln. It mattered
little to us what language he might employ on special occasions; it mattered little
to us, when we fully knew him, whether he was swift or slow in his movements;
it was enough for us that Abraham Lincoln was at the head of a great movement,
and was in living and earnest sympathy with that movement, which, in the nature
of things, must go on until slavery should be utterly and forever abolished in the
United States.

When, therefore, it shall be asked what we have to do with the memory of Abraham Lincoln, or what Abraham Lincoln had to do with us, the answer is ready,
full, and complete. Though he loved Caesar less than Rome, though the Union
was more to him than our freedom or our future, under his wise and beneficent
rule we saw ourselves gradually lifted from the depths of slavery to the heights
of liberty and manhood; under his wise and beneficent rule, and by measures
approved and vigorously pressed by him, we saw that the handwriting of ages, in
the form of prejudice and proscription, was rapidly fading away from the face of
our whole country; under his rule, and in due time, about as soon after all as the
country could tolerate the strange spectacle, we saw our brave sons and brothers
laying off the rags of bondage, and being clothed all over in the blue uniforms of
the soldiers of the United States; under his rule we saw two hundred thousand
of our dark and dusky people responding to the call of Abraham Lincoln, and
with muskets on their shoulders, and eagles on their buttons, timing their high
footsteps to liberty and union under the national flag; under his rule we saw the
independence of the black republic of Hayti, the special object of slaveholding
aversion and horror, fully recognized, and her minister, a colored gentleman, duly
received here in the city of Washington; under his rule we saw the internal slave-
trade, which so long disgraced the nation, abolished, and slavery abolished in the
District of Columbia; under his rule we saw for the first time the law enforced
against the foreign slave-trade, and the first slave-trader hanged like any other
pirate or murderer; under his rule, assisted by the greatest captain of our age,
and his inspiration, we saw the Confederate States, based upon the idea that our
race must be slaves, and slaves forever, battered to pieces and scattered to the

four winds; under his rule, and in the fullness of time, we saw Abraham Lincoln, after giving the slaveholders three months' grace in which to save their hateful slave system, penning the immortal paper, which, though special in its language, was general in its principles and effect, making slavery forever impossible in the United States. Though we waited long, we saw all this and more.

Can any colored man, or any white man friendly to the freedom of all men, ever forget the night which followed the first day of January, 1863, when the world was to see if Abraham Lincoln would prove to be as good as his word? I shall never forget that memorable night, when in a distant city I waited and watched at a public meeting, with three thousand others not less anxious than myself, for the word of deliverance which we have heard read to-day. Nor shall I ever forget the outburst of joy and thanksgiving that rent the air when the lightning brought to us the emancipation proclamation. In that happy hour we forgot all delay, and forgot all tardiness, forgot that the President had bribed the rebels to lay down their arms by a promise to withhold the bolt which would smite the slave-system with destruction; and we were thenceforward willing to allow the President all the latitude of time, phraseology, and every honorable device that statesmanship might require for the achievement of a great and beneficent measure of liberty and progress.

Fellow-citizens, there is little necessity on this occasion to speak at length and critically of this great and good man, and of his high mission in the world. That ground has been fully occupied and completely covered both here and elsewhere. The whole field of fact and fancy has been gleaned and garnered. Any man can say things that are true of Abraham Lincoln, but no man can say anything that is new of Abraham Lincoln. His personal traits and public acts are better known to the American people than are those of any other man of his age. He was a mystery to no man who saw him and heard him. Though high in position, the humblest could approach him and feel at home in his presence. Though deep, he was transparent; though strong, he was gentle; though decided and pronounced in his convictions, he was tolerant towards those who differed from him, and patient under reproaches. Even those who only knew him through his public utterances obtained a tolerably clear idea of his character and his personality. The image of the man went out with his words, and those who read them, knew him.

I have said that President Lincoln was a white man, and shared the prejudices common to his countrymen towards the colored race. Looking back to his times and to the condition of his country, we are compelled to admit that this unfriendly feeling on his part may be safely set down as one element of his wonderful success in organizing the loyal American people for the tremendous conflict before them, and bringing them safely through that conflict. His great mission was to accomplish two things: first, to save his country from dismemberment and ruin; and second, to free his country from the great crime of slavery. To do one or the other, or both, he must have the earnest sympathy and the powerful co-operation of his loyal fellow-countrymen. Without this primary and essential condition to success his efforts must have been vain and utterly fruitless. Had he put the abolition of slavery before the salvation of the Union, he would have inevitably driven from him a powerful class of the American people and rendered resistance to rebellion impossible. Viewed from the genuine abolition ground, Mr. Lincoln seemed tardy, cold, dull, and indifferent; but measuring him by the sentiment of his country, a sentiment he was bound as a statesman to consult, he was swift, zealous, radical, and determined.

Though Mr. Lincoln shared the prejudices of his white fellow-countrymen against the negro, it is hardly necessary to say that in his heart of hearts he loathed and hated slavery. The man who could say, "Fondly do we hope, fervently do we pray, that this mighty scourge of war shall soon pass away, yet if God wills it continue till all the wealth piled by two hundred years of bondage shall have been wasted, and each drop of blood drawn by the lash shall have been paid for by one drawn by the sword, the judgments of the Lord are true and righteous altogether," gives all the needed proof of his feeling on the subject of slavery. He was willing, while the South was loyal, that it should have its pound of flesh, because he thought that it was so nominated in the bond; but farther than this no earthly power could make him go.

Fellow-citizens, whatever else in this world may be partial, unjust, and uncertain, time, time! is impartial, just, and certain in its action. In the realm of mind, as well as in the realm of matter, it is a great worker, and often works wonders. The honest and comprehensive statesman, clearly discerning the needs of his country, and earnestly endeavoring to do his whole duty, though covered and blistered with reproaches, may safely leave his course to the silent judgment of time. Few great public men have ever been the victims of fiercer denunciations than Abraham Lincoln was during his administration. He was often wounded in the house of his friends. Reproaches came thick and fast upon him from within and from without, and from opposite quarters. He was assailed by Abolitionists; he was assailed by slaveholders; he was assailed by the men who were for peace at any price; he was assailed by those who were for a more vigorous prosecution of the war; he was assailed for not making the war an abolition war; and he was most bitterly assailed for making the war an abolition war.

But now behold the change: the judgment of the present hour is, that taking him for all in all, measuring the tremendous magnitude of the work before him, considering the necessary means to ends, and surveying the end from the beginning, infinite wisdom has seldom sent any man into the world better fitted for his mission than Abraham Lincoln. His birth, his training, and his natural endowments, both mental and physical, were strongly in his favor. Born and reared among the lowly, a stranger to wealth and luxury, compelled to grapple single-handed with the flintiest hardships of life, from tender youth to sturdy manhood, he grew strong in the manly and heroic qualities demanded by the great mission to which he was called by the votes of his countrymen. The hard condition of his early life, which would have depressed and broken down weaker men, only gave greater life, vigor, and buoyancy to the heroic spirit of Abraham Lincoln. He was ready for any kind and any quality of work. What other young men dreaded in the shape of toil, he took hold of with the utmost cheerfulness.

> A spade, a rake, a hoe,
> A pick-axe, or a bill;
> A hook to reap, a scythe to mow,
> A flail, or what you will.

All day long he could split heavy rails in the woods, and half the night long he could study his English Grammar by the uncertain flare and glare of the light made by a pine-knot. He was at home on the land with his axe, with his maul, with gluts, and his wedges; and he was equally at home on water, with his oars, with his poles, with his planks, and with his boat-hooks. And whether in his flat-boat on the Mississippi river, or at the fireside of his frontier cabin, he was a man of work. A son of toil himself, he was linked in brotherly sympathy with the sons of toil in every loyal part of the Republic. This very fact gave him tremendous power with the American people, and materially contributed not only to selecting him to the Presidency, but in sustaining his administration of the Government.

Upon his inauguration as President of the United States, an office, even when assumed under the most favorable conditions, fitted to tax and strain the largest abilities, Abraham Lincoln was met by a tremendous crisis. He was called upon not merely to administer the Government, but to decide, in the face of terrible odds, the fate of the Republic.

A formidable rebellion rose in his path before him; the Union was already practically dissolved; his country was torn and rent asunder at the centre. Hostile armies were already organized against the Republic, armed with the munitions of war which the Republic had provided for its own defence. The tremendous question for him to decide was whether his country should survive the crisis and flourish, or be dismembered and perish. His predecessor in office had already decided the question in favor of national dismemberment, by denying to it the right of self-defence and self-preservation—a right which belongs to the meanest insect.

Happily for the country, happily for you and for me, the judgment of James Buchanan, the patrician, was not the judgment of Abraham Lincoln, the plebeian. He brought his strong common sense, sharpened in the school of adversity, to bear upon the question. He did not hesitate, he did not doubt, he did not falter; but at once resolved that at whatever peril, at whatever cost, the union of the

States should be preserved. A patriot himself, his faith was strong and unwavering in the patriotism of his countrymen. Timid men said before Mr. Lincoln's inauguration, that we had seen the last President of the United States. A voice in influential quarters said "Let the Union slide." Some said that a Union maintained by the sword was worthless. Others said a rebellion of 8,000,000 cannot be suppressed; but in the midst of all this tumult and timidity, and against all this, Abraham Lincoln was clear in his duty, and had an oath in heaven. He calmly and bravely heard the voice of doubt and fear all around him; but he had an oath in heaven, and there was not power enough on the earth to make this honest boatman, back-woodsman, and broad-handed splitter of rails evade or violate that sacred oath. He had not been schooled in the ethics of slavery; his plain life had favored his love of truth. He had not been taught that treason and perjury were the proof of honor and honesty. His moral training was against his saying one thing when he meant another. The trust which Abraham Lincoln had in himself and in the people was surprising and grand, but it was also enlightened and well founded. He knew the American people better than they knew themselves, and his truth was based upon this knowledge.

Fellow-citizens, the fourteenth day of April, 1865, of which this is the eleventh anniversary, is now and will ever remain a memorable day in the annals of this Republic. It was on the evening of this day, while a fierce and sanguinary rebellion was in the last stages of its desolating power; while its armies were broken and scattered before the invincible armies of Grant and Sherman; while a great nation, torn and rent by war, was already beginning to raise to the skies loud anthems of joy at the dawn of peace, it was startled, amazed, and overwhelmed by the crowning crime of slavery—the assassination of Abraham Lincoln. It was a new crime, a pure act of malice. No purpose of the rebellion was to be served by it. It was the simple gratification of a hell-black spirit of revenge. But it has done good after all. It has filled the country with a deeper abhorrence of slavery and a deeper love for the great liberator.

Had Abraham Lincoln died from any of the numerous ills to which the flesh is heir; had he reached that good old age of which his vigorous constitution and his temperate habits gave promise; had he been permitted to see the end of his great work; had the solemn curtain of death come down but gradually—we should still have been smitten with a heavy grief, and treasured his name lovingly. But dying as he did die, by the red hand of violence, killed, assassinated, taken off without warning, not because of personal hate—for no man who knew Abraham Lincoln could hate him—but because of his fidelity to union and liberty, he is doubly dear to us, and his memory will be precious forever.

Fellow-citizens, I end, as I began, with congratulations. We have done a good work for our race to-day. In doing honor to the memory of our friend and liberator, we have been doing highest honors to ourselves and those who come after us; we have been fastening ourselves to a name and fame imperishable and immortal; we have also been defending ourselves from a blighting scandal. When now it shall be said that the colored man is soulless, that he has no appreciation of benefits or benefactors; when the foul reproach of ingratitude is hurled at us, and it is attempted to scourge us beyond the range of human brotherhood, we may calmly point to the monument we have this day erected to the memory of Abraham Lincoln.

In *Oration by Frederick Douglass Delivered on the Occasion of the Unveiling of the Freedmen's Monument In Memory of Abraham Lincoln* (Washington, DC: Gibson Brothers, 1876).

## H. CORDELIA RAY, "Lincoln," a Poem Written for Dedication of the Freedmen's Monument, Washington, DC, April 14, 1876

*The daughter of Charles B. Ray, a New York newspaper editor and abolitionist, Cordelia Ray (c.1850–1916) worked as a public school teacher for several years before pursuing a career as a poet. She was invited to compose the following poem that was read at the dedication of Thomas Ball's Freedmen's Monument and published with Frederick Douglass's speech at the event (see above). Ray's praise poem intended no critique but provided an encomium characteristic of the unveiling spirit. Ray writes that Lincoln was born with a divine purpose and gave his life to fulfill it. To mark the centennial of Lincoln's birth in 1909, Ray published a revised version of her poem that eliminated references to the unveiling of the monument and instead begins with the lines: "We lift the curtain of the past to-day/ And chase the mists and stains of years away/ Once more, O martyred chief, to gaze on thee,/ The worth and purpose of thy life to see" (AANB; H. Cordelia Ray, Poems [New York: The Grafton Press, 1910]).*

To-day, O martyred chief, beneath the sun
We would unveil thy form; to thee who won
Th' applause of nations for thy soul sincere,
A loving tribute we would offer here.
'T was thine not world to conquer, but men's hearts;
To change to balm the sting of slavery's darts;
In lowly charity thy joy to find,
And open "gates of mercy on mankind."
And so they come, the freed with grateful gift,
From whose sad path the shadows thou didst lift.

Eleven years have rolled their seasons round,
Since its most tragic close thy life-work found.
Yet through the vistas of the vanished days
We see thee still, responsive to our gaze,
As ever to thy country's solemn needs.
Not regal coronets, but princely deeds
Were thy chaste diadem; of truer worth
Thy modest virtues than the gems of earth.
Staunch, honest, fervent in the purest cause,
Truth was thy guide; her mandates were thy laws.

Rare heroism, spirit-purity,
The storied Spartan's stern simplicity,
Such moral strength as gleams like burnished gold
Amid the doubt of men of weaker mould,
Were thine. Called in thy country's sorest hour,
When brother knew not brother—mad for power—
To guide the helm through bloody deeps of war,
While distant nations gazed in anxious awe,
Unflinching in the task, thou didst fulfill
Thy mighty mission with a deathless will.

Born to a destiny the most sublime,
Thou wert, O Lincoln! in the march of time,
God bade thee pause and bid the oppressed go free—
Most glorious boon giv'n to humanity.
While slavery ruled the land, what deeds were done!
What tragedies enacted 'neath the sun!
Her page is blurred with records of defeat,
Of lives heroic lived in silence, meet
For the world's praise; of woe, despair and tears,
The speechless agony of weary years.

Thou utterest the word, and Freedom fair
Rang her sweet bells on the clear winter air;
She waved her magic wand, and lo! from far
A long procession came. With many a scar
Their brows were wrinkled, in the bitter strife,
Full many had said their sad farewell to life.
But on they hastened, free, their shackles gone;
The aged, young,—e'en infancy was borne
To offer unto thee loud paeans of praise,—
Their happy tribute after saddest days.

A race set free! The deed brought joy and light!
It bade calm Justice from her sacred height,
When faith and hope and courage slowly waned,
Unfurl the stars and stripes, at last unstained!
The nations rolled acclaim from sea to sea,
And Heaven's vault rang with Freedom's harmony.
The angels 'mid the amaranths must have hushed
Their chanted cadences, as upward rushed
The hymn sublime: and as the echoes pealed,
God's ceaseless benison the action sealed

As now we dedicate this shaft to thee,
True champion! in all humility
And solemn earnestness, we would erect
A monument invisible, undecked,
Save by our allied purpose to be true
To Freedom's loftiest precepts, so that through
The fiercest contests we may walk secure,
Fixed on foundations that may still endure,
When granite shall have crumbled to decay,
And generations passed from earth away.

Exalted patriot! illustrious chief!
Thy life's immortal work compels belief.
To-day in radiance thy virtues shine,
And how can we a fitting garland twine?
Thy crown most glorious is a ransomed race!
High on our country's scroll we fondly trace,
In line of fadeless light that softly blend,
Emancipator, hero, martyr, friend!
While Freedom may her holy sceptre claim,
The world shall echo with Our Lincoln's name.

In *Oration by Frederick Douglass Delivered on the Occasion of the Unveiling of the Freedmen's Monument In Memory of Abraham Lincoln* (Washington: Gibson Brothers, 1876). The text follows H. Cordelia Ray, *Lincoln* (New York: J. J. Little, 1893).

## GEORGE WASHINGTON WILLIAMS, *A History of the Negro Race in America*, 1882

*A native of Pennsylvania, Williams (1849–1891) served in the army during and after the Civil War. Following military service, Williams studied for the ministry, became interested in African American history, and was the first Black man elected to the Ohio legislature. Williams spent several years researching his history of African Americans. He also published a history of African American soldiers during the Civil War and urged that a monument honoring Black soldiers be erected in Washington. In the following excerpt, Williams claimed Lincoln was not an abolitionist and made it clear the Emancipation Proclamation was strictly a war measure. Williams further noted that Lincoln was initially opposed to the government taking coercive policy measures to settle the slavery issue, as he was for gradual, compensated emancipation. Despite the proclamation's limitations, Williams believed it marked slavery's death knell, and in calling upon Black men to serve in the military it also paved the way for African American citizenship (AANB).*

---

But the proclamation was a harmless measure. *First*, it declared that the object of the war was to restore "the constitutional relation between the United States and each of the States." After nearly two years of disastrous war Mr. Lincoln declares the object of the war. Certainly no loyal man had ever entertained any other idea than the one expressed in the proclamation. It was not a war on the part of the United States to destroy her children, nor to disturb her own constitutional, comprehensive unity. It must have been understood, then, from the commencement, that the war begun by the seceding States was waged on the part of the United States to preserve the *Union of the States*, and restore them to their "constitutional relation."

*Second*, the proclamation implored the slave States to accept (certainly in the spirit of compromise) a proposition from the United States to emancipate their slaves for a *pecuniary consideration*, and, by their gracious consent, assist in *colonizing* loyal Negroes in this country or in Africa!

*Third*, the measure proposed to free slaves of persons and States in rebellion against the lawful authority of the United States Government on the first day of January, 1863. Nothing more difficult could have been undertaken than to free *only* the slaves of persons and States in *actual* rebellion against the Government of the United States. Persons in *actual* rebellion would be *most* likely to have immediate oversight of this species of their property; and the owners of slaves in the States in *actual* rebellion against the United States Government would doubtless be as thoroughly prepared to take care of slave property as the muskets in their rebellious hands.

*Fourth*, this emancipation proclamation (?) proposed to pay out of the United States Treasury,—for all slaves of loyal masters lost in a rebellion begun by slave-holders and carried on by slave-holders!

Under the condition of affairs no emancipation proclamation was necessary. Treason against the United States is "levying war against them," or "adhering to their enemies, giving them aid and comfort." The rebel States were guilty of treason; and from the moment Fort Sumter was fired upon, every slave in the Confederate States was *ipso facto* free!

But it was an occasion for rejoicing. The President had taken a step in the right direction, and, thank God! he never retracted it. [ . . . ]

Even this proclamation—not a measure of humanity—to save the Union, not the slave—left slaves in many counties and States at the South. It was a war measure, pure and simple. It was a blow aimed at the most vulnerable part of the Confederacy. It was destroying its corner-stone, and the ponderous fabric was doomed to a speedy and complete destruction. It discovered that the strength of this Sampson of rebellion lay in its vast slave population. To the slave the proclamation came as the song of the rejoicing angels to the shepherds upon the plains of Bethlehem. It was like music at night, mellowed by the distance, that rouses slumbering hopes, gives wings to fancy, and peoples the brain with blissful thoughts. The notes of freedom came careering to them across the red, billowy waves of battle and thrilled their souls with ecstatic peace. Old men who, like Samuel the prophet, believing the ark of God in the hands of the Philistines, and were ready to give up the ghost, felt that it was just the time to begin to live. Husbands were transported with the thought of gathering to their bosoms the wife that had been sold to the "nigger traders"; mothers swooned under the tender touch of the thought of holding in loving embrace the children who pined for their care; and young men and maidens could only "think thanksgiving and weep gladness."

The slave-holder saw in this proclamation the handwriting upon the walls of the institution of slavery. The brightness and revelry of his banqueting halls were to be succeeded by gloom and sorrow. His riches, consisting in human beings, were to disappear under the magic touch of the instrument of freedom. The chattel was to be transformed into a person, the person into a soldier, the soldier into a citizen—and thus the Negro slave, like the crawling caterpillar, was to leave his grovelling situation, and in new form, wing himself to the sublime heights of free American citizenship!

George Washington Williams, *A History of the Negro Race in America*, 1882, 2 volumes (New York: G. P. Putnam's Sons, 1882), Volume 2: 270–271, 274.

## EMMANUEL K. LOVE, Emancipation Day Address at Savannah, Georgia, January 2, 1888

*A former slave who was serving as a Baptist minister in Savannah, Love (1850–1900) offered a corrective to what he perceived as undue adulation of Lincoln. In quoting from Lincoln's August 22, 1862, letter to Horace Greeley*

*and referencing Lincoln's offer in the Preliminary Emancipation Proclamation
that rebels could keep their slaves if they resumed their allegiance by January
1, 1863, Love emphasized that Lincoln's primary objective was to preserve the
Union. For Love, Massachusetts senator Charles Sumner deserved more credit
than Lincoln for championing the cause of freedom, while Confederate president
Jefferson Davis received praise for having the fortitude to refuse Lincoln's offer
and thus make emancipation possible. Though the Emancipation Proclamation
was a momentous event, Love believed it marked only a beginning (Sandy D.
Martin, "E. K. Love [1850–1900]," New Georgia Encyclopedia, https://www
.georgiaencyclopedia.org/articles/arts-culture/e-k-love-1850–1900).*

We are brought together to-day to celebrate the Emancipation Proclamation.
That was the greatest event that has occurred in our history in this country. [...]

No man is more willing to honor the means which God used in our emancipation than I—but I am not willing to give any man more honor than I candidly
believe he deserves. Our people have learned to think that Abraham Lincoln
was the greatest champion of our cause. But such is not true. The thing that
was uppermost in the mind of Mr. Lincoln was the salvation of the Union. So
far as Mr. Lincoln was concerned the Emancipation Proclamation was purely a
war measure—for he would "save the Union with or without freeing the slaves."
From this single statement, it must be clear to you that our freedom was not first
in Mr. Lincoln's mind, yet I thank God for Mr. Lincoln for his election which
had much to do with kindling the fire between the two sections which resulted
in a bloody war whose crimson stream washed away the black stain of slavery.
I thank God for Charles Sumner, whose persistent efforts, sweeping influence,
true patriotism and far seeing sagacity almost compelled Mr. Lincoln to issue the
Emancipation Proclamation which we celebrate to-day. We have never had a truer
nor abler friend than Charles Sumner. I honor Mr. Lincoln, but I honor Charles
Sumner more. I thank God for that brave man and soldier Jeff Davis. I thank God
for his election. Had the Southern Confederacy placed a coward at its head, we
would not have been freed as the results of that four years of bloody war. If Jeff
Davis had not been a brave, great man fighting from what he conceived to be, a
principle of right and justice (although he was wrong) he would have accepted
Lincoln's offer of surrender in ninety days. If he had accepted, it is hard for me to
see from a human standpoint how or when we would have been freed. The odds
were against Jeff Davis. He confronted a greater army than his, far more skilled
in the science of war and far more skilled in the manufacture of arms and with
all the power the shattered government had at its back. This would have been
a sufficient inducement for, perhaps any body but Jeff Davis to have accepted
Mr. Lincoln's inglorious offer. I call it inglorious from my stand point, for had

Jeff Davis accepted it I do not see how I could have been freed. The truth of it is that God was using both Abraham Lincoln and Jeff Davis to bring to light this child of freedom the birth of which we celebrate to-day. Our past is shrouded in shame, degradation, ignominy, ignorance, outrages on our virtue and inexplicable suffering. The Emancipation Proclamation has only served to check some of this treatment. In many instances the suffering has only been changed in form. Emancipation only gave us the key to greatness, but did not make us great.

In *Oration Delivered on Emancipation Day, January 2nd, 1888* (Savannah, GA: n.p., 1888), 1, 2, 3.

## WILLIAM S. SCARBOROUGH, Remarks at Ohio Republican League Club Lincoln Banquet, Columbus, Ohio, February 13, 1888

*Born a slave in Georgia, Scarborough (1852–1926) attended Atlanta University before graduating from Oberlin College. A scholar of Greek and Latin, Scarborough taught at Wilberforce University and published books and articles on classical philology. Scarborough eventually became president of Wilberforce and was active in Republican politics. The following was delivered at the Ohio Republican League's first banquet held to commemorate Lincoln's birthday. The only African American speaker at the event, Scarborough responded to the toast: "Why I am a Republican." For Scarborough, Lincoln made freedom and progress possible for Black people. Not only did he praise Lincoln, but he also made it clear why African Americans must remain loyal to the Party of Lincoln. Scarborough's position on the Republican Party was orthodoxy among African Americans until the advent of the New Deal in the 1930s (DANB).*

---

Mr. Chairman—If there ever existed in the minds of any the slightest doubt concerning Abraham Lincoln's "lofty courage and loftier faith in God and in the final trial of right," the solemn invocation with which he closed the grandest of his executive acts, the emancipation proclamation, should dispel the last lingering trace. Countless men have lived and died who were more polished, more brilliant, more learned, but none with loftier aims, purer motives, warmer heart, deeper sense of responsibility of trusts confided to their care, greater love of justice, more unflinching courage, more abiding faith in right.

Abraham Lincoln was a grand man because the inherent qualities inseparable from grandeur of character, from grandeur of soul, were ingrained in every fiber of his being. No hero that faced unmoved the cannon's mouth ever towered higher; for he bore himself with the calm intrepidity of a soul lifted far above this world, though every day of life was passed beneath the awful shadow of impending danger, though he knew the venomous hate and rage of incensed rebeldom dogged every footstep. Yet he fearlessly faced it all, braving it by repeated acts which could but increase the malice of his country's foes. At last their concentrated venom found vent in the assassin's bullet, and Abraham Lincoln, whose memory we honor tonight, died a martyr's death—a victim to his own fearless and uncompromising patriotism, his unyielding determination that right, not might, should prevail. We mourn him as we ever must. His memory will remain imperishably engraven upon the nation's heart with that of Washington, Grant and Garfield. Still, with gratitude, we thank God that the bullet which laid him low was not sped on its terrible errand till his great life-work was done. Before the hand of that God-fearing man was made cold in death, it had set the seal to what was to be the most brilliant star in the diadem of the martyred hero. He lived to see what his hand had accomplished—the yoke lifted and fetters struck from 4,000,000 human beings, and the South's most cherished institution, human slavery—the blackest, foulest, most brutal system that ever disgraced a civilized nation—crushed and swept out of existence from the face of our fair land. He had called forth a whole race to stand up as freemen and had paved the way for those glorious amendments which crown our American Constitution, clothing the beings, brutes but yesterday, with humanity's unalienable rights—manhood, citizenship and the ballot.

Gentlemen, it was that act, the emancipation proclamation, which gave birth to all of the negro's opportunities in the following quarter century and made it possible for me to have the privilege and honor of standing before you tonight. Every step which the colored race has taken toward the high planes of intelligence, culture, character, dignity and power is centered therein. Human judgment was not at fault, the voice of the people of the United States did not err when with no uncertain sound the great majority spoke as one man and chose Abraham Lincoln as the nation's chief; for he was a fit leader and commander for the party which placed him at the head of the nation, the party which was and is and ever will be the party of principle, of right, of justice, of broad humanity, the greatest and grandest party that ever wielded power in empire or republic—the Republican party of these United States. And because the platform of this party, of which the great emancipator was chief, rests upon such broad, firm and enduring foundations, gentlemen of the Ohio Republican League, I boast tonight with you of being a Republican. With the memory of more than a century of degradation behind me in the past, the knowledge of the broad fields of opportunities spread out in the present and the vision of the boundless possibilities in the perspective of the future, I can be nothing else.

If further reasons are demanded I would say:

I am a Republican because every right, privilege and honor that I can claim today is due to the party which upheld the hands of the revered Lincoln in every act during those perilous years, to the part under whose leadership conquests were made and final victory won, without which the negro's freedom would have been a short-lived mockery; to the party in whose ranks have ever been found indomitable champions of the slave—noble men, such as the silver-tongued Phillips and the fiery Garrison, the invincible Sumner and the fearless Chase, our own eloquent Douglass, with the martyred Lovejoy and grand old John Brown.

I am a Republican because that party not only suppressed the rebellion, but out of the darkness of mourning and adversity, brought the sunshine of rejoicing and prosperity in which both North and South, white and black, native and alien, were invited to share alike; because I, too, as an American citizen, have a pride in that "national honor and national faith" which that party was the one to uphold throughout the hours of the nation's struggle and perplexity.

I am a Republican because it is the party which believes intelligence and piety to be the pillars of our national greatness; because it has ever taken decided grounds in favor of universal education; because its heroes and heroines planted school-house and church close upon the foot-steps of the advancing armies long ere the clashing swords and whizzing bullets ceased their ghastly music—noble men and women who sowed then the seed of the harvest of today's intelligence and who are still spreading the light of knowledge in the benighted South.

I am a Republican, because to be anything else is to clasp hands directly or indirectly with the bitterest foe the colored man has ever had—Democracy; to give any influence to a party which has opposed the rising manhood of the race at every step; to sustain by my vote and voice the party which disfranchises today the negro in the South; to give my sanction to all the lawless acts of intimidation, violence and suppression of votes—bull-dozing, shotgun and fraud—the arguments and policy of the Democratic party; in short, to ally myself to thugs, robbers, rascals. There is no middle ground. Mugwump or Independent, Prohibitionist or Labor, he who divides the Republican vote aids but Democracy.

Again, I am a Republican because to make political alliance elsewhere would be to prove myself the veriest ingrate that ever trod the face of this green earth, the meanest poltroon that ever exhibited his moral weakness to the gaze of the public—deserved to be hissed and spit upon by those who I had deserted, and treated like a fawning cur, with inward scorn and contempt, by those whose cause I should espouse.

I am not free to leave the grand old party, the one which has aided the negro all along the line in his battles against caste and prejudice, for his rights. I say I am not free, and yet no one is more so; for I possess the birthright of every man— freedom to do the right, the only true freedom. All other is false.

*Daily Ohio State Journal* (Columbus), Feb. 14, 1888.

## JOHN MERCER LANGSTON, Memorial Day Address at Washington, DC, May 30, 1891

*A native of Virginia, Langston (1829–1897) grew up in Ohio and graduated from Oberlin College. He practiced law, was active in the abolition movement, and in 1855 he became the first African American to hold elected office when he won election as clerk for his Ohio township. During the Civil War, Langston recruited Black soldiers, and during Reconstruction he held a position with the Freedmen's Bureau and helped create the law school at Howard University. Prominent in Republican politics, Langston served as minister to Haiti during the Hayes administration and was the first African American member of Congress from Virginia. Shortly after his term in Congress ended, Langston delivered an address on Memorial Day at Lincoln Park, where Thomas Ball's Emancipation Group had been dedicated in 1876. Though his tenure in Congress was very brief, one of the bills Langston proposed would have made the birthdays of Lincoln and U. S. Grant national holidays. Langston's reverence for Lincoln is evident in the speech below, where he expresses his gratitude for Lincoln and refers to him as the "angel of emancipation." While Langston gave thanks to Lincoln for issuing the Emancipation Proclamation, he was deeply concerned that African Americans were not being treated as equal citizens (ANB; John Mercer Langston, From Virginia Plantation to National Capitol* [Hartford: American Publishing Company, 1894]).

---

The ground on which we stand is holy. Here is the monument erected by the freed people, to commemorate his memory, who gave them their liberty; to perpetuate their estimate and appreciation of such gift; to testify of their profound and abiding devotion and loyalty to the country and government, which sustain and promote their general welfare, by every legitimate means at their command. The Goddess of Liberty beholds, in her vast range of vision throughout our country, this day, no gathering, whose place of assembly is more sacred than ours! The spirit of Lincoln is here! The angel of emancipation guards this consecrated spot. [ . . . ]

We are no longer things! We are no longer beasts of burden! Ours is not today, the condition of slaves! We are freemen! We are citizens! We are voters! We have a country, our home, the land of our nativity, for which we may live, and for which we may die! We have a government for whose maintenance we are responsible! We have free institutions, the inheritance given us by our fathers, which we cherish and value; and which we must hand down to our posterity, unimpaired in their complete integrity and glory!

As Americans, citizens of the United States, we have the deepest interest in everything which pertains to our country. No question of peace, no question of war, no matter of national, or international concernment, which respects this great, matchless nation of ours, is without importance to us. The achievements of the great men and women of the country, the accomplishments of science, art and industry; reform and progress in State and Church; the cultivation and growth of literature; the development and support of genius and talent in every field of thought and labor; the maintenance and promotion of exalted individual and national, moral and religious character are all subjects, in which we have the gravest concern, and to advance which we are under the most serious obligation. Here the ground which we occupy, is that which is common to our fellow citizens; and the rule of duty and obligation is identical and of equal commanding force, whether rights are concerned or services enjoined. [...]

If we go hence, returning to our homes and our daily occupations, accepting these doctrines really, our souls animated with their teachings, our meeting here today shall be of the largest benefit to us, while our conduct in such regard shall illustrate our love of country, our appreciation of liberty, and our admiration of him whose name is to every true American the synonym of emancipation itself. All hail, Lincoln and emancipation!

*New York Age* (New York), June 13, 1891.

## PETER H. CLARK on Lincoln and Emancipation, May 18, 1892

*To draw attention to the alarming number of lynchings, a committee of African American men in St. Louis drafted a circular letter that called on Black people and their friends to gather in churches on May 31 and devote the day to fasting and prayer. The letter was signed by several prominent African American leaders, including Frederick Douglass, Booker T. Washington, and Henry McNeal Turner. Some, however, objected to a line in the letter that credited God for the Emancipation Proclamation because He had "forced" it "from the unwilling hand of Abraham Lincoln." Hale G. Parker, the sole African American commissioner to the upcoming World's Fair in Chicago, objected to this language and publicly criticized the circular. As a member of the committee that drafted the circular, Clark (1829–1925) felt compelled to respond. Prior to moving to St. Louis, Clark had been a pioneering schoolteacher, editor, orator, and leader in the Cincinnati African American community. No stranger to controversy, Clark was known for his unorthodox political positions that included support for emigration, socialism, the Democratic Party, and opposition to school integration for fear that it would result in Black teachers becoming unemployed. His response to Parker indicated that he believed African Americans owed no debt of gratitude to Lincoln, and the episode reveals the controversy that disputes over*

*Lincoln's legacy could arouse (Nikki Taylor,* America's First Black Socialist:
The Radical Life of Peter H. Clark *[Lexington: University Press of Kentucky,
2013];* Plaindealer *[Detroit, MI], May 20, 1892).*

---

The words "forced from the unwilling hand of Abraham Lincoln the Emancipation proclamation" are what chiefly arouse Mr. Parker's wrath, and they are, I presume, the chief "mistakes of fact" to which he alludes.

Upon the point Mr. Lincoln himself should be good authority, and he says in the proclamation itself that it was issued "upon military necessity." There is no pretense of justice or humanity. Mr. Lincoln was too honest for that. Nor did he in the original draft invoke the blessing of Almighty God upon what was a purely selfish act. The invocation was interlined at the suggestion of Mr. Chase.

What a man does from necessity, is presumably done against his will; and a man may fairly be said to be unwilling to do that which he has only done, because driven by necessity. We therefore think ourselves justified in saying that the proclamation was forced from the "unwilling hand of Abraham Lincoln."

It is notorious that Mr. Lincoln repeatedly said: "If I can save the Union without destroying slavery, I will save the Union." In a letter to Mr. Hodges, of Kentucky, he declares that he countermanded the emancipation proclamations of Generals Fremont and Hunter, and forbade the enlisting of the blacks, because the ["]indispensable necessity had not arisen." According to Mr. Henry Watterson, Mr. Lincoln said at the Hampton Roads conference with the commissioners of the seceding States: "Write 'Union' at the top of this paper, and you can write under it whatever you please." What he expected them to write may be inferred from the sentence in this inaugural address. That sentence reads thus: "I understand a proposed amendment has passed Congress to the effect that the Federal Government shall never interfere with the domestic institutions of the States, including that of persons held to service[.] I now depart from my purpose not to speak of particular amendments to say that holding such provision to be now implied in constitutional law, I have no objection to its being made express and irrevocable.["] Mark the words "express and irrevocable." That Mr. Lincoln considered the war between the States a 'white man's war' is shown by his refusal to permit the enlistment of colored men, because the "indispensable necessity" to consider the idea of giving the ballot to the black man, be looked at it from the standpoint of the white man's interests and said: "Perhaps the ballot in the hands of the black man may some day serve to keep the jewel of freedom in the American family." [...]

Mr. Lincoln had opposed slavery upon economic grounds, he proved that it did not pay, and because of that won the prize. He was undoubtedly an anti-slavery man, but all anti-slavery men were not friends to the Negro. [...]

Mr. Lincoln was a great, good, and humane man. He was, by nature, merciful to man and beast. But in that crisis in our National affairs he considered himself representative of those people who were both anti-slavery and anti-Negro.

It was only when compelled by dire "military necessity" that he enlisted colored men and g[a]ve them their freedom.

He was above all else an honest man, and I believe that were he alive to-day he would say, "Let the truth be told. Let no fulsome flattery shade the page of history."

"Parker's Interview," *Plaindealer* (Detroit, MI), May 27, 1892.

## FREDERICK DOUGLASS, Address at Lincoln Birthday Celebration, Brooklyn, New York, February 13, 1893

*Douglass accepted an invitation to speak at the Brooklyn Union League Club's fourth annual Lincoln Day dinner in February 1893. Other speakers that evening included Henry L. Wayland, an editor and Baptist minister from Philadelphia, and Stephen V. White, a former member of the US House from New York, but Douglass was the star attraction and he did not disappoint. This address, coming just two years before Douglass's death, proved to be his last major address on his relationship with Lincoln. Douglass had become very frustrated with the course of race relations since Reconstruction, to the point where in an 1888 speech he proclaimed emancipation a "stupendous fraud." He nevertheless retained a warm place in his heart for Lincoln. For Douglass, Lincoln was nothing less than the "great man" of the nineteenth century, and he regaled the audience with reminiscences of his three meetings with Lincoln at the White House. In particular, Douglass took pride in being a friend of Lincoln and noted that during their second meeting in 1864, Lincoln kept Governor William A. Buckingham of Connecticut waiting. Douglass's account of "breaking the ice" by getting into the White House reception and paying his respects to Lincoln on Inauguration Day, 1865 is particularly poignant. In praising Lincoln for his statesmanship and apparent lack of prejudice, Douglass noted that Lincoln was in the "hearts of all of us" and expressed a plaintive desire to see someone of his stature at the helm of state during a period when lynchings, Jim Crow laws, and disfranchisement were becoming commonplace for African Americans in the South.*

---

Gentlemen,—I beg to remind you at the outset that reminiscences are generally tedious. I hope you may find mine an exception to the general rule, though I fear the contrary, for speakers are often more interesting and eloquent about what they do not know, than about what they do know. (Applause.) It is impossible for me, and perhaps for anybody else, to say anything new about Abraham Lincoln. (Applause.) He is in the minds and hearts of all of us. We know him and know of him, as we know of no other great man of our century. (Applause.)

I had the good fortune to know Abraham Lincoln personally and peculiarly. I knew him, not on the side visible to the free, rich and powerful, but on the side which he presented to the unfortunate, the defenseless, the oppressed and the enslaved. (Applause.) It is something to know how a man will deport himself to his admitted equals, but more to know how he will bear himself to those who are recognized as his inferiors. (Applause.) It is this knowledge of Mr. Lincoln upon which I depend for any interest, value or significance of my story to you this evening.

Of course, and on general principles, it is a great thing for any man of whatever condition, to know a great man. For a truly great man is ever a rebuke to pride and selfishness in the strong, and a source of strength to the weak and unfortunate. The memory of such a great man is ennobling to men already noble, and we shall all feel better for reviving and keeping alive the memory of such a man tonight. (Applause.) [. . .]

Among the circumstances in which I deem myself most fortunate, is that of having seen many great men. They have not been of one country or of one continent alone. I have seen such men in England, and I have seen them in this republic. I have seen men of whom we have all heard; men who stood only a little lower than the angels.

They were great and god-like men, divinely equipped and commissioned from on high to serve the highest needs of mankind. They were not only uplifted men, but they were uplifting men; men whose range was far above all that is little, low and mean; but I have met with no such man, at home or abroad, who made upon my mind the impression of possessing a more godlike nature, than did Abraham Lincoln. (Cheers and applause.)

Greater men than he intellectually there may have been, but to my mind, measuring him in the direction of the highest quality, of human goodness and nobility of character, no better man than he has ever stood or walked upon this continent. (Cheers.) But you did not ask me for my opinion of Mr. Lincoln. You asked me for my recollections of him, and these I shall proceed to give you.

It may be that the conditions surrounding Mr. Lincoln when I first met him had something to do with the exalted impression I received of him. It is one thing to see a man in prosperity, and another thing to see him in adversity. It is one thing to see him surrounded by hardships, difficulties and dangers, and it is another thing to see him in his hours of ease and prosperity. [. . .]

The sea was not smooth, the sky was not bright, the wind was not fair, when I first met and measured Abraham Lincoln. It was in the darkest hours of the late war. There was much in the situation to make men anxious. It was a time to make the boldest hold his breath. No man could tell, at that time, whether the cause of the country would be saved or lost. I certainly was concerned, not only for the cause of the country, but for the cause of the slave; a cause for which I had given the best energies of my soul, the best years of my life, and the deepest longings of my heart. (Applause.)

The leaders of the rebellion were, at this time, especially fierce, bold and defiant. They had, in the pride of their power, scorned to accept the terms of peace that Mr. Lincoln had, a few months before offered them, whereby they might have saved the lives of men on both sides, North and South, and their slavery in the bargain.

But it was not only the rebels in arms at the South, but also the disloyal men at the North, who complicated the problem, and gave Mr. Lincoln much cause for anxiety. Our forces in the field were diminishing. Recruiting was becoming difficult and well-nigh impossible. The draft was being resisted. Loyal black men were being murdered in the streets of New York. Asylums and houses of black people were being burned in resentment of the draft and of the continuance of the war. Besides, the Administration was being fiercely assailed by the press, the platform and the pulpit of the North. Out of this darkness and storm the soul of Lincoln shone with a light all the more clear, calm and steady. (Applause.)

I first saw Mr. Lincoln in the early summer of 1863. I had a special object in seeing him at this time. I had been engaged in raising two regiments of colored men in Massachusetts, the Fifty-fourth and Fifty-fifth. Two of my sons were in those regiments. Jefferson Davis had taken notice of these colored soldiers and had notified the country that colored men taken in arms would not be treated as prisoners of war by the Confederate armies, but would be shot or hanged in cold blood, or sold into slavery. It was about this barbarous threat, in part, that I went to Washington to see Abraham Lincoln.

It required some nerve to approach the Chief Magistrate of the nation for such a purpose at such a time. I did not know how he would receive a man of my complexion, or whether he would receive me at all. I was not a member of Congress, a United States marshal, a Minister and Consul-General to Hayti, an elector at large, or even a citizen of the United States. I was still under the ban of the Dred Scott decision. So I felt it a bold thing for me to enter the White House and presume to talk with the President of the United States. Besides, I had no one to introduce me. Happily I was soon relieved at this point. I met with the late Senator Samuel Pomeroy (three cheers for Pomeroy), a good and true man, with whom I had become acquainted during the border ruffian war in Kansas, in connection with John Brown (cheering) and he kindly consented to accompany me to the White House and introduce me to Mr. Lincoln. It was a daring thing even for him, Senator though he was, to walk the streets of Washington with me at that time. To do so was to invite insult.

This done I went to the Executive Mansion, not however, without much solicitude as to how I should deport myself; how I should order my speech, and how
this great man in his exalted office would be likely to receive and treat a man of my
condition. The result was altogether at variance with my fears. I had not been an
instant in the presence of this great man before all apprehensions were dispelled.

I saw before me a man, a great man, a tall man physically, and I was not long
in discovering that I was in the presence of a great man mentally. I also made the
discovery that it is much easier to see and converse with a great man than with a
small man; with a big man than with a little one. (Laughter and applause.)

I found Mr. Lincoln seated in a low chair and surrounded on all sides by
unbound books and papers which I thought he had been overhauling.

As I approached, he began to rise to receive me, and he continued to rise, higher
and higher, till I found myself looking up to him, and he looking down upon me.
He gave me a welcome which was none too much nor too little; but just enough
to make me at ease.

First, I began to talk of myself, as I have been doing this evening. I told him
what I had been doing. He blandly put an end to it all by saying: "Mr. Douglass,
you need not tell me who you are. I know who you are. Mr. Seward has told me all
about you." Brought thus to a standstill, I proceeded with the object of my visit:

I said: "Mr. President, I have been recruiting colored troops; and if you want
me to succeed, I must be able to assure them that colored soldiers while in the
service shall have pay equal to that of white soldiers. Secondly, that when they
shall perform acts of bravery in battle, which would secure promotion to white
soldiers, the like promotion shall be accorded colored soldiers. Thirdly, that if
the threat of Jefferson Davis is carried out, you, President Lincoln, will retaliate
in kind." (Good! Good!)

Feeling myself now perfectly free to say to Mr. Lincoln all that I thought on
the subject, I supported my demands, as best I could, with arguments to which he
calmly and patiently listened, not once interrupting me, and, when I had finished,
he made a careful reply, covering each proposition that I had submitted to him.

He admitted the justice of the demand for equal wages and equal promotion
to colored soldiers; but reminded me that, for the moment, there were causes
for delay in its execution. He called my attention to the necessity, at that critical
time, of avoiding any shock to the prejudices of the white soldiers, and told me
of the many objections there were to making colored men soldiers; of the doubts
entertained of them; of how it was first proposed that they should be employed
simply as laborers; that they should be clothed in a peculiar and inferior uniform;
that they should not bear arms, but that they should work in trenches, with pickax
and shovel; that, as time went on, they were thought worthy to be soldiers, but
were not to take the field like other soldiers. They were only to hold fortified positions in sickly places, after those places should be captured by white soldiers. He

thought it was a great thing that they could be armed and uniformed as soldiers at all. He held, however, that in time, the first two points I had insisted upon would be conceded; that colored soldiers would be equally paid and equally promoted.

But when it came to the matter of retaliation, the tender heart of the great President appeared in the expression of his eyes, and in every line of his careworn countenance, as well as in the tones of his appealing voice. "Ah!" said he, "Douglass, I cannot retaliate. I cannot hang men in cold blood. I cannot hang men who have had nothing to do with murdering colored prisoners. Of course, if I could get hold of the actual murderers of colored prisoners, I would deal with them as they deserve; but I cannot hang those who have had no hand in such murders." (Applause.) I was not convinced that Mr. Lincoln's logic was right; but I was convinced that Mr. Lincoln himself, was right. (Applause.)

I could, and did, answer Mr. Lincoln's arguments; but I was silenced by his overmastering mercy and benevolence. I had found a President with a heart—one who could, even in war, love his enemies; and that was something. In parting, he said: "Douglass, never come to Washington without calling upon me." And I never did.

Though neither of the objects sought were immediately obtained, I was full of faith in the man, and felt sure that he would do what he could to secure justice to our soldiers, and protection to the lives of colored prisoners. I saw Mr. Lincoln several times after this interview and found him ever the same large-hearted man as when I first met him. At one time during the war he sent for me, to consult as to how to get more slaves into our lines. He had offered them freedom and protection, but he said that they were not coming in fast enough.

While we were talking over the matter, Gov. Buckingham, the war Governor of Connecticut (applause), was announced, and I at once arose, and asked leaved to withdraw, saying to Mr. Lincoln: "I must not stay to prevent your interview with Gov. Buckingham." Instead of allowing me to leave, he said to the messenger, in his peculiarly high and honest voice: "Tell Gov. Buckingham to wait. I am talking with my friend, Douglass." (Applause.)

In this interview President Lincoln told me to devise some plan by which to get more slaves within our lines, and to submit my plans to him. I did so; but it was never after necessary to put the plan into operation. Our rapid successes, and the increasing intelligence of the slaves concerning the new departure of the loyal people and Government, in their favor, brought the freemen into our lines much faster than the means we had could care for them.

I have often said that Mr. Lincoln was the first great public man with whom I could talk for hours without being once reminded, either by way of compliment or condescension, of my color.

Perhaps this statement was a little too strong; but it seemed true when I made it. The impression I designed to make was that Mr. Lincoln said and did nothing during our interview that reminded me in any way of our difference in color. He not only invited me to see him at the White House, but he invited me to tea with him at the Soldiers' Home (applause); and convinced me that he was far above the prevailing prejudices of his countrymen.

I found Mr. Lincoln different from my expectation of him, not only in his kindness to me, but also in his manners, which were very different from the current representation of them. He had been described as wanting in dignity; as jocose, and fond of telling witty stories. [...]

But I am bound to say of President Lincoln that it was never my lot to find him in any such mood. His whole deportment was a contradiction and a rebuke to everything like levity or merrymaking. He was not only intensely in earnest, but sadly in earnest.

The dimmed light in his eye, and the deep lines in his strong American face, told plainly the story of the heavy burden of care that weighed upon his spirit. I could as easily dance at a funeral as to jest in the presence of such a man. I felt that his heart was occupied with the thought of his imperiled country and of its brave sons, imperiled and dying on the battlefield. I was present at the beginning of President Lincoln's second term, and witnessed his second inauguration. I saw and followed his carriage that day from the White House to the Capitol. [...] For some reason, or for no reason, I was oppressed with a dread foreboding as I followed his carriage. The fear was upon me that Mr. Lincoln might be shot down on his way to the Capitol, and it was a great relief to me when the trip was safely ended. I know not why, but I felt that there was murder in the air of Washington. No hint had then been given that an organized band of assassins was hiding in the dark places of the city, seeking the life of Mr. Lincoln.

I stood near the steps of the east front of the Capitol when Mr. Lincoln appeared and had the oath of office administered to him by Chief Justice Chase. I heard his remarkable, memorable, and I might say, wonderful speech on that occasion. To me he seemed more the saint and prophet, in his appearance as well as in his utterance, than he did the President of a great nation, and the Commander-in-Chief of its army and navy. To understand that brief speech of Mr. Lincoln's we must remember that he had been fiercely and bitterly criticized from at least three different quarters. He had been assailed by Northern Democrats for making the war an abolition war. He had been denounced by the Abolitionists for not making it an abolition war. He was denounced for not making peace at any price, and again, for not prosecuting the war with more vigor. He answered all his critics with the following brief sentence: "Fondly do we hope, fervently do we pray, that this mighty scourge of war will soon pass away. (Applause.) Yet, if God wills that it continue until all the wealth piled by the bondman's two hundred and fifty years of unrequited toil shall be sunk, and until every drop of blood drawn by the lash shall be paid by another drawn with the sword, as was said three thousand years

ago so till it must be said, 'The judgments of the Lord are true and righteous altogether.' " (Applause.) This was said in a voice of deep solemnity, bordering upon
inconsolable sadness; but a voice as firm as the everlasting hills, and as pure and
clear as the "brave old overhanging sky." There seemed at the time to be in the
man's soul the united souls of all the Hebrew prophets. I was much relieved when
the President returned in safety to his room in the Senate, for I was, all through
his speech, haunted with the thought that he might be murdered before he could
finish what he had to say.

In the evening I attended Mr. Lincoln's inaugural reception. It was a new experience for Washington, a new experience for me, and a new experience for the
country, to see a person like myself present on such an occasion. (Applause.)

I was once in Albany, in company with that princely philanthropist, the late
Hon. Gerrit Smith, and was invited with him to dine with E. C. Delavan, an eminent gentleman of that city. I was about declining to accept this invitation when
the greathearted Gerrit Smith said, "Oh yes, Douglass, go! Some one must break
the ice." (Laughter.) Well, I did go, and did break the ice, and I have been breaking ice ever since (laughter), and some of it pretty hard and thick ice. Having
witnessed the inauguration of Mr. Lincoln in the morning, my colored friends
urged me to attend the inauguration reception at the Executive Mansion in the
evening. Here, indeed, I found solid ice to break, for no man of my "race, color,
or previous condition," had ever attended such a reception, except as a servant or
waiter. I did not look upon the matter lightly, either subjectively or objectively. To
me it was a serious thing to break in upon the established usage of the country,
and run the risk of being repulsed; but I went to the reception, determined to
break the ice, which I did in an unexpectedly rough way.

When myself and companion presented ourselves at the door of the White
House, we were met by two sturdy policemen, who promptly informed us that
we could not be allowed to enter, and when we attempted to enter without their
consent, they pushed us back with some violence. I was, however, determined
not to be repulsed, and forced myself and lady inside the door, despite the guard.
But my trouble was not ended by that advantage. A policeman inside met us and,
with a show of friendliness, said to us, "Oh, yes; come this way! come this way!"
Thinking that he was about to conduct us to the famous East Room, where the
reception was proceeding, we followed the lead of our new, red faced, burly,
blue-coated friend; but just when we thought that we were entering, we found
ourselves being conducted through an outside window on a plank for the exit of
visitors. (Laughter.)

I never before knew so exactly what is meant by "walking the plank." (Laughter.) I said, "This will not do!" To a gentleman who was passing at the moment
I said, "Tell Mr. Lincoln that Frederick Douglass is at the door and is refused
admission." I did not walk the plank, and, to the policeman's astonishment, was

especially invited into the spacious East Room, and we found ourselves in a bewildering sea of beauty and elegance (applause), such as my poor eyes had never before seen in any one room, at home or abroad. High above every other figure in the room, and overlooking the brilliant scene, stood the towering form of Mr. Lincoln, completely hemmed in by the concourse of visitors passing and taking his hand as they passed. The scene was so splendid, so glorious, that I almost repented of my audacity in daring to enter.

But as soon as President Lincoln saw me I was relieved of all embarrassment. In a loud voice, so that all could hear, and looking towards me, he said, "And here comes my friend, Frederick Douglass!" (Good! Good!) I had some trouble in getting through the crowd of elegantly dressed people to Mr. Lincoln.

When I did succeed, and shook hands with him, he detained me and said, "Douglass, I saw you in the crowd today, listening to my inaugural address. How did you like it?" I replied, "Mr. Lincoln, I must not stop to talk now. Thousands are here, wishing to shake your hand." But he said, "You must stop. There is no man in the United States whose opinion I value more than I do yours. How did you like it?" (Applause.) I said, "Mr. Lincoln, it was a sacred effort," and passed on, amid some smiles, much astonishment and some frowns. And this was the last time that I heard the voice and saw the face and form of honest Abraham Lincoln.

A few weeks later he fell before the bullet of the assassin. His murder was the natural outcome of a war for slavery. He fell a martyr to the same barbarous and bloody spirit which now pursues, with outrage and vengeance, the people whom he emancipated and whose freedom he secured. Did his firm hand now hold the helm of state; did his brave spirit now animate the nation; did his wisdom now shape and control the destiny of this otherwise great Republic; did he now lead the once great Republican party, we should not, as now, hear from the nation's capital, the weak and helpless, the inconsistent and humiliating confession that, while there are millions of money and ample power in the United States Government to protect the lives and liberties of American citizens in the republics of Hayti and far off Chili, and in every other foreign country on the globe, there is no power under the United States Constitution to protect the lives and liberties of American citizens in any one of our own Southern States from barbarous, inhuman and lawless violence. (Applause.)

The *Standard Union* (Brooklyn, NY), Feb. 14, 1893.

## E. W. S. HAMMOND, "Lincoln on the Negro," May 11, 1893

*A native of Baltimore, Hammond's (1850–1920) career as a Methodist minister spanned a half century and included stints at churches in Ohio, Kentucky, Indiana, and Tennessee. In 1892, he was elected editor of the* Southwestern

Christian Advocate, *a Methodist newspaper based in New Orleans that served African Americans in the southwestern states but also reached a White audience. After a four-year term as editor, Hammond returned to the pulpit and was dean of Walden University in Nashville. In this piece, Hammond addressed statements that Lincoln had made during the 1858 Lincoln-Douglas Debates, which remain among the most frequently quoted and controversial remarks he ever made. Hammond's source text is unknown, as the paragraph he quoted merged material from both Lincoln's opening remarks and his rejoinder at the Charleston debate. By the 1890s, advocates of the segregation and disfranchisement of African Americans were using Lincoln's words from 1858 in an effort to prove he was not an advocate of racial equality. For Hammond, the key question was whether Lincoln's actions during his presidency, particularly the Emancipation Proclamation, outweighed what he had said during the 1850s ("Colored Pastor's Funeral to be Held Tomorrow," Indianapolis Star, May 11, 1920).*

---

It goes without saying that the colored people of these United States regard Abraham Lincoln as one of the greatest benefactors of the human race. Indeed many regard him as the divinely appointed Moses who led them out of the Egypt of slavery into the Canaan of freedom. But there are those who would have us believe that Mr. Lincoln was an enemy to the Negro, that he did not believe that he was capable of citizenship, and that he was unworthy of the great boon of freedom.

Some diligent explorer has unearthed the following as among the utterances of the great statesman:

"I am not in favor of Negro citizenship. If the State of Illinois had the power to make a Negro a citizen, I should be opposed to the exercise of it. I am not, nor ever have been, in favor of bringing about in any way the social and political equality of the white and black races. I am not, nor ever have been, in favor of making voters or jurors of Negroes, nor of qualifying themselves to hold office, nor to intermarry with white people; and I will say in addition to this that there is a physical difference between the white and black races which I believe will forever forbid the two races living together on terms of social and political equality."

Mr. Lincoln might have said those things, but we have reasons to doubt his sincerity. If we are to place any stress upon his oft repeated assertions of interest in the Negro, there is reason to suspect that such utterances as are attributed to him in the above quotation were merely effervescent coruscations of political deception.

Against all these objections stands the fact that Mr. Lincoln was president of these United States during the most terrible sanguinary strife of modern times, when the whole question of slavery might have been decided otherwise; that he issued the great proclamation which brought freedom and citizenship to more than four millions of bondsmen. Granting the utmost charity to human weakness, these facts will adequately condone for any rash utterances which might have been made previous to this great event.

*Southwestern Christian Advocate* (New Orleans), May 11, 1893.

## CHARLES W. ANDERSON, Address on the Emancipation Proclamation, Chicago, February 12, 1895

*A native of Ohio, Anderson (1866–1938) was a noted orator and one of the most prominent African American federal office holders during the early twentieth century. Active in the New York Republican Party, Anderson held patronage positions with the state government in Albany until President Theodore Roosevelt appointed him a collector of internal revenue in 1905. Anderson remained in the position until Woodrow Wilson removed him from office. President Harding reappointed Anderson as a collector of internal revenue, and he held the position until shortly before his death. In 1895, Anderson was invited to deliver a speech in response to a toast to the Emancipation Proclamation at the annual Lincoln Day banquet of the Chicago Marquette Club. Noting that everyone knew Lincoln's life "by heart," Anderson gave a well-received tribute to the Great Emancipator, while at the same time, he reminded his White audience that the work Lincoln had begun would remain unfinished until all Americans were accorded justice and afforded an equal opportunity to succeed ("An Ohio Boy Serves Seven Presidents," Cleveland Gazette, Feb. 5, 1938).*

I most heartily thank the Marquette Club for the considerate courtesy which prompted it to invite to this board a representative of a people who can claim a closer relationship with him whose natal day we celebrate tonight than can be claimed through ties of race or consanguinity. [ . . . ]

I should like to utter a word or two of tender, reverential regard for the man who preserved this grand scheme of government, who renewed its self-respect, who saved it with his brains and sanctified it with his blood, who loved it with a perfect love and defended it with a pure devotion—that first of human beings, Abraham Lincoln. Feeling as I do the veneration of a mourner and the gratitude of a child, I fear I am incapacitated for speaking of Mr. Lincoln, save with words of eulogy. And while I know any words of eulogy that I might pronounce would be inept, yet eulogy it will surely be if I but speak the simple truth. While I am conscious that I could not impartially analyze his character, I rejoice to know that he was one of those rare characters in which analysis discloses nothing that affection would conceal. It would be equally useless to review the story of his life, for the world knows that by heart. It is the pride and possession of every American citizen, rich and poor, black and white, without distinction and without exception. [...]

Abraham Lincoln needs neither marble nor parchment to perpetuate his memory. Every colored schoolhouse is his monument, every colored boy is his eulogy. [...]

There hangs upon the walls of the State Library at Albany a document upon which are traced words worthy of immortality—words that proclaimed the Caucasian free forever and the negro forever free, the Emancipation Proclamation. For, my friends, as long as black men were sold in this country white men were slaves, as abject and helpless in many respects as ever were lashed to the wheels of a Roman chariot. When Mr. Lincoln freed the blacks of the South he manumitted the whites of the North [...].

In every house from Maine to Mexico where lives a colored family you will find food in the larder, a Bible on the table, and a picture of Lincoln on the wall. These figures show their steady, sustained radical achievement during a time when 99 per cent of the trades and business pursuits were closed against them [...].

The great shield of Phidias was said to be so thoroughly inwrought with the name of the artificer that when broken in the rough clash and shock of battle every fragment would bear the immortal patronymic. So it should be with the grand fabric of our scheme of government. Justice should be so interwoven in its texture that in each separate State, or in all the combined States, whether we look at them "distinct like the billows or one like the sea," this imperishable principle should everywhere salute the eye. Then, and not till then, will the purpose of Mr. Lincoln's proclamation be fulfilled and the dreams of the sages be fully realized. Then beneath the same flag, on the same soil, obeying the same laws, and speaking the same tongue will live men of different colors and creeds in one common bond of interest and affection of sympathy and purpose, forming one common community and sending up to heaven the unmatched harmonies of national gladness, peace, and prosperity. [...]

I, for one, do not believe that the dead "have died in vain." I do not believe that the rich blood that fertilized so many well fought fields was wasted and the lives laid down from Bull Run to Gettysburg were squandered. [...] I have great faith in the American people, and believe in the survival of that spirit which has exercised an influence wider than our language and mightier than our laws, an influence greater than our wealth and grander than our power, the spirit of the emancipation proclamation.

"It Is the Basis of All Liberty," *Chicago Tribune*, Feb. 13, 1895.

## BOOKER T. WASHINGTON, Address at the Union League Club, Brooklyn, New York, February 12, 1896

*The leader of Alabama's Tuskegee Institute since its founding, Washington (1856–1915) attracted national fame for his Atlanta Exposition address in 1895 and received even more invitations to speak outside of the South before predominantly White audiences, such as the Union League Club of Brooklyn. Speaking at a Lincoln birthday celebration in 1896, just three years after Frederick Douglass had addressed the same organization on Lincoln's birthday (see above), Washington made the first of a consistent stream of speeches in tribute to Lincoln. Washington recalled being one of the enslaved, with his mother praying that Lincoln would be successful in emancipation. Washington, nonetheless, referred to Lincoln as the emancipator of the entire nation. This view of emancipation encompassed all inhabitants, as Washington believed the Emancipation Proclamation had freed both Blacks and Whites because labor, commerce, and freedom were inextricably linked. Washington suggested that the country had already borne the fruit of Lincoln's leadership, and it is owed that the work be completed, especially in the South, where the clear reverberations of enslavement haunted everyone. Washington pledged the everyday support of African Americans to vindicate Lincoln's proclamation.*

---

You ask what the Great Emancipator found a piece of property and left an American citizen, to speak of Abraham Lincoln. My first acquaintance with our hero and benefactor is this: Night after night, before the dawn of day, on an old slave plantation in Virginia, I recall the form of my sainted mother bending over a batch of rags that enveloped my body, on a dirt floor, breathing a fervent prayer to Heaven that "Marsa Lincoln" might succeed, and that one day she and I might be free; and so on your invitation I come here to-night, Mr. President, to celebrate with you the answer to those prayers. But be it far from me to revive the bitter memories of the past, nor would I narrow the work of Abraham Lincoln to the black race of this country—rather I would call him the Emancipator of America—the liberator of the white man North, the white man South; the one who in unshackling the chains of the Negro, has turned loose the enslaved forces of nature in the South, and has knit all sections of our country together by the indissoluble bonds of commerce. To the man in the North who cherished hatred against the South, Lincoln brought freedom. To the white man who landed at Jamestown years ago, with hopes as bright and prospects as cheering as those who stepped ashore on Plymouth Rock, Lincoln for the first time gave an opportunity to breathe the air of unfettered freedom; a freedom from dependence on others' labor to the independence of self-labor; freedom to transform unused and dwarfed hands into skilled and productive hands; to change labor from drudgery into that which is dignified and glorified; to change local commerce into trade with the world; to change the Negro from an ignorant man to an intelligent man; to change sympathies that were local and narrow into love and good will for all mankind—freedom to change stagnation into growth, weakness into power; yea, to us all, your race and mine, Lincoln has been a great emancipator. [ . . . ]

But all is not done, and it remains for us, the living, to finish the work that Lincoln left uncompleted. You of the great and prosperous North, still owe a serious and uncompleted duty to your less fortunate brothers of the white race South, who suffered and are still suffering the consequence of American slavery. What was the task you asked them to perform? Returning to their destitute homes after years of war, to face blasted hopes, devastation, a shattered industrial system, you ask them to add to their burdens that of preparing in education, politics and economics, in a few short years, for citizenship, four or five millions of former slaves. That the South, staggering under the burden, made blunders that in some measure there has been disappointment, no one need be surprised.

The 4,000,000 slaves that Lincoln freed are now nearly 8,000,000 freemen. That which was three hundred years in doing, can hardly be undone in thirty years. How can you help the South and the Negro in the completion of Lincoln's work? A large majority of the people Lincoln freed are still ignorant, without proper food, or property, or skill, or correct habits; are without the requisites for intelligent and independent citizenship. The mere fiat of law could not make a dependent man independent; it could not make an ignorant voter an intelligent voter; it could not make one man respect another man. These results come by beginning at the bottom and working upwards; by recognizing our weakness as well as our strength; by tangible evidences of our worthiness to occupy the highest positions. Unfortunately too many of my people, because of ignorance, began at the top instead of the bottom; grasped for the shadow instead of the substance. We have spent time and money in attempting to go to Congress and State Legislatures, that could better have been spent in becoming the leading real estate dealer or carpenter in our county. We have spent time and money in making political stump speeches and in attending political conventions, that could better have been spent in starting a dairy farm, or truck garden, and thus have laid a material foundation on which we could have stood and demanded our rights. [ . . . ]

Yes, in answer to your proclamation, Father Abraham, we are coming 8,000,000 strong—we are coming by the way of the college, by the way of agriculture, the shop, the factory, the trades, the household arts. With this foundation, if God is right and the Bible is true, there is no power that can permanently stay our progress.

You cannot graft a fifteenth century civilization into a twentieth century civilization by the mere performance of mental gymnastics. You cannot convert a man by abusing him. The mere pushing of knowledge into the heads of a people, without providing a medium through the hands for its use, is not always wise. The educated idle man is more dangerous than the ignorant idle man. An educated man standing on the corners of your streets with his hands in his pockets, is not one whit more benefit to society than an ignorant man in the streets with his hands in his pockets. It is only as the black man produces something that makes the markets of the world dependent on him for something, will he secure his rightful place. [...]

Nor shall we be lacking in the exercise of the higher virtues. In 1840 one of my race was sold from Virginia into Georgia. After serving his master in slavery for twenty years, seeing his children sold, his wife subjected to the lash and other hardships, at the command of Lincoln he became a freeman. Conditions reversed themselves. By industry and economy the ex-slave secures a comfortable home, educates and trains his children along industrial lines; he becomes prosperous and independent. In the meantime, his former master and mistress grow infirm, have reverses, going down till poverty and want are reached. The black man, the ex-slave, hears of the condition of his former owners, and at great expense and inconvenience finds his way to them. Grasping them by the hand, he lets them know that the past is forgotten, tells them of his prosperity and future hopes. This black man brings his former owners to his own home, builds for them a neat cottage, nurses them, feeds them, warms and protects and cheers them into happiness and contentment. This, this, my friends, is an example of the true emancipation; let white men, North and South, strive to match it, to excel it, if they can.

This is the new emancipation we seek to bring about at Tuskegee; to emancipate the white man to love the Negro; to emancipate the Negro to love the white man; to emancipate the Negro into habits of thrift, skill, economy and substantial character; to teach the Negro if another man is little, he can be great; if another man is mean he can be good; if others hold malice, he can cultivate charity. Thus rising day by day in stepping on our dead selves, we hope to help the black and the white man bring about that larger, that higher emancipation.

*Address of Booker T. Washington, Principal of Tuskegee Normal and Industrial Institute [...]*
*Before the Union League Club (n.p., 1896).*

## HARRIET TUBMAN, Statement on Abraham Lincoln, July 1896

*One of the most famous participants in the Underground Railroad, Tubman (c.1820–1913), whose birthname was Araminta Ross, was a leading advocate for both racial and gender equality. After running away from a Maryland plantation, she aided the escape of enslaved persons, and served the Union cause during the Civil War as a spy and scout for the army. Tubman was active in the women's rights movement after the war, and the following statement is from an interview conducted in the same year that she attended the convention that formed the National Association of Colored Women. Although Tubman was initially a critic of Lincoln, after meeting with Sojourner Truth in 1864, she was persuaded to change her mind. For Truth's meeting with Lincoln, see above (ANB; Milton C. Sernett,* Harriet Tubman: Myth, Memory, and History *[Durham: Duke University Press, 2007], 161–162).*

---

When asked if she had ever met Lincoln she replied, "No, I'm sorry now, but I didn't like Lincoln in dem days. I us 'd go see Missus Lincoln but I never wanted to see him. You see we colored people didn't understand den he was our frien'. All we knew was dat de first colored troops sent south from Massachusetts only got seven dollars a month, while de white regiment got fifteen. We didn't like dat. But now I know all 'bout it, an' I'se sorry I didn't go see Massa Lincoln.

" 'Twas Sojourner Truth tole me Massa Lincoln was our frien'. Den she went to see him, and she tanked him for all he had done for our peoples. Massa Lincoln was kind to her, and she had a nice visit with him, but he tole her he had done nuffin himself; he was only a servant of de country. Yes, I'se sorry I didn't see Massa Lincoln and tank him."

Rosa Belle Hoyt, "A Heroine in Ebony," *The Chautauquan* 23, no. 4 (July 1896): 462.

## JULIUS F. TAYLOR, Critique of Lincoln and the Emancipation Proclamation, August 7, 1897

*Taylor (1854–1934) began publishing a weekly newspaper, the* Broad Ax, *in Salt Lake City, Utah in 1895. A staunch Democrat, Taylor was not one to mince words as he questioned African American loyalty to the Party of Lincoln and sought to disabuse people of the notion that Lincoln was the Great Emancipator. In this critique, Taylor highlights the limitations of both the preliminary and final Emancipation Proclamations, notes Lincoln's support for colonization, and asserts that if Black people feel indebted to someone for their freedom, credit should be accorded to Jefferson Davis. In 1897, Taylor relocated the* Broad Ax *to Chicago, where he continued to publish the newspaper until 1931 (Michael S. Sweeney, "Julius F. Taylor and the* Broad Ax *of Salt Lake City," Utah Historical Quarterly 77, no. 3 [Summer 2009]: 204–221; "Julius F. Taylor, Veteran Editor of* Broadaxe, *Dies," Chicago Defender, May 19, 1934).*

---

If all members of our race were only broad-minded enough to banish from their minds all their prejudices and handkerchief-head ideas while they are engaged in perusing the proclamation which President Lincoln promulgated on September 22d, 1862, they will observe that Mr. Lincoln gave Jefferson Davis and his associates one hundred days to consider whether or not they would accept his (the President's) proposition, which reads as follows, that if the people residing in the States and parts of States, which were then in rebellion against the United States, would be represented in both branches of the United States Congress by the first day of January, 1863, by representatives chosen thereto at elections held prior to that time, namely January 1st, 1863, that they, the people residing in such States and parts of States, would be permitted to resume all of their former Constitutional relations with the Federal Government.

Now, it is just as plain as your nose on your face, that Abraham Lincoln had no more idea or intention of liberating the members of our race from bondage at that time, September 22d, 1862, than he had of taking wings and flying to heaven.

While we never did pretend to know very much, nevertheless we are of the opinion that this is the height of presumption upon the part of any one, be they black or white, rich or poor, high or low, to give expression to sentiments respecting Mr. Lincoln's friendship for the negro which would not harmonize with the sentiments expressed in his reply to Horace Greeley's letter of August 19th, 1862. In short, all honest men must absolutely refrain from trying to convey the idea to the members of our race that President Lincoln issued his first proclamation for no other purpose than to proclaim freedom to all the negroes.

Before passing on to the consideration of the second proclamation we wish to remind all of our brethren who are scattered throughout the civilized world, that if they conscientiously believe that they are really under lasting obligations to some one for the freedom which they now enjoy, they had better bestow the greater portion of their gratitude and affection upon Jefferson Davis, for it was owning to his bullheadedness that the negro finally succeeded in becoming a full fledged American.

In other words, President Lincoln tried every imaginary scheme which his great mind was capable of conceiving, and he worked night and day for the purpose of getting Jefferson Davis to accept his proposition. But he was unsuccessful in all his negotiations with Mr. Davis and his associates, and the result was that Mr. Lincoln was compelled to give up all hope of saving the Union without interfering with slavery.

It will be observed that at the expiration of the one hundred days, which was January 1st, 1863, that President Lincoln had decided to adhere to his policy of endeavoring to save the Union by giving freedom to part of the slaves, and allowing others to remain in bondage.

The second proclamation did not liberate the slaves of West Virginia, Missouri, Kentucky, Tennessee, Maryland or Delaware. Neither did it confer freedom upon the slaves residing in fourteen counties of Louisiana, including the city of New Orleans. Neither did it change the status of the slaves in the seven leading counties of Old Virginia, including the cities of Norfolk and Portsmouth. It is fair to presume that more than one half of the slaves did not gain their liberty through President Lincoln's Proclamation.

There is another fact which we must not lose sight of, i.e., the war began between the North and the South during the month of April, 1861, but notwithstanding this fact Mr. Lincoln did not request the negro to assist in helping to fight for his own freedom until after the first day of January, 1863.

We must also remember that the President did not fail to inform the world in plain black and white, that military necessity impelled him to turn against the white brethren of the South. And it was not on account of the great love which he entertained for the negro.

Shortly after the first day of January, 1863, Mr. Lincoln requested the members of Congress to aid him in his colonization scheme, and Congress acceded to his demands by appropriating $100,000. This vast sum was to be expended in helping to colonize ex-slaves. But the greater portion of it was squandered by the President's political schemers and speculators, who succeeded in coaxing a few deluded blacks to accompany them to a new land, which flowed with milk and honey. But these poor, misguided people were transported to a wretched sand pit, known as Cow Island, on the coast of Hayti, where they ended their miserable existence. And that was the practical finale [...] of Abraham Lincoln's great colonization scheme.

"Our Review," *Broad Ax* (Salt Lake City, UT), Aug. 7, 1897.

## IDA B. WELLS-BARNETT, Emancipation Day Address at Decatur, Illinois, September 22, 1899

*A leader of the highest order for all her adult life, Wells-Barnett (1862–1931) was primarily known for her ongoing campaign against lynching, centrality to the National Association of Colored Women, and leadership in Chicago's civil rights movement. She was directly involved in several Emancipation Day celebrations, including Chicago's commemoration of the fiftieth anniversary of the Emancipation Proclamation, but her address at Decatur, Illinois, in 1899 is the most thorough report available of her remarks at such occasions. Though Lincoln was not the focus of her speech, she offered an expansive interpretation of the Emancipation Proclamation that concentrated on the opportunities the document afforded. She urged her African American listeners to vindicate Lincoln's act by having self-confidence, organizing, securing education, and taking initiative in establishing institutions that would provide jobs in their communities. The* Decatur Review *reported that she also criticized President McKinley for failing to take action against lynching and stated that African Americans had paid their debt to the Republican Party long ago and should vote for the candidates that best served their interests ("Mrs. Barnett's Talk,"* Decatur Review, *Sept. 23, 1899).*

---

Mrs. Ida Wells Barnett, the well known colored lecturer of Chicago, made a talk which was one of the best addresses ever made to the colored people of the city. She is a speaker of great force and personality, and her ideas are expressed in a manner which carries with them conviction and inspiration. She spoke to the colored people as a sister deeply interested in their lives and welfare and urged upon them the necessity of action in their own behalf if they ever hoped to become a power and gain their rights, socially and politically. She especially urged the need of education and organization. "Do not be content," she said, "to always fill menial positions. You say that it is no use to fit yourself for higher positions in the business and educational world because you are barred from making use of your attainments in that direction by race prejudice. This is not altogether true. The feeling against the race is strong but you can win the respect and confidence of the world in such a manner that you will command positions and places worthy of your efforts. First fit yourself for any occupation in life and then if it is not given to you the fault is not yours but belongs elsewhere. If you are ready when the opportunity comes you will find that it is not lack of opportunity entirely, and that merit will win. Teach the world to have confidence in you by showing confidence in yourselves. So long as you refuse to have confidence in the colored physician, lawyer and distrust your own people just so long will the world distrust you. Do not make the mistake of thinking that the more you are like the white people the more respect they will have for you. Do not try to blot out the characteristics which God has given you to make you a distinctive people. Make men and women proud of you as a race and make them respect your black face and wooly hair.

"Organization is needed more than anything else. Not only in this city and state but in the nation you will fail to get concessions until you are a power and can command them. Make yourselves a power. Stand as a solid phalanx and support men and institutions who will do the right thing by the colored people. Demand not only your rights as citizens but demand that the hanging, shooting and burning of your race be stopped. Do not wonder that men despise you when you sit by idly and allow all this and vote to put the party in power who will not only tolerate it but refuse to right the wrong that is done. Organize for safety and protection and you will find plenty of good white friends to help you and encourage you in the stand you have taken.

"Another thing I would have you consider is the matter of economy. Save the dimes and the dollars. If you have them to spend, spend them in a way to help your own people. Do not depend on the white people for employment. Band together and go into business for yourselves. Establish institutions for the purpose of giving employment to your own people. The more serious problems may be solved by beginning with this one which rests with each individual. Save your dimes and dollars and put them together for the advancement of your own interests. My message to you is to equip yourselves to enter the race of life, educate yourselves, organize yourselves into strong bodies, have confidence in yourselves as individuals and as a race and you will find that you have won the right to expect that all men will willingly give you what is your own."

"Mrs. Barnett's Address," *Decatur Herald*, Sept. 23, 1899.

## PAUL LAURENCE DUNBAR, "Lincoln," 1899

*A native of Ohio and the son of a Civil War veteran, Dunbar (1872–1906) was the most well-known African American poet of the late nineteenth and early twentieth centuries. He composed this poem for a collection of poetry to commemorate Lincoln that featured contributions from Walt Whitman, Herman Melville, John Greenleaf Whittier, and James Russell Lowell. Dunbar praised Lincoln by crediting him with bringing peace out of the Civil War's ravages with his wisdom, caring, and words.*

Hurt was the Nation with a mighty wound,
And all her ways were filled with clam'rous sound.
Wailed loud the South with unremitting grief,
And wept the North that could not find relief.
Then madness joined its harshest tone to strife:
A minor note swelled in the song of life
Till, stirring with the love that filled his breast,
But still, unflinching at the Right's behest
Grave Lincoln came, strong-handed, from afar,—
The mighty Homer of the lyre of war!
'Twas he who bade the raging tempest cease,
Wrenched from his strings the harmony of peace,
Muted the strings, that made the discord,—Wrong,

And gave his spirit up in thund'rous song.
Oh, mighty Master of the mighty lyre!
Earth heard and trembled at thy strains of fire:
Earth learned of thee what Heav'n already knew,
And wrote thee down among her treasured few!

In M. A. DeWolfe Howe, *The Memory of Lincoln* (Boston: Small, Maynard & Company, 1899), 65.

## ELIZABETH THOMAS, Reminiscence of Abraham Lincoln, 1900

*Thomas (c. 1830–1917) resided on land in Washington that the government appropriated to construct Fort Stevens during the Civil War. As Confederate soldiers reached the outskirts of Washington in July 1864, Thomas was an eyewitness when Lincoln visited the fort and came under enemy fire. Thomas resided at the site of the fort for the remainder of her life and was a popular figure in the Washington community, particularly with visitors to the fort whom she entertained by telling the story of her encounter with the president. Although the federal government failed to make good on Lincoln's promise of compensation, she remained proud of her connection to Lincoln and kept a portrait of him in her home. The following version of her story is taken from an interview by William Cox, a fellow resident in the Fort Stevens neighborhood who led an effort to construct a monument to Lincoln at the fort and purchased land from Thomas for this purpose ("Unveil Lincoln Stone," Washington Post, Nov. 8, 1911; "Fort Stevens, An Interesting Link of the Capital's War Defenses," Evening Star [Washington, DC], Dec. 22, 1912; "Mrs. Thomas Dead," Washington Bee [Washington, DC], Oct. 20, 1917).*

---

The soldiers camped here at this time were mostly German. I could not understand them, not even the officers, but when they began taking out my furniture and tearing down our house, I understood. In the evening I was sitting under that sycamore tree—my only house—with what furniture I had left around me. I was crying, as was my six-months'-old child, which I had in my arms, when a tall, slender man, dressed in black, came up and said to me, "It is hard, but you shall reap a great reward." It was President Lincoln, and, had he lived, I know the claim for my losses would have been paid.

William V. Cox, "The Defenses of Washington," *Records of the Columbia Historical Society, Washington, DC*, vol. 4 (1901): 138.

# ARCHIBALD H. GRIMKE, "Abraham Lincoln," March 1900

*Born a slave in South Carolina, Grimke (1849–1930) was the nephew of noted abolitionists Angelina Grimke Weld and Sarah Grimke. After graduating from Lincoln University in Pennsylvania and Harvard Law School, Grimke practiced law, edited a newspaper, served as a diplomat, and played an active role in the civil rights movement. The following essay reflects Grimke's strong identification with the abolitionist movement through not only familial connections but also his own scholarship, as he had written biographies of Charles Sumner and William Lloyd Garrison. Grimke sought an honest assessment of Lincoln by placing him in a comparative context, and urged African Americans to offer their own bold interpretations of the past. Grimke went on to help found the NAACP and served as president of the Washington, DC branch of the organization (ANB; Dickson D. Bruce Jr., Archibald Grimke: Portrait of a Black Independent [Baton Rouge: Louisiana State University Press, 1993]).*

---

It seems to me that it is high time for colored Americans to look at Abraham Lincoln from their own standpoint, instead of from that of their white fellow-citizens. We have surely a point of view equally with them for the study of this great man's public life, wherein it touched and influenced our history. Then why are we invariably found in their place on this subject, as on kindred ones, and not in our own? Are we never to find ourselves and our real thought on men and things in this country, and after finding them are we to deny to them expression, for fear of giving offence? Are we to be forever a trite echo, an insignificant "me too" to the white race in America on all sorts of questions, even on those which concern peculiarly and vitally our past, present and future relations to them? Is it due to some congenital race weakness, or to environment, to the slave blood which is still abundant in our veins, that we rate instinctively and unconsciously whatever appertains to them as better than the corresponding thing which appertains to ourselves, and count always what we receive from them, although vastly inferior in quantity and quality, as immensely superior to that which we give in return? Are we never to acquire a sense of proportion and independence of judgment, but must go on with our own brains befuddled with the white man's prodigiously magnified opinion of himself and achievements? I hope not; I do most devoutly pray not. For if we are ever to occupy a position in America other than that of mere dependents and servile imitators of the whites, we must emancipate ourselves from this species of slavery, as from all others. And the sooner a beginning is made in this regard the better. With whom then can we more appropriately begin this work of intellectual emancipation than with Abraham Lincoln, the emancipator? It will, therefore, be as a member of that race for whom he performed, incidentally, the grandest act of his life, that I shall now speak of this illustrious man. [. . .]

At no time before or after his election to the Presidency, was Abraham Lincoln a friend of the slaves in the same sense, as was William Lloyd Garrison, or anything like it, for a simple and sufficient reason.

Mr. Lincoln did not take part broadly as a man, in the slavery struggle in America, but rather as a white man, and more particularly still as a white man belonging to the non-slaveholding section of the Union. The abolition of slavery was never his life purpose, which was, as it related to this subject, limited strictly to restriction of the evil to the Southern States, and exclusion of it from the national territories. Like the great majority of Americans he entertained in the abstract, for the self-evident truths of the Declaration of Independence, unmeasured respect and veneration, yet when it came to conduct, those self-same truths were powerless to affect his action, any more than if they had been mere "glittering generalities." His devotion to the Constitution, with all of its slave compromises, amounted to idolatry, and for the Union with its shameful inequality and oppression of the blacks, he felt the most passionate attachment, as to the acme and *summum bonum* of everything worthy and wise on earth.

The right of the slave to freedom had no more practical weight with him, or with the North, when set over against the peace or prosperity, or preservation of that Union, than would have had, if such a thing was possible, the right to freedom of the imaginary inhabitants of Mars. What was true of Mr. Lincoln was emphatically true of the section of the country represented by him, with a few shining exceptions, such as the old abolitionists, for whom alone the principles of the Declaration of Independence possessed any practical moral obligations or value. The Negro as a human being did not count with the people of the North before the war, any more than so many cattle, and since that time, he has not counted with them as much as so many aliens. It is as a social or political factor that the North has ever allowed itself to think about the Negro, or to act in respect to him, and then only when his existence happened in some way to touch injuriously its pocket or its power.

There is no doubt whatever that during the first year of the war, and of Mr. Lincoln's administration, that he was bent on saving the Union without liberating the slaves. He was strangely slow and reluctant to change his policy on this question, strangely averse from abating one jot or tittle of the laws on the national statute book in favor of the masters. He had set out determinedly to maintain the Union with slavery, and in the pursuit of this purpose he turned, during that time, neither to the right nor to the left. [. . .]

The slaves, in these circumstances, had no more chance of freedom with Lincoln, while this mood of his lasted, than they had with the head of the Southern Confederacy. It was the stern logic of events which forced the President to change his mood and abandon his original position. When he struck slavery at last, his primary object was not to free the slaves, but to save the Union.

*[Grimke then offers a parable of the Civil War as a conflict between five brothers, three in a non-slave owning north and two in a slave owning south, for control of an island.]*

Two years passed, and the end of the war among the brothers was not in sight. This made the three brothers of the North very sad, for they did not like to fight. They loved peace, but they loved the old Union, and their right to the whole island, even more than they loved peace. Up to this time they had been very jealous in guarding the right of their two brothers to their slave, but perceiving then that alone they were not strong enough to conquer them and maintain the indivisibility of the island, they bethought them of calling to their assistance the poor slave, whom they had always despised and grievously wronged, to fight with them for their island. Well, in their extremity they hailed him and offered him freedom. But so little did they, in reality, wish to give him freedom, that they gave his masters instead from September to January to make up their minds to cease fighting, to abandon their design to divide the island, and to return with their slave into the old arrangement, by which the five brothers were to occupy and govern the island in common. Fortunately for the slave the two brothers laughed this offer to scorn, and went on fighting right lustily. Then as a last resort, and as an act of dire necessity, the three brothers gave the slave his freedom, put arms in his hands, and with his aid they beat the two brothers in the South, destroyed their government, and preserved the integrity of the island.

To whom think you, in the parable, is gratitude due, from the slave to the three brothers, or from them to him? When you have guessed aright the answer to this riddle, reader, you will understand the exact part which Mr. Lincoln enacted in the freedom of the slaves, and the plain motive which underlaid and actuated his famous Emancipation Proclamation. Let us render unto him the things which are justly his, and unto the Negro and the old abolitionists the things which are justly theirs. Truth is better than error. Let us have truth!

Was Abraham Lincoln a great American? Yes, certainly. Was he one of the greatest of American statesmen? Yes, assuredly. Was he a great philanthropist? No. Was he a great friend of human liberty and the Negro, like Garrison, Sumner and Phillips? No, a thousand and one times, no! For the sake of truth let us answer "yes" every time where "yes" agrees with the facts of history and "no" where simple honesty forbids any other reply. And then let us be done, once and forever, with all this literary twaddle and glamour, fiction and myth-making, which pass unchallenged for facts in the wonder-yarns which white men spin of themselves, their deeds and demigods.

*Howard's American Magazine* 4, no. 8 (March 1900): 352–358.

## ELIZABETH KECKLY on Lincoln, 1901

*Although the publication of* Behind the Scenes *ended Keckly's (1818–1907)—*
*or Keckley's—friendship with Mrs. Lincoln (see above), that did not diminish*
*her admiration of President Lincoln, as evidenced by the following comments*
*that she made in an interview with Smith D. Fry, a Washington, DC, historian*
*and correspondent for the* Los Angeles Times. *When Fry interviewed Keckly*
*she was living in straitened circumstances in Washington after having taught*
*sewing at Wilberforce University in Ohio. Keckly considered Lincoln a friend,*
*and her horrific experiences as a slave led her to have a deep appreciation of the*
*significance of the Emancipation Proclamation even though she had purchased*
*her own freedom prior to Lincoln's act. Keckly believed only those who had been*
*enslaved could fully comprehend the meaning of emancipation. While Keckly*
*had likened Lincoln to Moses in her book, here she characterizes him as the*
*Man of Sorrows who welcomed death. Fry's interview was published in several*
*newspapers during the summer of 1901.*

---

Abraham Lincoln was a good friend of mine; but he never knew what a good
friend of his I was, and have ever been. [ . . . ]

I was Mr. Lincoln's friend, am his friend now, and will always protect his memory, by keeping my mouth closed concerning the many things which he unhappily suspected or imagined were going on around him officially and unofficially.
I was born a slave, but bought my freedom, and so was under no obligations to
Mr. Lincoln for emancipation. But I loved him for his kind manner towards me
and for his great act of giving freedom to my race. I know what liberty is, because
I remember what slavery was. When I was a young woman, modest as any young
woman, I was stripped to the waist and flogged into insensibility. This was done
more than once, simply on the pretext that "my spirit must be broken." I know
what undeserved suffering was inflicted upon the slaves. Therefore I know what
emancipation meant. You who have never suffered cannot understand the full
meaning of liberty. I was as good a girl as ever lived; and I wanted to live as good
women live; but I was compelled to become a mother without marriage. Oh,
yes, I know what slavery was. Consequently I have almost worshipped Abraham
Lincoln. He was as kind and considerate in his treatment of me, as he was any
of the white people at the White House. In that he manifested consistency of
his belief that all human beings are created equal in the sight of God. He arose
every morning as a good man, and he went to bed every night as a God-fearing,
Christian man. They say that servants do not reverence their masters because
they know their weaknesses, as the rest of the world cannot know them. But
no servant failed to respect and revere that grand man of God, and man of the

common people. His life was pure. I cannot say that of all whom I knew in those days. [...]

I know and I know it well, that so unhappy was that great man, so tired of life and its burdens, that if he could have expressed an opinion concerning the work of the assassin, he would have said: "I am glad that it is all over." He was always ready for death, and I knew him so well that I have always felt that death was welcome to him when it came.

Smith D. Fry, "Lincoln Liked Her," *Paxton Daily Record* (Paxton, IL), July 1, 1901.

## "The Negro's Natal Day," February 1904

*The* Voice of the Negro *commenced publication in Atlanta in January 1904, and soon acquired a reputation as one of the leading African American periodicals. The* Voice *published essays and poems on a variety of topics, including pieces on Lincoln from prominent African American leaders. John W. E. Bowen (1855–1933) of the Gammon Theological Seminary served as editor while Jesse Max Barber (1878–1949), a recent graduate of Virginia Union University, served as the managing editor. Under Barber's guidance, the* Voice *rejected the accommodationist position of Booker T. Washington and became identified with W. E. B. Du Bois's Niagara Movement. After the* Voice *ceased publication in 1907, Barber attended dental school, became active in the civil rights movement in Philadelphia, and worked to keep the memory of John Brown alive. In this early editorial, the editors make clear the continuing relevance and significance of Lincoln and the Emancipation Proclamation for African Americans (ANB; Walter C. Daniel,* Black Journals of the United States *[Westport, CT: Greenwood Press, 1982]).*

---

Abraham Lincoln, the Emancipation Proclamation and the Negro are the three most suggestive words of the last half of the Nineteenth Century. In fact it may be said that the history of the Republic cannot be adequately written without giving large space to the discussion of the life, character, and achievements of this great Commoner of the Nation; to the high conception, purpose, and statesmanship of that second greatest state paper of the nation and to the pathetic history of the American Negro. These three will always be linked together. The Negro looks upon the first day of January as his natal day. The whole nation should celebrate it as the day when the freedom proclaimed in the Declaration of Independence became a living reality to the whole people. The South should take special pride in the day that celebrates its deliverance from the blighting curse of slavery.

*Voice of the Negro* 1, no. 2 (Feb. 1904): 73.

## WILLIAM A. SINCLAIR, *The Aftermath of Slavery*, 1905

*Born a slave in South Carolina, Sinclair (c.1856–1926) graduated from Howard University and the Andover Theological Seminary before serving as a missionary for the American Missionary Association. A member of late nineteenth century civil rights organizations and a founding member of the NAACP, Sinclair published* The Aftermath of Slavery *in 1905. This work is not generally known; most suggest that the history of African Americans by George Washington Williams in 1882 was the first scholarly history of Blacks, followed by Carter G. Woodson's* The Negro in Our History *in 1922. Sinclair's work appeared at a time of Jim Crow segregation and disfranchisement of African American voters throughout the South. These practices were enforced with lynching, while some White supremacists asserted that Lincoln shared their views. Sinclair sought to make it clear that Lincoln was anything but a White supremacist by citing his March 1864 letter to Michael Hahn and his final public speech as evidence that he supported Black voting rights. For Sinclair, the Emancipation Proclamation represented the Black man's "charter of liberty," and he believed Lincoln's adamant refusal to abandon or modify the proclamation illustrated the strength of his commitment to both Black freedom and Black citizenship. The implication of Sinclair's argument is clear: if Lincoln were alive he would use the power of the federal government to guarantee equal protection under the law for all citizens (AANB).*

---

Efforts at reconstruction were also made under [Lincoln's] direction in Louisiana, with promising results, and in Arkansas and Florida with tentative though not very substantial results. To Governor Hahn of the reconstructed government of Louisiana, Lincoln wrote in March, 1864, advising that the ballot should be given to the colored men: "Let in, as for instance, the very intelligent, and especially those who have fought gallantly in our ranks. They would probably help in some trying time in the future to keep the jewel of liberty in the family of freedom."

This was probably the first utterance from a responsible source in favor of bestowing the ballot on the colored people of the South. It shows to splendid advantage Lincoln's great and noble heart. For the war was still in progress and destined to last, no one knew how long. It did continue for over a year longer. Lincoln's renomination and re-election were hanging in the balance. Serious reverses in the field might have defeated either or both. He was far in advance of the public opinion of the nation. For at this time it was not at all likely that a single Northern state could have been carried on the simple question of negro suffrage. Yet he plainly, positively, unmistakably indicated suffrage for the colored man as a part of his policy in reconstructing the Southern states. His generous nature, his great and noble heart, would have it known that the colored men "who have fought gallantly in our ranks" can be trusted to "help in some trying time in the future to keep the jewel of liberty in the family of freedom."

These words of Lincoln are dwelt upon because they are of deep significance and add to our opinion of his greatness, his fame, when it is considered that the validity of the Emancipation Proclamation was at that time a much debated question. Many strong and learned loyal men in the North doubted the legal right or power of the President alone, even as a war measure, to destroy or confiscate property by proclamation, especially when that property was beyond the control of the government. The slaves were at that time property; they were also, with unimportant exceptions, within the bounds of the Confederacy and beyond the control of the government. Could the President alone, by mere proclamation, legally destroy and confiscate property which his government did not possess? Would Congress, the people, and the Supreme Court finally sustain him?

This question, pressed by influential sources in the North, weighed heavily on Lincoln. But he was equal to this, as he was to every emergency in the greatest conflict in history. He found strength and comfort in the "higher law" that "the negro was a man, and that no man was good enough to own another man and appropriate the fruits of his labor." And there was the feeling "that slavery drew the sword against the nation and that it should perish by the sword." To the realization of this "higher law" he hoped to bring the nation.

So important and pressing was this question that Lincoln dealt with it in his message to the Congress in December, 1864. In this message the President said: "While I remain in my present position I shall not attempt to retract or modify the Emancipation Proclamation. Nor shall I return to slavery any person who is free by the terms of that Proclamation or by any of the Acts of Congress. If the people should, by whatever mode or means, make it an executive duty to re-enslave such persons, another, and not I, must be their instrument to perform it."

Here is more than a veiled threat, it is an open defiance. Lincoln had just been re-elected to the presidency in November, a month before the message was sent to Congress; and he distinctly tells Congress and the people that he would give up the presidency rather than relinquish the principles of his Emancipation Proclamation; that he would resign his office rather than "return to slavery any person who is free by the terms of that proclamation or by any of the Acts of Congress."

Up to this date the Emancipation Proclamation was the only charter of liberty for the colored people in the South; and the all-important point is, that Lincoln regarded this as sufficient to enable the negroes to wear the uniform of a United States soldier, to be commissioned as officers, to be treated the same as white soldiers, to be protected as prisoners of war, to have common rights, and to vote at the ballot-box.

President Lincoln's deep solicitude for the colored soldiers, his profound interest in them, his unqualified respect for and appreciation of their invaluable services, and his determination that they should receive their full mete of justice, are made manifest in his state papers, public addresses and letters. [...]

He threatened retaliation, should the Confederates shoot black soldiers when captured, instead of treating them as prisoners of war. He refused to exchange a single Confederate soldier until colored soldiers were recognized by the Confederate government. [...]

[O]n the 11th of April, 1865, just four days before his death, and two days after General Lee's surrender, he made his last public address, favoring, as a start in the right direction, the reconstructed government which the loyalists had organized in Louisiana, abolishing slavery, adopting the Thirteenth Amendment, providing schools for black and white alike, and providing for the franchise for the colored people. [...]

If Lincoln was willing, as he proved to be, to use the great power of the United States government to guarantee that "the *black* soldier should have the same protection as the *white* soldier," then it defames his hallowed memory, and libels his nobility of heart to insinuate that he would not use the same powers to guarantee to the black citizen the same protection under the law as the white citizen. To him the Emancipation Proclamation meant freedom for the colored people; and freedom meant citizenship; and citizenship the ballot.

William A. Sinclair, *The Aftermath of Slavery: A Study of the Condition and Environment of the American Negro* (Boston: Small, Maynard & Company, 1905), 46–49, 54–55.

## JESSE MAX BARBER, "Abraham Lincoln and the Negro," February 1905

*Barber (1878–1949) had accepted the position as managing editor of the* Voice *shortly after graduating from Virginia Union University. As the following indicates, Barber believed in the importance of keeping history alive through remembrance. While he urged the celebration of Lincoln's birthday, Barber also noted that Lincoln did not favor racial equality to the extent that White abolitionists, such as William Lloyd Garrison and Wendell Phillips, did. In paying tribute to Lincoln, Barber quoted from both of Lincoln's inaugural addresses. Barber would later take an active role in commemorating the life of John Brown (ANB).*

---

The celebration of the birthday of this greatest American commoner cannot fail to develop the spirit of loyalty to the Nation and gratitude to God for its marvelous preservation. America had two natal days, both days of blood and providential ordering, July 4th, 1776 and January 1st, 1863. On the former, George Washington emerged as the embodiment of the American colonial spirit; on the latter, Abraham Lincoln rises up as the true spirit of the new republic and its greatest representative. The birthday of this man is removed but a few days from this historic event in which he is the central moving figure.

Mr. Lincoln was not a lover of the Negro. He could not be classed with Garrison, Wilson, Sumner and Phillips and a host of philanthropists whom the South called negrophobists and whom it hated with a love-hate. But Lincoln loved truth and justice. He was humanitarian to the core and he despised the cruelty of slavery. His first appearance into public notice was when he gave utterance to a mortal antipathy to the brutalities of slavery as he saw them in New Orleans and expressed the hope of having an opportunity of "hitting a hard blow to slavery." When he was inaugurated the first time as President, he attempted to calm the frenzied South with this laconic and statesmanlike declaration in his inaugural. "The property, peace and security of no section are to be in anywise endangered by the new, incoming administration." This sentiment was upheld by nearly all of the Union Generals. Fremont and Phelps and a few subordinates did not subscribe to it.

Four years pass in rapid and painful succession and the destiny of the nation is fairly settled and the same old war President takes a second time the oath of office and in language that still thrills with deep pathos and lofty faith he says "If God wills that this mighty scourge of war continue until the wealth piled up by the bondmen's two hundred and fifty years of unrequited toil shall be sunk and until every drop of blood drawn by the lash shall be paid with a drop of blood drawn by the sword, as was said three thousand years ago, so still it must be said, 'the judgments of the Lord are true and righteous altogether.' " Who can deny the hand of a directing providence leading this war President on?

A grateful Negro race moved by the spirit of genuine appreciation for this noble spirit and his far reaching Emancipation Proclamation erected his monument in bronze in Lincoln Park, Washington, D.C., at a cost of $17,000.

The celebration of his birth serves to revive the memory of his historic deeds that preserved the nation by emancipat[ing], both whites and blacks from the tyranny and brutality of slavery and that opened to the complex nation the history destined for it by the God of nations.

*Voice of the Negro* 2, no. 2 (Feb. 1905): 127–128.

## MARY CHURCH TERRELL, Address on Abraham Lincoln, New York, February 13, 1905

*A native of Tennessee, Terrell (1863–1954) graduated from Oberlin College and taught school prior to devoting her life to the civil rights movement. She was an advocate of woman's suffrage and had completed a term as the first president of the National Association of Colored Women when she delivered the following address to the Women's Henry George League in New York City to commemorate Lincoln's birthday. President Theodore Roosevelt was also in New York on this date and delivered an address on Lincoln to the Republican Club. Although Terrell agreed with Roosevelt and others that Lincoln was a laudable historical figure, she focused on the usable lessons that his life and times offered. Terrell saw alarming parallels between Lincoln's era and the challenges that African Americans faced during Roosevelt's presidency. Although Lincoln was honest, wanted a peaceful if postponed emancipation of the enslaved, and promised slaveholders they would be properly paid for providing freedom by 1900, he was rebuked, and more drastic measures were required. Just as defenders of slavery refused to do what was right, Terrell believed Southern Whites were repeating this behavior with lynching, disfranchisement, Jim Crow laws, and other practices. She hoped that Roosevelt would follow Lincoln's example and rise to the challenge. Terrell was active in the Republican Party and continued to fight for equal rights for the remainder of her life. In her eighties she played a leading role in ending segregation in Washington, DC (ANB).*

---

A little more than forty years ago this country was plunged into war. It was a civil war[.] And if one bloody conflict is more horrible and shocking than another, it is when brothers close together in deadly embrace with their hands at each other's throats. The war was waged solely to preserve the Union, it is said. Indeed the great Liberator himself emphasized that, when he replied to Horace Greely, who had criticized his action relative to the question of slavery in an editorial of the New York Tribune. "If I could save the Union without freeing any slave, I would do it"; said Abraham Lincoln. "and if I could do it by freeing all the slaves, I would do it; and if I could do it by freeing some and leaving others alone, I would also do that. What I do about slavery and the colored race, I do because I believe it helps to save the Union; and what I forbear, I forbear because I do not believe it would help to save the Union." But the same great and good man, whose birthday we commemorate to night declared just as emphatically on another occasion that the rebels who were fighting to destroy the Union were striving to prove that this government was built upon the foundation of human slavery rather than upon the foundation of human rights. Without slavery, he said in one of his messages, "the rebellion could never have existed; without slavery, it could not continue."

A little more than forty years ago there were 4 millions of bondmen in the United States, men, women and children, groaning under a yoke too bitter and too galling to be described. And that, too, as monstrous and incredible as it will appear to future generations in a country which owes its very existence to the unconquerable love of liberty in the human heart.

The man during whose administration the bloody civil strife commenced was no god of war from whose nostrils the smoke and flame of battle flashed, but he loved peace as dearly as [he] loved his life. If it had been possible for Abraham Lincoln with his warm and tender heart to secure an honorable peace and thus avert the awful throes through which his beloved country passed by giving his own life, he would gladly have sacrificed himself, I am sure. But it was not in Abraham Lincoln's power to prevent the Civil War. He tried to do so with all his heart, soul, mind and strength. But the Rebellion came because it was God's will that it should[.] It ended in victory for the Union and for the freedom of the poor, oppresed, long-suffering slave, just as the Father of all colors, and classes of men intended it should. The heart of no man was filled with a greater joy or with gratitude to the Creator more profound and sincere than wa[s] Abraham Lincolns, at the triumph of justice and right.

In my humble opinion no one has ever done full a[n]d complete justice to th[e] breadth and depth and graces of Abraham Lincoln's character. And although I know I should fail miserably, if I tried to [pay] a fitting tribute to this great man still if my thoughts were not directed into another channel nothing would afford me more pleasure than attempt a eulogy of him and his good deeds in the few minutes allotted me by the kind generous friends to whom I am indebted for the honor and privilege of addressing you to night.

Instead of devoting myself exclusively to a eulogy of the man whose name has been and will always be inseparably connected with the emanc[i]pation of the race with which I am identified, I shall call your attention to a few of the lessons which it seems to me the life and times of Abraham Lincoln teach.

The more I compare the conditions in the U.S. which obtained before the Civil war with those which present themselves in this country to day, the more deeply impressed I become with the striking similarity which these two periods afford. For this reason nothing is more sorely needed in the United States to day than a careful review of the lessons which that great catastrophe taught[.] [...] [O]ne has only to compare the pitiable condition of the men, women and children of African descent who were slaves in 1861 with the servile, humiliating and degrading position occupied by their descendants to day to observe the striking similarity between the status of bondmen forty years [ago] and the so called freedom of the present time.

When I see a might host of broad-minded, justice-loving and generous hearted American citizens consent to the crimes committed against defenseless people, consent to the awful barbarities perpetrated upon them[,] consent to the various kinds of injustice to which even the worthiest representatives of this unfortunate people are almost daily subjected [to] consent, I say by the silence on this subject which they religiously observe, I involuntarily think of the multitudes of loyal American citizens and good Christians who detested and loathed slavery before the war, but who deemed it unwise publicly to express their convictions and protest. But the points of similarity between the two periods under consideration are not exhausted, until the character of the man who was president forty years ago is compared with the distinguishing traits of that other great man who presides over the destiny of the nation to day.

The tried integrity and the incorruptible honesty for which Abraham Lincoln was noted are the most conspicuous virtues possessed by Theodore Roosevelt today[.] In comparing the evils which ran riot here forty years ago with those which bring disgrace upon the nation to day, it is a comfort to note that honors are easy, so to speak, when the virtue of the two men occupying the highest gift in the nation during the two periods compared are evenly balanced and so fully matched are concerned.

Since the two periods which have just been compared are so strikingly similar both in the problems presented and the public affected, it behooves us carefully and conscientiously to study the lessons taught by the stirring and tragic past, so that we may use them as guides in considering some of the serious conditions which confront us to day. If the events which transpired before the war and precipitated it teach one lesson more than another, it is that tolerating wrong, temporizing with injustice and long forbearance with evil doers are sure to bring sorrow and shame to the nation which makes this fatal mistake. Putting off till tomorrow the correction of national evils which should be made to day is simply deferring a little the day of wrath which is sure to com[e.] And when the day of rectification and retribution finally dawns, the difficulty of throttling evils grown great and strong is invariably increased a thousand fold.

Delay is dangerous. Delay is w[i]cked. Delay means death are the words of warning written upon the page of history of this country from the day the Declaration of Independence was signed, until Fort Sumter was fired upon by rebel guns. The French Revolution taught France the folly of delay in redressing wrongs of the oppressed and Russia is learning that same lesson to day & God forbid that our Beloved Country should make the mistake which can be atoned for only in blood.

Long before [Lincoln] declared that a nation cannot be half slave and half free, the truth and force of this axiom was doubtless felt by many thoughtful Americans in the very depths of their hearts. But the axe was not laid at the roots of the upas tree which spread its baleful shade over our beloved land, because it was not expedient to interfere with the peculiar institution which flourished in the South. With an optimism which it is difficult for any one who has studied national evils to understand there were many sanguine souls who prophesied that the evil would finally destroy itself, that slavery would die a natural death. Nobody knew better than Abraham Lincoln how frail was the foundation on which the ultimate extinction of slavery was based. In one of the greatest speeches which he ever delivered he showed that the framers of the constitution firmly believed that slavery would die a natural death, but that instead of expiring it was spreading itself like the green bay tree and taking on new life and increased strength day by day. But in spite of the facts which everybody could see, there were not wanting sanguine soul[s] in those days who worked themselves up into such a frenzy of prophecy concerning the ultimate extinction and the natural death theory that they beheld in their minds eye a glorious company of slaveholders voluntarily laying the shackles of their slaves at glad Columbia's feet. Again, there were some who did not delude themselves into the belief that such a monster as slavery would die of diminution, who saw the nation's peril and who tried to aver[t] the impending catastrophe by the invention of pleasant little schemes of freeing the slaves to which the masters would readily agree. Chief among the earnest souls who exhausted their mental resources in planning for the peaceful emancipation of the slave was the great and good Abraham Lincoln himself. Nothing that human ingenuity could invent o[r] human thought devise to compass this end did Abraham Lincoln leave undone and [u]ntried. If you will only promise to free your slaves some time in the future, he plead, you shall not lose a cent. You may keep your slaves for thirty seven years, he continued. You need not emancipate them until the first day of January 1900, he coaxed, and you shall be paid for every bondman which the 8th census shows you owned.

This will not work a hardship upon anybody he argued with all the persuasiveness and ardor of which he was capable, for if you will but adopt the proposition, the majority of the masters who would be most seriously affected by the emancipation of the slaves will not live to see it come to pass. So far as the slaves are concerned, he said, even though it seems rather hard that those now living will not enjoy freedom, still, they will have the satisfaction of knowing that their posterity will be free, while they themselves will be spared many of the ills which sudden emancipation would inevitably bring. But none of these things moved the men who lived upon the sweat of their dark brother's faces and who insisted upon their traffic in human souls. With the blind unreasonableness and the stiff-necked obstinacy for which the oppressor in all a[g]es and climes has been noted, the slaveholder galloped to his own undoing and ruin.

But, my friends, it is an ill wind which blows nobody good, and it is a very mean and selfish sort of an evil which is altogether bad. When I think that instead of having been born into freedom, instead of having enjoyed the blessing of liberty all my life, I should have had up to date but five years of freedom and would probably be learning my A.B.C's, when I think also that instead of possessing my only child, a little girl but six years old, I might be hunting for her to night, not knowing where or to whom she had been sold, if the slaveholders had accepted the proposition to retain their slaves for 37 years with ample compensation in t[h]e end, I must confess I rejoice in the providential blindness and the beneficent obstinacy which afflicted the South. For the sak[e] of peace and in order to avert the war not only did Mr. Lincoln advocate emancipation with compensation, but he committed himself to colonization as well. This latter concession was to relieve the minds of the good people in the North, who feared that if the slaves were emancipated, they would sweep down upon them in hordes and fairly cover the land. In order to allay the fears of the North, Mr. Lincoln promised to send the colored freedmen to Hayti, or to Liberia or to the Spanish-American colonies, in fact, he promised to send them anywhere and everywhere but to his Satanic Majesty below. But neither compensation nor colonization, single or combined satisfied the South. Every suggestion which Mr. Lincoln or any other patriot made was received with ridicule or scorn. [. . .]

Colored men are supposed to be free to day, and yet by the notorious disfranchisement acts which have been adopted by nearly every State in th[e] South, the freedmen of 1905 have no more rights of citizenship no more than did the slaves whom Abraham Lincoln liberated forty years ago. Almost every child knows that the present political power of the South which makes one white man of that section equal to seven in the North is derived from thousands of Colored men from [whom] the right of citizenship has been violently torn. And yet, if one dares to call attention to these illegal political practices, he is accused of waving the bloody shirt, or of stirring up sectional strife, than which nothing could be more criminal. Public wrath is no longer turned against the sinner, but against him, who calls the sinner to account. Moreover, the South can poke all manner of fun at the North, make faces at it and call it very naught[y] names, and it would never occur to anybody but an inmate of an asylum for lunatics or imbeciles to even suggest that the South was stirring up sectional strife. But let anybody be brazen and bold enough to declare that the fundamental law of the land should be respected and the right of citizenship be withheld from no one on account of race and color; that the shooting and burning alive of men and women, whose only crime in many instances is the color of their skin, and the so called best citizens of the section in which lawlessness so generally prevails, shake their fists at the North and roar with rage that their liberty is being attacked and they want to be let alone.

When one hears the eloquent apostrophes [to] liberty which emanate from a section in which that priceless boon is denied to a whole race of human beings, thousands of whom are intelligent and worthy of respect, he is forcibly reminded of the comment upon liberty which Abraham Lincoln once made. "The world," said he ["]is in want of a good definition of the word liberty. We all declare ourselves to be for liberty, but we do not all mean the same thing. Some men mean that a man may do as he pleases with himself and his property. With others, it means that some men can do as they please with other men and other men's labor. Each of these things is called liberty,["] said Mr. Lincoln, although they are entirely different. ["]To give an illustration", he continued, ["]a shepherd drives the wolf from the throat of his sheep, when attacked by him, and the sheep, of course, thanks the shepherd for the preservation of his life; but the wolf denounces him as despoiling the sheep of his liberty—especially["] said Mr. Lincoln, ["]if it be a black sheep."

In addition to the Disfranchisement system, the Jim Crow Car Laws, the Convict Lease System, the Contract Labor System[,] lynching and white capping the South expresses the liberty [which] is so highly prized by curtailing the educational facilities of colored children. Again and again efforts have been made to divide the taxes so that only so many schools shall be established and maintained for colored children as the taxes paid by colored people themselves will support. [...]

And yet the South says that in dealing with the race problem it must be left alone, just as it did when abolition was agitated fifty years ago. Commenting upon this insistent demand made by the South Mr. Lincoln asked in his Cooper Union speech in this city, "What will satisfy the South? We must not only let them alone, but we must convince them that we do let them alone. This we know by experience is no easy task.["] He then proceeded to enumerate the various arguments he had used to persuade the South that he had not intended to interfere with it, calling the attenti[o]n of the people of that section to the fact that nobody had ever been detected in the act of interfering with it. But Mr. Lincoln reluctantly admitted that all his efforts to convince the South that it was being let alone had been futile and vain. The only way to convince the South that it was being let alone he declared, ["]is to cease to call slavery wrong, and join them in calling it right. And this must be done thoroughly, done in acts as well as in words." In this diagnosis of the distemper whi[c]h afflicted the South fifty years ago, Mr. Lincoln proved himself to [be] a physician and a philosopher of surpassing skill. The state of mind which made it impossible for a slave holder to listen to reason, when slavery was discussed before the war has been inherited by their descendants, when they discuss the race problem to day. The South is still laying all its troubles with colored people on the North, and nobody will ever be able to convince the South that it is being let alone, unless it is permitted to treat the colored people of that section with all the indignities which it wishes to inflict without being called to account.

Prior to the War of the Rebellion Mr. Lincoln declared that the ringleaders of the confederacy against the [government] had been assiduously debauching the mind of the Sou[th] for 30 years, inventing ingenious sophisms by which the right thinking people of that section were deceived and misled. In the war waged by the South upon the liberty of colored people since their eman[cipation], the same method has been pursued by the South for the past 20 years. By a little exaggeration of the colored man's vic[es], by a studied suppression of proofs of his unparraled advancement, by a judicious use of epithets, such as the scarecrow of social equality, the bugaboo of negro domination and others which mislead and poison the public mind, by a watchful and searching skepticism with respect to evidence in favor of the colored man and a convenient credulity with respect to every report or tradition which can be used to prove the colored man's depravity, the South has almost succeeded in convincing the world that it is a martyr and the colored man is a brute. The rapidity with which the South has poisoned the mind of the North against colored people and has succeeded in withdrawing from us the sympathy of those who were once our best friends and who openly boasted of that fact is a splendid tribute to the persuasiveness, persistency[,] plausibility and power of the South, while it resembles nothing so much as skillful trick of legerdemain.

In addition to the ingenious sophisms invented to [bend?] the public mind the traducers and detractors of my race do not hesitate to circulate falsehoods, whenever that will help carry their point. Among the slanders against the colored people of the United States none is more unfounded and more false than that lynching in the South is in the halls of Congress, in periodicals of all descriptions and in the press, distinguished southern gentlemen whose words carry great weight are continually declaring that assaults upon white women by colored men are the cause of most of the lynching in the South. And that, too, in face of the statistics compiled by white men which show that out of every hundred colored men who are lynched from 75 to 85 are not even accused of what is so falsely and maliciously called the usual crime. And among the 12 or 15 out of the hundred who are accu[s]ed many are absolutely innocent of the crime.

And the public mind is debauched to day as Abraham Lincoln declared it was before the war. [. . .] The President of this great Republic is told that the governors and citizens of certain States despise him and can never forgive him, because he said uncomplimentary things about the great and good president of the Confederacy. We are asked to pick and choose the choicest terms when referring to what Abraham Lincoln called that bastard Confederacy, the purpose and mission of which was to strangl[e] or shoot the Union to death. Shades of Grant and Lincoln and Sherman, and the thousands of brave soldiers who fell on the field of battle in your country's defense, where in the world are we, and to what other fatal error [d]o we tend? [. . .]

In conclusion, let me appeal to your patriotism and your [. . .] sense of right and justice to prevent, so far as in each one of you may lie, the destruction of the glorious temple of liberty which the Pilgrim fathers labored so earnestly to build and Abraham Lincoln strove so heroically to preserve.

Mary Church Terrell Papers, Microfilm Reel 21 (Washington, DC: Library of Congress).

## T. THOMAS FORTUNE, Address on Lincoln, Montclair, New Jersey, February 16, 1906

*Born a slave in Florida, Fortune (1856–1928) attended Howard University and settled in New York, where he worked in the newspaper business. From 1887 to 1907, he was an owner and editor of the* New York Age, *a weekly newspaper that Fortune made nationally prominent. Though he was a close associate of Booker T. Washington, Fortune steered an independent political course and helped found the National Afro-American League in 1890, which advocated civil and political rights. From 1923 until his death, he worked as an editor of the* Negro World, *the newspaper of Marcus Garvey's Universal Negro Improvement Association. The following address was given at a Lincoln Day event sponsored by the Literary Union of Montclair, New Jersey. In reviewing the major events in Lincoln's political life, Fortune emphasized Lincoln's consistent opposition to slavery and desire for compensated emancipation. While the Emancipation Proclamation was Lincoln's greatest achievement, Fortune made it clear that Lincoln adopted this policy as a war measure to preserve the Union only after other options had been attempted (AANB).*

---

Ninety-seven years ago a man was born who was to know sorrow and be acquainted with grief. Few men in modern or ancient times were born in lowlier surroundings or in more unpromising conditions than Abraham Lincoln, and no man reached higher station or exercised a larger or more wholesome or more masterful influence upon a great people. Indeed, he was a master influence of his times and helped to shape that history which had been culminating since the foundation of the Government. [...]

The magnificent educational advantages now within reach of nearly every boy in the Republic were absolutely beyond the reach of anyone a century ago. It was only the extreme rich who could afford to give their children the inestimable benefits of a liberal education. The poorest black boy in the South, indeed, enjoys better opportunities to secure such education than he who gave a race by the stroke of his pen their freedom and opportunity. If he possessed but few books it is true that he thoroughly mastered their contents. [...]

In 1831, when he became of age, he made another trip to New Orleans. [...] What he saw of slavery at New Orleans at this time, as upon his previous visit, intensified his antipathy to slavery and the manifest injustice of permitting the slave labor of the South to come into competition with the free labor of the North. [...]

Following the preconceptions gathered in his two trips to New Orleans and the impulse which moved him in 1837 as a member of the Illinois Legislature, in

Congress Mr. Lincoln voted to consider anti-slavery petitions, and on January 16th, 1849, he introduced a bill in the House of Representatives to abolish slavery in the District of Columbia. His measure carried with it compensation to slave owners. This was one of his hobbies. In the last agonies of the great Rebellion, when the assassin's dagger hung suspended over his head by a thread as slender as that which held the sword of Damocles, he still adhered to it. But the inevitable fiat of destiny brushed aside such rubbish, not as a matter of equity but of exigency, of war, of victory. He was eminently just in all his views. He would not rob the slave master to enrich the slave, nor would he rob the slave to enrich the slave master. He recognized that the institutions of slavery had been sanctioned by the Government and slavery binding and sacred. Although he abhorred the institution of slavery, he still had an Anglo-Saxon's reverence for plighted obligation, the inviolability of contract. [...]

With this mastery of law, with his philosophical intuitions, with his instinctive love of and sympathy with the broadest forms of freedom, Mr. Lincoln undoubtedly must have been convinced, as he expressed it years after, that this Republic could not exist half slave, half free. [...]

Mr. Lincoln was not only a politician but a statesman and a philosopher as well. He knew men, he revered the Constitution and human liberty and a Republican form of Government he believed to be inseparable. With Sumner, he believed that it was better to be in the right with a minority of one than with a majority of ten thousand. Here was the strength of the man, here is where he rose above common humanity, here is where he towered above the masses and became their leader, because he was greater than they. [...]

As the war progressed the sentiment in favor of the total extinction of slavery rose to a mighty clamor. In legislatures, in newspapers and from thousands of rostrums, and by petitions without number, demand was made upon the Government to free the slaves, but Mr. Lincoln seemed not to be moved. He prosecuted the suppression of the Rebellion under the greatest difficulties. He had enemies to the right of him, enemies to the left of him, enemies before him and enemies behind him. He was compelled to pursue a course which should satisfy all the conflicting forces which it was necessary for him to use. The employment of Afro-Americans in the war and the abolition of slavery were questions upon which the Nation had not fully determined. It was the purpose of his to move in advance of public opinion. The dangers were so imminent and portentous that he could only hope to control public sentiment in favor of the Government by interjecting no further element of discord into the situation. In dealing with these two questions he displayed the highest arts of statesmanship. He moved as public opinion justified him to move. When General Butler proposed to use slaves as contrabands of war he found himself restrained by the President. When General Fremont issued a provisional proclamation of emancipation he found it revoked by the superior authorities at Washington. When Horace Greeley, assuming the dictatorial voice of command common to journalists, demanded that the President take more advanced ground upon these questions, Mr. Lincoln told him bluntly that it was none of his purpose to preserve slavery or to destroy it; that it was his supreme purpose to save the Union; that if he could save the Union by freeing some of the slaves he would do it; that if he could save the Union by freeing all the slaves he would do it; but that, in any event, saving the Union was the main object he had in view.

The letter in which these sentiments occurred was dated August 22, 1862, and yet on January 1, 1863, the emancipation proclamation was issued. It falls to the lot of few men to have such a magnificent opportunity as Mr. Lincoln had to link his name so gloriously and so indelibly with freedom's holy cause. [...]

This proclamation, promulgated on the 1st of January, 1863, following fast upon the battle of Antietam, was the greatest achievement of a life which had been conspicuous for moral and intellectual excellence. It rounded out and emphasized the consistency of his statesmanship. As a modest legislator, standing upon the threshold of his career, he stood up in his place in the legislature of Illinois and opposed some pro-slavery resolutions introduced by a Democratic member; fifteen years after, as a member of Congress, he not only voted to receive anti-slavery petitions, but on the 16th of January, 1849, he introduced a bill in the House of Representatives to abolish slavery in the District of Columbia; fourteen years later, as President of the United States and as the crowning act of his political life, he issued the emancipation proclamation which broke the shackles of four million five hundred thousand fellow-creatures. [...]

In all his utterances, as in all his public conduct, Abraham Lincoln stood close to the pulsing heart of humanity, the great mass of mankind, whose lot it is to labor ceaselessly and to hope in vain for that relief which comes not. His sympathies took in all the Union. The equality of manhood was the chief foundation stone of his Democracy. The chief sentiment of his speech at Gettysburg was the touchstone of his patriotism. [...]

He was great in heart, great in head, great in soul. He made the world better for his living and the poorer for his dying. But that which he did for the Nation and for humanity will only pass away when men shall cease to reverence moral grandeur, to respect intellectual pre-eminence and to idolize a patriotism broad as Democracy, as comprehensive as Republicanism.

*New York Age* (New York), Feb. 22, 1906.

## REVERDY C. RANSOM, Address on Abraham Lincoln, circa 1907

*A native of Ohio, Ransom (1861–1959) became an AME minister after he graduated from Wilberforce University. In addition to serving as a pastor at churches in Pennsylvania, Ohio, Illinois, and New York, Ransom was an advocate for social justice and civil rights. He participated in the Afro-American Council, the Niagara Movement, and the NAACP, and organized institutions in Chicago and New York that served the underprivileged. One of the most prominent figures in the AME Church during the early twentieth century, Ransom served as editor of the AME Review and was elected a bishop in 1924. Internal evidence, such as the reference to the controversy between the San Francisco Board of Education and Japanese government, suggests that Ransom made the speech earlier than the February 1912 date indicated in the collection of Ransom's speeches from which it is taken. Like many, Ransom expressed his admiration for Lincoln and deemed him a hero worthy of immortality, yet contrary to those who criticized Lincoln for his rigid adherence to the Constitution and placing preservation of the Union above all else, Ransom deemed these Lincoln's most worthy attributes. Ransom's speech contributed to the ongoing debate over what Lincoln would have done regarding civil rights if he had lived to finish his second term in office and by extension what he would do if he were still living. This was becoming an increasingly vital aspect of his legacy especially as Southern states routinely violated the Fourteenth and Fifteenth Amendments and used Lincoln's words from the 1850s to justify racial segregation. Ransom argued that these amendments were natural products of the Emancipation Proclamation—a document firmly grounded in constitutional authority as a necessary war measure—and a person with Lincoln's convictions would not hesitate to enforce them* (AANB; Anthony A. Pinn, ed., Making the Gospel Plain [Harrisburg, PA: Trinity Press, 1999]).

The fame of Abraham Lincoln does not diminish, the outlines of his character do not grow dim. His figure looms large against the horizon of the multiplying years which forever widen the distance that separates him from us. [...]

Among the select company of our immortals, Lincoln has a proud pre-eminence. This nation founded by the sword of Washington, the statesmanship of Adams, Jefferson and their compeers, and the diplomacy of Franklin, was preserved to posterity by the sublime courage, wisdom and patriotism of Abraham Lincoln.

The carrying power of a man's life is the test of his greatness, and the true measure of the value of his service to mankind. The great majority of men are not perceptibly influential beyond the generation in which they lived and labored, some reach into the generation immediately succeeding, still fewer emerge from the mist of a century, only a few belong to the ages. In the world's pantheon of deathless names, Abraham Lincoln is written high among those who have achieved immortality.

The life of Lincoln is a source of perennial interest and inspiration. Biography, that most fascinating form of literature, has in him a subject more attractive than has been portrayed by the poets or dramatists of any age. The world will never tire of the life-story of the poor boy of the back-woods of Kentucky, the boatman on the Mississippi, the Black Hawk warrior, the rail splitter, the invincible antagonist of Stephen A. Douglas; the strength and calmness of that figure, who, with the marks of cheerful sadness stamped upon his visage, guided our ship of state in safety through the greatest crisis that ever came upon this or any other nation.

He believed in God. He bore himself aloft, amid friends and foes, with a spirit of patience and forgiveness akin to that of the Son of God.

In a little more than forty years after the passing of Lincoln are found men, even an occasional colored man, who seek to impugn the motives that prompted him to emancipate the slaves. These either misinterpret, or have never read his letter to Horace Greeley Aug. 22, 1862, in which occurs the following passage: "My paramount object is to save the Union, and not either to save or destroy slavery. If I could save the Union without freeing any slave, I would do it; if I could save it by freeing all the slaves, I would do it; and if I could do it by freeing some and leaving others alone, I would also do that."

Abraham Lincoln lived inside the boundaries of the Constitution. He did not chafe at their restraints; he sought neither to extend nor curtail them. He regarded his oath of office—to support and defend the constitution—as something sacred, a pledge to the American people to be kept, a vow to God not to be broken. [...]

Great as was the hatred of Lincoln for the institution of slavery, he loved the integrity of his country more. But the act of Emancipation once performed—"as a necessary war measure, for the suppression of actual armed rebellion against the authority and government of the United States"—he firmly stood for the maintenance of the freedom of the former slaves.

Despite much recent talk both in Congress and the press, as to who is the greatest friend the Negro ever had in the White House, let the truth of history enlighten us. Abraham Lincoln was the first, and, I had almost said, the last President who did not only preach, but practiced, "the square deal for every man." In his annual message of Dec. 6, 1864, President Lincoln said: "While I remain in my present position I shall not attempt to retract or modify the Emancipation Proclamation; nor shall I return to slavery any person who is free by the terms of that proclamation or by any of the acts of Congress. If the people should, by whatever mode or means, make it an executive duty to re-enslave such persons, another, and not I, must be their instrument to perform it." [...]

As Lincoln refused to retract or modify the Emancipation Proclamation, or an act of Congress, by the term of which any person then free should be returned to slavery, so no president in these reactionary times, should permit citizens having the right to vote under the Constitution to be disfranchised. For indeed this is a greater peril within the nation, than the threat of Japan over the California school question, is from without. Lincoln neither ignored nor temporized with an issue vital to the Constitution, but met it squarely, with dignified calmness and wisdom. It almost verges on the sacrilegious to compare present day methods of meeting executive responsibilities, with those which characterized the presidential career of Abraham Lincoln. [...]

Some of the men who sought to destroy this government are today busily engaged, both in and out of Congress, seeking to nullify or destroy the legitimate fruits of the war which Lincoln carried to a successful conclusion for the preservation of the Union. They and their Northern sympathizers see in the work of the period of reconstruction nothing but blunders, and a desire to punish and humiliate further the South; they see a great menace to the nation in the Fourteenth and Fifteenth Amendments. They assume to be able to read the mind of Mr. Lincoln and to tell how the great emancipator would have opposed the enfranchisement of the freedmen. Lincoln is quoted as being opposed to the subsequent legislation which is the legitimate offspring of the work to which he dedicated himself and for which he fell a martyr at the hands of an assassin. It is perhaps idle to speculate as to what Mr. Lincoln would have done had he occupied the presidential chair during the period of reconstruction. But knowing Mr. Lincoln's character as we do, we may be assured that he who stood with bared head for hours on Pennsylvania Avenue to pass in review the Negro regiments returning with the gleaming bayonets which had riveted forever the rebellious states into the fabric of the Union, would never have denied them the right of political sovereignty in a nation they had so valorously assisted in saving from destruction. If any set of men on the face of the earth had imbibed his spirit it was the enlightened statesmen who framed, and the patriotic citizens who approved the enactment of the Fourteenth and Fifteenth Amendments to the Constitution.

No event in American history since the foundations of the government were laid, is destined to wield such a powerful influence over the future of this nation as Lincoln's Emancipation. Its potentialities are limitless. Out of it have arisen problems that taxed to the utmost the statesmanship of the period of reconstruction; out of it have arisen questions which call for the wisdom of the best brain of the church and the school, the sociologist and the moral philosopher. There is to-day a disposition to ignore and avoid the questions which take their rise from this proclamation. But we had just as well seek to ignore the gathering force of a tornado, or the rumbling warnings of an earthquake, as to seek to avoid the resistless current of the events which flowed from that immortal document. The former slave and his descendants are free.

Reverdy C. Ransom, *The Spirit of Freedom and Justice: Orations and Speeches* (Nashville: A. M. E. Sunday School Union, AMEC Publishing House, 1926), 26–30.

## W. E. B. DU BOIS, Address Delivered at Hull House, Chicago, Illinois, February 12, 1907

*When Du Bois (1868–1913) delivered the following address on Lincoln's birthday at the Hull House in Chicago, he was a professor at Atlanta University and one of the principal leaders of the Niagara Movement that had been formed as an alternative to Booker T. Washington's accommodationism. Du Bois lauded Lincoln as the preserver of the country, and the man who extinguished enslavement even though he was not an abolitionist when he became president. Focusing on character rather than the details of Lincoln's biography, Du Bois made the case that his example illustrated how one born into society's mudsill class could become great and lead a country to greatness. According to Du Bois, Lincoln was both clear-sighted and capable of enormous growth. In Lincoln he saw a member of the authentic aristocracy—those who represented society at its best. As such, Lincoln set societal standards with his vision of soul; his understanding of himself; and his willingness to be a martyr. Lincoln thus epitomized the American ideal of a genuine aristocracy based on democratic ideas.*

---

It is to be my pleasure to speak to you about Abraham Lincoln. I do not want simply to recall to your minds the facts of his life, but rather to make you realize that broader fact of his character, and of the meaning of that character for our good in America today. For after all the thing that interests human beings and ought to interest them is not the place of a man's birth and death, and the little every day things he did, but rather his whole attitude towards life—what life meant to him and what he made out of life: because in the whirl and mystery of this world we ever strain our eyes for and seek an interpreter, some one who will tell us truly what living really is. You all know that Abraham Lincoln was a great American, that he was born 98 years ago today in the state of Kentucky—the son of a woman whose father had never married her mother and that he came in shame and frailty an illegitimate into the world. And this woman's boy worked with his hands, studied at night and became a lawyer with a little country practice. He went into politics, became known throughout this state and then in a crisis was suddenly called to be chief magistrate of the nation at the time of its greatest and most fearful need; there he became the man who preserved the American union, swept slavery from the United States and is looked upon as Lowell has said even today, as "the First American."

When now a man has accomplished so much has woven himself so boldly and wonderfully into the history of a great land, you and I who sit and look at life and try to interpret its meaning must ask first of all, What sort of man was he? And when we ask that we have an answer, in this case, which does not coincide with

many of our preconceived ideas. When we think of greatness, we think unconsciously of greatness in every thing, of lofty bearing, of wonderful training, of
high position, of great respect. But if we think of Abraham Lincoln we have few
or none of these things. He was to be sure a tall man, but he was not a man of
particularly impressive bearing; he was on the contrary, a homely man. We like
to use that adjective in speaking of him; a face hard and heavily carven, without
refining lines, with blunt, even harsh speech—a man unpolished in his ways,
whose clothes did not fit, whose personal appearance did not suggest neatness
nor refinement—a man who had in many ways something of vulgarity; a man
who was always telling jokes, many of which would not always pass muster in
good society. Not only that, but he was not what the world calls a pushing man.
He was a slow man—a dreamer—a man who liked to loaf around country stores,
looking for the unexpected thing. He was not a man that saved much. He was
always poor—poor when he began, poor during his life, poor when he died. And
then, climax of all, he was not a happy man. Sorrow was written across his face,
a sort of curious never absent melancholy. Jovial he was to be sure, at times, but
never light-hearted or glowing with the thought or experience of the happy life.

Now when we think and know a character of this sort, it cuts across many of
our most favored preconceptions. Here is a great man, one of the world's greatest men, who did not for instance belong to the best society—who did not have
the higher training—who did not pursue the busy life—who did not become
wealthy and happy. On the other hand there is no doubt of his greatness and that
this consisted of a few simple things. The first was his clear sightedness—the way
that he could brush aside cobwebs of convention and of difficulty and see with
perfect clearness the right and justice and logic of life. But he did not always see
the right at first, and in that very fact lies his second claim to greatness and that
is his capacity for growth. He was not a man that could boast that he had held his
opinions for twenty and thirty and forty years. There are some men that can boast
of this; and woe to them and woe to the world that holds them! If in the lapse of
ten or twenty years a man has not capacity for growth and has not received enough
of knowledge to make him change the most of his opinions, then he is indeed a
hopeless case. But Abraham Lincoln not only had this capacity for growth, this
capacity to receive the new knowledge as it came, but had it in so wonderful a
degree that he became a leader of men.

He was not for instance an abolitionist when he became president. He dis-
liked slavery, but like most of us in the case of disagreeable things he was willing,
if not eager, to let it severely alone. Once, however, it dawned on him that this
land could not exist half slave and half free and once he realized that his was the
power to break the paradox, then he turned suddenly and led the very leaders
into freedom; and finally, not only did he have this peculiar clearness of vision at
critical times, so that the truth grew and blossomed in his soul, but he had too a

certain simple greatness of energy and decision that enabled him to put his whole life and soul into realizing the truth when he once saw it, a perfect capacity for sacrifice.

Now when we have enumerated these things as characteristic of the greatness of Abraham Lincoln, then every one feels like asking, What do we care if he did not belong to the best society? So much the worse for the best if it could not receive and recognize this greatest American. What do we care if his clothes did not fit him, if he was awkward always and vulgar sometime, if after all he had that great soul that ruled above all awkwardness of body, and that perfect purity, that clearness of mind, to which the little vulgarities of his manners hung loosely as evidence that they did not belong there? What do we care if he was poor, so long as he was rich in the capacity for gaining knowledge? And if he had not what the world called an education, then the pity of it is that the world has not revised its attempts at human training. Thus our first thought is on seeing and hearing and learning of a man like Abraham Lincoln to have rather a mean contempt for a world that does not seem altogether responsible for him, which did not know him nor recognize him until he had become great and indeed until he was dead. And yet we must not pass too hurried judgment on the world; we must remember that the world is groping, painfully groping, after certain great ideals and that when the ideal itself suddenly flashes across the sky it may not recognize it because of the very pain of its own struggle. But one thing it must do, watching the ideal when it comes to know it and watching its own struggle it must realize how far behind we are in our struggles toward the best and what it is that is wrong with our ideals. Therefore as I have said, I want to consider the character of Abraham Lincoln and to consider the ideals that we have here in America and ask what it is in Lincoln's life and character that may teach us to have better and greater and more successful ideals. That brings me to say that, after all, the things for which we strive and upon which we pour a certain contempt now and then because our striving seems so vain, are the things toward which every human society must strive.

I have said that Abraham Lincoln never belonged to the best society. Why the impatient ones ask insistently: What kind of a world is it whose best reject the best—who receive King Leopold of Belgium and reject Abraham Lincoln? The reply is: If the best society does this the fault is not solely with them; it lies heavily on you and on me. When the social elect pour contempt upon your effort and upon my effort, upon the greatness of Socrates and Jesus Christ, upon the greatness of Frederick Douglass and Abraham Lincoln for *that very reason* we must not pour contempt upon the ideal of a *best* in society. We must simply say that we have not yet found the right criterian, we have not yet risen to that great view which enables us to make in our social world a real aristocracy. [ . . . ]

Judged by his ancestors Abraham Lincoln had a chance in the world, only in the 19th century. If he had lived probably in any century before that, the Door of

Opportunity would have been miserably closed in his face; not because of lack of desert on his part, but simply because his father and his mother, his grandfather and grandmother were not people of distinction or indeed of any great worth. In this respect, therefore, today we live in a new century and in a new land. We need to congratulate ourselves that through pain and through blood and terrible striving, the world has at last come to a time when it is willing to accept a man upon his merit even though he did not have a distinguished father or grandfather—even though his mother was nameless! [. . .] But if we have reached this vantage ground where we can say: "Look to the man and his deeds and not to somebody else, in judging him," how necessary it is that we should fight to keep this advantage open to the world, to our brothers and to our sisters. And yet there are tendencies against which I warn you; there are times coming even here in the Twentieth century, when if an Abraham Lincoln should rise in the United States and if he should be a Jew in race or a Japanese in color, or a Negro in descent, that he would be judged not by the greatness of his soul or the clearness of his vision or the saneness of his judgments, but that his soul would be pressed and shut out of the republic of the civilized, simply because of his race or his color or the previous life of his ancestors. So that today we are fighting to leave the path open, the Door of Opportunity wide for men who come of humble birth and humble beginning. But this is not all. The choice of the chosen is ours. If we were today then choosing those persons who should represent our best society, we think we would choose at least in theory men like Abraham Lincoln and Benjamin Franklin and Alexander Hamilton. [. . .] The real difficulty then lies with us. If we really believe men of the type of Abraham Lincoln to be the best sort of men for this world, then our best society would by our own vote and judgment hold such men. But it is because of our heart of hearts we never have reached the height of even appreciating a character like Lincoln's that we give this form of aristocracy to those persons who represent in their lives that which we really worship. [. . .]

In the second place the thing that is perhaps the most striking about Abraham Lincoln and the thing which puzzles us most is the fact that while he was an uneducated man he was yet a man of wonderful training. [. . .] There again our first thought is to pour contempt upon education and systems of education and to say that Abraham Lincoln stands as a living proof of the futility of trying to do in schools what schools cannot do. Abraham Lincoln got his education, where? He got it in his work; he got it in his dreaming; he got it in his reading. He was not a college man; he was not a high school graduate; he was, as I have said, not what you call today an educated man. Yet we study some of his wonderful speeches as specimens of the most exquisite English. We follow his foresight as giving us examples of the best thinking and we look upon his character as one of the simplest and purest which the world has known. Now this matter of training is of especial interest to us. Many of you here are waiting for the finishing of your life's training; others are hesitating as to how to train boys and girls; are wanting so far as possible to give them the correct vision of life and they wonder how it shall be done. On the other hand we must of course recognize at once that simply because our schools do not turn out men of peculiar facility of mind and balance of training which Abraham Lincoln had, that does not necessarily mean that they are a failure. But on the other hand we must ask ourselves are our schools conducted to give to the world such kind of minds in any degree as Lincoln possessed. Young men and women who are able to see clearly the truth of life because in the first place they have had experience in clearness of thought and because in the second place they know something of what the world has thought.

Here again the teaching of Lincoln's life ought to impress us with the fact that it is thinking itself and not methods of thought—it is the souls of children and not the bricks of school houses that make the true measure of education. And the more we consider this, the more we remember that boys and girls who come through our schools too often face the world befuddled and bewildered with anything but clear thinking, with anything but accurate knowledge. Why? Some would have us think that our methods are bad or our teachers unlearned, and often there is some thing of truth in this. But the main difficulty—a difficulty against which Lincoln warns us in words and deed is our own hurry and rush. We seek to turn out the finished article in fully-trained boys as we turn out so much cloth. America today stands for hurrying and rush and work. We call ourselves a hustling nation. We do or we try to do a great deal more in a day than the average person in other lands, in other ages have done. But when we look at the life of this first American we see something that gives us pause. Why was it that Lincoln thought so clearly? It was first of all, because he *thought* and because he gave himself leisure to think. Many are the stories that they tell of him stretched out doing nothing, loafing here and there, whittling a stick, looking leisurely at the world. He *thought*. And that is one thing that the average American today does not do. That is one thing we do not do in our schools. The poor, hurried, worried children get no time to think, get no time to get acquainted with themselves. We then, as Americans, must take pattern of Lincoln and remember that before all, we must get acquainted with ourselves. [...] Abraham Lincoln's life gives us little sense of hurry. And yet Lincoln, as the world has known him, has been one of the world's great workers. And the reason is clear; if the human soul gets time to think and expand how much better it can work. Not that it always will work; many a man of the Lincoln type has loafed and dreamed his life away without ever putting it to the test of deeds. Many a nation has had the leisure that America lacks and squandered it. [...]

Now it is often said that if things were balanced in this world and were as they ought to be, that there would be greatly increased happiness. And yet I do not doubt that many men looking upon that sorrow carven face of Abraham Lincoln and remembering how hard he toiled to be a man and how great a man he made, will say, If such a man had such a life of grief and sorrow, what is the use of trying? Of the sorrows that Abraham Lincoln reaped there is no doubt. First there was the sorrow of his narrow and sordid youthful surroundings; then there was the sorrow of political defeat; after that came the sorrow of misapprehension; of being half-buried, of being patronized by men whose superior he was and knew he was. Then there was the sorrow of responsibility; if anything went wrong during those fearful years of war and turmoil, Abraham Lincoln was responsible for it; if anything went right, somebody else reaped the laurels and the praise. And then above all, there was the lonely sorrow of the lonely soul sitting above the world without companionship, little understood, who must suffer and be silent. He did not even have the solace of a wife who knew and sympathized with his great soul. His family life was not what we like to picture as ideal family life. He was alone, peculiarly alone. Is this then the rightful reward of the life of a man who came up in spite of adversity, who worked his way through the turmoil of life and did his duty? There are people who say, Yes, we ought to be glad to suffer for the good; but it seems to me that that is the wrong interpretation to put upon a life of this sort. [ . . . ]

To Abraham Lincoln the voice came. He was a martyr not so much in his death as in his life. It was in his life that he was crucified for the good.

We have then learned in the life of Abraham Lincoln the finer ideals of what is best in society, a clearer knowledge of the need of time in education, and a realization of the fact that life cannot be all hurry and work. We must have the leisure to know and feel, to realize our own selves. We have learned that wealth does not necessarily give leisure nor work happiness, but that while out of wealth and work must come happiness to the mass, it is often at the sacrifice of the life and well-being of single great individuals who are willing to offer themselves for the good of the world. If this is the meaning of the life of Abraham Lincoln what particular duty lies before us today? Here we are representing many lands and many nations coming from all the ends of the earth, showing forth in our faces, our life and thought the history of all that mass of men what make up human life today. We have come to a land of ideals, and we are here because of these ideals, and those ideals had their finest fruition and greatest presentation in the life and character of Abraham Lincoln. And if therefore, we have seen and known in America something to love and live for, then we must try and see that the ideals which Abraham Lincoln typified, the ideals on which America was founded be not lowered on account of us, suffer in no way because of our neglect, but by our coming and our being here, by our joint heritage in this vast and wonderful country, these ideals must grow greater and purer and better. Perhaps few of you realize that today the things for which Abraham Lincoln stood are as I have said in danger. In the first place the very type of man that he was, the simple, poorly bred, vulgar, but honest and great-hearted man is passing from the American stage. We have in his stead a man far better in looks, nicer, sleeker, shrewder, richer. Not only that, but we have growing up in this country, slowly, surely the idea that the world is not for everybody; that the world and its opportunities belong to a certain class of favorite individuals and while the class of the claimants today in America is still recognized as being much larger than the people of the Middle Age thought or the people of some European lands think, yet nevertheless it is a restricted class to which all human beings are not permitted. Then too, there is growing up in America the idea that we must be careful how we train children, that if their heritage is to be narrow and not the full, free, broad heritage toward which Abraham Lincoln looked they must be trained for their narrow heritage; that it is the business of most people to work and not to think and therefore we must make little provision for their thinking, and that above all, we must go on accumulating and heaping up wealth because the greatness of America lies in its richness. Now unless you and I are very careful we will find ourselves carried away by this philosophy and in being carried away we shall lose our appreciation for a man like Abraham Lincoln. Let us, therefore, set our faces like flint against the new-old growing but the dangerous philosophy. Let us insist that "All men are created free and equal." Let us say that the best society of America, no matter what the daily newspapers may tell us, consists of that company of the educated and the thoughtful and the true who are trying to make the world better. That unto all human souls the door of training must be opened just as far as the toil for bread and butter will allow, and that the accumulation of wealth in America and the deterioration of soul that goes with it, far from measuring our greatness, measures our shame. It is the most sinister thing that is happening today. I would leave with you then this thought: Thinking of the great man who nearly a century ago was born in circumstances as humble as any of ours, let us emulate his example, so far as we may with our narrow gifts, let us keep his ideals and let us make America still a land where men like Abraham Lincoln may flourish and be recognized—a land of opportunity and of opportunity not simply to the rich, but to the poor, not simply to the Gentile, but to the Jew, not simply to the white, but to the black, a land of opportunity for *all men*, and for all women, too.

W. E. B. Du Bois, "Abraham Lincoln," *Voice of the Negro* 4, no. 6 (June 1907): 242–247.

## WILLIAM MONROE TROTTER on Commemorating the Lincoln Centennial, January 18, 1908

*A native of Ohio, Trotter (1872–1934) was the son of a Civil War veteran and a graduate of Harvard University. Trotter was editor and publisher of* The Guardian, *a seminal newspaper in Boston that helped further his activism for equal rights. A critic of Booker T. Washington's accommodationist approach, Trotter helped found the Niagara Movement and the National Equal Rights League. Like Frederick Douglass and others before him, Trotter realized the important connection between African American commemoration of Lincoln and advancing the cause of civil rights. In this editorial, Trotter indicated his support for a bill in the Massachusetts legislature to celebrate the Lincoln centennial. While noting that African Americans had special reasons for honoring Lincoln, Trotter did not hesitate to mention Lincoln's alleged objection to racial equality. Nonetheless, he urged that the South's effort to claim Lincoln be resisted, so that he be remembered for his advances toward recognizing Black citizenship. Trotter is perhaps best known for his campaign against the film,* The Birth of a Nation, *and for a confrontational meeting at the White House with President Woodrow Wilson, where Trotter strenuously objected to Wilson's policy of segregating federal employees (ANB).*

---

The bill of Rep. Mock for a state celebration of the centennial of Abraham Lincoln is a good one, and one which should receive the support of every patriotic citizen. The Colored citizens, especially should be forward in urging its passage. This is not because they are Colored, but because President Lincoln's work had to do with the abolition of the slavery which was practiced against Colored people. A still stronger reason is that celebrations for such a man as Lincoln can be of benefit to the cause of freedom today, a cause in which the Colored citizen is especially interested by reason of the denial of equal citizenship to them more than to any other class.

We are not unmindful of the compromise position Lincoln took as to saving the Union with slavery if necessary or if possible even. We have in mind the claim he was against the equality of the races. But since the white south seeks to quote Lincoln as upholding them, since he is regarded in the north as a great and noble man and therefore his views are influential, that gives an additional reason why we should claim him as for equality of citizenship for the Colored American. There are substantial grounds for doing so and it is unwise to give the south any advantage. Then by manifesting a strong interest in a public manner for the passage of the bill it will be the more easy to have the exercises to recognize Lincoln's work for freedom, and to secure decent recognition of Colored citizens OF THIS STATE in the exercises.

Editorial on the celebration of Lincoln's birthday in "Proposed Mass. Lincoln Centennial," The *Guardian* (Boston), Jan. 18, 1908.

## MAUDE K. GRIFFIN, "Lincoln—Man of Many Sides," April 1908

*A resident of New York City, Griffin (fl. 1902–1909) contributed fiction and non-fiction pieces to the* Colored American Magazine *and was active in literary and charitable organizations, including a nursery for Black children that she helped found. Focusing on Lincoln's character, Griffin details several attributes worthy of both adulation and emulation. While looking forward to the upcoming Lincoln centennial and the role African Americans should have in it, Griffin believed Lincoln was a figure of such transcendent greatness that rather than celebrate him on a single day, he was worthy of study and remembrance each day.*

No name in history has a greater hold upon the confidence and hearts of the American people than that of Abraham Lincoln. No name so perfectly combines the highest principles of our citizenship. [ . . . ] It is undeniably true that the best achievements of all administrations combined since the day of Lincoln, have set no standard of national development higher than that indicated by his teachings and his ideals.

It is a glowing tribute to the character of the great American "Man of Sorrows" that his fame grows greater as time lengthens the distance between his day and ours. The nation not only reveres his memory, it loves the man. It ought not be extravagant to say that the time will come when no particular day shall mark the celebration of his birth and achievements. It would better typify our patriotism if every day American children might study in schoolrooms the lofty character of Lincoln and be inspired by it. [ . . . ]

One cannot call the roll of imperial greatness without mentioning the name of Abraham Lincoln. He was a great soul and it might better be said of him than of Cromwell: "He was a man for all ages to admire and honor in proud remembrance."

He was neither well nor greatly born; tradition even has it that he came from that class known in the South as "poor whites," though this is promptly listed with the legion wrongs of history. Lincoln himself was not ashamed of his humble birth; the memory of it is lost in the years of immeasurable greatness; it has endeared him to, rather than estranged him from the hearts of the people whom he sought to serve.

The career of the man embodies a singular study in versatility. He was a farmer, soldier, lawyer, orator, statesman, man. By circumstance he was a farmer, a calling that made him representative of the land of his nativity. Patriotism made him a soldier, and elective training developed him into a lawyer-orator-statesman. By Providence and fealty to duty he was liberator of a race, savior of a republic and martyr.

Lincoln's successes in life were of his own making, hence there is none who can pluck a laurel from his brow or lessen the measure of his fame. The indomitable will that overcame the drawbacks of obscurity and debt in the beginning of his public career made him a stranger to discouragement in the violent political and personal struggles of after years, though his opponents in most instances were better and more favorably known than himself. There were times when even his warmest supporters and closest friends were doubtful of his ability and fearful of his judgment, but he held them by his simplicity and sincerity and was always able to prove himself worthy of their confidence.

His service in the army was of short duration, but his experience in the Black Hawk war showed him a genius of originality and organization. In war he was fearless. In peace, when the responsibilities of the Government were upon him and the gloom blackest, he was heedless of danger where right was involved. He worked silently and persistently, never losing faith, but fighting to win.

What visions of greatness, power and fame the word statesmanship inspires! yet, how quietly Lincoln qualifies himself for this honor by his ability to discover the trend of events and shape the course of national affairs in harmony therewith. Abraham Lincoln was pre-eminently a statesman. He believed in and unflinchingly advocated the preservation of the Union and the abolition of the great "moral, social and political wrong" of slavery. A difference of opinion by those whose counsel he respected most never altered a deep-rooted conviction and he never looked upon the past with regret nor to the future with misgivings. When his position is considered and the odds against which he struggled numbered, it is faint praise to say that no nation has produced a man of more astute statesmanship than Lincoln. He practiced none of the questionable diplomacies too frequently associated with the politics of our time. He loved the truth, lived it and by its power gained his conquests.

And withal he was a man—gentle, tender and true. He loved humor and was himself a wit. Indeed the world will never exhaust its fund of "Lincoln stories." He could frequently bring himself to make a joke at the expense of a friend. But it was impossible for him to wound the feelings of anyone; if to lighten the heart of even a little child required a personal sacrifice, this he gladly made, gladly and without any show of condescension. He had no little lordiness, but possessed the dignified demeanor of manhood that is nobler than genius. Typifying the highest and best in American development, he started humbly and grew grandly, rising not above his place but to it.

Next year marks the centennial of Lincoln's birth. Certainly there is not one colored American in this broad land who will not enter into the spirit of the proposed celebration with a spirit of tenderest reverence and most intense patriotism.

*Colored American Magazine* 14, no. 4 (April 1908): 188–89.

## HIGHTOWER T. KEALING, "Lincoln's Birthday—The Great American Day," January 1909

*A native of Texas, Kealing (1859–1918) was educated at Straight University and Tabor College. He worked as a school principal prior to being appointed editor of the A. M. E.* Church Review *in 1896. The official journal of the African Methodist Episcopal Church, the A. M. E.* Church Review *began publication as a quarterly in 1884. As the nation prepared to mark the centennial of Lincoln's birth, Kealing published an editorial that proclaimed the great importance of this day by likening it to a secular Christmas and the "New Year's Day of American liberty." For Kealing, Lincoln's crowning achievement was the destruction of slavery, yet he predicted it would require another hundred years for the wounds from this sin to heal. While the landscape was already dotted with several monuments to Lincoln, Kealing called for a national monument in his memory to be erected in Richmond, Virginia—the last city outside of Washington that he visited and where he demonstrated his willingness to treat the defeated rebels as erring members of the family. In 1910, Kealing resigned as editor and accepted the presidency of Western College in Quindaro, Kansas, where he remained until his death ("A Race Leader Gone,"* Kansas City Sun, *March 2, 1918).*

---

Next month (February) marks the anniversary of the birth of Abraham Lincoln.

It is a sacred day—a kind of secular Christmas which calls not for gifts of toys, but for devout thanksgiving to God that the epochal man in American history was the bestower, under God, of the greatest of all gifts to man—freedom.

Slavery wronged the Negro in that it took from him the commonest right belonging to humanity—equality of opportunity to develop his individual soul powers and live his own responsible life; it wronged the white South in that it diverted the energy belonging to self-development into holding another down, with the consequent lagging in material as well as spiritual growth; it wronged the whole nation in that it stultified it and made it ridiculous in putting forth claims to being the home of the oppressed and the nursery of freedom while men groaned in chains over its fairest section.

Slavery is dead, thank God; but like any other case of violation of Divine law we do not get rid of the penalty immediately by ceasing the practice. It will take a hundred years more before this land will have recovered from the effects of its great sin—a hundred years of race suspicion, of inharmony and the sequelae of political injustice and chicanery that always follow distortion of moral perception and the sin of degrading another man. [. . .]

Abraham Lincoln comes as near being America's patron saint as a Protestant country can have. The whole nation now pedestals him, even those who once pilloried him. He is great in the prescience which saw and the prevision which prepared for destroying the greatest barrier to realizing our declared ideal; he is great in withstanding a great sin without hating the sinner; he is great in the patience which made him bide his time and seek constitutional methods of relief before resorting to force; he is great in finding ways to do the needed thing even against the mummified inertness of great predecessors who had declared that this nation had no power of self-defense in the face of progressing disintegration.

There are Lincoln monuments many—one of the most impressive we saw in Edinburgh, Scotland—but the real national monument has yet to be erected and when it is, it will be in Richmond, Virginia, where the tired face of the noble Preventer of national suicide was last seen outside of Washington as he showed himself to the people that they might see that his had been the chastisement of an elder brother.

Let February be the beginning of the American year; let February 22 be remembered with acclaim while all faces turn with pride toward Mount Vernon; but let February 12 be the New Year's Day of American liberty and let Kentucky and Illinois, mother and foster mother, respectively, lift their proud faces to receive the gratulations of their sisters who count them blessed for the kind of dust that entered into the son they nurtured.

*A. M. E. Church Review* 25, no. 3 (January 1909): 335–336.

## SILAS X. FLOYD, Address at Emancipation Day Celebration in Augusta, Georgia, January 1, 1909

*A native of Augusta, Georgia, Floyd (1869–1923) was a graduate of Atlanta University, children's book author, poet, Baptist minister, and school principal when he delivered the following address at Augusta's Emancipation Day celebration. Fearing that an increasing number of African Americans preferred to forget their past and criticize Lincoln, Floyd argued for the importance of celebrating Emancipation Day and honoring Lincoln. While Lincoln came from humble origins and possessed common sense rather than a towering intellect, Floyd believed his work in freeing the slaves and preserving the Union made him nothing less than the second greatest person in history after Jesus Christ. In reflecting on the status of African Americans at the centennial of Lincoln's birth, Floyd hoped that God would soon send someone to finish Lincoln's work (AANB).*

———————

The day we celebrate is the most glorious day in American history. No date in the annals of America outshines or can outshine January 1, 1863; and no event in the life of the American Republic overshadows or can overshadow the issuing of Abraham Lincoln's immortal edict of emancipation. Two years after issuing the Proclamation Lincoln himself said concerning it that it was the central act of his administration and the greatest event of the nineteenth century.

Of course, my fellow citizens, there are other days in our national history that are significant and that are worthy of patriotic celebration; as, for example, Independence Day, Washington's birthday, Lincoln's Birthday, Forefather's Day, and other similar days; but in my judgment, the grandest day in American history is Emancipation Day. Certainly, so far as the negroes in America are concerned, no day holds or ought to hold a higher place in their hearts.

But—and I regret to say it—there are some colored people who know so little what important factors tradition and sentiment are in the lives and characters of races and individuals that they are not willing to enter heartily into the observance of Emancipation Day. Many of our own race affirm that we have no right to celebrate this day, while others declare that we ought to try to forget that our race was once enslaved in this country. Did you ever see, my friends, a Confederate veteran who desired to forget that he once wore the grey, or who was unwilling to teach his children that he once proudly marched in battle behind Lee and Gord[o]n, behind Jackson and Johnston? Did you ever hear of a Union soldier who was ashamed of the part which he took in the Great war, or who felt humiliated to tell his children about it? And don't you remember that, when the children of Israel under the matchless leadership of Moses were on the march from Egypt, the home of their servitude, to Can[aa]n, the Land of Promise—don't you remember that, after they had safely crossed the Red Sea, the Lord commanded them to set up memorial stones by which the event should be remembered with joy in all time to come by themselves and their children? And yet some of the negroes wish to forget all about slavery—all about the past—and stoutly maintain that we have no right to be celebrating each year the day that brought freedom to our race. I do not know what you think or how you feel concerning these members of our *race*, and I beg that you will pardon me for not saying publicly what I think of them; but I will say, on the broad and general proposition as to the observance of this day, I will say—and I say it out of a full and honest heart—may God forget my people when they forget this day.

Today, with your kind permission, I shall talk to you about Abraham Lincoln. It is fit and proper on this forty-sixth anniversary of the issuing of the emancipation proclamation that we should discuss the life and character of Abraham Lincoln, because this year marks the one hundredth anniversary of the great Emancipator's birth.

I regret to say that there are some colored people here and there who do not revere the memory of Abraham Lincoln as they should; who feel that, after all, Lincoln was not so great a friend of the negro; that he loved the Union more than he did the race; and that he finally freed the colored people not so much because of love in his heart but only as a fit and necessary war measure. Ah, me! that, forty and six years after Lincoln's death, with all the history of those terrible times spread out before us like an open book, and with ample time for calm, deliberate and dispassionate judgment—Ah, me! that it should be necessary before an audience of negro Americans to defend the memory of Abraham Lincoln! It is no reflection upon Mr Lincoln's good name that this happens to be true, but it is only another evidence of the perversity of human nature. Lincoln was assailed enough in his life-time—assailed on your account and on mine—Lincoln was assailed enough in his life-time for empty headed negroes to spare him from denunciation now that he has entered into the grave. I say "empty-headed" advisedly, for most of the adverse criticism of Abraham Lincoln that we hear from a few negroes in these days and times, results from emptiness—ignorance [. . .].

Most of the biographers of Abraham Lincoln agree in saying that Abraham Lincoln was not an able man intellectually. It is safe to say that in intellect he was nothing more than the average American in the walk of life in which the nation found him. Of course he had a perfect comprehension of the leading principles of constitutional government; and then he could talk well—he had a homely, straight forward mode of reasoning; he posses[sed] considerable aptness without elegance of expression; he had a marked readiness of illustrations; and he also had quick intuitions that gave the element of shrewdness. But there was nothing in his intellect that eminently distinguished him. Now what did this man do? [. . .] He presided over and guided to a successful issue [the] most gigantic national struggle that the history of the world records. He called to his aid the best men of the time—the strongest men, the most intellectual men, without a jealous thought that they might overshadow him. He managed to control their jealousies of each other and compelled them to work harmoniously. He sifted out from weak and infected material men worthy to command our armies and lead them to victory. He harmonized conflicting claims[,] interests and policies, national and international, and in four years time absolutely annihilated the military power of a rebellion that was thirty years in preparation and that had in its armies the whole military population of a third of the Republic and at its back the entire resources of the men in arms and the producing power of 4,000,000 slaves. The destruction of the military power of the rebellion was Abraham Lincoln's special work. This work he did so thoroughly that no chief magistrate for centuries to come will be called upon to repeat the process. He found the nation weak and tottering to destructi[o]n. He left it strong, feared and respected by all the nations of the world.

And in addition to all this, he brought emancipation to 4,000,000 negro slaves. If he had done no more than this, he would have secured for himself the fairest fame it has ever been the fortune of a good man to win. To be regarded and remembered through all coming time as the Liberator of a race; to have one's name embalmed in the memory of an enfranchised people and associated with every blessing they enjoy and every good they may achieve, is a better fame than the proudest conqueror can boast.

The destruction of the rebellion and the destruction of slavery are the two great achievements on which the fame of Abraham Lincoln will rest in history; but no man will write the history of these achievements justly who shall not reveal the nature of the power by which they were wrought out. The history which shall fail to show the superiority of the wisdom of an honest, humble Christian heart over commanding and cultured intellect will be a graceless libel on Abraham Lincoln's fame. [...] Abraham Lincoln was not a preeminently intellectual man, but he was preeminently a man with an humble Christian heart—and the things that Lincoln did he was enabled to do not because he was a man of commanding intellect but because he had common sense, because he was honest, and because above all he was willing to listen to and to be guided by the still small voice of God. In all ages, in all times, and among all people, God Almighty has always raised up men to work His will and to bring to pass his wondrous plans for the amelioration of mankind. [...] Tried by this doctrine of divine inspiration where in all the world shall we find an example so impressive as Abraham Lincoln[?] He was born as lowly as the son of God, in a hovel; reared in squalor and penury, with no gleam of light or fair surroundings; without name or fame or official training; snatched from obscurity late in life; raised to supreme command at a supreme moment; and intrusted with the destiny of a nation. The great leaders of his party were made to stand aside, the most experienced and accomplished public men of the day were compelled to take back seats—were sent to the rear, while this fantastic figure was led by unseen hands to the front and given the reins of power[.] During four years, carrying with them such a weight of responsibility as the world never witnessed before, he filled satisfactorily—filled as possibly no other man of the time could have filled—the vast space allotted to him in the eyes and actions of mankind. How did he do it? He was inspired of God. From first to last Abraham Lincoln was sent of God, baffling the wit of man to fathom, defeating the machinations of the world, the flesh and the devil, until his work was done, and then he passed from the scene as mysteriously as he had come upon it. And he was not—for God took him! When we take into consideration all the things that he said and all the things that he did—when we recall how wise he was, how merciful, how just, how patient, how forgiving, how pure, how kind and loving he was, and how few mistakes of judgment he made—and then when we think of his origin—how lowly it was—and of his training—what little promise of distinction or greatness it gave—and then when we remember how he safely guided the old Ship of State safely through deep waters and through a very storm of hell, and righted her at last in the old current of the Union with all of her colors still flying, and how he brought light and liberty to four million slaves—when we take into consideration all these things, we are compelled to say that, next to Jesus Christ, Abraham Lincoln was the greatest and best man that the world has ever known. Washington, Gladstone, Bismar[c]k, Cromwell, William of Orange, Napoleon Bonaparte, Julius Caesar—all these, it is possible to measure by ordinary standards or rules of greatness; but Abraham Lincoln was in a class by himself; he was the most individual man the world has ever seen, and the best example, outside of Holy Writ, of a man divinely inspired. [ . . . ]

On the 22nd of July, 1862, Lincoln sent word to the members of his cabinet that he wished to see them. [ . . . ] Mr. Lincoln opened a drawer, took out a paper and said: "gentlemen, I have called you together to notify you what I have determined to do. I want no advice. Nothing can change my mind." He then read the proclamation of Emancipation. With a few minor additions to the document, and with the decision on a part of the cabinet that the president would wait for a victory in the field before giving it to the world, the meeting was over, and the members went their way. [ . . . ] On the 22nd of August of the same year—after Lincoln wrote his celebrated letter to Horace Greeley, in which he stated that his object was to save the Union[,] that he would save it with slavery if he could; that if it was necessary to destroy slavery in order to save the Union, he would; in other words, he would do what was necessary to save the Union. This letter disheartened, to a great degree, thousands and millions of the friends of freedom. They felt that Mr. Lincoln had not attained the moral height upon which they supposed he stood. And yet, when that letter was written, the Emancipation proclamation was in his hands and had been for thirty days, waiting only a favorable opportunity to give it to the world.

Thus far, my fellow-citizens, I have shown you that Abraham Lincoln was like Jesus Christ both in his birth and in his life; and I flatter myself by saying that the parallel is so plain that no one can fail to see it. It only remains for me to show that Abraham Lincoln was like Jesus Christ in his death. You will remember that Jesus Christ was ["]a man of sorrows and acquainted with grief." You know full well that his public ministry was one of toil and trial. He bore the world's burdens; he was touched by the world's sorrows; and he suffered and died for the sins of the world. [ . . . ] I am not appealing to any superstiti[o]us feeling, nor drawing an irreverent comparison. I am merely noting a remarkable coincidence. President Lincoln took the helm of state amid the storms of war. For four years he suffered the anguish his situation imposed; he mourned with the mourners; and he wept and prayed for the deliverance of his people. But finally on a bright Sabbath morning in April, 1865, Lee surrendered the rebel hosts to Lincoln's captain and the war ended. The news flew on the wings of lightning all over the land. It was a day or national rejoicing—the first really happy day of the loyal people of America in four long years. Now this first happy day for the nation—the first really happy day in President Lincoln's whole official life chanced to fall on the "Palm Sunday" of 1865. The next Friday—"Good Friday"—Lincoln was shot! Mere coincident; mere accident; no—no don't talk such nonsense to me. No other explanation is possible or plausible, when we undertake to speak of Abraham Lincoln's life than to say that he was the sent of God; and, when we think of his death, which came at the apex of his fame in five short days after he had accomplished the thing where unto God had called him, we can only say that we believe that God reserved that kind of death for him in order that he, like the Master, might wear throughout unending eternity a martyr's crown.

Jesus died for the sins of the world. Lincoln died for the sins of the American nation. And of him it may be truly said as was of Jesus, "He was wounded for our transgressions, he was bruised for iniquities; and with his st[r]ipes we are healed.["] [. . .]

I've hope for the future of my race in this country because I believe that underneath us are the everlasting arms of the great Jehovah. God who raised up Lincoln will easily raise up others in his own time and in his own way to defeat the plots and plans of the enemy and finish the great work which Lincoln began when he penned under divine inspiration. Let us falter not; let us fear not. God is in heaven and all is well.

And now I have done. What more need be said, what more could be said, on this holy, happy day? I ask you two questions in closing. In view of what he was and in view of what he did, I ask you how can any man, white or black North or South, hate the name of Abraham Lincoln? And in view of what he was and what he did for the colored people, I ask you how can any colored people refuse his homage to Abraham Lincoln's memory[?] And now as I take leave of you my prayer for you, for myself and for my race is that God may make us worthy of the memory of Abraham Lincoln.

*Georgia Baptist* (Augusta), Jan. 7, 1909.


## GEORGE L. KNOX, "Celebrating in Memory of Lincoln," January 2, 1909

*Born a slave in Tennessee, Knox (1841–1927) moved to Indiana after the Civil War and prospered first as a barber and later as an owner and manager of barbershops in Indianapolis. He was active in Republican politics and acquired* the Freeman *in 1892. As managing editor and publisher, Knox made the* Freeman *one of the country's most prominent and highly regarded Black newspapers. Knox worried that African Americans were becoming forgetful about the past, largely out of a desire to put the memory of slavery behind them. As the*

*nation prepared to celebrate the centennial of Lincoln's birth, he argued that*
*Lincoln must be remembered and celebrated, regardless of what may or may*
*not have motivated him to issue the Emancipation Proclamation. Knox used*
*allusions to the Bible and popular poems by Oliver Goldsmith ("The Deserted*
*Village") and Leigh Hunt ("Abou Ben Adhem") to help make the case that*
*Lincoln and African Americans were so interconnected that it was imperative*
*to craft a usable past by appropriating Lincoln's image ("George L. Knox,"*
Indianapolis Recorder, *Sept. 3, 1927; Willard B. Gatewood Jr., ed.,* Slave and
Freeman: The Autobiography of George L. Knox *[Lexington: University*
*Press of Kentucky, 1979]).*

---

September or January will do, just so we remember the immortal emancipation. In the years gone by there was a tendency to get away from the fact of slavery.
Abraham Lincoln, the civil war and the rest of it were "neglected to the limbo of
forgotten things." The thoughtful had begun to fear for his memory, feeling that
in the rush to get on and with the disposition to put the past behind in order to
get on, that a "sacrilege" might be committed through willful neglect. In more
recent years a decided change has been noted. And we are sorry to admit that
the change has not been so much of the natural promptings of the heart as it has
been due to a pressure from without, and which is becoming more and more
noticeable. This will be construed as a reflection or a restriction on the race; it is
all of that—reflection or restriction, and fully justified by what has been, or has
not been. The idea is to do what we can in forcing more respect for past beneficial
agencies.

To pursue the case a trifle further; there have been those who had it that Lincoln was not such a friend of the Negroes after all, and that he did what he did
because he had to. The question will not be argued here; suffice to say that he was
a benefactor, whether of chance or design. A homely saying is, that we should not
look a gift horse in the mouth. Perhaps Mr. Lincoln's administration did not set
out with the direct intent of freeing the Negroes. But, like every other happening
in every other administration previous or subsequent, it was responsible for what
happened. Had it been a calamity, a panic or anything else, it would have been
chargeable. Those unmuzzled individuals and shortsighted, to boot, "had ought
to" muzzle up and put on glasses.

We cannot add to the glory of Lincoln, likewise his detractors cannot do injury.
As Bulwer Lytton would say, he carved out an empire for himself which the praises
of men cannot widen nor can their condemnation make less. His services to the
Negro are incalculable, his services to the country are incalculable, his services to
humanity are incalculable. If we are wise we will not stop to analyze the where-
ases and the wherefores, but chime in the mighty chorus of him who stands with

the few liberators of all times. Mr. Lincoln did not come to the presidency with any set program; he and his party were for the obstruction of slavery. They came knowing that its death knell was to be sounded, but did not suspect it nearly so soon. [ . . . ]

Then take the life of Lincoln long before he was called from the wilds of Illinois. He was found battling on humanity's side. He chose to support that party which had small voice in governmental affairs, but big with potentialities, and because in the cause of right. All the time, at any time, in Congress, out of Congress Mr. Lincoln stood for a free soil. In truth, he was more interested in free soil than the Negroes. Incidentally he believed them human; had compassion for them out of his great nature, but he was not enamored of them. He at no time was associated with the liberation movements, excepting as his party declared. His vote in Congress was on the Negro's side, assuring that when forced to choose he was consistent.

As the years go by, leaving in accentuation their generations of mankind, it is becoming more and more evident that Mr. Lincoln was one of the evenest tempered, mildest mannered men that ever graced a "ruler's" chair. He only, it appears, was fitted for the work that fell to him, for the ordeal he underwent in accomplishing it. Ever on the defensive, his opposers forced him to be aggressive. He came to the presidency as an Isaiah might have, might have prophesied as sheep to the shamble— "opening not his mouth." Once when in the bitterness of despair he was known to have asked of himself: Abraham Lincoln are you a dog? He also would have had the cup pass from him. But if destiny has any part in human affairs, Abraham Lincoln was its child. It may not be generally known that he insisted from his youth up that he would be President some day. It seems strange. Yet when we think that most ambitious youth declare at least to themselves the same, it is not so strange after all, excepting the fact that it was Abraham Lincoln, so modest, so retiring, so devoid of the ego who said it. He had but few declarations to give out concerning himself, then to think that he announced that he would be President some day—there are things and ways past finding out.

Lincoln spent his time in preparation; he depended largely on himself for information—his schooling; he was his own teacher and had no fool for a scholar. He was a Saul in all respects, towering with men of the schools above men by his rare good sense and splendid [j]udgment. Speaking of the village preacher in his "Deserted Village," Goldsmith has it, that those who came to scoff remained to pray. Thus when our Lincoln came, taunts and gibes followed him. The press, whether friend or foe, bubbled forth in merriment at the lean, lank, gawky son of the wilderness that had come to "court." But that same destiny, or whatever influence, or his godlike mien and disposition soon put to rout the gainsayers and scoffers. It became apparent that a worthy successor of Washington, Adams, Jefferson was at the front of American affairs. His wisdom, wit, philosophy were ready, first handed, from a master mind. The "rude, uncouth, ungainly" was rich in the requirements of his office. He saw men as from an eminence, a distinction soon learned. Every day added unto him; his country plunged in war, he was yet the idol, and when the ballots of the second election were counted he again was the Abon Ben Adhem—his name leading all the rest.

He fell at his post as it were; most dastardly deed, but a glorious finale of the work he was "sent" to do. One cannot help recall the death of the One greater who was spared until His mission was ended. The parallelism of the foremost two is indeed striking. Without the beautiful story of the cross we would not see nearly so much in Jesus Christ. That he fell in the cause is the evidence that counts. It appeals to men—He gave his life. The Negro race can feel proud that the memory of Abraham Lincoln is entwined about their establishment. The total world lauds him, placing him second to none of the sons of men saving One—he who wore the impress of divinity. So much civil life and liberty never sprang up before at the behest of one man. The influence of the act ran the world around—bidding despondent man lift up as water the drooping plants. The world lamented his passing; it loved him for his virtue. His physical defects, whatever they may have been, were at last beautiful neath the halo of civil consecration. His death the last stanza of the poem of his life was the most awful and beautiful climax.

*Indianapolis Freeman*, Jan. 2, 1909.

## Selections from the *American Missionary*, February 1909: Thomas S. Inborden, George W. Henderson, William Pickens, Kelly Miller, Etta M. T. Cottin, Archibald H. Grimke, and John M. Gandy

*The* American Missionary *was the official organ of the American Missionary Association (AMA), an organization founded by abolitionists in the mid-nineteenth century to proselytize through the establishment of churches and schools abroad and in the United States. In addition to having a presence in Africa, the AMA played an important role in founding and sustaining schools throughout the South during Reconstruction. To commemorate the Lincoln centennial, several African Americans who had either benefited from AMA institutions or were otherwise involved in educating Black students were asked to provide their reflections on Lincoln and the Emancipation Proclamation. Their responses were published in a special issue that was devoted to celebrating the one hundredth anniversary of Lincoln's birth.*

*[Thomas S. Inborden, "Abraham Lincoln."*

*Educated at Oberlin College and Fisk University, Inborden (1865–1951) was employed by the AMA and serving as principal of the Normal Agricultural and Industrial School in Enfield, North Carolina when he wrote the following. At the time of the Lincoln centennial a debate was taking place concerning an appropriate national monument to honor Lincoln. Inborden indicated that most African Americans would not have an interest in such a monument for fear of negative repercussions, but he believed that all African Americans revered Lincoln and deemed their freedom, as conferred by the Emancipation Proclamation, a sufficient Lincoln monument. While Lincoln had given freedom to the enslaved, Inborden suggested that more work needed to be done in order to achieve justice and equality. If the country followed Lincoln's principles, then Inborden believed there would not be a so-called "Negro Problem" (Ralph Hardee Rives, "Inborden, Thomas Sewell, 6 Jan. 1865–10 Mar. 1951," https://www.ncpedia.org/biography/inborden-thomas-sewell)].*

It has been suggested that a highway costing many millions of dollars, similar to the old English roads, be built by the United States Government [. . .] This road to be known as the Lincoln Way. Another has suggested that a new State be created called Lincoln. Still others would dig a great canal from the Atlantic Ocean to the Mississippi River and call it the Lincoln Canal. All this to perpetuate the memory of Abraham Lincoln.

From an economic point of view nothing would be more valuable to the traveling public and especially to the farmers who might be permitted to use the road; from an educational point of view nothing would be more inspiring to the youth of our country than the art and science displayed in the construction and decoration of such a highway.

Whether a State is created and named or a canal dug or a great public highway built, nine-tenths of the Negroes of this country will never know, and it will not appear too unpatriotic to say, they will not care very much for fear that it will afford another opportunity for adverse legislation against them, but *ten-tenths* of the American Negroes will hold in sacred honor and perpetuate to their children forever the name of their emancipator—*Abraham Lincoln*. They may not know Barnard's statuary from the Egyptian Sphinx, but they know that this pioneer from the West, this man who educated himself by the light of the pine torch, who could split more rails than any other man in his community, whose home-spun clothes and rural appearance readily identified him with the common people, attained the highest eminence in the gift of the nation and that he had the courage of his convictions to sign the emancipation proclamation which gave them the liberty of American citizens.

They need no other monument, they ask for no insignia of greatness more enduring than the spirit of brotherhood and justice that inspired the thought of total emancipation for these dependent subjects.

The signing of that sacred document was an awful test of character. It was an expedient never before tried in the history of any race. It was faith joining hands with the eternal. It was also an opportunity that comes to only a few men. [ . . . ] Well and truthfully might he say in substance that if any one act should make him immortal in the annals of time it would be that of signing the Emancipation Proclamation. With a steady head, a sympathetic heart and a prophetic vision, he, with one stroke of the pen, built the monument which time itself cannot erase.

He knew better than any one else from his high vantage ground all that this act would mean to a desolated and disrupted country. He knew of the condition of these millions of subjects of this Southern Aristocracy, their ignorance and their absolute dependence for the necessities of daily life. He knew what their freedom would entail to the nation. He arose, not oblivious to the signs of the times, and truth triumphed majestically.

Well may it be said that this emancipation was an exigency of war. God is the author of the exigencies of war as much as he is of the exigencies of peace. If his will, power and spirit cannot be transmitted by men through the exigencies of peace let it be welcomed by them through the exigencies of war. Freedom has come and, theoretically at least, all the opportunities that could come to a civilized people. Let us thank God and take courage.

What of the present and future? Almost a half century has passed in the history of our freedom. Four millions have more than doubled. We have lived, shall we say in the enemies' country? No, they are not enemies who, after four years of the hardest struggle known to civilization find themselves bereft of their dearest possessions—their sons, their former subjects, their horses, their cattle, their homes, their social institutions, their cause, all gone except their bare acres, are willing to divide these acres and their products with their former subjects that they too may have a livelihood. Suffice it to say, as a testimonial to this fact, that there are over seven hundred thousand farms operated by Negroes whose combined value is almost five hundred millions of dollars. No, they are not enemies who, from their scanty earnings, have shouldered their own educational burdens and have helped us to shoulder ours to the extent of nearly sixty millions of dollars.

The few discordant notes in our legislative halls have not caused the race to lose heart, but rather to fight more courageously for every right guaranteed by the Constitution and vouchsafed by a chivalrous people. The disruptions in many sections of our country, occasioned by the community environment itself an environment of vice, laziness, and shiftlessness, and of inequality in the execution of justice, have not always been sanctioned by legislative authority. They are sincerely deprecated by the best people in both races.

The progress made in virtue, in intelligence, in the stable qualities of citizenship, in the acquisition of lands, homes, school and church property, and in business of various kinds, is most remarkable. From their past achievements there is no better guarantee of the worth of the emancipated race to this nation.

Lincoln was not mistaken in his interpretation of the signs of the times. He knew that to compromise meant simply to postpone the evil day. It always does when principle is at stake. He had faith in the future of these people. They have moved forward along all lines with such phenomenal strides that they have given rise to what is now called a "Problem." If the nation, including particularly the individual States, had but followed the principles established by this great emancipator, the principle of exact justice and equality for every citizen before the law, there would have been no problem. As it is this problem will never be solved until righteousness and the spirit of God brings the nation back to these first principles.

*[George W. Henderson, "Lincoln the Emancipator."*

*Born a slave in Virginia, Henderson (1850–1936) was educated at the University of Vermont, Yale Divinity School, and the University of Berlin. He was serving as dean of the Divinity School at Fisk University when he wrote the following defense of Lincoln and the Emancipation Proclamation. At a time when White supremacists were claiming Lincoln as a kindred spirit, Henderson noted that Lincoln was the first president who called for Black citizenship, including the right to vote. Henderson also emphasized the important role the Declaration of Independence played in shaping Lincoln's views on racial equality and how these views changed during the course of his political career. While some were calling for African Americans to leave the United States and cited Lincoln as an authority, Henderson argued that colonization was a corollary to Lincoln's initial proposal for gradual emancipation, while Black citizenship was the corollary to his expertly timed Emancipation Proclamation. For Henderson, the key question for the nation to answer in 1909 was whether Lincoln was right in believing African Americans were suitable for American citizenship as opposed to being deported. After leaving Fisk, Henderson spent several years as a professor at Wilberforce University (Xenia Daily Gazette [Xenia, OH], Feb. 6, 1936).]*

It is well for the country to pause on the centennial anniversary of Lincoln's birthday and consider anew his achievements as a statesman, and the principles which inspired and guided him in the midnight darkness through which he led the nation, with such singular wisdom and success. This is the unique distinction of having been the Emancipator of a race. In the character and magnitude of his task and in the difficulties overcome, he ranks with Moses, and there is no third name to be placed by their side. He differed from the great Hebrew leader, in that he freed, not his own, but an alien race and sealed his work with his life-blood. Both are world figures because both are identified with the cause of human liberty, which is the concern of universal humanity.

Like all truly great political leaders, Lincoln the man was father of Lincoln the statesman; statesmanship was but the method by which he impressed upon his country the profound convictions of his heart.

Lincoln's fame rests chiefly upon the Proclamation of Emancipation. That instrument, however, only conferred liberty, and not citizenship. It is not so generally remembered that he was the first public man of note to suggest Negro citizenship, including the elective franchise.

The Edict of Freedom became embodied in the Thirteenth Amendment passed and ratified in his own lifetime, the suggestion of citizenship subsequently became the basis of the Fourteenth and Fifteenth Amendments. Yet we are frequently told that, had he lived, the policy of reconstruction which rests upon this principle would have been fundamentally different.

The student of Lincoln's life will not fail to note the difference between his attitude toward the subject of the colored man's civil and political rights, in the beginning of his public career, and his position at the time of his death. The processes of the growth of his convictions are of profound interest. At the very first, he took his stand not solely upon the Constitution, but upon the Declaration of Independence. In his view the former was an attempt, more or less imperfect, to organize the Government so as to realize practically the great central truth—universal liberty—proclaimed in the latter. The Declaration was to him a kind of Bible; its sentiment of equality as therein defined was like a divine oracle. In the statement of this principle the authors of the Declaration had expressed "their understanding of the justice of the Creator to all his creatures," who had sent nothing into the world, stamped with the divine image, "to be trodden on and degraded and imbruted by its fellows." And only a few days before his first inauguration, as if forewarned of the destiny in store for him, he declared in the Hall of Independence, in Philadelphia, that if the country could not be saved without surrendering this principle he would rather be assassinated on the spot.

Few men acted more consistently on this principle—one thing at a time and that always the fundamental thing. Liberty was every man's birthright; to withhold it was an offense against the divine justice; political rights, on the other hand, was a subject for legislation. Moreover, history furnished substantially no light upon the question, whether the colored people could maintain such rights against the tremendous American prejudice, which seemed then to be gaining strength daily. A man of lofty ideals he was, yet pre-eminently sensible and practical, the least faulty in judgment said Charles A. Dana of any man he ever knew.

Of an open mind, events were his teachers; no false pride of consistency prevented his changing his position when convinced that he was mistaken. But it must not be supposed that Lincoln believed it possible for the colored people to maintain their liberty in this country, with no choice in the making of its laws. Nor is it conceivable that a mind so logical, so keen in its insight into human nature, could even have held the theory that the ballot could be given or withheld according to the mere pleasure of those in power. It might be regulated, but never denied; it was a corollary of liberty itself. Hence Lincoln's first proposed solution of the dilemma was colonization in Africa. He had in mind the Hebrew Exodus. This was a part of his scheme for gradual Emancipation. But when, in the providence of God, he was compelled to give freedom to the slaves upon military necessity, he turned to the idea of Negro citizenship in America, and suggested a qualified suffrage. Events had convinced him of its practicability, its justice he had probably never seriously doubted. And among the causes which effected this change of position, the conduct of the colored people themselves, under this severe ordeal through which they were passing, was the chief factor. He was deeply impressed by their patriotism, with the gallantry of the soldiers on the battlefield, which falsified the predictions of their enemies and the misgivings of their friends; and with the orderly and admirable behavior of the people after freedom had been given them. These manifestations of character and native ability were a gratifying surprise and full of promise. And to his just and discriminating mind, these people were worthy of the mantle of American citizenship. How generously he acknowledged the obligations of the country to the colored soldiers, without whose services he said the war could not have been successfully prosecuted.

Of Lincoln's first great act—giving liberty to the slave—there is probably now little or no question. Of the second—the suggestion of political equality—there is much division of opinion and the answer is still somewhat in suspense. It is clear that he did believe they could live as freemen in America without the ballot; it is equally clear that he believed a qualified suffrage might be safely granted them. Possibly, as some claim, Reconstruction under him would have taken a milder form; it is equally certain and more, the fundamental principle would have been substantially the same. Was Lincoln right? Have not the colored people in the progress of these forty-three years since his death justified his faith and indicated the soundness of his judgment? What answer will America give? He believed his country would be just; will it? He believed the only alternatives were colonization or the ballot; which shall it be? Our President-elect says the latter. Let us hope that this is the voice of the American people and that Lincoln's promise in the great Edict of Freedom that the Government would maintain it will be sacredly kept. Let the two sections of the country come together by all means, but not over the grave of the colored man's political rights. That would be building a house on sand.

Strange to say, I have heard speakers, white and colored, say that the Proclamation was a mere act of expediency, forced upon Lincoln by the necessities of the war, contrary to his personal convictions, his sole object being to save the Union. They seem not to know that this duty to save the Union gave him his only authority for striking slavery. His supreme merit as a statesman lies in having struck the blow at the psychological moment, when public opinion was ready to support him. Had he struck earlier or later, failure would have resulted. No statesman ever believed more profoundly in the Brotherhood of man in its Christian sense. His life-work may be summed up in a few words. Southern leaders, incited by Senator Douglas and the Supreme Court, took the colored man out of the Declaration of Independence and the Constitution of the United States, in fact, even out of the category of humanity; Lincoln put him back and raised him to the dignity of American citizenship, thereby removing the most serious menace to the existence and perpetuity of the Republic.

[William Pickens, "What Would Lincoln Do?"

*Best known for his work as a field secretary of the NAACP in the 1920s and 1930s, Pickens (1881–1954) was a professor of Latin at his alma mater, Talladega College, when he wrote the following. Like many, Pickens wondered what Lincoln would do if he were alive in 1909. According to Pickens, Lincoln was a multifaceted historical figure who maintained contradictory views on racial equality during the course of his political career. The key for Pickens was Lincoln's ability to evolve and change his position as he learned more and thought more about a question. For Pickens, Lincoln's sharp intellect and desire to be on the right side of an issue were what motivated him to alter his views rather than capriciousness or a desire for popularity. Given these character traits, along with his belief in the inherent evil of slavery, and consistent support of Black economic rights, Pickens provided a strong indication of what Lincoln would do about the race problem (AANB).]*

"If my name ever goes into history it will be for this act."

That is what Abraham Lincoln thought of his Emancipation Proclamation, whatever others may think of it, and what he said, he thought should take precedence to what others might say they think that he thought.

This Proclamation of Emancipation, which Lincoln issued as a war measure and the substance of which the Government of the United States has since made into law, naturally gave rise to new problems, which have lasted until our day, and will last. It is the condition of the life of government as of individual life, that the solution of one problem creates another.

What would Lincoln think and say and do in reference to this new race problem, which his life and acts more than those of any other one man helped to create? Of course, we cannot know; we can only judge from his thoughts and sayings and acts in past cases where the principle was about the same. He stuck to the main issue, and made a sophistical antagonist seem ridiculous. He had the happy faculty of preventing the opponent from dodging the real question, thus shifting the ground of controversy. When he argued that all men ought to be free, then as now, men tried to shift the question from one concerning the freedom of black people to one concerning the intermarriage of black and white people.

He replied: "It does not follow that because I would not have a Negro woman for a slave, I therefore want her for a wife." He made the opponent ridiculous; he said that if Judge Douglas and his friends were afraid that they could not resist the temptation of marrying Negroes if Negroes were free, that he was in favor of Illinois laws against intermarriage *for the sake of Judge Douglas and his friends.* [...]

When Lincoln appealed to the Declaration that all men are born "free and equal"—the plain implication being equal in the right to life, liberty and the fruits of honest endeavor—the sophist immediately began to show that men are not "equal"; that some are fat and some lean, some long and some short, some dull and some bright, some good and some bad, shifting the entire question. But Lincoln pinioned his adroit antagonist upon this thrust: "In the right to eat the bread, without the leave of anybody else, which his own hand earns, he (the Negro) is my equal, and the equal of Judge Douglas, and the equal of every living man." When the Supreme Court of the United States, in the case of Dred Scott, practically declared that there was no possible way for a slave ever to get his freedom except by the will and act of the master, Lincoln went straight to the heart of the absurdity by observing that it was singular for a court to hold "that a man never lost his right to his property that had been stolen from him, but that he instantly lost the right to himself if he was stolen."

On what can we best base an opinion as to what Lincoln would think and do in our day? We cannot base it on any special regard for the black man: he had no special love for the Negro above his love for other men. It cannot be based on any superior knowledge possessed by him: there are many men in public life to-day who have more accurate knowledge, especially about the Negro, than Lincoln ever could have had. We have simply to rely upon what we know of the honesty of his mind, which was always ready to give up an old opinion whenever it found a better one. In reference to the Negro there is hardly any opinion which Lincoln did not once hold, except, perhaps, the right to make the Negro a slave. Who knows that his opinion for freedom was not a developed opinion? He was once ready to support the "black laws" of Illinois; he had schemes for colonization and deportation, until shown their utter impracticableness; he thought that Negro soldiers would not fight until they actually fought; he thought that in a state of freedom the Negro race might die out, "catch cold and die," as he expressed it; and in reference to the Negro and the ballot, his opinions ran the whole gamut. In Illinois he had declared for an all-white vote, with the Negro as a free substratum; during the war he advised the loyal party in Louisiana to extend the elective franchise so as to include some of the people of color; and the friends of freedom recount with triumph how, before his end, he declared that all men of all races have an equal right to self-government, and that he said, that whatever opposition he may have given to the cause of freedom, was opposition to the will of God. This capacity to learn—to learn from events—to hold his opinion always subject to revision—to be actually controlled by the increasing light and the evolving truth—was what made him the statesman of his day. He once remarked, "My policy is to have no policy." He waited upon events, and we can say of him, as was said of a French statesman, that "time was his prime minister."

This willingness to change was not fickleness and weakness. It was the true attitude of an honest seeker. He was [al]ways seeking to get onto the right side of the question or the controversy, for he believed, as he said, that "right makes might." He was not trying to get the whole world on *his* side, but he was trying to get himself on the *right side*, trusting that God and the great Human Heart would be found on that side. This characteristic is clearly shown in his reply to a clergyman, who remarked to Lincoln that he hoped that "the Lord is on our side of the struggle." Lincoln replied: "The Lord is always on the side of right. I hope that I and this nation are on the Lord's side."

He was a patriot statesman; although he abhorred slavery in his own inclination, he was wise enough to see that the question of slavery was subordinate to the immediate object of saving the Union. "If slavery is not wrong, nothing is wrong," he declared as his private opinion; but it was his public duty and his oath to save the Union, regardless of slavery. His logic and clear seizure of the main point stood him in good stead against the overzealous Abolitionist on the one hand, while on the other hand, as soon as the interests of Negro freedom and the interests of the Union coincided, the same unchanged and consistent logic answered those who assailed him on constitutional grounds. He reasoned, every clause and provision of the Constitution is sacred and inviolate, just as every limb of the human body is sacred and inviolate, but the surgeon may amputate the limb if the loss of the limb is necessary to the salvation of the whole life.

He doubtless took great pleasure in finding his personal inclination and his public duty thus coincident. He believed that the opportunity was his to do a great service to his countrymen and to humanity at large. He was not endeavoring to bring a curse, but a blessing, upon slaveholders. Not the least part of his abhorrence to slavery was inspired by the inroads which he saw it making upon the healthy thinking, and consequently upon the liberties, of white men. He said that he was opposed to slavery because it compelled white men in their efforts to defend it, to attack the very foundations of human liberty itself, and even to assail the Declaration of Independence. He said, "In giving freedom to the slave, we assure freedom to the free, honorable alike in what we give and what we preserve."

This last argument he would doubtless apply to-day to every phase of the question of the rights and the liberties of the American Negro.

[*Kelly Miller, "The Genius of Abraham Lincoln."*
*Born to an enslaved woman in South Carolina, Miller (1863–1939) was educated at Howard University and Johns Hopkins University before becoming a professor at*

*Howard in 1890. Miller spent over forty years at Howard, where he taught math and sociology and served as dean of the College of Arts and Sciences. While most African Americans placed the Emancipation Proclamation at the top of Lincoln's list of accomplishments and others criticized him for framing the proclamation as a war measure, Miller argued that Lincoln's genius rested on the preservation of the Union (ANB).]*

One hundred years ago Abraham Lincoln was born amidst a lowly life. There is none other than the Son of Man to whom the great Messianic prophecy applies with such pointed pertinency. He grew up as a root out of dry ground. He had no form nor comeliness that we should desire him. He was a man of sorrows and acquainted with grief. The haughty and supercilious hid, as it were, their faces from him. He was wounded for our transgressions and bruised for our iniquities. With his stripes we are healed. He was cut out of the land of the living. Yet he has had his portion with the great and shared the spoils with the strong. [...]

Abraham Lincoln was a genius of the first order. He dwelt on the "radiant summit." He had not so much a message to deliver as a mission to perform. And yet, without learning, he could portray his meaning in such clear and lucid language, that the critics of elegant speech were constrained to say: "Few men ever spoke as this man speaks."

He saw the whole equation while others were engrossed in a single factor. He had faith where others wavered; he had knowledge where others had faith. He realized the substance of things which others hoped for; he had abundant evidence of things which others could not see. He more clearly than any other man of his day comprehended the axiom that the whole is greater than any of its parts. "Let us preserve our cherished institution," said the South. "Let us free the slave," said Garrison. "Let us make the North and West free soil," said Seward. But Lincoln said: "Let us save the union!"

He was more patient than the rest, because he had a greater vision. He was merry when others seemed sad; when others were frivolous, he was sober.

Loyalty and reverence are the chief traits of genius. Lincoln was loyal and reverent. Loyalty to principle and loyalty to loyalty form the key-note of a new ethical doctrine recently proclaimed by Professor Royce of Harvard University. Lincoln had lived this doctrine long before Royce wrote it. His chief mission was to preserve the union and to reinterpret its beneficence to mankind. There was no other wise enough and sane enough to do the work he did. He was chiefest among thirty millions.

The preservation of the union was the chief contribution to human progress made during the nineteenth century. Who can depict the result had the union been destroyed? [...] In the fullness of time, at the psychological moment, Abraham Lincoln appeared upon the stage. The man and the hour had arrived. "If thy right eye offend thee, pluck it out and cast it from thee: it is better that thine eye should perish than that thy whole body should be cast into hell." The chief object of social, as of physical surgery, is to save the body. The hasty surgeon delights to show his skill and is eager to operate for every irritating symptom. What cares he if the patient dies since the operation was successful. "Free the slaves, free the slaves," insisted Sumner and Stevens and Wilson, voicing the sentiment of the great anti-slavery forces back of them. So loud and so persistent was this demand that Lincoln would have lost his patience had it not been inexhaustible. The reformers said, "You must do it because it is right;" the politicians said, "You must do it because it is expedient." And yet the great Lincoln waited, till the freeing of the slaves, though inherently an act of justice, would best inure to the preservation of the union, which was the chief burden of his heart. It was not because of vacillation or indecision of character or of indifference to the claims of human freedom that he acted thus, but because he fully understood the relation of parts to the whole. He had the steadiness and poise of knowledge. He knew and knew that he knew. He was not swerved from the illumined tenor of his way by importunity of friend or denunciation of foe. Finally, at the calculated crisis of affairs, the proclamation was issued, merely as an incident of a larger policy. This document was the greatest charter of human liberty ever penned by the hand of man. This single concrete achievement serves beyond all others to fix his place in [the] temple of fame. It loses nothing of moral grandeur because of its subordinate purpose. The subsequent amendments to the Constitution flowed from it as corollaries from the leading proposition.

Although less fervent in his mode of advocacy than the more ardent reformers, he was nevertheless intensely devoted to the principles of liberty.

He was too large to be a special pleader, even for so worthy, and at the time so popular a cause as the freedom of the slave.

Lincoln saved the union and abolished slavery from its borders. Herein consists his undying fame. He was cut short in the midst of his great powers. [ . . .] Had Lincoln lived, asks the idle speculator, would he have risen to the level of the exigencies growing out of the great conflict? Why need we venture a reply? We know what he did, and that is enough.

*[Etta M. T. Cottin, "The Great Emancipator."*

*A native of Georgia, Cottin was principal of Cotton Valley School in Fort Davis, Alabama. For Cottin, Lincoln was a Christlike figure who brought redemption to four million slaves with his Emancipation Proclamation. Recalling that the annual meeting of the AMA had been held in Galesburg, Illinois the year before, she reflected on the debate that Lincoln and Stephen Douglas held there in 1858. It was there that Lincoln expressed his hatred of slavery and asserted that Blacks were entitled to all rights in the Declaration of Independence. Cottin gave Lincoln full credit for breaking the chains of African American enslavement but believed only they could fully understand the entire meaning of that event.]*

No one can read the act of Emancipation by President Lincoln without joy and patriotic pride. That act not only opened the door of hope to the black people of this country but to all slaves in the world. It did more; it awakened the conscience of the Christian world. Men everywhere saw slavery in a new light. They began to feel that there is significance in the brotherhood of man and the fatherhood of God.

President Lincoln through much travail gave the answer to the faithful prayers which for centuries the untutored Negroes and Christian philanthropists had sent to the throne of God. Is it not wonderful that the Great Ruler of the destinies of nations should have chosen such an agent for a deed so unprecedented? Abraham Lincoln it is said "floated into the White House on a Mississippi flat-boat." His humble origin reminds me very much of the birth of Christ. His emancipation act was the redemption of a people. Said he, "And upon this act, sincerely believed to be an act of justice, warranted by the Constitution upon military necessity, I invoke the considerate judgment of mankind and the gracious favor of Almighty God."

To celebrate the hundredth anniversary of the birth of such a man is most appropriate. It may be that this great man did not realize in his early experience that God was raising him up for just such a purpose. His was the nation's sacrifice, and ours the priceless gain. "He gave himself for us." It was fitting that the American Missionary Association should, in this year 1908, hold its annual meeting in the State of Illinois at Galesburg, for it was in that State and in that city that his famous debate with Judge Douglas was held. Mr. Lincoln made it plain then that he hated slavery with a perfect hatred, and that the Negro was included in the Declaration of Independence, and had a right to "life, liberty and the pursuit of happiness," and that this nation could not long remain "half slave and half free." As I stood recently and looked at the place where Judge Douglas and Mr. Lincoln debated, one for and the other against slavery, I thanked God that right prevailed. [ . . .] Christ suffered and died for the redemption of the world. Lincoln's life brought the redemption of four million Negroes from the cruel bonds of slavery. Surely this was a part of God's great plan.

No one but the Negro can realize just the full meaning of Lincoln's proclamation. Who can doubt the wisdom as well as the justice of it when he marks the progress of the colored people on the one hundredth anniversary of the Emancipator's birthday?

*[Archibald H. Grimke, "Abraham Lincoln and the Fruitage of His Proclamation."*
*After graduating from Lincoln University and Harvard Law School, Grimke (1849–1930) served as US consul at Santo Domingo, and authored biographies of William Lloyd Garrison and Charles Sumner. Here, he makes the point that in 1858 Lincoln firmly believed the nation could not survive divided over the slavery issue, yet he sought to prevent the further expansion of slavery rather than abolish it in states where it*

*already existed. Grimke postulates that Lincoln epitomized the conflicting views of*
*the North, and that his fealty to the Constitution kept him in an ambivalent position*
*regarding slavery during the first two years of the Civil War. When Lincoln determined*
*that ending slavery was indispensable to preserving the Union, he moved forward with*
*emancipation. Notably, Grimke brands this decision as the "psychologic moment" in*
*the war, as well as for Blacks and the nation. The Emancipation Proclamation did not*
*complete the process of freeing the enslaved, and it therefore had to be followed by the*
*Thirteenth, Fourteenth, and Fifteenth Amendments. Though the facts of Black life did*
*not correspond to such advancements in freedom, Lincoln laid the foundation for its*
*possibilities (ANB).]*

Five years before he signed the Emancipation Proclamation, Abraham Lincoln
had made the memorable declaration that a house divided against itself cannot
stand; that the American nation could not endure half slave and half free, but that
it would ultimately become either all slave or all free. He stood in 1858 not for the
abolition of slavery, but for its restriction. The movement to make the republic
all slave was at the time well under way on the part of the South. The counter
movement on the part of the North to check this movement was well under way
also. These counter movements were coming into frequent collisions, the one
with the other, and the sound of strife was filling the land with growing discord
and hate between the two halves of the Union. The right to hunt fugitive slaves
in any part of the free States had become a law. The old slave line of thirty-six
degrees, thirty minutes had disappeared from the map and Kansas had become a
battle ground where freedom and slavery were grappling for mastery. Yes, it was
becoming clear enough in the light of the fierce struggle which was in progress
in 1858, that a house divided against itself could not stand; that the nation could
not endure half slave and half free, for the slave half was fighting desperately to
make it all slave and the free half was fighting desperately likewise to keep itself
free, to overcome the rising slave tide which was flowing from the South with
increasing volume and violence. Such was the situation in 1860.

All that the Republican Party in that year hoped to achieve by the election of
Abraham Lincoln was restriction, not the extinction of slavery. There was to be no
more slave soil and no more slave states. Where slavery was at the time, established
by law, there it was to be respected by the North, by the rest of the nation. But
within those limits it was to be strictly confined; within those limits it was to be
forever walled in upon itself and isolated from the rest of the nation. Not another
inch of the national domain was to be conceded to it. All its claims and clamor in
respect to the same, to the contrary notwithstanding. This was the supreme issue
between the sections in the Presidential election of 1860. The slave half of the
union asserted its equal right with the free half under the Constitution to settle
upon this land, and this the free half met with denial and resistance at the polls.

With the triumph of the North at the polls, and of its policy of slavery restriction, the South seceded from the old union with its dual and mutually invasive labor systems and established a new union, founded on a single labor system, namely, slavery, which was declared to be its chief corner stone. Mr. Lincoln was more than any other man of his time the embodiment of the feelings of his section. He was the incarnation of its reverence for the old union with its mutually conflictive industrial ideas and interests. His devotion to the Constitution with its slave clauses amounted almost to idolatry, and kept him hesitant and conservative in respect to the subject of slavery during the first two years of the War of the Rebellion. His task as President, as he understood it, was to save this old union, this old Constitution intact—to do so at any cost—with slavery, if that could be done, but without it, if necessary.

When at the end of two disastrous years of war he perceived that the preservation of this old union and Constitution depended on the destruction of slavery, he proclaimed freedom to the slaves. It was the psychologic moment not only in the progress of the war, but in the life of a race and of the nation also. For the Emancipation Proclamation not only broke the back of the rebellion and abolished chattel slavery in the States then in rebellion, but it was the initial act of reconstruction of the republic with its dual labor systems and of its conversion into a new union with a single system of free labor. It is the peculiar glory of this great man that he not only foresaw clearly that this old union could not endure half slave and half free, but that it was given to him in a terrible crisis of its existence to perform an act which was the first of a series of great acts which are to establish free labor as its chief corner stone.

The Emancipation Proclamation being an act of war and without universal application, had to be followed by the Thirteenth Amendment of the Constitution which abolished slavery and involuntary servitude in the republic forever. But when it was found by the free States that this great act of itself fell far short of the work of rendering the country wholly free, the new freed men were invested with citizenship. Still, the movement toward freedom seemed to lag, to stop short of the consummation of industrial unity, of the establishment for it of a single labor system, and so the Fourteenth Amendment was followed by the Fifteenth, which conferred suffrage on the blacks. [...] It is the glory of Lincoln that he laid, as the chief cornerstone of our reconstructed union, free labor. His great act yet awaits the hands which shall lift into place in the new American edifice the splendid capstone of industrial and political equality and fair play for all men regardless of race, for all labor, whether white or black or brown.

*[John M. Gandy, "Mr. Lincoln's Real Attitude Toward the Negro."*
*A native of Mississippi and graduate of Fisk University, Gandy (1870–1947) spent*
*over forty years at the Virginia Normal and Industrial Institute (today's Virginia State*

*University), first as a professor of Classics, and then as president of the college from 1914 to 1943. Gandy offered a nuanced interpretation of Lincoln, as he noted that Lincoln had no particular concern for Black people, believed physical differences prohibited social and political equality between the races, and initially advocated colonization. Despite these convictions, Lincoln also thought it was wrong to enslave anyone, and asserted that African Americans were entitled to the natural rights vouchsafed by the Declaration of Independence—life, liberty, and the pursuit of happiness. While the Emancipation Proclamation was motivated solely by a desire to preserve the Union, Lincoln nevertheless destroyed slavery. In abandoning plans for colonization and believing Blacks had natural rights, he was more progressive than most White men of his era. Gandy further noted that President Theodore Roosevelt and President-elect William Howard Taft seemingly shared Lincoln's view on natural rights, yet he doubted that African Americans would be able to realize these rights without exercising political rights (Henry Louis Gates Jr. and Kwame Anthony Appiah, eds.,* Africana: The Encyclopedia of the African and African American Experience, *2nd ed., 5 Volumes [Oxford: Oxford University Press, 2005]).]*

Mr. Lincoln possessed a very sympathetic nature. In few instances, however, did he allow his feelings to get the better of his judgment. In no case was this true where great principles were at stake and far-reaching results were to follow. The great questions of his times teeming with sectional interests and pregnant with emotions he deliberated upon with the coolness and quietude of a philosopher, and with the breadth of view and disinterestedness that proved him to be a great statesman. Such questions blocked the straight path of reason of some other men both North and South, rendered accurate and unbiased judgment impossible and fired them to thoughtless and rash acts. Like William Lloyd Garrison and John Brown he advocated the emancipation of the Negro, but unlike them his motives prompting to such an attitude ran out to the Negro, the Slaveholder and the Union. He was not a sentimentalist. That the slave was a black man and was regarded as an inferior type of the human family had little to do with his anti-slavery ideas and feelings. It was a conviction of his that all men should be free; and since the Negro is a man, he too should enjoy the blessings of freedom. To enslave him was in Mr. Lincoln's opinion a positive moral wrong, since it prevented the development of possibilities implanted by the Creator and turned his energies and efforts to the enjoyment and happiness of others; and since every man has a right to the enjoyment of the results of his own efforts, and to eat the bread earned by the sweat of his own face.

The preservation of the Union was of more vital concern to Mr. Lincoln than any other public question. He had neither right, he said, nor inclination to interfere with slavery where it then existed; but he did oppose its spread to the territories, more for the welfare of the Union than for the benefit of the slave. He was willing to free all the slaves, or to keep them in bondage; or to free a part and to keep the other part in bondage to save the Union. He loved the Union more than he did either white or black men. The pressure coming from the Abolitionists of the North to emancipate the slaves did not move him one whit from this attitude. Though he believed in gradual emancipation, "Military Necessity" furnished the motive that struck an immediate deathblow to slavery.

What should be done with the Negro after Emancipation? What place should he hold in the political and social life? [. . .] It is interesting in the light of this to know what Mr. Lincoln thought and felt regarding these questions. His first impulse was that all Negroes should be sent to Africa. He dismissed this idea, however, as impracticable on the ground that the financial condition of the country would not allow it; nor could the Negro withstand the ravages of the climate, want and destitution on the Liberian coast. He denied political and social equality to the Negro on the ground that the great physical differences between the races would never allow it. He did not appeal to reason and judgment to justify his denial, but turned to universal feeling which, he said, would never permit.

Mr. Lincoln was willing, however, to grant the rights designated in the Declaration of Independence; the right of life, liberty, and the pursuit of happiness. [. . .] Thus what Mr. Lincoln would grant to the Negro is much more valuable than what he would deny him. If these natural rights could be secured in their full significance and ideality, the Negro's hopes and aspirations would be realized. It is doubtful, however, whether these natural rights can ever be fully secured and guarded without the possession at the same time of political rights.

At the time when the Negro was held in disfavor, when he was ignorant and showed little promise of mental and moral capabilities and when Mr. Lincoln had political aspirations and had to exercise caution in what he said and did, it must have taken good courage and deep convictions to express ideas that were held in derision and contempt by the majority of white men.

*American Missionary* 63, no. 2 (Feb. 1909).

## FRED R. MOORE, "Lincoln and the Negro," February 1909

*Born a slave in Virginia, Moore (1857–1943) grew up in Washington, DC, and worked for the Treasury Department. He was an associate of Booker T. Washington, and after moving to New York, he became involved in banking, served as secretary of Washington's National Negro Business League, was active in the Republican Party, and worked as an editor of the* New York Age. *In 1905, he became editor of the* Colored American Magazine, *one of the leading African American monthlies. As the nation celebrated the centennial of Lincoln's birth, Moore offered high praise by editorializing that no White man had done more*

*for African Americans than Lincoln. In extolling the Emancipation Proclama-*
*tion, Moore contrasted it with recent efforts to disfranchise Blacks and suggested*
*that if more White politicians followed Lincoln's example the path to progress*
*for African Americans would be clearer (DANB).*

---

Apropos of the memory of Lincoln let us say that no white man ever born in the United States has had the opportunity to do as much for the Negroes of the country as Abraham Lincoln, and no white man has ever done more for them. Lincoln had the opportunity to do the race a good service and he lost no time in the act. His emancipation proclamation had "no strings" to it, no grandfather attachments, no property qualifications, but was a clean cut, fee simple deed to four millions or more Negroes to freedom in the land they loved and in the foremost nation of modern times. Negroes can never say enough in praise of Lincoln; and his acts toward them, as compared with some other presidents of the United States are the mountain unto the mole hill.

If we had more Lincolns in the white race the Negro's progress in this country would not be beset with so many obstacles. Lincoln showed what a white man in power can do for a Negro if he wills to do so.

*Colored American Magazine* 15, no. 2 (Feb. 1909): 71.

## SYLVANIE F. WILLIAMS, "Abraham Lincoln and Emancipation," February 1909

*Williams (1855–1921) was an educator and activist in New Orleans. She worked as a school principal and was a member of the National Association of Colored Women. Williams noted that the Republican Party was not formed for the purpose of abolishing slavery, yet she credited Lincoln for having the heart to issue the Emancipation Proclamation and classified him with other abolitionists. In recalling the first Emancipation Day commemoration in New Orleans, Williams claimed that while Lincoln had freed the bodies of African Americans, intellectual emancipation remained a work in progress. For Williams, having knowledge of history and race pride were essential. Keeping the memory of the past alive by commemorating events such as Lincoln's birthday and Emancipation Day were therefore important aspects of this process.*

---

Forty-six years ago a chain forged in 1619 was suddenly snapped with a reverb[er]ation heard around the world. This chain was composed of many links, some strong, others weak, yet all of them firm enough to hold in bondage four millions of God's creatures [. . .].

All honor to the man who had the moral courage to break that chain, forged and strengthened by the strongest of all cements, the cement of public opinion. The longer we think of the act, the more heroic seems the deed, and the more inclined are we to believe that the man was created for the occasion. That he was an instrument in the hands of God for the accomplishment of a destiny which had been slowly advancing to its culminating point.

It has been said that the emancipation was merely a war measure. Granted. For we all know that the Republican party was not formed for the purpose of abolishing slavery, but to prevent its expansion into the territories. True a number of enthusiasts were preaching abolition, many believed that it would eventually come; but the populace would not have been aroused against the system had it not been for the enforcement of the Fugitive Slave Law of 1850 and the Kansas-Nebraska Bill of 1854 [...].

But the capture of runaway slaves and the possible extension of slavery into Northern territory, were the spurs that turned sentiment into action and Lincoln was the instrument designed by the Almighty Power to accomplish the deed.

What President can you call to mind from Jackson to Lincoln, who would have ventured to risk it? And what one, from Lincoln to Roosevelt, who would have dared to do it? And after forty-six years, we to-day, stand in awe at the stupendous intellect, and the unflinching courage of the man, neither allured by ambition, nor deterred by the fear of unpopularity, who could dare to liberate, to turn loose upon the community, four millions of human beings, endowed with memory, feeling, passions and ignorance.

Four millions human beings cast upon an unknown world, upon their own resources, without a guide, without a purpose, almost without their knowledge and certainly without their consent. Imagine for an instant, if you can, what a catastrophe if four millions of vessels were cut adrift upon the vast expanse of the ocean without a pilot, a rudder, or an anchor. What a series of frightful disasters, shipwrecks and appalling accidents we would be called upon to record. Search the annals of history to find a parallel of such a mighty upheaval of existing forces; such an earthquake of established opinion and customs, that have been adjusted with so little disastrous results.

Surely the Almighty did answer the prayer which the immortal Lincoln enunciated in the last clause of the emancipation proclamation, wherein he says: "Upon this act, sincerely believed to be an act of justice, warranted by the Constitution upon military necessity, I invoke the considerate judgment of mankind and the gracious favor of Almighty God."

Lincoln's prayer has been answered, for the act has already received the gracious favor of Almighty God, and every day brings nearer and nearer the considerate judgment of mankind. True, he was helped and sustained by a noble band of devoted men, who rejecting the theory that whatever was expedient was right, turned to the most sacred cause of that liberty, for which men have died on the scaffold, or on the battlefield, who persevered with a singleness of purpose and spotless devotion never before witnessed in American politics, until their principles were adopted by the Nation.

All honor to those departed stalwart captains of freedom's hosts, Lincoln, Garrison, Phillips, Seward, Chase, Fessenden, Douglas[s] and Sumner. To Sumner no less than to Lincoln should every heart on Emancipation Day be turned [...].

In the celebration of the forty-sixth anniversary, my mind reverts to the first Emancipation celebration which I witnessed in 1864 or 65, I do not know which. But I do know that I witnessed the first parade in honor of the Emancipation. Soldiers led the van and soldiers closed the rear, but the emancipated were the center of the parade as well as the center of interest. [...]

They were free to take up the larger life, free to shoulder their own life's burdens. They had not yet learned the bitter lesson, "that there is only one way to the land of freedom, down the banks of labor, through the waters of suffering."

Alas! some have not learned it yet, but that is the lesson the race must learn sooner or later. Emancipation! Oh, blessed word! But emancipated from what? Lincoln, by a stroke of the pen, emancipated four millions of human beings from chattel slavery. But who did? Who will? In fact, who can emancipate a people from the thralldom of sin, vice, ignorance and folly?

Does it not clearly follow that we have some work to do? The body is free, but how about the mind, the intellect? Are we able to soar above the petty strifes, the small jealousies, the little frictions caused by the angels of our undisciplined passions and follies? Are we emancipated from our own prejudices against the race? Have we a sympathetic chord that thrills with pride at the achievements of each other or swells with indignation when injustice is meted out to our fellow men? [...]

Let us then sow the seed of race pride by telling in song and story, every act of heroism, every deed of bravery, every item of interest connected with the history of the race, and there is no better way of beginning than by celebrating every recurring anniversary of the Emancipation celebration, and the Centennial of Abraham Lincoln.

*Colored American Magazine* 15, no. 2 (Feb. 1909): 96–100.

## HARRY C. SMITH, "Lincoln in a True Light," February 6, 1909

*A native of West Virginia, Smith (1863–1941) served as editor of the Cleveland Gazette for nearly sixty years. As a member of the Ohio legislature in the 1890s, Smith had introduced an anti-lynching bill that became a law and helped revise the state's civil rights statute. Smith offered a corrective to the fulsome praise that was being heaped on Lincoln as the nation prepared to celebrate the centennial of his birth. He reminded readers that Lincoln had placed the Union above all else, including slavery, and he asserted that while Lincoln was the greatest of all Americans, White abolitionists, such as Charles Sumner and Wendell Phillips, had been greater friends to African Americans. Smith's willingness to be critical of Lincoln remained consistent throughout his editorial career (AANB).*

---

President Lincoln's emancipation proclamation was a war measure, pure and simple. It was forced from him by the obstinacy of the rebellious south, which in the fall of 1862 refused to "lay down its arms within the 90 days" given by President Lincoln. He revoked the emancipation proclamations issued prior to his, by Gens. Hunter and Fremont, and as a result relieved the latter of his command of the Missouri, thereby sending him to an early and untimely grave and also doing what really ruined him financially. One will read the history of Lincoln's life "from birth to death," and fail to find therein sufficient to justify our placing him in a class with Sumner, Garrison, Phillips, Beecher and their kind of aggressive friends of the race. Never the less, Abraham Lincoln was a great man, but not the greatest friend of OUR race, by a good deal. He is, however, the greatest American that has ever lived, with the possible exception of George Washington, because he (Lincoln) saved the Union. He said he would do so, at any cost—half slave and half free; or all slave, or all free. And he saved it, all free. This was his one all-absorbing object from the very beginning, and it was wholly devoid of consideration for, or sentiment as to the iniquitous institution of slavery or any other national evil. Lincoln so expressed himself emphatically, and repeatedly. What he did for this country—saving the Union, including the freeing of it from slavery, is what makes him great in history and the minds of people generally. It is well however, that we understand his greatness and not continue to make the mistake persisted in ever since January [1], 1863, and credit the martyred president with the heart-interest, feelings and motives in the anti-slavery movement that prompted such men as Sumner, Garrison, Phillips, Lovejoy, Greel[e]y and others and that characterized their action to the end.

*Cleveland Gazette*, Feb. 6, 1909.

## JAMES H. MAGEE, Address at Lincoln Centennial Commemoration, Springfield, Illinois, February 12, 1909

*A native of Illinois, Magee (1839–1912) was an educator, minister, author, and prominent leader of the Black community. Active in the Republican Party, he was the first African American to be on the party's central committee in Illinois. In 1909, Magee lived in Springfield, where he held patronage positions in state government, was head of the Illinois Colored Historical Society, and had recently been president of a vocational school modeled after Booker T. Washington's Tuskegee Institute. The following was delivered at an African American celebration of the Lincoln centennial in Springfield. The one hundredth anniversary of Lincoln's birth occurred just six months after a riot in which a mob lynched two Black men and destroyed several Black homes and businesses. These events in Lincoln's hometown prompted a national call for a civil rights meeting on Lincoln's birthday that resulted in the founding of the NAACP. The Lincoln Centennial Association held a banquet in Springfield on the evening of February 12, 1909, that featured speeches from William Jennings Bryan and the French and British ambassadors. The Lincoln Association had invited Booker T. Washington to speak at the event, and while he was unable to attend, other Blacks were not welcome to purchase tickets for the banquet. Springfield African Americans therefore organized their own celebration that was held at St. Paul's AME Church. In his address, Magee noted that African Americans had fought for their country from the time Crispus Attucks was killed in the Boston Massacre to the Civil War and up to the more recent conflict against Spain. He proclaimed Lincoln's greatness and expressed his dismay that an event purporting to honor his memory would exclude those people whom he freed (Roger Bridges, "James H. Magee: Triumph Over Adversity,"* Illinois History Teacher *10, no.1 [2003]: 36–40).*

---

Looking backward one hundred years we behold the advent into the world of a mighty character, whose mission should accomplish a mighty work which shall endure until the archangel of God shall record the last syllable of time. Abraham Lincoln was as surely used as an instrument of Almighty God in setting at liberty 4,000,000 bond men, women and children, as was Moses in leading the children of Israel from Egyptian bondage. We are here tonight to do homage to the memory of this great man; great in goodness and good in greatness, whose life and character means more to the colored people of America than to any race or nationality in the world. For this race whose fetters were broken by the edicts of the emancipation proclamation, like the man of Nazareth, his life was sacrificed that the bonded black man and woman might be free. Jesus Christ, the Son of God, 1909 years ago gave up his life that the world might be free. We pay homage to the greatest man that ever lived except the God-man Jesus Christ, who died to redeem all mankind from the bondage of sin and the curse of the broken law. Looking forward we behold this race of ours, changed from chattels to free men and free women, with all the concomitant blessings of freedom, which are life, liberty and the pursuit of happiness, which means happy homes, happy children, joyful hope springing eternal in the human breast; to acquire and enjoy the good things of this world—the Eden home of mankind. Again looking forward one hundred years from this natal day, we behold another Lincoln celebration by the great-grandchildren of those who celebrate this centenary. America shall have grown to be the center of civilization, mental and moral culture. Prejudice shall have been banished as a myth and relegated to the dark days of "Salem witchcraft." The gospel of "malice toward none and charity toward all" shall have regenerated and changed the mental attitude of all towards the poor and despised on account of race, color or previous condition of servitude. [ . . . ]

The black man has been loyal to this country from the revolution with Crispus Attucks, the first black martyr to fall in defense of this country. One hundred and eighty-seven thousand black troops went into the civil war to fight for freedom and the Union. From Fort Pillow to Petersburg, Va., they fought valiantly until victory perched upon the banners of the Union army. At San Juan Hill the matchless black battalion saved the day of victory and enabled the intrepid and dauntless Theodore Roosevelt to become president of the United States. And now after all this the colored people are not good enough to mingle their presence with the "I am holier than thou" at the celebration of the one hundredth anniversary of the great emancipator, whose life work as president made it possible for even American white people to have a United States of America.

We colored people love and revere the memory of Lincoln for what he has done for us. He wrote the emancipation proclamation that made us forever free. And he enforced it by the United States army. Yes, we love the name of Abraham Lincoln, for his name is synonym for the freedom of wife, husband and children, and a chance to live in a free country, fearless of the slave catcher and his bloodhounds. We would that every colored man, woman and child in these United States could be brought together in one great procession in yonder cemetery, where lies the sacred dust of the great emancipator. I would rather be one of that number of black devotees than toastmaster at a so-called "Lincoln banquet" at $25 per. [ . . . ] Lincoln was a plain man, a true friend to the poor and humble, in the walks of life. His greatness came to him because of two important factors or acts in his life. He conquered rebellion and freed 4,000,000 slaves. Hence the true union loving white people of all parties and the colored people of this country are the only fit and worthy subjects to do honor to the memory of the greatest American, Abraham Lincoln.

*Illinois State Register* (Springfield), Feb. 13, 1909.

## BOOKER T. WASHINGTON, Address at Republican Club of New York, February 12, 1909

*Washington (1856–1915) had spoken in New York on Lincoln's birthday in 1896, just one year after his famous address in Atlanta, yet his speech at the New York Republican Club on the centennial of Lincoln's birth received widespread publicity and acclaim. Washington's acceptance of the invitation to speak at the banquet held in the ballroom of the Waldorf Astoria Hotel compelled him to decline an invitation to be one of the featured orators that same evening in Springfield, Illinois (Washington spoke in Springfield on Lincoln's birthday the following year). In his remarks, Washington hailed Lincoln as the Great Emancipator, while at the same time, appealed for sectional reconciliation by noting his Southern heritage and insisting that the Emancipation Proclamation freed Whites as well as Blacks. For Washington, the best way to honor Lincoln's memory was to imitate him. In Lincoln, Washington saw a hero who appealed to all races and classes, and commemorating him could therefore serve as a means to foster racial harmony. Washington's speech was well received by both Whites and Blacks. Fred R. Moore, editor of* Colored American Magazine, *published Washington's address and appended a note at the end that stated: "This address should be in every Negro home."*

---

You ask that which he found a piece of property and turned into a free American citizen to speak to you tonight on Abraham Lincoln. I am not fitted by ancestry or training to be your teacher to-night for, as I have stated, I was born a slave.

My first knowledge of Abraham Lincoln came in this way: I was awakened early one morning before the dawn of day as I lay wrapped in a bundle of rags on the dirt floor of our slave cabin by the prayers of my mother, just before leaving for her day's work, as she was kneeling over my body earnestly praying that Abraham Lincoln might succeed, and that one day she and her boy might be free. You give me the opportunity here this evening to celebrate with you and the nation the answer to that prayer.

Says the Great Book somewhere, "Though a man die, yet shall he live." If this is true of the ordinary man, how much more true is it of the hero of the hour and the hero of the century—Abraham Lincoln! One hundred years of the life and influence of Lincoln is the story of the struggles, the trials, ambitions and triumphs of the people of our complex American civilization. Interwoven into warp and woof of this human complexity is the moving story of men and women of nearly every race and color in their progress from slavery to freedom, from poverty to wealth, from weakness to power, from ignorance to intelligence. Knit into the life of Abraham Lincoln is the story and success of the Nation in the blending of all tongues, religions, colors, races, into one composite nation, leaving each group and race free to live its own separate social life, and yet all a part of the great whole.

If a man die, shall he live? Answering this question as applied to our martyred President, perhaps you expect me to confine my words of appreciation to the great boon which, through him, was conferred upon my race. My undying gratitude and that of ten millions of my race for this and yet more! To have been the instrument of Providence through which four millions of slaves, now grown into ten millions of free citizens, were made free, would bring eternal fame within itself, but this is not the only claim that Lincoln has upon our sense of gratitude and appreciation.

By the side of Armstrong and Garrison, Lincoln lives to-day. In the very highest sense he lives in the present more potently than fifty years ago; for that which is seen is temporal, that which is unseen is eternal. He lives in the 32,000 young men and women of the Negro race learning trades and useful occupations; in the 200,000 farms acquired by those he freed; in the more than 400,000 homes built; in the 46 banks established and 10,000 stores owned; in the $550,000,000 worth of taxable property in hand; in the 28,000 public schools existing with 30,000 teachers; in the 170 industrial schools and colleges; in the 23,000 ministers and 26,000 churches. But above all this, he lives in the steady and unalterable determination of ten millions of black citizens to continue to climb year by year the ladder of the highest usefulness and to perfect themselves in strong, robust character. For making all this possible Lincoln lives.

But, again, for a higher reason he lives to-night in every corner of the Republic. To set the physical man free is much. To set the spiritual man free is more. So often the keeper is on the inside of the prison bars and the prisoner on the outside.

As an individual, grateful as I am to Lincoln for freedom of body, my gratitude is still greater for freedom of soul—the liberty which permits one to live up in that atmosphere where he refuses to permit sectional or racial hatred to drag down, to warp and narrow his soul.

The signing of the Emancipation Proclamation was a great event, and yet it was but the symbol of another, still greater, and more momentous. We who celebrate this anniversary should not forget that the same pen that gave freedom to four millions of African slaves, at the same time struck the shackles from the souls of twenty-seven millions of Americans of another color.

In any country, regardless of what its laws say, wherever people act upon the idea that the disadvantage of one man is the good of another, there slavery exists. Wherever in any country the whole people feel that the happiness of all is dependent upon the happiness of the weakest, there freedom exists.

In abolishing slavery Lincoln proclaimed the principle that, even in the case of the humblest and weakest of mankind, the welfare of each is still the good of all. In re-establishing in this country the principle that, at bottom, the interests of humanity and of the individual are one, he freed men's souls from spiritual bondage; he freed them to mutual helpfulness. Henceforth no man of any race, either in the North or in the South, need feel constrained to fear or hate his brother.

By the same token that Lincoln made America free, he pushed back the boundaries of freedom everywhere, gave the spirit of liberty a wider influence throughout the world, and re-established the dignity of man as man.

By the same act that freed my race, he said to the civilized and uncivilized world, that man everywhere must be free, and that man everywhere must be enlightened, and the Lincoln spirit of freedom and fair play will never cease to spread and grow in power till throughout the world all men shall know the truth, and the truth shall make them free.

Lincoln in his day was wise enough to recognize that which is true in the present and for all time: that in a state of slavery and ignorance man renders the lowest and most costly form of service to his fellows. In a state of freedom and enlightenment he renders the highest and most helpful form of service.

The world is fast learning that of all forms of slavery there is none that is so hurtful and degrading as that form of slavery which tempts one human being to hate another by reason of his race or color. One man cannot hold another man down in the ditch without remaining down in the ditch with him. One who goes through life with his eyes closed against all that is good in another race is weakened and circumscribed, as one who fights in a battle with one hand tied behind him. Lincoln was in the truest sense great because he unfettered himself. He climbed up out of the valley where his vision was narrowed and weakened by the fog and miasma, on to the mountain top where in a pure and unclouded atmosphere he could see the truth which enabled him to rate all men at their true worth. Growing out of this anniversary season and atmosphere, may there crystallize a resolve throughout the nation that on such a mountain the American people will strive to live.

We owe, then, to Lincoln, physical freedom, moral freedom, and yet this is not all. There is a debt of gratitude which we, as individuals, no matter of what race or nation, must recognize as due Abraham Lincoln—not for what he did as Chief Executive of the Nation, but for what he did as a man. In his rise from the most abject poverty and ignorance to a position of high usefulness and power, he taught the world one of the greatest of all lessons. In fighting his own battle up from obscurity and squalor, he fought the battle of every other individual and race that is down, and so helped to pull up every other human who was down. People so often forget that by every inch that the lowest man crawls up he makes it easier for every other man to get up. To-day, throughout the world, because Lincoln lived, struggled, and triumphed, every boy who is ignorant, is in poverty, is despised or discouraged, holds his head a little higher. His heart beats a little faster, his ambition to do something and be something is a little stronger, because Lincoln blazed the way.

To my race, the life of Abraham Lincoln has its special lesson at this point in our career. In so far as his life emphasizes patience, long-suffering, sincerity, naturalness, dogged determination, and courage; courage to avoid the superficial, courage to persistently seek the substance instead of the shadow, it points the road for my people to travel.

As a race we are learning, I believe, in an increasing degree, that the best way for us to honor the memory of our Emancipator is by seeking to imitate him. Like Lincoln, the Negro race should seek to be simple, without bigotry and without ostentation. There is great power in simplicity. We, as a race, should, like Lincoln, have moral courage to be what we are, and not pretend to be what we are not. We should keep in mind that no one can degrade us except ourselves; that if we are worthy, no influence can defeat us. Like other races, the Negro will often meet obstacles, often be sorely tried and tempted; but we must keep in mind that freedom, in the broadest and highest sense, has never been a bequest; it has been a conquest.

In the final test the success of our race will be in proportion to the service that it renders to the world. In the long run, the badge of service is the badge of sovereignty.

With all his other elements of strength, Abraham Lincoln possessed in the highest degree patience and, as I have said, courage. The highest form of courage is not always that exhibited on the battlefield in the midst of the blare of trumpets and the waving of banners. The highest courage is of the Lincoln kind. It is the same kind of courage, made possible by the new life and the new possibilities furnished by Lincoln's Proclamation, displayed by thousands of men and women of my race every year who are going out from Tuskegee and other Negro institutions in the South to lift up such fellows. When they go, often into lonely and secluded districts, with little thought of salary, with little thought of personal welfare, no drums beat, no banners fly, no friends stand by to cheer them on; but these brave young souls who are erecting school houses, creating school systems, prolonging school terms, teaching the people to buy homes, build houses, and live decent lives, are fighting the battles of this country just as truly and bravely as any persons who go forth to fight battles against a foreign foe.

In paying my tribute of respect to the Great Emancipator of my race, I desire to say a word here and now in behalf of an element of brave and true white men of the South who, though they saw in Lincoln's policy the ruin of all they believed in and hoped for, have loyally accepted the results of the Civil War, and are to-day working with a courage few people in the North can understand, to uplift the Negro in the South and complete the emancipation that Lincoln began. I am tempted to say that it certainly required as high a degree of courage for men of the type of Robert E. Lee and John B. Gordon to accept the results of the war in the manner and spirit which they did, as that which Grant and Sherman displayed in fighting the physical battles that saved the Union.

Lincoln, also, was a Southern man by birth, but he was one of those white men, of whom there is a large and growing class, who resented the idea that in order to assert and maintain the superiority of the Anglo-Saxon race it was necessary that another group of humanity should be kept in ignorance.

Lincoln was not afraid or ashamed to come into contact with the lowly of all races. His reputation and social position were not of such transitory and transparent kind that he was afraid that he would lose them by being just and kind, even to a man of dark skin. I always pity from the bottom of my heart any man who feels that somebody else must be kept down or in ignorance in order that he may appear great by comparison. It requires no courage for a strong man to kick a weak one down.

Lincoln lives to-day because he had the courage which made him refuse to hate the man at the South or the man at the North when they did not agree with him. He had the courage as well as the patience and foresight to suffer in silence, to be misunderstood, to be abused, to refuse to revile when reviled. For he knew that if he was right, that the ridicule of to-day would be the applause of to-morrow. He knew, too, that at some time in the distant future our Nation would repent of the folly of cursing our public servants while they live and blessing them only when they die. In this connection I cannot refrain from suggesting the question to the millions of voices raised to-day in his praise: "Why did you not say it yesterday?" Yesterday, when one word of approval and gratitude would have meant so much to him in strengthening his hand and heart.

As we recall to-night his deeds and words, we can do so with grateful hearts and strong faith in the future for the spread of righteousness. The civilization of the world is going forward, not backward. Here and there for a little season the progress of mankind may seem to halt or tarry by the wayside, or even appear to slide backward, but the trend is ever onward and upward, and will be until some one can invent and enforce a law to stop the progress of civilization. In goodness and liberality the world moves forward. It goes forward beneficently, but it moves forward relentlessly. In the last analysis, the forces of nature are behind the moral progress of the world, and these forces will crush into powder any group of humanity that resists this progress.

As we gather here, brothers all, in common joy and thanksgiving for the life of Lincoln, may I not ask that you, the worthy representatives of seventy millions of white Americans, join heart and hand with the ten millions of black Americans— these ten millions who speak your tongue, profess your religion—who have never lifted their voices or hands except in defense of their country's honor and their country's flag—and swear eternal fealty to the memory and the traditions of the sainted Lincoln. I repeat, may we not join with your race, and let all of us here highly resolve that justice, good will and peace shall be the motto of our lives? If this be true, in the highest sense Lincoln shall not have lived and died in vain.

And, finally, gathering inspiration and encouragement from this hour and Lincoln's life, I pledge to you and to the Nation that my race, in so far as I can speak for it, which in the past, whether in ignorance or intelligence, whether in slavery or in freedom, has always been true to the Stars and Stripes and to the highest and best interests of this country, will strive to so deport itself that it shall reflect nothing but the highest credit upon the whole people in the North and in the South.

*Colored American Magazine* 16, no. 4 (April 1909): 235–240; typescript in Booker T. Washington Papers (Washington, DC: Library of Congress), Microfilm Reel 410.

## JAMES L. CURTIS, Address on Centennial of Lincoln's Birth, February 12, 1909

*A native of North Carolina, Curtis (1870–1917) graduated from Lincoln University in Pennsylvania and the Northwestern University Law School. A successful lawyer in New York, Curtis was appointed minister to Liberia in 1915 and remained in that position until his death. On the centennial of Lincoln's birth, Curtis paid tribute to him as the greatest man since Jesus Christ. Like Christ, Lincoln was a martyr who possessed a heart big enough to embrace all. Curtis offered a spirited defense of the Emancipation Proclamation as the real pathway to African American progress, and he urged his audience to seize the opportunity Lincoln's actions afforded by settling for nothing less than equality under the law ("U.S. Minister Curtis Buried," New York Age, Nov. 29, 1917).*

Since the curtain rang down on the tragedy of Calvary, consummating the vicarious sacrifice of Jesus of Nazareth, there has been no parallel in history, sacred or profane, to the deeds of Abraham Lincoln and their perennial aftermath.

For two hundred years this nation writhed in the pain and anguish of travail; and as a happy sequel to this long night of suffering, in the dawn of the nineteenth century, she bore a son who was destined to awaken a nation's somnolent conscience to a monstrous evil; to lead a nation through a fierce siege of fratricidal strife; to strike the shackles of slavery from the limbs of four millions of bondsmen; to fall a victim to the assassin's bullet; to be enshrined in the hearts of a grateful nation; and to have an eternal abode in the pantheon of immortals.

Abraham Lincoln! What mighty magic is this name! Erstwhile it made the tyrant tremble on his throne and the hearts of the down-trodden leap for joy.

Now, over the chasm of two score years, it causes the drooping hopes of freemen to bud anew, and the smoldering embers of their ambition to leap into flame.

With talismanic power, it swerves the darts of hate and malice aimed at a defenseless race, so that though they wound, they do not destroy. With antidotal efficacy, it nullifies the virus of proscription so that it does not stagnate the blood nor paralyze the limb of an up-treading and on-going race.

When the nation was rent in twain, Lincoln, the propitiator, counselled conciliation. When the States of the South sought to secede, Lincoln, the concatenator, welded them into a solid chain, one and inseparable. When brother sought the life of brother and father that of son, Lincoln, the pacificator, advised peace with honor. When the nation was stupefied with the miasma of human slavery, Lincoln, the alleviator, broke its horrid spell by diffusing through the fire of war the sweet incense of liberty.

The cynic has sneered at the Proclamation of Emancipation. The dogmatist has called the great Emancipator a compromiser. The scholar, with the eccentricity peculiar to genius, has solemnly declared that the slaves were freed purely as a war necessity and not because of any consideration for the slave. The undergraduate, in imitation of his erudite tutors, has asserted that the freedmen owe more to the pride of the haughty Southerner than to the magnanimity of President Lincoln. But the mists of doubt and misconception have been so dissipated by the sunlight of history, that we, of this generation, may clearly see the martyred President as he really was.

All honor to Abraham Lincoln, the performer, not the preacher; the friend of humanity, the friend of the North, the friend of the South, the friend of the white man, the friend of the black man; the man whose heart, like the Christ's, was large enough to bring within the range of its sensibilities every human being beneath the stars. The man who, when God's clock struck the hour, swung back on its creaking hinges the door of opportunity that the slaves might walk over its portals into the army and into new fields of usefulness in civil life.

One hundred years have rolled into eternity since freedom's greatest devotee made his advent on this earth. One hundred years, as but a moment compared with the life of nations; yet, changes in our form of government, in the interpretation of our laws, in the relation between the North and the South, in the status of the Negro, have been wrought, that were beyond the wildest dreams of Lincoln. And wonderful as have been these changes to our advantage, in the acquisition of property, in moral and mental development, in the cultivation of sturdy manhood and womanhood, yet, all these have come to us as a direct result of the labors of Lincoln, who, with the ken of a prophet and the vision of a seer, in those dark and turbulent days, wrought more nobly than he knew.

In Alice Moore Dunbar, ed., *Masterpieces of Negro Eloquence* (New York: The Bookery Publishing Company, 1914), 321–324.

# JOHN W. E. BOWEN SR., Address at Lincoln Centennial Commemoration, Chicago, February 12, 1909

*Born a slave in New Orleans, Bowen (1855–1933) was a Methodist minister, educator, and among the first African Americans to obtain a PhD. After receiving his PhD from Boston University, Bowen served at churches in Baltimore and Washington before accepting a teaching position at Gammon Theological Seminary in Atlanta. While at Gammon, Bowen became active in the civil rights movement, helped found the* Voice of the Negro, *and served as president of the institution. He continued to teach at Gammon until shortly before his death. The following was delivered in Chicago at a centennial celebration of Lincoln's birth that an African American committee in the city organized. Bowen paid tribute to Lincoln as the Great Emancipator and argued that Lincoln envisioned African Americans as having the same rights as White citizens. For Bowen, the great challenge for African Americans was to overcome both the legacy of slavery and racial stereotypes. Referring to the "mud puddles" of Africa and the ignorance of ex-slaves was provocative, but Bowen believed the fight for equality and the struggle to overcome racial prejudices must be fought by African Americans themselves. There was no longer a Lincoln, and Bowen therefore urged his audience to "liberate yourselves" (ANB).*

---

Even the schoolboy of to-day may easily interest an audience upon any phase of the life and deeds of Abraham Lincoln. It is not a difficult task, therefore, to gain attention, for the life of the man is full, his deeds are permanent, and his character is far-reaching in the superb and dominating elements that are appreciated by all mankind. I take it that the best thing to do on this occasion is to call your attention to some of the fundamental ideas that crystallized into deeds of the immortal Lincoln.

The name of Abraham Lincoln and the Emancipation Proclamation should be spoken with one breath. It is impossible to separate them. But there is more to the Emancipation Proclamation in its essence and truth than the mere removing of the shackles of the slave, and the freeing of man from between the plough handles to enter the battle of life. Larger results were contemplated by Lincoln than the liberation of dumb driven cattle from between the plough handles of the South. Mightier results were before him than merely to see four millions of ignorant and stupid blacks set free upon this American continent. His thought reached beyond the liberation of hand and foot. He who knocks the manacles from the wrists of the slave has done a great thing; but that is only the beginning of the work of emancipation. Utter, complete emancipation, not only of hand and foot, but of mind and heart, and a complete amalgamation into the body politic as a citizen of the mighty Republic, is the ultimate hope and the larger result to be looked forward to as the outcome of the emancipation of the slave.

We have come to a period in the discussion of this question when we must regard truth and not sentiment; when we must see fact and logic, and not be driven by whim. No race can be fully set free by shot and shell. Gunpowder cannot liberate a man in the truest and fullest sense of the term. Shot and shell make a beginning; but freedom is not "of the earth, earthy." Abraham Lincoln represented the American nationality—the American nationalism,—a mighty thought.

We have the proudest Republic under the sun. It is a Republic not composed of *white* men nor of *black* men, but of *men*, free men. Freedmen do not make a Republic. This is a Republic of men—free men, in the broadest sense of the term. The removal of the shackles is only the beginning of the mighty battle in life wherein the slave is to be ultimately redeemed and incorporated into the body politic as a factor in the life of the American nation. [ . . . ]

I am not afraid to use a term here which I can explain satisfactorily to any thinking man. Lincoln's idea and the idea of the broadest statesman was that the liberated slave should ultimately become amalgamated with the American Republic and become a member of this great nation. For, as he said, "The nation cannot long survive, permanently survive, one half free and one half slave." Even so, likewise, it cannot permanently survive with a great body of freedmen that have no right and title in the Republic as citizens to help direct its life and establish its destiny.

The American negro must understand that he must enter the battle of life and fight to-day the mightiest battle on the face of the globe. No man in the flesh has ever had such a conflict before him. It is the most difficult and the most dangerous undertaking on this footstool. For, look at the conditions that have surrounded him. He came from between the plough handles, with only a knowledge of ploughing. He was thrown into the lap of this mighty Christian civilization, and he was given the right of citizenship—a fearful boon to confer upon any unprepared man in any Republic. For the man who has the right to vote, has the right to be voted for.

I have no hesitancy in saying that it was hazardous at the time to place in the hands of these ignorant ex-slaves the ballot. Hear me through upon this dangerous question. I recognize that I am now walking upon eggs. I also recognize that there are some eggs that should be walked upon.

Look, if you please, at the pedigree of the ancient black slave. What did he have behind him? The story is a pathetic one. It is one that is full of sorrow and of intense interest. From the mud puddles of Africa, in the Providence of God he was dragged as it were, with hooks of steel, and transplanted upon this American continent. There was nothing back of him of which he could be proud—no illustrious pedigree. [ . . . ]

I dare not step back one foot lest I fall into the pit from which God Almighty, through Abraham Lincoln, digged me. Even now, with the memory of my ancestors illuminating my brain, I can hear the pathetic wail of the bloodhound that tracked them through the South. I have no kings and prophets back of me. No queens illuminate the firmament of my history. No men who wrote constitutions and laid the foundations of a government are back of me.

Who am I? The blue-eyed Saxon has his history written; the black-eyed Hamite will write his. He has been made; I am going to make somebody. "He is a descendant; I am an ancestor!" It is my business since the Proclamation has been written, to take hold of the mass of my ignorant people of the South—docile, tractable, easily moulded and easily guided—and mould them, and make a mighty people out of them. [...]

In this mighty country we have a Republic that is based, not upon the color of the skin but upon a national idea. Nationalism makes a Republic, and not blood or color. [...] Blood may make a race or an ancient nation, but blood does not make a Democracy [...] We must struggle for the preservation of the nation, the building up of one homogeneous nation; not homogeneous in its blood but homogeneous in its Nationalism. [...]

This celebration of the hundredth anniversary of the birthday of the great, martyred War President is observed all over the country, and we believe that ultimately we shall have a nation in this country that is united in its faith, in its zeal, in its absolute equality of political prerogatives, in its great purpose to make this the proudest nation on the face of the earth.

Just one other thought and then I am through. You must remember that in the City of Chicago, in the great State of Illinois, you have your part to do in this great battle. You have greater privileges than we have in the black belt of Alabama. Every door is open to you. You have yet to show in the years to come that you can wring out of your privileges the large good that we have wrung out of our disadvantages. In university life, in trades, in the accumulation of wealth, in the building of an honest character, in the making of men in face of difficulty without being discouraged, in meeting opposition without taking to the woods, you have yet to show that you can surpass your brethren on the plains of Texas.

I believe that we shall ultimately conquer in this great battle of life. We have great problems before us—great questions are under discussion. The negro should become a participant in the discussion and contribute to the life of the nation. I am glad of this privilege to bring this word of encouragement to you from the far South, from the land where you think it is extremely hard. Yes, it is hard, in some places. You have opportunities here that I sometimes covet, but I would prefer to ride in a box car in the South as a *man* doing something, fighting a battle, to riding in a palace car up here and generally doing nothing else.

You must liberate yourselves; you must not have anything more done for you. Legislation cannot make men, it can only prepare the way for the development of men. Law never makes one man equal to another man; there is no such thing as equality of manhood, and the American nation does not believe in this figment. You cannot make me believe that a certain black man is equal to a certain white man; and you would have a hard job to persuade me that a certain white man is equal to a certain black man. [...]

I believe that a man must make himself superior. You must make yourselves, you must liberate yourselves. Brain, cultivated brain, educated brain, skilled hands, a divine heart, a noble purpose, lofty ideals, the vision that reaches to the White Throne, make men—nothing else. You must not measure the man by the color of his skin. Great as Abraham Lincoln was, he was not great because he was white. He was great because he had a great soul in him.

In Nathan William MacChesney, ed., *Abraham Lincoln: The Tribute of a Century, 1809–1909* (Chicago: A. C. McClurg & Co., 1910), 91–98.

## CORA J. BALL, "On Lincoln's Centennial," February 13, 1909

*The daughter of formerly enslaved persons, Ball (1879–1956) was a native of Quincy, Illinois, who taught at the city's segregated Lincoln School and had contributed poems to African American newspapers in Chicago and Springfield when she composed the following to mark the Lincoln Centennial. As the nation celebrated Lincoln, Ball paid tribute to him as a martyr for the cause of justice, yet given the struggles African Americans faced, including those in Lincoln's home state, where Jim Crow prevailed in many areas, and a mob had recently killed Black residents near the site of Lincoln's home in Springfield, she wondered whether his sacrifice had been in vain. Ball's sober assessment of the centennial suggested that it was all too easy to honor Lincoln with words instead of actions that upheld his principles. Ball married Jonas Moten, an educator, and continued to publish fiction and poetry in prominent periodicals such as* The Crisis *and* Opportunity. *She and her husband moved to Los Angeles in the 1940s, where she worked as a newspaper editor and was active in various civic organizations for the remainder of her life ("Many Mourn as Death Calls Cora B. Moten,"* California Eagle *[Los Angeles, CA], July 19, 1956).*

---

Lincoln, thou who gave to manhood
Right to earn its manhood's due;
Thou, who pledged to woman's honor
Right to keep that honor true.

Martyred for a Nation's sinning
Is thy sacrifice in vain,
Are the noble things you stood for
Doomed to obloquy and shame?

Seest thou, with thy clearer vision,
How thy high ideals and pure,
Things thou gav'st thy very life for
Stir the Nation's heart no more?
Seest thou wrongs thou wouldst have righted,
Done with none to cry them shame;
Wrongs that stain the Nation's honor,
Wrongs that make thy work in vain?

Lincoln, Lincoln, stone and story,
Vaunting praise and martial song,
Cannot take the place of Justice,
Cannot make a right of wrong.
What are words but empty honors
If they grow not into deeds;
What, to thee a Nation's homage
Lest thy wise thought it heeds?

Tho' today the Nation praise thee,
Shirne thy dust in costly tomb,
Set thy name among its heroes,
Write thy praise in rhythmic rune;
Truer, aye, and dearer, vastly,
Is the praise of honest deeds
Wrought through love for weaker brothers
For some frailer human's needs.

The *Forum* (Springfield, IL), Feb. 13, 1909.

## FRED R. MOORE, "Lincoln Day and the White Folks," March 1909

*As the nation celebrated the centennial of Lincoln's birth in 1909, editor Moore (1857–1943) observed that February 12, which had traditionally been a day for African Americans to commemorate, was increasingly being celebrated by Whites who evinced little interest in remembering Lincoln as the Great Emancipator and sought to exclude Blacks from their Lincoln Day events. The most notorious example of this occurred in Lincoln's hometown of Springfield, Illinois (see address of James H. Magee above).*

---

The anniversary of Lincoln's birth was more generally celebrated this year than ever before. Not alone perhaps because it was the one hundredth anniversary, but because the white people are beginning to think more of Lincoln's character and work. Heretofore Lincoln's birthday has been left to the freedmen to celebrate. They have had to sound his praises as martyr, statesman, liberator; but this year the whites have outeralded Herod in their celebration of Lincoln's birthday. They in many places grew so intensely fond of him that Negroes were barred from not only speaking at many of their meetings, but at the Union League Club in Brooklyn, New York, it is stated that the colored waiters who wanted to hear what the orators would say about Lincoln were told to hie to the kitchen. After considerable persuading and apologies the dinner was served, but very sullenly. Probably next time this club will have foreign white waiters who will not be so sensitive about hearing what is said of Lincoln, who is no more to them than any other dead American. In Springfield, Ill., Lincoln's home town, the whites refused the Negroes admission to the exercises, and thus created some little stir. So after all the white man is beginning to admire Lincoln, but he wants to do the job by himself with no sandwiching in with the very bondmen that Lincoln set free.

What a contrast, what strange things happen in this life anyway?

*Colored American Magazine* 15, no. 3 (March 1909): 135.

## THOMAS NELSON BAKER, "Speech of Lincoln," March–April 1909

*Born a slave in Virginia, Baker (1860–1940) was educated at the Hampton Institute, Boston University, and Yale Divinity School, and he received a PhD in philosophy from Yale in 1903, becoming the first African American to obtain a doctorate in this discipline. Baker served as a Congregational minister in Pittsfield, Massachusetts, from 1901 until his death. In this tribute, Baker offered a mystical Lincoln who listened to a voice that told him to write the Emancipation Proclamation. As a former slave, Baker was grateful to Lincoln, even though Lincoln believed in the supremacy of his own race and valued the preservation of the Union above all else. Baker reminded his audience of the progress African Americans had made since emancipation and implied that work remained to ensure that they were able to exercise the rights of equal citizenship (George Yancy, "Thomas Nelson Baker: The First African American to Receive the Ph.D. in Philosophy," Western Journal of Black Studies 21, no. 4 [1997]: 253–260.)*

---

One hundred years ago today there was born in the Southland in the state of Kentucky a little child that was destined to become the emancipator of a race and the savior of a nation. Unlike Washington, the Father of his Country, this little child was born not with "a silver spoon in his mouth," but with an ax in his hand. From his seventh to his twenty-third year "he was almost constantly handling this most useful instrument." It was with "this most useful instrument" that he cut his way into the White House. It was during this ax period of his life that he won for himself the name "Honest Abe."

And it was during this period of his life that he received his first call. As like Abraham of old "he obeyed and went out not knowing whither he went." He was always more or less superstitious. As a boy he dreamed dreams, saw visions and heard voices. [...] It was one day while splitting rails that a voice called him, "Abraham!" And he said, "Here am I." And the voice said: "Stop splitting rails— lay aside the ax, take up the pen and learn how to write." And he did so. And the same faithfulness which he had manifested in using the ax, he manifested in using the pen. He was still "Honest Abe." And he learned to write as by divine command.

It was during this pen period of his life that he received his second call. One day while faithfully using his pen "without stopping to consider what personal results might come to himself," the Voice called a second time—"Abraham!" And he said: "Here am I." And the Voice said: "Go into your closet and write the Emancipation Proclamation." And immediately he "conferred not with flesh and blood" but went away with God to himself alone and wrote one of the most wonderful documents ever penned by man. When he called his cabinet together this is a part of what he said to them:

"When the rebel army was at Frederick, I determined as soon as it was driven out of Maryland to issue a proclamation of emancipation such as he thought most likely to be useful. I said nothing to anyone, but I made the promise to my Maker. The rebel army is now driven out, and I am going to fulfil that promise."

It was the fulfilling of that promise by Abraham Lincoln which he made to himself and to his Maker that makes [it possible for me to be here] to night and address you as "fellow-citizens." The fulfilment of that promise broke the chains not only from my father's hands, but also from the hands of my mother who bears this night upon her body the marks of the slave driver's whip. And not only from my father's hands but from these hands it broke the chains which were fastened upon them before I was born into the world. But that is not all. The fulfilment of that promise broke the chains not only from the hands of my people but from the hands of your people. It emancipated not only my people and me but it emancipated your people and you. Emerson says: "If you put a chain around the neck of a slave the other end fastens itself around your neck." Slavery degraded your race more than it degraded my race.

They tell us that the American Negro is dying out. About forty years ago Abraham Lincoln emancipated four millions of slaves. They have had no foreign immigration to increase their numbers but today they number about ten millions. They are dying out, but they are dying out at a mighty "poor rate."

I stand here tonight proud of my race—proud of its past—for they were the best slaves the world ever saw, and I believe they will yet give us the best citizens the world has ever seen. I am proud of its present state of progress, for no race has ever in the history of the world done so well under like circumstances. They began with nothing, but today the Negroes of the South own four hundred thousand farms, and two hundred thousand homes. And many of these homes will compare well in intelligence, morality, and religion with the best homes of this nation. The Negroes of this country own land equal to the combined areas of Belgium and Holland. Intellectually they have no need when compared with other races to be ashamed. Representatives of the race have taken the highest academic degrees from the best universities of the nation. And best of all they show an unusual capacity of soul to forgive and forget wrongs that have been and are still done against the race.

But do not misunderstand me. I do not understand that Abraham Lincoln was any special friend to the Negro. He was not any special friend to the Negro. He was something better than that—he was a special friend of God. It was not that he loved his own race less but it was that he loved truth, justice and fair play more. Abraham Lincoln believed in the superiority of his own race. He did not consider the Negro his equal esthetically, morally or intellectually but he did believe that in the right to life, liberty and the pursuit of happiness, in the right to eat without leave of any one the bread earned by his own hand, the Negro was the equal of himself, the equal of Judge Douglas and the equal of any living man. And because slavery denied the Negro his right and equality of opportunity, Lincoln hated slavery from his youth up with a perfect hatred.

But it is well known that President Lincoln had no intention or desire to interfere with slavery "either directly or indirectly." And when he did interfere with it he was driven to it. It took God a long time to make him see that he could not be the savior of the Union without first becoming the emancipator of the slaves. Some are born great, and some achieve greatness, and some have greatness thrust upon them. Abraham Lincoln was born great. We once thought of him as belonging to what is known as the "poor white trash of the South." He was born poor, but not trashy. There was nothing trashy about Abraham Lincoln. He had in his veins the best blood in the world. "Blood will tell." The best blood is the blood that does the best under given circumstances. Abraham Lincoln achieved greatness and he had greatness thrust upon him. Lincoln is doubtless the world's greatest emancipator and this greatest greatness was thrust upon him.

*Alexander's Magazine* 7, no. 5–6 (March–April 1909): 244–245.

## JOSEPHINE SILONE YATES, "Lincoln the Emancipator," April 1910

*An educator, author, and activist, Yates (1859–1912) was born in New York and attended schools in Philadelphia and Rhode Island before accepting a position at Lincoln University in Jefferson City, Missouri. Yates was the first woman to be appointed a professor at Lincoln, where she taught for eighteen years between 1889 and 1910. She was also active in the women's club movement and served as president of the National Association of Colored Women from 1900 to 1904. The following analysis of Lincoln's emancipation policy was published at the end of Yates's second stint at Lincoln when she was serving as chair of the English and History Departments (ANB).*

---

Historical records present to us an unbroken line of illustrious heroes, lofty in thought, dignified in speech, marvelous in action. Thus Greece has her Pericles; Rome, her Caesar; France, a Napoleon; England, a Wellington; Russia, Alexander II; the United States, her Lincoln; and here was the noblest Roman of them all, for in him were combined in an unusual manner the requisite elements to lead a people to honorable victory.

Each year fresh laurels and immortelles are placed, figuratively speaking, upon the brow of this martyred hero, Abraham Lincoln. And why this honor? Perhaps, that is best answered by reviewing, in part, that chapter of American history enacted between 1861 and 1865 which has special reference to the Emancipation Act—a chapter more thrilling and exciting than the pages of the most highly wrought fiction. The conditions surrounding the great American Republic during this time were such as to require the greatest skill, caution, sagacity, in the administration of government, from financial, patriotic and military standpoints; and the famous message of December 1st, 1861, showed that Lincoln, inaugurated March 4th of the same year, had carefully canvassed the situation; and that, among other things, slavery, *versus* emancipation, had received from him its full share of attention.

His keen judgment foresaw that the relation of this vexed question to the civil war was daily producing rapidly increasing complications; and by the phraseology of the message, in this particular, he evidently hoped to prepare the people to meet existing conditions, and the possibilities of others yet more startling [...].

It was, however, absolutely necessary that Lincoln, the man, who believed in the brotherhood of man and that all men were created free and equal, should lose himself in Lincoln, president of the United States, whose first duty it was to preserve the union, if possible. This duty, imperative, right and just, he never forgot [...].

Cautiously feeling the public pulse, he first proposed emancipation through the voluntary action of the states, hoping thus to render unnecessary the compulsory military form which Fremont and his followers had advocated and attempted; and he believed, that under the pressure of war necessities the border states might be induced to support this idea, if the general government would pay their citizens the full property value of the slaves that they were asked to liberate. Working along this line, on the sixth of March, 186[2], he sent to both the House and the Senate, a special message recommending the adoption of the following resolution: "Resolved, That the United States ought to co-operate with any state which may adopt gradual abolishment of slavery, giving to such state pecuniary aid to be used by such state in its discretion, to compensate for the inconvenience, public and private, produced by such change of system."

Mr. Lincoln had fully considered the criticisms that would follow concerning the expense of the proposed plan, and in letters, public and private, discussed it. [...] He recognized that the right of emancipation in these states was entirely in their hands; and he made his proposition, not as a threat, but as the shortest and easiest way of ending the war, by eliminating its dominant cause. [...]

About the middle of May of the same year, General Hunter, who had been sent to command the Department of the South, issued an order of military emancipation on the ground that slavery and martial law in a free country are incompatible [...].

This incident further complicated affairs, and [in] May 1862, the president issued a proclamation, declaring Hunter's order entirely void. "But," he continues, "I further make it known that whether it be competent for me as commander-in-chief of the army and navy to declare the slaves of any state free, and whether at the time, in any case, it shall have become a necessity, indispensable to the maintenance of the government, to exercise such supposed power, are questions which, under my responsibility, I reserve to myself." The signs of the times as now everywhere exhibited, both on the field and in private life, left a wonderful impress upon the long Congress, assembled from December 2d, 1861, to July 17th, 1862; and a series of anti-slavery measures were perfected and enacted which completely revolutionized the policy of the general government. [...]

Four months had now elapsed since the policy of compensated abolishment had been proposed, and with the exception of these great advances in legislation, no practical results had been reached. Meanwhile war, bloody-handed war, hourly was sapping the life of the nation and forcing conditions which could not be indefinitely prolonged.

Lincoln's anti-slavery policy during this time was, and has been widely assailed, even by his friends, but before passing any sweeping criticism upon his acts or utterances it is at least reasonable to consider the difficulties of the situation, the national crisis, the strength of the opposing forces, his official duty.

The issue of constitutional government is extremely delicate and a more aggressive leader would have worked irrevocable damage. The *necessity* of the hour was a *firm, cautious controlling hand,* able to avoid, on one side, the Scylla of rash experiment; on the other, the Charybdis of increasing rebellion.

That necessity was supplied in the person of the sagacious Lincoln; and those acts or utterances, which to the impassioned, or to the casual observer, seemed those of a mere temporizer, when viewed in the calm, clear light of historical evidence, are shown to be very important links in a chain of action that was in complete harmony with a satisfactory and justifiable method of procedure.

Accordingly, on the 12th of July, 1862, Lincoln again convened the delegates from the border slave states and read a second carefully prepared appeal to them, to accept compensation for slaves in their representative states, hoping thus to create a popular public sentiment for a policy which he considered afforded a plain, practical solution of the national difficulty; but this effort toward emancipation by compensation was no more fruitful in results than the former had been, and the defeat of this plan, coupled with McClellan's disastrous Richmond Campaign, doubtless caused Lincoln to decide upon a policy of military emancipation somewhat sooner than he otherwise would have done.

Three hundred thousand volunteers had been called for. A complete rearrangement of military officers was necessary, if, as he had previously declared, he intended to maintain the contest to ultimate triumph. He thoroughly believed, and afterward stated, that in a Republic, public opinion is the talisman which works the wonders of statesmanship. The hour was now propitious in this respect, and he soon decided in his own mind to give notice of his intention to emancipate the slaves, and to supply the deficiency of military strength from the ranks of the slave population of the South.

The confidential announcement of his plan was made to Secretary Seward, July 13, 1862, at which time Lincoln earnestly dwelt upon the gravity, importance, and delicacy of this matter; and on the 22d of July, he read to his cabinet a draft of a proclamation [...]. The discussion of the proposed proclamation by the Cabinet members was long and varied, and, at Secretary Seward's suggestion, that its issuance be postponed until it could be given to the country supported by military success, i.e., on the eve of an important victory, instead of, as was then the case, among the greatest disasters of the war, the President assented, and put the draft of the proclamation aside for a more auspicious moment. [...]

[T]he Union forces achieved a victory at Antietam, and buoyed up by this event, Lincoln seized an early opportunity to fulfill a solemn vow which he had made, and to make public the policy he had decided upon two months before. September 22d, all of the members of the Cabinet met at the White House, and to them he stated his determination to announce an emancipation proclamation, and that the victory in Maryland concerning which he had made a solemn vow to God, indicated to him his duty in the matter. [...]

The proclamation contained four leading propositions, the most important of which from many points of view previously have been stated; i.e., the announcement of military emancipation of all the slaves in states in rebellion, on the first day of January, 1863. The proclamation was heartily endorsed not only by nearly every free state governor, but by nearly two-thirds of the loyal representatives in the House. [...] On the 31st of December, 1862, Mr. Lincoln collected the notes, manuscript, and data which his Cabinet advisers brought him, and on the afternoon of that day carefully revised the entire body of the proclamation, completing it on New Year's Day, January 1st, 1863, with a hand already weary from observing the usual executive custom of hand-shaking on that day.

Thus did the final proclamation, duly signed, attested, and deposited in the official archives, materialize and become one of the great documents of history, as deciding the fate of a race, the life of a nation, a principle of government, a question of primary human rights; and, followed up, as it was, by the ratification of the Constitutional Amendment of 1865, by which slavery was forever abolished from the United States and all places subject to the laws thereof, this proclamation was, in truth, a most important step in the progress of the human mind toward a perfect, intellectual liberty, an absolute emancipation. [...]

And, while American Negroes in common with patriotic American citizens of whatever race and nationality, celebrate "The Glorious Fourth," to commemorate deliverance from political bondage; while the sturdy sons of New England unite to give praise to the Pilgrim Fathers for casting off the thralldom of religious bondage; it is, for obvious reasons, pre-eminently fitting that we, as a people, annually meet on Lincoln's natal day to do honor to this national hero who gave his life to a noble cause; and, as each circling year whirls round the day we celebrate, let us bring more than tribute of words. Let us be able to show courageous hearts, noble deeds, creative genius, monuments of science and art, all of those qualities and results which determine the standard of an advanced manhood and womanhood; that shall we prove, that he who wrote, "I trust I have made no mistake in my emancipation policy," "builded better than he knew."

A. M. E. Church Review 26, no. 4 (April 1910): 335–344.

## HENRY MCNEAL TURNER, "Reminiscences of the Proclamation of Emancipation," January 1913

*Turner (1834–1915) was a bishop in the AME Church when he offered the following reminiscence to mark the semi-centennial of the Emancipation Proclamation. Turner's warm memory of being in Washington when Lincoln issued the final Emancipation Proclamation provided a striking contrast to his reputation for being a harsh critic of the United States. After serving as a chaplain in the army during the Civil War and as a member of the Georgia legislature during Reconstruction, Turner became so disgusted with the state of race relations that he advocated Black emigration to Africa. While Turner offered a very positive assessment of Lincoln in 1913, just a few years prior he had been roundly condemned for reportedly denouncing the American flag as a "contemptible rag" and claiming hell was a better place for African Americans than the United States. Though Turner claimed he had been misquoted, he asserted that there was "not a star in the flag that the negro could claim or that recognized his civil liberty and unconditional manhood more than if it was a dirty rag." Turner could celebrate the Emancipation Proclamation and the man who issued it, while at the same time, lament that the work of emancipation remained unfinished (ANB; "Turner Denies He Cursed Flag," Atlanta Constitution, Feb. 24, 1906).*

---

We are now upon the verge of the fiftieth anniversary, since the Immortal Abraham Lincoln, then President of the United States, by the grace of God hurled against the institution of American slavery the thunderbolt which had been smelted in the furnace of fair play, justice and eternal equity. [...]

The Civil War between the states was then in full blast, and the seeming odds were at that time in favor of the Confederate forces, or to use a familiar term, "the rebel army." The agitation of enlisting colored soldiers was engaging public attention. Israel Church was only a couple hundred yards from the United States Capitol, where mighty speeches were being made in the United States Congress in favor of enlisting colored men in the Union army. [...]

In 1862, on the 22d day of September, Mr. Lincoln issued a proclamation that in a hundred days, unless the rebel army disbanded, and the several Southern states resumed their relation to the general government, he would declare the slaves in all the states free with a few local exceptions. The newspapers of the country were prolific and unsparing in their laudations of Mr. Lincoln. Every orator after reviewing in their richest eloquence, concluded their speeches and orations by saying, "God save Abraham Lincoln," or "God bless our President." [...]

In the great Union Cooper Hall in New York City, a colored man leaped and jumped with so much agility when the proclamation was read that he drew the attention of every man and woman, till Mr. Lincoln's proclamation was scarcely listened to. [...] Whites and blacks realized no racial discriminations. On the first day of January, 1863, odd and unique conditions attended every mass-meeting, and the papers of the following day were not able to give them in anything like detail. Like before sunset Israel Church and its yard were crowded with people. The writer was vociferously cheered in every direction he went because in a sermon I tried to deliver I had said that Richmond, the headquarters of the Southern Confederacy, would never fall till black men led the army against this great slave-mart, nor did it fall and succumb to the general government till black men went in first. [ . . . ]

Seeing such a multitude of people in and around my church, I hurriedly went up to the office of the first paper in which the proclamation of freedom could be printed, known as the "Evening Star," and squeezed myself through the dense crowd that was waiting for the paper. [ . . . ] The third sheet from the press was grabbed for by several, but I succeeded in procuring so much of it as contained the proclamation, and off I went for life and death. Down Pennsylvania Ave. I ran as for my life, and when the people saw me coming with the paper in my hand they raised a shouting cheer that was almost deafening. As many as could get around me lifted me to a great platform, and I started to read the proclamation. I had run the best end of a mile, I was out of breath, and could not read. Mr. Hinton, to whom I handed the paper, read it with great force and clearness. While he was reading every kind of demonstration and gesticulation was going on. Men squealed, women fainted, dogs barked, white and colored people shook hands, songs were sung, and by this time cannons began to fire at the navy-yard, and follow in the wake of the roar that had for some time been going on behind the White House. Every face had a smile, and even the dumb animals seemed to realize that some extraordinary event had taken place. Great processions of colored and white men marched to and fro and passed in front of the White House and congratulated President Lincoln on his proclamation. The President came to the window and made responsive bows, and thousands told him, if he would come out of that palace, they would hug him to death. Mr. Lincoln, however, kept at a safe distance from the multitude, who were frenzied to distraction over his proclamation.

I do not know the extent that the excitement in Russia led to, when the humane Emperor proclaimed the freedom of twenty-two million serfs, I think in 1862, but the jubilation that attended the proclamation of freedom by His Excellency Abraham Lincoln, I am sure has never been surpassed, if it has ever been equaled. Nor do I believe it will ever be duplicated again. Rumor said that in several instances the very thought of being set at liberty and having no more auction blocks, no more Negro-traders, no more forced parting of man and wife, no more separation of parents and children, no more horrors of slavery, was so elative and heart gladdening that scores of colored people literally fell dead with joy. It was indeed a time of times, and a half time, nothing like it will ever be seen again in this life. Our entrance into Heaven itself will only form a counterpart. January 1st, 1913, will be fifty years since Mr. Lincoln's proclamation stirred the world and avalanched America with joy, and [on] the first day of next January, 1913, our race should fill every Church, every hall, and every preacher regardless of denomination should deliver a speech on the results of the proclamation.

A. M. E. Church Review 29, no. 3 (Jan. 1913): 211–214.

## JAMES WELDON JOHNSON, "Father, Father Abraham," February 1913

*Writer of the historic Negro National Anthem, NAACP leader, poet, and anthologist before the New Negro Movement, Johnson (1871–1938) published this poem to commemorate both Abraham Lincoln's birthday and the fiftieth anniversary of the Emancipation Proclamation. Only five stanzas, Johnson's poem is a part of the vindicationist tradition certifying that African Americans had demonstrated their capabilities without the yoke of enslavement. Johnson pays gratitude to Lincoln for the enormous gift of freedom, and requests he bless Blacks again from his guaranteed place in heaven, intimating that struggles continue.*

---

Father, Father Abraham,
To-day look on us from above;
On us, the offspring of thy faith,
The children of thy Christlike love.

For that which we have humbly wrought,
Give us to-day thy kindly smile;
Wherein we've failed or fallen short,
Bear with us, Father, yet a while.

Father, Father Abraham,
To-day we lift our hearts to thee,
Filled with the thought of what great price
Was paid, that we might ransomed be.

To-day we consecrate ourselves
Anew in hand and heart and brain,
To send this judgment down the years:
The ransom was not paid in vain.

Father, Father Abraham,
To-day send on us from above
A blessing of thy gentle strength,
Of thy large faith, of thy deep love.

*The Crisis* 5, no. 4 (Feb. 1913): 172.

## WILLIAM H. LEWIS, Speech before the Massachusetts General Assembly, February 12, 1913

*A native of Virginia, Lewis (1868–1949) graduated from Amherst College and the Harvard Law School. While a student, Lewis became known for his talent as a football player and was the first African American to make the All-American team. After graduation, Lewis practiced law in Boston and served as an assistant coach for the Harvard football team. When Lewis was invited to address the Massachusetts General Assembly in commemoration of Lincoln's birthday and the fiftieth anniversary of the Emancipation Proclamation, he was an Assistant Attorney General of the United States, which at the time was the highest federal position held by an African American. Referring to himself as belonging to a liberated race, Lewis paid homage to Lincoln for that freedom, and maintained he epitomized what an emancipator should be. Lewis's awe of the sixteenth president was reflected in an unabashed view of him. For Lewis, Lincoln remained a living presence, as he suggested the voice of Lincoln was yet speaking to anyone who had the heart to listen and by following his words the nation could complete the unfinished work of emancipation. While Lewis lamented the treatment of African Americans, he also sought to vindicate Lincoln's act by detailing the progress Blacks had made in the half-century since emancipation. Like Lincoln, Lewis made a distinction between civil rights and social equality, as he believed that providing equal opportunities to African Americans would end the practice of passing and limit intermarriage (AANB).*

---

You have invited me, as a member of the liberated race, to address you upon this Lincoln's Birthday in commemoration of the 50th Anniversary of the Emancipation Proclamation. Words would be futile to express my deep appreciation of this high honor, however unworthily bestowed. [. . .]

To-day is the anniversary of the birth of Abraham Lincoln, the preserver of the Union, the liberator of a race. "The mystic chords of memory," stretching from heart to heart of millions of Americans at this hour, "swell the chorus of thanksgiving" to the Almighty for the life, character, and service of the great President.

Four brief, crucial years he represented the soul of the Union struggling for immortality—for perpetuity; in him was the spirit of liberty struggling for a new birth among the children of men.

"Slavery must die," he said, "that the Union may live."

We have a Union to-day because we have Emancipation; we have Emancipation because we have a united country. Though nearly fifty years have elapsed since his martyr death and we see his images everywhere, yet Lincoln is no mere legendary figure of an heroic age done in colors, cast in bronze, or sculptured in marble; he is a living, vital force in American politics and statecraft. The people repeat his wise sayings; politicians invoke his principles; men of many political stripes profess to be following in his footsteps. We of this generation can almost see him in the flesh and blood and hear falling from his lips the sublime words of Gettysburg, the divine music of the second inaugural and the immortal Proclamation of Emancipation. We see this man of mighty thews and sinews, his feet firmly planted in mother earth, his head towering in the heavens. He lived among men but he walked with God. He was himself intensely human, but his sense of right, of justice, seemed to surpass the wisdom of men. A true child of nature, he beheld the races of men in the raw without the artificial trappings of civilization and the adventitious circumstances of birth or wealth or place, and could see no difference in their natural rights.

"The negro is a man," said he, "my ancient faith tells me that all men are created equal."

As a man he was brave yet gentle, strong yet tender and sympathetic, with the intellect of a philosopher, yet with the heart of a little child. As a statesman he was prudent, wise, sagacious, far-seeing and true. As President he was firm, magnanimous, merciful, and just. As a liberator and benefactor of mankind, he has no peer in all human history. [ . . . ]

I have observed with aching heart and agonizing spirit during the last twenty years not only the growing coldness and indifference on the part of our people to the fate of the Negro elsewhere; but here in our own city the breaking up of the old ties of friendship that once existed between people of color and all classes of citizens, just after Emancipation; the gradual falling away of that sympathy and support upon which we could always confidently rely in every crisis. I have watched the spirit of race prejudice raise its sinister shape in the labor market, in the business house, the real-estate exchange, in public places, and even in our schools, colleges, and churches. [ . . . ]

National Emancipation was the culmination of a moral revolution, such as the world has never seen. [ . . . ] So for fifty years since Emancipation, there has been more or less conflict over the Negro and his place in the Republic. The results of that conflict have in many instances been oppressive and even disastrous to his freedom. Many things incidental to Emancipation and vital to complete freedom are unfortunately still in the controversial stages. The right of the Negro to cast a ballot on the same qualifications as his other fellow citizens is not yet conceded everywhere. Public sentiment has not yet caught up with the Constitution, nor is it in accord with the principles of true democracy. The right of the Negro to free access to all public places and to exact similar treatment therein is not universal in this country. He is segregated by law in some sections; he is segregated by custom in others. He is subjected to many petty annoyances and injustices and ofttimes deep humiliation solely on account of his color.

The explanation of this reactionary tendency sometimes given is that the Negro is only a generation from slavery. It should not be forgotten that individuals of every other race in history have at some time been held slaves. [. . .] No race has a right to lord it over another or seek to degrade it because of a history of servitude; all have passed through this cruel experience; the history of the black race is a little more recent, that is all. The fact of slavery, therefore, should not impose the slightest limitation upon the liberty of the Negro or restriction upon his rights as a man and citizen.

The one great phase of the race question agitating the country to-day is that of intermarriage and miscegenation. It is a serious question; it is a vital question. No one will deny the right of any man to protect his family stock, or the right of a group to preserve its racial integrity. The facts show, however, that laws, however stringent, will not accomplish it. I submit for the serious consideration of the American people that the only danger of infusion from the Negro side is simply one thing, and that is summed up in one word "injustice." Why is it that thousands of colored men and women go over to the other side, "pass" as we say? It is for no other purpose than to escape the social ostracism and civic disabilities of the Negro. Why is it that we see so many pathetic attempts to be white? It is simply to escape injustice. In a country where every opportunity is open to the white, in business, in society, in government, and the door shut against or reluctantly opened to the black, the natural unconscious effort of the black is to get white. Where black is a badge of an inferior caste position in society, the natural effort of the black is to find some method of escape. I do not advocate intermarriage; I do not defend miscegenation. The same thing is true to-day as it was true in the time of Lincoln. In his debates with Douglas in 1858, he noted "that among the free States, those which make the colored man the nearest equal to the white have proportionally the fewest mulattoes, the least amalgamation."

I submit therefore, that the only sure way to put an end to this tendency or desire, so far as the Negro is concerned, is to accord him all his public and political rights and to treat each individual upon his merits as a man and citizen, according to him such recognition as his talents, his genius, his services to the community or the state entitles him. Make black, brown, yellow, the "open sesame" to the same privileges and the same opportunities as the white, and no one will care to become white.

Upon this day which commemorates the emancipation of the black and the larger freedom of the white race, the redemption of the state and the birth of a new nation, I would bring to you a message not of blackness and despair but of hope [. . .].

Emancipation redeemed the precious promises of the Declaration of Independence. It rid the Republic of its one great inconsistency, a government of the people resting upon despotism; it rescued the ship of state from the rocks of slavery and sectionalism, and set her with sails full and chart and compass true once more upon the broad ocean of humanity to lead the world to the haven of true human brotherhood. [. . .] "In giving freedom to the slave we insured freedom to the free." In a country where all men were free none could be slaves. Emancipation raised labor to its true dignity and gave a new impetus to industry, commerce, and civilization. [. . .]

What of the Negro himself? Has he justified Emancipation? The statistics of his physical, intellectual, and material progress are known to all. He has increased his numbers nearly threefold. [. . .] He has reduced his illiteracy to thirty per cent. He owns nearly $700,000,000 worth of property including nearly one million homes. He has shown that his tutelage in American civilization has not been vain; that he could live under the most trying and oppressive conditions.

Three milestones in his progress have been reached and passed:

First: The North and South agree that the abolition of slavery was right and just.

Second: The people of the North and South agree that every industrial opportunity shall be given to the Negro.

Third: The right of the Negro to be educated and the duty of the state to see to it that he has every opportunity for education are established. Public opinion has settled forever the right of the Negro to be free to labor and to educate. These three things constitute no slight advance; they are the fundamental rights of civilization.

The prophecy of Lincoln has been fulfilled, that Emancipation would be "An Act, which the world will forever applaud and God must forever bless." [. . .] The American Negro in freedom has brought new prestige and glory to his country in many ways. [. . .]

The history of the world has no such chapter as the Negro's fifty years of freedom. *The duty of the hour is to unshackle him and make him wholly free.* When the Negro is free from the vexatious annoyances of color and has only the same problems of life as any other men, his contribution to the general welfare of his country will be greater than ever before.

Whatever be his present disadvantages and inequalities, one thing is absolutely certain, that nowhere else in the world does so large a number of people of African descent enjoy so many rights and privileges as here in America. God has not placed these 10,000,000 here upon the American Continent in the American Republic for naught. There must be some work for them to do. He has given to each race some particular part to play in our great national drama. I predict that within the next fifty years all these discriminations, disfranchisements, and segregation will pass away. Antipathy to color is not natural, and the fear of ten by eighty millions of people is only a spook of politics, a ghost summoned to the banquet to frighten the timid and foolish.

I care nothing for the past; I look beyond the present; I see a great country with her territories stretching from the rising to the setting sun, with a climate as varied as a tropical day and an Arctic night, with a soil blessed by the fruits of the earth and nourished by the waters under it; I see a great country tenanted by untold millions of happy, healthy human beings; men of every race that God has made out of one blood to inherit the earth, a great human family, governed by righteousness and justice, not by greed and fear—in which peace and happiness shall reign supreme. [ . . . ]

With the widening of men's visions they must realize that the basis of true democracy and human brotherhood is the common origin and destiny of the human race; that we are all born alike, live alike, and die alike, that the laws of man's existence make absolutely no distinction. [ . . . ]

God grant to the American people this larger view of humanity, this greater conception of human duty. In a movement for democracy, for social and industrial justice, for the complete Emancipation of the Negro from the disabilities of color, Massachusetts must now, as in the past, point the way. If we fail here, with traditions and history such as are ours behind us, can we succeed elsewhere? The Great Emancipator speaks to us at this hour and furnishes the solution for all our race problems. "Let us discard all this quibbling about this man and the other man, this race and the other race, and the other race being inferior and therefore must be placed in an inferior position. Let us discard all these things and unite as one people throughout this land, until we shall once more stand up declaring that 'all men are created equal.'"

God grant that the American people, year by year, may grow more like Lincoln in charity, justice, and righteousness to the end that "the government of the people, for the people, by the people, shall not perish from the earth."

In Alice Moore Dunbar, ed., *Masterpieces of Negro Eloquence* (New York: The Bookery Publishing Company, 1914), 409–424.

## W. E. B. DU BOIS, Address to Commemorate the Fiftieth Anniversary of the Emancipation Proclamation and Lincoln's Birthday, Chicago, February 12, 1913

*An intellectual and civil rights leader from the late nineteenth century to his death a day before the 1963 March on Washington for Jobs and Freedom, Du Bois (1868–1963) was both a critic and supporter of Abraham Lincoln. When Du Bois delivered the following speech in Chicago to commemorate the fiftieth anniversary of the Emancipation Proclamation and Lincoln's birthday, he was serving as Director of Publicity and Research for the recently formed*

*NAACP and editor of* The Crisis, *the organization's magazine. Du Bois's address focused on Lincoln's adherence to democratic principles and faith in the popular will. For Du Bois, Lincoln's legacy was keeping American democracy alive by privileging the "real people," and trusting in their ability to understand the slavery issue and reach the conclusion that it must be abolished. Lincoln's example was all the more relevant during a time when Du Bois feared Americans were losing their faith in democracy, especially in the South, where Blacks had been systematically disfranchised through a series of contrivances that subverted the Fifteenth Amendment. Du Bois provided statistics to illustrate how much more a White man's vote counted in the South than in the North. In singling out three notorious White supremacists, Governor Coleman L. Blease of South Carolina, US Senator Benjamin R. Tillman of South Carolina, and US Senator Hoke Smith of Georgia, Du Bois raised the specter of an oligarchy replacing the democracy that Lincoln had fought and died to preserve.*

---

Abraham Lincoln has always been looked upon as one who in a peculiar way represented the mass of the American people. Perhaps this fact more than any other single thing has saved the traditional American faith in democracy. When we have been tempted, as we so often have been, to lose faith in the effectiveness of any appeal to the popular vote—when we have sneered at the shifty politicians whose ears are ever to the ground listening intently for any far off rumble of the popular whim or will, or when in angry disquiet we have arisen the morning after election to find things all gone wrong—then we remember on days like this, that gaunt and simple man, scrawny and uncouth, and yet so strangely and compellingly human, who kept his ear to the ground and believed in the ultimate sanity of the American people.

Where is it then, that we almost insensibly and yet instinctively draw the line between the demagogue and Abraham Lincoln? Our nation is today full of men—shrewd, far-seeing men—who are straining every nerve, using every means of prediction and measurement, to anticipate the popular demands of tomorrow. We not only do not hail them as great—rather we despise them as something less than small, and although the future may reverse our severe judgment in some cases, as it did the judgment of many wise men in the case of Lincoln, yet on the whole we are painfully certain and unwillingly certain that our judgments in the main are only too correct.

The real righteousness in the case of Abraham Lincoln lay in his intense belief in the wisdom, the sanity and the good will of the masses of men. This is not today a wide spread belief. Publicly it is, of course, wise to profess it, and most of us do, but privately one hears and talks of the foolishness of the average run of men, their peculiar lack of brains, and their remarkable desire to do wrong and to be wrong. Here then is a distinct difference of opinion between the average man of the world today and Abraham Lincoln. [...]

Now and then, however, we catch anxious glimpses of agreement with Lincoln. Those who go down to the sea in ships—who go down to the writhing, struggling mass of men, not casually, but continuously, eternally—in school and settlement, in social brotherhood, come back to us with face ablaze and soul on fire. [...]

It is the widening and deepening of such experience which is today becoming the antidote for our loss of faith in democracy. We are continually learning that it is not the east side of New York or the West Side of Chicago that is solely or even mainly responsible for the worst failures of our civilization. Indeed, we have come to see with Abraham Lincoln that the real problem of democratic government is strangely like the problems of former monarchy. [...]

Now, the courtiers and courtesans of democracy are even more numerous than those of monarchy, and Abraham Lincoln knew it. He was ever pushing and striving to get to the real people, whose reign is truly by the grace of God. The great life work of Abraham Lincoln was to clear a path to this throne,—to allow the people to know just what slavery meant, and what it did not mean. His legacy to you and to me was to keep that path open. To make democracy effective in America, by giving it a basis in the untrammelled expression of every sane soul which has reached years of responsibility. He said—and it was perhaps, his greatest, most comprehensive word—no man is good enough to rule his neighbor without his neighbor's consent. He was determined that this nation should be a free nation in the sense that every man, as a man, should have the right to sit in judgment on the acts of his fellow men.

Now this implied then, and it implies now tremendous faith in the masses of men. Some have even affected to believe that it means that the people can do no wrong. Abraham Lincoln never believed this and never said it. To him and to all sane thinkers Democracy is not an end, it is a means. If you allow each man to sit in judgment on the acts of his fellows, then his fellows have laid on them the tremendous duty and responsibility of justifying their acts and intentions before the intelligence of every voter. If the voter is ignorant and vicious his judgment will be dangerous. If he is intelligent and decent his judgment will be worthy, but this is also true if appeal is made to one king or a few oligarchs, and Abraham Lincoln believed, and the world is steadily moving toward his belief, that the wider you make this appeal to men, the deeper you drive the foundations of civilization. The mass of men may and do go wrong, but they go wrong less seldom than any one man, or than any group of men selected by any possible method of choice.

If we believe this, and as Americans and sharers in the priceless legacy left by this great and good man, we must believe it—then the practical question before us this day is: Are we walking in the path which Abraham Lincoln blazed? Are we determined that this nation shall not be an oligarchy, half slave and half free, but a democracy based on the franchises of all men—and all women, regardless of their wealth, or their race or the color of their grandfathers?

I fear few Americans realize how far we have already strayed from the Democracy of Abraham Lincoln, and how far the sins which they load on the back of popular government in America are in reality the sins of those who are determined to thwart any expression of the popular will. Some of us have seen the deep-seated disease of irresponsible oligarchy in the power of corporate wealth, and the ruthless manipulation of government by shrewd and conscienceless men. But I want tonight to call attention to another wide spread flouting of democracy, which you are disposed to ignore because you think it merely a local and racial issue which can be settled without reference to the main problems of democratic government in America. [...] I want to prove to you by a few simple figures, in order that you may realize that what is often called simply a Negro problem is the same problem of American Democracy at which Abraham Lincoln worked, and which still fronts us, and will front us until we settle it right.

We have just passed through a presidential election, and after long delay the official returns are in. I invite your attention to a few of these figures. In that election the State of Alabama and the State of Minnesota each having about the same population, each cast twelve electoral votes. But while it took 300,000 voters to cast these votes in Minnesota, it took only 100,000 to cast the same number in Alabama. Florida and Maine each had six electoral votes, but 50,000 Florida voters exercised exactly the same power as 130,000 voters in Maine. Again, Georgia and New Jersey each have fourteen electoral votes, but it took over 400,000 voters in New Jersey to equal 120,000 in Georgia. So, too, less than 80,000 voters in Louisiana cast the same number of electoral votes as 365,000 votes in Kansas, while 63,000 voters in Mississippi had as much power as 215,000 in Rhode Island and Oregon.

But you are, of course, interested in your own state, and you will doubtless be pleased to know that whereas it requires in the state of Abraham Lincoln 1,150,000 voters to cast its electoral vote that it takes only 224,000 voters to wield exactly the same power in the state of Governor Blease and Mr. Tillman, the bailiwick of Senator Hoke Smith, and the state of Florida together.

Outside of any question of color, race or slavery this is a condition that no democracy can allow to go on and live. When eight states deliberately disfranchise so many of their White and Black citizens that an oligarchy of less than a million voters can wield the same power as nearly three million voters elsewhere in the country, the very foundations of democracy are in danger. When the Minnesota voter places one ballot in the box the Alabama voter places three. It takes seven New Jersey votes to balance two in Georgia, while in Louisiana two men can out vote nine in Kansas.

Do you realize that you cannot appeal to the American people today? Do you realize that between you and the sovereign American democracy stands this entrenched oligarchy? Do you realize that one man in the former slave states has more political power than any three in Illinois[?] [...]

This rotten borough system is destroying the very vitals of American democracy. It is giving to the least prepared section of our country a power over social legislation which is simply overwhelming. [...] Now is the time to stop it. Now is the time to use reason and law and appeal to the better part of men north and south to remove this menace to Abraham Lincoln's democracy. The National Association for the Advancement of Colored People, in whose behalf I speak tonight, is the organization of American citizens without regard to race, sex or section, which is trying to say to all Americans, "Now is the accepted time—here lies your bounden duty."

*Broad Ax* (Chicago), Feb. 15, 1913.

## BOOKER T. WASHINGTON, Address at Rochester, New York, February 12, 1913

*While W. E. B. Du Bois seized the occasion of delivering a speech on Lincoln's birthday in 1913 as an opportunity to question the disfranchisement of African Americans in the South, Washington (1856–1915) devoted much of his 1913 Lincoln Day address to detailing the progress that had been made in the half-century since Lincoln had issued the Emancipation Proclamation. As the titular leader of African Americans since his "Atlanta Compromise" address in 1895 and the death of Frederick Douglass that same year, Washington welcomed the opportunity to speak in a town where Douglass lived for twenty-five years. A consistent theme in Washington's tributes to Lincoln was his desire to vindicate Lincoln's decision and prove that Blacks had made the most of their freedom. At Rochester, Washington assured his audience that African Americans had become more like Whites than recent European immigrants. Additionally, in the face of expectations to the contrary, he claimed African Americans had become largely self-sufficient. Interestingly, Washington concluded with the notion that freedom must be won; it cannot be given. The work Lincoln commenced would therefore not be finished until Blacks had the same opportunities as Whites to rise and were accorded equal treatment under the law.*

I am grateful for the opportunity to speak before this distinguished body on the anniversary of the birth of the Great Emancipator of my race. I have always felt that as a race we could best manifest our gratitude to Abraham Lincoln and the other friends of the white race who so nobly and bravely contended for our freedom not by contenting ourselves to sing their praises, but by proving day by day that we could suc[c]eed as American citizens. And when I say success, I do not mean success in external things of life, but success in the ordinary daily affairs of life. [...]

During our fifty years of freedom we have been subjected to some pretty severe tests, and in meeting these tests it should always be remembered that our progress as a race is measured by the progress of the American white man by whose side we live. We have proven our ability both in a state of slavery and in a state of freedom to increase in numbers. A few hundred years ago twenty members of the race were brought into this country as slaves. By importation and by natural increase, at the end of slavery we had multiplied to about four millions of people. At the present time we number about ten millions, and the race is still increasing at about the same rate that the people of Great Britain are increasing in numbers.

Unlike many alien races, we have not stood aside and refused to accept and use the American white man's ideas of civilization, but we have eagerly sought after, absorbed and used these ideas, so that aside from his color the American Negro is more like the native white man than most foreign races that come upon our shores. The American Negro prepares and eats his food just as the white man does. He wears the same kind of clothes, speaks the same language, professes the same religion, and loves and honors the same flag.

The most difficult lesson that the Negro has had to learn during his fifty years of freedom has been that of respect for labor with the hand. Naturally when we came out of slavery the idea was pretty prevalent among us that it was disgraceful for an educated man to use his hands in ordinary labor. It required years of hard and patient effort on the part of such institutions as Hampton Institute, the Tuskegee Institute and others to bring the American Negro to the point where he would feel that it was just as honorable for an educated man to work in the shop, laundry or kitchen as it was to preach the gospel or teach school. [...] This I consider the most important evidence indicating Negro progress that we can point to. [...]

We have proven, too, that we can get property and keep it, not so much as an end but as a means toward the higher civilization. It means a great deal, it speaks much in behalf of the white people of this country as well as the Negro himself that a race beginning practically with no property fifty years ago now owns and pays taxes upon at least 20,000,000 acres of land. [...]

When Mr. Lincoln freed us only 3 per cent of the American Negroes could either read or write. At the present time practically 70 per cent of the American Negroes can both read and write. [...]

Despite what we hear about crime among colored people, a careful and impartial investigation will reveal the fact that the Negro is not more criminal than is true of other races in the same relative stage of civilization. [...] I should be the last, however, to apologize for the Negro criminal. We must have fewer such characters in the future than we have had in the past. But in all parts of the country in an increasing degree the Negro is becoming a sober, law-abiding citizen, and in proportion as he gets education, learns the dignity of labor, and owns property and becomes a tax-payer he will in a still great measure cease committing crime.

In this connection I am glad to say that during the last twelve months we have had fewer lynchings and mobs in the South than we have for twenty years, excepting one other year. All this indicates that both the Negro and the Southern white man are learning to respect law. [. . .]

We are proving to the world, too, that it is possible for the American Negro and the American white man to live upon the same soil in large numbers side by side in peace and friendship. This I say despite the occasional outbreaks of disgraceful lynchings and mobs which indicate racial friction. It must be remembered when considering the two races in the South that we have a tremendous territory covered by about nine million black people and over twenty million white people, and wherever you have practically thirty million people living on the same territory there is likely once in a while to be trouble, but in proportion as the Southern white man and the Southern Negro get education and get higher ideas of civilization we are going to have less lawlessness and fewer mobs.

Only a little while ago I was called into the State of Mississippi to a Negro municipality to take part in the formal opening of a large cotton seed oil mill that had been built by black hands and by the capital of the black people of Mississippi at a cost of about $100,000. [. . .] The man at the head of this movement was a former slave of Jefferson Davis, Isaiah T. Montgomery.

We have proven, too, that we can support ourselves from a material point of view in a state of freedom. I know that there were not a few in this country fifty years ago who said to Abraham Lincoln that the Negro would neither feed, clothe nor shelter himself in a state of freedom, consequently he would prove a constant burden upon the pocketbook of the nation, but during all the years of freedom since the days of reconstruction the American Negro has never called upon the American Congress to appropriate a single dollar to be used to provide for us either food, clothing or shelter. In all these fundamental matters we have cared for ourselves and mean to do so in the future; the only calls we have made upon the generosity of the public have been for money with which to provide for ourselves education, the same kind of call that all races and nations have a right to make upon the generosity of the public.

Lastly, we have learned that freedom in its broadest and deepest sense can never be a bequest, it must be a conquest.

All, however, is not done. I am not deceived as to the present nor as to the future. Before my race will be thoroughly upon its feet, before satisfactory conditions will be thoroughly established as between white people and black people in the South there remains years of hard, patient work for both races. We must still bear in mind that a very large proportion of our Southern population, black and white, are still in ignorance, unused to the higher and better things of American civilization. Our work will not be done until there is a good public school lasting either nine or ten months every year placed at the door of every white and black child in the South. Our work will not be done so long as in any state there is lynching or the prevalence of mob law. Our work will not be done so long as the chief executive of any state boasts of the fact that he encourages or permits mob law to flourish in his state. Our work will not be done so long as in any portion of the country one man feels that in order for him to appear rich another man must be kept in poverty. Our work will not be done until all the laws in every state are conceived in righteousness and executed in absolute justice regardless of race or color.

Booker T. Washington Papers, Microfilm Reel 411 (Washington, DC: Library of Congress).

## JOHN H. MURPHY SR., "A Government for the People," July 5, 1913

*The year 1913 marked not only the fiftieth anniversary of the Emancipation Proclamation but also the fiftieth anniversary of the Battle of Gettysburg and Lincoln's Gettysburg Address. As over fifty thousand veterans of both the Blue and Gray gathered at Gettysburg for a reunion to mark the occasion, the editor of the* Afro-American, *John H. Murphy (1840–1922), also a Civil War veteran, worried that the hard-fought victory achieved in the war was being squandered. As Murphy surveyed the situation, he drew a direct connection between the desire for sectional reconciliation that the Gettysburg reunion symbolized and the state of affairs in the South. Murphy concluded that only by following the words Lincoln had spoken at Gettysburg could the situation be rectified (ANB).*

———

Just at this particular time, when so much is being said and done in reference to the fiftieth anniversary of the great battle that turned the tide of the Union armies and finally resulted some few years later in the ultimate victory of the government over the revolutionists of the south, a few words in reference to the notable utterance of President Lincoln on the occasion of the dedication of the former battlefield into a National Cemetery for the burial of those who lost their lives in that horrible conflict may not be out of place.

Said President Lincoln, among other things:

"It is rather for us to be here dedicated to the great task remaining before us, that from these honored dead we take increased devotion; that we here highly resolve that these dead shall not have died in vain; that this nation under God shall have a new birth of freedom; and that government of the people, by the people, for the people shall not perish from the earth."

We are wondering whether Mr. Lincoln had the slightest idea in his mind that the time would ever come when the people of this country would come to the conclusion that by the "People" he meant only white people. No one can look over the conditions in the Southland as they prevail today and come to any other conclusions than that "government of the people, by the people, for the people," means anything else but government for all the people by the WHITE people. In not one southern state, whether formerly in rebellion or otherwise, but that the government is in the hands of the white people, and is administered solely for the benefit of the white people. The teeming millions of Negroes in the South are not considered when it comes to a question of government, only so far as the white people of that section may feel inclined.

Today the South is in the saddle, and with the single exception of slavery, everything it fought for during the days of the Civil War, it has gained by repression of the Negro within its borders. And the North has quietly allowed it to have its own way. Even now notwithstanding the preelection promises of the President and his sponsors, in almost every department of the government in Washington, the Negro is beginning to feel the effects of the South holding the reins of government.

The Negro has been loyal all the way through, even under the most adverse circumstances. And when Mr. Lincoln called for Negro volunteers, the call came back to him with the answer: "We are coming Father Abraham, one hundred thousand strong." And they came and fought and died, and their blood consecrated almost every battlefield from the Potomac to the Gulf. Today that blood is crying from the ground in every Southern State. Will the voice be heard? If it is not heard, little will the great reunion of the "Blue and Gray" on the battlefield of Gettysburg, or elsewhere do towards carrying this great country on and on to the highest pinnacle of civilization.

Rather will it be like others who have passed away and have gone, and whom scientists are today digging up from the dust of centuries. Its name will be "Ichabod," and will be written in letters of infamy to be read of by generations yet to come.

It would be wise, just at this juncture, to study well the words of the immortal Lincoln and in order that the government of the people, by the people and for the people shall not perish from the earth, to recall the fact that at least part of the people of this country are Negroes and at the same time human beings, and civilized human beings at that; struggling towards the light, as God has given them to see the light.

The *Afro-American* (Baltimore, MD), July 5, 1913.

# RICHARD R. WRIGHT SR., Address at the Emancipation Proclamation Exposition, Philadelphia, Pennsylvania, September 14, 1913

*Born to enslaved parents, Wright (1855–1947) was a graduate of Atlanta University and the president of the Georgia State Industrial College for Colored Youth when he delivered the following address at the opening of an exposition in Philadelphia that was held to commemorate the fiftieth anniversary of the Emancipation Proclamation. Wright had been unsuccessful in his efforts to obtain federal funding for a national exposition, but this did not deter some states and several towns and cities from holding their own commemorative events. Harry W. Bass, the first African American member of the Pennsylvania legislature, helped persuade fellow lawmakers to appropriate funds for the event in Philadelphia. Wright's speech exemplifies the ambivalence and complexity of responses to Lincoln, for he hailed the greatness of Lincoln's proclamation and elevated it to the same level as the Declaration of Independence, yet he also pointed out its limitations and made it clear that preservation of the Union was Lincoln's chief aim. Wright celebrated an unfinished emancipation, as he noted the lack of recognition accorded to Black veterans at the recent Blue-Gray reunion held on the Gettysburg battlefield and suggested that a nation that permitted Blacks to be segregated, disfranchised, and lynched was not fulfilling the principles of either Jefferson's Declaration or Lincoln's proclamation (David W. Blight,* Race and Reunion: the Civil War in American Memory *[Cambridge, MA: Belknap Press of Harvard University, 2001]; AANB).*

---

It must be acknowledged that it is a happy coincidence that where the cradle of American Liberty had its basis, we meet to celebrate the Fiftieth Anniversary of the Emancipation Proclamation of the American Negro. It is also very singular, indeed, that the author of the Declaration of Independence and the author of the Emancipation Proclamation were both Southern men. This may not be significant in the progress of American liberty or Negro liberty, but it is worth stating. I verily believe that the Emancipation Proclamation is as much a fact in American life as the Declaration of Independence. Each was in some measure the outgrowth of the stress of the demands of war. We must believe, however, that as long as the Declaration of Independence stands, so long will stand the Emancipation Proclamation. Perhaps there are here today few men who were acquainted with Abraham Lincoln, the Hamlet of the great American drama of the nineteenth century. But there is none here who does not regard the great emancipator as the Negro's benefactor, America's hero and one of the world's chief humanitarian[s].

In making this statement with reference of the Emancipation Proclamation, it is not to be contended by the most ardent admirer of Mr. Lincoln that it was his chief purpose on subscribing to the oath as President of the United States to so manage his administration, whether with or without war, to bring about the Emancipation of the slaves. Reliable historical information confirms the opinion that it never was Lincoln's purpose to emancipate the slaves contrary to the laws of his country. I fully believe had not the salvation of the Union and the extremities of the war demanded it, the Emancipation Proclamation would not have been issued by Abraham Lincoln, certainly not at the time it was issued. The fiat of war drove him irresistibly to the issuance of his provisional proclamation on September 22, 1862 and of the Emancipation Proclamation [on] January 1, 1863. He said to those who were in arms, if you will lay down your arms, I will not emancipate your slaves by the edict of war, but if you do not lay down your arms against the American Government, in every state where the (so-called) rebellion exists, the slave shall be forever free.

Had the God of Freedom so ruled that the southern men had laid down their arms, the Emancipation Proclamation would not have been issued, but, perhaps, it is not superstitious to declare that there is a Divinity that shapes our end, rough hew them as we may. Long, long before the Civil War it was plainly written in the Book of Fate that slavery was doomed. In admitting this, it is unnecessary to pluck a single laurel from the brow of the great emancipator. Whether or not he was master of his own fate, he alone can tell. Suffice it for us to know and the world to give praise that he was the author of one of the world's greatest events of the nineteenth century.

Notwithstanding this, we believe that in the course of events, slavery would have gradually become extinct in America. [...] But whether by the logic of events or by the necessities of war, the Emancipation Proclamation is an event which stirs the hearts of all true men. We rejoice that it came and came no later than it did come.

The Gettysburg celebration was a great occasion and fifty thousand men were there from all sections of the country to honor it. Bivouacking there upon America's greatest battlefield dedicated by Lincoln to human liberty, the gray and the blue united and renewed their allegiance to the old flag. There were probably not present many of the two hundred thousand Negro soldiers who liberated by the edict of America's greatest President had helped make the majority of the side of the Union and to save the jewel of liberty in the diadem of freedom. Be this as it may, we are not going to grumble or quarrel about this slight on this occasion. Despite this we too love the old flag. We have fought for it in every war for American liberty. Its ample folds may have not always been broad enough to protect us even upon American soil, which has been well nigh drenched with our blood [...]. We have patience, the patience of Lincoln, but we expect to enjoy all the rights, privileges and immunities accorded to any other American citizen; we are patient, but we have "Jim Crow" cars and "Jim Crow" steamboats and "Jim Crow" hotels; we are patient, but we know we are treated unjustly when we are disfranchised and denied participation as voters and office holders in the government of our country, both State and Nation; we are patient, but we feel keenly the insults, sneers, and rebuffs of our more fortunate fellow citizens. We wonder how long can our government afford to deny to our criminal and unfortunate, protection and trial by the courts of the land.

Nevertheless, we shall not despair, although we know that our status in American life is at present very precarious; although we know that on this fiftieth anniversary of our Emancipation Proclamation, it is difficult to say just where we are and whither we are tending.

*New York Age*, September 18, 1913.

## THEOPHILE T. ALLAIN, Address to Commemorate the Fiftieth Anniversary of the Emancipation Proclamation, Decatur, Illinois, September 23, 1913

*The son of a White planter and an enslaved woman, Allain (1846–1917) was a Louisiana landowner and Republican member of the state legislature prior to moving to Illinois. Over four hundred African Americans from Decatur and surrounding communities gathered to commemorate the fiftieth anniversary of the Emancipation Proclamation and hear Allain's speech. In addition to offering high praise for Lincoln, Allain argued that former slaves in the United States had made more progress since their emancipation than former serfs in the Russian Empire. The measures introduced during the 1913 session of the Illinois General Assembly that Allain referred to at the end of his address were bills that would have prohibited interracial marriages. Robert R. Jackson, the lone African American member of the legislature, helped defeat these proposals. While Allain praised Governor Edward F. Dunne for opposing these measures, the governor had also vetoed a bill that would have prevented racial discrimination in cemeteries (DANB; Decatur Herald [Decatur, IL], Sept. 24, 1913).*

---

All the races and nations take one day out of 365 days in the year to celebrate the grandest epoch in the achievements of their race and their best efforts, and we, the colored people of the United States of America, take September 22, 1862, and January 1, 1863, as our day to celebrate our freedom. [ . . . ]

Mr. Chairman, Ladies and Gentlemen, there are five great epochs in my mind before and since the coming of our Lord Jesus Christ, which precede our emancipation and our achievements as compared with the other nations the world over.

First, among the things in the Bible which goes before us and our work is to be found in the first book of Moses, 12th chapter of Genesis, when God Almighty sent Abraham to find the Promised Land, the land of Canaan, which he did. Second, the second epoch in the Bible which goes before our achievements is to be found in the second book of Moses, called Exodus, when God Almighty in the 20th chapter, gives to Moses the Ten Commandments, which now illuminates the world as a guide to mankind.

Third, the third epoch which is much greater than all of our work is what took place one thousand nine hundred and thirteen years ago—the birth of our Lord Jesus Christ in Bethlehem of Judea.

Fourth, the fourth epoch, which is greater than all of our work, was when as you will find in the sixth chapter of Matthew, when our Lord Jesus Christ gave to the world Our Lord's Prayer, commencing at the sixth verse to the ninth verse inclusive, and His Commandments are in the fifth chapter of Matthew, Jesus Christ's Sermon on the Mount.

Fifth, the fifth epoch is Lincoln's birth and his prayer at Gettysburg, and Meade's success in winning the battle of Gettysburg, because God Almighty heard Abraham Lincoln's prayer and gave him the victory of his army at Gettysburg July 1, 2 and 3, 1863. Mr. Chairman, I see before me here a large number of the men of the Grand Army of the Republic, the grandest organization of the earth, and I want to say to you and those you represent, that on behalf of all of the American Negroes I thank you for what you have done on the field of battle, because without you and those living and dead, there would have been no celebration here today.

You men of the Grand Army of the Republic, the whole country loves you, because you won your honors upon the field of battle. Teach your boys and your girls that from 1619, when the first negroes were brought over here by the white people, white men and negroes have fought side by side, bled and died together that this country under God would be what it is today, the grandest on earth. You may hear some foolish things by irresponsible people, but believe me when I tell you that if any nation should ever make the mistake and fire on your flag, the American flag, we, the Negroes, will furnish any morning before breakfast, one-half million of black soldiers who will sing as they did at San Juan Hill: "There will be a hot time for all comers this day." You Grand Army men represent the whites and we of the colored people represent the blacks; let us drop a tear upon the regretted memories of the past, and blot them out forever.

Read what Lincoln said at Gettysburg November 19, 1863, five months after the three days' battle, the grandest ever fought on earth. [...]

*[Here Allain recited the Gettysburg Address in its entirety.]*

My fellow citizens, had Robert E. Lee succeeded, the Southern Confederacy would have been established, the union divided, slavery would have been continued, and no celebration would have been held here today. Abraham Lincoln, God bless his dear soul! Friends, if I had the ability, the education and the language to do so, I would bind my happiest and brightest thoughts into bouquets and place those bouquets upon his grave and upon his monument; wrap his record in the American flag and write upon his breast his first and second Emancipation Proclamations, and salute him with the thirteenth, the fourteenth and the fifteenth amendments to the Constitution of the United States of North America. [ . . . ]

And now, Mr. Chairman, in behalf of the 10,500,000 Negro men and women living in the United States and who are true to its honor and to its flag, I want to say that when in aftertimes, when the petty revolutions of society and the bloody conflicts of the battlefields are forgotten, the coming Negro boys and girls, the men and women of our race that will come after us, and will take our places in this grand and noble republic, will build monument after monument all over the states of the union and will put upon its and their peaks that man who sits on the left hand and with Jesus Christ on the right hand of God, transmitting to all in aftertimes the record of his virtues and of his achievements [ . . . ].

The czar of Russia in 1861 emancipated 14,000,000 Russian white slaves, or serfs, and how does their history compare with our achievements and all facts reported by white historians in Europe and in this country? If our two leaders, Booker T. Washington and W. E. B. DuBois could have taken part in the writing of the history, results may have been different as to our part, or showing in the final history, as they are made up today. Ladies and gentlemen, please look at this bug as I lift up the chip. The 14,000,000 serfs pay taxes on $500,000,000 of property as we find in Russian history, reduced their illiteracy from 90 per cent in 1861 to seventy per cent in 1910, the last census, a reduction of twenty per cent in forty-nine years, with three acres of land given to each person in 1861, which multiplied by fourteen gives 42,000,000 acres of land in 1861. The negroes in the United States, 4,000,000, with no land given to them in 1863, with ninety per cent of illiteracy against them, in 1910 paying taxes on $700,000,000 worth of property, reduced their illiteracy to thirty per cent, a reduction of sixty per cent in forty-seven years. This is, on illiteracy, forty per cent the best of the Russian serf and $200,000,000 the best of them as to property on which taxes are paid. [ . . . ]

And I would like to say here and to make it plain that all laws that were introduced in the 1913 session of the Illinois General Assembly were defeated because of the influence of the state administration and because of the effect and intent of those bills were against the interest and the rights of the colored men and women of this state, and you well know that influence of this state administration gave to the colored, an appropriation of $25,000 to celebrate their fifty years of freedom and of their work and of their grand achievements in fifty years.

*Address of Ex-Senator T. T. Allain*, n.p. (1913).

## OLIVIA WARD BUSH-BANKS, "Abraham Lincoln," 1914

*Bush-Banks (1869–1944) grew up in Rhode Island and was of African and Native American descent. She taught drama in Boston, Chicago, and New York, and was a poet associated with the Harlem Renaissance. Her tribute to Lincoln appeared in her second published volume of poetry that included poems honoring Frederick Douglass, William Lloyd Garrison, and William Carney, an African American Civil War soldier and recipient of the Medal of Honor. In the immediate wake of the fiftieth anniversary of the Emancipation Proclamation, Bush-Banks offered a celebratory poem that acknowledged Lincoln as the architect of Black emancipation. As "a Martyr for the cause," he will live forever in their memories, and divine approbation has been his reward (ANB).*

Like some gigantic, lofty forest tree,
Shorn of its leafy garment in the storm,
With roots secure deep-fastened in the earth,
Where naught can rob it of its noble form,
So stood this man, strong in his sense of right,
Who faltered not, whose courage never failed,
Within the Nation's heart, his image stands
For aye;—because o'er Wrong he had prevailed.

More than a friend, or brother, then was he,
In very truth, a Martyr for the Cause,
Unflinching in his zeal-opposing wrong,
Defending bravely God's own Righteous laws.
For, out of hard almost unyielding rock,
Did he not hew a passage for our way?
Did he not cause the darkness to disperse,
Did we not see the dawning of the day?

Live ever in our memories, great soul.
Tho' passed beyond the pale of human sense,
Thy work well done, hath found its just reward,
Divine approval is thy recompense.

In *Driftwood* (Providence, RI: Atlantic Printing Co., 1914), 29.

## GRAND HOUSEHOLD OF RUTH, Resolution on
## Equal Suffrage, August 1915

*At its annual meeting held at Poughkeepsie, New York, a branch of the Grand Household of Ruth, the women's auxiliary to the United Order of Grand Odd Fellows, invoked Lincoln's image as the Great Emancipator to advocate passage of a woman suffrage amendment to the New York Constitution. The resolution refers to a letter that Lincoln penned in 1836, which announced that he was seeking re-election to the Illinois legislature. Although the resolution places Lincoln's statement in quotation marks and emphasizes his endorsement of women's rights, Lincoln's actual words were: "I go for admitting all whites to the right of suffrage, who pay taxes or bear arms, (by no means excluding females.)" The constitutional amendment was defeated in the November referendum, yet the resolution is testament to the malleability of Lincoln's memory and the way in which African American women fashioned Lincoln into not only the emancipator of their race but also as a would-be emancipator of women (Collected Works, 1:48).*

---

Whereas, the women of New York are seeking political emancipation at the hands of the men of the state by a constitutional amendment giving the right of suffrage to women, to be voted on November 2, 1915, and

Whereas, It is as unjust to subjugate people on account of sex as on account of color; and

Whereas, the women of our race are largely wage-earners in industry and their labor needs the protection of the ballot; and by the successful passage of the suffrage amendment we will be able to vote on equal terms with men without hindrance by reason of race, color, or sex; and

Whereas, the Great Emancipator, Abraham Lincoln, whom we all revere as the liberator of our race, preached equality for all, men and women alike, and said, "I go for all sharing the privileges of the government who assist in bearing its burdens BY NO MEANS EXCLUDING WOMEN!" [...]

Be It Resolved, That the Household of Ruth endorses the cause of woman suffrage and urges our husbands, brothers, sons and friends to help win our political emancipation by voting on the Woman Suffrage Amendment, November 2, 1915.

The *Freeman* (Indianapolis), August 28, 1915.

## RICHARD W. GADSDEN, Address on Lincoln's Birthday, Savannah, Georgia, February 12, 1918

*A graduate of Atlanta University, Gadsden worked as a school principal in Savannah from 1902 until his retirement in 1947. The following was delivered at a Lincoln birthday celebration held at the St. John Baptist Church. As the United States sent troops to France for the ostensible purpose of making the world safe for democracy, Gadsden paid tribute to Lincoln as a global symbol of democracy. Echoing the famous Frontier Thesis of Frederick Jackson Turner, Gadsden argued that Lincoln's frontier upbringing ideally suited him to preserve democracy in the United States and serve as an inspiration to others. In pointing out that African American soldiers were playing an important role in saving democracy in Europe, despite being denied its benefits at home, Gadsden anticipated former Atlanta University professor W. E. B. DuBois's noted editorial from 1919, "Returning Soldiers" ("Tribute Paid Retiring Savannah School Head," Pittsburgh Courier, Aug. 2, 1947).*

---

Abraham Lincoln was born at a time when the rigors and hardships of the backwoods living had become accentuated in his ancestors and it was impossible for him to escape the solid, simple, hardy heritage which was his. [ . . . ]

The three-sided house, the pile of leaves on which he slept, his deerskin pants and coonskin cap and moccasins for shoes, represent days of straitened circumstances.

The school days were as scant as everything else, for he could spare only a few days from work to attend school. His father at one time was so hard-pressed that he had to hire him out to one of his neighbors for two dollars a week.

He had three books, Bunyan's Pilgrim's Progress, Robinson Crusoe and the Bible. [ . . . ] Lincoln lay on his stomach and by the light from a lightwood knot, learned by heart his few books. [ . . . ]

You will pardon me, I know, for referring to the time when our fore-parents were whipped if they were found with a book in their hands, but yet, some of them learned under such adverse circumstances. [ . . . ]

From the beginning he had the experience with the common people. He knew their joys, their expectations, their suffering, their hardships. He knew these things in the only way they can be known. He saw the worst phases of slavery and was fitted by nature to be the champion of the common people and the emancipator of the slave. The experiences he had at home, in school, in the field, on the boat, in the post office, as surveyor, as rail-splitter, made him the pre-eminent democrat of the world, efficient, courageous, persistent and righteous. [ . . . ]

Every picture of Abraham Lincoln is unsatisfactory to somebody, because he was a man of many-sided personality. He possessed the strength of a giant, the energy of a superhuman, the features of a Socrates. He was ugly and gawkey, but he also possessed the gentleness and kindness of a woman and there was something in him that was soft to the point of sadness. [...]

He was elected by the new party styled the "Black Republicans" because they included Negroes in their party, and were determined to contend for their freedom.

The abolitionists and the pro-slavery faction were waging a bitter contest, men were being killed and property was being destroyed and the country was being lined up on the question of slavery, and finally brother lined up in battle array against brother and when the smoke of the conflict rose from the battlefield a great army had been defeated and two great questions had been decided, the right of the states to secede and the right of one individual to hold another as slave.

Unfortunately when the battle died away and men were anxious to think soberly of the past and hopefully of the future, some men yet unable to throw off the bitterness of former days and the man who had spent so many days in sad contemplation upon the limits to which men's prejudices lead them was to become the victim of an assassin's bullet. Thus ended the life of the world democrat.

May be the question arises in our minds: why should people stop yearly to do honor to men whose voices are still and who move no more amongst us? The man whom we honor today was a different man from other men. He was a great man measured by all the rules of greatness. He possessed the king becoming graces; he was patient, charitable and knew his neighbor. He believed in the multitude and he knew and loved the common people.

But why do we turn aside and uncover our heads, and pronounce eulogies upon Abraham Lincoln? Ordinarily we answer, because he freed our forefathers. This would be sufficient reason, if it were all. To confine his greatness to the emancipation would be to circumscribe his greatness and minimize our claim upon him.

The life of this great man from the earthen flood in a most humble home, reared of such primitive parents to the popularity of a great nation, nay, even to the highest honor his countrymen could give him, was all a preparation of him and a consummation of destiny to make him by birth, by hardship, by every experience the fittest and best exponent of democracy. The only lasting and safe government is the government of the people, for the people and by the people.

In these parlous times when almost the whole world seems ablaze and in the travail of the birth of a new idea of government, Abraham Lincoln looms large indeed because of his definition of democracy, and the wise men of earth and the people, the common people are all recognizing that the divine right to rule resides not in kings, emperors and princes lounging complacently in gilded palaces, but everybody everywhere is accepting and fighting for democracy—for the rule of the people by themselves.

Even we Negroes, the most mistreated, the most insulted, the most down-trodden and at the same time the most courageous, the most forgiving and apparently the most forgetting and patriotic people under democracy's sun, are fighting to make it safe for the world.

Whenever and however democracy comes the Negro will be the largest beneficiary, not as a free gift, but as an award which comes to him for valiant service rendered shoulder to shoulder with men and his red blood will continue to help make the red stripes of Old Glory.

Abraham Lincoln, a love of the people, the common people. He was our friend. He was a democrat and we cherish his memory.

*Savannah Tribune* (Savannah, GA), Feb. 23, 1918.

## EDWARD A. JOHNSON, Speech on Lincoln's Birthday in the New York State Assembly, Albany, New York, February 12, 1918

*A former slave and native of North Carolina, Johnson (1860–1944) worked as a teacher, wrote a history of Black soldiers in the Spanish-American War, and served as dean of the law school at Shaw University before moving to New York. Johnson practiced law, was active in the Republican Party, and in 1917, he became the first African American member of the New York State Assembly. During his single term in the legislature, Johnson led a successful effort to revise the state's civil rights law that expanded the places of public accommodation where racial discrimination was prohibited. While it might have been fashionable in some circles to criticize Lincoln and point out the shortcomings of the Emancipation Proclamation, Johnson would not hear of it ("Edward Austin Johnson," The Journal of Negro History 29 [Oct. 1944]: 505–507).*

Mr. Speaker and gentlemen of the Assembly: I think no one in this house can feel prouder of Lincoln than myself. I, as the Speaker has just told you, was born a slave in the State of North Carolina, in the town of Raleigh, its capital. The emancipation proclamation emancipated me. We had eleven children in our family. Those eleven children also would have been slaves but for the emancipation proclamation. My father was a slave and my mother was a slave. They were all emancipated through the proclamation of this great man—Abraham Lincoln.

So that you can readily understand I have a great deal of feeling on a day like this, and I do not know, in the last twenty years, when Lincoln's birthday has passed, without my saying something somewhere in reference to that great character.

I know that he has been criticized, and some have attempted to say that his efforts in behalf of the slaves were not sincere, but done purely as a war measure;

but looking at the matter from all sides I believe that that position is not true—that Lincoln was sincere in his efforts and his success in emancipating the slaves. He did it at a time when he did not have to do it. His whole party was against him. [...] Not only his own party but the other parties were against him at the time, and I believe that he did it from the consciousness of his duty.

There is a story told about him that on one occasion, when he went down on one of those boats to New Orleans, that there he witnessed the sale of a slave girl—he witnessed the improprieties and the indignities that were shown her, the familiarities by the slave dealers, and he went back home and told his people that if ever it came his opportunity to strike the institution of slavery a blow that he would strike it a hard one.

That blow was struck in the emancipation proclamation of 1863. We do not credit it to Karl Marx or to any other body or personage whatsoever—it was Lincoln's act and Lincoln's deed. The world has grown great on account of it, and America has become the beacon light of liberty of the whole world.

What have these people done since slavery to vindicate the justice of the emancipation proclamation? Have they made good? You have them owning in the states of this country over 276,000 farms. They have over 38,000 school teachers, thousands of professional men, both in medicine and in law and in dentistry and in other fields; one has been register of the treasury of the United States, they have been ministers to the different countries, and in no instance do I know of one that has betrayed his trust or profession or proved recreant to the great duties that were imposed upon him. They have made a good record.

They have accumulated in dollars and cents, which cannot be the criterion of all that is good perhaps, and yet it is a measure in a certain sense of civilization and prosperity—they have accumulated $800,000,000 of property according to the census.

They have fought and bled in every war for America's independence and America's glory, from Crispus Attucks, who fell in Boston in 177[0], the first man to fall in the war of the revolution [...].

In the war of the rebellion they furnished 180,000 troops, who marched for the freedom of themselves and the freedom of America. [...]

They have been brave, they have been willing, and in this present conflict there are enlisted 735,000 brave black boys that are going to Europe or wherever they are called.

I am coming down to the political question again. Let me say that in my district there are only about 3,200 colored voters out of a voting population of 10,500. I got nearly twice as many white votes as I got colored votes in that district. I have their recommendation. It was perfectly natural that the colored people should vote for me as representing them and representing their ideas, but it might not be natural for the white people to vote for me unless I represented their ideas as expounded by Lincoln, and as he had in mind, when he emancipated the slaves. So that the endorsement they gave me I bring here, and I come representing that district as a vindication of the righteousness of Lincoln's deed and of Lincoln's proclamation, not to slack away from Lincoln, not to deviate from his ideas that were real and courageous, but like the colored flag bearer in the Spanish-American war, who went at one time ahead of his companions, who, when an officer said to him, "Bring the flag back, bring the flag back," answered: "I will not bring the flag back, you come up to the flag."

And that is where I stand today, asking you gentlemen here, in behalf of a race that you know as well as I do hasn't all the opportunities and all the privileges and all the advantages that some others may have in this great republic, for justice. But I believe that the heart of the republic is right, and that the best brain and the best ideas of the republic are right, and that they are going to vouchsafe to us as colored people our rights, the same as to other people, and that, as the colored flag bearer said you are going to come up to the flag of Lincoln and not have his flag or any other flag brought back to you.

Gentlemen, I thank you for hearing me this long, and I know you will pardon me if I have trespassed on your valuable time, but I can feel as you do not feel and I can know as you do not know, and I can appreciate as you do not appreciate, and I can love Lincoln and love his memory as perhaps no man in this house can, and it pains me that any man following any doctrine, any tenet, should fail to stand up and voice his sentiments for the great embodiment of all that is good in America and all that is good in the world, so far as freedom and liberty are concerned, as can be embodied in the ideas of one man and that man Abraham Lincoln. Let it not occur again. I thank you. (Great applause.)

*State Service: An Illustrated Monthly Magazine* 2, no. 3 (March 1918): 39–41.

## ALICE DUNBAR-NELSON, "Lincoln and Douglass," 1920

*A native of New Orleans, Dunbar-Nelson (1875–1935) was educated at Straight College and Cornell University. She worked as a teacher, and while known for being married to Paul Laurence Dunbar, Dunbar-Nelson attained recognition as a literary figure in her own right. In addition to publishing poems and short stories, Dunbar-Nelson was a journalist and editor who compiled two volumes of African American oratory. The following essay is taken from the second volume she edited, and it links Lincoln with Frederick Douglass. Though the exact birthday of Douglass is unknown, she suggests he was born in February. Referring to both as emancipators, Dunbar-Nelson acknowledges the influence of Douglass on Lincoln's growth, as he pushed Lincoln to follow his best self by supporting Black citizenship and economic self-sufficiency. She believes that while it is important for Black youth to celebrate Lincoln and know his Gettysburg Address, it is equally appropriate to celebrate Douglass and know his speeches, for the speeches of Douglass are just as timely as those of Lincoln because America has not changed its attitudes toward Blacks (ANB).*

———————

Frederick Douglass once said: "Any man may say things that are true of Abraham Lincoln, but no man can say anything that is new of Abraham Lincoln." If that were true in the past century, in the early seventies, how much more it is true today, when over a century has passed since the hero of America opened his eyes in a log cabin of Kentucky.

It is eminently fitting and proper that we, as Americans, celebrate the birth of the man who, by a single stroke of his pen—albeit, a reluctant stroke—gave the Negro the right to stand with his face to the sun and proclaim to the world, "I am a man!" It is our right and our duty to commemorate his birth, to mourn his death, to revere the twelfth of February as a holiday, to come together to lay laurel wreaths on his tomb. But we Americans of the darker skin have another day as dear to us as the twelfth of February, less well known, perhaps, but which we should acclaim with shouts of joy, even as we acclaim the day which has grown familiar by long usage. That day is the birthday of Frederick Douglass.

Lincoln and Douglass; Douglass and Lincoln! Names ever linked in history and in the hearts of a grateful race as the two great emancipators, the two men above all other Americans, fearless, true, brave, strong, the western ideal of manhood. Is it not fitting that their natal days should come within a few hours of each other? Is it not right that when the Negro child lifts its eyes to the American flag on Lincoln's day he should, at the same time, think of the man whose thunderous voice never ceased in its denunciation of wrong, its acclamation of right, its spurring the immortal Lincoln to be true to his highest ideals; its sorrowful wail when he seemed to fail the nation? Verily, on this day of days we of the darker hued skin have a richer heritage than our white brothers—ours the proud possession of two heroes, theirs of but one.

Every school boy in the nation knows Abraham Lincoln—his gaunt figure, his seamed and pain lined face, with its sweetness and patience, are familiar to their eyes. His life, with its romance of poverty and toil, its tragic sorrow and tragic end, are as close to the heart of the nation as the stories of the Bible and the Christ-child. The utterances of Lincoln, the anecdotes of his life, the whimsical stories of his early days and his quaint humor furnish a never ending theme of interest to the American school boy. His sublime speeches; the delicate pathos of his first inaugural address; the splendid, stern, yet tender beauty of the second inaugural address are recited from thousands of school platforms annually, while the Gettysburg speech is as well known in America as the Lord's Prayer and the

Beatitudes, and I deem it no sacrilege to say that in point of literary beauty it stands with them. It is graven in bronze in the national cemeteries, on school walls, in the halls of colleges and universities. It is recited semi-annually by the majority of the school boys in the country, and it is right that it should be, for is not Lincoln the nation's idol, the American ideal?

Yet how many Negro youths in the land know as much of the ideal of Negro manhood, Frederick Douglass? If Lincoln is the American idol, so is Douglass the Negro's idol. If Lincoln's was a romance of life, with its toilsome youth culminating in a splendid manhood, attaining the highest gift which the nation could bestow, how much more is Douglass' life a romance? The slave, beaten, starved, stripped, fleeing from slavery at the most deadly peril, to become in his later manhood the guest of nobles and kings, the cynosure of the nation's eyes, the friend of this same Lincoln, the great man of the century? If Lincoln's utterances are inspiring, calling in clarion notes for right and justice and truth, so much more are Douglass' inspiring to us, calling for manhood and strength and power. [ . . . ]

The Negro youth of the land recites the Gettysburg speech, and it is right that he should do so; but does he know Douglass' "What to the Slave is the Fourth of July?" The Negro youth of the land admires Lincoln's Second Inaugural address, but does he know Douglass' splendid tribute to the man who wrote the Second Inaugural address, when the freedmen of this country erected the Lincoln monument at Washington? The Negro youth rolls over his tongue the witty epigrams of the mighty Lincoln, but has he been made familiar with some of the pithy aphorisms of his own Douglass?

But, I hear you say, Lincoln's speeches were for all time: Douglass' for the period in which slavery existed; Lincoln addressed an entire nation: Douglass only a limited portion. Not so. What Douglass said was true today, as it was in his own day. If America were guilty in holding slaves, she is no less guilty in her attitude towards the men whose fathers were slaves. If the conscience of the nation needed quickening in 1860, how much more so does it need quickening in this year?

Lincoln reached the zenith of his fame only to be struck down in cold blood by the ruthless hand of an assassin. Douglass lived to an honored age, to die in the ful[l]ness of love and fame and admiration. It was the sad duty of Douglass to pay the tribute of a grateful and sorrowing race to the name and fame of the Emancipator. While the nation mourned, aghast, at the heinousness of the crime, while North and South alike agreed in the execrations which were hurled at the assassin, there was the humble, child-like Negro race, whose shackles he had struck off, bowed in dumb misery at the spectacle of his one and only true white friend, cold in death. It seemed a wise dispensation of Providence that one of that race could come forward fearlessly and lay the tributes of his people on the prostrate form. [ . . . ]

Lincoln and Douglass; Douglass and Lincoln! We honor them both today, but more than the mere men, we honor their impress on our own people. We glean from their lives lessons of worth, but more than from their lives we learn from their characters what we need to make our own strong, and of their characters the two lessons which we most need we may take to heart—moral honesty and moral courage. [...]

My friends, we do well to gather here today to honor the memory of Abraham Lincoln; we do better to remember his great contemporary, Frederick Douglass. The twelfth of February is to us, as Americans, a sacred occasion—the fourteenth of February is to us, as Negroes, a no less holy day. When the race which shares with us this great country lays its laurel wreaths on the tomb of Lincoln, we, of the dark-hued skin and saddened eyes, must lay our palms on the grave of Frederick Douglass. Both heroes are ours to remember, to extol, to revere, to emulate.

Lincoln and Douglass; Douglass and Lincoln! May their names ever be welded into one memory in the hearts of every Negro in the land!

In Alice Moore Dunbar Nelson, ed., *The Dunbar Speaker and Entertainer* (Naperville, IL: J. L. Nichols & Co., 1920), 197–203.

## HUBERT H. HARRISON, "Lincoln and Liberty—Fact Versus Fiction," March 1921

*Born on the island of Saint Croix, Harrison (1883–1927) immigrated to the United States in 1900 and settled in New York City, where he became affiliated with the Socialist Party, worked as a journalist and lecturer, and was in the forefront of the New Negro movement. In 1920, he became an editor of the* Negro World, *the newspaper of Marcus Garvey's Universal Negro Improvement Association. In a four-part series on Lincoln, Harrison questioned Lincoln's support for racial equality and critiqued the motives and limitations of the Emancipation Proclamation. In offering what he believed was an honest, accurate assessment of the measure, Harrison hoped it would lead Blacks to question their loyalty to the Republican Party and help spur a movement for African American political and intellectual independence (AANB).*

---

Personally, I believe that Abraham Lincoln was the greatest President that the United States had up to his time. I believe that his record still remains as that of the greatest President that America has had down to our time. But greatest and (may I coin a word?) "goodest" are not necessarily the same. The current opinion of Abraham Lincoln as a god is not supported by the facts, and I shall try to present some of these facts, sticking to those relating to ourselves. [...]

I shall endeavor to show that Lincoln was not an Abolitionist; that he had no special love for Negroes; that he opposed the abolition of the Domestic Slave Trade and favored the Fugitive Slave Law; that he opposed citizenship for Negroes; that he favored making slavery perpetual in 1861; that he denied officially that the war was fought to free the slaves; that he refused to pay Negro soldiers the same wages that he paid the white soldiers; that without these Negro soldiers the North could not have won the war; that the Emancipation Proclamation was issued, not for the slaves' sake, but solely as an act to cripple the army of the South; and finally, that it did not abolish slavery and was not intended to. [ . . .]

During the first year and a half of the war the white working men of England and Europe made repeated requests to Lincoln to declare that the freedom of the Negro slaves was one of the objects of the war. Karl Marx and the working men of Great Britain particularly urged him to do this, pointing out that the Tories of England were making capital of the fact that they could not get their cotton and were stirring up trouble to get England into the war on the side of the Confederacy. [ . . .] And even [s]o—even though their requests were backed up by such big men in America as Moncure D. Conway, [ . . .] and Horace Greeley—even though the support of the Liberal parties of Europe hung in the balance, Abraham Lincoln was so wedded to his view (which is not the view currently ascribed to him) that he would not say that the war was a war to free the slaves, but insisted instead in saying again and again that the war was not a war to free slaves.

Greeley was impatient at this attitude of the President. He held that it was an ignoble Morality—the morality of the slick politician—and he had the courage to write an open letter to the President in which he stated that point of view. In his letter replying to Greeley's, Lincoln said, among other things: [ . . .]

"My paramount object in this struggle is to save the union and is not either to save or destroy slavery. If I can save the union without freeing any slave, I would do it. If I can save it by freeing all the slaves, I would do it, and if I could save it by freeing some and leaving others alone, I would also do that"—and I might add parenthetically that that is exactly what he did. [ . . .]

I wish to say here that it is a very sensible reason which Mr. Lincoln gives. It is statesmanlike and it merits approval for statesmanship. But since "you cannot eat your cake and have it, too" it effectually disposes of any claim to the Negroes' gratitude on the grounds of high moral altruism and benevolence. [ . . .]

When Jefferson Davis and the men of the South saw that Negroes were fighting against them, they issued proclamations saying that if they captured any Negroes they would treat them, not as soldiers captured in war, but as "niggers"; they would lash them; they would sell them further South into slavery to hoe corn and tend cotton.

Mr. Lincoln knew this. The proclamations were reproduced in the papers of the North. It was then clear that the black soldier in fighting ran a risk that the white soldier did not run. He practically fought with a halter around his neck. Yet in the face of this, Mr. Lincoln and Mr. Lincoln's government went back on their pledged word and offered to the Negro soldiers half the wage which they had promised in the proclamations issued to call soldiers into the Union ranks. They were good enough to stop bullets—they were men there—but when it came to the recompense they were only "niggers" in the opinion of Lincoln and his Republican government. When Frederick Douglass and the delegation of black men went to him to protest against this—and Frederick Douglass had a son in the Fifty-fourth Massachusetts—Mr. Lincoln said he "could not afford to antagonize the sentiment of the white people of the country" on a matter of simple justice—common honesty bona fides; keeping one's publicly pledged word.

Mr. Lincoln could not afford to antagonize the popular sentiment of the white people of the country. So these men were to be given half pay. [. . .] After a year and a half, representatives of Massachusetts, Rhode Island and Connecticut, by pounding and pounding in Congress, got the government to vote the Negroes the same pay as the other soldiers [. . .].

For the last two points we go to the text of the Emancipation Proclamation itself. If the South had agreed to return to the Union Lincoln would never have issued the Emancipation Proclamation. He says so in correspondence which I cannot quote here. They are official exchanges of explanations between himself and several officers of the government. But I stand here on the text of the document itself. [. . .]

Note that Abraham Lincoln says in this document that he is doing this "as a fit and necessary war measure," as a measure which he explains later was to bring Negroes into the ranks of the army, as a measure which was intended to take the slaves who were working on the Southern plantations away from them by letting them know that they were free and that they could run away without risk of being sent back, "as a fit and necessary war measure." He says later that "this measure is warranted by the Constitution upon military necessity." And what does that measure provide? It provides that the slaves shall be declared free only in those States that are in rebellion. [. . .] Why the exceptions? Because the Northern troops were in control in these sections and it was not needed there "as a fit and necessary war measure." He was not declaring a freedom measure—he was declaring a war measure; he was tearing the tools of war out of the hands of his enemy. That and only that was Abraham Lincoln aiming at. You see how truly he spoke when he said that if could only win the war by freeing some of the slaves and leaving the others bound to servitude he would do that. And I remarked at the time that that was exactly what he did do. [. . .]

I make no claim to have given the results of profound scholarship. It is our shame that the facts were right there on the surface. But we have no interest in these matters. We talk about learned men and "bookish" people, and we leave information to them. Whereas, information of this sort—information such as I have presented here tends to affect the practical political life of our people, and the way in which they cast their votes. That certainly is a sufficiently practical matter and we have let it go. We have lived in lies; lulled ourselves in the luxury of lies told us by white people and black politicians who were feeding out of their hands.

The character of Abraham Lincoln is a great character, but it is not what we have been told. Abraham Lincoln was not a friend of freedom. Abraham Lincoln was not a friend of Negroes. Abraham Lincoln was not an altruist, and it is high time that we Negroes of today who boast of our education and culture should be aware of this simple historical fact. It is time that we Negroes should do our own historical work instead of taking our food pelican-wise from the white people's pouch. And when we do this we will have rectifications to make as vital as those I have made here on the relation of Lincoln to liberty. For, while we patter about race emancipation we will still be brain-bound to the white man's mental products and his invented interpretation of our people to the world in which they live. And that is, after all, a more hopeless slavery than physical bondage could ever be.

*Negro World* (New York), March 5, 12, 19, 26, 1921.

## CARTER G. WOODSON, *The Negro in Our History*, 1922

*Woodson (1875–1950) was serving as editor of the* Journal of Negro History *and director of the Association of the Study of Negro Life and History when* The Negro in Our History *was published, generally acknowledged as the first scholarly general history of African Americans. A chapter is devoted to the Civil War. Contrary to the Lost Cause interpretation, Woodson believed slavery was the cause of the conflict, and despite Lincoln's initial reluctance to interfere with slavery in the states where it already existed, and his support for colonization, Woodson insisted that Lincoln remained essentially antislavery. Although Lincoln hesitated in allowing Blacks to serve in the army, Woodson emphasized the contributions these soldiers made once Lincoln authorized their enlistment. Woodson asserted that the Emancipation Proclamation was the key constitutional question of the war, and while Lincoln was unsure for a considerable time whether he had the authority to free slaves, he issued the proclamation after important Union victories. When Woodson began to commemorate Negro History Week in 1926, he selected the month of February because of its connection to the birthdays of Lincoln and Frederick Douglass (AANB).*

Against all temporizing and compromising efforts to placate the mad proslavery advocates, Lincoln persistently warned his fellow-countrymen. He early saw that the country had by its continuation of the policies of the pro-slavery party decided upon a fatal course of winking at a terribile evil. [ . . . ]

When the war broke out, the President of the United States openly declared that it was not his purpose to interfere with the institutions of the South, meaning of course, that he had no desire to attack slavery in those commonwealths in which it existed. The South, on the other hand, anxious to win favor abroad and knowing how it would harm its cause in foreign countries to have it said that it had undertaken a war to promote slavery, declared its position one of self-defense to maintain its right to govern itself and to preserve its own peculiar institutions. Negroes, therefore, were not to be freed and of course were not to take part in the war, as it was considered a struggle between white men. This does not mean, however, that Abraham Lincoln had lost sight of the fact that he had been elected by a party opposed to the extension of slavery, nor that he ceased to put forth efforts, whenever possible, to check the institution as he had formerly declared. After the war had been well begun and it was evident that such efforts as the peace convention could not succeed, Lincoln took up with the border States the question of setting the example of freeing the Negroes by a process of gradual emancipation.

Before the war had proceeded very far, however, the Negroes came up for serious consideration because of the many problems which developed out of the peculiar situation in which they were. In the first place, there were in the North free Negroes who were anxious to do their share in defeating the purposes of the Confederate States, knowing that the success of their cause meant the perpetuation of slavery. There were in the North, moreover, white men who were of the opinion that free Negroes should share a part of the burden entailed by waging the Civil War. Furthermore, as soon as the invading Union armies crossed the Mason and Dixon line into the South, disturbing the plantation system and driving the masters away from their homes, the Negroes were left behind to constitute a problem for the army. There arose the question as to what was the status of such Negroes. Nominally they were slaves, actually they were free, but there was no law to settle the question. A few slaves who had been taken over by the Union armies from persons in rebellion against the United States, were confiscated by virtue of the legislation providing for this disposition of such property of the Confederates. Yet there were Negroes who did not wait for the invading armies but, when their masters had gone to the front to defend the South, left their homes and made way to the Union camps. [ . . . ]

Lincoln, therefore, soon accepted the policy of using the slaves in this capacity, receding from his former position of thinking that should the slaves be given any encouragement to leave their homes they might start a servile insurrection, and in promoting such he would weaken himself in his hold on the North. [ . . . ]

It was arranged also to send a number of these Negroes from the congested districts in the loyal States as fast as opportunities for their employment presented themselves. [. . .] Several schemes were set forth to transport this population, and when this number was still further increased by the thousands of Negroes emancipated in the District of Columbia in 1862, Abraham Lincoln himself thought to get rid of these freedmen by promoting a scheme to colonize them in foreign parts.

To carry out this plan as he desired, he sent a special message to Congress expressing the necessity for Congressional action in the way of an appropriation to finance such an enterprise. [. . .] In the beginning it became evident that only two countries, Liberia and Haiti, each of which were settled by Negroes, were willing to admit these refugees. But the Negroes themselves, because of their prejudice against Liberia and the unsuccessful effort at colonization in Haiti, did not care to emigrate to those countries. Favorable replies, however, finally came from the Island of A'Vache. The government immediately planned to send a colony to that settlement by virtue of an appropriation made by Congress. Bernard Koch approached the government and induced the authorities to make with him a contract for the transportation of Negroes to this island. [. . .]

Accordingly a number of Negroes were sent to this island in the year 186[3], but owing to the unfavorable conditions and their lack of initiative, unusual suffering ensued. It was necessary for the Government, because of the many complaints received therefrom, to send a special investigator to report on the situation, and finally, on account of his unfavorable report, to dispatch a transport to bring the emigrants back to the United States.

Lincoln, however, remained fundamentally an antislavery man in spite of this untoward enterprise, but he religiously adhered to his gradual emancipation schemes. He would not permit the antislavery sentiment of the country to force upon him the policy of instant emancipation. As there were in the field generals availing themselves of every opportunity to weaken the slave power, much vigilance had to be exercised to avoid extreme measures which might embarrass the Federal Government. [. . .]

Congress passed sweeping confiscation acts by virtue of which the armies could take over slaves, and, in 1862, Lincoln came forward with the Emancipation Proclamation, declaring that after the first of January in 1863 all slaves in those parts of the country where the people might remain in rebellion against the United States, should be declared free. [. . .]

The most important constitutional matter coming up during the Civil War was that of the Emancipation Proclamation itself. Lincoln had for some time wondered whether or not he had such authority, and long hesitated to issue this mandate declaring free all the Negroes in the districts then in rebellion against the United States. Fremont, Hunter and Butler, in charge of Union armies, had undertaken to do this, but had to be restrained. One of the members of Lincoln's cabinet was of the opinion that he had no such power and that such a step would doubtless do more harm than good. In the end, however, just after a number of encouraging Union victories, the Emancipation Proclamation was issued and had its desired effect, but to become legal it had to be fortified by the Thirteenth Amendment.

Carter G. Woodson, *The Negro in Our History* (Washington, DC: The Associated Publishers, Inc., 1922), 215, 221, 223, 225–228, 230–231, 237–238.

## ROBERT R. MOTON, Address at the Dedication of the Lincoln Memorial, Washington, DC, May 1922

*Educated at the Hampton Institute in his native Virginia, Moton (1867–1940) was a protégé of Booker T. Washington and succeeded him as head of the Tuskegee Institute following Washington's death in 1915. By virtue of his high-profile position at Tuskegee, Moton had many important contacts, including former president and then Chief Justice William Howard Taft, who, as chairman of the Lincoln Memorial Commission, invited Moton to speak at the dedication ceremony on May 30. Taft asked Moton to submit his speech in advance, so that its length could be reviewed, as there was a strict time limit of fifteen minutes. Moton accepted Taft's invitation and sent him a draft of the speech. After Taft reviewed the draft, he requested that Moton cut five hundred words and advised that "in making the cut you give more unity and symmetry by emphasizing tribute and lessening appeal." Taft did not offer specific recommendations and instead simply expressed his hope that Moton understood the occasion was not "one for propaganda." Moton responded that he had "already made certain changes in the address along lines of your suggestion" and he was also making further revisions. Some of the changes Moton made are quite illuminating, and the text that follows is Moton's draft along with the revisions that substantively altered the tone and content of his speech. In the interest of fostering sectional reconciliation, the Lincoln Memorial was designed to honor Lincoln as the savior of the Union rather than as the Great Emancipator. The ceremony explicitly appealed to this sentiment by having Civil War veterans from both sides represented. In his remarks at the occasion, Taft claimed the memorial symbolized the "restoration of the brotherly love" between North and South, while President Warren G. Harding reminded the audience that emancipation was merely a means to fulfill Lincoln's goal of preserving the Union. In a further act of rejecting a view of Lincoln as the Great Emancipator and champion of equal rights, African American members of the audience were ordered to a segregated section. This nod to Jim Crow provoked protests from the Black press and the local branch of the NAACP. Taft responded to this outcry in disbelief and claimed no such order for segregation had come from him (correspondence between Moton and Taft and documents concerning the controversy over the segregated dedication ceremony are in the William Howard Taft Papers [Washington, DC: Library of Congress]).*

---

When the Pilgrim Fathers set foot upon the shores of America in 1620, they laid the foundations of our national existence upon the bed-rock of liberty. From that day to this, liberty has been the watchword, liberty has been the rallying call, liberty has been the battle-cry of our united people. In 1776, the altars of a new nation were set up in the name of liberty and the flag of freedom unfurled before the nations of the earth. In 1812, in the name of liberty, we bared our youthful might, and struck for the freedom of the seas. Again, in '61, when the charter of the nation's birth was assailed, the sons of liberty declared anew the principles of their fathers and liberty became co-extensive with the union. In '98, the call once more was heard and freedom became co-extensive with the hemisphere. And as we stand in solemn silence here today before this newly consecrated shrine of liberty, there still come rumbling out of the East the slowly dying echoes of the last great struggle to make freedom co-extensive with the seven seas. Freedom is the life-blood of the nation. Freedom is the heritage bequeathed to all her sons. For sage and scholar, for poet and prophet, for soldier and statesman, freedom is the underlying philosophy of our national existence.

But at the same time, another influence was working within the nation. While the Mayflower was riding at anchor preparing for her epoch-making voyage, another ship had already arrived at Jamestown, Virginia. The first was to bear the pioneers of freedom, freedom of thought and freedom of conscience; the latter had already borne the pioneers of bondage, a bondage degrading alike to body, mind and spirit. Here then, upon American soil, within a year, met the two great forces that were to shape the destiny of the nation. They developed side by side. Freedom was the great compelling force that dominated all and, like a great and shining light, beckoned the oppressed of every nation to the hospitality of these shores. But slavery like a brittle thread in a beautiful garment was woven year by year into the fabric of the nation's life. They who for themselves sought liberty and paid the price thereof in precious blood and priceless treasure, somehow still found it possible while defending its eternal principles for themselves, to deny that same precious boon to others.

And how shall we account for it, except it be that in the Providence of God the black race in America was thrust across the path of the onward-marching white race to demonstrate not only for America, but for the world whether the principles of freedom were of universal application. From the ends of the earth were brought together the extremes of humanity to prove whether the right to life, liberty and the pursuit of happiness should apply with equal force to all mankind.

In the process of time, these two great forces met, as was inevitable, in open conflict upon the field of battle. And how strange it is that by the same over-ruling Providence, the children of those who bought and sold their fellows into bondage should be the very ones to cast aside ties of language, of race, of religion and even of kinship, in order that a people not of their own race, nor primarily of their own creed or color, but brethren withal, should have the same measure of liberty and freedom which they enjoyed.

What a costly sacrifice upon the altar of freedom! How costly the world can never know nor estimate. The flower of the nation's manhood and the accumulated treasure of two hundred and fifty years of unremitting toil: and at length, when the bitter strife was over, when the marshalled hosts had turned again to broken, desolated firesides, a cruel fate, unsatisfied with the awful toll of four long years of carnage, struck at the nation's head and brought to the dust the already wearied frame of him, whose patient fortitude, whose unembittered charity, whose never failing trust in the guiding hand of God had brought the nation, weltering through a sea of blood, yet one and indivisible, to the placid plains of peace. On that day, Abraham Lincoln laid down his life for America, the last and costliest sacrifice upon the altar of freedom.

We do well to raise here this symbol of our gratitude. Here today assemble all those who are blessed by that sacrifice. The united nation stands about this memorial mingling its reverent praise with tokens of eternal gratitude: and not America only, but every nation where liberty is loved and freedom flourishes, joins the chorus of universal praise for him, who with his death, sealed forever the pledge of liberty for all mankind.

But in all this vast assemblage, there are none more grateful, none more reverent, than those who, representing twelve millions of black Americans, gather with their fellow-citizens of every race and creed to pay devout homage to him who was for them, more truly than for any other group, the author of their freedom. There is no question that this man died to save the union. It is equally true that to the last extremity he defended the rights of states. But, when the last veteran has stacked his arms on fame's eternal camping ground; when only the memory of high courage and deep devotion remains to inspire the noble sons of valiant fathers; at such a time, the united voice of grateful posterity will say: the claim of greatness for Abraham Lincoln lies in this, that amid doubt and distrust, against the counsel of his chosen advisors, in the hour of the nation's utter peril, he put his trust in God and spoke the word that gave freedom to a race, and vindicated the honor of a nation conceived in liberty and dedicated to the proposition that all men are created equal.

But someone will ask: Has such a sacrifice been justified? Has such a martyrdom produced its worthy fruits? I speak for the Negro race. Upon us, more perhaps than upon any other group of the nation, rests the immediate obligation to justify so dear a price for our emancipation. In answer let me review the Negro's past upon American soil. No group has been more loyal. Whether bond or free, he has served alike his country's need. Let it never be omitted from the nation's annals that the blood of a black man—Crispus Attucks—was the first to be shed for the nation's freedom; and first his name appears in the long list of the nation's martyred dead. So again, when a world was threatened with disaster and the deciding hand of America was lifted to stay the peril, her black soldiers were among the first to cross the treacherous sea; and when the cause was won, and the record made of those who shared the cruel hardship, these same black soldiers had been longest in the trenches, nearest to the enemy and first to cross their border. All too well does the black man know his wrongs. No one is more sensible than he of his incongruous position in the great American republic. But be it recorded to his everlasting credit, that no failure on the part of the nation to deal fairly with him as a citizen has, in the least degree, ever qualified his loyalty.

*[The last sentence was revised to shift the burden of failure from the nation onto African Americans: "But be it recorded to his everlasting credit, that no failure on his part to reap the full reward of his sacrifices has ever in the least degree qualified his loyalty or cooled his patriotic fervor."]*

In like manner has he served his country in the pursuits of peace. From the first blows that won the virgin soil from the woods and wilderness to the sudden, marvelous expansion of our industry that went so far to win the war, the Negro has been the nation's greatest single asset in the development of its vast resources. Especially is this true in the South where his unrequited toil sustained the splendors of that life which gave to the nation a Washington and a Jefferson, a Jackson and a Lee. And afterwards, when devastating war had levelled this fair structure with the ground, the labor of the freedman restored it to its present proportions, more substantial than before.

While all this was going on, in spite of limitations within and restrictions without, he still found the way to buy land, to build homes, to erect churches, to establish schools and to lay the foundations of future development in industry, integrity and thrift. It is no mere accident that Negroes in America after less than sixty years of freedom own 22,000,000 acres of land, 600,000 homes and 45,000 churches. It is no mere accident that after so short a time Negroes should operate 78 banks, 100 insurance companies, and 50,000 business enterprises representing a combined capital value of more than $150,000,000. Neither is it an accident that there are within the race 60,000 professional men, 44,000 school teachers and 400 newspapers and magazines; that general illiteracy has been reduced to twenty per cent. Still the Negro race is only in the infancy of its development, so that, if anything in its history could justify the sacrifice that has been made, it is this: that a race that has exhibited such wonderful capacities for advancement should have the restrictions of bondage removed and be given the opportunity in freedom to develop its powers to the utmost, not only for itself, but for the nation and for humanity. Any race that could produce a Frederick Douglass in the midst of slavery, and a Booker Washington in the aftermath of reconstruction has a just claim to the fullest opportunity for development.

*[In the revised version, the last sentence was altered to vindicate the act of emancipation and a new sentence was added to conclude the paragraph: "Any race that has produced a Frederick Douglass in the midst of slavery, and a Booker Washington in the aftermath of reconstruction has gone far to justify its emancipation. And the nation where such achievement is possible is full worthy of such heroic sacrifice."]*

But Lincoln died, not for the Negro alone, but to vindicate the honor of a nation pledged to the sacred cause of human freedom. Upon the field of Gettysburg he dedicated the nation to the great unfinished work of making sure that "government of the people, for the people and by the people should not perish from the earth." And this means <u>all</u> the people. So long as any group within our nation is denied the full protection of the law; that task is still unfinished. So long as any group within the nation is denied an equal opportunity for life, liberty and the pursuit of happiness, that task is still unfinished. So long as any group is denied the fullest privilege of a citizen to share both the making and the execution of the law which shapes its destiny—so long as any group does not enjoy every right and every privilege that belongs to every American citizen without regard to race, creed or color, that task for which the immortal Lincoln gave the last full measure of devotion—that task is still unfinished. What nobler thing can the nation do as it dedicates this shrine for him whose deed has made his name immortal—what nobler thing can the nation do than here about this shrine to dedicate itself by its own determined will to fulfill to the last letter the lofty task imposed upon it by the sacred dead?

More than sixty years ago he said in prophetic warning: "This nation cannot endure half slave and half free: it will become all one thing or all the other." With equal truth, it can be said today: no more can the nation endure half privileged and half repressed; half educated and half uneducated; half protected and half unprotected; half prosperous and half in poverty; half in health and half in sickness; half content and half in discontent; yes, half free and half yet in bondage.

My fellow citizens, in the great name which we honor here today, I say unto you that this memorial which we erect in token of our veneration is but a hollow mockery, a symbol of hypocrisy, unless we together can make real in our national life, in every state and in every section, the things for which he died. This is a fair and goodly land. Much right have we, both black and white, to be proud of our achievements at home and our increasing service in all the world. In like manner, there is abundant cause for rejoicing that sectional rancours and racial antagonisms are softening more and more into mutual understanding and increasing sectional and inter-racial cooperation. But unless here at home we are willing to grant to the least and humblest citizen the full enjoyment of every constitutional privilege, our boast is but a mockery and our professions as sounding brass and a tinkling cymbal before the nations of the earth. This is the only way to peace and security at home, to honor and respect abroad.

Sometimes I think the national government itself has not always set the best example for the states in this regard. A government which can venture abroad to put an end to injustice and mob-violence in another country can surely find a way to put an end to these same evils within our own borders. The Negro race is not insensible of the difficulties that such a task presents; but unless we can together, North and South, East and West, black and white, find a way out of these difficulties and square ourselves with the enlightened conscience and public opinion of all mankind, we must stand convicted not only of inconsistency and hypocrisy, but of the deepest ingratitude that could stain the nation's honor. Twelve million black men and women in this country are proud of their American citizenship, but they are determined that it shall mean for them no less than for any other group, the largest enjoyment of opportunity and the fullest blessings of freedom. We ask no special privileges; we claim no superior title; but we do expect in loyal cooperation with all true lovers of our common country to do our full share in lifting our country above reproach and saving her flag from stain or humiliation. Let us, therefore, with malice toward none, with charity for all, with firmness in the right as God gives us to see the right—let us strive on to finish the work which he so nobly began, to make America the symbol for equal justice and equal opportunity for all.

*[Moton completely revised the final third of his speech and replaced the last four paragraphs with the seven paragraphs that follow. Instead of citing the Gettysburg Address and emphasizing the "unfinished work" of emancipation, Moton instead focused on healing the wounds and divisiveness of the Civil War. The tone was also considerably altered in the revised version, as Moton deleted the strong language about the nation remaining divided and the suggestion that failure to finish the work of emancipation made the Lincoln Memorial seem like an act of hypocrisy.]*

But Lincoln did not die for the Negro alone. He freed the nation as well as a race. Those conflicting forces planted two hundred and fifty years before had slowly divided the nation in spirit, in ideals and in policy. Passing suddenly beyond the bitterness of controversy, his taking-off served more than war itself to emphasize the enormity of the breach that had developed between the sections. Not until then was there a full realization of the deep significance of his prophetic words:—"This nation cannot endure half slave and half free."

That tragic event shocked the conscience of the nation and stirred a great resolve to establish forever the priceless heritage so dearly bought. From that day, the noblest minds and hearts, both North and South, were bent to the healing of the breach and the restoration of the union. With a devotion that counted neither personal loss nor gain, Abraham Lincoln held steadfastly to an ideal for the republic, that measured at full value, the worth of each race and section, cherishing at the same time the hope under God that all should share alike in the blessings of freedom. Now we rejoice in the far-seeing vision and the unswerving faith that held firmly to its single purpose even in the midst of reproach, and preserved for all posterity the integrity of the nation.

Lincoln has not died in vain. Slowly through the years that noble spirit has been permeating every section of our land and country. Sixty years ago he stood in lonely grandeur above a torn and bleeding nation, a towering figure of patient righteousness. Today his spirit animates the breasts of millions of his countrymen who unite with us to pay tribute to his lofty character and his immortal deed.

And now the whole world turns with anxious heart and eager eyes toward America. In the providence of God there has been started on these shores the great experiment of the ages—an experiment in human relationships where men and women of every nation, of every race and creed are thrown together in daily contact. Here we are engaged, consciously or unconsciously, in the great problem of determining how different races can not only live together in peace but cooperate in working out a higher and better civilization than has yet been achieved. At the extremes the white and black races face each other. Here in America these two races are charged under God with the responsibility of showing to the world how individuals, as well as races, may differ most widely in color and inheritance, and at the same time make themselves helpful and even indispensable to each other's progress and prosperity. This is especially true in the South where the black man is found in greatest numbers and the two races are thrown in closest contact. And there today are found black men and white who are working together in the spirit of Abraham Lincoln to establish in fact, what his death established in principle—that a nation conceived in liberty and dedicated to the proposition that all men are created equal, can endure.

As we gather on this consecrated spot, his spirit must rejoice that sectional rancours and racial antagonisms are softening more and more into mutual understanding and effective cooperation. And I like to think that here today, while we dedicate this symbol of our gratitude that the nation is dedicated anew by its own determined will to fulfill to the last letter the task imposed upon it by the martyred dead: that here it highly resolves, that the humblest citizen of whatever color or creed, shall enjoy that equal opportunity and unhampered freedom, for which the immortal Lincoln gave the last full measure of devotion.

And the progress of events confirms this view. Step by step has the nation been making its way forward in the spirit of the great Emancipator. And nowhere is this more true than in that section which sixty years ago seemed least in accord with his spirit and purpose, yet at this hour, in many things, is leading the rest of the nation toward fulfillment of his hopes.

Twelve million black Americans share in the rejoicing of this hour. As yet, no other name so warms the heart or stirs the depths of their gratitude as that of Abraham Lincoln. To him above all others we owe the privilege of sharing as fellow-citizens in the consecration of this spot and the dedication of this shrine. In the name of Lincoln twelve million black Americans pledge to the nation their continued loyalty and their unreserved cooperation in every effort to realize in deeds, the lofty principles established by his martyrdom. With malice toward none, with charity for all we dedicate ourselves and our posterity, with <u>you</u> and <u>yours</u>, to finish the work which he so nobly began, to make America an example for all the world of equal justice and equal opportunity for all.

Robert R. Moton Papers, Library of Congress, Washington, DC.

## GEORGIA DOUGLAS JOHNSON, "To Abraham Lincoln," 1922

*One of the major poets associated with the Harlem Renaissance, Johnson's (18??-1966) brief but powerful tribute to Lincoln appeared in her second volume of poetry that was published the same year the Lincoln Memorial was dedicated. For Johnson, Lincoln's memory will always have a special place in the hearts of African Americans. As a longtime resident of Washington, Johnson witnessed the Memorial's construction and was inspired by the inscription on the wall behind Daniel Chester French's statue of Lincoln:*

> *In This Temple*
> *As In The Hearts of the People*
> *For Whom He Saved The Union*
> *The Memory of Abraham Lincoln*
> *Is Enshrined Forever*
> *(ANB).*

---

Within the temple of our heart
Your sacred memory dwells apart,
Where ceaselessly a censor swings
Alight with fragrant offerings;
Nor time, nor tide, nor circumstance
Can dim this grand remembrance,
And all the blood of Afric hue
Beats in one mighty tide—for you!

In *Bronze: A Book of Verse* (Boston: B. J. Brimmer Company, 1922).

# W. E. B. DU BOIS, Editorials on Abraham Lincoln, July 1922 and September 1922

*Du Bois (1868–1963) served as editor of* The Crisis, *the monthly journal of the NAACP, from its inception in 1910 until 1934. In the wake of the dedication of the Lincoln Memorial in Washington, Du Bois published a very brief editorial in the July issue that described Lincoln as a poor, coarse, illegitimate White boy who enjoyed ribald stories. Despite Lincoln's unappealing outward appearance, Du Bois believed the interior Lincoln was conflicted yet large enough to embody profound inconsistencies. This nuanced though seemingly irreverent analysis provoked such a controversy that Du Bois felt compelled to clarify his position. In the September issue he therefore published "Again, Lincoln," a lengthier explanation of his views that expressed regret at having offended ardent Lincoln fans and reminded them that all humans are flawed. He wondered why there was even a need for heroes to be perfect. Du Bois indicated his respect for Lincoln was based on his efforts to reconcile personal contradictions regarding African Americans. After quoting from remarks Lincoln made during his debates with Stephen A. Douglas in 1858, Du Bois concluded there was no finer human in the nineteenth century.*

---

Abraham Lincoln was a Southern poor white, of illegitimate birth, poorly educated and unusually ugly, awkward, ill-dressed. He liked smutty stories and was a politician down to his toes. Aristocrats—Jeff Davis, Seward and their ilk—despised him, and indeed he had little outwardly that compelled respect. But in that curious human way he was big inside. He had reserves and depths and when habit and convention were torn away there was something left to Lincoln—nothing to most of his contemners. There was something left, so that at the crisis he was big enough to be inconsistent—cruel, merciful; peace-loving, a fighter; despising Negroes and letting them fight and vote; protecting slavery and freeing slaves. He was a man—a big, inconsistent, brave man.

*[The September response follows:]*

We love to think of the Great as flawless. We yearn in our imperfection toward Perfection—sinful, we envisage Righteousness.

As a result of this, no sooner does a great man die than we begin to whitewash him. We seek to forget all that was small and mean and unpleasant and remember the fine and brave and good. We slur over and explain away his inconsistencies and at last there begins to appear, not the real man, but the tradition of the man—remote, immense, perfect, cold and dead!

This sort of falsehood appeals to some folk. They want to dream their heroes true; they want their heroes all heroic with no feet of clay; and they are astonished, angered, hurt if some one speaks the grim, forgotten truth. They can see but one motive for such digging up of filth, for such evil speaking of the dead—and that is prurient love of evil.

Thus many of my readers were hurt by what I said of Lincoln in the July CRISIS.

I am sorry to hurt them, for some of them were tried friends of me and my cause—particularly one like the veteran, wounded at Chickamauga and a staunch defender of our rights, who thinks my words "unkind and uncalled for."

First and foremost, there comes a question of fact. Was what I said true or false? This I shall not argue. Any good library will supply the books, and let each interested reader judge. Only they should remember that, as one of my naive critics writes, "I know that there are among his early biographers those who say something to the same effect"; but against these he marshals the later words of those who want to forget. I leave the matter there. If my facts were false, my words were wrong—but were my facts false?

Beyond this, there is another and deeper question on which most of my critics dwell. They say, What is the use of recalling evil? What good will it do? or as one phrases, "Is this proper food for your people"? I think it is.

Abraham Lincoln was perhaps the greatest figure of the nineteenth century. Certainly of the five masters,—Napoleon, Bismarck, Victoria, Browning and Lincoln, Lincoln is to me the most human and lovable. And I love him not because he was perfect but because he was not and yet triumphed. The world is full of illegitimate children. The world is full of folk whose taste was educated in the gutter. The world is full of people born hating and despising their fellows. To these I love to say: See this man. He was one of you and yet he became Abraham Lincoln.

Some may prefer to believe (as one correspondent intimates) that he was of Mayflower ancestry through the "Lincolns of Hingham!" Others may refuse to believe his taste in jokes and political maneuvers and list him as an original abolitionist and defender of Negroes. But personally I revere him the more because up out of his contradictions and inconsistencies he fought his way to the pinnacles of earth and his fight was within as well as without. I care more for Lincoln's great toe than for the whole body of the perfect George Washington, of spotless ancestry, who "never told a lie" and never did anything else interesting.

No! I do not love evil as evil; I do not retail foul gossip about either the living or the dead; but I glory in that crucified humanity that can push itself up out of the mud of a miserable, dirty ancestry; who despite the clinging smirch of low tastes and shifty political methods, rose to be a great and good man and the noblest friend of the slave.

Do my colored friends really believe the picture would be fairer and finer if we forgot Lincoln's unfortunate speech at Charleston, Illinois, in 1858? I commend that speech to the editors who have been having hysterics. Abraham Lincoln said:

> I will say, then, that I am not, nor ever have been, in favor of bringing about in any way the social and political equality of the white and black races—that I am not, nor ever have been, in favor of making voters or jurors of Negroes, nor of qualifying them to hold office, nor to intermarry with white people; and I will say in addition to this, that there is a physical difference between the white and black races which I believe will forever forbid the two races living together on terms of social and political equality. And inasmuch as they cannot so live, while they do remain together there must be the position of superior and inferior, and I, as much as any other man, am in favor of having the superior position assigned to the white race.

This was Lincoln's word in 1858. Five years later he declared that black slaves "are and henceforward shall be free." And in 1864 he was writing to Hahn of Louisiana in favor of Negro suffrage.

The difficulty is that ignorant folk and inexperienced try continually to paint humanity as all good or all evil. Was Lincoln great and good? He was! Well, then, all evil alleged against him are malicious lies, even if they are true.

"Why should you wish to hold up to public gaze those defects of character you claim he possessed, knowing that he wrought so well?"

That is the very reason for telling the Truth. That is the reason for painting Cromwell's mole as it was and not as some artists conceive it ought to have been.

The scars and foibles and contradictions of the Great do not diminish but enhance the worth and meaning of their upward struggle: it was the bloody sweat that proved the human Christ divine; it was his true history and antecedents that proved Abraham Lincoln a Prince of Men.

*The Crisis* 24, no. 3 (July 1922): 103; no. 5 (Sept. 1922): 199–201.

# National Association of Colored Women, Speeches and a Resolution Commemorating Abraham Lincoln, 1923–1924

*Founded in 1896, the National Association of Colored Women (NACW) supported a variety of causes, including woman suffrage, temperance, and antilynching legislation. The NACW was also very active in preserving and commemorating the past, as the organization had recently raised funds to pay off the mortgage and restore the home of Frederick Douglass in Washington, DC. In 1923, the NACW led a successful fight against the efforts of the United Daughters of the Confederacy to erect a "Black Mammy" monument in Washington. The following documents indicate that members of the NACW also took a keen interest in using Lincoln's image to advance the objectives of their organization.*

[M. Cravath Simpson (1860–1945) was serving as president of the Massachusetts State Union of Women's Clubs when she addressed that organization at its Lincoln-Douglass Day meeting in Boston on February 11, 1923. A longtime activist in a variety of women's clubs and equal rights organizations, Simpson's speech discussed the efforts of the NACW to preserve Douglass's home and urged African Americans to follow his example by not being afraid to fight for their rights. Simpson was concerned about the recent resurgence of the Ku Klux Klan and lamented the failure of Congress to approve an anti-lynching bill, yet she believed that if leaders in Washington simply enforced Lincoln's interpretation of the Declaration of Independence, true equality could be achieved. For Simpson, Lincoln's vigorous defense of the Declaration in his June 1857 speech in response to the US Supreme Court's ruling in Dred Scott, made it just as significant as his famed Gettysburg Address (The National Notes 25, no. 8 [May 1923]: 6–7; Sarah Deutsch, Women and the City: Gender, Space, and Power in Boston, 1870–1940 [New York: Oxford University Press, 2000], 112; Joan Marie Johnson, "'Ye Gave Them a Stone': African American Women's Clubs, the Frederick Douglass Home, and the Black Mammy Monument," Journal of Women's History 17, no. 1 [2005]: 62–86).]

Would to God such a man as Abraham Lincoln stood today at the head of affairs in Washington! He would make the Congress know that while they had closed their eyes to the Constitution of the United States and will not enforce its laws, that the Declaration of Independence still stands.

He would repeat to them the definition of the Declaration of Independence which to my mind is as great a speech as his Gettysburg address; listen, I think you will agree with me. "Its authors meant it to be as thank God, it is now proving itself—a stumbling block to all those who in after times might seek to turn a free people back into the hateful paths of despotism. They knew the proneness of prosperity to breed tyrants and they meant when such should reappear in this fair land and commence their vocation they should find left for them at least one hard nut to crack. They meant to set up a standard for free society which should be familiar to all, and revered by all, constantly looked to, constantly labored for and even though never perfectly attained constantly approximated and thereby constantly spreading and deepening its influence and augmenting the happiness and value of life to all people, of all color everywhere."

This was defined in a speech by Abraham Lincoln at Springfield, Illinois, J[une] 26, 1857, over sixty-six years ago. Is it to be wondered at one never hears it spoken of? I feel safe in saying that not a man in either house of Congress knows it ever was delivered. I doubt if the present incumbent of the White House knows anything about it. You never hear the Declaration of Independence spoken of today and why? Because white Americans do not like the tone of the words.

*[Edith Tiffin Stewart (1886–1956) was a resident of Moline, Illinois and president of the Illinois Federation of Colored Women's Clubs when she delivered a welcome address to the delegates who assembled at Chicago in August 1924 for the NACW's biennial national meeting. Like Simpson, Stewart was active in a variety of women's organizations and drew inspiration from Lincoln, whom she characterized as a martyr to the cause of equal opportunity for all humankind (Broad Axe [Chicago], Aug. 9, 1924; The Dispatch [Moline, IL], July 27, 1950; Rock Island Argus [Rock Island, IL], March 3, 1956).]*

A new human ideal appears to be taking possession of the world, the ideal of common humanity. It is not enough for us that here and there a rare saint attains it, it is not enough that the results of civilization is accomplished for a few. We demand life for ourselves and for every human being. Our entire society is being transformed by the desire to give every man, woman and child all opportunity and life in striving for life, happiness, culture, intelligence, helpfulness and all ends of life that are worth seeking.

At a single bound our memory is swept back to one who became a martyr for this new ideal, back to the great Emancipator, Abraham Lincoln who suffered martyrdom for the cause of human liberty, launched one of the greatest social problems known to civilization and engaged the attention of the human race. And out of the night the black woman raised high her head as a dainty bouquet of rare and sweet scented flowers, culled from the heart and mind resplendent virtues, those virtues that make a race glorious. Our one regret is that a pilgrimage cannot be made to the blessed shrine of this great hero where all that remains of this sacred body slumbers in the bosom of mother earth in the city of Springfield.

*[During its 1924 convention in Chicago, the NACW passed a resolution that recommended September 22—the anniversary of Lincoln's Preliminary Emancipation Proclamation—be observed as a day to honor Lincoln's memory. Further, it encouraged all organizations to come together in a non-partisan way to renew pledges for human rights on that day. The resolution was an effort to further assert African American claims to Lincoln's legacy and to commemorate Lincoln as a symbol of freedom and equality at a time when many White Americans focused on Lincoln as a nationalist savior of the Union. In accordance with the resolution, members of the NACW helped organize a 1924 Emancipation Day program that was held in Chicago's Lincoln Park*

*where Augustus Saint-Gaudens's statue of Lincoln is located ("Ask Memorial Day to Honor Lincoln," Chicago Defender, Sept. 20, 1924; Minutes of the Fourteenth Biennial Convention of the National Association of Colored Women [1924], 38, Records of the National Association of Colored Women's Clubs, Microfilm Edition, Reel 1 [Bethesda, MD: University Publications of America, (1993) 1994]; "Lincoln, Emancipator to Be Honored Today," Chicago Tribune, Sept. 22, 1924).]*

Whereas, Lovers of Liberty throughout the world deservedly honor the memory of Abraham Lincoln, but President Lincoln is specially dear to Colored people as "The Great Emancipator;" and

Whereas, Lincoln's birthday, February 12, and January 1, "Emancipation day," are both holidays, hence on those dates it is hard for Colored people to pay sufficient homage to his genius; therefore be it

Resolved, By the National Association of Colored Women assembled in 14th biennial convention in Chicago:

This association recommends that September 22 be annually utilized, especially by Colored People, as a date well suited to honor Lincoln's memory. On September 22, 1862, President Lincoln issued his preliminary proclamation of emancipation stating that on January 1, 1863, "All slaves . . . shall be free."

The National Association of Colored Women further urges all Colored men's and women's organizations to cooperate in a non-partisan way to make this Lincoln day a success. White people are cordially invited to do likewise, both North and South. Schools are requested to participate. It is suggested that the Republican and Democratic national committees use their influence to promote this event, as Lincoln is no longer a "Party Man" but "Belongs to the Ages."

Lincoln statues and memorials in various cities should be made shrines to which all citizens can make their pilgrimages.

## LANGSTON HUGHES, "Lincoln Monument: Washington," March 1927

*Hughes (1901–1967) was a student at Lincoln University in Pennsylvania when he took inspiration from the relatively new Lincoln Memorial in Washington and composed the following poem. In a previous poem, the oft-anthologized "The Negro Speaks of Rivers," Hughes had imagined the young Lincoln taking a flatboat down the Mississippi to New Orleans, where he encountered slavery, and according to legend, vowed to abolish it. Here, Hughes juxtaposed the silence of Daniel Chester French's sculpture with the voice of Lincoln that continued to speak. In a few lines, Hughes conveys the enduring symbolic power of Lincoln (Langston Hughes, The Big Sea: An Autobiography [New York:*

*Alfred A. Knopf, 1940; reprinted, New York: Hill and Wang, 1993]; Arnold Rampersad, The Life of Langston Hughes, vol. 1 [New York: Oxford University Press, 1986]).*

————————

Let's go see old Abe
Sitting in the marble and the moonlight,
Sitting lonely in the marble and the moonlight,
Quiet for ten thousand centuries, old Abe.
Quiet for a million, million years.

Quiet—

And yet a voice forever
Against the
Timeless walls
Of time—
Old Abe.

In Arnold Rampersad, ed., *The Collected Poems of Langston Hughes* (New York: Vintage Classics, 1995), 103, first published in *Opportunity*, March 1927.

## CHARLES CHESNUTT, Address to the Harlan Club, Cleveland, Ohio, February 14, 1928

*Among the first African American novelists and short story writers with a national reputation, Chesnutt (1858–1932) marked Lincoln's birthday with an address to an organization of Black lawyers. Recalling his opportunity to view Lincoln's body as it passed through Cleveland on the way to Springfield in 1865, Chesnutt defended Lincoln and the Emancipation Proclamation from critics who argued that Lincoln issued the proclamation only as a measure to win the Civil War. Chesnutt argued that Lincoln's opposition to slavery and his desire to fulfill the promise of equality in the Declaration of Independence were sincere and consistent throughout his political career. Most significantly, Chesnutt pointed out that Lincoln was not compelled to issue the Emancipation Proclamation, and while it was framed as a necessary war measure, the Union cause would have prevailed without it. During an era when it was increasingly popular to debunk heroic figures, Chesnutt noted that Lincoln was free from scandal, and unlike some of his predecessors in office, he did not abuse Black women. In exposing himself to the threat of assassination, Lincoln was both martyr and emancipator.*

————————

Mr. President, members of the Harlan Cub, ladies and gentlemen:

It is eminently fitting that this group should celebrate the memory of Abraham Lincoln, for without Abraham Lincoln, unless some other man with equal ability had performed his task, such a group as this would not have been possible.

The pulpits, the forums, the newspapers and the air have been full of eulogies of Lincoln for the past week. They have stressed his patience under harsh and unmerited criticism, his far-seeing statesmanship, his kindliness, his sense of humor, his services in saving the Union. He has grown with the passing of the years to heroic stature. But whatever he did and however he did it, the greatest thing that he did was to emancipate the slaves, and therefore I am going to speak of him as Lincoln the Emancipator. There are those who insist, and some of them are cynics of our own, that Lincoln issued the Emancipation Proclamation solely as a war measure, and with no particular regard for the humanitarian side of the question. That is no more true than that the Civil War was fought on the issue of States' Rights alone, as Southern historians would have the rising generation believe. Horace Greeley characterized the Civil War correctly as the war to perpetuate slavery, from the Southern standpoint, and it might have been equally well described from the Northern standpoint as the war to abolish slavery. We are told that the question was purely an economic one, a battle between free and slave labor. I am quite sure that Wendell Phillips, William Lloyd Garrison, John Brown, Parker Pillsbury, Frederick Douglass and the rest of the Abolitionists whose labors culminated in the Civil War, were vastly more concerned about the inhumanity of the institution than about the competition of free and slave labor. I am quite sure that Julia Ward Howe's famous Battle Hymn of the Republic, the trumpet strains of which I never hear without emotion, was not inspired by any abstract economic principle. [. . .] I first heard that hymn sung when it meant something, for I was born here in Cleveland, a hot bed of patriotic Unionism, just four years before the breaking out of the Civil War, and lived as a small child through that fearful conflict, in which my father participated. And when the War came to its righteous end, thousands, nay, millions of good people thanked God as much for the abolition of slavery as for the preservation of the Union.

I think the briefest study of the life and utterances of Abraham Lincoln will demonstrate, [. . .] [he] believed in the equality of man, and, as to any man of such belief, that slavery was abhorrent to all his instincts. It is the text of his Gettysburg Address. One of his most quoted statements was, quoting from the Scripture: "A house divided against itself cannot stand," to which he added that "this Republic cannot endure half slave and half free."

"Four score and seven years ago," he began his Gettysburg Address, "our fathers brought forth upon this continent a new nation, conceived in liberty and dedicated to the proposition that all men are created equal." And before that, on July 7, 1863, he characterized the Southern revolt as "a gigantic rebellion, at the bottom of which is an effort to overthrow the principle that all men are created equal."

In the series of debates between Lincoln and Stephen A. Douglas, on the extension of slavery, he showed himself an orator of the first rank, and proved conclusively that he hated slavery.

When I was about eight years old I walked past the body of Lincoln as it lay exposed under a black catafalque in the southwest corner of the Public Square, in front of the old Forest City House, now the Cleveland Hotel. [...]

The opportunity to abolish slavery as a war measure was one which Lincoln welcomed. He wanted to save the Union, not solely as a Union, but as a free nation where the equality of man should prevail. Of course he was sworn to observe the Constitution and the laws of the United States, and that Constitution and those laws recognized slavery as an established institution, and it was necessary under those circumstances to resort to the device of a war measure in order to abolish it. But he did not have to abolish slavery. The abolition of slavery undoubtedly shortened the war, but I have no slightest doubt that the Union forces would have defeated the South without it. They had the men and the money, and "God," said Napoleon, "is always on the side of the strongest battalions." Had the war been won without the abolition of slavery, it would have been difficult to abolish it. It would have become or would have continued to be the football of politics, as it had been for a generation. Lincoln saw the opportunity to rid the country of this incubus, and he seized it, and from us, of all men, his memory is entitled to gratitude and veneration.

Lincoln was an all-around man. He had a keen sense of humor. He loved a good story, and was not unduly particular about the theme of the story. [...]

But whatever criticism might be directed to Lincoln's taste in stories, he lived a pure life. He had no Negro women to play with, like Washington and Jefferson and Hamilton and most of the founding fathers, as the phrase goes. No sexual scandal ever soiled his fame. No bastard daughter of his ever defamed her sire. His administration was not besmirched with graft and peculation of government funds. True, some army contractors became unduly rich, as they always do, but there were no Teapot Dome scandals. He gathered around him a cabinet of the wisest and ablest and most liberal men of his generation.

And again we venerate his memory, not only as the Emancipator, but also as the Martyr, because his assassination was the direct sequel of the abolition of slavery. True, he fell at the hands of a fanatic, but every martyr is a victim of fanaticism, sometimes camouflaged as religion, sometimes as justice, sometimes as patriotism. [...]

We love Lincoln, the honest, wholesome, lovable man of the common people—Honest Old Abe. We celebrate the birth of Lincoln, the great Emancipator, the exponent of human equality. We venerate the memory of Lincoln the Martyr, who died for humanity, just as did Savonarola or John Huss, or even the Master himself.

Gentlemen, those are my sentiments, and frankly, I should not think much of any American colored man who did not share them.

Fisk University, John Hope and Aurelia E. Franklin Library, Special Collections, Charles Chesnutt Papers, Box 11, Folder 2.

## Walter White, "If Lincoln Were Here," Radio Address on Lincoln's Birthday, February 12, 1929

*Walter White (1893–1955) served as the executive secretary of the National Association for the Advancement of Colored People during much of the 1930s and 1940s. In 1929, he gave a radio address on Lincoln's birthday that was broadcast by WOV in New York. For the theme of his address, White chose to imagine what Lincoln would think if he were alive in 1929. In this way, White linked Lincoln to the mission of the NAACP and adapted Lincoln's image to advance the cause of racial equality. Designating Lincoln as one of the greatest men ever, White emphasized that the strength of Lincoln's views evolved over time. White made several observations about Negro progress since Lincoln, despite the simultaneous evidence of resistance to it, and cited numerous examples of the NAACP waging successful struggles against caste and prejudice.*

---

We honor today Abraham Lincoln, born 120 years ago. [. . .] Born of a father who was an ignorant and shiftless carpenter and of a mother from the poor white class of Kentucky this man was destined to become one of the great men of all time and with Charles Darwin, one of the two greatest figures of the nineteenth century.

With a meagre education Abraham Lincoln passed through the various stages of shop-keeper, postmaster, surveyor, stump speaker, lawyer and legislator on to the halls of Congress and eventually to the Presidency of these United States. It was destined that to him should be given the opportunity to strike the death blow at the greatest evil of modern times—human slavery. It will perhaps be interesting to note for a moment that Lincoln's convictions against slavery as a moral wrong and an economically unsound system did not spring up suddenly but instead were a matter of slow growth. During his second term in the Illinois legislature he and another member wrote one of the first protests against slavery. This protest was voiced against certain pro-slavery resolutions which had passed the legislature. Concerning them Lincoln said that it was his belief "that the institution of slavery is founded on both injustice and bad policy but that the promulgation of abolition doctrines tends rather to increase than to abate its evils."

Three years later Lincoln's heart was touched when he saw twelve Negro slaves chained together on a steamboat headed southward on the Mississippi river and of this spectacle he later wrote "that sight was a continued torment to me." As a member of Congress he introduced a bill to abolish slavery in the District of Columbia but no action was taken upon that bill nor is there any record that Lincoln strongly advocated its passage.

In 1852 in the course of a eulogy of Henry Clay he spoke strongly "against a few but an increasing number of men who, for the sake of perpetuating slavery, are beginning to assail and to ridicule the white man's charter of freedom, the declaration that 'all men are created free and equal.'" [...] With extraordinarily clear thinking, simplicity of phrase, unimpassioned but forceful and direct style Lincoln's words served definitely to crystallize the scattered sentiment against human bondage. In one of his speeches delivered in 1854 Lincoln declared "Most governments have been based practically on the denial of the equal rights of men ... Ours began by affirming those rights. They said, some men are too ignorant and vicious to share in government. Possibly so, said we; and by your system you would always keep them ignorant and vicious. We proposed to give all a chance; and we expected the weak to grow stronger; the ignorant wiser and all better and happier together." Later, he declared, "The doctrine of self government is right—absolutely and eternally right ... If the Negro is a man, is it not to that extent a total destruction of self government to say that he, too, shall not govern himself! When the white man governs himself, that is self-government; but when he governs himself and also governs another man, that is more than self-government—that is depostism. ... No man is good enough to govern another man without that other's consent. ... Allow all the governed an equal voice in the government, and that only is self-government." Shortly before his election to the Presidency Lincoln in an address at Independence Hall in Philadelphia, defended the Constitution of the United States and, more accurately than he knew, foretold the fate which was destined for him because of his advocacy of the principles couched in our federal constitution. He spoke in that address of those things which had held the United States together as a confederation of separate bodies. "It was not the mere matter of separation of the colonies from the motherland, but that sentiment in the Declaration of Independence which gave liberty not alone to the people of this country but hope to all the world for all future time. It was that which gave promise that in due time the weights would be lifted from the shoulders of all men, and that all should have an equal chance. ... Now, my friends, can this country be saved on that basis? If it can, I will consider myself one of the happiest men in the world if I can help to save it. ... But if this country cannot be saved without giving up that principle, I was about to say I would rather be assassinated on this spot than surrender it."

I do not need to rehearse here the occurrences of those stormy years leading up to the election of Lincoln to the Presidency, of the firing upon Fort Sumter, of the bloody years of civil war. I do not need here again to tell of the sacrifice made not simply that Negro slaves should be free from bondage but that Lincoln's dream of these United States living up to its fundamental principles of freedom for all its citizens should come true. As we today look back down the years we wonder now that there should have been any doubt as to the wisdom of Lincoln's words but as we read the speeches of those who opposed him and who bitterly assailed him, we gain some idea of the terrific forces which are lined up against the other. Yet, when we look about us today it is not so hard to re-create the atmosphere of the years just before, during and after the Civil War. The work which was begun by Abraham Lincoln is yet far from finished. While we celebrate today the 120th anniversary of Abraham Lincoln's birth, we celebrate also the 20th birthday of the organization which came into being to complete the work of the great emancipator—the National Association for the Advancement of Colored People.

Twenty years ago today a small group of white and colored people, stirred and horrified by a bloody race riot in Springfield, Illinois, the old home of Abraham Lincoln, met in New York City to discuss means by which Lincoln's ideal of justice for all men regardless of color could be consummated. [...]

I am asked today to speak on the subject "If Lincoln Were Here." If the great emancipator were alive today what would he find? On the positive side he would see that in contrast with the four million Negroes in the United States during his lifetime there are today upwards of twelve million. Against twelve thousand homes owned by colored people in 1866, today seven hundred thousand homes are owned. Against twenty thousand farms operated in 1866, a half century later one million farms are run by Negroes. Seventy thousand businesses stand against twenty-one hundred in 1866; a total wealth of Negroes of two billion dollars stands against twenty million at the close of the Civil War. Illiteracy has been reduced largely through the efforts of Negroes themselves from 90% to 10%. [...]

Against this what are the handicaps and problems yet to be solved? The Negro is yet the victim of lynching mobs. Within the last 46 years 4,962 human beings have been hung by lawless mobs and in some instances have been burned at the stake. As midnight approached on December 31, 1928, a mentally defective Negro convict in Mississippi who had killed a convict camp boss for beating him was taken by a mob, paraded for seven hours through various parts of the state and then, in the presence of a mob of six thousand men and women, was slowly burned to death. [...]

In many states of the south where upwards of nine million Negroes yet live, Negroes are denied access to the ballot box and the 14th and 15th amendments to the constitution are flouted with impunity. Negroes are discriminated against in colleges and universities when they seek training. In industry the Negro is usually the last to be hired and the first to be fired when there is necessity for cutting down the number of employees. In many states of the south where Negroes must pay the same taxes as others from seven to fifteen times as much is expended for the education of white children as for Negroes. Over and above all of these physical disabilities is the caste and color prejudice by means of which those who seek to keep the Negro down are able to prevent decent and fair minded people even from knowing what the facts really are.

It was to meet this situation that the National Association for the Advancement of Colored People was brought into being. During the twenty years of its existence it has had a most extraordinary record. It initiated and continued the only organized and unremitting campaign against the evil of lynching which has been waged. [ . . . ]

[S]o has the Advancement Association opposed disfranchisement of Negroes. A considerable voteless class can be and will be exploited, mobbed and denied opportunity with impunity; and those who debar that class from access to the polls as guaranteed by the federal constitution injure themselves in that oppression always works evil upon the moral fibre of the oppressor as well as upon the privileges and immunities of the oppressed. [ . . . ]

In these and other cases the Advancement Association has struggled primarily for the Negro but in a larger sense it has struggled also for the vindication of the fundamental tenets of the American government.

NAACP Papers, Group I, Box 421, Part 11, Series B, Reel 35 of Microfilm Edition (Washington, DC: Library of Congress).

## LAMAR PERKINS, Address in the New York State Assembly, Albany, New York, February 12, 1930

*A native of Georgia, Perkins (1896–1973) was a graduate of Lincoln University and Harvard Law School. After serving in the army during World War I, he began practicing law in New York City. In 1929 he was elected to the New York State Assembly and served a single term. Perkins remained active in the Republican Party and was appointed an assistant attorney general by Governor Thomas Dewey in 1944. Perkins was selected to address the New York Assembly on Lincoln's birthday, and he used the occasion to invoke Lincoln's name in the cause of universal freedom and equality. In praising Lincoln's head and heart, Perkins noted Lincoln's global significance and asserted that Lincoln's place in the hearts of his countrymen had only grown with the passage of time.*

To-day we celebrate the birth of a great American. Among that grand array of notables which the Nation has sired he takes the place of its foremost son. In all the annals of this country there is no one who so fittingly portrays its character—its virgin strength, the grim struggle of its pioneer existence, its unequaled opportunities, its daring ideals, its glorious achievement. It might well be said that his life was itself the great American Epic.

Those finer qualities of head and heart were in him so happily blended that he stood alone, almost lonely in his greatness. Of the humblest origin, he knew well the heart of humanity. At all times his hand was on the pulse of the people. Yet for all his love for the people he never stooped to the level of the demagogue. His most stirring popular appeals were flavored with simple justice and homely wisdom. In that darkest hour of the Civil War when the Nation was wrapped in despair and gloom hung like a pall over the country, and the people North and South were loud in their condemnation of him, he maintained that calmness of purpose, that unwavering determination unshaken to the end.

That with the passing years his character becomes increasingly impressed not only in the hearts of his fellow countrymen but looms larger and larger on the horizon of the world is a clear and powerful attestation to the greatness of this man. I would not call him the great emancipator. That would limit his greatness to a single act. I would not call him the Great War President, lest his memory be associated only with the horror of bloodshed. I would not even call him the Saviour of his country, lest his greatness rest with the verdict of a single people. Rather would I call him that rare gift of God to man, a fine soul encased in common clay, an understanding heart in the body of a prophet.

Abraham Lincoln is not to be taken as a dim figure out of the past whose influence was only upon an era now past and gone. His influence is a vital living force today. He made a contribution to statesmanship that was at once unique and simple, yet incomprehensible to but a few of his day. Into the cold harsh methods of war and statecraft he injected the policy of kindliness to his enemies, tolerance for the opinions of those who differed with him, a belief that freedom of all men should be a reality, an accomplished fact, that war should be only a terrible last resort, that the eyes of mankind should look forward to the day when men might live as brothers. He was the first man in history who realized fully that there can be no hope of peace on earth unless all men are free.

Our American Commonwealth is at once the test of the modern trend of government and a supreme challenge to civilization. In this country we have living side by side men of every race and creed on earth, men who are as different as men can be. Yet we all propose to live in peace and harmony allowing every individual the freest possible self expression compatible with the safety of his neighbor. This Nation is itself the hope of mankind. [ . . . ]

The nations of the world today are in conference seeking a means to reduce the implements of war. At the instance of America this first step toward peace among men was made, which is only one step in the general movement to the end of universal peace and the brotherhood of man. This movement will succeed and can only succeed by a recognition by these powers of that policy and prophecy of Lincoln that part of the people can not remain free and part slave. Each Nation must sacrifice some of its desire for self-aggrandizement. Each Nation must allow every other Nation the same opportunity for self-expression that it desires for itself. The powers of the world in taking even this first step in the consummation of Lincoln's ideal justifies us in saying of him "Thou art mighty yet, thy spirit walks abroad."

The greatness of Lincoln must rest more upon the quality of his soul rather than upon his intellect, as great as that was. He possessed the understanding heart that the wisest man prayed for. The prejudices and hatreds that have filled the world from the beginning of time have been caused by a lack of understanding between men. When men consult together misunderstandings and prejudices vanish. When men really know each other they begin to see and appreciate those finer qualities that they see in their friends. The hope of the world is that men will ultimately gather at the council table with their enemies.

As this lonely figure of the past dedicated himself to a task of freedom and salvation, let us dedicate ourselves to a furtherance of that task and pledge our lives that men, all men, shall be free, not only of the physical bonds of slavery, but also free of those sinister mental forces of misunderstanding and misconception. Let us resolve that no man is free unless all men are free, that no man is safe unless all men are safe, that the Universal Brotherhood of Man shall in each of us find at all times a champion, that we, as Americans, shall forever keep alive the spirit of that immortal man as the guiding force of our Nation and the hope of mankind.

*Journal of the Assembly of the State of New York* (1930), 333–335.

## SAMUEL A. HAYNES on Lincoln and Emancipation Day, January 7, 1932

*A native of Belize, Haynes (1898–1971) served in World War I, and was involved with Marcus Garvey's Universal Negro Improvement Association prior to immigrating to the United States in the early 1920s. He worked as a journalist and editor and was involved in the civil rights movement. Haynes was also a proponent of decolonization, and one of his poems became the lyrics for Belize's national anthem. In this column for the* Philadelphia Tribune, *Haynes challenged the image of Lincoln as the Great Emancipator and compared him unfavorably to two men who had led unsuccessful slave insurrections: Nat Turner and John Brown. Haynes also cited Frederick Douglass's famous quote about African American allegiance to the Republican Party "ship" as he questioned this continued loyalty and suggested that it went hand-in-hand with uncritical praise of Lincoln. In viewing these practices as antiquated, destructive relics of the past, Haynes anticipated a shift in African American support from the Republican Party to the Democrats that would soon become evident at the national level (Silvaana Udz, "Haynes, Samuel Alfred," in* The Dictionary of Caribbean and Afro-Latin American Biography, *edited by Franklin W. Knight and Henry Louis Gates Jr. [New York: Oxford University Press, 2016]).*

---

The annual celebration of Emancipation Day brought forth the customary mass meetings, silver tongue orators, reading of the Declaration of Independence, and tribute to Abraham Lincoln. I am yet to be convinced of the genuine value of this annual pastime. These mass meetings are nothing but hot air pow-wows. The Declaration of Independence is idyllic, but its relationship to the aspirations of black Americans is foreign. Lincoln was a great American, not a great emancipator. If he were the humanitarian he is reputed to have been he would have emancipated the slaves on the basis of human justice rather than national expediency. I have the highest regard for any man, white or black, who rose from obscurity to the highest rung of the human ladder as Lincoln did. I cannot, however, applaud Lincoln as a superman; as the great white savior of the poor benighted slaves. The eulogy is but a phantasm of the historians.

Emancipation of the slaves was inevitable.

The presence of Lincoln was not a prerequisite. Had the bondage continued by popular choice, innumerable insurrections would have ensued and historians would have immortalized the courageous efforts of John Brown and Nat Turner as memorable triumphs rather than defeats. Lincoln, as President, was custodian of the nation's honor. Slavery jeopardized that honor.

It was his duty to go the limit in protecting it. He risked nothing, sacrificed nothing. When he weighed the welfare of the nation against the welfare of the slave traders and slave owners he exhibited a weakness common to most white leaders who must decide between human justice and national well being. Brown and Turner, unlike Lincoln, did not eschew the slavery issue. They did not patronize. They struck a course which incurred the wrath of their countrymen. To white America they were traitors; to God and humanity, conquering heroes. If we are going to make a saint of Lincoln let us at least be consistent and extend the honor to John Brown and Nat Turner, who had no regrets for their human benevolence.

A man steals your purse. The police recovers it. The magistrate sends the culprit to jail. Would you immortalize the magistrate because he did his duty as a public servant? Let it be borne in mind, too, that the Republican party was born out of the issue of slavery. The Negro made it; it did not make the Negro. It is time we read history with light and understanding. When we cleave to the tradition which gave us the slogan, "The Republican Party is the ship, all else the sea;" when we worship blindly at the shrine of Lincoln, we but behave like dumb driven cattle. That we persist in fetish adoration of the two is proof sufficient that the shackles which once borne our body are now securely fastened to our brain.

Editorial in the *Philadelphia Tribune*, Jan. 7, 1932.

## WILLIAM E. LILLY, *Set My People Free: A Negro's Life of Lincoln*, 1932

*A native of Tennessee, Lilly (1878–1948) graduated from the Howard University Law School and eventually settled in Chicago during the 1920s, where he established a successful law practice. As the first African American to write a book-length biography of Lincoln, Lilly emphasized the importance that the slavery issue played in forming Lincoln's political and moral views. In focusing exclusively on Lincoln's pre-presidential career, Lilly devoted attention to events that were often overlooked in favor of Lincoln's wartime achievements. As the following excerpts indicate, Lilly attached much significance to Lincoln's 1837 protest against slavery in the Illinois General Assembly, as he believed it exceeded even the Emancipation Proclamation for its moral courage. Lilly also deemed Lincoln's proposal for gradual, compensated emancipation in Washington, DC as the single greatest act of his brief career in Congress. For Lilly, Lincoln's commitment to ending slavery and preserving the Union made him a more pragmatic and ultimately more successful alternative to the radical abolitionists ("Atty. William E. Lilly, Lincoln Authority, Dies," Chicago Defender, June 5, 1948).*

———————————

Now there is a resolution before our Illinois Legislature. It strongly condemns the abolitionists, bewails the hurt they are doing to the slaves. Strange solicitude is this. It was adopted January 20, 1837, by a vote of 77 to 6. Lincoln and five others have seen fit to vote against it. Their reasons are not set forth. Six weeks later a resolution of protest signed by Dan Stone and A. Lincoln is spread on the journal of the House. It proceeds as follows: "We believe the institution of slavery is founded both on injustice and bad policy, but that the promulgation of abolition doctrines tends to increase rather than to abate its evils." This resolution, brief in verbiage but comprehensive in scope, differs from the abolitionists as to the possible results of their efforts, but has no condemnation for them; and if it does not condemn the slaveholders in person, it is a complete indictment of the system of slavery based both on morals and sound policy. Others, whether in high place or low, whether President of this American land or some humble laborer, might grope uncertainly during the next twenty-three years for a fixed policy with which to face the terrific storms of passion that were to sweep over the nation. This young man being barely twenty-eight, had announced the base on which he pitched his battle against that monstrous iniquity, and so firm was this base that never after did he need to change or shift his position.

This resolution of protest has an especial interest for us of a later day because it sets forth the ground upon which was to be waged slowly but effectively, for more than a quarter of a century, the struggle that was to end in the destruction of chattel slavery. As an important state paper it has been strangely overlooked, both by the historians and the hundreds of Lincoln biographers. This is the more strange since the man who has been recognized as the foremost of Americans adhered to its terms with singular fidelity, not only in the days of his obscurity when he was still striving for recognition in Illinois, but in that later day when the word of Abraham Lincoln carried beyond the bounds of that State and even to the farthest ends of America. Both in word and action all his after life in politics and statecraft was in accord with this resolution, set out in his twenty-eighth year. Whether we consider it as far-seeing calculation or unvarying consistency, it is probable that the like has not been witnessed either before or since in American annals.

Whether Dan Stone, a lawyer already well known in his district and profession, or Abraham Lincoln, still a mere student in that profession, drew the resolution, we do not know. But we do know that it outlined the course of action that was to be followed by the latter with regard to the paramount issue that confronted the American people through all the days that saw the rise of Lincoln from the place of member of the Legislature to that which saw him as President of the United States.

This will be readily seen by an examination of the three paragraphs of the resolution devoted to declaring the views of the two bold signers of the paper. The paper is divided into five paragraphs containing less than a hundred and fifty words. The first, we have already seen. The second declares "that Congress under the Constitution, has no power to interfere with the institution of slavery in the existing States." There was nothing new or startling in this pronouncement. It was in accord with the settled opinion of the day and questioned only by the more extreme abolitionists.

The third paragraph asserts, "that Congress has the power under the Constitution to regulate slavery in the District of Columbia, but that it ought not to be exercised unless at the request of the people of the District of Columbia." Here in this proposition that resolution has reached dangerously controversial ground, and has taken square issue with the resolution sent as an ultimatum by the Legislature of Alabama to the various northern States. It constituted in settled fact the field on which was to be waged a hundred civic battles in the various State legislatures, the Congress of the United States, and in all the courts of the land, even to the final court of appeals, in the vain effort to find a solution for a problem that had no solution save that which would be finally found on a hundred battle fields. [...]

That was the first of three great outstanding acts against slavery, forming a mighty trinity connecting the three periods of the manhood of Lincoln, and however much applause the world has given to the third of these acts, and however tremendous the results that followed the Emancipation Proclamation, there is much reason to feel that in true moral grandeur it is this first of the trinity of acts that ranks highest.

The act to abolish slavery in the District of Columbia was a carefully drawn measure with features that were expected to draw votes from all sections of the country. It was introduced following a debate full of bitterness over another bill for the freeing of the slaves of the District, more sweeping in its tenor and less calculated to command sufficient votes to be enacted into law. It is likely that the hatreds generated in the debates on this first bill made it impossible to carry through the second, despite the provisions that it had been hoped would receive favorable consideration even from the slave-holding group. After designating classes that were not thereafter to be held in slavery in the District, which included slaves not already owned by residents, and unborn children, the bill went on to permit those coming into the District in an official character to bring and retain their domestic servants, without being controlled by the pending measure, and then provided that children born to slave mothers after January 1, 1850, should be held for service as apprentices to a specified age, during which suitable support and education was to be provided them.

It appears that Lincoln had studied closely the measures that had been presented in Great Britain and other lands for abolishing slavery in their dominions, and provision was made as in them for compensating the owners of the slaves. Here was a measure broad enough to have given reasonable satisfaction to all, and that offered a sound basis for eliminating the brutal system from all the land; but the irritated slave-holders would hear of no plans that contemplated making a truth of certain traditions as to liberty and equality that had in the first period of the nation been highly popular. So was rendered futile the peaceful efforts of a man always inclined to peace to solve a problem that was to confront him at another day, when he would be compelled in its solution to have recourse to the method of blood and iron. [...]

With none of the fiery impulsiveness that made some of these men [abolitionists] ready to strike down the thing, regardless of all other results, Lincoln's determination to destroy slavery was probably more fixed than theirs. His practical mind, however, made him instinctively know that men possessed of great riches would never give it up because of some moral argument. He had no thought of destroying the Union over slavery, and he had no thought of allowing the South to go its way with its wealth of slaves. In both these propositions he found himself differing with many of the extreme abolitionists like Garrison and Phillips. Strange as it may seem, these with many of their group who had been so prodigal of words that certainly helped bring on the storm, now, when the first rude gusts of secession blew heavily from the South, were ready that the South should go its way. Phillips talked flippantly, of speeding the "parting guest;" Greeley, at first would have "let the erring sisters depart in peace." Whittier, the Quaker, true to the peaceful tenets of his group, would do likewise. Had these men their way, slavery would have continued indefinitely for nine-tenths of the colored people. In bidding the "erring sisters go their way in peace" these abolitionists would have gotten rid of slavery in the Union, but left it firmly fixed where practically all the slaves were; that is in the seceding States. But the man in Springfield, knowing this, thought always of ending a great wrong, and not merely of getting it out of his and their house. Fortunately for millions of colored people his wiser counsel prevailed, though at the cost of the most destructive war ever seen on the western continent.

William E. Lilly, *Set My People Free: A Negro's Life of Lincoln* (New York: Farrar & Rinehart, 1932), 53–56, 129–132, 259–260.

## ROBERT L. VANN, "The Patriot and the Partisan," Speech Delivered in Cleveland, Ohio, September 11, 1932

*Vann (1879–1940) was editor of the* Pittsburgh Courier, *one of the most influential African American newspapers. By 1932, Vann had become disillusioned with the Republican Party and switched his allegiance to the Democratic Party. According to Vann, Republicans had taken Black support for granted and had not adequately responded to the Great Depression. Vann also felt snubbed when he did not receive a plum patronage appointment after campaigning for Republicans during the 1920s. His address at Cleveland was widely publicized, and as Vann's biographer argues, it "rocked the nation's black community." Vann asserted that African American reverence of Lincoln and loyalty to the Republican Party were based on ignorance. He believed African Americans owed no debt of gratitude to a political party that had done little more than exploit them. Without stating it explicitly, Vann essentially suggested that the notion of Lincoln as Great Emancipator was a myth, and he predicted that African Americans would be turning their portraits of Lincoln to the wall and voting for Democrats in the upcoming elections. Vann's speech was widely circulated,*

*and prompted a delegation of Black Republicans, led by Roscoe Conkling Sim-*
*mons, to meet with President Herbert Hoover at the White House. While some*
*African Americans followed Vann's advice in 1932, the major shift to the Demo-*
*cratic Party occurred in 1936. Vann received an appointment in the Roosevelt*
*administration as an assistant in the attorney general's office (Andrew Buni,*
Robert L. Vann of the Pittsburgh Courier: Politics and Black Journalism
*[Pittsburgh, PA: University of Pittsburgh Press, 1974], 188).*

---

A patriot is defined by our accepted dictionaries [as] one who loves his country,
and, specifically, one who loves his country and zealously supports its authority
and interests. Patriotism is the love of country, devotion to the welfare of one's
country; the passion inspiring one to serve one's country.

Partisanism, by the same authority, is defined as being the adherence to a
party or faction,—specifically, one having the character of blind or unreasonable
adherence to a party,—one blinded by partisan zeal.

It is self-evident that a patriot occupies a higher and more important status with
respect to his country than a partisan. Patriotism is above partisanism. Patriotism
seeks first to serve the country, and the patriot, the true patriot, loves his country
and zealously supports its interests. [...]

Next in importance to the preservation of one's country is the government of
that country, and for convenience, governments are established by the people,
to be operated for the people with the consent and support of the people. [...]

The Republican party came into power through the use of a purely political
issue based upon purely economic reasons. Back in the 50'[s], the great economic
question of the cost of production in two separate sections of this country brought
forth the political issue of free labor, known as slave labor. [...] Out of this economic question evolved the political issue of slavery. Abraham Lincoln, in his
famous address at Cooper Union, New York City, disclosed himself the man best
fitted to expound the issue. And upon this political issue of slavery the Republican
party laid its foundation and successfully built its superstructure. We all know
the history of the war. In the language of the politicians of those days, it was a
war to free slaves, but in the language of the bankers, financiers and economists,
it was a war to equalize the cost of production of commodities manufactured in
this country[...].

Out of that war rose triumphant the Republican party. The Negro as a slave
was let loose, without a penny, to find his way amid a civilization then ripening
into the highest form of intelligence, culture, and financial power, known to the
world. [...] The political issue of slavery had triumphed, and out of it a political
party was born, and this political issue was made the battle cry of freedom in every
national election from 1858 until 1900. [...] There stood the black man, free, but

helpless, staggered by the realization of a long-prayed-for freedom, but helpless, nevertheless, in his penury and ignorance. What a picture this must have been. All of the beauty of devotion of slave to master had been destroyed. All of the compassion and love of master for slave had been rooted out. Slave and master were set in antagonistic opposition, one against the other. No longer the lullaby of the black mammy rang through the great house; and no longer did her black breast furnish nourishment to the tender youth of her former master. [...]

Negroes in those days felt that the Republican party was the ship and all else the sea. A black orator became famous for that very phrase. They felt that Abraham Lincoln had been given to this country by God Himself and, in many places, Lincoln enjoyed a reverence at the hands of black people akin to that of Jesus Christ Himself. The political issue of slavery was forever held aloft, and Abraham Lincoln was the man who carried the flag and on it were inscribed "Emancipation, Freedom, Equality," and under this banner for decade after decade, Negroes, without rhyme or reason, swore by the Republican party and swore at everything else, political, under the sun. The Negro literally sold his soul to the Republican party.

But this was only natural. A helpless and ignorant people, snatched as overnight from bondage and thrust, with little or no educational preparation, into high governmental authority, were jubilant with joy. Their cup ran over with gratitude, and they were so absorbed with their new surroundings and their sudden ascendancy to power that they never thought to figure out either for themselves or for their progeny the reason why. But what a price we have paid for that joy!

It was also perfectly natural and human that former masters should look with disdain and scorn upon a governor who yesterday was a slave. [...] Every thrust intended for the victorious North found its way into the heart of a black man in the South. [...] Today, there are white boys and girls and Negro boys and girls in this country who have a dislike, akin to hatred, for each other, and they don't know why. They can find the reason in the selfish history of the Republican party. [...]

This is the burning, ugly truth—the burning, ugly cause of most of our woes. It can only be told by the few surviving victims who lived through that unparalleled period known as the Reconstruction. The Republican party amended the Constitution [...] to protect the man who had furnished the successful political issue during the period of the war. [...] [T]he Republican party declared that the black man had his protection. He had been made a part of the citizenry of this great country. He had been clothed with authority and surrounded with the power of his government, and that government was the Republican party. Year after year, Negroes marched to the polls and with heads erect and eyes fixed upon the image of Abraham Lincoln, they voted the Republican ticket wherever and whenever they could get their hands upon a ballot. Abraham Lincoln was the symbol of freedom. His name was synonymous with liberty, and he was the embodiment of all things Republican. For years, for decade after decade, the Negro of this country has monotonously supported a government by the Republican party. What else could be expected of people who were unable to fathom the economic reasons behind a political issue? What else could be expected of a people whose conception of political success was political office? What else could be expected of a people whose hearts and minds were so confused that they were unable to discriminate between patriotism and partisanism? To them patriotism was service not to their country, but to the party that had selected them as the convenient political issue in an economic crisis.

Today, Negroes fifty years and older still believe that slavery was abolished out of the full heart and compassion of the Republican party; but, ah, my friends, there are Negroes today between the ages of eighteen and forty who know that the Negro was never liberated from slavery by the Republican party because slavery was wrong, or because the Republican party loved the Negro more than it loved its country. There are Negroes today within the sound of my voice who know that the abolition of slavery was brought about through a political issue purely and solely to relieve an economic crisis. So long as the Republican party could use the photograph of Abraham Lincoln to entice Negroes to vote a Republican ticket, they condescended to accord Negroes some degree of political recognition. But when the Republican party had built itself to the point of security, it no longer invited Negro support. It no longer gave Negroes political recognition. [ . . . ] After the administration of President McKinley, political patronage for the Negro began definitely and gradually to decline [ . . . ] What has followed in the last twenty years? The Thirteenth, Fourteenth and Fifteenth amendments have been forgotten and not a voice has been raised, except as a gesture, in defense of the violations of these amendments. [ . . . ]

Instead of encouraging Negro support, the Republican party, for the past twelve years, has discouraged Negro support [ . . . ] [T]he Republican party, under Harding, absolutely deserted us. The Republican party under Mr. Coolidge was a lifeless, voiceless thing. The Republican party under Mr. Hoover has been the saddest failure known to political history. [ . . . ] I know, out of my own experience, that the Republican party looks upon the black man today as the most expensive and costly liability enumerated among its many[ . . .].

The Republican party has drifted away from its original moorings. The party designed to serve all the people has been transformed into a party which serves only the few. The patriot finds himself unable to enjoy the pursuits of happiness because a partisan government has betrayed him [ . . . ] We have seen ourselves ignored, deceived, hoodwinked, and ballyhooed, only to awake to find that we have been robbed in the house of our friends. [ . . . ]

I see in the offing a horde of black men and women throwing off the yoke of partisanism practiced for over half a century, casting down the idols of empty promises and moving out into the sunlight of independence. I see hordes and hordes of black men and women, belonging to the army of forgotten men, turning their faces toward a new course and a new party. I see millions of Negroes turning the pictures of Abraham Lincoln to the [w]all.

*Pittsburgh Courier*, Sept. 17, 1932.

## CARTER G. WOODSON, "Abolitionists Worried Lincoln," November 24, 1932

*The following essay from Woodson (1875–1950) further reinforces the importance of 1932 as a pivotal year for African American perceptions of Lincoln. As many Blacks left the Party of Lincoln and joined the Democratic Party, this shift in allegiance was accompanied by a rejection of the image of Lincoln as a friend and benefactor. Written in the wake of the presidential election in which Franklin Roosevelt defeated President Herbert Hoover, Woodson's piece was a non-partisan effort to contextualize Lincoln and correct inaccuracies that had been published and uttered during a heated political campaign. The pre-eminent African American historian of his era, Woodson believed that Lincoln must be judged by the standards of his own time. While Lincoln placed the Union before emancipation and initially supported colonization, Woodson noted that the Union had to be preserved for slavery to be completely abolished, and he argued that Lincoln's views on race evolved to the point where he had abandoned colonization and advocated limited Black voting rights. For Woodson, Lincoln's views on race bore little resemblance to White supremacists of the early 1930s.*

The election has passed now, and what I shall say cannot be construed as having any political intent. I am not a politician and would not have walked a mile to throw the election either way, if my vote had such significance, for the two degenerate major parties, being practically alike, merely contend for the opportunity to do the same thing. [. . .] In the interest of truth, however, I want to register an objection to the way Negroes especially have recently referred to Abraham Lincoln during the campaign.

I do not think of misfits and opportunists like Hoover and Roosevelt in connection with Lincoln; and yet I do not consider Lincoln a martyr in the sense in which I regard John Brown. Lincoln was a practical man; and while he said and did some things which we condemn today, he must be judged by the standards of his time.

Practically all statesmen who advocated the abolition of slavery believed that the Negroes when freed should be colonized abroad. If they remained in this country, these reformers thought they should have the status of free Negroes of that time. This meant that they could own property and make contracts to labor, but they should not sit on the jury, serve in the militia, vote, or hold office. This is precisely what the South tried to do with the freedmen in 1865, and the North interfered and made the Negro a voter and an officeholder. Lincoln, as his record will show, however, was far ahead of this conservative position and he developed further in the other direction during the Civil War.

Negroes of today severely criticize Abraham Lincoln for his inaction and hesitancy in matters respecting the emancipation and recognition of the race; and they, therefore, laugh at the idea of recording him in history as the "Great Emancipator." Lincoln often expressed his contempt for abolitionists like Sumner and Stevens. They worried him by urging the instant liberation of the "d—d niggers." He repeatedly said that he would save it without slavery. His chief purpose was to save the Union. Lincoln countermanded the emancipating orders of Butler, Fremont and Hunter. Lincoln could not easily come to the position of immediate emancipation. He had thought only of gradual and compensated emancipation to be completed by the year 1900.

With respect to Negroes after they became free, moreover, he was not very liberal. He did not care to have Negro soldiers in the Union Army, and when finally all but forced by circumstances to admit them, he did not desire to grant them the same pay and the same treatment accorded white soldiers. He believed, moreover, that Negroes, if liberated, should be colonized abroad, inasmuch as they could not hope to remain in this country and become socially and politically equal to white men.

Lincoln's attitude was made clear in 1862, when after the liberation of the Negroes in the District of Columbia, he summoned certain of their group to urge them to emigrate. "And why," said he, "should the people of your race be colonized and where? Why should they leave this country? You and we are different races. We have between us a broader difference than exists between almost any other two races. Whether it is right or wrong I need not discuss, but this physical difference is a great disadvantage to us both, as I think. Your race suffers very greatly, many of them, by living among us, while ours suffers from your presence. In a word we suffer on each side. If this is admitted, it affords a reason why we should be separated."

Lincoln, however, should not be unsympathetically condemned as the Negro's enemy who sought to exterminate slavery because it was no economic handicap to the white man. It must be remembered that Lincoln was not elected on an abolition platform. His party had merely repudiated the Dred Scott decision and opposed the extension of slavery. Lincoln, himself, had borne eloquent testimony against mob rule, lynching and slavery throughout his career. In Congress he had worked for gradual and compensated emancipation, and he had kept his plan before the slave States as the best solution of their problem.

To say that he would save the Union with or without slavery does not necessarily show a lack of interest in emancipation. No one will hardly think that emancipation would have had much of a chance if the Union had been lost. It succeeded with the Union saved.

In his hesitancy as to emancipation and the arming of the Negroes there may be evidence of statesmanship rather than lack of interest in freedom and democracy. As he often well said, the main thing was to win the war. Everything depended upon that. Had Lincoln immediately declared the Negroes free and turned them armed upon their masters he would have lost the war. Many of the people in the border slave States who were kindly disposed to the Union, were never the less pro-slavery.

A considerable number of the people in the free States, moreover, especially the "Copperheads" in the Northwest, objected to the "coercion" of the South. They would have risen in protest against anything resembling a servile insurrection. The war was not an effort to free slaves. Lincoln, as President of the United States, could not carry out his own personal plans. In a situation like this an executive must fail if he undertakes a reform so far ahead of the time that his very co-workers cannot be depended upon to carry out his policies.

The abolitionists were a small minority. Men had to be gradually brought around to thinking that immediate emancipation would be the proper solution of the problem. There was much fear that such a radical step would lead to interracial war. For this reason Lincoln and others connected deportation with emancipation. As the experiment had not been made, the large majority of Americans of Lincoln's day believed that the two races could not dwell together on the basis of social and political equality. A militant minority of the descendants of these Americans do not believe it now. The abolitionists themselves were not united on this point.

Lincoln, moreover, gradually grew into the full stature of democracy. Observing finally that the Negroes would remain permanently in this country, he urged upon the States in process of reconstruction to make some provision for the education of the freedmen and suggested that the right of franchise be extended to those who were intelligent and owned property. Whatever Lincoln did was what he thought best for all concerned. He was not prejudiced against any race in the sense that men are today. Frederick Douglass said that Lincoln was the first white man he ever met who did not say or do something to make him feel that he belonged to a different race.

*Atlanta Daily World*, Nov. 24, 1932.

## WILLIAM LLOYD IMES, "A Negro's Tribute to Lincoln," Radio Address on Lincoln's Birthday, February 12, 1935, Station WMCA, New York

*A native of Tennessee, Imes (1889–1986) was educated at Fisk University, the Union Theological Seminary, and Columbia University. He worked as a Presbyterian minister, served as president of Knoxville College, and was a member of the NAACP board of directors when he delivered the following radio address on Lincoln's birthday. The NAACP often produced special radio programs on Lincoln's birthday as a way of explicitly connecting memories of Lincoln with interracial cooperation and the ongoing struggle for civil rights. Imes began his address by paying tribute to Arthur Spingarn (1878–1971), a White man who served as chair of the NAACP's legal committee and was president of the organization from 1940 to 1966. Imes not only enlisted Lincoln in the cause of civil rights but also that of international peace and justice. Despite President Franklin Roosevelt's support, the Senate refused to ratify US participation in the World Court in early 1935. Denouncing those who opposed the World Court as demagogues, Imes cited a Bible verse (Luke 11:47) to illustrate the hypocrisy of those who claimed to honor Lincoln yet acted contrary to his principles. Clearly, Imes hoped listeners would accept his depiction of Lincoln as an exemplar of the principles that animated the work of the NAACP.*

It is a pleasure to speak not alone on the birthday of one of the greatest of Americans, but on the same evening when numbers of our fellow-citizens are honoring one who still lives among us, and whose innate modesty and self-effacement would rather continue the service of that still-handicapped race which Lincoln freed, than to accept all the testimonials which the world could give. I refer to Mr. Arthur Spingarn, whose distinguished service to the National Association for the Advancement of Colored People is one of the finest examples of modern interracial chivalry we are ever likely to see.

My theme is that of a tribute to the immortal Lincoln. But what person is sufficient to add further lustre to his name? To be called the "Saviour of His Country" at once tells his character in terms which give his life sacramental and cosmic meaning. There can be no higher honor nor greater service than that.

I honor Lincoln because he was just. Springing from the common soil of humanity, without the artificial trappings of convention and pretentious aristocracy, he became just what one would expect, a man to whom power could be safely entrusted, because he was simply human, and knew instinctively that if ever justice should be attained for all the people, it must be attained for "the man farthest down" as well. So far removed from the specious philosophy of caste was he that he put to shame those who sought special privilege, and he began a great tradition of non-political democracy, the influence of which has never ceased since his day. And this was because he was just. He freed the slaves because they were men and women, made in the image of God, and his act was not pity, nor sentiment, but honest and decent justice, so that he might stand unabashed in the clear sunlight of truth.

I honor Lincoln also because he never was patronizing in his attitude toward the lowly. If there is one thing from which twelve millions of citizens of color suffer most today, it is from the perhaps sometimes well-intentioned, but utterly mistaken and foolish policy of stronger and abler racial groups looking with condescension upon them, feeling that they are only children, and need the guidance and overlordship of others in every sphere. We feel this in business, in education, in religion; in fact, there is not a single phase of American life that does not reveal it. In the great Southland, it is evidenced by the very degrading social system of segregation, and in the North it is still in evidence, not only by a sort of subtle and unofficial segregation, but also by a philanthropy that deadens the abilities and dwarfs the development of these highly capable and useful fellow-citizens of color. Lincoln would never have done the follow-up of his emancipation of the slaves in such a stupid way. He had the common sense never to belittle nor patronize his fellow-men.

I honor Lincoln because he was discerning. He saw beneath the superficialities of life down to its real substratum. When his advisers counselled headstrong measures, he went slowly and carefully; when they insisted upon retaliation and revenge toward the slaveholding and slavery-sympathizing elements of our country, he knew that one greater than any of us, black or white, said: "I say unto you, 'Love your enemies, do good to them that persecute you,'" and he both believed and practiced his Bible better than most churchmen of his day, South or North.

It was this discernment that kept him both firm in every right measure for preserving the Union, and yet that never led him into the vicious and short-sighted policy of "getting even with" those whose ways he could not approve. A smaller man would have ruined his opportunity to save the nation by his pettiness, but above all else, Lincoln was never mean and petty. He could not live in the small backyard of prejudice and selfishness, where so many of us still are content to reside, I am ashamed to say, seventy years after his martyrdom.

But, towering above most other great things in the life and character of Lincoln you and I may well honor him that he was, in the best sense of a much-abused word, a great leader. Now there are leaders and leaders, and no cry is more insistently heard in our world of 1935 than the one which clamors for leadership. Part of this clamor is sincere, but a very large part is quite definitely insincere. What we need in our leadership today, as in all ages before us, is the assurance of both commanding ability, and crystal-clear honesty in dealing with all our fellow-men.

Leadership based upon hatred of race or class will not endure, and Lincoln knew it. So far different was he from most of our so-called leaders of today, that it seems almost blasphemous to mention him in the same breath with them. Everywhere today we are beset with these false leaders in America and in the world. They use our pulpits, our radio stations, our senate halls, our newspapers and everything else they can control to try to sway our multitudes into mob action, into cheap and easy ideas of success, or of pseudo-patriotism, or of that brand of Americanism which means the continued privilege for the few at the expense of the many. And when any of us of the common people, white or black, rebel against this demagogy, we are called dangerous and radicals, and all the rest of the bogey names that can be conjured up. Well, we are in excellent company! Lincoln was called these names and worse by the time-servers of his generation, and somehow even our demagogues of this day appeal to Lincoln, when, if Lincoln were really here again, and were to do the exact things he did in 1863, they would be ready to re-enact his assassination. "Ye kill the prophets, and then build monuments to them."

Truly great leaders like Lincoln are Heaven's kind gift to mankind, if only we can discern through them the way in which humanity must march forward in order to bring a righteous world-order to pass. And this we are endeavoring to do, even with faltering steps, in this year of God's grace. No wonder the descendants of those whom Lincoln's proclamation outwardly freed are uniting with millions of others in this commonwealth to honor his memory.

What Lincoln would have done to make for an international order, based upon that same understanding and goodwill which characterized his domestic policy of government, can never be fully known. But of this we may be sure. If such a decision as that which came before our government recently had come before a mind like Lincoln's, in reference to a World Court for enlightened counsel and high-minded action in the field of arbitration, he would hardly have taken the narrow and selfish view. And while we of the race Lincoln emancipated regret the apparent short-sighted and isolationist policy that for the present, at least, has prevailed, we cannot be surprised, for any nation that calmly tolerates the steady outrage of barbarous lynching of human beings, its citizens, mainly those of color, can scarcely be morally prepared to sit in a World Court, or take any other part looking toward a better world order.

And so, Lincoln, we honor you! But be sure that we do not dare boast that we have yet caught up with you! When your justice, your humanity, your high-mindedness, your hatred of sham, and your sacrifice shall really be understood, then will shine forth a greater America, and a part of that America will be the children and children's children of both slaves and freedmen who trod the wine press with God and you!

William Lloyd Imes Papers, Box 6, Special Collections Research Center, Syracuse University Libraries.

## EUGENE GORDON on Lincoln, Boston, Massachusetts, February 1935

*A native of Florida, Gordon (1891–1974) enlisted in the army during World War I and rose to the rank of second lieutenant. After the war, he worked as a journalist for the* Boston Post *and eventually became an editor for the* Post— *one of the first African Americans to serve as an editor for a White newspaper. Frustrated by the state of race relations and disillusioned that the service of African Americans in the First World War did not lead to greater progress, Gordon joined the American Communist Party in the early 1930s and lived in the Soviet Union during the mid-1930s, where he worked for the* Moscow Daily News. *After returning to the United States, Gordon continued to work as a journalist and essayist. The following piece questioned Lincoln's reputation as the Great Emancipator and offered a Marxist critique of Lincoln's Republican Party. To support his argument that Lincoln opposed civil rights for African Americans, Gordon cited George S. Merriam's* The Negro and the Nation *(1906) (AANB; Chicago Defender, Sept. 15, 1934).*

---

Abraham Lincoln, as a mythical figure, is of recent origin. During his lifetime and shortly after his death so much truth was written about him that it is amazing how the myths grew up. The fact is, the fanciful tales about Lincoln's being the black man's savior did not originate until the Republican party originated them.

I do not intend to go into a discussion of the Republican party, but simply to point out that this party of Northern capitalists, feeling the need of the colored man's loyalty, invented the tale of "The Great Emancipator." Until then everybody had taken Lincoln for just what he was—a clever politician and a tool of the young capitalist class. [ . . . ]

Abraham Lincoln was not "The Great Emancipator," since, although he signed the Emancipation Proclamation, which liberated black workers from chattel slavery, he did nothing actually to make them free. In fact, he opposed actual freedom.

Lincoln was a politician who served his party faithfully. That, of course, was the Republican party, recently organized to carry out the wishes of the people who wanted to check the spread of slavery. The party represented the interests of the growing young capitalist class. Unless slavery was abolished, capitalism could never spread throughout the great American continent. Slavery was a holdover from feudalism; capitalism was new and vital and strong. It was the society of the future; whereas, slavery represented a social order that had already been buried everywhere except in the Southern part of the United States.

When Lincoln, therefore, seemed to hate slavery, he was reflecting the attitude of the class which controlled his party. When he seemed to waver, to vacillate, in his attitude toward the South, it was because the Republican party itself wavered. He could not act independently of his bosses, the men who furnished money to keep the Republican party going.

Some of the abolitionists did not understand these facts. They accused Lincoln of weakness. One of his most persistent accusers was Horace Greeley, editor of the New York Tribune. Greeley published an open letter in his paper, entitling it, "The Prayer of Twenty Millions."

During the course of this letter, Greeley suggested that Lincoln write to the United States ministers in Europe and ask them to say candidly "whether the seeming subserviency of your policy to the slave-holding, slave-upholding interest, is not the perplexity, the despair of statesmen and of parties, and be admonished by the general answer!"

Greeley forgot that Lincoln was acting that way because the Republican party did not want to hurt the South too much. To free the slaves would be a severe blow to the South, "Therefore," said the Republican party, "don't even threaten to do that until every other device has failed." Lincoln obeyed his orders. He was a good party man. [ . . . ]

Did Lincoln actually say that he was not in favor of giving black men the kind of freedom white men enjoyed? If so, then he was really against real freedom for the blacks, wasn't he? If he did, he was against equal rights for colored people, wasn't he? But how could the Great Emancipator be against equal rights for those whom he emancipated? If we remember that he emancipated the slaves only because he thought that act would weaken the South, we can understand how he could have opposed actual liberation for the colored people. [ . . . ]

Not only did Abraham Lincoln believe the black man to be inferior to the white man, but, like the rest of the Republicans of his time, "he disclaimed any disposition," says Merriam, "to agitate against the fugitive slave law; as to practical restriction, he had nothing to urge except exclusion from the territories."

When he declared, later on, that he did not believe the nation could exist half slave and half free, he meant just this: that a capitalist society could not exist side by side with a bastard feudalism. One of them had to be crushed. Bastard feudalism was crushed, because vigorous young capitalism was stronger.

All this happened when Lincoln was running against Stephen A. Douglas for Senator. Two years later Lincoln was elected President. His views on slavery and the black man did not improve, so far as the records show.

Frederick Douglass, whose mother was a slave, but whose father was a white man, was about eight years younger than Abraham Lincoln. A judicial balancing of their lives side by side shows Douglass to be in every way a greater man than Lincoln. The very fact that Lincoln did not believe in the full equality of white men and black men, that he was not personally concerned whether the great masses of blacks were ever truly liberated, marked him as Douglass's inferior.

And if Lincoln-Day orators among our "leaders" today absurdly claim Lincoln as the black man's great emancipator, Douglass, who knew him and had every opportunity to eulogize, was never guilty of such a blunder. [...]

During this week, when more will be said in praise of Lincoln than of Douglass, it would pay every worker, black and white, to learn something more of the early history of both of these men [...] We need such heroes as Douglass in our present-day struggle for our liberation and for the liberation of all workers from the yoke of capitalist oppression.

Editorial in the *Afro-American* (Baltimore), Feb. 23, 1935.

## ARTHUR W. MITCHELL, Address in the US House of Representatives, June 1, 1936

*Mitchell (1883–1968) was the first African American member of the Democratic Party to be elected to the US House of Representatives. A native of Alabama, Mitchell practiced law, moved to Chicago, and defeated Oscar De Priest, the first African American member of Congress from a northern state, in the 1934 congressional elections. As the first African American Democrat in Congress, Mitchell symbolized the shift in Black allegiance from the Republican Party that occurred during the Great Depression in response to President Franklin Roosevelt's New Deal. Mitchell was a frequent target of Republicans who believed Blacks that voted Democrat were betraying their loyalty to the Party of Lincoln. The following address was delivered in response to a speech by John M. Robison, a Republican member of the House from Kentucky. Robison had attacked Mitchell for making a speech on April 22 that explained why African Americans should support the Democratic Party. Robison took issue with Mitchell's assertion that Lincoln was not elected to abolish slavery. For Mitchell, whatever debt African Americans owed to the Party of Lincoln had been paid in full (ANB).*

---

To begin with, I may say that when I stood here on the 22d of April I read Abraham Lincoln's own speech, and I read every word that he used discussing the question of the abolition of slavery and the paragraph which he took from the Republican platform of 1860, and I defy any man, living or dead, to show the contrary. [...]

What have we done here this morning? We have listened to a typical Republican campaign speech. We have listened to the speech that has been made by Republicans to my people for 70 years, and all the while they have kept us in political slavery, and now one of my colleagues from Kentucky Mr. [John M.] Robison has the audacity to wish to continue that kind of political slavery. [...]

I should like to remind the gentleman that the Negro of 1936 is not the Negro of 1870, 1880, and 1890, but a new Negro with political vision and ambition. He has struggled for political freedom, and it will do your cause no good to go back to 1860 and wave the red flag before our faces. We have too long tried you and your party, to our sorrow.

For 70 years we followed you blindly; for 70 years we perpetuated you in power; and for 70 long years you promised relief, and forgot your promises the minute you found yourself in office. You have had your day with the Negro vote.

Granting that all you contend is true—and I say it is not—has not the Negro paid you for what you did for him in 1861, 1863, and 1865? Is it your idea that because he was liberated during the administration of a Republican President he must still vote your ticket as a matter of gratitude, with his eyes closed toward his present and future needs? I deny that this should be the requirement of any party. Does not 70 years of unbroken loyalty to you and your party even up the debt, or is it your contention that this party loyalty you are claiming is to be an eternal thing? Can you not cease to talk about what your party did 70 years ago, and tell the aspiring youth of this country what your party proposes to do in 1936 and the years to follow? Do you think we are so blind and so dumb as to be led again to the political slaughter by Republicans seeking to hold office, whose record insofar as we are concerned is a chain of broken promises reaching across three-quarters of a century? [ . . . ]

I repeat to you, my friends, what I said April 22 are the words of Abraham Lincoln. Lincoln said himself he did not expect to interfere with slavery where it existed. I was making no particular attack on Abraham Lincoln. I take second place to no person from Kentucky or any other State in admiring that great states-man, but I deny that he is President now, and that his party has by its political conduct bound me or my people to follow their lead blindly.

Abraham Lincoln has been dead 70 years. If the gentleman does not know it, there are people who know that when he lived he was a politician like all the rest of us. He worked to get into office. He served in this House. He served in the legislature of his State. He served in various offices. He even served in the Presidency of the United States, and he made no effort to free the Negro until 1863, almost 2 years after he came into the Presidency, and I am told, and those who have read the story know, the difficulty that Republicans and Democrats alike throughout this country, who believed in the abolition of human slavery, had in getting him to sign the emancipation proclamation, which was not signed until January 1, 1863. If he and his party were so bent on freeing the Negro, why did they have to wait all those 2 years to start about it? [ . . . ] Abraham Lincoln had to free the Negroes in order to bring conscripts into the Army to save that situation. [ . . . ]

We have the story of the man's work, we have the story of the man's life, and we know that Democrats as well as Republicans joined the Union Army and fought to preserve this Union. [...]

We shall not take either party all together upon its past record; we shall deal with both parties as they show an interest in us and deal with us in 1936. For my part there is no question in my mind but that the Democratic Party, as constituted today, offers the Negro by far the best opportunity in this country, and I shall use all the influence and all the power that I possess to drive this truth home to the Negroes in this country.

Today the Negro refuses to stand by you simply on 60-year-old promises still unfulfilled. Until you make good the promises that you have made from the last 70 years, we shall try new political fields not marked "G.O.P." [...]

The Republican Party has conjured with the name of Lincoln long enough. Lincoln has been dead for 70 years, and his party as the party of human rights died years ago.

*Congressional Record, 74th Cong., 2d Sess., 8551–8552.*

## GRACE EVANS, Remarks at Emancipation Day Celebration, Connersville, Indiana, September 22, 1936

*Evans (1893–1952) was active in a variety of organizations, including the Republican Party and the Indiana Federation of Colored Women's Clubs, and she served as president of the NAACP branch in her hometown of Terre Haute. The following report on an Emancipation Day celebration indicates that not all African Americans left the Republican Party to join the Democrats in the 1930s. Indeed, Mrs. Evans felt very strongly that the Party of Lincoln remained the only true bulwark protecting civil rights and she credited Lincoln's Emancipation Proclamation for being responsible for those rights she now enjoyed. In Mrs. Evans's view, the Democratic Party still represented slavery and racial oppression rather than the promise of a New Deal, and she was not about to remove Lincoln's portrait from her wall ("Grace Wilson Evans, Ind. Clubwoman Dies," Indianapolis Recorder, June 14, 1952).*

At a celebration here September 22, staged by a group of alleged Negro Democrats commemorating the 74th anniversary of the Emancipation Proclamation, Mrs. Grace Evans, Terre Haute, Ind., state president of the Federation of Colored Women's Clubs, made an impassioned plea that changed the trend of the entire meeting.

Following the Rev. Chas H. T. Watkins, New Deal enthusiast and pleader for Communism, the New Deal and other radical changes in our governmental set-up, Mrs. Evans was introduced and immediately captivated her audience. She went directly into the crux of her subject with the poignant declaration that, "Democrats and Communists cannot tell you about Lincoln and emancipation, but I can. As a Negro woman upon the wall of whose home Abraham Lincoln, by his acts, made it possible for a marriage certificate to be hung, and that my little brown baby boy could bear the name of his father, legitimately instead of being bastarded as was the case under Democratic chattel slavery and oppression, I can tell you about this man and Emancipation.

"Lincoln by a stroke of his pen backed by armed forces to preserve the Constitution, made it possible for me to rightly enjoy the cherished rights of citizenship, and enabled me to stand before you today and intelligently say to you that our constitutional rights, abrogated by Democratic mountebanks, must be guaranteed by a Republican electorate. And that this mockery of attempting to drape his memory in the crepe of economic slavery and proscription, fostered by these alleged Democrats, is an insult to that sacred memory and our intelligence."

The meeting held here in the home town of Raymond Springer; Republican Candidate for Governor, was attended by approximately 1000 citizens, most of whom were women. Instead of being a Democratic rally as planned, Mrs. Evans' address turned it into a Republican stampede.

In "Mrs. Evans the Speaker," *Negro Star* (Wichita, KS), Oct. 16, 1936.

## HARRY C. SMITH, Editorial Critical of Lincoln, February 20, 1937

*In this editorial, Smith (1863–1941) sought to correct those who placed Lincoln in the same category as William Lloyd Garrison and other abolitionists by citing John G. Nicolay and John Hay's Abraham Lincoln: A History (1890) to support his assertion that Lincoln placed the preservation of the Union above all else.*

---

We believe that the best history of the martyred president, Abraham Lincoln, was written by his secretaries, John Nicolay and John Hay. The history ran as a serial in the Century magazine for many months, years ago, and prior to its publication in book form. There is absolutely nothing in it to show that Lincoln was an abolitionist, tho he did not approve slavery.

During the progress of the War of the Rebellion, General Hunter, in command of the Department of South Carolina, issued an emancipation proclamation, declaring a free man every slave to enter his department. This was revoked by President Lincoln. Subsequently Gen. John C. Fremont, "The Pathfinder," also issued an emancipation proclamation for the Department of Missouri, over which he presided. This, too, was revoked by President Lincoln and the General relieved of his command. Sept. 22, 1862, President Lincoln issued his emancipation proclamation and served notice on the rebellious South that if it did not lay down its arms within a specified time (60 or 90 days), the proclamation would go into effect on the first day of January, 1863. On different occasions, prior to this announcement, as a result of wordy bombardments from such abolitionists as William Lloyd Garrison, Wendell Phillips, Horace Greeley, Lovejoy and others, President Lincoln had said that saving the union was PRIMARY with him and emancipation, secondary; that he intended to save the union with or without slavery. The foregoing statements are historical facts and easily verified. Nevertheless, the martyred President, in spite of them, is undoubtedly the greatest white American. There can be no question as to this.

Editorial in the *Cleveland Gazette*, Feb. 20, 1937.

## Selections from WPA Slave Narratives, 1936–1938

*In 1936, the Federal Writers' Project under the Works Progress Administration (WPA), a program that was part of President Franklin Roosevelt's New Deal, began to record interviews with persons who had once been enslaved. A standard questionnaire was devised for the interviews in 1937, and one of the questions asked was what the person thought of Abraham Lincoln. Records of the interviews were processed by the Writers' Unit at the Library of Congress. As the responses that follow indicate, informants offered diverse and quite vivid impressions of Lincoln. Interviewers were instructed not to influence informants with their own points of view and to record the stories "without excessive editorializing." Even with these guidelines, an additional directive to avoid terms such as "darky" and "nigger" indicated the bias inherent in a project conducted by predominantly White interviewers in the Jim Crow South of the 1930s. As B. A. Botkin, the chief editor of the project observed, there are "obvious limitations" of this material. In addition to the biases and sometimes flawed techniques of interviewers, the informants were recalling events decades after they occurred, and may have crafted their responses to conform with what they thought the interviewer wanted to hear. Despite these caveats, these records provide valuable knowledge of slave life from those who experienced it. Informants offered unique perspectives on Lincoln that not only reveal his importance as a symbol but also situate him within African American folk culture. Some of the persons interviewed by the WPA spoke a variation of the English language derived from the strength and uniqueness of their enslaved experiences, including absence of formal education. All languages are dialects; no one can be universal, and for more than fifty years, this form of speech and writing has been termed Black English or Ebonics. It is a sophisticated melding of the English language, Black class locus, and the ascendant speech patterns of the communities in which they lived. These interviews are therefore presented as they appear in the compiled volumes, and readers should bear in mind John W. Blassigame's observation that each WPA interview "had two authors, the person who asked the questions and the person who answered them" (John W. Blassingame, ed.,* Slave Testimony *[Baton Rouge: Louisiana State University Press, 1977], xlvi). For analysis of these sources, see John Barr and David Silkenat, " 'Serving the Lord and Abe Lincoln's Spirit': Lincoln and Memory in the WPA Narratives,"* Lincoln Herald *115, no. 2 (2013): 75–97.*

---

### William Henry Towns (Vol. 1: Alabama, 389, 392–393).

Some say dat Abe wan't intrusted so much in freein' de slaves as he was in savin' de union. Don' make no diff'ence iffen he wan't intrusted in de black folks, he sho' done a big thing by tryin' to save de union. [ . . . ] I thinks that Abe Lincoln was a mighty fine man even if he was tryin' to save their union. I don't like to talk 'bout this that have done happened. It done passed so I don't say much 'bout it, specially de Presidents, 'cause it might cause a 'sturbance right now. All men means well, but some of 'em ain't broadminded 'nough to do anythin' for nobody but themse'fs. Any man that tries to help humanity is a good man.

### Mary Colbert (Vol. 4: Georgia, Part 1, 224).

Now I am going to tell you the truth as I see it. Abraham Lincoln was an instrument of God sent to set us free, for it was God's will that we should be freed.

### Jefferson Franklin Henry (Vol. 4: Georgia, Part 2, 192).

Now that its all been over more than 70 years and us is had time to study it over good, I thinks it was by God's own plan that President Abraham Lincoln sot us free, and I can't sing his praises enough.

### Sam Mitchell (Vol. 14: South Carolina, Part 3, 203).

Did I ebber hear ob Abraham Lincoln? I got his history right here in my house. He was de president of de United States that freed four million slave. He come to Beaufort befo' de war and et dinner to Col. Paul Hamilton house at de Oaks. He left his gold-headed walking cane dere and ain't nobody know de president of de United States been to Beaufort 'till he write back and tell um to look behind de door and send um his gold-headed walking cane.

**William Pratt (Vol. 14: South Carolina, Part 3, 279).**

I think Abraham Lincoln didn't do just right, 'cause he threw all the negroes on the world without any way of getting along. They was helpless. He ought to have done it gradually and give them a chance to get on their own.

**Mary Wallace Bowe (Vol. 11: North Carolina, Part 1, 150–151).**

In dem days dey wuz peddlers gwine 'roun' do country sellin' things. Dey toted big packs on dey backs filled wid everythin' from needles an' thimbles to bed spreads an' fryin' pans. One day a peddlar stopped at Mis' Fanny's house. He was de uglies' man I ever seed. He was tall an' bony wid black whiskers an' black bushy hair an' curious eyes dat set way back in his head. Dey was dark an' look like a dog's eyes after you done hit him. He set down on de po'ch an' opened his pack, an' it was so hot an' he looked so tired, dat Mis' Fanny give him er cool drink of milk dat done been settin' in de spring house. All de time Mis' Fanny was lookin' at de things in de pack an' buyin', de man kept up a runnin' talk. He ask her how many niggers dey had; how many men dey had fightin' on de 'Federate side, an' what was she gwine do if de niggers was set free. Den he ask her if she knowed Mistah Abraham Lincoln.

'Bout dat time Mis' Virginia come to de door an' heard what he said. She blaze up like a lightwood fire an' told dat peddlar dat dey didn't want to know nothin' 'bout Mistah Lincoln; dat dey knowed too much already, an' dat his name wasn't 'lowed called in her house. Den she say he wasn't nothin' but a black debil messin' in other folks business, an' dat she'd shoot him on sight if she had half a chance.

De man laughed. "Maybe Mr. Lincoln ain't so bad," he told her. Den he packed his pack an' went off down de road, an' Mis' Virginia watched him 'till he went out of sight 'roun' de bend.

Two or three weeks later Mis' Fanny got a letter. De letter was from dat peddlar. He tole her dat he was Abraham Lincoln hese'f; dat he wuz peddlin' over de country as a spy, an' he thanked her for de res' on her shady po'ch an' de cool glass of milk she give him.

When dat letter come Mis' Virginia got so hoppin mad dat she took all de stuff Mis' Fanny done bought from Mistah Lincoln an' made us niggers burn it on de ash pile. Den she made pappy rake up de ashes an' th'ow dem in de creek.

**Rev. Squire Dowd (Vol. 11: North Carolina, Part 1, 268).**

Abraham Lincoln was a father to us. We consider him thus because he freed us.

**Thomas Hall (Vol. 11: North Carolina, Part 1, 361).**

Lincoln got the praise for freeing us, but did he do it? He give us freedom without giving us any chance to live to ourselves and we still had to depend on the southern white man for work, food and clothing, and he held us through our necessity and want in a state of servitude but little better than slavery. Lincoln done but little for the Negro race and from [a] living standpoint nothing. White folks are not going to do nothing for Negroes except keep them down.

### Charlie Davenport (Vol. 9: Mississippi, 38).

I reckon I was 'bout fifteen when hones' Abe Lincoln what called hisself a rail-splitter come here to talk wid us. He went all th'ough de country jus' a-rantin' an' a-preachin' 'bout us bein' his black brothers. De marster didn' know nothin' 'bout it, 'cause it was sorta secret-lak. It sho' riled de Niggers up an' lots of 'em run away. I sho' hear'd him, but I didn' pay 'im no min'.

### Mattie Lee (Vol. 10: Missouri, 225–226).

I think a lot of Abe Lincoln. I have often thought how hard it was to give up his life, for de United States. But Christ died for to save de world and Lincoln died to save de United States. And Lincoln died more Christlike dan any other man dat ever lived.

### Rhody Holsell (Vol. 10: Missouri, 194).

I believe it would been better to have move all de colored people way out west to dem selves. Abraham Lincoln wanted to do dis. It would have been better on both races and dey would not have mixed up. But de white people did not want de "shade" taken out of de country. Many of de bosses after de freedom couldn't stand it and went in de house and got a gun and blew out his brains. If Lincoln had lived he would have separated us like dey did de Indians. We would not have been slaughtering, burning, hanging, and killin' if we had been put to ourselves, and had our own laws. Many a person is now in torment because of dis mixup.

### H. B. Holloway (Vol. 2: Arkansas, Part 3, 295).

I was looking right in Lincoln's mouth when he said, "The colored man is turned loose without anything. I am going to give a dollar a day to every Negro born before emancipation until his death,—a pension of a dollar a day." That's the reason they killed him. But they sure didn't get it. It's going to be an awful thing up yonder when they hold a judgment over the way that things was done down here.

### Margret Hulm (Vol. 2: Arkansas, Part 3, 357–358).

I remember Mr. Lincoln. He came one day to our house (I mean my white folks' house). They told me to answer the door and when I opened it there stood a big man with a gray blanket around him for a cape. He had a string tied around his neck to hold it on. A part of it was turned down over the string like a ghost cape. How was he dressed beneath the blanket? Well, he had on jeans pants and big mud boots and a big black hat kinda like men wear now. He stayed all night. We treated him nice like we did everybody when they come to our house. We heard after he was gone that he was Abraham Lincoln and he was a spy. That was before the war.

### John Johnson (Vol. 2: Arkansas, Part 4, 94).

It was Abraham Lincoln whut wanted to free the black race. He was the President. The first war was 'bout freedom and the war right after it was equalization. The Ku Klux muster won it cause they didn't want the colored folks have as much as they have.

### George Conrad Jr. (Vol. 13: Oklahoma, 44).

Abraham Lincoln was a smart man, but he would have done more if he was not killed. I don't think his work was finished.

### Alice Douglass (Vol. 13: Oklahoma, 74–75).

Abraham Lincoln gits too much praise. I say, shucks, give God the praise. Lincoln come thoo' Gallatin, Tennessee and stopped at Hotel Tavern with his wife. They was dressed jest lak tramps and nobody knowed it was him and his wife till he got to the White House and writ back and told 'em to look 'twixt the leaves in the table where he had set and they sho' nuff found out it was him.

### Octavia George (Vol. 13: Oklahoma, 114).

Abraham Lincoln! Why we mourned three months for that man when he died! I wouldn't miss a morning getting my black arm band and placing it on in remembrance of Abraham, who was the best friend the Negroes ever had. Now old Jeff Davis, I didn't care a thing about him. He was a Democrat and none of them mean anything to the Negro. And if these young Negroes don't quit messing with the democratic bunch they are going to be right back where we started from. If they only knew as I know they would struggle to keep such from happening, because although I had a good master I wouldn't want to go through it again.

### Mattie Logan (Vol. 13: Oklahoma, 191).

I think Lincoln was a mighty good man, and I think Roosevelt is trying to carry some of the good ideas Lincoln had. Lincoln would have done a heap more if he had lived.

### Stephen McCray (Vol. 13: Oklahoma, 209).

I wish Lincoln was here now. He done more for the black face than any one in that seat.

**Hannah McFarland (Vol. 13: Oklahoma, 211).**

I didn't care much 'bout Lincoln. It was nice of him to free us, but 'course he didn't want to.

**Bob Maynard (Vol. 13: Oklahoma, 225–226).**

I think Abe Lincoln was next to de Lawd. He done all he could for de slaves; he set 'em free. People in the South knowed they'd lose their slaves when he was elected president. 'Fore the election he traveled all over the South and he come to our house and slept in old Mistress' bed. Didn't nobody know who he was. It was a custom to take strangers in and put them up for one night or longer, so he come to our house and he watched close. He seen how the niggers come in on Saturday and drawed four pounds of meat and a peck of meal for a week's rations. He also saw 'em whipped and sold. When he got back up north he writ old Master a letter and told him he was going to have to free his slaves, that everybody was going to have to, that the North was going to see to it. He also told him that he had visited at his house and if he doubted it to go in the room he slept in and look on the bedstead at the head and he'd see where he'd writ his name. Sho' nuff, there was his name: A. Lincoln.

**Easter Wells (Vol. 13: Oklahoma, 321).**

God worked through Abraham Lincoln and he answered de prayers of dem dat was wearing de burden of slavery. We cullud folks all love and honor Abraham Lincoln's memory and don't you think we ought to?

**John Williams Matheus (Vol. 12: Ohio, 72).**

I think Abraham Lincoln was the greatest man that ever lived. He belonged to no church, but he sure was a Christian. I think he was born for the time and if he lived longer he would have done lots of good for the colored people.

**Nan Stewart (Vol. 12: Ohio, 91).**

One ob my prized possessions is Abraham Lincoln's pictures an' I'se gwine to gib it to a cullud young man whose done bin so kind to me, when I'se gone.

In *Slave Narratives: A Folk History of Slavery in the United States from Interviews with Former Slaves*, 17 volumes (Washington, DC: Library of Congress, 1941).

## AARON H. PAYNE, Address at Lincoln Day Dinner, New York, February 12, 1940

*A native of Louisville, Kentucky, Payne (1901–1994) was a graduate of Howard University and the University of Chicago Law School. He began practicing law*

*in Chicago during the mid-1920s, and was invited to speak at the 1940 Lincoln
Day dinner at the National Republican Club in New York City. This was the
same organization that Booker T. Washington had addressed on the centennial
of Lincoln's birth in 1909. Payne was active in Republican politics, and his speech
sought to regain African American allegiance to the Party of Lincoln, as many
Black voters had shifted their support to the Democratic Party in response to
President Franklin D. Roosevelt's New Deal. Payne reminded his audience of
what Lincoln and the Republican Party had done for African Americans and
argued that the Democratic Party had been no friend to Blacks in the South.
The concluding paragraph of the speech is a quotation from Lincoln's Second
Inaugural Address. Payne's speech was carried over the radio and was so well
received that the Republican Party distributed it as a pamphlet for the 1940
presidential campaign. Payne continued to practice law and was active in the
NAACP and Urban League (Chicago Defender, Feb. 24, 1940; Aaron H.
Payne Papers, University of Illinois at Chicago).*

---

Mr. Chairman, Ladies and Gentlemen, Fellow Republicans: Some years ago
the beloved Booker T. Washington of Tuskegee was one of your speakers. He
was universally accepted as the accredited spokesman for his people. He richly
merited this distinction. He has no successor, but the cause of Republicanism
and the love of Abraham Lincoln were no stronger in his heart then, than in mine
now.

Our perspective is not yet far enough removed for *all of us* to see clearly and
fully appreciate the true stature of Lincoln—but each passing year increases our
estimate of his greatness. He was so humbly born that the most destitute could
not envy the condition of his birth; he failed so often that few would desire his
fortune.

He succeeded to the Presidency during a period of great domestic unrest;
Civil War was imminent; the fate of the Union was in the balance.

And in the end, so bitter was his cup that even those opposed to him prayed
that it would pass him by.

The whole pattern of his life seems to have been shaped by an exacting destiny
to one end, definite and divine, and that end accomplished, the curtain fell.

His untimely death left the wounds of war to be healed by those less wise than
he. Therein lies the real tragedy.

Lincoln, more clearly than any other of his day, keenly "divined where between
men to erect the monumental mark dividing just reverence for authority from
just resistance to abuse."

With sincerity of purpose and humility of spirit, he undertook the task he felt
ordained by God to do.

The part that Lincoln played in the cause of freedom bound the Negro to the Republican Party with ties of affection and gratitude.

Of late years the ties have weakened—all recognize the change—but few agree upon the cause.

There are those who charge the Negro with ingratitude. Those who have undergone recent political conversion claim that ours is not now the party of Abraham Lincoln.

Neither is wholly right.

Both the Party and the Negro have come along so fast since the Civil War, that a feeling grew in the one that they were not needed, and in the other that they were not wanted.

The time has now come for us to put our house in order.

The Negro needs the Republican Party as long as the Democrats of the South believe that we have no rights they are bound to respect.

The Republican Party needs the Negro, not only for his political support, but what is more, to forever keep alive the ideals whereupon freedom lives.

Because of slavery the Republican Party was conceived, and in advancing the rights of man, the Republican Party achieved its highest attainment. In supporting the Republican Party, the Negro attained his highest political and economic development.

Each has an undisputed claim upon the other.

We know, that it is not now, and never has been, the policy of the Democratic Party to admit the Negro into its folds on terms of political equality. No one is more fully aware than are we that the Democratic Party is the party of race and class.

Are we, who have escaped the oppressive conditions of the South to vote approval of the party responsible for the conditions from which we fled?

Are we to be no longer mindful of those we left behind?

Those who now stand on the pinnacle of temporary advantage and control the destiny of this nation, now seek our support. They can not sustain their present advantage without it.

To my people who have been persuaded into the Democratic Party by petty patronage and relief, I direct this plea: You are now in position to demand of that Party fairer consideration than has ever been accorded you. Let the Democratic Party first demonstrate genuine concern for your welfare by respecting the plain mandates of the Constitution of our country which guarantees to you certain rights and privileges without regard to race, creed, or color.

Demand that for every Negro democratic vote you cast in the North, they shall give you one in the South.

Demand in exchange for your vote, the abolition of the Jim Crow system and all that it connotes in unfairness and degradation.

In short, demand everything for the Negro in the South that the Republican Party keeps open for us in the North.

If they turn you down, and you know they will, tell them that you have thought it over, and you just "Don't want to go to Heaven with that Crowd."

Tell them that you are going to support the Republican Party this time as of old, because you are convinced that the present Republican leadership is sincerely determined to bring to pass a fulfillment of the assurances and rights promised and guaranteed by the Declaration of Independence and the Constitution of the United States.

Remember it is only in the Democratic South that the despicable system of peonage continues to exist, and remember further, that it exists with the full approbation of that Party which now seeks your support.

I cannot contend that the Republican Party has measured up to the full extent of its possibilities in assisting the Negro to realize his highest economic and civil development, but I call upon you to realize that every *law directly beneficial* to the Negro has been placed upon the statute books of his nation by the Republican Party, and that every law designed to deprive the Negro of his rights guaranteed under the Constitution, has been enacted by the Democratic Party.

If the decision of this forthcoming election rested in the hands of the Negro in the South, there is no doubt as to what the outcome would be!

Seventy-five years have passed since the death of Lincoln—years that have witnessed unparalleled material development in America.

In the rapid and amazing progress of our material development, the social order has been permitted to fall farther and farther behind.

The social order and material development must be brought abreast, for the source of our present difficulties is generally recognized in the failure of the social order to advance step for step with our material development.

To achieve this most necessary result a man of unusual merit must soon be found to point the way.

The record shows that our difficulties have been aggravated during the past seven years rather than relieved; that our moral and spiritual fiber has been weakened beyond belief; that our national prestige suffers among the nations of the world.

The Negroes of America are no less interested in these problems than are you. Dislocated industry has thrown great masses of us upon the charity of the Government, upon relief.

No matter what you may hear to the contrary, we are not content with the miserable existence afforded by a regimented, vote-buying, coercive, dole-relief program. We wish to occupy a dignified relationship to our fellows. We may not fully realize all the connotations and implications of the words "individual initiative and free enterprise," but we stand with our fellow-citizens of all classes and conditions when we ask for a free opportunity to do a man's work, in a work-a-day world, unfettered by economic entanglements which consign most of us to an existence not far removed from abject penury and want.

We wish, and we call upon you who hold the torch of Liberty that Lincoln held so high, to help open to us equality of opportunity in education and employment. We call upon you for safety from mob-violence. We call upon you for the protection of our ballot, the greatest defense of freemen everywhere.

Nearly a hundred years ago this nation faced greater and more difficult problems.

The then existing political parties attempted to compromise with principle. This was their undoing.

A new political party was born, pledged to the fundamental principles that gave life to America.

Joseph Medill, a young man of twenty-nine, out of the Middle West, called this new party "Republican."

He, more than any other, made Lincoln's nomination possible.

The Emancipator was caught up in the tide of changing opinion and elected.

The great truth that all men are by right entitled to be free was in dispute.

Today, time has combined with reason as to that truth and it is universally accepted in principle, if not in practice.

With but three exceptions since Lincoln, the Republican Party has controlled the National Government.

Those three exceptions have each furnished a tragic interlude.

It is for you to determine whether or not the Republican Party shall again seize the opportunity to adjust our internal differences by delegating leadership to one who has proved his courage, his honor, and his ability.

This man should be one who knows that the primary function of government is to protect the person and property of the governed, that these interests are inseparable and that only the gullible are deceived when interest is arrayed against interest, religion against religion, or race against race.

He should understand that every racial group in America is so inextricably interwoven into the fabric of this nation's life that benefits secured separately are ultimately to the disadvantage of all[.]

That what is injurious or unfair to one finally affects us all; that where the purpose of the law is not orderly fulfilled—in every instance where equal justice is denied, the victim suffers—but the social order suffers more[.]

That whenever and wherever constituted authority is superseded by force and violence, society is degraded.

The man to be chosen for this leadership will be wise enough to realize that there has *never* been a "Race Problem" in America or anywhere else—only *"Human problems" that exist everywhere.*

The Republican Party has such a man. Call him forth—elevate him.

Washington, and the founding fathers, proclaimed and defined liberty for America. Lovejoy, Medill and Lincoln were the instruments in pointing the way to its partial realization. They were the apostles of a new faith in man's relation to his fellowman.

In the solution of our present problems and difficulties the Republican Party assumes the responsibility and leadership in rebuilding this nation in the spirit and faith of Lincoln—

"With malice toward none, with charity for all; with firmness in the right as God gives us to see the right—let us strive on to finish the work we are in; to bind up the nation's wounds;—and do all which may achieve a just and lasting peace among ourselves, and with all nations."

*The Republican Party and the Negro* (Washington, DC: Republican National Committee, 1940).

## CLAUDE MCKAY, "Lincoln—Apostle of a New America," February 13, 1943

*A major poet of the Harlem Renaissance, McKay (1889–1948) wrote an essay to commemorate Lincoln's birthday in 1943. He contended that Lincoln was a visionary who realized the future success of the United States was dependent upon industrialization, and therefore the feudalism of the South had to be destroyed. In forging a strong, united, modern industrialized nation, Lincoln accomplished far more than liberating the slaves, for McKay believed Lincoln liberated the country from outmoded social and economic institutions. Lincoln's vision surpassed that of both abolitionists and defenders of slavery in that it was a unique combination of realism and idealism. Penned when the outcome of the Second World War remained in doubt, McKay's essay suggested the United States was well-poised to defeat Nazi Germany due to the nation fulfilling Lincoln's progressive vision, whereas if the South had prevailed in the Civil War, the country would be an antiquated relic like Russia under the czars.*

---

Abe Lincoln's greatness as a man and as President has been glorified by the pregnant bigness of his time. In the eighteen fifties the United States needed a sterling leader as much as it did in the seventeen seventies. And the pivotal significance of Kansas and Nebraska in the struggle of free labor versus slave labor, with abolitionists opposed to slavocrats and Horace Greeley, William Lloyd Garrison, John Brown, Uncle Tom's Cabin and Young Republicans, representing the militant new industrial society against the feudal system of Tory Democrats—all converged upon Abraham Lincoln to find national expression in his sane, balanced, soil-flavored voice.

Now Lincoln's eyes must have gazed far beyond the horizon into the expansion and the future of the United States. And those eyes saw clearly that if this nation were dominated by the feudalism of the South, that the United States arteries would harden and its expansion checked. And so Lincoln declared, in his speech of nomination for the Senate in 1858: "A house divided against itself cannot stand. This government cannot endure permanently half slave and half free."

Yet he disassociated himself from the impetuous John Brown and Horace Greeley and all those whose actions would have resulted in a split nation, leaving the South immersed and smug with its backward system. For Lincoln had glimpsed the glory of the United States moving forward as a single nation, subduing the Northwest and the Far West, with its ships ploughing the oceans. And as Lincoln's eyes saw more clearly he grew stronger in spirit and greater in stature. Perhaps it was the inner revelation, the hidden mysticism of the profound mind that urged him on to emerge as the great American apostle of the Industrial Revolution. [...]

At that epoch the slavocrats of the South with its impossible romantic attitude of life aspired to the leadership of the nation. Yet there were signs on every side that the burgeoning new age needed a new outlook, new blood, a new system of popular education, which the South did not possess and could not create. Then in 1860 Lincoln challenged the South and decreed the complete exclusion of slavery from the new territories. From compromise and tolerance Lincoln had moved out boldly at the opportune moment to take the leadership of the nation, and war between the North and the South was inevitable. [...]

We like to speak of Lincoln as the great Emancipator in thinking of the liberation of Negro slaves. But Lincoln was a much greater emancipator than that. It was the whole American nation he liberated to measure itself and take its stride as a leader in the general progress of the world. And Lincoln himself had no illusion about the situation, for he possessed the mind of a seer. Lincoln saw that the old South was hell-bent on Secession and he knew that a separate Southern nation of slaves and slaveholders within the United States would be inimical to the interests of the entire nation, free whites as much as Negro slaves. And so in his first message to Congress he described the conflict as "a people's contest, a struggle for maintaining in the world that form and substance of government whose leading objective is to elevate the condition of man . . ." And in his reply to Horace Greeley, who had attacked him on the issue of slavery, Lincoln said: "My paramount object in this struggle is to save the union and is not to save or destroy slavery." [...]

If the reactionary Southern states had won in the Civil War, this nation might have remained cramped and stagnant and backward as Czarist Russia. And so the grandeur of Abraham Lincoln is godlike as one sees him in his true perspective—a backwoodsman, self-educated, self-made, honest, but vacillating, a dreamer, a pioneer in overalls, epitomizing the spirit of the new America stepping out in the race among the nations of the industrial age.

Many of the loud-mouthed demagogues in high places in the eighteen fifties had no understanding of the real issues involved, just as many today do not, as the American nation faces another great crisis. But in my humble opinion America's stake in this war is greater than any nation's. The composition of the American population and its economy place this nation in a position of unalterable opposition to the Nazi idea of a "new order." It is interesting to imagine on Abraham Lincoln's birthday, how he in sharp and clear phrases might have presented the basic facts of this plain truth to all of the American people, with the knowledge that idealism is like a castle in the air if it is not based upon a solid foundation of social and political realism.

*The New Leader* (New York), Feb. 13, 1943, 4.

## MARCH ON WASHINGTON MOVEMENT, Press Release Regarding the Celebration of Lincoln's Birthday, February 14, 1943

*A. Philip Randolph (1889–1979) was one of the primary architects of the March on Washington Movement (MOWM), an organization formed in 1941 for the purpose of protesting segregation. A planned march on Washington was canceled after President Franklin Roosevelt issued Executive Order 8802 prohibiting racial discrimination in war-related industries. The MOWM continued to pressure the government, and the following press release was inspired by an interfaith, interracial ceremony that had been held at the Lincoln Memorial in Washington on Lincoln's birthday in 1943. It is suggested that a Lincoln Memorial Pilgrimage become part of the annual celebration of his birthday. In appropriating Lincoln as a symbol of civil rights and interracial harmony, the MOWM envisioned hundreds of celebrations taking place on Lincoln's birthday wherever a Lincoln monument was located. These annual events would serve to assess the ongoing progress of Lincoln's cause of an integrated society. The release was also signed by Benjamin F. McLaurin (1906–1989) who worked with Randolph in the Brotherhood of Sleeping Car Porters and was secretary of the MOWM.*

Dear Editors,

Abraham Lincoln, if he were alive, would have liked what happened last Friday in Washington, before the great statue erected in his memory. At two o'clock on the afternoon of February 12th a little group of clergymen climbed the steps leading to the Memorial. They represented the three faiths: Protestant, Catholic, and Jewish. Three of them were colored and three were white. They came to execute a symbolic act of interfaith and interracial unity; to say by their presence that the brotherhood of the spirit transcends doctrinal differences; that there can be no bar of race, creed, or color in the service of democracy. Then, as they stood bowed in the columned court before the statue, the rich voices of the Howard University Glee Club poured forth noble music, "The Battle Hymn of the Republic" and "Go Down Moses."

Could there have been a more fitting observance of the Great Emancipator's birthday? We have reason, all of us, I think, to be grateful to the participants in this ceremony and especially to the enlightened and courageous clergymen who sponsored this ceremony [...].

Why should not a Lincoln Memorial Pilgrimage become a permanent feature of the day? Already the Protestant churches have set aside Sunday, February 14th as "Race Relations Sunday." Why should not Lincoln's birthday itself be made the occasion not merely for a symbolic ceremony participated in not merely by Negroes but by other minority groups as well as by the progressive spiritual leaders of the majority groups which have an equal stake in the ending of race discrimination, the building of interracial unity and peace? Why should not Lincoln's Birthday be made the occasion for an annual review and re-appraisal of the progress made toward completing that great task of Emancipation which Lincoln began?

Next year I hope that we shall have not one such ceremony, but hundreds, all over America, wherever there is a statue of Lincoln, and wherever groups of enlightened citizens of both races, both churchmen and laymen, can be brought together to re-affirm Lincoln's high faith and to advance the cause he served.

I should welcome correspondence with readers who think this is a practical idea and would like to bring it to fruition. We are,

Your faithful servants,
A. Philip Randolph
B.F. McLaurin

A. Philip Randolph Papers, Box 26, Microfilm Reel 22, Library of Congress, Washington, DC.

## ROSCOE CONKLING SIMMONS, Address to a Joint Session of the Illinois General Assembly, February 13, 1944

*A native of Mississippi, Simmons (1878–1951) was a graduate of the Tuskegee Institute who worked as a journalist and was recognized as one of the leading orators of his day. Simmons was among the most visible African Americans in the Republican Party, as he played an active role in numerous campaigns. In 1932, he seconded the renomination of President Herbert Hoover at the Republican convention, and led a delegation of African Americans to the White House that met with the president just prior to the election. Simmons remained a loyal Republican while many African Americans became Democrats during the 1930s. In 1944, Simmons accepted an invitation to address the Illinois General Assembly as part of its commemoration of Lincoln's birthday. Lincoln had served four terms in the Illinois legislature, and in the midst of World War II, Simmons offered Lincoln as a symbol of freedom and unity. At a time when Whites were focusing more on Lincoln as a savior of the Union and less on emancipation, Simmons memorialized Lincoln as the Great Emancipator. For Simmons, Lincoln's greatest achievement was the Emancipation Proclamation, and Thomas Ball's monument to Lincoln in Washington was therefore greater than Augustus Saint-Gaudens's statue of Lincoln in Chicago's Lincoln Park. While Simmons noted that Lincoln was not an abolitionist, he was as much a martyr to freedom as Elijah Lovejoy and John Brown (AANB).*

---

I am asked to speak of the works of the noblest representative of the human race that has lived—, Abraham Lincoln. I attempt no speech on his character; his works speak his character—, actions, deeds, not words. [...]

Our great writer, Emerson, said that Mr. Lincoln is the true history of the American people—father of the country. As I speak I attach myself to his name for through me he worked his works. Mr. Lincoln, as Emerson says, is the true history of the American people and father of his country, but he is even more; he is the true history of the Free Man, father of the Free World.

I am not to detail the life of Mr. Lincoln. Gentlemen of the Assembly know more of the routine of that life than I, maybe. On the illustrious rolls of this House his name is found; therefore, you are second to Parliament in history.

When Mr. Lincoln and your illustrious fathers met here millions sank in slavery, chained, hopeless. When they met together the unity of the Revolution had been dissolved, and our great men stood in array against one another. The end seemed near; the house about to fall.

Within 30 years, but three short decades, after Mr. Lincoln appeared at Vandalia he had lit the torch of hope and lifted it in the long ugly night of despair; had for the first time in history created and brought forth a new people, and where your fathers saw their government torn and distracted, he left a nation made new by his hands; now indivisible, the only nation of free men that has thus far been known.

Here I might well rest, but his memory is more precious than all the jewels of sea and cave and mountain, and so I venture a few steps further.

Bear with me for no word of mine shall here spoil the tenderest of themes or darken the noblest of occasions. I come in gratitude, not to boast, not to remonstrate the grievous hour, but I am here that for a moment the great people that produced Mr. Lincoln through you their children, may meditate his life, while I, who sprang from his hand, must remain content to triumph only in his death! [...]

But I am told by Va[chel] Linds[a]y, truly a poet, that oft in the bewitching hours of mid-evening he has passed Mr. Lincoln on the familiar ways of this city, feeling the warm breath of his presence as he brushed him by; that he is not always at Oak Ridge.

He is not there now; I feel his presence beside me here as I tremble to try a few words in his name.

I say I shall be brief, for no fit encomium can be spoken of Mr. Lincoln; certainly not by me, and I offer no biography filled more with the author than with Mr. Lincoln. What he said, what he did, this is my simple speech.

The words of Stanton hold good. Looking upon his dying, then his dead face, tears coursing cheeks unaccustomed to watery grief, exclaimed "Now he belongs to the ages." No; the ages belong to Mr. Lincoln and his fame cannot be spoken in any known language.

This greatest of men followed no path ever trod before; voiced thoughts never heard before; did what had never been done before and cannot be done again.

You know the story—, Kentucky, home of such of my ancestors as I here speak of—, February 12, 1809; the straw mattress; floor for the be[d]stead; mud fireplace; the lampless, windowless cabin; no doctor, nor the tender hand of woman to comfort his mother's anxious hour.

Then the end, April 15, 1865, Washington, the morning after his assassination on my account. Time published no notice of his birth, but his death was spoken around the world, and you find it on the bulletin board of eternity among important events that may be counted on the fingers of the hand.

Between his birth and his death, by his sayings, his deeds, his dreams, fears that cleansed and doubts that fortified his soul; between the hesitant moments that clouded his thoughts and his conversion that fell like sunbeams upon every loyal Union bayonet, Mr. Lincoln had produced a revolution that rolled out of Virginia to bleed the world.

Absence of loved ones from your firesides testify that that Revolution proceeds today over every known sea, across every known land, while the soul of awakened man reaches for Lincoln, for it was from his almost divine lips that first we heard the doctrine—"under God; new birth of freedom; government of the people!"

Ministers of war now speak Mr. Lincoln's name; linger over his matchless words, but he is not there. He, too, heard of territories, states, divisions and partitions; heard of the stoutest line in the history of conflict, superior to any breastwork thrown up in modern war, that of Mason and Dixon, that divided men on principles. "There is no line," said Mr. Lincoln, "straight or crooked upon which to divide."

Mr. Lincoln meditated such matters, and strove to persuade the people, but each day increased the grief that shook the times and his generals were pressed on the bloody fields.

Suddenly Mr. Lincoln reexamined the scene; withdrew into his chambers, alone with his thoughts. He arose from prayer, and painted on his banner one word, "MAN." From that hour all was bright. [...]

The first monument erected to Mr. Lincoln's memory stands in Lincoln Park, Washington. It was unveiled in 1876. You love St. Gauden's, where Lincoln stands in magnificent relief, as if to speak. You see it in Lincoln Park, Chicago.

But the truest story of Lincoln in stone, truer than the Rail Splitter, is Ball's, the one I speak of. There stands Lincoln above the kneeling slave, who lifts to his tender, noble face chains freshly broken on the fettered hand.

Under St. Gauden's you might carve these words, "Gettysburg—the Great Speech." But under Ball's, worthy of Phidias, carve words far nobler,—"Man's GREATEST DEED."

Former slaves erected that monument in Washington. In the presence of President Grant, his Cabinet, the Senate, the House and the Supreme Court, Frederick Douglass, the noblest slave ever set free, and the first sight of whom put Emancipation in Mr. Lincoln's heart, dedicated that monument in one of the great speeches of our language.

It was here that Douglass declared:

"An[y] man can say things that are true of Abraham Lincoln, but no man can say anything that is new of Abraham Lincoln."

True then, true now. You search Lincoln as you search the prophets and the apostles, not for new things but for gifts that are ageless.

If you will erect still another monument to Lincoln, something grander than the Memorial in Washington, looking down the Mall towards the Capitol; call, if you can, another Douglass, to speak his greatness; let its base rest on the ancient rock, and let its summit pierce the vaulted blue, affording rest for the eternal starry pilgrimage, and yet the genius of Abraham Lincoln would remain unspoken and his attainments but feebly honored.

The noblest mind in thought and vision, St. Paul, finds that there are two bodies, one natural, the other s[p]iritual. Thus, except for six gentlemen, whose title is guaranteed by Lincoln, the kinship of this distinguished company with Lincoln is natural, in blood, tribe, features long distinguished to human advancement; prejudices.

But there are those to his bloody wounds natural only in the genesis of man. Yet, as for his works of wonder and the flow of soul[s] which overran the world, they, and I with them, are first in line of descent. Unworthy of bequest, yet I am his spirit heir.

Vain but tender is the wish of many that they could have seen Lincoln; could have heard a voice chorded to subdue the tumult or raise the mournful spirit. You see Lincoln as I stand here among his great people, by them summoned to speak his deeds. He fell that I might at this time rise in this place, the beginning of his works, and testify that he lived, and that you might see him again.

No finished phrase is mine, and unworthy may be the speech, but nevertheless you hear Mr. Lincoln, for where once I was voiceless he bade me speak, and where once a people knew only the language of bondage, he built around their cause, and their cause alone, eloquence more noble than any reported from the classic past.

Half dozen events tell Mr. Lincoln's life; his marriage to a slaveholder's daughter, the best blood of Kentucky, who hated slavery and, though unhonored for her feat, stood with him on the bridge the whole voyage as he rode the heavy sea of fate; his "house divided" speech; the debate with Douglas, where Nature, pitted against Art, pinned it on its bosom as a decoration; Cooper Union, where he assumed intellectual leadership of the Union; Presidency, the War and discovery of Grant; Emancipation.

Take away either and you have an incomplete Lincoln. His fame rests on all; the quality of immortality only on one, the Proclamation. All words and thought, each act and deed that had gone before led to the Proclamation. Recollection of him by those permitted to live in his time; every story told, each history attempted of him by unending affection, centers in this Document, which was issued without model and must remain without imitation.

These were the marks of Mr. Lincoln, fear and worship of God; sympathy for the Slave, love of the Union, but we never cease to wonder at either the purity of his reasoning or the power of his word. [. . .]

Mr. Lincoln was product of the prairies, the oak, the willow bending to catch music from the tireless brook; the steadfast forest; fields of grain laughing with both joyful rain or approach of cloudless day; the Big Muddy and the Sangamon; the starry messengers nightly fresh with tidings from his Maker; these were his instructors.

He was the patient student, for he felt himself called and ordained. "If God has a part for me" he said—"and I think He has, I believe I am ready." [. . .]

Shall I speak of Mr. Lincoln as lawyer? With Mr. Lincoln the law was but a school where wit might feel the whetstone and reason meet the test. You read books on Mr. Lincoln, the politician. With Lincoln politics was but the convenient door by which he entered on the tragic stage.

Garrison had declared[,] "I will not retreat one single inch and I will be heard." And he set up his imposing stone in Boston. "I will try for a hearing," said Lincoln, and repaired to the stump, in his day the only university of the people[.]

The blade of war his hand refused; yet there he sits in the White House the lonely strategist of conflict. If not warrior, can we call him philosopher? His heart had been shaped in righteousness ere his eyes opened upon his world; so neither the maybe nor the perhaps of philosophy could his mind corrupt or stay his fateful course.

Ah! Jove, the forked lightning in his hand,
And thunders rolling at his command.

That invention charmed the pagan past, but your fathers witnessed Lincoln's living exploit. They saw him convoke the elements when he encountered on the guiltless prairies the hostile giant advancing to meet his challenge; saw him aim and hurl the sto[ne]; then turn his unfaltering steps towards Washington.

"Defeat" cried Springfield, but he knew he had conquered. Genius is man trusted with judgments of God and knows no defeat.

A thousand books each tell a thousand stories on how Mr. Lincoln rose to the Presidency. Mr. Lincoln did not rise to the Presidency. The day of his birth the Presidency tarried in a Kentucky cabin. A star bright with cheer lingered above the silent mountains but there was none to catch its sign.

He could not escape the presidency. He accepted it from forces unseen that none could resist and lifted it to a prophecy that none could hinder.

He found the presidency a voice of state and left it the voi[c]e of liberty. It became seat of war; he made that war a victorious one by seeming not to make but only to accept war. South Carolina seceded not from the Union but from Lincoln. You have here not a figure, something earthy, only of the soil.

Mr. Lincoln was a principle; an article of faith walking in the flesh.

To reach the presidency Mr. Lincoln entered Washington under guard, lest his enemies slay him, with our nation in fear and the world in doubt. His task done, and now having been slain, his body left Washington for Springfield with every sleepless star a guard of honor, with a now new nation in tears and the world in mourning.

Write a thousand titles to choose a name,
Only Lincoln's brings a blush to the cheek of fame.

Columbus discovered America; Lincoln disclosed what America was discovered for—, the New World,—land of promise, hidden on the map by its Creator, where, the season having arrived, peoples and colors, scattered like seed over the measureless fields of time, would be gathered together again, the golden harvest of the restored brotherhood of man.

As with the New World, so with Mr. Lincoln, he was hidden by his Creator until that New World, was ready to proclaim new things for the new man. Only his World and only his times could have produced Abraham Lincoln. [...]

In 1860 at Leavenworth Mr. Lincoln, speaking to a free soil audience, thought John Brown guilty of treason; saw nothing at Harper's ferry except idle dream and an old man's folly. But within him his natures rose in struggle.

A few brief years and Lincoln himself had suffered death in the cause that led John Brown over the mountains; the cause that kept Lincoln in the stir and ferment that produced the Lincoln you see at the Second Inaugural, where he was more sublime than at Gettysburg; almost as sublime as the day of his goodby to Springfield.

Virginia hanged John Brown in the name of tradition. Crying Virginia's motto—"sic semper tyrannis["]—a son of the Dominion, seized by an evil dream, slew Mr. Lincoln in the name of revenge.

John Brown on the scaffold opened the Civil War; [f]alling under the steel of revenge Mr. Lincoln closed it. Divinity sprinkled the blood of the fanatic on the crown of the martyr.

Some men of God are called by one name; some by another, but at the beckon of necessity you see them step forth, David with a throne, St. Paul with a kingdom without a throne, Lincoln with neither kingdom nor throne, but no less skilled and no less attended by company fearful to speak of.

Deny, if you will, that what Lincoln called "purposes of the Almighty" step into human affairs, that they take notice of events, and in the dr[e]am of existence arranges no scenes, selects no actors; deny that winge[d] messengers bear judgments above the courts of human quarrels. [...]

Mr. Lincoln's greatest achievement was the connection he established between his people and divine favor. I sit in no judgment here, but fondly ask, Have you lost it or do you have it?

If the people who established our nation had done nothing than afford the stage for Abraham Lincoln, still you must call them as I know them to be, the foremost people in the long record [of] human endeavors. Beneath the rock at Plymouth was discovered the pregnant soil whence sprang the flower of freedom; Lincoln its bloom, fairer than any in the story of the flowers of manhood.

He lived serene amid the storms. Gone now 80 years, yet the world that marvelled at his words now calls his name but to wonder at his amazing skill.

He still remains beyond the grasp of his countrymen. The people rescued from irons and placed in the society of the free still struggle to become worthy even of his name.

The resolute people of our great South, from whom he snatched the wretched slave still struggle to utter words that forgive. Yet they tell you he did more for them than for the slave. The prophet, however, thrives on contradiction, for a painting of Mr. Lincoln hangs on the walls of the office of the Governor of Mississippi.

From Mississippi Jefferson Davis issued his challenge; from Illinois Lincoln accepted. Davis, rich; Lincoln, poor; Davis born in a mansion; Lincoln in a hut; Davis, culture and education; Lincoln, untaught, his graces entirely native; in the arena they met, with what results you know, these two, both natives of Kentucky, born around seventy miles apart. Tell me, sirs, is all this but a happening, or do I see the eternal, unstayed Hand resting on the scene?

I say Mr. Lincoln remains ungrasped, unreached. Sons of the gallant men who fought for him, and even many of their gall[a]nt fathers, the moment of his withdrawal, saw the ardor of his cause cool in the breat[h] of triumph.

We meet in time of war to speak of Mr. Lincoln, a war called the greatest of conflicts. But you have in this bloody quarrel no issue to excuse the vulgar claims of war. Gentlemen, if war can summon a single virtue, the greatest war freemen ever fought was conducted by Mr. Lincoln; a war fought in one land, between peoples of one blood, of one language, a common ancestry; fought under two leaders, both great soldiers, Grant and Lee, both products of West Point; a war fought to determine a question left unsettled by fathers of both the soldiers in blue and those in grey.

Every story of Abraham Lincoln begins and ends with two achievement[s], preservation of the Union; freedom of the slave. [...]

Slaves pressed Mr. Lincoln in the streets of Richmond, eager to touch his great cape. They knelt at his feet. His great, kind, hand resting on the brow of an aged mother, looking up at him, he said, "Don't; rise; kneel only to God. You and I owe all to Him."

To Chase Mr. Lincoln said, "I made a solemn vow before God, that if Lee was driven back I would crown the result by the declaration of freedom to the slave." Lee was driven back, and Mr. Lincoln called for his pen.

"The signature looks a little tremulous," he said, "for my hand was tired, but my resolution was firm."

And so the Slave was freed. What loosed he when he freed the Slave? He unbound wings of genius; uncaged the lark; unchained a mind which jewels the story of the West; lent science the knowing eye, the patient, tender hand to woo Nature of her cherished secrets, and where warmth and glow were absent in the cold chambers of intellectual excellence, Mr. Lincoln set free laughter, lovely joy and the soft, unfailing speech of human kindness.

What freed he? He freed the noble South and restored its great people to the heritage of the Revolution from which a cruel vanity bewitched them.

Not every slave set free by Mr. Lincoln was a free man. Fetters do not make the slave nor broken chains the man. Thousands freed by Lincoln's pen were hereditary slaves. You see their offsprings now, often found where chance has led them, loaded with words, standing amid confusions of books, assaulting with thick-tongued jabber the memory of their benefactors.

Gratitude, sirs, is the only flower natural to a free man's heart. A black man who speaks slightly of his Emancipator has escaped chains that he deserves.

In the Old State House Mr. Lincoln talked to a few friends during the campaign of 1860. He said: "Douglas don't care whether slavery is voted up or down, but God cares, and humanity cares, and I care." So it should be with this people brought into life by Mr. Lincoln, now engaged in a struggle classic among the fights of time, though Senates and academies oppose them, if God cares, all is well.

Mr. Lincoln was a seer. In 1864 he wrote Governor Hahn of Louisiana to extend the franchise to loyal people of color. "They," he wrote, ["]would probably help in some trying time to come, to keep the jewel of liberty in the family of freedom.["]

Eighty years after you see them, in a trying time; gone and glad to go, almost a million, wherever assigned, sons of this people, wounded, yet fighting on, asking no questions; heavy at heart, yet singing on; cast aside, yet pressing on, not a star on their shoulder but the star of Lincoln on their brow, keeping that jewel of liberty in the family of freedom.

Self-schooled, yet Mr. Lincoln's words were awaited by the pomp of erudition; not an abolitionist, yet he alone abolished slavery; not a grammarian, yet his epistles, letters and immortal papers are the standard of classic utterance; not a rhetorician, yet he vanquished the adversary in every encounter on the fields of discussion; but a fire-light student of law, yet peerless as an advocate; axe-wielder, yet as tender as Summer's first rose blushing at the caress of the vagrant breeze. This is Mr. Lincoln, product of American slavery.

The day following Mr. Lincoln's election Wendell Phillips, voice of New England, spoke in Tremont Temple. "If," he said, ["]the telegraph speaks the truth, for the first time in our history the Slave has chosen a President of the United States."

God had cast the slave's vote. Have you a moment to examine the slave? He in the entire story of the Union, whether of Jefferson or Webster, Franklin or Samuel Adams, poet or Senator; whether Lee in defeat or Grant in triumph; whether Jefferson Davis fleeing his capital or Lincoln saying, "I want to see Richmond,"—it is all the same.

Around a Slave, Crispus Attuck[s], the Revolution opened, as the lettered stone in Boston tells you; around the Slave the Rebellion opened and closed, as you see in every souvenir of Abraham Lincoln.

Books cannot contain nor speech tell of the works of Mr. Lincoln. Sentences from his sayings search every secret place of the being; almost every word a jewel that sparkles on the breast of time. [ . . . ]

At Alton Lovejoy opened the martyrdom of freedom. Out of Springfield went Lincoln to complete it. In between rose John Brown. Phillips said that behind the curtain that went [up] and down on Lincoln always stood John Brown. Behind Brown, then, and hovering over Lincoln, you see Lovejoy. Martyrdom is a covenant between God and His interpreters.

Mr. Lincoln quoted no authors to adorn his story; his faith invented its own literature, but Jefferson was his man—, the Declaration[,] the Virginia Statute, the Northwest [Ordinance]. "He was the first man," spake Mr. Lincoln, "who had the foresight and the capacity to introduce into a revolutionary document an abstract truth applicable to all men." Mr. Lincoln made that truth concrete; let [u]s walk and live. Jefferson set the nation down on paper!

Mr. Lincoln set the nation up; shaped it; made it work. He amended the Declaration; widened the Statute; kept the Northwest free soil for a place on which to stand and war on slave soil. Patrick Henry supplied the words to lift a king from his seat; Washington unsheat[h]ed the sword and kept it bright even in the night of Valley Forge.

For his cause Lincoln furnished the language that upset all thrones; trusted the sword to Grant. Only a few miles from Yorktown where Cor[n]wallis gave up in the Revolution, the Rebellion collapsed at Appomattox. With liberty all places are common ground.

About to unveil the picture of Mr. Lincoln in London, Lloyd-George said, "In a moment you will see the best known historical face in the Anglo-Saxon world."

Mr. Lincoln's face is the best known face in any world. In life he was Anglo-Saxon; in death he escaped nationality. Go through any gallery and the guide hands you a book by which to tell who hangs yonder. Lincoln's is the only face in the history of mankind that needs no guide. He is far-off in frame and face, and from a canvas he spreads something of breath and always seems to speak.

His wisdom surpasses that of any man who yearned to advance a cause in human progress. The curse and sight of bondage he stored in his heart, and when he drew the treasure forth, he spoke not his feelings, but only of the Union. He knew the temper of his people and left them with their thoughts.

"I shall not disturb slavery," he said, "but let it rest where it is." The war came, bursting, not upon him, but upon the people, for he had said war would come.

Then like dawn gradually breaking away from the grasp of night, so by degrees Mr. Lincoln began the unfolding of his heart. "Must save the Union; lay down your arms," he said. But heedless the foe pressed across the fevered fields.

Then, as the full day calls to the Sun to light its appointed way, Mr. Lincoln unbosomed his treasured hopes to the gaze of the world, "The time has come," he said; "I thought thirty years ago it would come.["] "I am here to do the will of God."

I remember his words at the first inaugural. "I am loath to close[," he] said. So now with me in this hour. I, too, would stay and continue with the man who alone bears the title of Emancipator, the highest title ever worn by mortal man.

Standing among the dead at Gettysburg Mr. Lincoln touched the loftiest point of all human eloquence:—"that we here highly resolve that these dead shall not have died in vain."

Let us, then, gathered to[d]ay in the shadow of his tomb, here highly resolve that Mr. Lincoln shall not have died in vain; that there shall be neither North nor South, East nor West, as he prayed and that every wound shall speedily be bound; and that, under his God, who prepared his speeches and guided his steps, his nation, having had in his death a new birth of freedom, shall now have a new birth of love and union of hearts, and all his people, those of his flesh and those of his spirit, shall become one in hope, one in faith and one [in] works worthy of Abraham Lincoln and acceptable to God.

Roscoe Conkling Simmons Papers, Harvard University Archives.

## JOEL A. ROGERS, "Lincoln Wanted to Deport Negroes and Opposed Equal Rights," February 26, 1944

*A native of Jamaica, Rogers (1880–1966) immigrated to the United States in 1906. He lived in Chicago, where he studied at the Art Institute and was a Pullman porter before eventually settling in New York. He worked as a journalist and wrote several popular books on African American history and the history of persons of African descent. His pamphlet,* The Five Negro Presidents *(1965) asserted that Lincoln's father was African American. In the midst of World War II, Rogers argued that Lincoln did not measure up to the likes of John Brown and other abolitionists when it came to supporting racial equality. Quoting from Lincoln's January 27, 1838, Lyceum Address, the September 18, 1858, debate with Stephen A. Douglas at Charleston, and the August 14, 1862, address on colonization, Rogers suggested that Lincoln's position on race helped fuel the arguments of leading White supremacists of the early twentieth century, such as author Thomas A. Dixon; Dr. Robert Shufeldt, a proponent of scientific racism; and Southern politicians James K. Vardaman, J. Thomas Heflin, and Theodore Bilbo (AANB).*

---

Abraham Lincoln was not only a great American, but one of the most illustrious figures of all time. He was wise and able. Without his leadership the North might have lost the war and slavery would not have ended when it did. His rise from lowliness to the heights of power will ever be an inspiration. More than all, he had a great soul. Negroes, in particular, owe him an immense debt.

Still, in spite of my great admiration for him, I cannot join in the blind, overfulsome praise usually showered on him this time of the year. To do that would be to overshadow the memory of certain other great Americans as Harriett Beecher Stowe, Frederick Douglass, Wendell Phillips, William Lloyd Garrison, Charles Sumner, Bishop [Gilbert] Haven and others, who, in my opinion, had a greater vision of right than Lincoln, and without whose constant prodding Lincoln might have fallen far short of what he did against slavery.

The simple truth is that Lincoln, like every other President before or since, showed by his actions, especially as regards the Negro, that he was a politician first and a humanitarian next. I have no doubt that a policy of having the affairs of state running smoothly has in most cases forced these Presidents to do what they did. But there is a world of difference between the psychology of any of these Presidents and that of John Brown, who was so convinced that he was right that he gave up his life for it. Would any of the Presidents have been willing to risk even his political prestige in so firm a stand for equal justice?

The great issue in Lincoln's time was the Negro. I shall give a few excerpts from his letters and speeches as published by Nicolay and Hay. Let anyone match them against what the abolitionists above mentioned said on the same subject.

Lynching: On the burning alive of a Negro named McIntosh, at St. Louis, Mo., in 1837, Lincoln spoke in great condemnation, but he made this amazing concession to the lynchers, "He (McIntosh) had forfeited his life by the perpetration of an outrageous murder upon one of the most worthy and respected citizens of the city, and had he not died as he did, he must have died by the sentence of the law in a very short time afterward. As to him alone it was as well the way it was." But is the action of a mob in burning alive a human being "ever as well" the way it is? Moreover, Lincoln was a lawyer and must have realized that when the mob steps in, the law steps out.

Segregation: "I will say then that I am not, nor ever have been, in favor of bringing about in any way the social and political equality of the white and black races ... that I am not nor have ever been, in favor of making voters or jurors of Negroes nor of qualifying them to hold office, nor to intermarry with white people; and I will say in addition to this that there is a physical difference between the white and black races which I believe will forever forbid the two races living together on terms of social and political equality. And inasmuch as they cannot so live, while they do remain together there must be the position of superior and inferior, and I as much as any other white man am in favor of having the superior position assigned to the white man."

But could not Lincoln have seen that the "physical difference" between the "races" had broken down to the extent that there were "blacks" as white as Lincoln himself—so white that it had become possible to kidnap white children in the North and in Europe and sell them as Negro slaves in the South, and that these whites could not prove they were white because of the whiteness of some of the "blacks?"

Deportation: Lincoln was firmly in favor of the deportation of Negroes. He wanted to get them out of America—anywhere, to Africa, to the West Indies, to Central and South America—anywhere provided he got them out. On August 14, 1862, when a delegation of Negroes waited on him at the White House he spoke in terms that almost seemed to blame the Negroes for the war. He said, "But for your race among us there could be no war, although many men engaged on either side do not care for you one way or the other. Nevertheless, I repeat, without the institution of slavery and the colored race, the war could not have existence. It is better, therefore, for us both to be separated." However, we find Lincoln saying a year later that without the aid of the Negro soldier, he would be "powerless" to save the Union.

So anxious was Lincoln to deport the blacks that he asked the Dutch, the British, the Haitians and Ecuador and Colombia to take them. Finally selecting Haiti, he had Congress vote him a first installment of $500,000 for the purpose and gave the matter into the hands of one Bernard Kock. Even when Kock was exposed as a worthless adventurer, Lincoln did not withdraw his commission. Kock, too, in his greed, made no provisions for housing the blacks on the desolate island of Vache, and the colony was a total failure.

More than 100 of the 450 Negroes sent died of privation and disease, and Lincoln had to send a ship for the survivors. But even that did not cure Lincoln of the deportation idea. In 1865, we find him, a few days before his death, planning to send the Negro veterans to dig the Panama Canal where they would have died like flies as did the French. No wonder Douglass said of him, "He is not our man."

I can barely touch on the subject here. Suffice it to say that what Lincoln said against equal rights for the Negro has been the very meat of the great Negro-haters as Tom Dixon, Vardaman, Heflin and Shufeldt. As for Bilbo, he wallows in it.

*Pittsburgh Courier*, Feb. 26, 1944.

## MARY MCLEOD BETHUNE, Address on Lincoln's Birthday, Washington, DC, February 12, 1945

*Founder of Bethune-Cookman College, creator of the National Council for Negro Women, and a member of Franklin Delano Roosevelt's Black Cabinet, Bethune (1875–1955) addressed the League for World Brotherhood during its celebration of Lincoln's birthday. Referring to him as a humanitarian who privileged common people, she stated Blacks were better off because Lincoln lived. Reflecting on his belief that Whites diminish their own freedom in making Blacks chattel slaves, Bethune reminded the audience that eighty years after the Civil War, Blacks were helping the United States achieve victory in World War II. At that particular time in history, Bethune believed Lincoln's Gettysburg Address held particular significance, and in addition to quoting from the speech, she imagined what Lincoln would say if he were alive in 1945. As Lincoln had articulated the purpose of the Civil War at Gettysburg, Bethune hoped that victory in World War II would make it possible for everyone to enjoy the Four*

*Freedoms President Roosevelt had articulated in his 1941 Annual Message to Congress: Freedom from fear; Freedom from want; Freedom of religion; and Freedom of speech (ANB).*

---

It is a happy privilege to share in the Lincoln's Day Celebration of The League for World Brotherhood. At this time when the world is sick,—suffering, because of human hatred, bitterness, and greed, it is fitting that an organization committed to world peace should note with appropriate exercises the anniversary of a great humanitarian, who dedicated his life to bringing freedom, love, understanding, and a spirit of brotherhood to the peoples of his native land, which he dearly loved. [...] The greatest Emancipator,—Christ,—early gave to the world an example of unselfish love for man,—giving Himself,—making the Supreme sacrifice, that men and women might be freed from the deadening effects of sin, vice, hate, greed, selfishness, and other soul destroying ideologies and practices. It was the Christ, too, who looked with compassion on a sin-sick world and said, "I am come that ye may have Life,—that ye may have it more abundantly." Lincoln, likewise looked on the suffering of great masses of the common people, and understanding their plight,—had compassion,—and became God's instrument in striking the slave shackles from the limbs of the Negro,—setting him free, that he might move into "Green Pastures." Tonight, I stand before you as a representative of fifteen million Negro men and women, who, because Lincoln lived,—they live, and know a better life. I express the gratitude of this host of black Americans for the life of Abraham Lincoln and pay humble tribute to his hallowed memory. [...]

The Better Life, men of all races seek, comes out of Brotherhood and Understanding; likewise Brotherhood and Understanding make for the full realization of the Better Life. If men and women of all races, all creeds, from all corners of the earth are to experience the satisfied living implied in the Better Life, we must lose ourselves in a oneness of spirit and thought [...].

It is equally important that we now plan for the difficult postwar days with their complex problems of racial, economic, and job adjustment. In one of his campaign speeches Lincoln made bold to say,

"In our greed-chase to make profit of the Negro, let us beware lest we cancel and tear to pieces even the white man's charter of freedom." [...]

It is the task of every American to work for the kind of America in which men of all races and creeds, shall have equality of opportunity, to enable each to enjoy the Four Freedoms.

In America, the gravest and most perplexing domestic problem is the relationship of whites and Negroes. It involves not only differences of race, but wider and more manifest dissimilarities in color and physical features. These obviously create bases for distinctions, discriminations and antipathies. In reaching a satisfactory solution to the problem, it is imperative that cooperation and encouragement should supplant old prejudices. The achievement of Negroes and their struggles for self-improvement should be recognized and appreciated. Both races need to learn that in America no one has rights without responsibilities. The interest of all races in the common good are identical. Race relations based on friendliness and understanding provide the only insurance against racial clashes, so eminent in the period of post-war adjustment.

All of us, regardless of color or racial origin, need to be taught common standards of self-respect, honesty, fairness, industry and forbearance, and above all, of mutual helpfulness. The experiences of the past have value chiefly as they aid in the understanding of the problems of the present. No help or healing can be derived from appraising past responsibilities or in apportioning of blame or praise.

Any observance of Lincoln's birthday would be incomplete without some reference to or quotation from his immortal Gettysburg Address. We, on the Home Front, would do well to "read, mark, learn, and inwardly digest" the many thoughts expressed in this great epic. "Four-score and seven years ago, our forefathers brought forth on this continent, a new Nation, dedicated to the proposition that all men are created equal." Lincoln went on to say, "Now we are engaged in a great civil war, testing whether that Nation, or any Nation so conceived and so dedicated, can long endure." If Lincoln were living today, he might say, "Now we are engaged in a great global war, testing whether that Nation or any nation so conceived and so dedicated can long endure."

We must continue to do our full part to assure the winning of the war. To this end the Negro in the armed forces and the Negro worker along the production lines are playing their parts well and effectively. Many lives are being sacrificed on the far-flung battlefields of Europe, in the South Pacific, and in the China hinterland. [...]

May we here tonight rededicate "Our lives, our fortunes, and our sacred honor," using the words of Lincoln.

"It is for us the living, rather, to be dedicated here to the unfinished work which they who fought here have thus far so nobly advanced."

"It is rather for us to be here dedicated to the great task remaining before us, that from these honored dead we take increased devotion to that cause for which they gave the last full measure of devotion; that we here highly resolve that these dead shall not have died in vain; that this nation, under God, shall have a new birth of freedom, and that government of the people, by the people, and for the people, shall not perish from the earth."

Mary McLeod Bethune, *Mary McLeod Bethune Papers*: 1922–1955, Microfilm Edition, Reel 2, Part I (Bethesda, MD: University Publications America, 1995).

## JOHN HOPE FRANKLIN, *From Slavery to Freedom*, 1947

*In his canonical first edition of* From Slavery to Freedom, *John Hope Franklin's (1915–2009) assessment of Lincoln begins with the verdict that he was anti-slavery. Ironically, perhaps, he then focuses on Lincoln's caution, as the president, to give serious attention to Blacks, in order to keep Border States in the Union and not test the ambivalence on race in the North. With Lincoln generally being cautious, Franklin asserts this is reflected in his proposal for gradual, compensated emancipation, as well as colonization. Lincoln, Franklin believes, had no ambivalence about the Emancipation Proclamation; even as a war measure, it had profound implications for a yet-new country.*

---

When President-elect Lincoln arrived in Washington late in February, 1861, the nation he was to administer during the next four years was rapidly falling apart before his very eyes. Already seven states in the lower South had seceded, and there was talk of the same momentous step in each of the other slave states. Even before his inauguration Lincoln conceived his most important and difficult task was stemming the tide of national disintegration. In his carefully worded Inaugural he condemned the Southern citizens—not states—who were in insurrection, and thus he may have won friends in the doubtful border states; but his words were hardly encouraging to abolitionists who felt that the time for words were over. Action was needed in their opinion to bring an end to an institution against which the Republican Party had taken a stand during the election campaign. But Lincoln had to move cautiously lest he offend the eight slave states that still remained in the Union. No amount of caution, however, could maintain peace indefinitely without surrendering the authority of the federal government in the South. When the time came to defend Fort Sumter, Lincoln acted promptly; but the defense of the Fort cost him four more slave states and plunged the country into Civil War.

Even if there had not been the problem of keeping the remaining slave states—Delaware, Maryland, Kentucky, and Missouri—in the Union, there were still many people in the North who would have recoiled from a war against slavery or for abolition. Lincoln not only had to mollify the border slave states, but also avoid any policy offensive to thousands throughout the North who had grown weary of the abolition movement. [ . . . ]

Lincoln feared that the border states would take exception to a policy of arming Negroes and that it would seriously alienate support in the North. He therefore gave no serious consideration to arming Negroes until the spring of 1862; and then it was forced on him.

As a result of considerable pressure from officers in the field, the acting Secretary of War authorized General Thomas W. Sherman in October, 1861, to "employ fugitive slaves in such services as they may be fitted for . . . with such organization as you may deem most beneficial to the service; this, however, not being a general arming of them for military service." [ . . . ] In the autumn of 1862, however, Lincoln permitted the enlistment of some Negroes. [ . . . ]

These months of vacillation on the treatment of runaway slaves, the relief of Negroes, and their military service had a disquieting effect on the status of the Negro during the Civil War. If the federal government would not take a stand to uphold him, he could expect little from private citizens. [ . . . ]

From the very beginning of the war there had been speculation as to whether or when the slaves would be emancipated. Northern Democrats were opposed and said unequivocally that slavery was the best status for the Negro. The abolitionists supported the Republicans in 1860 principally because their platform was antislavery; and they demanded that the party fulfill its pledge by setting the slaves free. Lincoln had to move cautiously, however, for constitutional, political, and military reasons. His views on emancipation were well known. As early as 1849 he had introduced a bill in Congress for the gradual emancipation of slaves in the District of Columbia, and in the ensuing decade he announced his position on several occasions. For the abolitionists, gradual emancipation was bad enough, but not even to take definite steps in that direction was unforgivable.

The whole matter caused Lincoln grave concern. As he evolved his plan of emancipation, he was viewed all the more unfavorably because he felt it necessary to restrain enthusiastic officers who emancipated slaves without his authorization. In 1861 General John C. Fremont proclaimed military emancipation in Missouri, but Lincoln had to modify his action in keeping with the Confiscation Act. In 1862 General David Hunter proclaimed that slaves in Georgia, Florida, and South Carolina were to be forever free. When Lincoln learned of this order ten days later, he immediately issued a proclamation nullifying it and reminding slaveholders that they could still adopt his plan of compensated emancipation.

President Lincoln was going ahead with this plan for the solution of the problem of the Negro in America. He hoped to achieve emancipation by compensating the owners for their human property; and then he looked forward to colonizing the Negroes in some other part of the world. In fall of 1861 he attempted an experiment with compensated emancipation in Delaware. He interested his friends there and urged them to propose it to the Delaware legislature. He went so far as to write a draft of the bill, which provided for gradual emancipation and another which provided that the federal government would share the expenses of compensating masters for their slaves. Although these bills were much discussed, there was too much opposition to introduce them.

More definite steps in the direction of emancipation were taken in the spring of 1862. In a special message to Congress, President Lincoln recommended that a resolution be passed announcing that the United States would cooperate with any state adopting a plan of gradual emancipation together with satisfactory compensation of the owners. He urged the congressional delegations from Delaware, Maryland, West Virginia, Kentucky, and Missouri to support his policy. They opposed it, however, because their constituents were unwilling to give up their slaves. [. . .] All over the North the abolitionists denounced Lincoln's plan of compensated emancipation.

Another of Lincoln's recommendations, which became law in April, 1862, provided for the emancipation of slaves in the District of Columbia. There would be compensation, of course, not exceeding $300 for each slave. A significant feature was the provision of $100,000 for the voluntary emigration of freedmen to Haiti and Liberia. Negro colonization seemed almost as important to Lincoln as emancipation. [. . .]

From June, 1862, the policy of the government toward emancipation took shape rapidly. On June 19, the President signed a bill abolishing slavery in the territories. On July 17, a measure became law setting free all slaves coming from disloyal masters into Union-held territory. Lincoln again called together Congressmen from the border slave states and told them that since slavery would be destroyed if the war lasted long enough, they should accept his plan of compensated emancipation. His plea fell on deaf ears. Having gone as far as he had, however, Lincoln considered emancipating by proclamation all slaves in rebellious states, an idea which he discussed with his Secretaries of State and Navy, Seward and Welles.

For two days, July 21 and 22, the Cabinet debated the draft of an emancipation proclamation which Lincoln read to them. Rebels were to be warned of the penalties of the Confiscation Act, reminded of the possibility of emancipating their slaves and receiving compensation, and all slaves in their possession on January 1, 1863, were to be set free. Only two cabinet members, Seward and Chase, agreed even in part with Lincoln's proposed proclamation; and Seward strongly advised him not to issue it until the military situation became more favorable. Apparently there was some hope, based on rumor, that the President would issue the proclamation in August; when it was not forthcoming, advocates of emancipation were sorely disappointed. [. . .] Interestingly enough, the President told one delegation that he could not free slaves under the Constitution, because it could not be enforced in the rebel states. Any proclamation would be about as effective, from Lincoln's point of view, "as the Pope's bull against the comet."

It was the Union victory at Antietam on September 17, 1862, that caused Lincoln to act. Five days later he issued a preliminary Proclamation. In this document he revived the possibility of compensated emancipation and said that he would continue to encourage the voluntary colonization of Negroes "upon this continent or elsewhere." The time had come, however, when more direct action was needed; so he proclaimed that on January 1, 1863, "all persons held as slaves within any State or designated part of the State, the people whereof shall be in rebellion against the United States, shall be then, thenceforward, and forever free."

The preliminary Proclamation, despite this critical reaction, captured the imagination of workingmen in many parts of the world who viewed it as a great humanitarian document, and whenever slaves learned of it they laid down their tools and took on the mantle of their newly-found freedom. By the end of December, 1862, the suspense attending the final Proclamation was so great that even before it was read it had assumed the significance of one of the great documents of all times. [. . .] President Lincoln set free all slaves except those in states or parts of states not in rebellion against the United States at that time. These exceptions, in addition to the four loyal slave states, were thirteen parishes of Louisiana, including the city of New Orleans, the forty-eight counties of Virginia which had become West Virginia, and seven counties in eastern Virginia, including the cities of Norfolk and Portsmouth.

Lincoln left no doubt of his justification for the Emancipation Proclamation. Twice he mentioned the military necessity of pursuing this course. He described it as a "fit and necessary war measure" for suppressing the rebellion which he could take by virtue of the power vested in him as Commander-in-Chief of the Army and Navy. In the last paragraph of the Proclamation he said that it was "sincerely believed to be an act of justice, warranted by the Constitution upon military necessity." He counseled the slaves, however, to abstain from all violence except in self-defense and to work faithfully for reasonable wages.

If the Proclamation of Emancipation was essentially a war measure, it had the desired effect of creating confusion in the South and depriving the Confederacy of much of its valuable laboring force. If it was a diplomatic document, it succeeded in rallying to the Northern cause thousands of English and European laborers who were anxious to see workers gain their freedom throughout the world. If it was a humanitarian document, it gave hope to millions of Negroes that a better day lay ahead, and it renewed the faith of thousands of crusaders who had fought long to win freedom in America.

John Hope Franklin, *From Slavery to Freedom* (New York: Knopf, 1948), 267–268, 273–280.

## ELLA BAKER, Emancipation Day Address, Atlanta, Georgia, January 1, 1947

*Baker (1903–1986) was a leading figure in the civil rights movement from the 1930s until the 1970s. As the United States entered the Cold War with the Soviet Union, Baker focused her address on the contradictions between American concerns for spreading and defending democracy around the globe while denying civil and political rights to African Americans. Though she spoke more about contemporary issues than the past, she noted that Black freedom was not part of*

*Lincoln's original purpose in waging the Civil War and credited Black soldiers for being largely responsible for securing emancipation. In offering a vision of emancipation that was international in its scope, Baker clearly believed that the work Lincoln had begun remained unfinished at home and abroad.*

———————————

America was warned Wednesday that it cannot maintain world leadership and a pretense to democracy while keeping freedom from some at home.

The oft-repeated admonition came with fresh vigor and electrification from Miss Ella Baker, former national NAACP branch director and organizer, in the Emancipation Day address at Big Bethel Church, an occasion for the formal launching of the annual membership drive.

Noting that the freedom of Negroes came as an incidental matter during the Civil War, that their emancipation was an inevitable act of President Abraham Lincoln, tied up with a larger crisis, and that had it not been for the participation of Negroes in Union Army activities emancipation probably would have been delayed, Miss Baker called upon American Negroes to constantly ally themselves with the cause of oppressed peoples everywhere and to assert themselves vigorously for their own rights.

According to the speaker, white Americans are being made to realize that their salvation and welfare are tied up directly with the advance of the Negro, that they cannot rise without letting the Negro rise. As an example, Miss Baker cited the drives in the South by the major labor unions, stating that the Negro wage level must rise to a liveable minimum if the white level is expected to do so.

Rationalization by white Americans as to Negro rights was pointed out as one of the greatest holdbacks to this nation's democracy. There is still confusion in the white man's thinking on many points of Negro freedom and privilege, she said. There is an attempt to praise the Negro and his advance from slavery on the one hand, on the other hand to justify the white man's treatment and handling of Negro rights, the speaker stated, asserting that the Negro must concentrate a great deal of his efforts on reviving a sense of moral consciousness in the white man.

"The fight for unionization concerns the businessman, the doctor, the lawyer and other professional folk," Miss Baker asserted, "because their fate is tied up directly with the fate of the working man. They cannot exist except with the money made by the working man." Further the speaker said they must identify themselves with the labor fight, as well as with other fights of oppressed people everywhere. College degrees don't count, Miss Baker pointed out, because there is a tendency to identify all Negroes together, hence they must work to pull themselves en masse up from the mire of second-class citizenship.

Negro leadership was hit for many times saying what white people want them to say, instead of saying what is needed and good for Negro people in general. "There is no salvation except through yourselves," Miss Baker asserted.

Rationalizing by Republicans in the current effort to rid the United States Senate of Theo. "The Man" Bilbo came in for a blast by Miss Baker. She said that news accounts of the past several days showed a tendency by Republican members of the Senate to try to dismiss the charges that Bilbo caused violence and discrimination against Negroes in the Mississippi primary election, by saying that other people and representatives in the South had said that Negroes should not vote. The speaker said it was a tragedy that men in the national house of Congress could not see to it that men like Bilbo speak for democracy.

Again asserting that America is on a road to self-destruction unless there is a rebirth of moral thinking, Miss Baker scoffed at the Jimmy [Byrnes] ilk who attempt to conduct free elections in Europe, while turning their backs on the elections of South Carolina and Georgia. "They cannot have democracy at home unless they give it to all," the speaker asserted. The world crisis today over whether the forces of fascism and totalitarianism shall beat down democracy sees the Negro to benefit or lose along with the majority rulers, the speaker noted, pointing out the similarity of the struggle with the Civil War when a national crisis was at hand.

No Negro leader in the last 50 years has made the sacrifices for freedom known by other leaders of color, such as the Indians of Asia, Miss Baker said, adding that many leaders of the American group attempt to rise so high that they cannot be touched.

Calling on white people to be "true friends" to the Negro minority, the speaker issued a challenge to those 84 years out of slavery to organize their fight, support the NAACP as a frontal organization, press for fair labor laws, better health conditions, a fair employment practice committee, anti-poll tax legislation and against every measure, proposal and practice designed to oppress the underprivileged. The Negro must quit looking for a saviour and work to save himself and wake up others about him, the speaker concluded.

In William A. Fowlkes, "U.S. Warned to Make Democracy Work at Home," *Atlanta Daily World,* Jan. 2, 1947.

## LUTHER PORTER JACKSON, "The Views of Abraham Lincoln on the Race Question," February 12, 1948

*Jackson (1892–1950) was a native of Kentucky who earned a PhD in history at the University of Chicago and taught for nearly thirty years at Virginia State University. Jackson's scholarship focused on African American history, with his major work being on free Blacks in Virginia prior to the Civil War. Jackson was active in the civil rights movement, particularly in advocating and organizing for voting rights. During the 1940s, Jackson published a column,*

*"Rights and Duties in a Democracy," for the* New Journal and Guide, *an African American newspaper in Norfolk. The following piece was prepared to mark Lincoln's birthday and was published in the* New Journal and Guide *on February 21. In analyzing Lincoln's position on civil rights, Jackson addresses what has become Lincoln's most infamous and oft-quoted statement on Black civil rights and observes that in 1858, Lincoln sounded much like contemporary White supremacists, such as Mississippi governor Fielding Wright, and US Senator James Eastland. For Jackson, the key question was whether Lincoln's views changed between 1858 and 1865.*

Since the day on which I write this article is Feb. 12th and it falls within Negro History Week, I deem it fitting to say something about Abraham Lincoln who was born on this day. It is especially fitting to say something about him now for the reason that his views on the race question have been dragged into the current controversy over the civil rights of Negroes in America. In this connection, a resident of Madison, Virginia recently had published in the Richmond Times-Dispatch a portion of a speech delivered by Lincoln at Charleston, Illinois, in 1858 in one of the famous Lincoln-Douglas debates. In a previous debate Douglas had accused Lincoln of advocating racial equality and of endeavoring to "abolition-ize" the whole country. In an effort to defend himself against this charge Lincoln spoke thus to Douglas:

> I will say, then, that I am not, nor ever have been in favor of bringing about in any way the social and political equality of the white and black races; that I am not, nor ever have been, in favor of making voters or jurors of Negroes, nor of qualifying men to hold office, nor to intermarry with white people; and I will say in addition to this, that there is a physical difference between the white and black races which I believe will forever [for]bid the two races living together on terms of social and political equality. And inasmuch as they can not so live, while they do remain together there must be the position of superior and inferior, and I as much as any other man am in favor of having the superior position assigned to the white race.

These utterances no doubt come as a distinct shock to the many people of today who have had no occasion to make a special study of Lincoln on these and other public issues. Here he advocates white supremacy in the same vein as Senator Eastland and Governor Wright of Mississippi are loudly advocating it now. In presenting this speech and others of Lincoln like it to my classes in American history here at Virginia State College, my students have remarked: "I am through with Lincoln."

In expressing these ideas Lincoln was no different from the average white American of the pre-Civil War period and no different from a host of such persons today. He had no liking whatever for William Lloyd Garrison and the militant abolitionists, for they were advocating the immediate emancipation of the slaves and they were preaching racial equality.

Within three years after making this speech Lincoln had become the President of the United States and in this capacity he faced the slavery question and the race question constantly. Did Lincoln while serving as President in 1861–65 retain his views of 1858 when he was merely running for high public office? Everybody knows that by 1863 Lincoln had changed his mind on the subject of the abolition of slavery by issuing the Emancipation Proclamation, but every one does not know that by 1864 he had also changed his mind considerably about Negroes exercising the right to vote. In this year the State of Louisiana, having been defeated by the union armies, was in the process of change from a state of the Confederacy to a state of the union. With respect to framing a constitution for the new state government and making provisions respecting who might vote, Lincoln wrote to Governor Hahn as follows:

> Now you are about to have a convention, which, among other things, will prob-
> ably define the elective franchise. I barely suggest for your private consideration,
> whether some of the colored people may not be let in—as, for instance, the
> very intelligent, and especially those who fought gallantly in our ranks. They
> would probably help in some trying time to come, to keep the jewel of liberty
> within the family of freedom.

Lincoln not only made this concession but also approved the provision in the constitution that the state legislature might allow Negroes to vote.

For an official of government to have a set of backward ideas at one time and to change them later is a mark of statesmanship of the highest order. Apparently it was the war which changed his mind. He went into the struggle thinking that the slaves should not necessarily have their freedom or aspire to citizenship. At the close of the struggle he was ready by degrees to make them voting citizens and enter political life. The war transformed the thinking of Lincoln and it appears that World War II has similarly affected the thinking of President Truman.

Luther Porter Jackson Papers, Box 66, Virginia State University Special Collections and Archives.

## WILLARD TOWNSEND, "Lincoln Did Not Envision 1952 in His Speech at Gettysburg," January 19, 1952

*A native of Ohio, Townsend (1895–1957) served in the army during World War I and was a graduate of the Royal College of Science in Toronto, Ontario. He worked as a redcap in Chicago, organized fellow redcaps into a labor union during the 1930s, and served as president of the organization for the remainder of his life. Active in civil rights organizations, such as the NAACP and National Urban League, Townsend offered an assessment of American democracy in the early 1950s and used Lincoln's Gettysburg Address as the measuring stick. Townsend asserted that if Lincoln were alive in 1952 he would be disappointed by the lack of equal opportunity and persistence of segregation. He added that the current war in Korea was being waged to vouchsafe democracy for its citizens, yet Blacks could not vote in the South. Pointedly, Townsend maintained that southern Whites, who were recipients of Lincoln's charity in 1865, had violated Lincoln's trust by preventing democracy from moving forward. While Townsend claimed Lincoln as an ally in the civil rights struggle, he noted that Senator Robert A. Taft of Ohio, known as "Mr. Republican" and a frontrunner for the Republican presidential nomination, had stated at a recent appearance in Durham, North Carolina that the federal government should not forcibly integrate southern schools (ANB).*

---

"Four score and seven years ago our fathers brought forth on this continent a new nation conceived in liberty and dedicated to the proposition that all men are created equal."

For more than three quarters of a century this introduction to Lincoln's Gettysburg address has been democracy's symbolic statement for children to memorize at school and the basis for demagogic addresse[s] by politicians when other arguments failed to arouse the voting populace.

If Lincoln were alive today and in the same frame of mind as when this speech was hurriedly written on the train to Gettysburg, he would have much cause for alarm at our great reluctance to accept the most elementary principle of our democratic way of life—the right of each person to enjoy freedom of opportunity.

Lincoln would question the future of American democracy if he had had the opportunity to have listened in a week or so ago in the city of Durha[m], N. C., and heard Senator Taft endorse the right of the state to maintain segregation.

Lincoln would cry out in shame at the spectacle of a free government and its institutions searching for ways to straddle this basic right of black southerners to educate their children in institutions, free from racial bigotry.

"Now we are engaged in a great civil war testing whether that nation, or any nation so conceived and so dedicated, can long endure. We are met on a great battlefield of that war. We have come to dedicate a portion of that field as a final resting-place for those who here gave their lives that that nation might live. It is altogether fitting and proper that we should do this. But, in a larger sense, we cannot dedicate, we cannot consecrate, we cannot hallow this ground. The brave men, living and dead, who struggled here have consecrated it far above our poor power to add or detract.

"The world will little note nor long remember what we say here, but it can never forget what they did here. It is for us the living rather to be dedicated here to the unfinished work which they who have fought here have thus far so nobly advanced.["]

Today we are engaged in another war in Korea to safeguard and extend democratic processes. While this is going on, millions of second class citizens in eight Southern states are disfranchised by statutes of infamy. Through this denial of elementary rights, the most reactionary elements in the South (and there are some fine democratic elements in the South) have reduced popular government to "plantation government."

These elements are elected year after year by less than five percent of the voters who are able to pay the poll taxes, and they represent only the interests of the tiny but influential minority in the South. The vote is small and it is easy for those "hoe-cake" politicians of the poll tax states to establish tight, unbeatable machines.

They acquire seniority on important congressional committees and maintain a strangle hold on national progress and decency. These recipients of the "charity" of Lincoln in 1865 have done more to nullify the ideals and vision of the "Great Emancipator" than any other section or division within the national community.

The cause of freedom and liberty, which the dead at Gettysburg dedicated their lives, today receives its mortal blows from the hands of Southern political autocracy. The alliance of this dangerous minority with another equally dangerous and vicious minority, Northern reactionary Republicans, is one great challenge to effective prosecution of our global war and a peace based on justice, freedom and security for all.

"It is rather for us to be here dedicated to the great task remaining before us—that from these honored dead we take increased devotion to that cause for which they gave the last full measure of devotion—that we here highly resolve that these dead shall not have died in vain, that this nation under God shall have a new birth of freedom, and that government of the people, by the people, for the people, shall not perish from the earth."

*Chicago Defender*, Jan. 19, 1952.

## RALPH J. BUNCHE, Address at the Lincoln Association of Jersey City, New Jersey, February 12, 1954

*After graduating from UCLA, Bunche (1904–1971) pursued a career in academia at Howard University and received a PhD from Harvard. He advised the US delegation that helped create the United Nations and attained international prominence as a diplomat for the UN. In 1950, he became the first*

*African American recipient of the Nobel Peace Prize for his role in negotiating a ceasefire in the 1948 war between Israel and its Arab neighbors. He also helped mediate other international conflicts and was actively involved in the civil rights movement at home. Bunche believed remembrance of Lincoln was important to both the civil rights movement and the cause of international peace. He spoke in Lincoln's hometown of Springfield, Illinois on Lincoln's birthday in 1951, and would later serve on the Lincoln Sesquicentennial Commission. The following address was delivered at the annual Lincoln Day dinner of the Lincoln Association of Jersey City, New Jersey. For Bunche, Lincoln was a symbol of freedom, democracy, and nationalism in the international struggle against Soviet communism and also an important ally in the domestic struggle to complete the work of the Emancipation Proclamation by making equality under the law a reality for all citizens (ANB).*

---

I am deeply appreciative of the invitation which brings me in your midst tonight. It is a privilege to attend this eighty-ninth Annual Dinner of the oldest and most venerable of all Lincoln Associations. With your permission may I congratulate, most earnestly, the officers and members of this Association—the oldest of its kind in the nation, which, through patriotic motivation, thus performs a rich service to our country and its people in memorializing and perpetuating the name, traditions and ideals of a man of rare greatness, a truly stalwart figure in our nation's history; indeed, one of the great men in human history.

It is with profound humility that I stand before you in the realization that we are here to venerate the name, and I trust, re-dedicate ourselves, to the principles and ideals of a man who was at once most humble and most inspired and inspiring among men.

I have no phrases at my command to do honor or justice to the greatness of Abraham Lincoln, whose name and deeds will remain in the minds of men as long as human history; whose profound thoughts expressed in eloquently simple words will endure as long as the conscience and memory of man; whose spiritual strength knew no bounds; whose simple humility shamed, and will ever shame, the falsely proud and the arrogant; whose vast tolerance was the embodiment of all that is conveyed by human brotherhood and compassion; whose scrupulous truthfulness is an eternal model for all leaders. Lincoln was a man of faith—faith born of tragedy and anguish. His pillars were love of God and neighbor, and where may stronger pillars be found?

But Abraham Lincoln was a man, not a god—and I trust that legend will never render him otherwise. He was fallible, as all men are. Historians tell us of his spells of melancholia; history records his moments of indecision, his groping, his bows to political expediency. In the crucial hours of decision, however, he found a boundless strength which flowed from his unwavering faith in people, in the "plain people," from the equalitarianism of the West in which he was reared, from his firm belief in the equality and dignity and essential goodness of man.

Lincoln, the leader, the immortal, today belongs to no party, to no partisanship. He belongs rather to the whole American people, whose unity today, indeed, is owed to him. In our entire history of great Americans, I believe Abraham Lincoln provides our most complete and satisfying symbol of leadership. For he was a man of the people; he never left them; despite his elevation to the highest position of the land, he never severed the roots that bound him to them. We have had many great leaders but never one who was so everlastingly identified with the people from whom he came. He was a humanist, of the heart as well as the intellect, for Lincoln reacted deeply to inequality and inhumanity wherever he encountered it. He was a nationalist, for to him the survival of the united nation claimed first priority. As President he was strong; when decisive action was required he knew how to act decisively and had the courage to do what had to be done.

Although in some circles today it has become a term of opprobrium, Lincoln was an intellectual—in the truest and finest sense, for his apparent approach to problems was to examine them from all directions and work out their solutions intellectually by the application of reason. Were he in our modern political arena he might well be called an "egghead," though there are some who might wish to disqualify him on grounds of poor spelling.

These are times in which it is especially useful and refreshing to read Lincoln. For though he stood alone at the helm of a nation in mortal peril, torn asunder by internal strife, he never lost hope and faith, he ever looked forward. He was an apostle of hope, not of doom. Although, through grim internecine strife, the meanest traits of his fellow men were brutishly revealed, his faith in men did not falter. His words maintain a perpetual freshness; his thoughts provide a true beacon. He looked always up, not down.

Read in the context of the contemporary world, his words often carry apt international significance.

In his First Annual Message on December 3, 1861, for example, Lincoln said:

"The struggle of today is not altogether for today; it is for the vast future also."

What could be more truly said of the world struggle today underway—the struggle of the concept of freedom and of the rights and dignity of the individual, to withstand the onslaughts of aggressive communism? Lincoln, I believe, would well understand the deep significance of this struggle, its ideological and human as well as its military implications. He would understand that this is a universal struggle for the minds and hearts of men; that peoples such as the vast millions in Asia, Africa and the Near East, who have known for centuries only misery and subjugation, and most of whom have had little opportunity to enjoy freedom, must be won to our cause by sincere compassion for their plight, by accepting them fully and equally as brothers. These are weapons as effective as armaments in reaching their understanding and in fortifying them against the blandishments of communism.

Lincoln would also, I think, instinctively understand the inevitability of our American role of leadership in the free world today. Because of our tremendous resources, our unparalleled productive process, our formidable military potential, and above all, our firm traditions of freedom, we could not do otherwise than to uphold the cause of freedom in the world and join hands with all those who believe as we do in the inalienable right of all men to be free of tyranny over mind or body. Indeed, this was implicit in a statement made by Lincoln in his speech at Springfield on June 27, 1857, when he said, prophetically:

"They {authors of the Declaration} meant to set up a standard maxim for free society, which should be familiar to all, and revered by all; constantly labored for, and even though never perfectly attained, constantly spreading and deepening its influence and augmenting the happiness and value of life to all people of all colors everywhere." [...]

The world being as it is, it should be clear to us that the cause of peace and freedom would be nobly served if the more favoured peoples will, without selfish motive or strings attached, extend generous and friendly encouragement to the less favoured as they advance along the difficult course of human progress. The costs, though heavy, would be insignificant alongside the costs of war. We in the West must also make certain that the notions of freedom, equality and the dignity of man are available for unrestricted export to the far corners of the earth; to yellow, brown and black men, as well as to white.

Of all Lincoln's legacies, none, it seems to me, could have greater significance today to our nation and to the peace and freedom loving world than his emphasis on unity.

Our traditional concepts and ideals, our democratic American way of life, are being challenged, more sternly than ever in our history, by an alien ideology. Never has the need been greater or more urgent for our maximum unity, our maximum strength, spiritual as well as material, our maximum faith in ourselves. We may fervently hope and pray that in these dangerous times unity will not fall prey to excessive partisanship; that our spiritual strength may not be sapped by cynicism; and that faith in ourselves will not retreat before fear, suspicion and bitter recrimination. As Lincoln well advised: "That union is strength is a truth that has been known, illustrated and declared in various ways and forms in all ages of the world. That great fabulist and philosopher, Aesop, illustrated it by his fable of the bundle of sticks; and He whose wisdom surpasses that of all philosophers has declared that a house divided against itself cannot stand." {Whig circular, March 1, 1843, I, 255.}

In the larger world, the need for unity among all peoples nurturing those ideals common to free men and those men who, still lacking it, nevertheless, aspire to freedom, is equally urgent.

The Charter of the United Nations provides a sure vehicle for all such peoples. Its fundamental principles and objectives are Lincolnesque in their clarity and simplicity and in their substance.

In the Charter of the United Nations the peace-loving peoples of the world express their fundamental faith in the dignity and worth of the human person, and commit themselves to the promotion of social progress and better standards of life in larger freedom. [. . .]

The 200 million people still remaining in colonial status find increasing sympathy and assistance from the international community toward the realization of their aspirations for self-government or independence, through the operations of the UN and the specialized Agencies [. . .].

Frequently though it has been said, it bears constant reiteration that the United Nations is man's greatest hope for peace. Admittedly, the United Nations, with its limited strength, is a thin enough thread on which to suspend humanity's future. But there is none stronger. In truth, there is no other. [. . .]

It is not, really, the United Nations as an organization to which I am devoted, but rather the ideals and objectives to which it is committed and which it perseveringly strives to implement. For how can civilization and mankind survive and progress unless we have peace; unless people are free; unless there is hope for progressively improving living standards for all people; unless there is morality and justice—international as well as national; unless racial and religious bigotries are eliminated and we can cultivate a true spirit of brotherhood among men? And how are we to serve these ends if we do not bring the nations together, the friendly and unfriendly alike, in the never-ceasing effort to bridge the gaps of difference by trust, understanding and goodwill? Is this United Nations way not the Christian way? Is it not the way Lincoln would have urged? Is there really any other? [. . .]

It will be understood, I know, that I especially, would not wish to conclude this talk, honoring the Great Emancipator's birthday, without some reference to the descendants of that multitude of hapless souls to whom Lincoln gave their freedom ninety-one years ago—a mere instant in human history, but a very long time in terms of the individual life-span. In these nine decades the American Negro has come a long way. There can be no question but that we are well on the way toward solution of that unfortunate heritage of our history, the problem of race relations. In this last decade, especially, thanks to enlightened citizens of all colors and creeds; the efforts of national and community organizations, Negro and inter-racial; the actions of the national Government and of many state governments and municipalities as well, remarkable progress has been made.

But if Lincoln could walk amongst us today, he would quickly discern the problem of race still persists, albeit in less aggravated form. I wonder what he might think. Even on the time chart of the gradualists, ninety-one years must appear as a tolerably long time in the solution of a society's purely human problem.

Obviously, it is only by continuing and resolute effort by all men and women of good will that the emancipation process begun by Lincoln can be completed. And its completion can mean only the realization of the goal of full and equal citizenship for all Americans irrespective of race or creed or national origin.

Clearly, this must be the goal, for the Negro citizen can never be content with anything less than his full birthright as a citizen, and no one who truly believes in our system could think otherwise. It is, indeed, a measure of the rapid advances that have been made that when our President today states that there must be no "second-class" American citizens there is widespread agreement. But when some were saying precisely this only a score of years ago it was considered "radical" and was shocking to not a few.

What the Negro American desires is as simple as it is fair. He asks that he be weighed and treated in the society on the same scale and basis as every other citizen; that he be accepted or rejected, not as a group on the automatic basis of his colour, but as an individual, in accordance with whatever merit he may possess.

I speak as an American to Americans. I am proud to be an American and I am devoted to my country and its way of life. I have enjoyed great benefits in this society and I am proudly grateful. I offer no apologies, therefore, when I state that the Negro American must enjoy all the rights and privileges and opportunities which are the priceless heritage of every American—and must accept all the obligations and duties and make all the sacrifices required of every citizen. [. . .]

I have unbounded faith in America and Americans. I know that the American conscience is sensitive, that in this society the sense of fairness and justice is deeply rooted, and the belief in democracy is genuine and fervent. I am confident, in this faith, that all racial and social injustice will be corrected.

But a society's ills are never self-healing. There must be alertness and determined action. The greatest enemy is usually citizens' indifference.

In this regard, you may be interested to know that the N.A.A.C.P. was recently inspired to initiate what is known as "The Fight For Freedom Fund," whose target is January 1, 1963, and whose purpose is defined in a pamphlet about to be issued as follows:

"Because of these unfinished tasks of Emancipation, the National Association for the Advancement of Colored People has dedicated the remaining years of the first century of freedom to the fulfillment of Lincoln's historic proclamation.

On January 1, 1963, the nation will celebrate the 100th anniversary of that proclamation.

By that time the N.A.A.C.P. intends to clean up the remnants of the heritage of slavery.

By that time, the Association hopes to have achieved full and unqualified citizenship for the 15,000,000 native Americans who compose the Negro group in this country.

By that time, the N.A.A.C.P. confidently expects that the Jim Crow signs which now deface America will have been relegated to the museums to be displayed along with the horse-drawn streetcars and other relics."

To expand and speed its work towards these goals, the N.A.A.C.P. is launching a campaign to raise a Fight for Freedom Fund of a Million Dollars a year until 1963, the end of the first century of freedom.

I imagine that Abraham Lincoln, could he be with us in this year of 1954, would warmly endorse that program—a program designed simply to make every American an American in full, to make of the American people a fully united people.

I can think of no better or more pertinent words with which to conclude this talk than with the immortal words with which Lincoln closed his Second Inaugural Address; for there is great work ahead of us to be done, nationally and internationally; it is our historic mission to ensure that it is done; in our own vital interest, and in the interest of peace and freedom and justice at home and abroad, it must be done. Lincoln said, in some of the noblest words I know:

"With malice toward none; with charity for all; with firmness in the right, as God gives us to see the right, let us strive on to finish the work we are in; . . . —to do all which may achieve and cherish a just, and a lasting peace, among ourselves, and with all nations."

May we as a nation & people never falter in this course.

Ralph J. Bunche Papers, Box 362, Folder 11, Library Special Collections, Charles E. Young Research Library, UCLA.

## MARY MCLEOD BETHUNE on Lincoln's Birthday, February 12, 1955

*Here, Bethune (1875–1955) extended her message on Lincoln from ten years earlier with an editorial on Lincoln's birthday that was written in the wake of the Supreme Court's landmark decision in* Brown v. Topeka Board of Education *(1954) that ruled segregated schools were inherently unequal and therefore unconstitutional. As some Southern politicians vowed to resist the court's decision, Bethune recalled Lincoln's difficult position during the Civil War when he sought freedom and justice for the enslaved while being severely criticized. Bethune was unequivocal about Lincoln's place in history. Picturing Lincoln as a common man who had faith in democracy, Bethune believed that all American citizens would see, in time, that just as those who criticized Lincoln's actions during the Civil War were foolish, the critics of* Brown *will one day be viewed*

*in the same light. Lincoln realized slavery had to end if the country was to sur-*
*vive, and he courageously issued the Emancipation Proclamation. In referring*
*to the* Brown *decision as "Lincoln-like," Bethune was optimistic that it would*
*be implemented, and claimed Lincoln as an ally in the cause for civil rights.*

---

Today, no one with any sense of history and of human values questions the greatness of Abraham Lincoln or the significance of his contribution to the race of mankind.

In his time, however, this man who said, "I certainly wish that all men could be free," had bitter enemies.

Lincoln took his stand with right and with truth; he identified himself with human justice. Hence, he became destined for greatness.

Knowing personal tragedy and sorrow, he bore also the pain of being at the center of a Civil War which he realized was inevitable that brothers not fight each other again in this land if all were to be free.

As we view the activities of Lincoln with the perspective of time, we realize that he did not jump at once into the main contribution he was to make to mankind. When it came time to take his stand on a controversial issue, Lincoln was ready.

Lincoln was down-to-earth. He wanted the slaves free; he wanted victory, but he wanted the people of the country to make up their minds on the issue. He believed they would decide to do the right thing.

Thus, with faith not only in God, but also in man, he, as has been said, "always addressed the intelligence of men, never their prejudices, their passion, or their ignorance." [...]

The President's soul was sorely tried at the rift which the War made in the Nation. It grieved him that men should fight over an issue he saw so clearly and which he knew at last all men would see, with the passage of time, as having only one just and fair solution.

Today Abraham Lincoln towers above his critics. Their hatred and their prejudice mark them as small men while Lincoln's tallness is characterized by courage and wisdom in human relations.

As we celebrate his birthday this year, our Nation is taking a further step in the direction of human liberty, justice and freedoms. The reason of the American people is being called upon to implement a quite Lincoln-like decision of our Court.

Again, history appeals to our intelligence, and not to our prejudice, our passion or our ignorance. Let us stand where Lincoln stood: "On the assumption that a democracy can think."

This is the hope of our Nation and the hope of mankind.

Editorial in the *Chicago Defender*, Feb. 12, 1955.

## ROY WILKINS, Radio Address to Commemorate Lincoln's Birthday, February 11 or 12, 1958

*Wilkins (1901–1981) was serving as the executive secretary of the National Association for the Advancement of Colored People when he gave this radio address to commemorate Abraham Lincoln's birthday in 1958. The connection between Lincoln's birthday and the founding of the NAACP was noted for strategic purposes. Acknowledging that Lincoln's views on race were being used by both civil rights supporters and segregationists, Wilkins admitted that some of Lincoln's statements, when taken out of context, seemed to reflect those of Hitler supporters, yet he asserted that most embodied a commitment to equality. If Lincoln were alive in 1958, Wilkins had no doubt where he would stand on the issue of civil rights. With the current Soviet threat, Wilkins saw the countervailing civil rights movement as a force to maintain the best of America's ideals.*

---

We celebrate today the 149th anniversary of the birth of Abraham Lincoln, the Great Emancipator. Today is also the 49th birthday of the founding of the National Association for the Advancement of Colored People which was organized for the purpose of making a reality of Lincoln's basic ideals of human brotherhood.

There was about Lincoln a universal quality which encompassed varying views on humankind. As is done with the Bible, quotations from his works are now being utilized by segregationists and white supremacists as well as by those of us who believe in equal rights for all.

Undoubtedly during the course of his lifetime Lincoln said many things which, if isolated, may seem to support the views of our contemporary disciples of Hitler. This is true, also, of certain segments of the Bible. But the sum total of Lincoln's letters and works, as of the Bible, clearly expresses his conviction that all men are entitled to life, liberty and the pursuit of happiness on equal terms. He would, as he forcefully declared, be neither slave nor master, but only another human being in a democratic society, sharing equally the rights, privileges and responsibilities demanded of membership in such a society.

It is now 93 years since the Great Emancipator was cut down by an assassin's bullet. Where would he stand on today's civil rights issue? Except for the slavery question, the issues of today are much as they were at the time of his death. Conditions, of course, have changed. The Negro of 1958 is not the freedman of 1865. Today he is literate, propertied and conscious of the denial of his rights. He is articulate and demanding of recognition as a citizen of a democracy. He is determined to eliminate the barriers which stigmatize him as something less than a full citizen. He cherishes both Lincoln's firmness in a crisis and his charitable instincts for those who would deny basic rights to Negro citizens. He wishes harm to none of his fellow Americans, but he is insistent upon his basic constitutional rights.

In what was, perhaps, his most famous remark, Lincoln declared that this nation cannot continue to exist half slave and half free. The Negro today holds with equal conviction that this nation cannot continue half segregated and half free. The constitutional principles of equality of citizenship must prevail in Mississippi as in Massachusetts, in South Carolina as in South Dakota. There cannot be one standard of citizenship in one state and another in each of the other 47 states. The rights of citizenship are universal throughout the length and breadth of our nation "conceived in liberty and dedicated to the proposition that all men are created equal."

Because the National Association for the Advancement of Colored People is also dedicated to the Lincolnian philosophy, it has worked ceaselessly for nearly a half-century to eliminate racial discrimination and segregation from all aspects of public life in our country. [...]

The need for this activity is even more urgent today than in Lincoln's time. As the leader of the free world, our country can no longer afford the handicaps and limitations of racial discrimination. Those who would continue this archaic practice undermine the unity and strength of our nation at home as well as our prestige abroad. Those who work to bring life and meaning to Lincoln's philosophy are strengthening our nation at home and enhancing its leadership among the millions of uncommitted peoples elsewhere. Now, as never before, we need the understanding and support of these people who are being wooed by the most powerful foe America has ever confronted.

As long as America keeps trying to attain its goals our temporary failures and setbacks will not loom too large in the eyes of fair appraisers; but if we stand still and refuse to go forward, if we mock and defy our laws, our proclamations and our ideals, we will influence our potential friends to incline an ear to the deceptive invitations of Moscow.

Of course, we must re-dedicate ourselves to Lincoln not merely because of the Soviet threat, but because equality and individual liberty form the bedrock of Western democratic society. If it is renounced, all that mankind hoped for from the new Western world will be lost. In a very real sense, then, the campaign of the Negro American for his democratic rights is a campaign to preserve the American ideal for all his fellow citizens.

NAACP Papers, Series III, Box A-255, Part 24, Reel 19 (Washington, DC: Library of Congress).

## MORDECAI W. JOHNSON, Address on Abraham Lincoln before the Michigan Legislature, Lansing, Michigan, February 12, 1959

*Educated at Atlanta Baptist College, the University of Chicago, and Rochester Theological Seminary, Johnson (1890–1976) served as a minister, was active in the NAACP, and became the first African American president of Howard University in 1926. A highly regarded orator, Johnson was invited to address the Michigan legislature on the 150th anniversary of Lincoln's birth. Focusing more on Lincoln's character rather than his accomplishments, Johnson identified five key traits that shaped his personality. Johnson's address is also notable for not focusing on either Lincoln as Great Emancipator or savior of the Union. Instead, Johnson offers a unique perspective by asserting that Lincoln's greatest quality was his pure heart that offered compassion towards White Southerners. For Johnson, Lincoln's expression of "malice toward none" in his Second Inaugural Address and the lenient terms of peace extended to the defeated rebels exemplify the depth of his compassion. Without directly mentioning contemporary events, it seems that Johnson hoped Lincoln's example of respecting all persons and his unwavering belief in the promise of equality in the Declaration of Independence would serve as an inspiration as Americans struggled over civil rights. Johnson retired as president of Howard in 1960 (ANB).*

---

I am deeply grateful to you for the privilege which you give me today of joining you in meditative appreciation of our great leader, Abraham Lincoln—the man whose name is the greatest of all names connected with popular government in the history of the World. I have come to you today, bearing in my heart a deep sense of personal indebtedness to this man, for I am a child of slaves. My father was a slave and my mother was born a slave. Both of them were set free by Abraham Lincoln. Along with the deep sense of debt which I bear in my heart toward him is another which is akin to it, namely, the sense of debt which I bear toward you and for your kindred in this State who, under the leadership of Abraham Lincoln, made so very large an investment of devotion and suffering in that cause which made it possible for us to be free. [...]

Of all the men in the public life of the World who have deeply impressed me in this respect, Abraham Lincoln is one who grows on my affections year by year. The qualities of his heart and mind are remarkable, beyond measure, in their fitness and power to sustain and to transform the institutions of the democratic public life. [...]

For the purposes of our meditation I want to divide the life of Abraham Lincoln into three periods. The first period, from 1809 to 1854, I would call the Period of Preparation during which his great personal powers were in the making. The second period, from 1854 to 1860, I would call the Period of Political Creation, in which, under great difficulties, he nourished and brought to leadership in the Nation a political vehicle of decisive power. The third period, from 1861 to 1865, the Period of Victorious Achievement, during which, under the pressure of violence, suffering and death he obtained the great political ends for which the World reveres him—the emancipation of the slaves and the preservation of the Union. [...]

[T]here was a whole lot more to the life of Abraham Lincoln in those first 45 years than he himself took time to mention. For in those 45 years this man developed by his own efforts one of the most powerful groups of qualifications for political leadership ever to be found in history. These are the qualities which made him the power that he was from 1854 to 1861, when he became President of the United States, and which led him in the years 1861 to 1865 to become the Emancipator of the slaves and the preserver of the Union.

Now what are these qualities? First of all, Abraham Lincoln developed in those early years a vivid and powerful ethical disposition which he made radically applicable to every human being whom he touched—whatever his race, color, creed, sex or national origin—and he extended it even to animals. He was especially sensitive in the presence of cruelty, either to men or animals, and often found it impossible to pass by an animal in distress. [...]

He was never able to look on cruelty complacently. He was never able to look at men and women who suffered from any unjust cause without feeling identified with them. This is where he got his great conviction that slavery was wrong, that the cruelty connected with slavery was wrong, that a cruel thing like this had no business to exist on this earth, and that somehow or other it ought to be done away with. There is no place on record where he ever said anything different from that. [...]

In the second place, Abraham Lincoln was a man who had a thorough grasp of the meaning of the Declaration of Independence, and he accepted the radically transitive universal ethics of that Declaration of Independence with all his heart. I do not mean merely that he accepted it intellectually. He accepted it as a part of his very being. [...]

In the third place, Abraham Lincoln acquired in early life a masterful power of communication. In all the history of public political speech there is no man in this country who ever had a greater power than Abraham Lincoln. It was an intellectual power, because he was a thoughtful man who gathered his facts and arranged his arguments with great care. He carefully studied grammar. He studied the language of the Bible and pondered it and absorbed it in his system. He studied mathematics, not in order that he might become a mathematician, but that he might reason precisely, consecutively and with a clear and powerful relatedness.

But there was something more than intellectual power in his speaking. There was a moral power and often persuasive moral beauty in what he said. He respected and loved the people to whom he was speaking. He believed in the capacity of the most ordinary man to understand the most profound ethical and political truths, if he needed them for his life. And when he spoke to such men he was not making an oration of words. He was speaking what he deeply believed. [. . .] Sometimes when he spoke his rugged, melancholy face would light up like a lamp and throw a glow of persuasive beauty to the very ends of the auditorium. People loved him, believed in him, flocked to him because he bought their allegiance with the gold of sincerity and clarity that came to them from a pure heart.

Another of his great qualities—the fourth—was his habituation of himself in his actions to simple and truthful relationships with individual human beings. You can see this nowhere better than in his practice of the law. If a client had a crooked or an unjust case, he would not take it if he knew it beforehand. [. . .] He was helpless to use his best powers in the presence of the necessity to defend cruelty or crookedness. But if you had an honest case, very often the first thing he would try to do was to see whether he could adjust it without going into court, and especially if the case involved cruelty and injustice, he would put his whole life and soul into that case. [. . .] He took it for the joy of setting things right, for the privilege of being vehicular toward the establishment of justice.

Along toward the end of this preparatory period of his life, the fifth quality developed within him, which is remarkable to think about: he developed a sense of having great unspent power and a sense of melancholy distress because that power in him had never had a chance to be used up fully in some great cause. He walked about conscious of that power and with the feeling that some day the occasion would arise when he would use it for everything that he had in him. He respected that occasion and looked toward it, afar off, with melancholy hope, and because he respected that far off occasion, he never would sell his powers cheaply. He would not sell them for money [. . .] And although he went to the State Capitol three times and to Congress once, as the elected representative of the people, he quit them both with very great dissatisfaction of heart, because he was occupying political power and moving about among men who accepted political power without having any great cause at stake. [. . .] He did not like it. He did not want it. He stayed at home, nourishing his powers, waiting for a great and worthy day to come. [. . .]

In the history of parties in this country there is nowhere a record of devotion superior to that which this man Lincoln put into the building of the Republican Party between the years 1854 and 1860. In this undertaking he subordinated entirely his personal ambition to hold political office. He saw with clear eyes that unless a party devoting its whole life unequivocally to the restriction of the growth of the slave system and the deliverance of the Union from the danger of dominance by that system, could be brought to effective power, no office would be fit to have. And so when public office was set before him again and again he would not take it. [...]

When he began this series of debates and speeches in the Illinois Senatorial campaign in 1858 he was scarcely known outside of Illinois. When he had completed them, the most intelligent and resourceful men on the Eastern seaboard sent for this man of the one horse towns and crowded Cooper Union in New York to hear him. If ever there were any of us who felt contemptuous toward a man of no University education—toward a poor man of no cultural family background and no University education—let us read again this speech produced by one who was called "the poor white trash." Let us read again his powerful putting together of historic facts; let us read again the masterful analysis of the arguments of the supporters of the slave system; let us observe again the intellectual power and moral sagacity with which he reduced the whole thesis of the slave masters to a demand that slavery henceforth be considered not only lawful but right. Then let us behold this gangling awkward son of the frontier, ignited from the depths of his being by moral conviction about the wrongness of slavery and its fateful danger to the Union, and with his rude melancholy face glowing with persuasive light, holding this great audience of intelligent and resourceful New Yorkers and easterners in all but breathless silence, as he commandingly called them to put aside everything and support this Republican movement with all their hearts to halt the onward march of this wrong and evil thing and to put it in a place where it could no longer imperil the life of the Union. Here indeed, once again from the humblest depths of life, there had come a man of intellectual, moral and spiritual power of the highest significance for all mankind. [...]

Now I come to the third and last period in the life of Abraham Lincoln. In this period I wish to concentrate attention entirely upon a quality which first appeared in the early days of his conflict with the slave system, but which reached its greatest development only in this third period; namely, his compassion toward the people of the South.

In the earliest days of Abraham Lincoln's fight against slavery he learned how to do what is almost impossible; how to fight an evil cause without entertaining malice and enmity toward the men who support that evil cause. He hated slavery but he never hated the slave owners or the people of the South as a group. When he agreed as he did agree that the Constitution required him to leave slavery alone in the southern States, he did not agree to this merely for the sake of taking a political position. He agreed to it because he believed in the righteousness of this position and because he intended to be loyal to it. Abraham Lincoln did not feel that the people of the South were different in any fundamental respect from the people of the North. He did not feel that they supported the slave system, because there was some peculiar element in their human make-up which inevitably required them to do this. He knew that the people of the South had not hatched the slave system. The people of the North were just as much responsible for the development of the slave system as the people of the South. Moreover, he knew that there were hundreds of thousands and even millions of white people in the South who held no slaves, and would like to get rid of the slave system, but now that the slave system had come to be the only working economic system in the South, they did not know how to get rid of it. He was not sure that he himself would know how to get rid of the slave system if he were then so situated in the South. Instead of hating the southerners, therefore, his compassion went out to them with a loving heart. [...] He wanted to keep them in the Union so that a Union committed by majority leadership to the proposition that all men are created free and equal could be decisively helpful to them in working out a way to overcome the slave system and to establish complete freedom from it in their institutions and in their hearts.

One of the most beautiful things about Abraham Lincoln's thinking during this period of his life was this; that although he was obliged to approve the taking of arms, and to justify and to carry through the killing of men in battle, never did he, under any circumstances, allow the actualities of war to alter his compassion for the people of the South or to harden him into hating them or into despising them. [...]

Not only did he persist in his compassion, he reached out his hand in loving solicitude, endeavoring to persuade them. "Brothers", he said in effect, "you have made a great mistake. You have seceded from the Union, which is precious to us all. You have taken up arms against your country in order to advance a cause which will destroy the Union. You would not have done this but for the evil influence of the system of slavery on your institutions and in your hearts. Come now, give up the slaves. I will have the government of the United States compensate you with money in full for every slave that you give up." This was the length to which compassion took him and held him until the day when he met the Captain of Eternity in a decisive way.

There came a time when the Union's cause had lost so many battles that it looked as if victory was going to be impossible. He saw, instead, that the pro-slavery armies, with the help of four and one-half million slaves, could possibly win the war, destroy the Union, and set up slavery permanently. [...] Down on his knees, he came to recognize that the hand controlling this war was not his own. [...] And on his knees Abraham Lincoln heard the Captain of Eternity and rose with a reverent determination to do it. On a day thereafter when he took his pen in hand to sign the Emancipation Proclamation which could, supported by the 13th Amendment, free all the slaves, and free the body and the soul of the South and of the Union from the curse of slavery, he found that his hand was trembling. "Wait, a moment," he is reported to have said to the man who was near him, "I am about to sign the most important paper that any man can sign in the World and my whole soul is in it. Let no trembling of my hand appear in this signature."

And so it came about that he who in all humility had seen no honorable way to deal with slavery except to halt its western progress while leaving it alone in the South—no doubt for years and years to come—now saw that God had given him the privilege to wipe it out entirely. And he did it with a heart full of gratitude and of trembling joy. [ . . . ]

With the armies moving toward victory and the people once again united, what did he do, when he came to his second inaugural address? [ . . . ]

What then did he do? His compassion was so deep and so thoughtful that instead of scorning and branding his brethren, instead of threatening and humiliating them, he put his arm around them in suffering and said, "This suffering that we are enduring together, we together have brought upon ourselves from the hands of a just God who is displeased with what both of us have done about slavery." The fact is that his compassion had deepened more than ever, for just a few days before the inaugural address he had once more sought to have his Cabinet promote a joint resolution in both Houses of Congress offering the southern States 400 million dollars in United States bonds, to be allotted among them in proportion to the property in slaves which each had lost. He saw the greatness of their suffering and his heart went out to them in their need. He wanted with all his heart to hasten their recovery, and to hasten their return to the Union. [ . . . ]

An assassin killed him. But what more could it mean to him to be physically shot down? For four long years he had been killed all the day-long by the continuing obligation to carry on a war against his brothers. For him to die was nothing. He knew all along that he was expendable and might have been killed at any time. [ . . . ] But today we all know that the Lord laid on him the iniquity of us all, that with his stripes we all were healed, and that with the four years of his dying and at length by his physical death, God redeemed this Union from slavery and purified her soul.

How beautiful upon the mountain are the feet of them that bear the glad tidings of emancipation, glad tidings of Union, but, above all, the glad tidings of a man inwardly driven by universal respect for all mankind, a man wholly committed to that Union which was "conceived in liberty and dedicated to the proposition that all men are created equal," a man masterful in sincere and simple communication of the truth, a man pure in his heart toward every individual human being with whom he came in contact, neglecting none, a man reverent of all his powers and using them up in a great Cause as if they were but wax under a lamp, a man unequivocal in his beliefs, diligent in his purposes to restrict and to overcome evil, but filled with a compassion so deep and beautiful that he always loved his very enemies.

Do you tell me that the history of the United States says that slavery was abolished and the Union was preserved by the victory of the Civil War? I tell you it is not so. There was one place in America where the slave was always free; there was one place in America where the Union was never broken—there in the heart of Abraham Lincoln. That is why we love him, black and white, North and South. That is why they love him in every Nation in the world. That is why they will love him a thousand years from today. For he was liberty. He was Union. He was freedom.

Mordecai W. Johnson Papers, Box 178–14, Manuscript Division, Moorland-Spingarn Research Center, Howard University, Washington, DC.

## CARL J. MURPHY, "Freedom Is Never a Gift," January 23, 1960

*Educated at Howard University and Harvard, Carl J. Murphy (1889–1967) succeeded his father, John Murphy Sr., as editor and publisher of the* Afro-American *in 1922. Active in the NAACP, Murphy used his newspaper to advocate for racial equality, and this experience undoubtedly influenced the following editorial. Contrary to what numerous speakers had asserted on previous Emancipation Days, the* Afro-American *opened a new decade by making it clear that rather than a gift, freedom had been earned by the sacrifices of African American soldiers who served in the Civil War. In addition to pointing out the limitations of the Emancipation Proclamation, the editorial claimed that it was only reified by the defeat of the rebellion and ratification of the Thirteenth Amendment. The implications of such an interpretation were clear, as any further advances in the freedom struggle would have to be fought for rather than received as a gift from a benefactor (AANB).*

---

When Lincoln issued the Emancipation Proclamation it was little more than a piece of paper.

It declared slavery at an end not in the North or in Maryland and Kentucky, but in the states then in rebellion against the United States.

If the North had lost the war, slavery would have continued for all the people set free by Lincoln's proclamation.

Real Emancipation came officially after the Union victory and congressional enactment of the 13th Amendment forever prohibiting slavery on American soil.

Freedom is never a gift. To be preserved it must be earned. Without the Civil War—four years of bloody strife—American slavery could not have been ended for all time.

Historians are prone to treat it lightly, but it is a fact, confirmed by official War Department records, that more than 200,000 of our ancestors fought for our freedom and the Union.

Of these, 68,178, or more than one-third gave their lives in the struggle for liberty, a higher percentage of casualties than any other recruits in the war. [...]

With these figures etched clearly in mind, it is difficult for us to ever think of Lincoln's proclamation of freedom for the slaves without the overshadowing remembrance of our fighting and dying in the Virginia wilderness, at [Chaffin's] Farm, at Fort Pillow, the Crater, Petersburg and the distinguished leadership of Grant and Sherman, Hunter, Howard, Butler, Higginson and Farragut.

For the first time many of us had a flag and a uniform and clothed with these we made Lincoln's piece of paper a living document.

Editorial in the *Afro-American* (Baltimore), Jan. 23, 1960.

## JACKIE ROBINSON, "Kennedy Not Another Lincoln," June 9, 1962

*The first Black Major League baseball player in the twentieth century, Robinson (1919–1972), was active in the civil rights movement throughout his life and was also heavily involved in politics as a supporter of the Republican Party. As a Republican, Robinson sought to keep the party firmly anchored to its Lincoln connection. Here he makes it clear that President John Kennedy did not measure up to Lincoln. Referring to the request Dr. Martin Luther King Jr. and the Southern Christian Leadership Conference (SCLC) made of Kennedy for a type of second Emancipation Proclamation which would abolish racial segregation, Robinson laments no such statement will be forthcoming.*

You may have read that, on May 17, the anniversary of the United States Supreme Court decision outlawing segregation in schools, President Kennedy received a petition signed by a group of prominent Americans. The petition asked the Chief Executive to issue an executive order on the basis of the Fourteenth Amendment to the Constitution, a sort of second Emancipation Proclamation. This Executive Order would outlaw all forms of racial segregation throughout the fifty states of the Nation.

The request made to the President was initiated by Dr. Martin Luther King and the Southern Christian Leadership Conference. Not only some [of] the most outstanding Negro leaders signed the original petition but also some noted white Americans who have proven over the years that they are on the side of equal justice—people like Mrs. Roosevelt.

We were honored to be asked by Dr. King and the SCLC to become one of the initiators of this petition, and, of course, we promptly agreed.

We agreed because we are in sympathy with the feeling that the President of the United States ought to have the courage and the integrity to rise above politics and reach the level of statesmanship. He should recognize that the United States has no right to pretend to be the leader of world democracy abroad until we straighten out at home some of the terrible violations of democracy and decency which occur.

We do not believe, however, that President Kennedy will sign such an executive order.

We give Dr. Martin King and SCLC credit for a valiant try. But we do not believe Dr. King himself believes that the President will sign such a sweeping executive order.

In Harlem, only a few evenings back, Dr. King spoke with his usual eloquence at a banquet in his honor. Dr. King noted that Mr. Kennedy the candidate, had promised to sign an executive order outlawing discrimination in housing—but that Mr. Kennedy, the President, now refuses to sign it until he believes it is "in the best interests of the country."

Dr. King knows, as the whole country knows, that Mr. Kennedy's real reason for evading this issue is that he is afraid of offending Southern politicians.

Dr. King declared in Harlem that "President Kennedy owes it to the nation to immediately sign an executive order banning discrimination in housing. He owes it to his own moral convictions and to the God he worships."

Further, Dr. King declared, should the President fail to do this, he is "betraying the cause of justice and his own campaign promises."

With President Kennedy refusing to keep a promise to outlaw discrimination in one area, housing, we have little [to] hope for in expecting him to sign an executive order outlawing all forms of discrimination.

We have received quite a few congratulatory comments on our recent column in which we asked the President why he couldn't get as angry in the interest of civil rights as he got in the steel situation.

The only time we recall the President getting mad about civil rights was when he showed a flare of temper because a reporter asked him if he was intending to keep his campaign promise by signing the anti-bias housing bill.

Don't get us wrong. We believe the President is a decent man, a man truly concerned about the race issue. We don't think, however, he has the courage of his convictions. If he would only keep his promises, stop worrying about Dixie and start backing up the sincere efforts of his brother, the Attorney General, we'd probably make a lot more progress.

Dr. King, in his appeal for a second Emancipation Proclamation, refers to the fact that Abraham Lincoln brought physical freedom of the Negro into being by a stroke of the pen.

If Mr. Kennedy does the same in the area of the Negro's total freedom it will be the biggest surprise of our life.

We think the President is a fine man, like we said.

But an Abraham Lincoln—he ain't.

*Chicago Defender,* June 9, 1962.

## MARTIN LUTHER KING JR., Draft of an Address to Commemorate Centennial of the Emancipation Proclamation at the Park Sheraton Hotel, New York, New York, September 12, 1962

*Though most have images of Dr. King (1929–1968) standing before the Lincoln Memorial and delivering his famous "I Have a Dream" speech during the 1963 March on Washington, few are aware of his speech the preceding September delivered at a centennial celebration of the Emancipation Proclamation in New York, where he spoke at the invitation of Governor Nelson Rockefeller. King indicated that the Declaration of Independence and the Emancipation Proclamation testify to the greatness of American civilization. Acknowledging that the challenges and setbacks this country has faced cannot obliterate the enduring impact of the proclamation, King saw no opportunism in Lincoln, though he admitted Lincoln vacillated before finally issuing the document. The proclamation redeemed the promise of the Declaration and contributed to Black self-emancipation, yet King also anticipated a theme he would address in his remarks before the Lincoln Memorial the following August when he urged that the most appropriate way to honor Lincoln and the centennial of the proclamation was for the entire nation to fully realize the promise of freedom.*

---

Mankind through the ages has been in a ceaseless struggle to give dignity and meaning to human life. It is that quest which separates it from the animal, whose biological functions and anatomical features resemble aspects of the human specie[s].

If our nation had done nothing more in its whole history than to create just two documents, its contribution to civilization would be imperishable. The first of these documents is the Declaration of Independence and the other is that which we are here today to honor, the Emancipation Proclamation. All tyrants, past, present and future, are powerless to bury the truths in these declarations, no matter how extensive their legions, how vast their power and how malignant their evil.

The Declaration of Independence proclaimed to a world, organized politically and spiritually around the concept of the <u>inequality</u> of man, that the liberty and dignity of human personality were inherent in man as a living being that he, himself, could not create a society which could last if it alienated freedom from man. The Emancipation Proclamation was the offspring of the Declaration of Independence using the forces of law to uproot a social order which sought to separate liberty from a segment of humanity. The principle of equality on which the nation was founded had to be reaffirmed in the flames of a scorching war until rededication to liberty was once again recorded in the Emancipation Proclamation.

Our pride and our progress could be unqualified if the story might end here. But history reveals that these documents were each to live lives of stormy contradictions, to be both observed and violated through social upheavals and spiritual disasters.

If we look at our history with honesty and clarity we will be forced to admit that our Federal form of government has been, from the day of its birth, weakened in its integrity, confused and confounded in its direction, by the unresolved race question. [...]

Our nation has experienced a ceaseless rebellion against the Declaration of Independence, the Constitution, the Emancipation Proclamation and the Supreme Court by one region. In the Revolutionary War powerful slave elements in the south fought with the British. The development of the nation to the west was complicated and hindered by the slave power, and only the holocaust of war settled the direction and character of our growth. But the rebellion against equality continued into the second half of the 19th century and into the 20th century, diminishing the authority of the Federal government and corroding its authority. It has contaminated every institution in our society in every year of our existence. Still today that single region of our country holds a veto power over the majority of the nation, nullifying basic constitutional rights, and in the exercise of its illegal conduct, retarding our growth. The south in walling itself off from the application of laws and judicial decrees behind an iron curtain of defiance, becomes a law unto itself. It is an autonomous region whose posture toward the central government has elements as defiant as a hostile nation. Only the undeveloped or primitive nations of the world tolerate regions which are similar, in which feudal autocrats or military governors have supremacy over the Federal power. It is a condition unknown to modern industrial societies except for our own. This is the source of the scorn expressed by African and Asian states when we lecture them on government while our own suffers from a glaring defect of sovereignty.

The unresolved race question is a pathological infection in our social and political anatomy, which has sickened us throughout our history. [...]

The imposition of inferiority externally and internally are the slave chains of today. What the Emancipation Proclamation proscribed in a legal and formal sense has never been eliminated in human terms. By burning in the consciousness of white Americans a conviction that Negroes are by nature subnormal, much of the myth was absorbed by the Negro himself, stultifying his energy, his ambition and his self-respect. The Proclamation of Inferiority has contended with the Proclamation of Emancipation, negating its liberating force. Inferiority has justified the low living standards of the Negro, sanctioned his separation from the majority culture, and enslaved him physically and psychologically. Inferiority as a fetter is more subtle and sophisticated than iron chains; it is invisible and its victim helps to fashion his own bonds.

Inequality before the law is so pervasive in the life of the Negro its detailing is impossible. We boast that ours is a government of laws, but every Negro knows a thousand examples in which law and government do not protect him. In the past weeks Christian churches were bombed or burned in a single community in Georgia. If a government building were bombed in Washington the perpetrators would be shot down in the streets. But if violence affects a Negro church, not all the agencies of government can find or convict the arsonists.

This is the essential texture of freedom and equality for the Negro one hundred years after the Emancipation Proclamation; and one hundred and eighty-six years after the Declaration of Independence.

This sombre picture may induce the sober thought that there is nothing to commemorate about the centennial of the Emancipation Proclamation. But tragic disappointments and undeserved defeats do not put an end to life, nor do they wipe out the positive, however submerged it may have become beneath floods of negative experience.

The Emancipation Proclamation had four enduring results. First, it gave force to the executive power to change conditions in the national interest on a broad and far-reaching scale. Second, it dealt a devastating blow to a system of slave-holding and an economy based upon it, which had been muscular enough to engage in warfare on the Federal government. It forced a change in which the area of maneuver enemies of the Constitution might deploy, was limited. Third, it enabled the Negro to play a significant role in his own liberation with the ability to organize and to struggle, with less of the bestial retaliation his slave status had permitted to his masters. Fourth, it resurrected and restated the principle of equality upon which the founding of the nation rested.

When Abraham Lincoln signed the Emancipation Proclamation it was not the act of an opportunistic politician issuing a hollow pronouncement to placate a pressure group.

Our truly great presidents were tortured deep in their hearts by the race question. Jefferson with keen perception saw that the immorality of slavery degraded the w[h]ite master with the Negro. He feared for the future of white children who were taught a false supremacy. His concern can be summed up in one quotation, "I tremble for my country when I reflect that God is just."

Lincoln's torments are well known, his vacillations were facts. In the seething cauldron of '62 and '63 Lincoln was called the "Baboon President" in the north, and "coward", assassin, savage, murderer of women and babies, and Lincoln the Fiend in the South. Yet he searched his way to the conclusions embodied in these words, "In giving freedom to the slave we assure freedom to the free, honorable alike in what we give and what we preserve." On this moral foundation he personally prepared the first draft of the Emancipation Proclamation, and to emphasize the decisiveness of his course he called his cabinet together and declared he was not seeking their advice as to its wisdom but only suggestions on subject matter. Lincoln achieved immortality because he issued the Emancipation Proclamation. His hesitation had not stayed his hand when historic necessity charted but one course. No President can be great, or even fit for office, if he attempts to accommodate to injustice to maintain his political balance.

The Emancipation Proclamation shattered in one blow the slave system, undermining the foundations of the economy of the rebellious south; and guaranteed that no slave-holding class, if permitted to exist in defeat, could prepare a new and deadlier war after resus[c]itation.

The Proclamation opened the door to self-liberation by the Negro upon which he immediately acted by deserting the plantations in the south and joining the Union armies in the north. [...] Beyond the war years the grim and tortured struggle of Negroes to win their own freedom is an epic of battle against frightful odds. If we have failed to do enough, it was not the will for freedom that was weak, but the forces against us which were too strong. It is significant in this connection that all our efforts from the Reconstruction onward to this morning's daily paper, the reporting and historical interpretation of our actions suffer the grossest corruption of truth. American historiography itself has been a victim of the unresolved race question and is yet to be purged of error if it is to be scientific history. [...]

We have spelled out a balance sheet of the Emancipation Proclamation, its contributions and its deficiencies which our lack of zeal permitted to find expression.

There is but one way to commemorate the Emancipation Proclamation. That is to make its declaration of freedom real; to reach back to the origins of our nation when our message of equality electrified an unfree world, and reaffirm democracy by deeds as bold and daring as the issuance of the Emancipation Proclamation. [...]

The Negro will never cease his struggle to commemorate the Emancipation Proclamation by making his emancipation real. If enough Americans in numbers and influence join him, the nation we both labored to build may yet realize its glorious dream.

There is too much greatness in our heritage to tolerate the pettiness of race hate. The Declaration of Independence and the Emancipation Proclamation deserve to live in sacred honor; many generations of Americans suffered, bled and died, confident that those who followed them would preserve the purity of our ideals. Negroes have declared they will die if need be for these freedoms, and many have, even in months just past. All Americans must enlist in a crusade finally to make the race question an ugly relic of a dark past. When the whole scope of American liberties encompasses this freedom then will the Emancipation Proclamation truly be commemorated in luminous glory and truth.

Originally viewed as a typescript, the King Center Digital Archive; see also "Address of the Reverend Dr. Martin Luther King," New York State Archives Partnership Trust, https:// www.nysarchivestrust.org/education/consider-source/browse-primary-source -documents/post-war-united-states/address-reverend-dr-martin-luther-king-jr.

## THURGOOD MARSHALL, Remarks on Commemoration of the Centennial of the Preliminary Emancipation Proclamation at the Lincoln Memorial, Washington, DC, September 22, 1962

*Commemoration of the centennial of the American Civil War was complicated by coinciding with the modern civil rights movement, or Second Reconstruction. Congress had created the Civil War Centennial Commission (CWCC) to organize commemorative events, yet much like the original intent of the Lincoln Memorial in Washington, the CWCC preferred a message that emphasized national unity rather than one that connected the centennial of the Emancipation Proclamation to the ongoing freedom struggle. The event to mark the one hundredth anniversary of Lincoln's Preliminary Emancipation Proclamation, held at the Lincoln Memorial, was a microcosm of these difficulties. The CWCC believed it had secured President Kennedy as the featured speaker, yet Kennedy backed out shortly before the ceremony, and some believed he did so for fear of alienating Southern Democrats. While Mahalia Jackson had been engaged to sing, civil rights leaders threatened to boycott the event when they learned no African American had been invited to speak. Thurgood Marshall (1908–1993), well known for his work with the NAACP, and recently appointed a judge to the US Court of Appeals, accepted an invitation to speak on very short notice. Although Marshall made no direct assessment of Lincoln in his speech, he was nonetheless clear regarding the importance of the Emancipation Proclamation. Marshall maintained its purpose was both to free the enslaved and provide them rights enjoyed by others. He reminded the audience it was their responsibility to support equal rights for all, as the Proclamation was the clearest expression of the Judeo-Christian ethic to protect human rights. In addition to Marshall, Adlai Stevenson, Nelson Rockefeller, and the poet Archibald MacLeish delivered remarks at the occasion, while President Kennedy recorded a message that was played during the event. The commemoration was broadcast on television, yet the sparse crowd in attendance was attributed to lack of enthusiasm from the African American community due to the failure to initially invite a Black speaker. To diminish such controversies in the future, the Kennedy administration sought to shift the responsibility of commemorating the centennial of the Emancipation Proclamation to the US Civil Rights Commission, but Congress did not appropriate funding for this purpose. However, the Civil Rights Commission was involved with an exhibit on the Emancipation Proclamation that opened at the National Archives in January 1963 (see Charles Wesley's remarks below). In 1967, Marshall became the US Supreme Court's first African American justice (Robert J. Cook,* Troubled Commemoration: The American Civil War Centennial, 1961–1965 *[Baton Rouge: Louisiana State University Press, 2007]; "Emancipation Program Attracts Only 3,000,"* Afro-American *[Baltimore, MD], Sept. 29, 1962; "Sharp Criticism Is 'Background Music' for Opening of Emancipation Exhibit,"* Afro-American *[Baltimore, MD], Jan. 19, 1963).*

---

It is an extreme privilege to participate in this commemoration of the 100th anniversary of the Emancipation Proclamation. This proclamation must be regarded as one of the historical documents basic to the protection of our human rights. We can all recite from memory sections of the Declaration of Independence, especially the phrase, "we hold these truths to be self-evident, that all men are created equal." Each year we pay honor to Bill of Rights Day in recognition of our Government's determination to protect the individual from Federal governmental tyranny. As a former justice of our Supreme Court stated:

"The very purpose of a Bill of Rights was to withdraw certain subjects from the vicissitudes of political controversy, to place them beyond the reach of majorities and officials and to establish them as legal principles to be applied by the courts."

The important purpose of the Declaration of Independence was carried forward by the Emancipation Proclamation.

The underlying purpose of that document was to not only free the slaves but also to give them the rights already enjoyed by all others. However, after the Civil War our Government found that this could only be accomplished by amendments to the Constitution. Thus, we added the 13th, 14th, and 15th amendments to our basic documents for the protection of human rights. These documents have been termed efforts toward codification of the Judeo-Christian ethic. The

Emancipation Proclamation is certainly the clearest expression of this doctrine. Indeed, the 13th, 14th, and 15th amendments carrying this principle over into enforcible constitutional law have been characterized by our Supreme Court as follows:

> "One great purpose of these amendments was to raise the colored race from that condition of inferiority and servitude in which most of them had previously stood into perfect equality of civil rights with all other persons within the jurisdiction of the States."

While the enforcement of the Civil War amendments as other constitutional provisions must remain with the courts, the realization of the equalitarian principles of the Emancipation Proclamation is the responsibility of all. We must, therefore, re-dedicate ourselves to the determination to recognize every American on his merit without regard to race, color, or previous condition of servitude.

*Congressional Record*, Oct. 1, 1962, 21580.

## EDITH SAMPSON, Address on the Emancipation Proclamation, circa 1962–1963

*A native of Pennsylvania, Sampson (1901–1979) graduated from the New York School of Social Work and Loyola University Law School. She practiced law in Chicago, worked as a state's attorney, became involved in the civil rights movement, served as a representative to the United Nations, and was a representative of the State Department overseas. A municipal judge in Chicago from 1962 until her retirement in 1978, Sampson served as secretary of the American Negro Emancipation Commission that the Illinois General Assembly created for the purpose of organizing events to mark the centennial of the Emancipation Proclamation. As part of her work on the commission, Sampson gave a series of speeches in 1962 and 1963. The following undated address was prepared for these occasions. Sampson provides a sobering consideration of the Emancipation Proclamation and places it in an international context. Though she says Lincoln's language in the Proclamation was dry, if not prosaic, and is clear regarding its limitations, she argues that its spirit was most important. That spirit of freedom resonated abroad, as she reminds her audience in the midst of the Cold War struggle against the Soviet Union and amidst the often self-congratulatory commemorations of the Civil War centennial, that Americans must do their utmost to act in a way that fulfills the promise of freedom in Lincoln's proclamation (AANB).*

Of all the keystone documents in our American tradition, none is so forbid-dingly stiff or legalistically narrow as the Emancipation Proclamation. In a formal, official language remote from the stirring cadences of his Gettysburg Address, Abraham Lincoln wrote:

"... as a fit and necessary military measure ... I, as Commander-in-Chief of the Army and Navy of the United States, do order and declare that on the first day of January in the year of Our Lord one thousand, eight hundred and sixty-three, all persons held as slaves within any state or states, wherein the constitutional authority of the United States shall not then be practically recognized, submitted to and maintained, shall then, thenceforward and forever, be free."

This limited writ did not even run to all of the states of the embattled Union. Maryland, Missouri, Kentucky, Delaware—in each the peculiar institution of slavery was endorsed by law, yet they were not affected by the letter of the proc-lamation because they were not then in rebellion.

And yet from the very start it was not the letter of the proclamation that mat-tered; it was the spirit of it, the spirit alone, that counted.

And from the very start the impact of that spirit was felt abroad just as it was at home.

England had wavered for months on the brink of recognizing and giving overt aid to the South, toward which she looked for cotton. But with the issuance of the Emancipation Proclamation, the Confederacy's last hope for British assistance was lost.

The British, who had long since abolished slavery in their own territory, might have justified support of the South if the North had kept insisting that only union, not slavery, was the issue of the Civil War. Once slavery was the open issue, though, as it had been the implicit one from the beginning, Britain's course was firmly settled. The rebellion was doomed.

I think we do well, this hundred years after, to remember that others overseas read the Emancipation Proclamation with intense interest, over our national shoulder, when first it was issued.

They have been reading it just so in the century since—and increasingly they have judged us on the degree and the quality of our adherence to the principles that brightly underlie its stiff and colorless words.

True enough, there are other nations even now that still tolerate slavery as an established institution. But these cannot be judged so strictly as we are, for they do not also have—as we most emphatically do—the professions of a dedication to liberty and equality written large in their national histories.

We said it once, openly, defiantly, in the Declaration of Independence: "We hold these truths to be self-evident—that all mean are created equal; that they are endowed by their Creator with certain unalienable rights; that among these are life, liberty, and the pursuit of happiness."

We said it over again, obliquely but still firmly, in the ringing central phrase of the Emancipation Proclamation: " . . . all persons held as slaves . . . shall then, thenceforward and forever be free."

What an immense word that is—free! Free from bondage, free from all shackles, physical, social, political, economic.

We cannot now afford to do less than live up to the fullest, richest implications of our commitment to freedom—freedom for all, without distinction or discrimination. Particularly, we cannot afford to do so in light of the accelerating revolution of rising expectations among the new nations of the world.

We would like to have those new nations as our friends. We would like for them to choose the democratic heritage of the West rather than the regimented heritage of an East that has done no more than substitute commissars for Czars.

But we must be mindful that they do not measure us only by the words we have set down in the national documents. They measure us, rather, by the ways in which we have—or in some cases have not—put those words to work.

We have come a tremendously long way in the hundred years since emancipation was proclaimed. Perhaps never before has a people made such giant strides forward as the American Negro has been able to make in the sometimes painful course of that century.

But we still have a tremendously long way to go toward complete fulfillment of the ideal of true liberty that animated the proclamation.

It is good that we should recall, on this occasion, the great progress that has been made. It will be even better if we also rededicate ourselves to the formidable task of further progress.

The eyes of the whole world are upon us, and the ears of the whole world hear what we have said—"shall then, thenceforward and forever be free." We dare not give less than our unstinting best.

Edith Sampson Papers, Folder 266, Schlesinger Library, Harvard University.

## BENJAMIN QUARLES, *Lincoln and the Negro*, 1962

*A native of Boston, Quarles (1904–1996) was educated at Shaw University and the University of Wisconsin, where he earned a PhD in history. A prolific scholar, who published several notable books over the span of more than forty years, Quarles spent much of his academic career at Morgan State University. His 1962 volume on Lincoln set the tone for future historians who grappled with Lincoln's ambivalence in his attitudes and policies toward African Americans. Acknowledging Lincoln's "masterly inactivity" on sensitive issues, Quarles contends that Lincoln personally abhorred slavery, yet had a greater commitment to the preservation of the Union and initially preferred gradual, compensated emancipation coupled with colonization. Quarles suggests that Blacks realized before Lincoln the possibilities and necessity of an emancipation proclamation, and in issuing it, Lincoln became a hero, father, and messiah for many. According to Quarles, African Americans played a vital role in creating a Lincoln image that helped shape the national popular perception of the Great Emancipator. In short, Lincoln became Lincoln because of Black people (AANB).*

———————

To the mass of Negroes, Lincoln had passed from history to legend even before Booth's bullet. The flesh-and-blood Lincoln paled before this legendary figure—a figure who came alive in the hopes and aspirations of colored Americans. "My mother used to talk much of Abraham Lincoln," wrote school Principal Joseph L. Wiley: "Though she had never seen him, she talked as if she had."

His Negro admirers are not to be blamed if they did not see Lincoln in the round—few people did, in his day or afterward. It is not so much that Negroes saw only one aspect of Lincoln's character as it was that, as a rule, only one aspect of Lincoln's complex and many-sided character ever seemed to present itself to an observer. To those who held communion with him, Lincoln, like nature, spoke a various language.

The Negro mirrors America, and his concept of the folklore Lincoln was a part of the general pattern. For Abraham Lincoln was destined for the number one spot in America's gallery of heroes. "We all know Lincoln by heart," said Frederick Douglass, a Negro contemporary. And, in a sense that Douglass would not have ruled out, that is how the American rank and file came to know Lincoln—by heart rather than by mind. He became a symbol, and hence a product of something more than memory alone.

If people's evaluation of Lincoln tended to be uncritical, it was not unimportant. Americans are the sum of the influences brought to bear upon them, and one of these influences has been the pervasive spirit of this towering figure who "came out of the wilderness, down in Illinois." In him, Americans realize themselves. He lives because he was a man the people loved. No other group symbolizes this deep affection as do colored Americans. They have not bothered to claim any superior devotion to his memory, yet it is a matter of historical record that they loved him first and have loved him longest.

In fine, Lincoln became Lincoln because of the Negro, and it was the latter who first reflected the image of the Lincoln that was to live. [ . . . ]

This lack of a clear-cut presidential policy was the result of design. On questions relating to the Southern Negro, Lincoln deliberately took his time. Tomorrow was good enough for him. His "make haste slowly" policy on Negro matters had various roots, among them his own mental make-up and his political sensitivity to public opinion.

To have congratulated Lincoln on never being rash would perhaps have brought him more inner pleasure than most compliments. Lincoln was not a man to act until after much winnowing and sifting, until he had taken time to view a question from all sides. He knew that in public life a reflective man was often considered weak-willed, but this risk he was prepared to run.

On matters relating to the Negro, Lincoln appeared to be slow because he was not an extremist. Essentially he was a man of the middle way, a moderate, one might almost say an extreme moderate. Lincoln thought of himself as an agent of reconciliation, an executive whose true function was to bring together conflicting parties in the hope that they could reach a common ground. Lincoln made policy only when other actions were exhausted.

The Lincoln of the White House years had deep convictions about the wrongness of slavery. But as Chief Magistrate he made a sharp distinction between his personal beliefs and his official actions. Whatever was constitutional he must support regardless of his private feelings. If the states, under the rights reserved to them, persisted in clinging to practices that he regarded as outmoded, he had no right to interfere. His job was to uphold the Constitution, not to impose his own standards of public morality.

As a constitutionalist Lincoln was dedicated to the preservation of the Union. [...] He was determined that the American experiment in democracy must not fail, and that such a government by the people "can long endure."

Lincoln's behavior on Negro questions not only was a product of his temperament but also reflected his sensitivity to public opinion. Lincoln always had his ear to the ground, trying to sense the mood of America, the things for which men would fight and die. [...]

Lincoln's habitual caution was reinforced by his belief that the nation's security was endangered by too early action on matters relating to the Negro. Looming large in Lincoln's thinking were the slaveholding states on the side of the North. These border states of Missouri, Kentucky, Maryland, and Delaware would fight to restore the Union. But as for slavery, they wanted it left alone, and they would almost rather lay down their arms than see it done away with. [...]

Kentucky-born Lincoln was aware of the attitude of the whites in the border states. He knew that to them it was an article of faith that any change in the status of the Negro would bring in its train all kinds of calamity. Lincoln knew that slaveholding communities lived in fear of the servile population running amok, and that in wartime the horrors of slave insurrection would become especially vivid. Lincoln did not want the border states to become alarmed about the loss or the behavior of their bondmen. Such fears might impel these states to join the Confederacy, and thus prolong the war.

This would never happen if Lincoln could prevent it. "I think to lose Kentucky is nearly the same as to lose the whole game," wrote he to Illinois Senator Orville H. Browning. [...]

In coping with an unfriendly attitude toward the Negro, Lincoln's difficulties were not limited to border-state inhabitants. In the large Northern cities the foreign-born, particularly the Irish-Americans and the German-Americans, lived in fear that the slaves, if freed, would leave the South and flood the manpower market with cheap black labor. In the Midwestern states there was a sizable number of immigrants from the Southern states, people who had brought with them the conviction that to be a Negro was to carry an inborn defect of race. To such persons any attempt to upgrade the Negro was contrary to the best interests of all concerned, including the black man himself.

In moving slowly on the Negro question, Lincoln was also influenced by his friendly feeling for the people of the Confederacy. He believed that many of them were really loyal to the Union, but that they had permitted themselves to be carried into the war. To free the Negro would be to punish these many well-intentioned Southerners whose only fault was a temporary lapse of judgment. Lincoln's sympathetic attitude toward the people below the Potomac, loyal or otherwise, made him hesitate to take any step that would widen the breach between the North and the South. If Lincoln hated slavery, he did not hate slaveowners; if he condemned the former, he refrained from abusing the latter. He wanted the South to free its slaves, but he felt that people outside the South should urge the measure "persuasively, and not menacingly."

Lincoln made no fetish of consistency. Hence his policy of "masterly inactivity" on Negro questions, like all of his policies, was subject to change. The influences that prompted him to go slow ran head on into counter influences. And as the war entered its second year, these forces for change began to gain strength and momentum.

Loudest of the voices for changing the status of the Negro were those of the abolitionists. In private life Lincoln had carefully side-stepped contacts with anti-slavery zealots, never even taking part in their war of words. [...]

Lincoln knew that these men of the Garrison-Phillips stripe had deep convictions about human brotherhood, and that they had no political favors to beg. But he also viewed them as men whose zeal outran their judgment. In running the country, as Lincoln knew, the give-and-take of compromise was essential. But to the reformer, compromise was a sin. Daily the Lincoln of the White House had to make choices between unpleasant alternatives. Perfectionism could be practiced only by men not burdened with the responsibilities of getting things done in government.

Ignoring the practical considerations that influenced Lincoln's course of action, the Negro and his friends besought the President to get on the freedom track. God's timetable, said Harriet Tubman, was faster than Lincoln's, and she predicted that "God won't let Massa Linkum beat de South till he do de right ting." [...]

The coolness of the border states toward compensated emancipation was particularly grievous to Lincoln, because it threw cold water on his other pet plan for the Negroes—to send them out of the country. Lincoln's plan of compensated emancipation rested on the assumption that the liberated slaves would not remain in America. It was not his intention to swell the free Negro population. In Lincoln's thinking, compensated emancipation was doomed unless it could be tied in with deportation. Such a tie-in was necessary to quiet the fears of the people in the North that their states would be "Africanized"—swamped by Negroes made free by the war.

Lincoln held the strong belief that colonization would accomplish a dual purpose: rid the South of human bondage and rid the country of the colored man. Slavery and the race problem would thus vanish simultaneously.

Lincoln's belief in Negro deportation was rooted in his reverence for Thomas Jefferson and his deep admiration for Henry Clay both of whom held similar views. The Lincoln of the 1850's had come to believe that it was to "our national interest to transfer the African to his native clime." He admitted that the task would not be easy, but he held that what colonization needed most was "a hearty will." [. . .]

Negroes could give themselves fully to glorifying the Emancipation Proclamation because they did not view it in the round. They had their own authorized version of the Lincoln Testament, and it could be summed up in the scriptural phrase "Out of the house of bondage." Focusing their thoughts on the proclamation's antislavery side, most Negroes ignored its other aspects. Had these Negroes read the document, they would have known that it was only a declaration, and that it applied only to those areas in rebellion, excluding Tennessee. Readers of the proclamation would have noted that Lincoln, ever highly fearful of slave insurrections, had urged Negroes to abstain from violence except in self-defense. On the more positive side, the proclamation expressed Lincoln's intention to enlist former slaves into the armed services. [. . .]

The esteem that Negroes had for the Emancipation Proclamation helped to make it one of the most far-reaching pronouncements ever issued in the United States. Negroes were instrumental in creating the image of the proclamation that was to become the historic image. For in its own day Lincoln's edict was destined to reflect the luster and take on the evocative power reserved only for the half-dozen great charter expressions of human liberty in the entire Western tradition. The proclamation soon assumed the role that Negroes had given it at the outset, and became to millions a fresh expression of one of man's loftiest aspirations—the quest for freedom. [. . .]

True enough, Lincoln had originally conceived of the proclamation as a measure for the self-preservation, rather than for the regeneration, of America. But the proclamation, almost in spite of its creator, changed the whole tone and character of the war. Negroes sensed this more quickly than did Lincoln. Long before he had ever dreamed of issuing an edict of freedom, Negroes had been hoping and praying for such a measure. Just as they were in advance of Lincoln in the time set for the proclamation, so they were in advance of him in a realization of the proclamation's broad implications for freedom in America. [...]

To some Negroes, Lincoln was the word made flesh. [...] The attitude of the Negro toward Lincoln had varied roots, among them hero worship, father image, and messianic deliverer. But whatever its origins, this high opinion of Lincoln gave to the Negro one inestimable boon—the feeling that he had a stake in America. And as the war moved toward its close, the Negro's sense of identity with the land of his birth grew deeper, nourished anew by its source—Abraham Lincoln. [...]

Lincoln was ever a growing man, but he did not fully perceive the role of the ballot as a source of protection for the former slave. What he did sense was that the South was not ready for Negro suffrage. He was almost equally sure that most of the people in the North had the same reluctance to give the ballot to the black man. Lincoln did not feel like compelling the South to do something that the North also had not got around to doing. [...] So great was Lincoln's popularity among the Negro rank and file that it was hardly affected by his go-slow policy on equal suffrage.

Benjamin Quarles, *Lincoln and the Negro* (New York: Oxford University Press, 1962), unpaginated foreword, 82–86, 108, 148, 150, 210, 230.

## JOHN HOPE FRANKLIN, *The Emancipation Proclamation*, 1963

*A native of Oklahoma, Franklin (1915–2009) was educated at Fisk University and Harvard, where he obtained a PhD in history. Franklin began his teaching career at historically Black colleges before accepting a position as chair of the history department at Brooklyn College. He later held positions at the University of Chicago and Duke University. One of the most accomplished historians of the twentieth century, Franklin published numerous books and articles, including a survey of African American history that became a standard in college classrooms. His 1963 work on the Emancipation Proclamation, published to coincide with the centennial of the document, argues that the proclamation is known well as a war measure, slippery as a measure of principle, and neglected as a document of freedom (AANB).*

The character of the Civil War could not possibly have been the same after the President issued the Emancipation Proclamation as it had been before January 1, 1863. During the first twenty months of the war, no one had been more careful than Lincoln himself to define the war as one merely to save the Union. He did this not only because such a definition greatly simplified the struggle and kept the border states fairly loyal, but also because he deeply felt that this was the only legitimate basis for prosecuting the war. When, therefore, he told Horace Greeley that if he could save the Union without freeing a single slave he made the clearest possible statement of his fundamental position. [. . .]

Lincoln saw no contradiction between the contents of his reply to Greeley and the contents of the Emancipation Proclamation. For he had come to the conclusion that in order to save the Union he must emancipate *some* of the slaves. His critics were correct in suggesting that the Proclamation was a rather frantic measure, an act of last resort. By Lincoln's own admission it was, indeed, a desperate act; for the prospects of Union success were not bright. [. . .]

The language of the Proclamation revealed no significant modification of the aims of the war. Nothing was clearer than the fact that Lincoln was taking the action under his authority as "Commander-in-Chief of the Army and Navy." The situation that caused him to take the action was that there was an "actual armed rebellion against the authority and government of the United States." He regarded the Emancipation Proclamation, therefore, as "a fit and necessary war measure for suppressing said rebellion." In another place in the Proclamation he called on the military and naval authorities to recognize and maintain the freedom of the slaves. Finally the President declared, in the final paragraph of the Proclamation, that the measure was "warranted by the Constitution upon military necessity." This was, indeed, a war measure, conceived and promulgated to put down the rebellion and save the Union. [. . .]

Despite the fact that the President laid great stress on the issuance of the Proclamation as a military necessity, he did not entirely overlook the moral and humanitarian significance of the measure. And even in the document itself he gave some indication of his appreciation of the particular dimension that was, in time, to eclipse many other considerations. He said that the emancipation of the slaves was "sincerely believed to be an act of justice." This conception of emancipation could hardly be confined to the slaves in states or parts of states that were in rebellion against the United States on January 1, 1863. It must be recalled, moreover, that in the same sentence that he referred to emancipation as an "act of justice" he invoked the "considerate judgment of mankind and the gracious favor of Almighty God." This raised the Proclamation above the level of just another measure for the effective prosecution of the war. And, in turn, the war became more than a war to save the integrity and independence of the Union. It became also a war to promote the freedom of mankind.

Throughout the previous year the President had held to the view that Negroes should be colonized in some other part of the world. And he advanced this view with great vigor wherever and whenever possible. He pressed the Cabinet and Congress to accept and implement his colonization views, and he urged Negroes to realize that it was best for all concerned that they should leave the United States. It is not without significance that Lincoln omitted from the Emancipation Proclamation any reference to colonization. It seems clear that the President had abandoned hope of gaining support for his scheme or of persuading Negroes to leave the only home they knew. Surely, moreover, it would have been a most incongruous policy as well as an ungracious act to have asked Negroes to perform one of the highest acts of citizenship—fighting for their country—and then invite them to leave. Thus, by inviting Negroes into the armed services and omitting all mention of colonization, the President indicated in the Proclamation that Negroes would enjoy a status that went beyond mere freedom. They were to be free persons, fighting for their *own* country, a country in which they were to be permitted to remain.

The impact of the Proclamation on slavery and Negroes was profound. Negroes looked upon it as a document of freedom, and they made no clear distinction between the areas affected by the Proclamation and those not affected by it. One has the feeling that the interest of the contrabands in Washington in seeing whether their home counties were excepted or included in the Proclamation was an academic interest so far as their own freedom was concerned. After all, they had proclaimed their own freedom and had put themselves beyond the force of the slave law or their masters. [...]

Slavery, in or out of the Confederacy, could not possibly have survived the Emancipation Proclamation. Slaves themselves, already restive under their yoke and walking off the plantation in many places, were greatly encouraged upon learning that Lincoln wanted them to be free. They proceeded to oblige him. [...]

Lincoln hoped that the proclamation would provide the basis for a new attitude and policy for Negroes. That all slaves would soon be free was a reality that all white men should face. "Those who shall have tasted actual freedom I believe can never be slaves, or quasi slaves again." He hoped, therefore, that the several states would adopt some practical system "by which the two races could gradually live themselves out of their old relation to each other, and both come out better prepared for the new." He hoped that states would provide for the education of Negroes, and he went so far as to suggest to Governor Michael Hahn of Louisiana that his state might consider extending the franchise to free Negroes of education and property.

Thus, in many ways the Proclamation affected the course of the war as well as Lincoln's way of thinking about the problem of Negroes in the United States. Abroad, it rallied large numbers of people to the North's side and became a valuable instrument of American foreign policy. At home it sharpened the issues of the war and provided a moral and humanitarian ingredient that had been lacking. It fired the leaders with a new purpose and gave to the President a new weapon. Small wonder that he no longer promoted the idea of colonization. Small wonder that he began to advocate education and the franchise for Negroes. They were a new source of strength and deserved to be treated as the loyal citizens that they were.

For the last hundred years the Emancipation Proclamation has maintained its place as one of America's truly important documents. Even when the principles it espoused were not universally endorsed and even when its beneficiaries were the special target of mistreatment of one kind or another, the Proclamation somehow retained its hold on the very people who saw its promises unfulfilled. It did not do this because of the perfection of the goal to which it aspired. At best it sought to save the Union by freeing *some* of the slaves. Nor did it do it by the sublimity of its language. It had neither the felicity of the Declaration of Independence nor the simple grandeur of the Gettysburg Address. But in a very real sense it was another step toward the extension of the ideal of equality about which Jefferson had written.

Lincoln wrote the Emancipation Proclamation amid severe psychological and legal handicaps. Unlike Jefferson, whose Declaration of Independence was a clean break with a legal and constitutional system that had hitherto restricted thought and action, Lincoln was compelled to forge a document of freedom for the slaves within the existing constitutional system and in a manner that would give even greater support to that constitutional system. This required not only courage and daring but considerable ingenuity as well. As in so many of Lincoln's acts the total significance and validity of the measure were not immediately apparent, even among those who were sympathetic with its aims. Gradually, the greatness of the document dawned upon the nation and the world. Gradually, it took its place with the great documents of human freedom.

John Hope Franklin, *The Emancipation Proclamation* (Garden City, New York: Doubleday, 1963), 136–140, 152–153.


## ST. CLAIR DRAKE, the Emancipation Proclamation Centennial Lectures, Chicago, January–February, 1963

*Educated at the Hampton Institute and the University of Chicago, where he received a PhD in anthropology, St. Clair Drake (1911–1990) was a professor and pioneering social scientist at Roosevelt University and later at Stanford University. He was the author of several books, including seminal works, such as* Black Metropolis *(co-authored with Horace Cayton) and* Black Folk Here and There. *In 1963, Drake delivered a series of lectures on the American Dream to commemorate the centennial of the Emancipation Proclamation. He offered a complex portrait of Lincoln who initially favored compensated emancipation, enforcement of the Fugitive Slave Act, and a constitutional amendment protecting slavery in the states from federal interference. For Drake, the key to Lincoln was his "capacity for sympathetic understanding and for growth" to the point where, by late 1863, his American Dream was very closely aligned to that of Frederick Douglass and other abolitionists. For Drake, Lincoln's American Dream anticipates the same dream Martin Luther King articulated later that year at the Lincoln Memorial in Washington (ANB).*

---

Abraham Lincoln, Kentucky-born and Illinois bred, rail-splitter who became a lawyer and then a national leader, honest to the bone and conscientious to a fault, was, himself, personally opposed to the existence of slavery anywhere upon the earth. But he felt that his election mandate did not include permission for him to express his personal wishes through the exercise of executive authority [ ... ].

During his first year and a half in office, Lincoln set himself two paramount tactical goals within a not too clearly conceptualized grand strategy. One was to prevent, at all costs, the defection of the border states. The other was to organize actual and incipient pro-Union groups within the seceded states, encouraging them to assume political control and to bring their states back into the Union. [ ... ]

One avenue of approach to the border states and the South in attempting to re-integrate them into the Union was to allay fears that the Federal Government would wipe out their $3,000,000,000 investment in slave property by uncompensated Emancipation, or would force any form of Emancipation upon them by Federal legislation or executive edict. Lincoln was quite prepared to give guarantees against the forcible and uncompensated extirpation of slavery where it already existed. In his first inaugural address he agreed to support the resolution which had been passed by Congress to so amend the Constitution as to make slavery legal forever in the South. He devised a scheme for compensated emancipation in Washington, D.C. and put it into operation, hoping that the border states would, themselves, follow the example of the nation's capital, and he was in favor of Federal funds being used to compensate owners in these states. He toyed with schemes for either deporting freed slaves or persuading them to [e]migrate—with Federal assistance, thinking that this would make emancipation more attractive to the white population of America. And, above all, he reaffirmed his willingness to enforce the fugitive slave act should the union remain "half slave and half free,"—to use Federal force to return all runaways to their masters. Extreme abolitionists denounced him. On one point Lincoln stood firm, however; he would never sanction the *extension* of slavery. [ ... ]

It was within this context of a war that was not going too well for the North that Emancipation was proclaimed—and was explicitly defined as a war measure taken to weaken the South by appealing to the slaves to desert their masters and to come over into the Union lines—to work and to fight for a Union victory. They were explicitly asked not to rise up in revengeful insurrection. [ ... ]

Lincoln was very frank about why he did what he did when he did it. [. . .] So he decided to forestall the playing of the South's 'ace in the hole,' for the slaves were already responsible for the food and services which kept the South a going concern and the South could recruit them to the army if necessary by offering them their freedom—and did actually discuss doing so later in the war. Lincoln called his cabinet together on July 22nd, 1862 and put a draft of the Proclamation upon the table. [. . .]

Myth and legend have grown apace about what happened between July and September when Lincoln decided he would wait no longer. One story to which Lincoln himself gave some support was that he pledged himself and his "Maker" that if the Union Army was successful at the battle of Antietam he was going to issue the Proclamation. It should be noted that when Lincoln spoke of his decision in this fashion he implied that he considered the Proclamation as more than a mere war measure, that he felt it was, in part, at least, an act of long delayed justice to the slaves, that it was the carrying out of an obligation which though second in importance to saving the Union, was nevertheless very important, if not urgent. Something had been happening to Lincoln during these months. [. . .]

There is no question but that abolitionist sentiment was growing. Lincoln knew it. He may have, in an ambivalent, but also very real way, welcomed it.

Lincoln was having trouble with his generals, too, on the abolition issue, particularly two of them, Butler in Virginia and Fremont in Missouri. Both of them felt that they should not only encourage the slaves in their combat areas to run away, but should put guns in their hands to aid the Union armies, not just mule whips and shovels. Lincoln called a halt to these premature acts of emancipation and enlistment. But at the same time, these unauthorized experiments had shown that Freedmen were willing and eager to work and to fight—perhaps not to restore the Union, but certainly to help free themselves and their families—and to destroy the system.

Whatever the influence of the mystical component may have been in Lincoln's coming to the point of no return on the Emancipation issue—and Lincoln did have a strong belief in Fate as well as in Providential Design—it is certain that he was also exercising that political "instinct" which served him so well on many occasions. He felt that the time was ripe, or to change the metaphor, that the iron was hot. He felt that not only would the Proclamation "stir up" the situation behind the Confederate lines, but that it would also put "new meaning" into the conflict for hundreds and thousands of Northerners, by turning it into a crusade against slavery. [. . .] By September 1862 Lincoln was ready to take the decision which would integrate his personal desire with the national calls. We have the feeling that he was happy to be able to do what he had always wanted to do anyhow.

But Lincoln was, as ever, cautious. The proclamation issued in September was not to take effect until January 1, 1863—after a hundred days. This gave time to feel the public pulse, in the North, in the South, and abroad. One could always withdraw it if that seemed best. [ . . . ]

Among the Negroes, however, the tempo of non-violent protest—simply by deserting the plantations—was stepped up, and there was a generally favorable reaction in the North. [ . . . ]

The Emancipation Proclamation was the end result of what the distinguished Negro historian, John Hope Franklin, in a book recently published by that name to celebrate the occasion, calls "precedents and pressures." Abraham Lincoln stands at the end of 244 years of American history, arising late in time, but in the fullness of time, to integrate and transmute those precedents and to respond as a sensitive instrument to those many and sometimes irritating pressures. The assassin's bullet in Ford's Theater on that terrible tragic Good Friday night in 1865 stilled all slanders and calumnies of his contemporaries and made him immortal. That bullet, too, mutes the criticism today of those who feel that he was over-cautious but who also pay him honor for his sincerity and singlemindedness. The emancipation process continues. [ . . . ]

The joint efforts of black men and women—and white—acting sometimes with violence and sometimes without it, sometimes within the framework of the law and sometimes in obedience to what they call the Higher Law, exerted the pressures that changed opinion in the nation and made it easier for Lincoln to act. Their courageous acts and those of the soldiers—black and white—who fought the Civil War wiped out the injustices of the past, and white men's acceptance of their guilt redeemed the sins of history. [ . . . ]

I spoke, too, of the man who gave his life for The Dream, the truly great and certainly never to be forgotten Abraham Lincoln. For him, like Jefferson, the right of *all* men to liberty was a sacred belief though not a consuming passion. For him, the saving of the Union was "the pearl of great price." When, however, he came to feel that the preservation of the Union demanded the freeing of the slaves, he not only acted, but also experienced a great sense of relief that his personal ideals and the national welfare now, at last, coincided. Yet, even then, Lincoln could not envision an America in which Negroes were integrated, and certainly not one in which they were amalgamated, or even just accommodated. Lincoln, too, fantasied about sending them away. Unable, however, to persuade the Freedman's leaders or the white Radical Abolitionists that Negroes should do the country the favor of withdrawing, and finally convinced that the cost of resettlement would be pro-hibitive, and perhaps motivated also by considerations of justice—a belief that they who gave their lives to save the Union have earned the right to be a part of it—he eventually and reluctantly accepted the idea that the ex-slaves were here to stay. He even suggested that a few intelligent ones should be given the vote immediately and that the masses should be prepared for the franchise and useful living by education.

Watching Negro soldiers massacred and immolated at Fort Pillow and hearing of their heroic deeds on other battlefields, conversing for the first time with illustrious illiterate Negroes such as Harriet Tubman and cultivated ones like Frederick Douglass, receiving the plaudits and almost the worship of thousands of ex-slaves as their "Father Abraham," Lincoln demonstrated his remarkable capacity for sympathetic understanding and for growth. What had once been mere "niggers" to him were now transformed into persons among whom he found a few friends. By the time Lincoln came to Gettysburg he was pleading for "a new birth of freedom" and his vision included portions of Garrison's dream and Sumner's dream, Fred Douglass' and Thad Stevens'. The American Dream had assumed expanded dimensions for him.

Fate spared Lincoln the agony of having to try to translate his new vision into reality during the post-Civil War period.

In *The American Dream: 100 Years of Freedom?* (Chicago: Roosevelt University, 1963), 5, 6, 7, 8–9, 32, 33–34.

## CHARLES H. WESLEY, Remarks at Opening of the Emancipation Proclamation Exhibit at the National Archives, Washington, DC, January 4, 1963

*Wesley (1891–1987), the fourth African American to receive a PhD from Harvard University, was a historian who taught at Howard University before becoming the president of Wilberforce University. He eventually became president of Central State University and served for many years as president of the Association for the Study of Negro Life and History. The author of numerous books and articles, Wesley was historical consultant to the US Commission on Civil Rights when he delivered the following address at the opening ceremony for an exhibit to mark the centennial of the Emancipation Proclamation. On the one hundredth anniversary of the Emancipation Proclamation, Wesley praised Lincoln for issuing a revolutionary document and supporting racial equality. Wesley also noted the contribution African Americans made in securing their freedom, and the ongoing challenge to complete the work of emancipation. Wesley shared the speakers' podium with Attorney General Robert Kennedy (ANB).*

The Emancipation Proclamation was a turning point in our history, which has a three-fold concept, with tremendous trends toward the fulfillment of the purposes of the founders of the nation. It was first a historical event. Second, an unusually famous document. And third, a continuing challenge.

As a historical event, Abraham Lincoln is seen at the crest of a wave of emancipation, preceded by manumissions, wills, deeds, flights, purchases, and self-willed actions, until Negro Americans increased to over a half-million free persons in 1860, most of whom had made themselves free. Lincoln should be seen in history standing upon the shoulders of abolitionists, black and white, supported by the strivings of thousands of pamphleteers, orators, insurrectionists, and non-violent endeavors culminating in the martyrdom of John Brown and five courageous Negroes at Harpers Ferry in 1859, whose souls went marching on with the singing armies of freedom. For the war was changed by the proclamation into a crusade for human freedom.

Abraham Lincoln was in this event a courageous president, whose travail of soul extended from his first inaugural address, March 4, 1861, when he declared: "I have no purpose, directly or indirectly, to interfere with the institution of slavery in the states where it exists." To July 22, 1862, when to the contrary, he read to his cabinet a first draft of a proclamation. To September 22, when he announced the Preliminary Proclamation, through the following one hundred days to January 1, 1863, when he dipped his famed pen and signed the proclamation, in part from personal conviction and in part for military, political, and international purposes.

As a document, the proclamation, despite its strict interpretation as a war measure by some historians, has become one of the famed proclamations of policy and program constructed for our temple of freedom in this transition from chattel slavery to citizen freedom. For as President John F. Kennedy has well said, "Abraham Lincoln performed one of the great acts of history." The proclamation can be ranked with other great milestones of freedom, such as Magna Carta of 1215 at rural Runnymede, and the Declaration of Independence of 1776 at the little village of Philadelphia then. But history, tradition, and interpretation have not kept these documents as the plain documents which they were in every line but that made them what they were to be in interpretation and value for the American Dream and now almost for the world.

Similarly, the Emancipation Proclamation, acclaimed contemporaneously as a revolutionary document, not only lifted the war aim to a higher moral level, but it has been growing with the passing years in significance. In the words of Frederick Douglass, "We have seen in its spirit a life and power beyond the letter." It has been dramatized beyond its Civil War purpose and has given breadth and depth to our democratic faith. For as Lincoln declared, "In giving freedom to the slave, we assure freedom to the free."

As a challenge, the proclamation has now come to a place of profound emphasis on freedom with its documentary image continuously enlarged. Its legal ineffectiveness was recognized immediately by critics, but this was made effective by the adoption of the Thirteenth Amendment and by the approval by Congress of its validity and conclusiveness of the Civil War proclamation. Lincoln knew also that they who would be free must themselves strike the blow. Therefore, the proclamation announced that colored Americans would be used militarily and they served with distinction in over 200,000 in number for the freedom of the nation as well as themselves. For slaveholders were as much in slavery to the system as were the slaves.

Before the war had ended, the Emancipator praised the challenge to the nation by Louisiana which had, as a first state, given, in Lincoln's own words, "the benefit of public schools equally to black and white, and empowering the legislature to confer the elective franchise upon the colored man." Public schools equally to black and white and the franchise. This challenge of freedom has existed prior to and from the Emancipation Proclamation until now, when slavery has given way to segregation, a child who has grown as strong as its slave parent.

The call is again for patriots who will give realism, not simply in words but to the tones and the overtones of the Emancipation Proclamation, this foundation document. And their work will live after them as patriots as Lincoln's did, for his work is one of the stones used in the building of the nation's temple of freedom.

Another stone has been the United States Supreme Court decision of 1954, based like the Emancipation Proclamation upon the nation's ideal of equality of opportunity. Attempts have been made to defeat both, one in history and one currently, but they have failed and are failing. The temple these patriots built will last while the ages roll, for that beautiful unseen temple is the nation's immortal soul.

As we enter the second century of emancipation, may this centennial celebration and this centennial review and exhibit of documents inspire us and others to reach for still another turning point in our history, where a stone will be laid to mark its place in the temple of freedom. As a result of which we shall continue to build with courage and determination the nation's immortal soul.

Transcription of remarks from a Voice of America broadcast of the event, available at the John F. Kennedy Presidential Library, Boston.

## DAISY BATES, "After 100 Years—Where Do We Stand?" An Address on the Emancipation Proclamation, Oklahoma City, Oklahoma, January 6, 1963

*A native of Arkansas, Bates (1914–1999) ran a newspaper in Little Rock with her husband and became president of the Arkansas NAACP in the early 1950s. For her role in assisting the Little Rock Nine in integrating Central High School, Bates became nationally known and celebrated. In January 1963, she spoke at events commemorating the centennial of the Emancipation Proclamation in*

*Jackson, Mississippi and Oklahoma City. Much like Booker T. Washington and previous Emancipation Day orators, Bates wondered whether Lincoln's act was in vain. While Washington pointed to African American economic progress, Bates drew a direct connection between the Emancipation Proclamation and the 13th, 14th, and 15th Amendments to the Constitution. For Bates, Lincoln's proclamation helped make James Meredith's integration of the University of Mississippi possible in 1962, yet she also noted the alarming extent to which the vestiges of slavery remained and the work that needed to be done in order to finish what Lincoln's document set in motion (AANB).*

---

ABRAHAM LINCOLN signed and issued the Emancipation Proclamation January 1, 1863, liberating—by law—all the slaves held in the Confederate States. The stroke of Mr. Lincoln's pen made the 13th, 14th and 15th Amendments to the Federal Constitution applicable to all alike.

And for a century, there has been no legal right to discriminate between people of different nationalities and color in these United States.

The United States was not first, and neither was it last to recognize the Christian, moral and scientific truth, that all men are created equal. We were not the pioneers of freedom.

The British people passed legislation in 1833. Brazil passed legislation in 1888. Slavery was still a concern during the first World War. And a form of slavery existed in the Soviet Union until about ten years ago.

So you can see, we were not the first, nor the last to recognize the sins of slavery. But, I am afraid that we are the last to abolish slavery through practice.

One hundred years after Abraham Lincoln signed the Emancipation Proclamation wiping out the legal basis for slavery, have we fulfilled the promise of freedom to every man?

We have merely wiped out through the Emancipation Proclamation, and in many instances, later through the efforts of the NAACP, in the courts of the land, the legal basis for slavery's existence.

Today, as we celebrate the 100th Anniversary of the signing of the Emancipation Proclamation destroying the legal aspects for bondage, many men in the United States, white as well as black are still held in slavery.

They are held in slavery by the illegal use of force, sanctioned by custom.

Man can be enslaved by the denial of an opportunity to earn a living in a free country.

Man can be enslaved by the denial of the opportunity to live and rear his children in the atmosphere he desires.

Man can be enslaved by the denial of the right to cast his vote for the candidate of his choice in a free election.

Man can be enslaved by the denial of the right to educate his children in the institution of his choice.

Man can be enslaved when they see whole areas of life closed to them, while opened to others.

In Little Rock, Arkansas in 1957, the whole world saw nine teenage children enslaved, because they were denied the right to an education in a public institution of their choice.

In Tennessee in 1960, Negroes by the thousands were enslaved and made foodless and homeless just because they wanted to exercise the right of franchise that the Federal Constitution says is theirs in their own home land.

Throughout the entire southland, including your own city, many young dark skinned Americans were enslaved, thrown in jail and fined, and subjected to all kinds of police brutality because they attempted to quench a thirst with a refreshing drink and appease an appetite with a hamburger in a place which had been licensed to serve the public.

In 1962 many white and black Americans were enslaved, mobbed and jailed by Southern Law Officers because they attempted to travel in America as free people—the kind of free people Abraham Lincoln's Emancipation Proclamation said legally, they were.

As late as October 1, 1962, the whole world had the opportunity to see just how the Emancipation Proclamation affected one lone Negro citizen in Mississippi when he attempted to further his education in his home state in the land that he had traveled foreign soil to protect.

This one instance is enough to make the signer of the Emancipation Proclamation turn over in his grave, and ponder the question as to whether his efforts were in vain.

No, Mr. Lincoln the Emancipation Proclamation was not in vain.

All evidence will point to the fact that it has not done entirely what it was aimed to do. But, it has served its purpose.

It made these United States recognize that it was religiously, morally and scientifically wrong for one man to claim the ownership of another. It paved the way for the courts to later interpret the Federal Constitution in a manner far different from those interpretations in the Confederate States.

There have been many changes, and some progress has been made during the first 100 years. But there is much to be done to finish the job.

Just how long it will take America to fac[e] up to the truth and make the Emancipation Proclamation a living reality instead of a documentary paper, depends entirely upon America.

In the struggle for full equality, there is no one organization or one Philosophy which can meet all the needs of leadership. Increasingly, THE GOVERNMENT—at all its levels—must supplement programs of self-help with services designed to accelerate the readiness of the non-whites to participate fully in the life of the Nation.

For every successful person, there are others equally qualified who, either because of forces beyond their control or social attitudes and institutions, never have the opportunity to prove themselves.

Many of us think that the basic problem of discrimination can be solved by singing praise of some Negro who has secured some first post—we are suffering from a delusion—many of these first are last—they are *not* followed by seconds and thirds.

The American Negro wants all the rights enjoyed by White Americans.

As we celebrate the Emancipation Proclamation, this is a time when we look back at the long road we have traveled, and at the steps which have made progress possible.

But it is also a time for looking forward—more important—to the day when every citizen will have a voice in his Government, when every family will live in decent housing of its own choice, when every child will have an equal chance to develop his abilities and when every worker will be employed on his merit.

Daisy Bates Papers, Special Collections, University of Arkansas Libraries.

## MALCOLM X, Speech at the University of California, October 11, 1963

*Fewer than two months after the historic March on Washington for Jobs and Freedom, Malcolm X (1925–1965) contested the view of Lincoln as the model White liberal. For Malcolm, White liberals were historically more a problem than a solution. If Lincoln and his Emancipation Proclamation had been authentic then Malcolm says there would have been no need for Dr. Martin Luther King Jr. to ask President John Kennedy to issue a second Emancipation Proclamation. This critique of Lincoln as a White liberal anticipated Lerone Bennett's more fully developed analysis.*

-------

The Civil War was fought on this continent, but not to free the Black slaves as is commonly taught in the white man's schools. The Civil War was actually fought to preserve the Union, to keep the country intact for white people. [. . .]

Historically in America, the white liberal has been the one always supposedly who has the solution to the race problem. An example: the leading white liberal in American history was supposed to be Abraham Lincoln. He's the one who has been dangled in front of our people as a god who brought us out of slavery into the promised land of freedom. Martin Luther King last year was begging

President Kennedy to issue another Emancipation Proclamation. If the Emancipation Proclamation of Abraham Lincoln was authentic and produced the results that it was supposed to and if it had been sincere, it would have gotten results. Then Martin Luther King wouldn't have to be begging for another proclamation of emancipation today.

In Bruce Perry, ed., *Malcolm X: The Last Speeches* (New York: Pathfinder, 1989) 63, 76.

## GWENDOLYN BROOKS, "In the Time of Detachment, in the Time of Cold, 1965"

*The first African American recipient of a Pulitzer Prize, Brooks (1917–2000) composed this poem to commemorate the centennial anniversaries of Lincoln's death and the end of the Civil War at a 1965 symposium in Springfield that was organized by the Illinois Civil War Centennial Commission. Interestingly, Brooks, who also served as the Poet Laureate of Illinois, would be converted to the Black Arts Movement by the younger poets of the late 1960s, and did not include this poem in published collections with Broadside Press and Third World Press, two Black presses for which she wrote after leaving Harper & Row. Brooks memorializes Lincoln as "The Good Man," even then in this country's time of detachment, evil, and hate. She entreats him to infuse his spirit of love to repair his land of the droughts and manias of the day. She even asks him to force his saving grace on Americans to show the way back to connections, sunlight, and rhyme.*

---

> The good man.
> He is still enhancer, renouncer.
> In the time of detachment,
> In the time of the vivid heathen and affectionate evil,
> In the time of oral
> Grave grave legalities of hate—all real
> Walks our prime registered reproach and seal!
> Our successful moral.
> The good man.
> Watches our bogus roses, our rank wreath, our
> Love's unreliable cement, the gray
> Jubilees of our demondom.
>
> Coherent
> Counsel! Good man! Good Lincoln! Abraham!—

Require of us our terribly excluded blue!
Constrain, repair your ripped, revolted land.
Put hand in hand land over.
Reprove
The abler droughts and manias of the day
And a felicity entreat.
Love.
Complete
Your pledges, reinforce your aides, renew
Stance, testament.

Or

Force our poor sense unto your logics! lend
Superlatives and prudence: to extend
Our judgment—through the terse and diesel day;
To
Singe! smite! beguile our own bewilderments away.
Teach barterers the money of your star!
Or
Retrieve our trade from out the bad bazaar.

In the time of detachment, in the time of cold, in this time
Tutor our difficult sunlight. Rouse our rhyme.

In *A Portion of That Field: The Centennial of the Burial of Lincoln* (Urbana: University of
Illinois Press, 1967), 1–2.

## JOHN HOPE FRANKLIN, "Abraham Lincoln and Civil Rights," an Address at Gettysburg National Cemetery, Gettysburg, Pennsylvania, November 19, 1965

*On the 102nd anniversary of Lincoln's Gettysburg Address, Franklin (1915–
2009) delivered an incisive speech at the Gettysburg National Cemetery where
he discussed Lincoln's contemporary relevance on the issue of civil rights. In the
long struggle over Lincoln's legacy, there has been much speculation over what
he would do if he were alive. Franklin pushed back against the pro-segregationist
White Citizens Council and others who appropriated Lincoln for their own
racist purposes. In doing so, Franklin mapped the growth of Lincoln's humanitarianism by detailing the shift in his attitude regarding African American citizenship and civil rights.*

I can think of no task more difficult for the historian or for any others who choose to make use of history than to enlist a figure from the dim past in the cause of some contemporary problem. This is not to suggest, of course, that the contributions of people and institutions in the past have no relevance for current problems and undertakings. Quite the contrary. We generally do not take history into account enough; and we tend either to ignore it or ignore its obvious lessons. But what is really difficult or even dangerous is to take an important figure—such as George Washington or Abraham Lincoln—and put him to work on some current task or problem that is greatly in need of support from such a figure. [ . . . ]

The best current example we have of this can now be referred to as the incident of February 10 of last year. On that date the Citizens Councils of America placed large advertisements in numerous newspapers across the United States. These advertisements purported to be a statement of the views of Abraham Lincoln, in his own words, on civil rights. By a most artful and clever selection of quotations, by taking some of them out of context, and by interpreting the whole thing in terms of their own philosophy and program, the Citizens Councils of America celebrated the birthday of the Great Emancipator by welcoming him into their camp. They reminded their readers, for example, that in 1858 Lincoln urged the separation of the white and black races, opposed Negroes as jurors or voters, and of course was dead set against intermarriage. The Citizens Councils thought that they saw great relevance for the present of Lincoln's position of 1858, and they made the most of it; much to the consternation of that great body of Lincoln supporters who thought that Lincoln should either be properly enlisted on the other side in the civil rights struggle or be permitted to rest in peace.

No one—not even the most ardent Lincoln fans from Illinois or Indiana, where we now find such emphasis on his boyhood days—or of Pennsylvania, where today we observe the anniversary of his immortal address—not any of this group would attempt to make a "tin god" out of Lincoln or, indeed, to wrench him out of the context of his times. While his views on slavery were ahead of most of his contemporaries, his views were more representative of his times. As early as 1837, when he was a fledgling member of the Illinois legislature, Lincoln had said "slavery is founded both on injustice and bad policy." Five years later he told a Cincinnati audience, "Slavery and oppression must cease, or American liberty must perish." One would not have expected the Citizens Councils of America to have quoted Lincoln here, for this did not quite fit their purposes. In his expressed view that there were racial differences and that whites and Negroes should be kept apart, Lincoln reflected the average view of the people of the United States at that time. And he was honest enough to express that view to any and everyone, including Negroes themselves.

The remarkable thing about Lincoln's views on race relations is not that he made statements in 1858 that the opponents of civil rights could use in 1964 or

1965. The truly remarkable thing is that as the years passed and as Lincoln's views on such matters underwent significant change, his pronouncements on race relations and civil rights came to be of no use to the Citizens Councils of this day and time. Indeed, between 1861 and 1865 Lincoln demonstrated a remarkable capacity for growth, for he was always looking for new ways to solve old problems. The changes that took place in the last four years of his life regarding his view of race and racial justice are greater and more significant than the changes on the same subject that the Citizens Councils and their predecessors have undergone in the last hundred years. The minds of those who would seek to make a racist of Abraham Lincoln are themselves twisted and deranged, and they have none of the capacity for growth that he exhibited.

As Lincoln grew in political experience and wisdom, after becoming President of the United States, he came to appreciate the moral as well as the political and military implications of the Civil War. This is why the Emancipation Proclamation is more than a political and military document. When, for example, he invited Negroes to enlist as soldiers in the Union Army—and more than 180,000 accepted his invitation—he knew he was asking them to perform one of the highest acts of citizenship—fighting to save their country. This would be the beginning, he hoped, of a new role and a new place for Negroes in American life. "Those who shall have tasted actual freedom," he said, "I believe can never be slaves, or quasi slaves again." Lincoln hoped, therefore, that the several states would adopt some practical system "by which the two races could gradually lift themselves out of their old relation to each other, and both come out better prepared for the new." Fearing that his own Proclamation of Emancipation might not lead to the manumission of all slaves, President Lincoln urged Congress to amend the constitution in a way that would provide for the abolition of slavery. When the Thirteenth Amendment was sent to the states for ratification, Lincoln said, "the amendment is a King's cure for all the evils. It winds the whole thing up."

What Lincoln really meant was that the Amendment completed the first stage of emancipation and started Negroes on the road to citizenship. There were other steps to be taken, and he was determined to assume responsibility in securing for Negroes all of their rights as citizens. Thus, when Louisiana undertook in 1864 to write a new constitution looking toward readmission to the Union, President Lincoln suggested to the provisional governor that Louisiana should take the next step by enfranchising at least the "very intelligent" Negroes and "especially those who have fought gallantly in our ranks. They would probably help, in some trying time to come, to keep the jewel of liberty within the family of freedom."

No one was more enthusiastic than President Lincoln about the bill creating the Freedmen's Bureau, and he was particularly pleased that it provided for the education of Negroes and for other means that would assist them in their difficult transition from slavery to freedom. On the same day that the bill passed both the

House and the Senate, March 3, 1865, the President gave his assent by signing it. There is no better evidence of his view that the rights of Negroes should be protected than by this prompt approval by President Lincoln.

The war-time President also left no doubt regarding his view that the economic well-being of the former slaves was all-important if they were to become responsible and stable citizens. He hoped, therefore, that they would be able to secure land of their own. That is why he sought to give the thrifty and industrious Negroes of Port Royal, South Carolina, an opportunity to purchase small farms. He ordered that the tax sales be in twenty-acre lots, at $1.25 per acre and with pre-emption rights for the occupants of the land, which in many instances, were Negroes.

During the final, fateful week of his life President Lincoln visited the fallen Confederate capital, Richmond, and was greeted by large throngs of Negroes. He stopped several times to speak to them. In one of these impromptu speeches the President is reported to have told Negroes, "you may rest assured that as long as I live no one shall put a shackle to your limbs, and you shall have all the rights which God has given to every other free citizen of this Republic." He then said that he must return to Washington "to secure to you that liberty which you seem to prize so highly."

He had so little time left. His remaining days were devoted largely to the formidable task of making the surrender at Appomattox a victory more certain. This was a task that involved more than binding up the Nation's wounds, and caring for those who fought the war and their dependents. It involved, as Lincoln had said, doing "all which may achieve and cherish a just and lasting peace among ourselves and with all nations."

Thus, by taking the initiative in setting the slaves free, in advocating the franchise for them, in urging education for the former slaves, in seeking to secure to them a measure of economic well-being, and in pledging himself to work for equal rights for all, Lincoln took his stand in behalf of civil rights for all Americans. Those who would understand this good and great man must first appreciate his broad humanitarianism and his adherence to principles of equity and justice. They must appreciate his capacity for growth in wisdom and understanding. They must themselves study his life with care and understanding. They will, then, discover that it is a remarkable distortion of his position and a crude disrespect for his service and his memory to enlist him in the cause of racism and discrimination. For, he said, as early as 1856, "The human heart is with us. God is with us. We shall again be able not to declare that 'all states as states are equal,' nor yet that all citizens as citizens are equal, but renew the broader, better declaration, including both these and much more, that 'all men are created equal.'"

John Hope Franklin Papers, Box W25, Rubenstein Library, Duke University.

## JULIUS LESTER, *Look Out Whitey, Black Power's Gon' Get Your Mama*, 1968

*A graduate of Fisk University, an activist, and an author perhaps best known for his children's books, Lester (1939–2018) published the following during the height of the Black Power Movement. Referring to African Americans as pawns in a White game, he suggests there is no reason for Blacks to be grateful to Lincoln, as it reinforces the myth that Whites have done a lot for them. Lester argues that if Lincoln had been a sincere friend to African Americans he would not have waited so long to issue the Emancipation Proclamation. For Lester, the Great Emancipator myth ignores Black agency in achieving their own freedom. Lester further noted that Lincoln blamed Blacks for the war and wanted to send them to Africa or Central America. Lester's critique reflected a desire to foster a sense of Black consciousness that would interrogate the very idea of a White savior (AANB).*

---

One of the bigger lies that America has given the world is that Lincoln freed the slaves, and that blacks should be grateful from can to can't because Mr. Lincoln was so generous. It is true that Lincoln affixed his signature to a proclamation giving the slaves their freedom and that the slaves, thereby, were free to "get hat." It is not true that Lincoln did so out of the goodness of his heart or that we have to be grateful to him. What does it matter why he did it? Isn't it sufficient that he did it? No, because white folks never miss an opportunity to tell us "what we did for you people. . . ." The black school-child grows up feeling half-guilty for even thinking about cussing out a white man, because he's been taught that it was a white man who gave us freedom. How many times has the photograph been reprinted of the small Negro boy staring up at the huge statue of Lincoln at the Lincoln Memorial? The photograph would mean nothing if the boy doing the staring were white. What is the catechism the black child learns from Grade One on? "Class, what did Abraham Lincoln do?" "Lincoln freed the slaves," and the point is driven home that you'd still be down on Mr. Charlie's plantation working from can to can't if Mr. Lincoln hadn't done your great-great-grandmama a favor. [. . .]

Blacks have no reason to feel grateful to Abraham Lincoln. Rather, they should be angry at him. After all, he came into office in 1861. How come it took him two whole years to free the slaves? His pen was sitting on his desk the whole time. All he had to do was get up one morning and say, "Doggonnit! I think I'm gon' free the slaves today. It just ain't right for folks to own other folks." It was that simple. Mr. Lincoln, however, like Mr. Kennedy (take your pick) and Mr. Eastland, moved politically, not morally. He said that if he could keep the Union together by maintaining slavery, he'd do it. If he had to free the slaves to keep the Union together, he'd do that, too. But he was in office to preserve the Union, not free the slaves. [...]

But Mr. Lincoln hadn't reckoned on US. Everywhere the Union army set foot, we showed up with our wives, children, aunts, uncles, grandparents, and anybody else who'd come. [...]

There were other factors operating which finally made Lincoln and the Union army take a pragmatic approach to blacks. With the general strike against the plantations by a half-million slaves, there still remained some three million on the plantations. Lincoln saw clearly that by freeing these he could cripple the South. Too, the Union was having a difficult time recruiting whites to fight the war. [...]

There were many factors which led to the Emancipation Proclamation, and it is not only misleading, but a lie, to depict Lincoln as the Great Emancipator. [...]

Once the slaves were free and the war over, everybody had the same question: What shall we do with the Negro. Lincoln had an interesting proposal. Send them back to Africa.

Julius Lester, *Look Out Whitey, Black Power's Gon' Get Your Mama* (New York: Grove Press, 1968), 57–68.

## LERONE BENNETT JR., "Was Abe Lincoln a White Supremacist?" February 1968

*A native of Mississippi, Bennett (1928–2018) graduated from Morehouse College and became an editor of Ebony magazine in the early 1950s. As an editor, Bennett contributed numerous articles on African American history, and authored several books. The argument that Lincoln was a White supremacist and "the leading white liberal in American history" was foregrounded at the conclusion of his 1964 book, The Negro Mood, and more fully developed in this 1968 essay that sparked much controversy and has influenced the debate over Lincoln ever since. Bennett asserted that the image of Lincoln as Great Emancipator was a myth, and that mythology was created and sustained by the "psychological needs of a racist society." Detailing Lincoln's views and practices as president, Bennett claimed Lincoln was forced to issue the Emancipation Proclamation, but that did not alter his views of Blacks. Suggesting that Lincoln did not completely overcome the racist environment of his upbringing, Bennett unfavorably compared him to White abolitionist contemporaries. Bennett weaved together elements that are present in earlier documents, but he does so in such a way as to provoke readers to abandon what he perceived as a harmful fantasy (AANB).*

The Presidential campaign was over and the victor was stretching his legs and shaking off the cares of the world in his temporary office in the State Capitol in Springfield, Ill. Surrounded by the perquisites of power, at peace with the world, the President-elect was regaling old acquaintances with hilarious stories of his early days as a politician. One of the visitors interrupted this entertaining mono-logue and remarked that it was a shame that "the vexatious slavery matter" would be the first question of public policy the new President would have to deal with in Washington.

The President-elect's eyes twinkled and he said he was reminded of a story. According to eyewitness Henry Villard, President-elect Abraham Lincoln "told the story of the Kentucky Justice of the Peace whose first case was a criminal prosecution for the abuse of slaves. Unable to find any precedent, he exclaimed at last angrily: 'I will be damned if I don't feel almost sorry for being elected when the niggers is the first thing I have to attend to.' "

This story, shocking as it may sound to Lincoln admirers, was in character. For the President-elect had never shown any undue interest in black people, and it was altogether natural for him to suggest that he shared the viewpoint of the reluctant and biased justice of the peace.

In one of the supreme ironies of history, the man who told this story was forced by circumstances to attend to the Negroes. And within five years he was enshrined in American mythology as "the Great Emancipator who freed the Negroes with a stroke of the pen out of the goodness and compassion of his heart."

Over the years, the Mythology of the Great Emancipator has become a part of the mental landscape of America. Generations of schoolchildren have memo-rized its cadences. Poets, politicians, and long-suffering blacks have wept over its imagery and drama.

No other American story is so enduring. No other American story is so com-forting. No other American story is so false.

Abraham Lincoln was *not* the Great Emancipator. As we shall see, there is abundant evidence to indicate that the Emancipation Proclamation was not what people think it is and that Lincoln issued it with extreme misgivings and reserva-tions. Even more decisive is the fact that the real Lincoln was a tragically flawed figure who shared the racial prejudices of most of his white contemporaries.

If, despite the record, Lincoln has been misunderstood and misinterpreted, it is not his fault. A conservative Illinois lawyer, cautious and conventional in social matters, Lincoln never pretended to be a racial liberal or a social innovator. He said repeatedly, in public and in private, that he was a firm believer in white supremacy. And his acts supported his assertions. Not only that: Lincoln had profound doubts about the possibility of realizing the rhetoric of the Declara-tion of Independence and the Gettysburg Address on this soil; and he believed until his death that black people and white people would be much better off separated—preferably with the Atlantic Ocean or some other large and deep body of water between them.

The man's character, his way with words, and his assassination, together with the psychological needs of a racist society, have obscured these contradictions under a mountain of myths which undoubtedly would have amused Lincoln, who had a wonderful sense of the ironic and ridiculous. The myth-makers have not only buried the real Lincoln; they have also managed to prove him wrong. He said once that it was impossible to fool all of the people all of the time. But his apotheosis clearly proves that it is possible to fool enough of them long enough to make a conservative white supremacist a national symbol of racial tolerance and understanding.

If the Lincoln myths were the harmless fantasies of children at play, it would be possible to ignore them. But when the myths of children become adult daydreams and when the daydreams are used to obscure deep social problems and to hide historical reality, it becomes a social duty to confront them. When, at the height of the summer rebellion season, President Lyndon B. Johnson said he intended to follow a Lincolnian course, Professor Vincent P. Harding of Spelman College rebuked him, pointing out in a letter to the New York Times that Lincoln's vacillating Civil War posture was a prescription for social disaster today.

Because, as Professor Harding suggested, we are environed by dangers and because we need all the light we can get; because Abraham Lincoln is not the light, because he is in fact standing in the light, hiding our way; because a real emancipation proclamation has become such a matter of national survival and *because no one has ever issued such a document in this country*—because, finally, lies enslave and because the truth is always seemly and proper, it has become urgently necessary to reevaluate the Lincoln mythology. The need for such a reevaluation has already been recognized in some scholarly circles. Some scholars have confronted the ambiguities of the Emancipation Proclamation and have suggested that Lincoln's reputation would be more securely based if it were grounded not on that document but on his services as leader of the victorious North. Analyzing the same evidence, David Donald said in *Lincoln Reconsidered* that perhaps "the secret of Lincoln's continuing vogue is his essential ambiguity. He can be cited on all sides of all questions." Donald was not quite correct, for Lincoln cannot be cited on the side of equal rights for black people, a fact that has discomfited more than one Lincoln Day orator. Commenting on Lincoln's determined opposition to a policy of emancipation, Professor Kenneth Stampp wrote: "Indeed, it may be said that if it was Lincoln's destiny to go down in history as the Great Emancipator, rarely has a man embraced his destiny with greater reluctance than he."

To understand Lincoln's reluctance and his painful ambivalence on the question of race, one must see him first against the background of his times. Born into a poor white family in the slave state of Kentucky and raised in the anti-black environments of southern Indiana and Illinois, Lincoln was exposed from the very beginning to racism.

It would have been difficult, if not impossible, for young Abraham Lincoln to emerge unscathed from this environment. By an immense effort of transcendence, worthy of admiration and long thought, Lincoln managed to free himself of most of the crudities of his early environment. But he did not—and perhaps could not—rise above the racism that was staining the tissue of the nation's soul.

It appears from the record that Lincoln readily absorbed the Negro stereotypes of his environment, for he ever afterwards remained fond of Negro dialect jokes, blackface minstrels and Negro ditties. "Like most white men," Professor Benjamin Quarles wrote, "Lincoln regarded the Negro as such as funny." More to the point, Lincoln, as Quarles also noted, regarded the Negro as inferior.

There is a pleasant story of Lincoln awakening to the realities of slavery on a visit to New Orleans in 18[3]1. According to the traditional account, an aroused Lincoln said: "If I ever get a chance to hit that thing {slavery} I'll hit it hard." Since the man who reported this statement did not accompany Lincoln to New Orleans, the story is of dubious value. More telling is the fact that Lincoln distinguished himself as a public official by a reluctance to hit slavery at all.

In the general literature, Lincoln is depicted as an eloquent and flaming idealist, whaling away at the demon of slavery. This view is almost totally false. In the first place, Lincoln was an opportunist, not an idealist. He was a man of the fence, a man of the middle, a man who stated the principle with great eloquence but almost always shied away from rigid commitments to practice. Contrary to reports, Lincoln was no social revolutionary. As a matter of fact, he was an archetypal example of the cautious politician who assails the extremists on both sides. It is not for nothing that cautious politicians sing his praises.

It should be noted, secondly, that Lincoln's position on slavery has been grossly misrepresented. Lincoln was not opposed to slavery; he was opposed to the *extension* of slavery. More than that: Lincoln was opposed to the extension of slavery out of devotion to the interests of white people, not out of compassion for suffering blacks. To be sure, he did say from time to time that slavery was "a monstrous injustice." But he also said, repeatedly, that he was not prepared to do anything to remove that injustice where it existed. On the contrary, he said that it was his duty to tolerate and, if necessary, to give practical support to an evil supported by the U.S. Constitution.

More damaging is the fact that Lincoln apparently believed that immediate and general emancipation would be a greater evil than slavery itself. Eulogizing Henry Clay on July 6, 1852, he associated himself with that slaveowner's colonization ideas and said that Clay "did not perceive, as I think no wise man has perceived, how it {slavery} could be at *once* eradicated, without producing a greater evil, even to the cause of human liberty itself." In other speeches of the same period,

Lincoln commended travel to black people and noted with admiration that "the children of Israel . . . went out of Egyptian bondage in a body."

A third point of significance is that Lincoln's opposition to the extension of slavery was a late and anomalous growth. In the 1830s and 1840s, in the midst of one of the greatest moral crises in the history of America, Lincoln remained silent and lamentably inactive. In his few public utterances on the subject in the 30s and 40s, he very carefully denounced both slavery and the opponents of slavery.

For many white Northerners, the most agonizing moral issue of the day was the fugitive slave law, which required all Americans to assist in the capture and return of runaway slaves. Many whites, some of them quite conservative, refused to obey the law. Others, more daring, organized an open resistance movement, moving runaway slaves from station to station on the Underground Railway.

Instead of aiding this effort, Lincoln opposed it, publicly announcing his support of the fugitive slave law. In a private letter to Joshua F. Speed in 1855, he said: "I confess I hate to see the poor creatures hunted down, and caught, and carried back to their stripes, and unrewarded toils, but I bite my lip and keep quiet."

Lincoln came down off the fence, rhetorically, in the 50s when the Kansas-Nebraska act reopened the whole question of the extension of slavery to the largely uninhabited territories of the West. This was, he said, a clear and present threat to free white men and to what he called "the white man's charter of freedom"—the Declaration of Independence. In his public speeches of this period, Lincoln was given to saying in the same speech that he believed in white supremacy as a practical matter and in the Declaration of Independence as an abstract matter of principle.

The Lincoln years in Illinois were years of oppression and reaction. Black people could not vote, testify against white people in court or attend public schools. It was a crime for free black people to settle in the state. Although Lincoln was a powerful figure in state politics for more than a quarter of a century, he made no audible protest against this state of affairs. In fact, he said he preferred it that way. When H. Ford Douglas, a militant black leader, asked Lincoln to support a movement to repeal the law banning black testimony, Lincoln refused.

In the famous series of debates with Stephen Douglas, Lincoln made his position crystal clear. He was opposed, he said, to Negro citizenship and to "the niggers and the white people marrying together." Speaking at Charleston, Illinois, on September 18, 1858, Lincoln said: "I will say, then, that I am not, nor ever have been, in favor of bringing about in any way the social and political equality of the white and black races; (applause) that I am not, nor ever have been, in favor of making voters or jurors of Negroes, nor of qualifying them to hold office, nor to intermarry with white people; and I will say, in addition, to this, that there is a physical difference between the white and black races which I believe will forever forbid the two races living together on terms of social and political equality. And inasmuch as they cannot so live, while they do remain together there must be the position of superior and inferior, and I as much as any other man am in favor of having the superior position assigned to the white race."

Lincoln grew during the war—but he didn't grow much. On every issue relating to the black man—on emancipation, confiscation of rebel land and the use of black soldiers—he was the very essence of the white supremacist with good intentions. In fact, Lincoln distinguished himself as President by sustained and consistent opposition to the fundamental principle of the Proclamation that guaranteed his immortality. Incredible as it may seem now, the man who would go down in history as the Great Emancipator spent the first 18 months of his administration in a desperate and rather pathetic attempt to save slavery where it existed. He began his Presidential career by saying he has neither the power nor the desire to interfere with slavery in the states. And he endorsed a proposed Thirteenth Amendment which would have guaranteed that slavery would never be molested in existing states and Washington, D.C.

"My policy," Lincoln said, "is to have no policy." In this famous statement, Lincoln was something less than candid. For he did have a policy and that policy was to win the war without touching slavery. "It is the desire of the President," Secretary of War Simon Cameron wrote a general on August 8, 1861, "that *all existing rights in all states be fully respected and maintained.*" When Lincoln's policy foundered on the reef of Southern intransigence, Lincoln complained sadly to a friend: "I *struggled* nearly a year and a half to get along without touching the 'institution.'..."

In accordance with the real policy of the Lincoln Administration, the War Department refused to accept black troops and Union generals vied with each other in proving their fealty to slavery. Some generals returned fugitive slaves to rebel owners; others said that if black slaves staged an uprising behind enemy lines they would stop fighting the enemy and turn their fire on their black friends. Union officers who refused to go along with the "soft-on-slavery" policy were court-martialed and cashiered out of the service. When, in August, 1861, General John C. Fremont emancipated Missouri slaves, Lincoln angrily countermanded the proclamation, telling Fremont's wife that "General Fremont should not have dragged the Negro into it..." A year later, when General David Hunter freed the slaves in three Southern states, Lincoln again countermanded the order, saying that emancipation was a Presidential function.

That this policy was changed at all was due not to Lincoln's humanitarianism but to rebel battlefield brilliance and the compassion and perseverance of a small band of Radical Republicans. Foremost among these men were Charles Sumner, the U.S. senator from Massachusetts; Wendell Phillips, the brilliant agitator from Boston; Frederick Douglass, the bearded black abolitionist; and Thaddeus Stevens, the Pennsylvania congressman who virtually supplanted Abraham Lincoln as the leader of the Republican party. As the war continued and as Northern casualties mounted, the Radical Republicans put events to use and mobilized a public pressure Lincoln could not ignore. Delegation after delegation waited on the President and demanded that he hit the South where it would hurt most by freeing the slaves and arming them. Lincoln parried the pressure with heat and conviction, citing constitutional, political and military reasons to justify his anti-emancipation stand. Lincoln usually expressed his opposition to emancipation in a troubled but polite tone. But he could be pushed across the border of politeness. When Edward L. Pierce urged the President to adopt a more enlightened policy, Lincoln, according to Pierce, exploded and denounced "the itching to get niggers into our lives."

The traditional image of Lincoln is of a harried and large-hearted man fending off "extremists of the left and right" only to emerge at the precise psychological moment to do what he had always wanted to do. This image clashes, unfortunately, with evidence which suggests that sudden and general emancipation was never Lincoln's policy.

Lincoln was given to saying that his constitutional duties prevented him from doing anything substantial to give point to his "oft-expressed *personal* wish that all men everywhere could be free." But it is obvious from the evidence that Lincoln's problems were deeper than that. For when his duty was clear, he refused to act. On several occasions he refused to take anti-slavery action which was mandated by Congress and he sabotaged some anti-slavery legislation by executive inaction. Somehow, duty, in Lincoln's view, almost always worked against the black man.

Lincoln defenders say that he resisted emancipation pressures because of his fear that premature action would alienate white supporters in Northern and Border States and endanger the prosecution of the war. But this view does not come to grips with the fact that Lincoln was *personally* opposed to sudden and general emancipation before 1861 and the further fact that he continued to oppose sudden and general emancipation after the circulating Proclamation proved that his fears were groundless. Nor does the traditional Lincoln apologia touch the mass of evidence—in Lincoln letters as well as in private and public statements—which shows that Lincoln was personally opposed to sudden emancipation on social and racial grounds.

It was not the fear of emancipation but the fear of what would happen afterwards that palsied Lincoln's hands. He was deeply disturbed by the implications of turning loose four million black people in a land he considered the peculiar preserve of the white man. He spoke often of "the evils of sudden derangement" and warned Congress against "the vagrant destitution which must largely attend immediate emancipation in localities where their numbers are very great." He said over and over again that it was his considered judgment that "gradual, and not sudden, emancipation is better for all." Count Adam Gurowski believed Lincoln was concerned about poor white fear of black competition. "Be sure," he wrote in a May 7, 1862, letter, "that Lincoln is at heart with Slavery. He considers that *emancipation is a job which will smother the free States. Such are his precise words.*"

Lincoln also feared racial conflict. Like many white liberals, he was consumed by fears of black violence. More than one visitor to the White House found him in agony over the possibility of a Nat Turner-like uprising behind the enemy's lines.

An additional factor in Lincoln's opposition to the principle of sudden emancipation was his racial bias. He considered black people unassimilable aliens. There was not, in his view, enough room in America for black and white people. He didn't believe white people would sanction equal rights for black people and he didn't ask white people to sanction equal rights for black people. Since he did not propose to confront racism, he told black people they would have to travel or accept a subordinate position in American life.

Insofar as it can be said that Lincoln had an emancipation policy, it was to rid America of slaves and Negroes. When he failed in his attempt to end the war without touching slavery, he fell back to a second plan of gradual and compensated emancipation extending over a 37-year-period. This was linked in his thinking with a companion policy of colonizing black people in South America or Africa.

As the pressure for emancipation rose, Lincoln argued passionately and eloquently for his plan of gradual emancipation and abrupt emigration. On August 14, 1862, he called a hand-picked group of black men to the White House and proposed a black exodus. In "a curious mixture of condescension and kindness," to use James M. McPherson's phrase, Lincoln told the black men that it was their duty to leave America. "You and we," he said, "are different races. We have between us a broader difference than exists between almost any other two races. Whether it is right or wrong I need not discuss, but this physical difference is a great disadvantage to us both, as I think your race suffer very greatly, many of them by living among us, while ours suffer from your presence."

Lincoln did not seek the opinions of his visitors. He did not propose, he said, to discuss racism, to debate whether it was founded on reality or justice. He was simply, he said, presenting a fact: white people didn't want black people in America and therefore black people would have to go. "There is," he said, "an unwillingness on the part of our people, harsh as it may be, for you free colored people to remain with us." The only solution, Lincoln said, was a black exodus. "It is better for us both," he said, " . . . to be separated." He proposed a black settlement on Central American land, "rich in coal;" and he asked his visitors to help him find black settlers "capable of thinking as white men."

Although Lincoln's plan received a generally hostile reception in the black community, he pursued it with passion and conviction. For several months after the signing of the Emancipation Proclamation, he was deeply involved in a disastrously abortive attempt to settle black people on an island off the coast of Haiti. When that venture failed, he shifted to the Southwest, conferring with contractors on the feasibility of settling black people in the state of Texas.

While Lincoln was trying to send black people away, Congress was busy emancipating. In the spring and summer of 1862, Congress forbade military officers to return fugitive slaves, authorized the President to accept black soldiers, and emancipated the slaves in Washington, D.C. Finally, on July 17, 1862, Congress passed the Second Confiscation Act, which freed the slaves of all rebels. This act, which has received insufficient attention in general media, was actually more sweeping than the Preliminary Emancipation Proclamation, which came two months later.

Lincoln followed Congress' lead slowly and grudgingly, signing most of these acts with evident displeasure. But the drift of events was unmistakable, and Lincoln changed steps, saying with great honesty that he had not controlled events but had been controlled by them. Conferring with the member of a congressional committee charged with drafting a plan for buying the slaves and sending them away, Lincoln urged speed, saying: "You had better come to an agreement. Niggers will never be cheaper."

Orthography apart, Lincoln caught here the spirit of the times. At that moment, in late July of 1862, the Union war effort was bogged down in the marshes of Virginia, and England and France were on the verge of intervening on the side of the Confederacy. At home, the heat was rising fast, fueled by mounting Northern casualties. Faced with mushrooming pressures at home and abroad, Lincoln reversed his course and "conditionally determined," to use his words, to touch the institution of slavery.

Lincoln adopted the new policy from necessity, not conviction. In public and in private, he made it clear that he was not motivated by compassion for the slaves. Taking his stand on the ground of military necessity, he said his new policy was designed to weaken Southern white men and to strengthen the hand of Northern white men. "Things," he said later, "had gone from bad to worse, till I felt we had reached the end of the rope on the plan of operation we have been pursuing, and that we had about played our last card." Lincoln said he was driven to the "alternative of either surrendering the Union, and with it, the Constitution, or of laying a strong hand upon the colored element."

There was truth in this, but it was not the whole truth. There is evidence that Lincoln was forced to adopt the new policy by political pressures. Edward Stanly, military governor of North Carolina, said Lincoln told him that "the proclamation had become a civil necessity to prevent the Radicals from openly embarrassing the government in the conduct of the war. The President expressed the belief that, without the proclamation for which they had been clamoring, the Radicals would take the extreme step in Congress of withholding supplies for carrying on the war—leaving the whole land in anarchy." Count Gurowski gave a similar version of Lincoln's metamorphosis and concluded, in a fine phrase, that Lincoln was literally "whipped" into glory.

Responding to a parallelogram of pressures, Lincoln issued a preliminary Emancipation Proclamation on September 22, 1862. In this document, he warned the South that he would issue a final Emancipation Proclamation in 100 days if the rebellion had not ended by that time. The proclamation outlined a future policy of emancipation, but Lincoln had no joy in the black harvest. To a group of serenaders, who congratulated him on the new policy, Lincoln said: "I can only trust in God I have made no mistake." To his old friend, Joshua F. Speed, Lincoln expressed misgivings and said he had "been anxious to avoid it." To Congressman John Covode of Pennsylvania, Lincoln explained that he had been *"driven to it,"* adding: "But although my duty is plain, it is in some respects painful. . . ." Still another visitor, Edward Stanly, received a dramatic account of Lincoln's resistance to a policy of emancipation. "Mr. Lincoln said," according to Stanly, "that he had prayed to the Almighty to save him from this necessity, adopting the very language of our Savior, 'If it be possible, let this cup pass from me,' but the prayer had not been answered."

On Thursday, January 1, 1863, Lincoln drank from the cup, and apparently he liked neither the flavor nor the color of the draught. When he started to sign the document, his arm trembled so violently, an eyewitness said, that he could not hold the pen. Lincoln, who was very superstitious, paused, startled. Then, attributing his shakes to hours of hand-shaking at a New Year's Day reception, he scrawled his name, saying he did not want the signature to be "tremulous" because people would say "he had some compunctions."

He had "compunctions."

Nothing indicates this better than the Emancipation Proclamation which is, as J.G. Randall and Richard N. Current indicated, "more often admired than read." Cold, forbidding, with all the moral grandeur of a real estate deed, the Proclamation does not enumerate a single principle hostile to slavery and it contains not one quotable sentence. As a document, it lends weight to the observation of Lincoln's law partner, William Herndon, who wrote: "When he freed the slaves, there was no heart in the act."

There wasn't much else in it, either. Rightly speaking, the Emancipation Proclamation, as Ralph Korngold wrote, was "not an Emancipation Proclamation at all." The document was drafted in such a way that it freed few, if any, slaves. It did not apply to slaves in the Border States and areas under federal control in the South. In other words, Lincoln "freed" slaves where he had no power and left them in chains where he had power. The theory behind the Proclamation, an English paper noted, "is not that a human being cannot justly own another, but that he cannot own him unless he is loyal to the United States."

The Proclamation argued so powerfully against itself that some scholars have suggested that Lincoln was trying to do the opposite of what he said he was doing. In other words, the suggestion is that the Emancipation Proclamation was a political stratagem by which Lincoln hoped to outflank the Radicals, buy time and forestall a definitive act of emancipation. This is not the place to review the political stratagem theory in detail. Suffice it to say that on the basis of the evidence one can make a powerful case for the view that Lincoln never intended to free the slaves, certainly not immediately.

Lincoln's post-Proclamation behavior lends substance to this view. For contrary to all logic, he continued to agitate against his own policy. On the eve of the Proclamation, he again recommended to Congress his favorite plan of gradual and compensated emancipation. And he continued, according to several witnesses, to doubt the wisdom of the Emancipation Proclamation. Three weeks after signing the document, he reportedly told Wendell Phillips that the Proclamation was a "great mistake." Two months later, he told Congressman George W. Julian that the Proclamation had "done about as much harm as good." In the following months, Lincoln repeatedly said that he still favored a gradual emancipation plan which contradicted the spirit of his own Proclamation.

To this bleak picture one should add in all justice that Lincoln can be quoted on both sides of the issue. He reportedly said later that the Proclamation and the arming of black soldiers constituted the heaviest blows against the rebellion. It should also be said that Lincoln, after a period of vacillation and doubt, helped to win passage of the Thirteenth Amendment, which made the paper freedom of the Proclamation real. Having said that, it remains to be said that Lincoln never fully accepted the fundamental principle of the Proclamation and the Thirteenth Amendment. As late as February, 1865, he was still equivocating on the issue of immediate emancipation. At an abortive peace conference with Confederate leaders at Hampton Roads, Virginia, Lincoln said, according to Alexander Stephens, that he had never been in favor of immediate emancipation, even by the states. He spoke of the "many evils attending" immediate emancipation and suggested, as he had suggested on other occasions, a system of apprenticeship "by which the two races could gradually live themselves out of their old relations to each other."

At Gettysburg, Lincoln shifted gears and announced a new policy of liberation and social renewal. America, he said, was engaged in a great war testing whether it or any other nation "conceived in liberty and dedicated to the proposition that all men are created equal" could long endure. The war, he said, would decide whether "government of the people, by the people, for the people" would perish from the earth. But 20 days later when he unveiled his own postwar policy, it was obvious that *all* meant the same thing to Lincoln that it had always meant: all white people. In his Proclamation of Amnesty and Reconstruction, Lincoln said he would recognize any rebel state in which one-tenth of the white voters of 1860 took an oath of allegiance to the United States and organized a government which renounced slavery. What of black people? Slavery apart, Lincoln ignored them. Incredibly, the commander-in-chief of the U.S. Army abandoned his black soldiers to the passions of Confederate veterans who feared and hated them. Lincoln barely suggested "privately" that it would be a good thing for Southern states to extend the ballot "to the very intelligent {Negroes}, and especially those who have fought gallantly in our ranks." But these were private sentiments, not public acts; and they were expressed in an extremely hesitant manner at that. Lincoln didn't require fair or equal treatment for the freedmen. In fact, he didn't make any demands at all. Reconstruction, Lincoln style, was going to be a Reconstruction of the white people, by white people and for the white people.

It seems that Lincoln never reconciled himself to the implications of emancipation. Shortly before his death, Lincoln summoned General Benjamin F. Butler to inquire about the possibilities of "sending the blacks away." According to Butler, he said, "I wish you would examine the question and give me your views upon it and go into figures as you did before in some degree as to show whether the Negroes can be exported." Butler went away and came back two days later with a sad story. "Mr. President," he said, "I have gone very carefully over my calculation as to the power of the country to export the Negroes of the South and I assure you that, using all your naval vessels and all the merchant marine fit to cross the seas with safety, it will be impossible for you to transport to the nearest place fit for them . . . half as fast as Negro children will be born here."

Lincoln's assassination and the aggressive dissemination of the "Massa Linkun myth" pushed the real Lincoln with his real limitations into the background. And black people were soon pooling their pennies to erect a monument to the mythical emancipator. When, on April 14, 1876, this monument was unveiled, with President U.S. Grant and other high officials in attendance, Frederick Douglass punctured the myths and looked frankly at the man. Douglass praised Lincoln's growth, but he also rehearsed his limitations.

*Truth* {Douglass said} *is proper and beautiful at all times and in all places, and it is never more proper and beautiful in any case than when speaking of a great public man whose example is likely to be commended for honor and imitation long after his departure to the solemn shades, the silent continent of eternity. It must be admitted, truth compels me to admit, even here in in the presence of the monument we have erected to his memory, Abraham Lincoln was not, in the fullest sense of the word, either our man or our model. In his interests, in his associations, in his habits of thought, and in his prejudices, he was a white man. He was preeminently the white man's President, entirely devoted to the welfare of white men . . . In all his education and feeling he was an American of the Americans.*

Speaking thus of interests and passion and public acts, Frederick Douglass, who knew Lincoln well, sounded the discordant notes of a national, not a personal tragedy. For, in the final analysis, Lincoln must be seen as the embodiment, not the transcendence, of the American tradition, which is, as we all know, a racist tradition. In his ability to rise above that tradition, Lincoln, often called "the noblest of all Americans," holds up a flawed mirror to the American soul. And one honors him today, not by gazing fixedly at a flawed image, not by hiding warts and excrescences, but by seeing oneself in the reflected ambivalences of a life which calls us to transcendence, not imitation.

*Ebony* 23, no. 4 (Feb. 1968): 35–42.

## HENRY LEE MOON, "Abraham Lincoln: A Man to Remember and Honor," February 1968

*A native of South Carolina, Moon (1901–1985) was a journalist, civil rights activist, and author of* Balance of Power *(1948), where he argued for the vital importance of the Black vote influencing elections. A longtime employee of the NAACP, Moon became editor of* The Crisis *in 1965. In the same month that Lerone Bennett's essay attacking Lincoln as a racist appeared, Moon published the following editorial in response to young Black "militants" whom he believed were expressing the same views as White bigots. In a period of Black Power and nationalism, Moon was concerned by this assault on Lincoln's image, as he believed it ignored Lincoln's anti-slavery convictions and policies to improve race relations. For Moon, Lincoln remained the Great Emancipator, the greatest of all presidents, and an international symbol of liberation (AANB).*

It is ironic that some of the apostles of the new cult of black "militancy" should now be adopting the view of the white bigots who maintain that Abraham Lincoln was essentially a racist espousing the evil doctrine of white supremacy. They would withhold from the Great Emancipator the respect, admiration and affection in which his memory is held by millions of people of all races and faiths.

In support of their contention, they cite certain statements of Lincoln, known to every student of the period, advocating segregation of the races, involving massive deportation of Negroes to Africa and affirming the primacy of saving the Union at whatever cost, including continued slavery. They fail to mention his historic deeds or his many anti-slavery statements.

Lincoln was, of course, a politician—one of the most consummate in the history of the nation, not excluding such able practitioners of the art of politics as Franklin Delano Roosevelt and Lyndon Baines Johnson. He was also a product of his era—a period in which the majority of white Americans condoned slavery and assumed white supremacy was unchallengeable.

However, there were in his generation, as now, political thinkers who clung tenaciously and uncompromisingly to their ideals and principles. They rejected any idea of the inequality of mankind and consistently demanded immediate and universal emancipation. Such were John Brown, William Lloyd Garrison, Frederick Douglass, Charles Sumner, Wendell Phillips and scores of others, not one of whom could be elected to a position of power in which they could effectuate their noble ideals. They, nevertheless, served a useful and essential service. Their agitation, propaganda and defiance aroused the nation to the horror of slavery and paved the way to the election of Lincoln, the politician and humanitarian.

Men are rightly judged by, and remembered and honored for, what they did in their finest hour, not by the mean compromises they may have felt called upon to make on the way to their destiny. Where would the country be today if any of the three pro-slavery presidential candidates—Douglas, Breckinridge or Bell—had been elected in 1860?

On the basis of his deeds, Lincoln is generally regarded as the greatest of American presidents not only in this nation which, at the supreme sacrifice, he preserved and in which he made possible "a new birth of freedom," but also in Africa and Asia, in Europe and South America, and wherever men live. His towering stature, a century after his assassination, remains undiminished despite the puny critics, black and white, now snarling at his heels.

*The Crisis* 75, no. 2 (Feb. 1968): 42–43.

## JOHN H. SENGSTACKE, "A New Lincoln," February 12, 1968

*A native of Savannah, Georgia, and graduate of Hampton Institute, John H. Sengstacke (1912–1997) was the nephew of the* Chicago Defender's *founder, Robert Abbott, and he began working for the newspaper in the early 1930s. Sengstacke became editor and publisher of the* Defender *after his uncle's death and further increased the circulation and national influence of the paper. One of the foremost leaders of African American journalism in the twentieth century, Sengstacke founded an association for Black newspapers and became the proprietor of additional newspapers, including the* Pittsburgh Courier. *By 1968, when Sengstacke responded to Lerone Bennett's* Ebony *article, the* Defender *was a daily newspaper with a reputation for being a leading voice in the civil rights movement. Based on Bennett's piece and the work of historian Stephen Ambrose, Sengstacke was persuaded that it was time to interrogate the myth of Lincoln as Great Emancipator (Robert Mcg. Thomas Jr., "John Sengstacke, Black Publisher, Dies at 84,"* New York Times, *May 30, 1997).*

---

The true image of Abraham Lincoln is finally coming through the mist of legends that surrounded him for over a century. The Negro and a large body of the

American people have been deceived for a long time by historians who deliberately concealed the true facts about the Civil War President.

The story about Lincoln freeing the slaves out of a great humanitarian impulse proves inconsistent with the facts that honest historical research has brought out. In a recent, incisive article on the Great Emancipator, the erudite senior editor of Ebony, Lerone Bennett, emphasized the point that Lincoln was a firm believer in white supremacy.

Bennett's assertion is not mere fantasy. He has convincing historical data to support his views. Other scholars with equal regard for the truth, have reached similar conclusions.

Known to history as the Great Emancipator, Lincoln believed—and often said—that it was impossible for white and black men to live together in Freedom. His only solution for America's greatest problem was for all the Negroes to return to Africa. In his Emancipation Proclamation he carefully drew the boundaries within which it would operate, and deliberately excluded all areas in which his armies had control. However, it should be recalled, as Dr. Stephen E. Ambrose, professor of history at Johns Hopkins University, observed that Congressional action and activities of certain generals had already freed thousands of Negroes, and would continue to be more important as a source of emancipation.

Lincoln revealed quite clearly his attitude toward the issue of slavery in his famous reply to save the Union, and if he could accomplish that by not freeing any slaves, he would free none.

To the common man today, Lincoln is the railsplitter, the ragged boy who rose to become President, the Great Emancipator who in the end suffered martyrdom. But there is considerable evidence that Lincoln was not alarmed at the extreme Southern doctrine that slavery was the natural condition of the working class. The old image of "Father Abraham" as a labor sympathizer, with his compassion for the suffering of the black slaves is being wiped out by modern historiography, thanks to Bennett and Ambrose.

Editorial in the *Chicago Daily Defender*, Feb. 12, 1968.

## NORMAN E. W. HODGES, *Breaking the Chains of Bondage*, 1972

*Educated at Fisk University, Yale University, and Columbia University, Hodges was one of several historians at the beginning of the 1970s who emphasized Black agency and offered a critique of mainstream historical perspectives. Of this group of new historians, Hodges's 1972 history of African Americans included the most extensive discussion of Lincoln and reflected the influence of Benjamin Quarles and Lerone Bennett. Hodges suggests "Lincoln's moral repugnance was never as strong as his racial and practical considerations," and that he took a "moderate" or "accommodationist" approach to slavery.*

———————

Some historians have recently taken a hard look at the legendary "Great Emancipator," especially with regard to his alleged views on slavery, equality, and the role of the freedmen in a non-slave-based American society. The Black writer and popular scholar Lerone Bennett, Jr. has done impressive research on the Lincoln period. He has asserted that the sixteenth president was equivocal towards Blacks; that Lincoln reflected the "racist" attitudes and responses of his White contemporaries on the question of social equality and integration. Bennett has pointed out that the Emancipation Proclamation did not, in effect, "emancipate," inasmuch as its provisions were restricted to those slaves in the enemy states over whom Lincoln had no effective jurisdiction. The slaves in the Border states were not covered by his proclamation, though they constituted one-fourth of the 4,000,000 Blacks in America. In fact, they were to continue in bondage until the passage of the Thirteenth Amendment in 1865. Of course, none of Bennett's conclusions were new, but they have caused a minor sensation in today's Black community because he stated them in sharp terms.

Lincoln claimed to have developed a moral repugnance for slavery long before he ascended to the presidency. He recalled, in a letter to an acquaintance, the torment he felt when he saw slaves in irons aboard a ship upon which he was travelling in 1841. Lincoln expressed the view that bondage was a "moral evil," in numerous speeches and writings. However, the new president was not an abolitionist. In point of fact, many abolitionists were skeptical of him because he had not been part of the movement.

While a member of the Illinois legislature in 1837, Lincoln had introduced resolutions that denounced slavery as a product of "both injustice and bad policy," but he also opposed abolitionism because he thought it "tends rather to increase than to abate its evils." Lincoln disagreed with the abolitionists' contentions that all slaves should be quickly freed without compensation to their owners and that the federal government had the right and duty to abolish bondage in the "slave" states. He did, however, oppose the extension of slavery into the territories, but the record amply proves that he was motivated by economic (and racist?) considerations. For example, he felt that slave labor would discourage poor Whites from settling in the West since Whites employment opportunities there would be endangered. It thus appears that Lincoln's moral repugnance was never as strong as his racial and practical considerations.

Abraham Lincoln took a distinctively "moderate" or "accommodationist" approach to slavery. He hoped that slavery could be gradually brought to an end in the South by providing compensation for slave masters willing to free their slaves. Lincoln thought that he could appeal to their pocketbooks, though such a view does not seem altogether reasonable since the Southerners resisted abolitionism precisely because they considered bondage profitable within their "cotton kingdoms." Nevertheless, Lincoln thought that his plan would lead to emancipation for all slaves by the close of the century.

Lincoln, moreover, was never an advocate of social equality for Blacks; in this, he simply reflected the sentiments of most contemporary politicians and citizens of the majority race. He had argued for the right of Blacks to enjoy the fruits of their labor. Yet it is not likely that he foresaw full economic equality for Blacks either—some historians have been eager to assert—since he clearly thought that the races should live apart, either in America or, preferably, elsewhere. It must be remembered that Lincoln was compelled to recognize the crucial role of slavery in the Civil War. He had originally not intended to wage the war as an abolitionist crusade: he had conceived of the war as a struggle to preserve the Union, not as a battle against slavery. Fortunately, Lincoln was forced to abandon his policy of keeping the Blacks in *status quo*—a practice that Benjamin Quarles, the Black scholar, has described as Lincoln's "hands-off-the-Negro" policy.

Blacks today rightfully charge that *all* Americans have been "miseducated" or "brainwashed" to some extent by the romantic legends with which most White historical figures have been endowed. Lincoln was always depicted in schoolbooks as the "Great Emancipator" who loved Blacks and thought that all men were equal in brotherhood. We were taught (or, rather, indoctrinated) that the Emancipator fought a great and bloody war in order to "free" the slaves. It is doubtful that Lincoln himself—if he was, indeed, "honest Abe"—would recognize the image presented by schoolbook mythology for so many generations! One does not wish to disparage Lincoln. His stature in history looms large. It is, however, an absolute obligation and duty for the sincere scholar to seek to wipe from the historical record all the concoctions and fabrications that tend to delude us concerning the past. Lincoln was a *man* not a *god*. He had opinions and prejudice and special interests, as do we all. We can understand the man and his times better, if we can view both from a realistic perspective.

Quarles has written that Lincoln faced both a war and a revolution and that "although one was military and the other social, they were interrelated." Faced with the social revolution, Lincoln formulated two plans, one for slaves and [an]other for free Blacks: (1) gradual and compensated emancipation for slaves—freeing them over a period stretching over 30 years and compensating their masters out of the national treasury; and (2) voluntary deportation of free Blacks—this plan would send Blacks out of the country to settle in "colonies" elsewhere. The affected slave owners were hostile to the first plan; quasi-free Blacks rallied against the colonization scheme.

Lincoln's position on colonization was in accord with his conviction that Blacks were not the social equals of Whites. He felt that the races should exist apart and that the White community would never accept Blacks in its midst as free men. Blacks, on the other hand, were not prepared to accept deportation—voluntary or involuntary—since they regarded America as their home, as a society built literally with the "blood, sweat, and tears" of their ancestors, themselves, and their slave brothers.

The Republican Party, it should be noted, had nominated Lincoln in 1860 for the presidency precisely because his views were moderate enough to conciliate the various factions within the party. [...] After Lincoln rejected an 1860 compromise proposal, by which Congress attempted to divide the territories between slavery and freedom, South Carolina became the first State to secede from the Union (it did so on December 20, the same day on which Lincoln repudiated the compromise proposal). Though adamant against the inclusion of slavery in the territories, Lincoln had vowed to permit the institution to continue in states where it was "legal," and to insure firm enforcement of the Fugitive Slave Act. [...]

We have noted that Lincoln believed the preservation of the Union to be the paramount issue confronting his new presidency. But the action of the Southerners at Fort Sumter on April 12, 1861, when South Carolina troops fired on the federal garrison, forced him to move to crush the rebellion. Even then his primary motive was to "preserve" the Union, which in the eyes of the rebels no longer existed. The President's position was that the Southern states could not secede. In point of fact, they had seceded—and on the issue of slavery. [...]

Though President Lincoln sent out a call for troops to fight in the war, he rejected the Blacks who flocked into recruiting stations to enlist. [...]

Lincoln was eventually compelled by events to turn to the recruiting of Black soldiers when the war failed to produce a quick victory for the Union side as he had hoped. [...]

Though Lincoln had ended slavery in the territories and in the capital and had, in effect, nullified the Fugitive Slave Act by granting freedom from slavery to Blacks crossing Union lines, millions of human beings remained in bondage. The President had scrupulously avoided taking steps to abolish slavery in the Border states, and the slaveholders there had not adopted his "gradual compensated emancipation" program. Lincoln had not dealt at all with the continued enslavement of Blacks in the South. He claimed that the Confederate states were still in the Union because the act of secession was illegal. Therefore, he would abide by his earlier pledge not to interfere with slavery in the states where it was legal. The President's thinking appears confused on this point. If the states were in rebellion, would not their "illegal" act seem to deprive them of the federal government's duty to adhere to practices established for its relations with law-abiding states? [...]

Lincoln explained that the illegal insurrection of the Confederate states had to be crushed and that the freeing of the slaves would insure Union victory. He did not doubt his constitutional power as wartime commander-in-chief of the armed forces to put down the rebellion by any means within his authority. The President intended to declare that all slaves in rebel areas would be free on the next New Year's Day.

Thus, in a preliminary proclamation on September 22, 1862 (a little more than a month following the Greeley attack), President Lincoln declared that slaves in areas of rebellion on January 1, 1863, "shall be then, thenceforward, and forever free." Later, on that fateful New Year's Day itself, he issued the final Emancipation Proclamation in which he said that freed Blacks "will be received into the armed service of the United States." [...]

To some, Lincoln had come to the great moment, after too great reluctance and agonizing slowness. He had issued the preliminary proclamation to alert the rebels to his future plan and to give them an opportunity to return voluntarily to the Union. He had promised that any state that returned to the Union prior to New Year's Day would be able to retain its slaves since it would no longer be in rebellion. Even with that inducement, the South angrily rejected the offer. Only then did Lincoln proceed to sign the final Emancipation document on January 1, 1863; then he called on the newly freed Blacks to work hard for wages, to abstain from unruly behavior, and to take the opportunity to serve in the military forces.

We have noted that the Proclamation had minimal impact upon the millions of slaves that it was meant to free. The three-quarters of America's slaves that the Proclamation "freed" lived outside areas under Union control. Furthermore, as we have noted, the much-heralded document was *not* addressed to the 1,000,000 slaves who lived in Border states and were, at least in theory, within the reach of Lincoln's authority. For military and political reasons, these hapless Blacks were to continue in wretched bondage until December 18, 1865, when the Thirteenth Amendment to the Constitution was adopted. [...]

Lincoln had always insisted that "readmission" to the Union for the rebel states would not be an issue. [...] He was prepared to pardon all these rebellious individuals, except for high Confederate officials who must, of course, be brought to justice.

Before the war had ended, Lincoln had drawn up a *Proclamation of Amnesty and Reconstruction* which contained his ideas for a moderate policy. Most Southerners would be given a general amnesty (pardon), provided they were willing to pledge future loyalty to the Union. The Union would recognize new state governments once persons equal in numbers to 10 percent of the vote cast in the 1860 elections had pledged loyalty, abolished slavery, and organized a state government.

Lincoln did not clarify his intentions regarding the freedmen in the proclamation. While he implied that the South should give the vote to Blacks of education and property (or to those who were military heroes), the President ignored the mass of Blacks, whom he probably considered unready for citizenship. He anticipated, however, that the federal government would aid the freedmen in the economic sphere.

Norman E. W. Hodges, *Breaking the Chains of Bondage* (New York: Simon and Schuster, 1972), 171–74, 177–178, 180–182, 192.

## ARVARH STRICKLAND, Remarks at the Abraham Lincoln Symposium, Springfield, Illinois, February 12, 1980

*A native of Mississippi, Strickland (1930–2013) was educated at Tougaloo College and the University of Illinois, where he earned a PhD in history. He taught at Chicago Teachers College (today's Chicago State University) before becoming the first African American faculty member at the University of Missouri in 1969. Best known for his* History of the Chicago Urban League, *Strickland also published an article, "The Illinois Background of Lincoln's Attitude toward Slavery and the Negro," and raised critical issues regarding Lincoln and race at a symposium in 1980. While he agreed that Lincoln was a racist according to the dictionary definition, he argued that the term is anachronistic when applied to Lincoln's time period. In assessing the work of Lerone Bennett, J. G. Randall, and Benjamin Quarles, Strickland urged that Lincoln be judged by his contributions (John L. Bullion, "In Memoriam: Arvarh E. Strickland [1930–2013]," Perspectives on History, November 13, 2013, www.historians.org/publications -and-directories/perspectives-on-history/november-2013/in-memoriam-arvarh -e-strickland).*

Certainly the concept [of] racism is an anachronism as we try to read the concept that we have now back to the Civil War era because our concept of racism has largely been shaped by the '60s. By the Kerner Report, for instance, and the concept of institutional racism that we now talk about as we deal with our policies on civil rights and affirmative action [...] and so we do have to keep in mind [...] that we are talking about something within a time context and the '60s have been very significant in this. But there are a couple of questions I would like to raise, or points [to] explore really, and that is one, to, you know, to ask the question, How do we look at the concept of racism? [...]

We speak of, I guess, the kind of dictionary definition [...]. [R]acism is simply assuming the inherent racial superiority or purity of one of a certain race and so we are not talking necessarily about prejudice and discrimination or hatred, and we are simply talking about the concept of believing one race is in some way superior to another. Well, when we draw that out, and I don't intend this to be a lecture on semantics, we do get this modern concept of racism and if we support institutions that further this kind of assumption we are dealing with institutional racism. [. . .] [W]e can all start with the premise Lincoln was a racist. There is no doubt about that. [. . .] Lerone Bennett's article [. . .] was nothing new, not surprising at all. This has been said over and over and over. It had been simply said in other context[s].

Now when I was a graduate student at the University of Illinois I read the unexpurgated version of J.G. Randall's *The Civil War and Reconstruction* and in that very scholarly volume, with some obvious problems that were later dealt with to some extent, Randall said that, you know, Lincoln was certainly not the abolitionist type; he was really moved toward emancipation reluctantly and all of the things that Bennett said basically, but Randall states quite emphatically that Lincoln believed slavery was morally wrong. This set him aside throughout—we get this.

David Donald, even as he is reconsidering Lincoln and trying to bring some corrective to Professor [Randall's] work, talks about Lincoln issuing the proclamation only as a war measure. When we look at the whole question of whether or not he was the Great Emancipator, you know, [. . .] through the years nobody ever claimed for Lincoln an unalloyed devotion to equality in all respects. [. . .] [W]e are looking for Lincoln the man.

I have no problems with legends and mythological heroes in history. I think that to see our great people as people is more important than to see them as heroes bigger than life that we can't relate to as human beings, and so to say all of that about Lincoln really to me does not diminish him as the Great Emancipator or the great president that he was.

There is another point I would like to speak to just briefly and that is [. . .] the role of blacks and Lincoln and race and the events of this period. Too often we as historians, we were trained this way and many of us never lose the weakness, [to] think of blacks in American history as a mass that had been acted upon and not as active participants in the history of this country. And if we don't take into consideration blacks as active participants during this period we lose a very significant point in the creation of the image of Abraham Lincoln and of the Emancipation Proclamation[.] [A]nd on this point I would like to refer [. . .] to another part of the work of Professor Benjamin Quarles whom I think does a better job than [Stephen] Oates and others in really helping us to understand Lincoln and his image and that of the Emancipation Proclamation. Frederick Douglass and other blacks understood the limits of the Emancipation Proclamation as soon as it was issued. There were some blacks who came out forthrightly and said, "This thing doesn't say anything," but Douglass said, "Oh yes it does, even though it does not do what we would like for it to do, we must proclaim it to be what we want it to be." And what black people were doing was making this document into a great document of freedom for Americans. They were doing to it what generations of Englishmen had done to the Magna Carta and what Americans had already begun doing to the Declaration of Independence and it was black people who saw the potential there and helped to do it. And also when we think of Lincoln the Great Emancipator, it was the black people who first proclaimed him that. They were those who, as Quarles said, loved him first and it was not as David Donald seemed to have thought through a naive childlike simplicity that they did it[.] [I]t was through an intentional use of symbol and the very essential concept of democratic life that this image was used and so I guess many blacks were as shocked [. . .] in the '60s when we, ourselves, started to try to destroy the image we had created historically. So I think we need to understand that as we try to understand Lincoln the Emancipator and his greatness there.

So I think that the simple point I want to make [. . .] is we need to keep in mind what we mean now by this anachronistic concept of racism and the things that we can simply take as givens in Lincoln: Lincoln's personality, his life, his work, and yet realize that this does not detract from the greatness of the man or of the contribution he made and, in fact, it makes him even more a model for us as human beings with all our weaknesses and foibles and everything else.

Typed transcript in Abraham Lincoln Association Papers, Box 110, Abraham Lincoln Presidential Library, Springfield, IL.

## MARY FRANCES BERRY, "Lincoln & Civil Rights for Blacks," Address at the Abraham Lincoln Association Banquet, Springfield, Illinois, February 12, 1980

*A native of Tennessee, Berry (1938– ) was educated at Howard University and the University of Michigan, where she earned a PhD in history and a JD from the law school. In addition to holding positions at academic institutions such as Howard University and the University of Pennsylvania, Berry was appointed to the US Civil Rights Commission in 1980 and served as the commission's chair from 1993 to 2004. The author of several books and articles, Berry offers an interpretation of Lincoln's views on African American civil rights and speculates on what Lincoln might have done if he had lived. Most significant is her reading of Lincoln as a pragmatist who viewed the Constitution as a flexible document. Berry analyzes Lincoln's statements from the 1850s that indicated his clear opposition to Black civil rights, yet she argues that circumstances and his own principles led him to gradually shift these views during the Civil War. Lincoln came to embrace not only emancipation and the enlistment of Black*

*soldiers but also Black suffrage. While there were politicians more advanced in*
*their views on racial equality, Berry notes that they could not have been elected*
*president (AANB).*

---

As we consider Lincoln, the successful leader and politician, dealing with the civil rights of Negroes, let us ask two questions. How much did he tell people what they wanted to hear, and how much did he give them a new sense of direction? Did he strike a proper balance between idealism and pragmatism? I believe he did. [...]

I want to focus in particular on Lincoln's actions and words on civil rights for the Negro.

As I do, I am reminded that the distinguished scholar James Randall, looking at constitutional aspects of Lincoln's policies, explained that much of the constitutional reasoning of those days was mere rationalizing. [...]

I find much to applaud in Randall's approach to history. Like Randall, I believe it is more insightful to ask how Lincoln's approach to the Civil War shaped our constitutional understanding than to ask how the Constitution limited policy alternatives available to Lincoln.

The really exciting constitutional inquiries, I believe, are finding out how adept the fathers were in picking and choosing from the Constitution's different rationales, and then ascertaining the purposes of the arguments, and analyzing the social effects of their goals. Whatever arguments evolved became accretions and part of the constitutional wisdom to be passed along. The real task, then, is not choosing between believing that politicians meant what they said about the Constitution and ignoring what they said, but analyzing both what they said and what they did in order to come up with interpretations of both. That is what we must do in considering Lincoln and the issue of civil rights for the Negro. [...]

Now, consistent with these perspectives on the ingredients for success as a politician and the role of constitutional argument in politics, what did Lincoln—who was not an altogether unsuccessful politician—say about civil rights for the Negro? What did he do and why, and how did he add to our constitutional and political wisdom?

What he said is well known to scholars and Lincoln buffs. In a speech at Peoria, Illinois, on October 16, 1854, he said:

> Free them, and make them politically and socially, our equals? My own feelings will not admit of this; and if mine would, we well know that those of the great mass of white people will not. Whether this feeling accords with justice and sound judgment, is not the sole question, if indeed, it is any part of it. A universal feeling, whether well or ill-founded, can not be safely disregarded. We can not, then, make them equals.

In attacking slavery:

> Let it not be said I am contending for the establishment of political and social equality between the whites and blacks. I have already said the contrary.

In a Springfield speech on June 26, 1857, Lincoln stated:

> Now I protest against that counterfeit logic which concludes that, because I do not want a black woman for a *slave* I must necessarily want her for a *wife*. I need not have her for either. I can just leave her alone. In some respects she certainly is not my equal; but in her natural right to eat the bread she earns with her own hands without asking leave of any one else, she is my equal, and the equal of all others.

Furthermore, he said, as he understood the intention of the authors of the Declaration of Independence:

> They did not mean to assert the obvious untruth, that all were then actually enjoying ... equality, nor yet, that they were about to confer it immediately upon them.... They meant simply to declare the *right*, so that the *enforcement* of it might follow as fast as circumstances should permit. They meant to set up a standard maxim for free society, which should be familiar to all, and revered by all: constantly looked to, constantly labored for, and even though never perfectly attained, constantly approximated, and thereby constantly spreading and deepening its influence, and augmenting the happiness and value of life to all people of all colors everywhere.

During the first Lincoln-Douglas debate, on August 21, 1858, at Ottawa, Lincoln stated:

> I have no purpose to introduce political and social equality between the white and the black races.... But I hold that ... there is no reason in the world why the negro is not entitled to all the natural rights enumerated in the Declaration of Independence, the right to life, liberty, and the pursuit of happiness.

And at the Charleston debate on September 18, he stated: "I am not nor ever have been in favor of making voters or jurors of negroes, nor of qualifying them to hold office, nor to intermarry with white people." As long as blacks lived in America with whites: "while they do remain together there must be the position of superior and inferior, and I as much as any other man am in favor of having the superior position assigned to the white race."

These statements were all made in the environment preceding the Civil War. Before the 1854 Peoria speech, Lincoln's statements concerned abolition, not civil rights, and of course Illinois opinion, even antislavery opinion, was against black voting. The issue was shaping opinion to end slavery—not obtaining political rights for blacks. First things first. But when he argued that the Constitution did not permit interference within the Southern states (as he pointed out in an October 3, 1845, letter to Williamson Durley), that use of the Constitution was "a paramount duty . . . due to the Union of the states," and not because no one could think of an interpretation of the Constitution that would have permitted interference.

In 1854, when he clearly stated that he did not mean to make blacks equal to whites, Lincoln was expressing a view that became new Republican Party doctrine. In the aftermath of the Kansas-Nebraska Act repealing the Missouri Compromise, he always pointed out that he would not interfere with existing slavery and would uphold the fugitive slave laws—these being essential for the maintenance of the Union—but that Congress could, under the Constitution, keep slavery out of the territories. He knew that Free Soilers and Republicans had to make clear over and over again that, although they were against the extension of slavery, they were not radically for civil rights for blacks nor for attacking the South in order to win in Illinois. [ . . . ]

When Stephen Douglas made a speech concerning the Dred Scott case in which he implied that anyone who opposed the decision was in favor of blacks being political and social equals of whites, Lincoln responded. He explained that Republicans respected the Court but would seek to overturn the decision. Mindful of the necessity for negating the idea that Republicans believed in black equality or amalgamation, Lincoln stated that a black woman had the natural right to eat the bread she earned but was not equal to him. He recognized that his constituency had a "natural disgust" for amalgamation and that the only way in which to prevent amalgamation was to oppose the spread of slavery and to propose the colonization of free Negroes. As he emphasized, the Declaration of Independence held out a promise for progress and improvement of mankind, but blacks could achieve that promise in this country or elsewhere. Colonization was a way of gaining support for the Republicans' antislavery goals.

Lincoln extended those views in the Lincoln-Douglas debates. To have done otherwise would have doomed the Republican party to defeat again in the 1860 election. Lincoln was being both popular and political. He explained the party position in terms that appealed to his listeners and that reflected their own views, but he proposed colonization as a way to set them thinking more positively about ending slavery. Lincoln's strategy proved its effectiveness when, with Hannibal Hamlin on the ticket, the Republicans attracted Illinois, Indiana, and Pennsylvania and won the election.

When the Civil War came, we find further evidence that Lincoln was a pragmatic, successful politician; in a series of events he gradually changed his posture toward civil rights for Negroes. As President, he moved to an emancipation policy in order to keep the border states in the Union. When circumstances led him to enlist blacks, he found authority for the action in the constitutional powers of Commander-in-Chief, recognizing that the interpretation of the Constitution can change with events. Therefore, "Measures, otherwise unconstitutional, might become lawful."

His was no static, dead-hand view of the Constitution. The Constitution was a changing, evolving document yielding to necessity. When slavery was on the way to ultimate extinction, then he could deal with civil rights issues. One can speculate that Lincoln's final public statement (in April, 1865)—supporting suffrage for those blacks who had served in the Army—was made because he feared, as Benjamin Butler said, "a race war . . . at least a guerilla war because we have taught those men how to fight." This, of course, is just speculation. We can, however, conclude—based on the pattern of his public statements—that Lincoln was flexible enough to change his political positions while remaining within the Constitution. His justifications for black soldiers and for emancipation itself, then, are evidence of his creative use of the Constitution. Lincoln and his advisers were very good lawyers.

Perhaps a man with Lincoln's pragmatism and flexible posture, with the threat to Republican party influence and the possibility of a race war, would have supported the Civil Rights Act of 1866, as his party did. Perhaps he would have supported Negro citizenship and all the other rights white citizens enjoyed. We should be mindful of Frederick Douglass's observation on the Emancipation Proclamation: Lincoln in his "peculiar cautious, forbearing and hesitating way, slow, but . . . sure" had emancipated slaves. "Events" said Douglass, "may be relied on to carry him forward in the same direction."

And events after the Proclamation did carry Lincoln forward in the same direction. Using Negroes as soldiers led logically, given the traditional association between citizenship and military service, to permitting Negroes to vote. [ . . . ] Lincoln's private and then public statements encouraging the vote for black soldiers after the war showed his understanding and pragmatism on the issue. If Lincoln could respond positively within the Constitution when emancipation was necessary, he could respond if voting became necessary, especially was this so given the Constitutional nexus between military service and suffrage. The bottom line in any consideration of Lincoln, however, is this: There were certainly men and women who were more advanced in their civil rights actions and views than Lincoln in 1860 and 1864, but they could not be elected President. [ . . . ]

Men had to be shown gradually that civil rights for the Negro was a proper solution to the post-emancipation status of black soldiers. Lincoln, moving into "the full stature of democracy," would have been equal to the task of generating that understanding.

*Journal of the Abraham Lincoln Association* 2 (1980): 46–57.

## VINCENT HARDING, *There Is a River*, 1981

*Educated at the City College of New York, Columbia University, and the University of Chicago, where he received a PhD in history, Harding (1931–2014) was a scholar, minister, professor, and community activist. In addition to holding academic positions, Harding wrote books on African American history, and composed much of Martin Luther King Jr.'s "Beyond Vietnam" speech. In the following excerpt from There Is A River, Harding points out the limitations of the Emancipation Proclamation and places great emphasis on the agency that enslaved people exercised during the Civil War. In a more nuanced fashion than Lerone Bennett, Harding suggests that the actions of the enslaved render the narrative of Lincoln as Great Emancipator a myth. While Harding admits that the Emancipation Proclamation, Attorney General Edward Bates's opinion on Black citizenship, and the federal government's willingness to accept Black men as soldiers were all significant, he argues that African Americans created their own freedom by running away and secured it by joining the ranks of the army and successfully fighting for it. Harding deems the Great Emancipator myth both inaccurate and deleterious, as it contributed to the historical feeling that Blacks must show gratitude to Lincoln for the gift of freedom (Margalit Fox, "Vincent Harding, Civil Rights Activist and Associate of Dr. King, Dies," New York Times, May 22, 2014).*

---

In September 1862 Abraham Lincoln, in a double-minded attempt both to bargain with and weaken the South while replying to the pressures of the North, finally made public his proposed Emancipation Proclamation. Under its ambiguous terms, the states in rebellion would be given until the close of the year to end their rebellious action. If any did so, their captive black people would not be affected; otherwise, the Emancipation Proclamation would go into effect on January 1, 1863, theoretically freeing all the enslaved population of the Confederate states and promising federal power to maintain that freedom.

What actually was involved was quite another matter. Of great import was the fact that the proclamation excluded from its provisions the "loyal" slave states of Missouri, Kentucky, Delaware, and Maryland, the anti-Confederate West Virginia Territory, and loyal areas in certain other Confederate states. Legally, then, nearly one million black people whose masters were "loyal" to the Union had no part of the emancipation offered. In effect, Lincoln was announcing freedom to the captives over whom he had least control, while allowing those in states clearly under the rule of his government to remain in slavery. However, on another more legalistic level, Lincoln was justifying his armies' use of the Confederates' black "property," and preparing the way for an even more extensive use of black power by the military forces of the Union. Here, the logic of his move was clear, providing an executive confirmation and extension of Congress's Second Confiscation Act of 1862: once the Emancipation Proclamation went into effect, the tens of thousands of black people who were creating their own freedom, and making themselves available as workers in the Union camps, could be used by the North without legal qualms. Technically, they would no longer be private property, no longer cause problems for a President concerned about property rights. [...]

In the North [...] [w]ord of Lincoln's anticipated proclamation had an electrifying effect on the black community there, but at the same time further removed the focus from the black freedom-seizing movement in the South. The promised proclamation now gave the Northerners more reason than ever to look to others for release, to invest their hope in the Union cause. Now it seemed as if they would not need to be isolated opponents of an antagonistic federal government. Again, because they wanted to believe, needed to hope, yearned to prove themselves worthy, they thought they saw ever more clearly the glory of the coming; before long, in their eyes the proclamation was clothed in what appeared to be almost angelic light. [...] Doubts from the past were now cast aside, for their struggle was unquestionably in the hands of Providence and the Grand Army of the Republic. The voice of God was joined to that of Abraham Lincoln. [...]

The unexpectedly harsh exigencies of war, the reluctance of whites to fight, the pressure from his generals, the unpredictable freedom activities of blacks in the South, and the constant demands from Northern black leaders—all had combined to convince Lincoln that the North must finally enlist black troops in the federal armies [...] [N]ear the end of November, Attorney General Edward Bates issued an official advisement, saying in part: "Free men of color, if born in the United States, are citizens of the United States." That war-created statement became the first federal admission of black citizenship. A little more than a month later, the Emancipation Proclamation was announced, followed by the first official national recruitment of black troops. Taken together, these three events—rising out of the bitter agonies and unexpected duration of the civil conflict, and inspired in large part by the powerful presence of tens of thousands of Southern blacks who had created their own emancipation—placed the bloody imprimatur of black struggle upon the federal government's pursuit of victory. [...]

[F]rom a certain legal point of view it could be argued that the Emancipation Proclamation set free no enslaved black people at all. Since by December 31, 1862, no Confederate state had accepted Lincoln's invitation to return to the fold with their slaves unthreatened, and since Lincoln acknowledged that he had no real way of enforcing such a proclamation within the rebellious states, the proclamation's power to set anyone free was dubious at best. (Rather, it confirmed and gave ambiguous legal standing to the freedom which black people had already claimed through their own surging, living proclamations.)

Indeed, in his annual address to Congress on December 1, 1862, Lincoln had not seemed primarily concerned with the proclamation. Instead, he had taken that crucial opportunity to propose three constitutional amendments which reaffirmed his long-standing approach to national slavery. The proposed amendments included provisions for gradual emancipation (with a deadline as late as 1900), financial compensation to the owners, and colonization for the freed people. In other words, given the opportunity to place his impending proclamation of limited, immediate emancipation into the firmer context of a constitutional amendment demanding freedom for all enslaved blacks, Lincoln chose another path, one far more in keeping with his own history.

But none of this could dampen the joy of the black North. Within that community, it was the Emancipation Proclamation of January 1, 1863, which especially symbolized all that the people so deeply longed to experience, and its formal announcement sent a storm of long-pent-up emotion surging through the churches and meeting halls. [...] In spite of its limitations, the proclamation was taken as the greatest sign yet provided by the hand of Providence. The river had burst its boundaries, had shattered slavery's dam. It appeared as if the theodicy of the Northern black experience was finally prevailing. For the freedom struggle, especially in the South, had begun to overwhelm the white man's war, and had forced the President and the nation officially to turn their faces toward the moving black masses. Wherever black people could assemble, by themselves or with whites, they came together to lift joyful voices of thanksgiving, to sing songs of faith, to proclaim, "Jehovah hath triumphed, his people are free." For them, a new year and a new era had been joined in one. [...]

Such rapture was understandable, but like all ecstatic experiences, it carried its own enigmatic penalties. Out of it was born the mythology of Abraham Lincoln as Emancipator, a myth less important in its detail than in its larger meaning and consequences for black struggle. The heart of the matter was this: while the concrete historical realities of the time testified to the costly, daring, courageous activities of hundreds of thousands of black people breaking loose from slavery and setting themselves free, the myth gave the credit for this freedom to a white Republican president. In those same times when black men and women saw visions of a new society of equals, and heard voices pressing them against the American Union of white supremacy, Abraham Lincoln was unable to see beyond the limits of his own race, class, and time, and dreamed of a Haitian island and of Central American colonies to rid the country of the constantly accusing, constantly challenging black presence. Yet in the mythology of blacks and whites alike, it was the independent, radical action of the black movement toward freedom which was diminished, and the coerced, ambiguous role of a white deliverer which gained pre-eminence.

In a sense, then, it was these ecstatic Emancipation Proclamation meetings which provided the first real shaping of the unlikely message that the God of the black community had used Abraham Lincoln as his primary agent of freedom— Abraham Lincoln, rather than those many, many thousands of Afro-Americans who had lived and died through blood baptism in the river. In the development of black struggle and black radicalism in America, the consequences of this mythology lasted long and created many difficulties.

Indeed, the consequences began to be evident immediately. Near the end of the Emancipation Proclamation, after Lincoln had counseled the enslaved black population "to abstain from all violence, unless in necessary self-defense," he added this paragraph: "I further declare and make known that such persons, of suitable condition, will be received into the armed service of the United States to garrison forts, positions, stations, and other places, and to man vessels of all sorts in said service." Thus Lincoln had inextricably bound the cause of black emancipation to the military role of black people in preserving his white-defined, white-controlled Union. In a sense, he was indicating which acts of self-defense were "necessary," clarifying why black freedom was being legitimized, preparing to move thousands of black men from the white domination of the Southern plantations to the white domination of the Northern armies.

Vincent Harding, *There Is a River* (New York: Random House), 1981, 232–237.

## CLARENCE THOMAS on Lincoln and the Declaration of Independence, 1987

*Thomas (1948–) was serving as chair of the Equal Employment Opportunity Commission when he published this essay that coincided with the bicentennial commemoration of the Constitution. The bicentennial sparked debate over the connection between slavery and the American Founding, with Justice Thurgood Marshall asserting that the framers of the Constitution produced a "defective" document because it protected slavery. Thomas instead argues in favor of a "Lincolnian" interpretation of the American Founding. Quoting from Lincoln's June 26, 1857 address in response to the Supreme Court's ruling in* Dred Scott, *Thomas holds that the natural rights philosophy in the Declaration of Independence established the United States on the principle of equality and the Constitution was designed to fulfill this ideal. Thomas laments the lasting influence of Chief Justice Taney's pro-slavery interpretation of the Constitution, while Lincoln's and Frederick Douglass's anti-slavery interpretation is a more accurate assessment of the original intent of the Founding Fathers. In 1991, Thomas became the second African American to serve as a justice of the US Supreme*

*Court, when he was appointed to the vacancy created by Justice Marshall's*
*retirement (Thurgood Marshall, "Reflections on the Bicentennial of the United*
*States Constitution," Harvard Law Review 101, no. 1 [1987]: 1–5).*

Our task as defenders of constitutional government and the heritage that is indispensable to its perpetuation requires us to challenge the *Dred Scott* decision. Major elements of Chief Justice Roger Taney's opinion continue to provide the basis for the way we think today about slavery and the founding, civil rights, ethnicity, as well as the way we think of the nation in general. To properly interpret the Constitution in these areas, it is necessary to consider the arguments of the most profound critic of *Dred Scott*, Abraham Lincoln. Both before (as in his Peoria address of October 16, 1854) and after the *Dred Scott* opinion, Lincoln elaborated on the central place of the Declaration of Independence to America. For Lincoln and for the Declaration, equality led to the principle of government by consent, limited government, majority rule, and separation of powers. The Declaration's *promise* of equality of rights obliged citizens to take this "standard maxim for free society," to be "constantly looked to, constantly labored for, and even though never perfectly attained, constantly approximated, and thereby constantly spreading and deepening its influence, and augmenting the happiness and value of life to all people of all colors everywhere." Lincoln's case against slavery insisted on the principle of equality as fundamental for America. The tolerance of slavery for some threatened the liberty of all.

Contrast these arguments with the extraordinary line of reasoning in Chief Justice Taney's 123-page opinion. [...] Taney had contended that in the Founders' view, Black men "had no rights which the white man was bound to respect." [...]

But the "jurisprudence of original intention" cannot be understood as sympathetic with the *Dred Scott* reasoning, *if* we regard the "original intention" of the Constitution to be the fulfillment of the ideas of the Declaration of Independence, as Lincoln, Frederick Douglass, and the Founders understood it. Such an understanding of original intention will keep it from deteriorating into a defense of constitutional sideshows such as "states' rights." Above all, we must cease accepting these crucial premises of Taney's opinion and the subsequent injustice: that no one in the founding generation "thought of disputing, or supposed to be open to dispute" the morality of slavery; and that public opinion at his time was more "enlightened" than earlier public opinion (in fact, the new belief in a "scientific" basis for racism *lowered* regard for Blacks).

It should certainly be troubling that Lincoln's version of the Declaration of Independence is not the standard one. It is as though the Southern arguments triumphed. But to accept Lincoln's interpretation of the American Founding is not merely to go with the winner, or indulge in a sentimental reminiscence about the Great Emancipator—it is Lincoln in the highest political office as an educator who guides us.

Certainly this Lincolnian understanding of the founding does not provide instant wisdom on the whole range of issues concerning Civil Rights, equal opportunity, and race relations. But to quote Lincoln again, from his "House Divided" speech, "If we could first know *where* we are, and *whither* we are tending, we could then better judge what to do, and *how* to do it." It is of absolute importance to preserve what is strongest in the original Civil Rights movement: its insistence that what it demanded is what America had always promised; the logic of American ideals *required* Civil Rights legislation. Accepting the Taney view of American history puts the Civil Rights tradition at odds with the American political tradition, an enmity that saps it of its greatest moral force. We should keep in mind the power of John Hope Franklin's recent description of slavery as "the most remarkable anomaly in the history of the country." Even a brief examination of the founding [. . .] provides ample evidence for Lincoln's interpretation.

"Toward a 'Plain Reading' of the Constitution—The Declaration of Independence in Constitutional Interpretation," *Howard Law Journal* 30, no. 4 (1987): 984–86.

## BARBARA JEANNE FIELDS, "Who Freed the Slaves?" 1990

*Educated at Harvard University and Yale University, where she earned a PhD in history, Fields (1947–) worked with the Freedmen and Southern Society Project and is currently a professor at Columbia University. Her essay that was published in the companion volume to Ken Burns's documentary film,* The Civil War, *reflects a historiographical trend that emphasizes social history and the vital role that African Americans had in securing their freedom. Fields contends that the actions of the enslaved forced Congress, the military, and President Lincoln to take action toward their emancipation. Fields further suggests that Congress acted before Lincoln in addressing the emancipation issue. Instead of Lincoln being the Great Emancipator, Fields believes that emancipation was a collaborative effort and the real credit should go to those who ran away from their masters and compelled the federal government to respond.*

---

Although Lincoln privately believed that slavery was wrong and wished it might be abolished, his public policy faithfully reflected the standpoint of those for whom the war was an issue between free, white citizens: between unionists and secessionists, between rights judged by free-soil northerners and rights claimed by slaveholding southerners. [. . .]

A black soldier in Louisiana, born a slave, dismissed with contempt those northerners, including Abraham Lincoln, who proposed to save the Union without disturbing slavery: "Our union friends Says the{y} are not fighting to free the negroes we are fighting for the union and free navigation of the Mississippi river very well let the white fight for what the{y} want and we negroes fight for what we want . . . liberty must take the day nothing Shorter." By the time that anonymous soldier's defiant manifesto, discarded on a street in New Orleans, was found by a policeman, Lincoln had been forced to recognize the truth it expressed. In issuing his final Emancipation Proclamation on January 1, 1863, Lincoln himself conceded that liberty must take the day, nothing shorter. Preserving the Union—a goal too shallow to be worth the sacrifice of a single life—had become a goal impossible in any event to achieve in that shallow form. [. . .]

What was true from the beginning—and clear to the wise—was not immediately clear to everyone, however. Shortsighted rebels expected to preserve slavery while fighting for independence. Equally shortsighted unionists believed that they could forever compromise the issue of the slaves' freedom to suit the convenience of white citizens. Abraham Lincoln carefully tailored his policies and his public pronouncements to protect such unionists from the truth. In December 1862, three months after announcing his intention to free slaves in the rebellious Confederacy, Lincoln proposed an unamendable amendment to the Constitution that would have postponed the final abolition of slavery in the United States until the year 1900.

Unlike Lincoln, the slaves harbored no illusion that a war to defeat secession could be anything but a war to end slavery. They knew ahead of Lincoln himself that he would have to take on the role of emancipator, and they acted on that knowledge before there was anything but blind faith to sustain it. Right after Lincoln's election, before even South Carolina had seceded, slaves deep in the South celebrated the coming jubilee. [. . .]

Even inevitable lessons do not necessarily come easy or cheap. Only gradually and at great cost did the nation at large learn that the slaves were more than property to be haggled over or offered as payment for the compromises of others. They were people: people whose will and intentions were as much a fact of the war as terrain, supplies, and the position of the enemy; people whose point of view must therefore be taken into account. The burden of teaching that lesson fell upon the slaves. Their stubborn actions in pursuit of their faith gradually turned faith into reality. It was they who taught the nation that it must place the abolition of slavery at the head of its agenda.

Officers and men of the armed forces were among the first to acknowledge practical reality, because it was they to whom the slaves first gained access. The deceptively simple first step in the process came when slaves ran away to seek sanctuary and freedom behind Federal lines, something they began doing as soon as Federal lines came within reach. And, unfortunately for Lincoln's plan to keep the question of union separate from the question of slavery, Federal lines first came within the slaves' reach in the border slave states that Lincoln was determined to keep in the Union at all costs. [...]

Once the slaves arrived, something had to be done about them. Deciding just what proved a ticklish matter, since every possible course—taking them in, sending them away, returning them to their owners, or looking the other way—threatened to offend some group whose goodwill the administration needed. Sheltering the fugitives would antagonize the loyal slaveholders, whose support underpinned Lincoln's strategy for holding the border slave states in the Union and perhaps wooing back to the Union some slaveholders within the Confederacy itself. But handing fugitives over to their pursuers would infuriate abolitionists. [...]

Lincoln did his best to evade the whole question, ordering his commanders not to allow fugitives within the lines in the first place. But orders could not stop the slaves from seeking refuge with Union forces; nor could orders prevent Union forces—out of altruistic sympathy with the fugitives' desire for freedom, pragmatic pursuit of military advantage, or a selfish desire to obtain willing servants—from granting the refuge sought. Whatever action military officials then took committed the government, visibly, to a definite policy concerning slaves and their owners. However politicians might strive to separate the war from the question of slavery, military men learned at first hand that the two were inextricably linked. [...]

Twice Lincoln's commanders embarrassed him publicly by moving ahead of him on the question of emancipation. In August 1861, General John C. Fremont proclaimed martial law in Missouri and declared free all slaves of secessionist owners. Fremont refused Lincoln's order that he amend the proclamation. Accordingly, Lincoln amended it himself and, after a decent interval, relieved Fremont of command and appointed General David Hunter to replace him. [...] In May 1862, General Hunter himself, by then transferred to command of the Department of the South (which included South Carolina, Georgia, and Florida), put Lincoln on the spot once more—and for higher stakes—by declaring slavery abolished throughout his department. This time the slaves at issue belonged not to loyal owners in loyal states but to unquestionably rebellious owners in the Confederacy itself. Upon Lincoln fell the onus—the disgrace, many believed—of abolishing Hunter's abolition, as he had abolished Fremont's.

While Lincoln, pursuing his own delicate political calculations, permitted himself the luxury of temporizing on the question, Congress took decisive action. [...] In August [1861], Congress passed an act confiscating slaves whose owners had knowingly required or permitted them to labor on behalf of the rebellion. The language of the act left unsettled whether or not such slaves became free [...] But for all its equivocation, the first confiscation act opened a door through which slaves fleeing military labor with the Confederate army could take the first step toward freedom; and it established a precedent for less equivocal actions to follow.

Before long, Congress proceeded from cautious first steps to much bolder ones. In March 1862, it adopted a new article of war that forbade military personnel—upon pain of court-martial—to return fugitive slaves to their owners. [...] In July 1862, over Lincoln's objections, Congress passed a second confiscation act that did what Fremont had tried to do in Missouri: it declared free all slaves whose owners supported the rebellion. In the same month, Congress authorized the enlistment of "persons of African descent" into military service. Above all else, it was military recruitment that doomed slavery in the loyal slave states. So far ahead of Lincoln had Congress traveled on the road to emancipation that, at the moment of its issuance, the final Emancipation Proclamation freed not a single slave who was not already entitled to freedom by act of Congress.

The initiative of the slaves forced Congress to act. Slaves could not vote, hold office, or petition for redress of grievances. They were not, in fact, citizens at all. But the war provided them a port of entry into the political system, a transmission belt to carry their demand for freedom from military lines to the highest levels of government, whether officials seated at the heights wanted to hear it or not. By touching the government at its most vulnerable point, the point at which its military forces were fighting for its life, the slaves were able to turn their will to be free into a political problem that politicians had to deal with politically. [...]

And although the second confiscation act and the Emancipation Proclamation turned the armed forces of the Union into an engine of liberation within the Confederacy, nothing but the unarmed force of the slaves themselves could prevent owners from seizing them again once the troops moved on. After all, the main business of the army and navy was fighting the war, not protecting the freedmen.

Whether in the loyal slave states of the Union or in the heart of the Confederacy, the slaves themselves had to make their freedom real. Thousands of slave men gained freedom for themselves and their families by enlisting for military service. Others, temporarily assigned by Confederate authorities to perform military labor away from home, returned to spread subversive news—about the progress of the war or about the Union's emancipation edicts—among slaves hitherto insulated from events in the outside world. When rebel owners fled, fearing the approach of the Federal army, many slave men and women refused to be dragged along. Instead they stayed behind to welcome the Union forces, taking over and dividing the abandoned plantation property and setting up their own households and farms. Deep in the Confederacy, where they could expect no help from Union forces, slaves forced concessions from mistresses left to manage plantations on their own. Mistresses were ardent Confederate patriots and the bedrock upon which slavery rested. But with routine disrupted and able-bodied white men away at war, many had no choice but to make terms when the slaves slowed the pace of work or demanded wages before they would work at all.

The slaves decided at the time of Lincoln's election that their hour had come. By the time Lincoln issued his Emancipation Proclamation, no human being alive could have held back the tide that swept toward freedom. How far the slaves' freedom would extend and how assiduously the government would protect it were questions to which the future would provide a grim answer. But, for a crucial moment, the agenda of the slaves merged with that of the government. The government discovered that it could not accomplish its narrow goal—union— without adopting the slaves' nobler one—universal emancipation.

In Geoffrey C. Ward, with Ric Burns and Ken Burns, eds., *The Civil War* (New York: Knopf, 1990), 178–181.

## LERONE BENNETT JR., *Forced into Glory*, 2000

*Published more than three decades after Bennett's (1928–2018) Ebony magazine article,* Forced into Glory *is a significant reworking and extension of that essay. Here, Bennett affirms Lincoln's vital significance in American cultural memory by suggesting that the identity of all Americans is connected to what each thinks about Lincoln, as he may be the "key to the American personality." Bennett also seeks to further deconstruct what he perceives as the myth of Lincoln as Great Emancipator. Not only does he detail Lincoln's various emancipation proposals, but he argues that none of them ever freed a single slave, and he thinks that Lincoln never completely abandoned the belief that slaves were property and slaveowners deserved compensation for their loss. While many had praised Lincoln's conviction that the Declaration of Independence applied to all men, regardless of race, Bennett demurs and reinforces his belief in Lincoln's racism by asserting that Lincoln's four readings of the Declaration did not question White supremacy.*

For although few newspapers print Great White Emancipator editorials on February 12, and although fewer scholars hold Lincoln up as a model of race relations, there is still a tendency to exaggerate his role in the abortive emancipation of African-Americans and to evade the true meaning and imperatives of the First Reconstruction [...].

This is *not* a biography: this is a political study of the uses and abuses of biography and myth, and it suggests, among other things, that your identity, whatever your color, is based, at least in part, on what you think about Lincoln, the Civil War, and slavery.

Lincoln or somebody said once that you can't fool all of the people all the time. By turning a racist who wanted to deport all Blacks into a national symbol of integration and brotherhood, the Lincoln mythmakers have managed to prove Lincoln or whoever said it wrong. [...]

[S]lavery was a crime against humanity and [...] there is no hope for us until we cross the great equator of our history and confront Lincoln, Lee and all the other participants on that level. I have compared Lincoln not with twentieth-century leaders but with the White men and women of his own time, and I have suggested that one of the reasons we are in trouble racially in this country is that we have systematically downplayed and suppressed the White men and women who, unlike Lincoln, really believed in the Declaration of Independence.

I have suggested finally that Lincoln is a key, perhaps the key, to the American personality and that what we invest in him, and *hide* in him, is who we are. [...]

The first article in the Lincoln Doctrine was that it was necessary for all good White men to support the Missouri Compromise and to stop arguing over "that unfortunate source of discord—Negro slavery". [...] This was a delicate agreement that required, Lincoln said, a spirit of compromise in both the South and the North—he meant the *White* South and the *White* North.

Above all else, it required, as Lincoln said elsewhere and almost everywhere, Northern Whites to defend the "right" of slaveholders to hold Blacks in slavery and to carry out their "duty" of returning fugitive slaves to their "rightful owners" to be whipped and rechained. To be fair, Lincoln never said the slaves should be whipped, but he had seen the Negro jails and whipping posts in the South and he knew—he had to know—that a runaway slave who was returned to [Henry] Clay or almost any other slaveholder was punished. [...]

Although Lincoln drafted his emancipation bills at different times to meet different situations, they share four features that throw new light on Lincoln and the Emancipation Proclamation.

1. None of the documents he issued or announced publicly, not even the famous Proclamation, emancipated a single slave outright.
2. With the exception of the Emancipation Proclamation, all required the government or the state to buy the slaves and compensate the slaveholders. [...] The fact that the Proclamation departed from this basic Lincoln principle in the beginning—Lincoln tried until the end to get his cabinet to approve a $400,000,000 compensation plan for slave-owners—is one of the strongest arguments against Lincoln's investment in it.
3. All required a period of apprenticeship controlled by the former slaveholders during which time, as Lincoln was fond of saying, the slaves and slaveholders could work themselves out of their old

relationship—on the slaves' time and at their expense. It will be said, of course, that the Emancipation Proclamation didn't provide for apprenticeship. Anybody who says that has not read the implementing provisions of Lincoln's Reconstruction plans, which provided for a period of apprenticeship. [...]

4. All were rebound emancipations, designed to provide a safer, more conservative alternative to emancipation plans that called for immediate emancipation or other moves Lincoln feared. The first emancipation was designed to supplant the Gott amendment and to defuse the explosive situation caused by its introduction. The Delaware bills were designed to outflank congressional critics and to defuse the situation created by Lincoln's revocation of General John Charles Frémont's emancipation decree. The last emancipation act was designed to neutralize the Second Confiscation Act and to outflank congressional critics who were calling for the use of Black soldiers and the immediate emancipation of the slaves of rebels in rebel states and so-called loyal states. [...]

Lincoln performed radical surgery on the Declaration, creating at least four different Declarations which he pulled out from time to time, depending on the audience, like cards from a marked deck.

Lincoln created the first Declaration, which we will call Declaration A, by elevating the real Declaration to a heaven high above the real world where it was not affected by slavery or Indian massacres or by anything White people did and did not do. Declaration A, the Declaration Lincoln never stopped praising and idolizing from afar, was pure, white, undefiled. It was, in Lincoln's words, "an abstract principle" about abstract, that is to say, unreal rights. [...]

The real Declaration, then, the Declaration to keep in mind when determining duties to subhumans who were not entitled to all the rights extended to the fully human Whites in the perfect Declaration, was Declaration B, which participated , in the real, profane world of slaves and nonWhites. [...]

Declaration B [...] was, in turn, divided into two declarations, Declaration C, based on the meaning of the words, and Declaration D, based on the venue. Declaration C said that the original Declaration created two classes of rights, certain unspecified nonnatural rights and the "natural" rights enumerated, i.e., the right to life, liberty and the pursuit of happiness. In Lincoln's specious reading, [...] Declaration C extended all rights, natural and nonnatural, to all Whites, whenever they came to America and however they came to America. What about Blacks? Because they were nonWhite and because they didn't come from Europe or a "white" land, they were only entitled, Lincoln said, to the "natural" rights and were excluded from equal political and social rights. [...]

In Declaration C, Lincoln created separate but unequal sections of the Declaration of Independence, and it is appalling that almost all scholars, all exceptions freely admitted, have, until this date, enthusiastically endorsed the concept.

Even here, however, we are dealing with a stacked deck. For although Lincoln's Declaration C gave Negroes and other "subhumans" certain natural rights in theory and in the abstract, it didn't in fact give any concrete Negro, as opposed to any abstract Negro, any concrete right in Illinois, where the Black Laws, with Lincoln's support, defined Blacks as subhumans, or in the slave states, where Lincoln's "necessities" nullified the provisions. It was only in new societies and in the creation of new states that this could be done. Hence, the fourth Declaration of Independence, Declaration D, the one that operated imperfectly in new states.

Even so, Lincoln was deceiving himself, and others, for he said in a statement that nobody quotes that *Negroes had no rights, natural or otherwise, that they could exercise anywhere in America.* This statement is so shocking that the best thing for us to do is to get out of the way and let Lincoln speak:

> *Negroes have natural rights, however, as other men have, although they cannot enjoy them here,* and even {Chief Justice Roger} Taney once said that "the Declaration of Independence was broad enough for all men." But though it does not declare that all men are equal in their attainments or social position, yet no sane man will attempt to deny that the African upon his own soil has all the natural rights that instrument vouchsafes to all mankind.

Here, then, ominously, is the White man's Declaration of Independence as defined by Abraham Lincoln, a Declaration defined by race and geography and blood, a Declaration that agreed practically with Roger Taney that Negroes had no civil and political rights in America that White men were bound to respect.

Lerone Bennett Jr., *Forced into Glory* (Chicago: Johnson Publishing Company, 2000), unpaginated preface and 219, 244, 313–315.

## HENRY LOUIS GATES JR., *Lincoln on Race and Slavery*, 2009

*A graduate of Yale University and Cambridge University, where he earned a PhD in English, Gates (1950–) has held academic appointments at Yale, Cornell, Duke, and Harvard. The director of the W. E. B Du Bois Institute for Afro-American Research at Harvard, Gates is the author and editor of numerous books and articles. In 2009, he published an anthology of Lincoln's writings on race and slavery that includes an extensive introduction from which the excerpts that follow are taken. Gates offers important insight in suggesting that slavery, race, and colonization were not of one piece in Lincoln's thinking and can be found in three separate discourses. Like Quarles, Gates believes Blacks have*

*been responsible for "confect[ing] an image" of Lincoln that has endured. Like
Du Bois, Gates sees Lincoln as a man of contradictions—a White supremacist
and a Great Emancipator—whose views on race evolved as he came into contact
with African Americans and realized the vital contribution that Black soldiers
played in winning the war (AANB).*

———————

One of the most striking conclusions that a close reading of Lincoln's speeches
and writings yielded to me was that "slavery," "race," and "colonization," were quite
often three separate issues for him. Sometimes these issues were intertwined in
Lincoln's thinking, but far more often they seem to have remained quite distinct,
even if we have difficulty understanding or explaining how this could have been
so. And this difficulty has led far too many scholars, I believe, when writing about
Lincoln's views on slavery, for example, to blur distinctions that were important
to him and to his contemporaries as they reflected upon the institution of slavery,
the status of African Americans both as human beings and as potential citizens in
the United States, and whether or not voluntary colonization was an inseparable
aspect of abolition.

In Lincoln's case, we can trace these three strands of thought clearly within
three distinct discourses that braid their way through his speeches and writings:
in his early and consistent abhorrence of slavery as a violation of natural rights, as
an economic institution that created an uneven playing field for white men, and
that dehumanized and brutalized black human beings; in the fascinating manner
in which he wrestled with the deep-seated, conventional ambivalence about the
status of Negroes vis-a-vis white people on the scale of civilization, his penchant
for blackface minstrelsy and darky jokes, his initially strong skepticism about the
native intellectual potential of people of color and the capacity of black men to
serve with valor in a war against white men; and, finally, his long flirtation with
the voluntary colonization of the freed slaves either in the West Indies, in Latin
America, or back in Africa. [ . . . ]

The Abraham Lincoln of the popular American imagination—Father Abraham, the Great Emancipator—is often represented almost as an island of pure
reason in a sea of mid-nineteenth-century racist madness, a beacon of tolerance
blessed with a certain cosmopolitan sensibility above or beyond race, a man whose
attitudes about race and slavery transcended his time and place. It is this Abraham
Lincoln that many writers have conjured, somewhat romantically—for example,
as Ralph Ellison often did—to claim for him and those who fought to abolish
slavery a privileged, noble status in the history of American race relations from
which subsequent, lesser mortals disgracefully fell away. [ . . . ]

Lincoln was no exception to his times; what is exceptional about Abraham
Lincoln is that, perhaps because of temperament or because of the shape-shifting

contingencies of command during an agonizingly costly war, he wrestled with his often contradictory feelings and ambivalences and vacillations about slavery, race, and colonization, and did so quite publicly and often quite eloquently. [...]

It is fascinating to trace how these three strands of Lincoln's thought about the status of black people in America manifested themselves in his attitudes about voluntary colonization [...] Lincoln favored colonization initially because of a genuine concern that blacks and whites could not live in social harmony. He continued to contemplate colonization for much of his term as president because of an equally genuine concern that the huge number of slaves who would ultimately be freed by the Thirteenth Amendment would never be accepted by the former Confederates and white people in the North, whither at least some of the former slaves would sooner or later migrate. [...]

When we consider Lincoln today, we tend to forget that we are reading him—indeed, conceiving of him—through an interpretive frame forged in part, ironically enough, by the uses to which his image was put by blacks long after he was dead, at least since Booker T. Washington created his "Onward" series of lithographs at the turn of the century, with a noble Lincoln, on one side, and a fierce Frederick Douglass, on the other, both blessing their stepchild and logical heir, Booker T. Washington. Moreover, we hear Lincoln's words through the echo of the rhetoric of the civil rights movement, especially the "I have a dream" speech of Martin Luther King, Jr. It is easy to forget that when Lincoln made a public address, he was speaking primarily—certainly until his second inaugural address—to all white or predominantly white audiences, who most certainly were ambivalent about blacks and black rights, if not ambivalent about slavery. [...] And we do both Lincoln and ourselves a grave disservice by attempting to elide his contradictory feelings and thought and actions about the future of slavery in the Republic, and the future of the Republic's slaves and former slaves. [...]

But what is clear is that Lincoln hated slavery, not only because of its brutality and inhumanity, but first and foremost because it constituted the theft of another person's labor—both the labor of the slave and that of the white men who had, in effect, to compete disadvantageously in the marketplace with slave labor—and he was exceptionally clear and forceful about saying so, as early as 1854. Indeed, Lincoln's central opposition to slavery seems to have been deeply rooted in this economic premise, rather than only or primarily stemming from humanitarian grounds. [...]

Lincoln could live with slavery if he had to, if this was the only way to preserve the integrity of the country he thought he had been elected to serve, a point that he had emphasized during his run for the presidency, even if, temperamentally, he was opposed to the institution itself, and thought that its containment to the slave states would, ultimately, force it to collapse, through gradual, compensated emancipation and voluntary colonization. [...]

And though he recognized the cost to the North of slave labor among the Southern troops, he still remained profoundly skeptical of the capacities of blacks to serve as useful soldiers [. . .] All that began to change, gradually if inevitably, in August of 1862. And it began to change, first and foremost, because Lincoln knew that the North was losing the war, and desperate—even heretofore unthinkable—measures now were called for. [. . .]

It seems perfectly reasonable to me that a man as brilliant as Abraham Lincoln, a man who loved the concept of country so much more than any single component of it, would have continued to wonder about the merits and efficacy of the colonization of the mass of these former black slaves. We underestimate Lincoln's commitment to reuniting the Union, at all costs, and diminish his complexity as a man still rooted deeply in his age and time when we romanticize him as the first American president completely to transcend racism and race. [. . .]

Lincoln remade himself as a proponent of black freedom, fully aware of how far he had come in doing so. We can do Lincoln no greater service than to walk that path with him, and we can do no greater disservice than to whitewash it, seeking to give ourselves an odd form of comfort by pretending that he was even one whit less complicated than he actually was.

Henry Louis Gates Jr., *Lincoln on Race and Slavery* (Princeton, NJ: Princeton University Press, 2009), xx, xxi, xxiii, xxiv–xxv, xxix, xxx, xxxiii, xxxiv, xxxvi–xxxvii, xxxviii, xxxix, xl, xli, xlii–xliii, xliv, xlvi, xlvii, lix, lxiii–lxiv.

## BARACK OBAMA, "What I See in Lincoln's Eyes," July 2005

*The forty-fourth President of the United States, Barack Obama (1961–) was in his first year as a member of the United States Senate when he wrote the following reflection on Lincoln. Using Alexander Gardner's February 1865 photograph of Lincoln as his inspiration, then-Senator Obama draws a parallel between Lincoln's hardscrabble upbringing and his own struggles as a young man in Illinois. While acknowledging the limitations of the Emancipation Proclamation and Lincoln's views on race, Obama, like Du Bois, finds these complexities and imperfections most appealing about Lincoln, for his determination to persevere and confront the issue of slavery reflects the very best in the American character.*

My favorite portrait of Lincoln comes from the end of his life. In it, Lincoln's face is as finely lined as a pressed flower. He appears frail, almost broken; his eyes, averted from the camera's lens, seem to contain a heartbreaking melancholy, as if he sees before him what the nation had so recently endured.

It would be a sorrowful picture except for the fact that Lincoln's mouth is turned ever so slightly into a smile. The smile doesn't negate the sorrow. But it alters tragedy into grace. It's as if this rough-faced, aging man has cast his gaze toward eternity and yet still cherishes his memories—of an imperfect world and its fleeting, sometimes terrible beauty. On trying days, the portrait, a reproduction of which hangs in my office, soothes me; it always asks me questions.

What is it about this man that can move us so profoundly? Some of it has to do with Lincoln's humble beginnings, which often speak to our own. When I moved to Illinois 20 years ago to work as a community organizer, I had no money in my pockets and didn't know a single soul. During my first six years in the state legislature, Democrats were in the minority, and I couldn't get a bill heard, much less passed. In my first race for Congress, I had my head handed to me. So when I, a black man with a funny name, born in Hawaii of a father from Kenya and a mother from Kansas, announced my candidacy for the U.S. Senate, it was hard to imagine a less likely scenario than that I would win—except, perhaps, for the one that allowed a child born in the backwoods of Kentucky with less than a year of formal education to end up as Illinois' greatest citizen and our nation's greatest President.

In Lincoln's rise from poverty, his ultimate mastery of language and law, his capacity to overcome personal loss and remain determined in the face of repeated defeat—in all this, he reminded me not just of my own struggles. He also reminded me of a larger, fundamental element of American life—the enduring belief that we can constantly remake ourselves to fit our larger dreams.

A connected idea attracts us to Lincoln: as we remake ourselves, we remake our surroundings. He didn't just talk or write or theorize. He split rail, fired rifles, tried cases and pushed for new bridges and roads and waterways. In his sheer energy, Lincoln captures a hunger in us to build and to innovate. It's a quality that can get us in trouble; we may be blind at times to the costs of progress. And yet, when I travel to other parts of the world, I remember that it is precisely such energy that sets us apart, a sense that there are no limits to the heights our nation might reach.

Still, as I look at his picture, it is the man and not the icon that speaks to me. I cannot swallow whole the view of Lincoln as the Great Emancipator. As a law professor and civil rights lawyer and as an African American, I am fully aware of his limited views on race. Anyone who actually reads the Emancipation Proclamation knows it was more a military document than a clarion call for justice. Scholars tell us too that Lincoln wasn't immune from political considerations and that his temperament could be indecisive and morose.

But it is precisely those imperfections—and the painful self-awareness of those failings etched in every crease of his face and reflected in those haunted eyes—that make him so compelling. For when the time came to confront the greatest moral challenge this nation has ever faced, this all too human man did not pass the challenge on to future generations. He neither demonized the fathers and sons who did battle on the other side nor sought to diminish the terrible costs of his war. In the midst of slavery's dark storm and the complexities of governing a house divided, he somehow kept his moral compass pointed firm and true. What I marvel at, what gives me such hope, is that this man could overcome depression, self-doubt and the constraints of biography and not only act decisively but retain his humanity. Like a figure from the Old Testament, he wandered the earth, making mistakes, loving his family but causing them pain, despairing over the course of events, trying to divine God's will. He did not know how things would turn out, but he did his best.

A few weeks ago, I spoke at the commencement at Knox College in Galesburg, Ill. I stood in view of the spot where Lincoln and Stephen Douglas held one of their famous debates during their race for the U.S. Senate. The only way for Lincoln to get onto the podium was to squeeze his lanky frame through a window, whereupon he reportedly remarked, "At last I have finally gone through college." Waiting for the soon-to-be graduates to assemble, I thought that even as Lincoln lost that Senate race, his arguments that day would result, centuries later, in my occupying the same seat that he coveted. He may not have dreamed of that exact outcome. But I like to believe he would have appreciated the irony. Humor, ambiguity, complexity, compassion—all were part of his character. And as Lincoln called once upon the better angels of our nature, I believe that he is calling still, across the ages, to summon some measure of that character, the American character, in each of us today.

*Time,* July 4, 2005, 74.

## BARACK OBAMA, Remarks at the Abraham Lincoln Association Banquet, Springfield, Illinois, February 12, 2009

*When James H. Magee spoke in Springfield on the centennial of Lincoln's birth (see above) he imagined that in one hundred years, on the bicentennial of Lincoln's birth, African Americans would be "a factor in our government," but perhaps even he would have been surprised that the first African American president was the keynote speaker in Lincoln's hometown on February 12, 2009. President Obama's administration coincided with important historical anniversaries from the Civil War era, including the sesquicentennial of the Emancipation Proclamation, yet his most significant remarks were delivered shortly after his presidency commenced when he paid tribute to Lincoln in the city where both men had served as members of the Illinois General Assembly. Obama had announced his candidacy for the presidency from the Old State Capitol in Springfield—the same building where Lincoln delivered the House Divided Speech that initially attracted Frederick Douglass's attention in 1858. Acknowledging that Lincoln had helped make his own story possible, President Obama focused his address on Lincoln's attachment to the Union rather than the Emancipation Proclamation. Having taken office during the most dire economic crisis since the Great Depression, Obama's appeal to Lincoln's faith in the Union was used to frame his own vision for aiding the nation's recovery.*

I served here for nearly a decade and, as has already been mentioned, this is where I launched my candidacy for President two years ago this week—on the steps—(Applause)—on the steps of the Old State Capitol where Abraham Lincoln served and prepared for the presidency.

It was here, nearly 150 years ago, that the man whose life we are celebrating today, who you've been celebrating all week, bid farewell to this city that he had come to call his own. And as has already been mentioned, on a platform at a train station not far from where we're gathered, Lincoln turned to the crowd that had come to see him off and said, "To this place, and the kindness of these people, I owe everything." And being here tonight, surrounded by all of you, I share his sentiment. But looking out at this room, full of so many who did so much for me, I'm also reminded of what Lincoln once said to a favor-seeker who claimed it was his efforts that made the difference in the election. (Laughter.) Lincoln asked him, "So you think you made me President?" "Yes," the man replied, "under Providence, I think I did." "Well," said Lincoln, "it's a pretty mess you've got me into." (Laughter.) "But I forgive you." (Applause.)

So whoever of you think you are responsible for this—(Laughter)—we're taking names. (Laughter.)

It's a humbling task, marking the bicentennial of our 16th President's birth—humbling for me in particular because it's fair to say that the presidency of this singular figure who we celebrate in so many ways made my own story possible.

Here in Springfield, it's easier, though, to reflect on Lincoln the man rather than the marble giant—before Gettysburg, before Antietam, before Fredericksburg and Bull Run, before emancipation was proclaimed and the captives were set free. In 1854, Lincoln was simply a Springfield lawyer who'd served just a single term in Congress. Possibly in his law office, his feet on a cluttered desk, his sons playing around him, his clothes a bit too small to fit his uncommon frame, maybe wondering if somebody might call him up and ask him to be Commerce Secretary—(laughter)—he put some thoughts on paper, and for what purpose we do not know: "The legitimate object of government," he wrote, "is to do for the people what needs to be done, but which they cannot, by individual effort, do at all, or do so well, by themselves."

To do for the people what needs to be done but which they cannot do on their own. It's a simple statement. But it answers a central question of Abraham Lincoln's life. Why did he land on the side of union? What was it that made him so unrelenting in pursuit of victory that he was willing to test the Constitution he ultimately preserved? What was it that led this man to give his last full measure of devotion so that our nation might endure?

These are not easy questions to answer, and I cannot know if I'm right. But I suspect that his devotion to the idea of union came not from a belief that government always had the answer. It came not from a failure to understand our individual rights and responsibilities. This rugged rail-splitter, born in a log cabin of pioneer stock; who cleared a path through the woods as a boy; who lost a mother and a sister to the rigors of frontier life; who taught himself all that he knew; and everything that he had was because of his hard work—this man, our first Republican President, knew better than anybody what it meant to pull yourself up by your bootstraps. He understood that strain of personal liberty and self-reliance, that fierce independence at the heart of the American experience.

But he also understood something else. He recognized that while each of us must do our part, work as hard as we can, be as responsible as we can, although we are responsible for our own fates, in the end, there are certain things we cannot do on our own. There are certain things we can only do together. There are certain things only a union can do.

Only a union could harness the courage of our pioneers to settle the American West, which is why Lincoln passed a Homestead Act giving a tract of land to anyone seeking a stake in our growing economy.

Only a union could foster the ingenuity of our framers—the ingenuity of our farmers, which is why he set up land-grant colleges that taught them how to make the most of their land while giving their children an education that let them dream the American Dream.

Only a union could speed our expansion and connect our coasts with a transcontinental railroad, and so, even in the midst of civil war, Lincoln built one. He fueled new enterprises with a national currency, spurred innovation, and ignited America's imagination with a national academy of sciences, believing we must, as he put it, add "the fuel of interest to the fire of genius in the discovery of new and useful things." And on this day, that is also the bicentennial of Charles Darwin's birth, it's worth a moment to pause and renew that commitment to science and innovation and discovery that Lincoln understood so well.

Only a union could serve the hopes of every citizen to knock down the barriers to opportunity and give each and every person the chance to pursue the American Dream. Lincoln understood what Washington understood when he led farmers and craftsmen and shopkeepers to rise up against an empire; what Roosevelt understood when he lifted us from Depression, built an arsenal of democracy, created the largest middle class in history with the GI bill. It's what Kennedy understood when he sent us to the moon.

All these Presidents recognized that America is—and always has been—more than a band of 13 colonies, or 50 states—more than a bunch of Yankees and Confederates, more than a collection of Red States and Blue States. But we are the United States. There isn't any dream beyond our reach—(applause)—there is no dream beyond our reach, any obstacle that can stand in our way when we recognize that our individual liberty is served, not negated, by a recognition of the common good.

That is the spirit we are called to show once more. The challenges we face are very different now: two wars; an economic crisis unlike any we've seen in our lifetime. Jobs have been lost. Pensions are gone. Families' dreams have been endangered. Health care costs are exploding. Schools are falling short. We have an energy crisis that's hampering our economy and threatening our planet and enriching our adversaries.

And yet, while our challenges may be new, they did not come about overnight. Ultimately they result from a failure to meet the test that Lincoln set. I understand there have been times in our history when our government has misjudged what we can do by individual effort alone, and what we can only do together; when we didn't draw the line as effectively as we should have; when government has done things that people can—and should—do for themselves. [ . . .]

It's only by coming together to do what people need done that we will, in Lincoln's words, "lift artificial weights from all shoulders {and give} an unfettered start, and a fair chance, in the race of life." That's all people are looking for, fair chance in the race of life.

That's what's required of us—now and in the years ahead. We will be remembered for what we choose to make of this moment. And when posterity looks back on our time, as we are looking back on Lincoln's, I don't want it said that we saw an economic crisis but did not stem it; that we saw our schools decline and our bridges crumble but we did not rebuild them; that the world changed in the 21st century but America did not lead it; that we were consumed with small things, petty things, when we were called to do great things. Instead, let them say that this generation—our generation—of Americans rose to the moment and gave America a new birth of freedom and opportunity in our time.

These are trying days and they will grow tougher in the months to come. And there will be moments when our doubts rise and our hopes recede. But let's always remember that we, as a people, have been here before. There were times when our revolution itself seemed altogether improbable, when the union was all but lost, when fascism seemed set to prevail around the world. And yet, what earlier generations discovered—and what we must rediscover right now—is that it is precisely when we are in the deepest valley, when the climb is steepest, that

Americans relearn how to take the mountaintop. Together. As one nation. As one people. (Applause.) As one nation. As one people. That's how we will beat back our present dangers. That is how we will surpass what trials may come. That's how we will do what Lincoln called on us all to do, and "nobly save the last best hope on earth." That's what this is, the last best hope on earth. Lincoln has passed that legacy onto us. It is now our responsibility to pass it on to the next generation.

Thank you, God bless you, and may God bless the United States of America. (Applause.)

https://obamawhitehouse.archives.gov/the-press-office/remarks-president-102nd
-abraham-lincoln-association-annual-banquet.

# CREDITS

# INDEX

abolitionism, Douglass on, 110–13

abolitionists: AL opposes, 377, 398–99, 423, 455, 491; compared to AL, 158, 229, 235, 282, 287, 368, 371–72, 376, 377, 398–99, 407, 411–12, 423, 489; critical of AL, 110, 113, 417–18; emancipation efforts of, 33–34; as heroes, 203, 368; morality of, 228, 360; their pressure on AL, 481–82, 484–86

Africa, potential colony in, 108–9. *See also* Liberia

African American citizenship: AL opposes, 215, 340, 355, 412, 422, 480, 499, 501; AL supports, 423, 473; Douglass's wish for, 110; and the *Dred Scott* decision, 96–97; Edward Bates's advisory on, 503; preparation for, 126, 219, 298–99; as a result of the Emancipation Proclamation, 199, 232–34, 271–72, 387; soldiers and, 6, 98, 273–74, 459, 463–64, 501, 503; and suffrage, 21–22, 234; withheld during Jim Crow, 240, 256. *See also* Fifteenth Amendment

African American missionaries, 102–3

African American newspapers and magazines, 11, 489; *Afro-American*, 8, 441; *Anglo-African*, 29, 32, 134, 160; *Broad Ax*, 221; *Chicago Defender*, 7, 489; *Colored American Magazine*, 283; *Douglass' Monthly*, 59; *The Elevator*, 45; *The Guardian*, 225–26; *Indianapolis Freeman*, 265; *Negro World*, 243,

339; *Pacific Appeal*, 45; *Pittsburgh Courier*, 372; *Voice of the Negro*, 231, 297

African Americans: ambivalence toward AL, 2, 4, 8–9, 215–16, 390–91; call to arms, 70–71, 80, 81, 324; and crime, 321–22; criticized for admiring Lincoln, 8, 372–76; discrimination in employment and education, 364–65; disenfranchisement of, 364–65, 395; excluded from AL's funeral procession in New York, 162–63, 170–71; as keepers of AL's memory, 184–85, 194–95, 217, 230, 234–35, 266–68, 269–71, 289, 335, 352, 357–58; material progress of, 291, 296, 304, 315, 321–22, 329, 335, 348–49, 364, 396; meet with AL, 42–44, 46–47, 111–13, 116, 126–28, 128–29, 136–38, 141–42, 142–44, 146–49, 209–14; passing as White, 89, 177, 314; prevented from enlisting, 34, 35, 50, 52–53, 58, 63, 65, 206, 493; and property ownership, 129–31, 132; reluctance to celebrate AL, 261–65; and the Republican Party, 9, 201–3, 224–25, 372–76, 402, 442; their agency in the struggle for equality, 5, 51, 81, 196–97, 229, 441–42, 502–5, 507–11; their patriotism and loyalty, 52, 52–53, 55, 83, 88, 295, 298, 328–29, 333–34, 335, 348, 351, 460; those who changed their minds about AL, 66–68, 89–90, 110–13, 135; violence against, 209, 224, 350, 364, 446.

sage to Congress, 177, 504; 1862 message to Congress on compensated emancipation, 11, 38–40, 40–42, 306, 417–18; 1864 Annual Message to Congress, 233, 247; first Annual Message to Congress, 36–37, 399, 427; order of retaliation for captured Confederate soldiers, 100; proclamation for a day of fasting and prayer, 34–36; Proclamation of Amnesty and Reconstruction, 113–14, 486–87, 494; proclamation revoking Gen. Hunter's emancipation decree, 45–46, 206, 287, 306, 377, 387, 417, 481, 509. *See also* Emancipation Proclamation; Preliminary Emancipation Proclamation

Lincoln, Abraham, speeches of: address at Sanitary Fair at Baltimore, 240–41; Address on Colonization, 48–51, 51–53; Cooper Union, 241, 373, 405, 438; 1838 Lyceum Address, 412; First Inaugural Address, 176, 235; House Divided Speech, 15–17, 184, 238–39, 280, 298, 360, 399, 507; last public address, 180, 234; in Peoria, 1854, 498–99; Second Inaugural Address, 8, 176, 211–12, 214, 235, 289, 398; in Springfield, 1857, 499; at a war meeting, 48. *See also* Gettysburg Address; Lincoln-Douglas debates

Lincoln, Mary, 177–81, 221

Lincoln Centennial: African Americans excluded from events, 288–89, 302; anticipated, 258; in Massachusetts, 255–56; in New York, 290–96; selections from the *American Missionary* about, 268–83

Lincoln Day: address by Booker T. Washington, 218–20, 290–96, 320–23; address by Charles W. Anderson, 216–17; address by Frederick Douglass, 207–14; address by Mary Church Terrell, 235–42; address by Thomas N.C. Liverpool, 184–85; address by T. Thomas Fortune, 243–45; address by W.E.B. Du Bois, 249–55; address by William S. Scarborough, 201–3; calls to celebrate, 234–35, 259–60, 308; celebrated by Republicans, 201–3; celebrations of, by African Americans, 184–85; co-opted by White Americans, 6, 301–2; as national holiday, 184; pilgrimage to Washington Monument on, 400; radio address by William Lloyd Imes, 7–8, 379–81

Lincoln Day centennial, 6, 11; African Americans excluded from, 288; Booker T. Washington's address on, 290–95; Fred

R. Moore on, 283–84; Harry C. Smith's critique of AL on, 286–87; Hightower T. Kealing on the importance of, 259–60; importance for African Americans, 258, 286; James H. Magee's address in Springfield, IL, 287–89; James L. Curtis's praises AL on, 295–96; John W.E. Bowen, Sr.'s address on AL as Great Emancipator, 297–300; poem by Cora J. Ball on, 300–301; poem on, 195–97; selections from *The American Missionary* on, 268–83; William Monroe Trotter on, 255–56

Lincoln-Douglas debates, 355; AL on racial equality, 215, 275, 355, 412, 422, 480–81, 499; AL professes hatred of slavery, 361; favors admission of slave states into the Union, 21; Frederick Douglass on, 15–17; in Galesburg, IL, 279

Lincoln Memorial: dedication of, 7, 345–52; Emancipation Proclamation commemoration event at, 448–49; inspiration for Langston Hughes, 358; Langston Hughes's poem on, 1; photograph of, 475; pilgrimage to, 400–401; and reconciliation narrative, 7–8

Lincoln Memorial Club, 184–85

*Lincoln's Proclamation*, 11

Liverpool, Thomas N.C., address on Lincoln's Birthday, 184–85

Logan, Mattie, 392

Louisiana: AL supports suffrage for African Americans in, 127, 177, 232, 355, 409, 423, 459, 466, 473; delegation from meets with AL about suffrage, 126–28; reconstruction efforts in, 234

Louverture, Toussaint, 119

Love, Emmanuel K., Emancipation Day address, 199–201

Lovejoy, Elijah, 409

lynching, 364; AL on, 412; and anti-lynching bill in Ohio, 286; call for day of prayer about, 205–7; Mary Church Terrell on, 241, 242; NAACP efforts against, 365

Magee, James H., address at Lincoln Centennial in Springfield, IL, 287–89

Malcolm X, on AL as a White liberal, 469–70

March on Washington Movement press release, 400–401

marriage, interracial: AL on, 274–75; bill against in Illinois, 327, 329; as a problem, 314

# Index

Pratt, William, 390

Preliminary Emancipation Proclamation: commemoration of, 357–58, 448–50; and compensated emancipation, 418; defense of, by C.P.S., 71–72; Ezra R. Johnson on, 69–71; Frederick Douglass on, 59–63; Henry McNeal Turner on, 66–68; issued, 182, 264, 307–8, 309; Philip A. Bell on, 58–59

proclamation for a day of prayer, 34–36

Proclamation of Amnesty and Reconstruction, 113–14, 120, 486–87, 494

Proctor, John, his letter to AL, 94–95

Purvis, Robert, address to Anti-Slavery Society, 96–97

Quarles, Benjamin, 1–2, 479, 492, 496; on AL as symbol, 9; on the image of AL to African Americans, 452–57

racism, and AL, 495–97

Randall, James G., 496, 498

Randolph, A. Philip, 400–401

Ransom, Reverdy C., address on Abraham Lincoln, 245–48

Ray, H. Cordelia, poem, 4, 195–96

Reconstruction: AL's plans for, 232–34; beginning of in AL's third Annual Message, 114; Emancipation Proclamation and, 281; Frederick Douglass on, 175–77; Proclamation of Amnesty and Reconstruction, 113–14, 120, 486–87, 494; and punishment for enslavers, 162

reconstruction, course of, if AL had lived, 248

Republican Party: African Americans' abandonment of, 9, 224–25, 369, 372–76, 384–86; African Americans' loyalty to, 201–3, 386–87, 393–98, 402; AL's work in building, 437–38; and campaign of 1858, 17–19; in Illinois, 16, 20, 22, 287–88; as insufficiently anti-slavery, 19–21, 30; its doctrine on racial equality, 500; Marxist critique of, 382–84; as party of "the white man," 32; radical abolitionists in, 481–82

Richmond, VA, AL's visit to, 150–52, 152–54, 154–55, 260, 408, 474

Robinson, Jackie, compares AL to John F. Kennedy, 442–44

Rogers, Joel A., critique of AL on equal rights, 411–13

Roudanez, Jean Baptiste, memorial to AL on suffrage for African Americans in Louisiana, 126–28

Russia, compared to the United States, 310, 329, 399

Rutter, Don Carlos, asks AL about land ownership in the Sea Islands, 129–31

Saint-Gaudens, Augustus, 404

Sampson, Edith, address on the Emancipation Proclamation, 450–52

Sanderson, Jeremiah B., address at emancipation jubilee in San Francisco, CA, 84–86

Scarborough, William S., Lincoln Day address, 201–3

Sea Islands, settlement by Freedmen, 129–31, 149–50

second Confiscation Act. *See* Confiscation Act of 1862

second Emancipation Proclamation, 442–43, 469–70

segregation: African Americans' support for, 391; AL's words used to support, 232, 246, 412, 433–34, 471, 488; at the dedication of the Lincoln Memorial, 345–46; at the Gettysburg reunion, 325; during Jim Crow, 7, 232, 313, 380; and proposed second Emancipation Proclamation, 442–43; in Washington, DC, 83

Sengstacke, John H., on the myth of AL as the Great Emancipator, 489–90

Seward, William H., 37, 42, 286; to AL about Frederick Douglass, 112, 210; and the Emancipation Proclamation, 307, 418; as a Republican, 17–18; views on slavery compared to AL, 277

Sherman, William T., 149

Simmons, Roscoe Conkling, address to the Illinois Assembly, 401–11

Simpson, M. Cravath, on AL and the Declaration of Independence, 356–57

Sinclair, William A., selection from *The Aftermath of Slavery*, 232–34

Slade, William, note to AL about recruitment of African Americans, 95–96

slave insurrections, 34, 148, 456

slavery: AL's hatred of, 516; expansion in the territories, 21, 25–26, 31, 97, 280–81, 285, 479–80; gradual abolition of, 38–40, 40–41, 326, 473, 482–83, 486; insufficient attention to, as a cause for the Civil War, 7, 19, 35, 61, 65, 133; natural death of, 238–39; roots of, in the formation of the Constitution, 87; and the slave trade, 33

**FRED LEE HORD** is a professor of Black studies and director of the Department of African Studies at Knox College. He is the editor of *I Am Because We Are: A Black Philosophy Reader* and *Reconstructing Memory: Black Literary Criticism*.

**MATTHEW D. NORMAN** is an associate professor of history at the University of Cincinnati, Blue Ash College.

**THE KNOX COLLEGE LINCOLN STUDIES CENTER SERIES**

*Herndon's Lincoln*
William H. Herndon and Jesse W. Weik;
edited by Douglas L. Wilson and Rodney O. Davis

*The Lincoln-Douglas Debates*
*The Lincoln Studies Center Edition*
Edited by Rodney O. Davis and Douglas L. Wilson

*The Civil War Diary of Gideon Welles, Lincoln's Secretary of the Navy*
*The Original Manuscript Edition*
Edited by William E. Gienapp and Erica L. Gienapp

*Herndon on Lincoln: Letters*
William H. Herndon; edited by Douglas L. Wilson and Rodney O. Davis

*Lincoln's Confidant: The Life of Noah Brooks*
Wayne C. Temple; edited by Douglas L. Wilson and Rodney O. Davis

*Knowing Him by Heart: African Americans on Abraham Lincoln*
Edited by Frederick Hord and Matthew D. Norman

The University of Illinois Press
is a founding member of the
Association of University Presses.

———————————————

Composed in 10.75/13 Arno Pro
with Brioso Pro display
by Kirsten Dennison
at the University of Illinois Press
Manufactured by Versa Press

University of Illinois Press
1325 South Oak Street
Champaign, IL 61820-6903
www.press.uillinois.edu